The Cambridge Companion to Durkheim

Long recognized as a foundational figure in the development of social scientific thought, Emile Durkheim's work has been the subject of intense debate over the years. This authoritative and comprehensive collection of essays re-examines the impact of Durkheim's thought, considering the historical contexts of his work as well as evaluating his ideas in relation to current issues and controversies. Eminent authorities in the field have contributed to this up-to-date overview, giving readers – both students and academics – a chance to engage directly with leading figures in the field about contemporary trends, ideas, and dilemmas. This volume reflects the cross-disciplinary application of Durkheim's theories and will interest scholars of anthropology, political science, cultural studies, and philosophy, as well as sociology. It is a landmark that redefines the relevance of Durkheim to the human sciences in the twenty-first century, highlighting in particular the significance of his insights for contemporary moral philosophy and his ever-growing centrality for cultural theory.

JEFFREY C. ALEXANDER is the Lydia Chavenson Saden Professor of Sociology, Yale University and Co-Director of the Center for Cultural Sociology.

PHILIP SMITH is Assistant Professor of Sociology and Associate Director of the Center for Cultural Sociology, Yale University.

THE CAMBRIDGE
COMPANION TO
DURKHEIM

EDITED BY

JEFFREY C. ALEXANDER

AND

PHILIP SMITH

CAMBRIDGE
UNIVERSITY PRESS

CAMBRIDGE UNIVERSITY PRESS
Cambridge, New York, Melbourne, Madrid, Cape Town, Singapore, São Paulo

Cambridge University Press
The Edinburgh Building, Cambridge CB2 2RU, UK

Published in the United States of America by Cambridge University Press, New York

www.cambridge.org
Information on this title: www.cambridge.org/9780521806720

© Cambridge University Press 2005

First published 2005

Printed in the United Kingdom at the University Press, Cambridge

A catalogue record for this book is available from the British Library

Library of Congress cataloguing in publication data
The Cambridge companion to Durkheim / edited by Jeffrey C. Alexander and Philip Smith.
p.   cm.
Includes bibliographical references and index.
ISBN 0 521 80672 0 (hardback) – ISBN 0 521 00151 X (paperback)
1. Durkheim, Emile, 1858–1917.   2. Durkheimian school of sociology.   3. Sociology.
1. Alexander, Jeffrey C.   II. Smith, Philip (Philip Daniel), 1964–
HM465.C36   2004   301′.092 – dc22   2004052649

ISBN 0 521 80672 0 hardback
ISBN 0 521 00151 X paperback
ISBN 13: 9780521806725 (hardback)
ISBN-13: 9780521001519 (paperback)

We would like to dedicate this book to
Morel Morton and Philippa Smith
our partners
and to the memory of
Philippe Besnard
the Frenchman whose pioneering contributions
to Durkheim scholarship have proven invaluable
to rethinking Durkheim and whose generosity as
a colleague and friend will be sorely missed.

CONTENTS

PREFACE AND ACKNOWLEDGMENTS

This collection has been a long time in the making. We thank the contributors for their patience. It was Catherine Max, then an editor at Cambridge, who proposed to us at some point in the late-1990s that there should be a Cambridge Companion to Durkheim. It was her successor, Sarah Caro, who saw this project through to completion several years later. We thank Sarah for her suggestions, both positive and critical, her steady faith in the project, and her continued support during its long developmental life. Isaac Reed prepared the chronology and bibliography in consultation with the editors. Tanya Goodman battled heroically with a copy-editing and coordination task of Olympian magnitude and kept the project on track in the final months before the typescript was submitted. Ann Fitzpatrick provided further secretarial and administrative assistance. The chapter by Philippe Besnard was translated by Philippa Smith. Susan Beer and Jackie Warren oversaw the final stages of production at Cambridge University Press.

Despite the great renaissance of Durkheim scholarship and Durkheim-inspired contemporary social science, the present volume is the first broad collection of original Durkheim scholarship to have been fostered in the United States in almost four decades. The whats, whys, and wherefores of this explosion of interest are topics we address in our introduction. If the structural preconditions for this text are disciplinary, the proximate causes are personal and biographical. One editor of this collection (Alexander) traces his first sympathetic contact with Durkheim back to Berkeley, to Leo Lowenthal and Robert Bellah, the latter of whose Durkheimain interest traces back to the earlier generation of W. Lloyd Warner and Talcott Parsons, who began their scholarly work less than a decade after Durkheim's death. The other editor (Smith) first encountered Durkheim through a reading of the classics of British structural-functionalist anthropology, Mauss, Hertz, and Victor Turner, as an anthropology undergraduate in Scotland at St Andrews and Edinburgh. The editors' mutual interest in Durkheim converged in Los Angeles during the late 1980s, at UCLA, and was nurtured locally by the members of the "Culture Club," nationally and internationally by a growing movement of cultural sociology, and particularly by our immediate Durkheimian collaborators – Steven J. Sherwood, Ron Eyerman, Roger Friedland, Bernhard Giesen, Ron Jacobs, Tim Phillips, Steven Seidman, Ken Thompson, and Brad West.

NOTES ON CONTRIBUTORS

JEFFREY C. ALEXANDER is the Lydia Chavenson Saden Professor of Sociology and co-Director of the Center for Cultural Sociology at Yale University. His books engaging with Durkheim include *The Antimonies of Classical Thought: Marx and Durkheim* (University of California Press, 1982), *Durkheimian Sociology* (Cambridge University Press, 1988, editor), *Differentiation Theory and Social Change* (Columbia University Press, 1990), and *The Meanings of Social Life* (Oxford University Press, 2003).

ZYGMUNT BAUMAN is Emeritus Professor of Sociology at the University of Leeds and the University of Warsaw. His more recent contributions include *Intimations of Postmodernity* (Routledge, 1991), *Postmodernity and its Discontents* (New York University Press, 1997), *Liquid Modernity* (Blackwell, 2000), and *Wasted Lives* (Polity Press, 2003).

ROBERT N. BELLAH is Elliott Professor of Sociology Emeritus at the University of California at Berkeley. He is author of *Tokugawa Religion* (Free Press, 1957) and *Beyond Belief* (Harper and Row, 1970) among other volumes. His most recent book is *Imagining Japan: The Japanese Tradition and its Modern Interpretation* (University of California Press, 2003). In 2000 Bellah was awarded the National Humanities Medal.

PHILIPPE BESNARD was Director of Research at the Centre nationale de la recherche scientifique. He is the author of *L'anomie* (PUF, 1987) and *Études durkheimiennes* (Droz, 2003), and the editor of *The Sociological Domain, the Durkheimians and the Founding of French Sociology* (Cambridge University Press, 1983). His contribution to this volume is one of his last published writings.

MARK S. CLADIS is Professor of Religious Studies at Brown University. He is author of *A Communitarian Defense of Liberalism: Emile Durkheim and Contemporary Social Theory* (Stanford University Press, 1992), *Public*

Vision, Private Lives (Oxford University Press, 2003), and editor of Oxford World Classics' edition of *The Elementary Forms of Religious Life* (Oxford University Press, 2001).

RANDALL COLLINS is Professor of Sociology at the University of Pennsylvania. His writings include *Conflict Sociology* (Academic Press, 1975), *The Credential Society* (Academic Press, 1979), *Interaction Ritual Chains* (Princeton University Press, 2004), and *The Sociology of Philosophies* (Belknap Press, 1998).

KAREN E. FIELDS is the translator of Durkheim's *The Elementary Forms of Religious Life* (Free Press, 1995) and author of *Revival and Rebellion in Colonial Central Africa* (Princeton University Press, 1985).

MARCEL FOURNIER is Professor of Sociology at the University of Montreal. His books include *Cultivating Differences* (Chicago, 1992, edited with Michele Lamont), *Lettres à Marcel Mauss* (Presses Universitaires de France, 1998, edited with Philippe Besnard), and *Marcel Mauss* (Fayard, 1994).

ROGER FRIEDLAND is Professor of Religious Studies and Sociology at the University of California, Santa Barbara. His books include *Powers of Theory* (Cambridge University Press, 1985 with Robert Alford), *Beyond the Marketplace* (Aldine de Gruyter, 1990 edited with Alexander Robertson), *Nowhere* (University of California Press, 1994 edited with Deirdre Boden), *To Rule Jerusalem* (Cambridge University Press, 2000, with Richard Hecht), and with John Mohr, *Culture Matters: Cultural Sociology in Practice* (2004).

GABRIELA GALESCU is a PhD candidate in the Department of Sociology at Cornell University. She is carrying out comparative research on the structure of occupational segregation by sex, race, and ethnicity in formerly socialist as well as (long-standing) market economies.

DAVID B. GRUSKY is Professor of Sociology and Director of the Program on Inequality at Stanford University. He is author (with Maria Charles) of *Occupational Ghettos: The Worldwide Segregation of Women and Men* (Stanford University Press, 2004), editor of *Social Stratification: Class, Race, and Gender in Sociological Perspective* (Westview Press, 2001), co-editor (with James Baron and Donald Treiman) of *Social Differentiation and Social Inequality* (Westview Press, 1996), and author of numerous articles on social class, occupational segregation, and social mobility.

ROBERT ALUN JONES is Professor of Religious Studies, History and Sociology at the University of Illinois, Urbana-Champaign. He is author of *Emile Durkheim: An Introduction to the Four Major Works* (Sage, 1986), *The Development of Durkheim's Social Realism* (Cambridge University Press, 1999), and is a former editor of *Études Durkheimiennes*.

ALEXANDER RILEY is Assistant Professor of Sociology at Bucknell University. He is the author of numerous articles on the Durkheimian sociology of religion and the co-editor (with Philippe Besnard) of the correspondence of Robert Hertz *Un Ethnologue dans les tranchées* (CNRS Éditions, 2002).

CHRIS SHILLING is Professor of Sociology at the University of Portsmouth. His books include *The Body and Social Theory* (Sage, 1993), *Re-Forming the Body* (Sage, 1997 with P. A. Mellor), *The Sociological Ambition* (Sage, 2001 with P. A. Mellor), and *The Body in Culture, Technology and Society* (Sage, 2004).

PHILIP SMITH is Assistant Professor of Sociology and Associate Director of the Center for Cultural Sociology at Yale University. His books include *The New American Cultural Sociology* (Cambridge University Press, 1998, editor), *Researching the Visual* (Sage, 2000 with Michael Emmison), *Cultural Theory: An Introduction* (Blackwell, 2001), and *War Stories: the Cultural Politics of Suez, the Gulf War and the War in Iraq* (Chicago, 2005). He is the author of various articles deploying and developing Durkheimian themes.

EDWARD A. TIRYAKIAN is Professor Emeritus of Sociology at Duke University. The author of *Sociologism and Existentialism* (Prentice-Hall, 1962) and numerous articles of Durkheimian sociology, his most recent volume is *Rethinking Civilizational Analysis* (co-edited with Said Arjomand, Sage, 2004).

CHRONOLOGY OF DURKHEIM'S LIFE

April 15, 1858	Born in Épinal, Lorraine
1870	German soldiers occupy Épinal
1874	Receives Baccalauréat en Lettres, Collège d'Épinal
1875	Receives Baccalauréat en Sciences, Collège d'Épinal
1879	Admitted to École Normale Supérieure
1880	Fustel de Coulanges becomes Director of the École Normale Supérieure
July 14, 1880	Takes part in Republican demonstrations in the streets of Paris
1880–91	Ferdinand de Saussure studies and teaches in Paris
1882	Passes aggrégation
October 1882	Begins teaching philosophy at Lycée de Puy (moves to Lycée de Sens in November 1882, and to Lycée de Saint-Quentin in February 1884)
1884	Begins work on *De la division du travail social*
1885–6	Visits German universities, including Berlin, Marburg, and Leipzig
October 1886	Returns from Germany, is appointed philosophy teacher at Lycée de Troyes
1887	Marries Louise Dreyfus; Appointed "Chargé d'un Cours de Science Sociale et de Pédagogie" at Bordeaux; gives first public lecture at Bordeaux, proposing to develop the new science of sociology in the course of teaching it
1889–90	Gives course, "Le Suicide"
1893	Publishes *De la division du travail social*
1894	Publishes "Les Règles de la méthode sociologique" in the *Revue philosophique*
1894	Gabriel Tarde appointed Director of Criminal Statistics office of the Ministry of Justice; Captain

xiv

	Alfred Dreyfus accused of spying, arrested, and found guilty of high treason
1894–5	Gives course, "La Religion," including his engagement with the texts of Robertson-Smith
1895	Publishes *Les Règles de la méthode sociologique* (book version includes modifications and a preface)
1895–6	Gives course, "L'Histoire du socialisme"
1896	Begins work on *L'Année sociologique*; appointed to full professor in social science, the first such post in France
1897	Publishes *Le Suicide*
1898	First volume of *L'Année sociologique* published
1898	Émile Zola publishes "J'accuse . . . !"
1899	President of France pardons Alfred Dreyfus
1900–1	Gives course, "Les Formes élémentaires de la religion"
1902	Appointed "Chargé d'un cours de Pédagogie" at the Sorbonne in Paris
1903	With Marcel Mauss, publishes "De quelques formes primitives de classification: contribution à l'étude des representations collectives" as the lead article in Volume VI of the *Année sociologique*
1906	Appointed to Chair of the Science of Education at the Sorbonne
1906–7	Gives course, "La Religion: Origines"
1907	In a letter to the director of the *Revue néo-scholastique*, recounts how the course of 1894–5 on religion, and the intellectual encounter with the works of Robertson-Smith, were a "revelation" that marks a break in his thinking
1909	Exchange with Levy-Bruhl; publishes "Sociologie religieuse et théorie de la connaissance" in *Revue de métaphysique et de morale*, which will become the introduction to *Les Formes élémentaires de la vie religieuse*
1912	Publishes *Les Formes élémentaires de la vie religieuse*
1913	Chair at the Sorbonne renamed Science of Education and Sociology
1913–14	Gives course, "Pragmatisme et Sociologie"
August 3, 1914	Germany declares war on France

1915	Son André sent to the Bulgarian front; publishes *Qui a voulu la guerre?*
1916	André Durkheim confirmed dead
Late 1916	Suffers a stroke leaving a meeting
November 15, 1917	Dies in Paris

I

PHILIP SMITH AND JEFFREY C. ALEXANDER

Introduction: the new Durkheim

What does Durkheim mean for social science and social theory today? This is a deceptively simple question. One way to attempt an answer is to put a deconstructive twist on the standard sociological literature about the production of culture and knowledge. It is commonplace within that field to suggest that authors produce texts to send messages to others. As participants in intellectual markets, writers strive to meet collegial expectations and hope to gain recognition in exchange (Collins this volume; Hagstrom 1965; Lamont 1987). Yet when an author's work has staying power beyond its immediate context, this being the very quality that distinguishes a truly great contribution, something much more intriguing happens. Readings proliferate that are unintended and unpredictable, with determinations that go far beyond those that could have been consciously anticipated by the maker of the original text. Time reverses the direction of influence. New contexts of interpretation come to rewrite texts as authors and theories are re-narrated for present relevance. Next, these critical interventions are themselves reworked and rethought. Eventually a layered field of immense dialogic activity is formed as words, ideas, their underlying structures of feeling and analytic choices accumulate and attach to the classical bedrock. It is precisely this sequential accretion of complexity and controversy that marks out the proper and full domain for inquiry into a great scholar. Because foundational texts and subsequent commentaries alike should be understood as social facts as well as a hermeneutic practice, we must give due attention to both scholarly intents and intellectual contexts. In thinking through questions about Durkheim and his legacy, we come to engage with others. These relate less to the cultural and intellectual preoccupations of other ages and more to those of our own.

So it is that this collected volume stands testament not only to Durkheim's posthumously evolving, and increasingly better understood, intellectual portfolio, but to current, pressing social and intellectual concerns. A marking stone that appears midway between the centennials of Durkheim's first (1893) and last (1912) major books, the *Cambridge Companion to Durkheim* captures not only the great French thinker's current incarnation, but also the challenges engaging contemporary social theory and the society in which it is circumscribed.

The many Durkheims and their fates

In the contribution that forms the next chapter of this volume, Marcel Fournier remarks on the enduring mystery of Durkheim as man and mind. Although he gave us clues and traces, we are left with a biography that is curiously elusive. The real "who" of Durkheim slips through our fingers. Socialist, positivist, establishment figure, Jew and, of course, sociologist – Durkheim was all of these but cannot be reduced to their sum, their boundaries, or even their dialogue. Durkheim's biography is a terrain that produces its own surplus. Much the same can be said for his thought, which exhibits a tension between promises of consistency and evidence of fragmentation. So it is that Philippe Besnard (this volume) demonstrates that Durkheim slips through the formalist intellectual grids that many have tried to impose on his conceptual universe. His concepts and typologies exhibit tantalizing geometries, but these never quite run in parallel, so we end up trying to hammer round pegs into square holes. Even at the level of the individual word or phrase it seems impossible to fix Durkheim's intent. As Karen Fields documents (this volume), Durkheim's carefully chosen vocabulary and expression is often intrinsically multivalent. This has thrown down a formidable challenge to translators for the past century, forcing them to make the toughest of interpretative choices. They have wrestled with Durkheim's thinking in the full knowledge that they do violence to its subtleties even as they attempt to be faithful unto it. If we can find this ambivalence in lived biography, in conceptual schemas and in the printed words of original text, it should come as no surprise that we can trace non-Euclidean contradictions in the vectors of Durkheim interpretations as these have arced through the last century and headed off towards new and uncharted vanishing points. Let's review this geometry and history.

Gathering up the scholarly missives left behind by earlier generations of Durkheim's admirers, one notes with irony that the great advocate of the social fact as an objective, external, ontologically unavoidable thing was unable to fix in hard stone his own interpretation. Durkheim the social scientist intended his texts to be closed, definitive and "writerly" in Barthes' (1975) terms. Yet, the tangled webs of Durkheim exegesis have demonstrated time and time again that his writings are open, suggestive and "readerly." As Karen Fields (this volume) illustrates, Durkheim's style, particularly in

The Elementary Forms of Religious Life (1912) is one of surprising complexity and literary creativity. Although highlighted in the problematic of translation, interpretative choices also confront native readers. Such textual qualities assisted a more sociological process in which Durkheim metamorphosed into a totem, a symbol whose diverse interpretations lay not only in his texts or volitions but also in less personal, more collective institutional and cultural determinations. It is precisely because he was blown hither and thither like a feather in the social, cultural, and theoretical winds of other epochs and agendas, precisely because he was readerly and not writerly, that Durkheim has passed down to us such a diverse, rewarding and ultimately surprising intellectual inheritance.

Even Durkheim's immediate survivors in France found themselves in possession of an ambiguous legacy. Alexander outlines the great tensions in Durkheim's early and middle period writings in this volume. It should not be surprising, then, that the disciples of *Année sociologique* pursued contradictory lines of inquiry that careened between more symbolic and more structural, more radical and more conservative lines of analysis. Notwithstanding the productivity of these scholars, and the fact that they were in positions of real influence, new followers of Durkheimian sociology were hard to recruit after the First World War. As Randall Collins remarks in this volume, Durkheim was stigmatized as a member of the "old guard." He became a lightning rod for dissatisfaction with centrist Third Republican politics and normativizing neo-Kantian philosophy. Zygmunt Bauman's contribution to this book demonstrates this line of interpretation continuing to resonate today, albeit with a postmodern shift in sensibility that exhibits the anxieties of our era.

Yet, as Alexander Riley elaborates in this volume, at the very same time that Durkheim was reviled as an Establishment figure, he became, perhaps unwittingly, the founder of a politically radical and intellectually iconoclastic school of surprising originality and scope. Ideas about the "impure sacred" were taken from *The Elementary Forms of Religious Life* (1912) (hereafter *Elementary Forms*) – where they make only a brief, inconsistent but provocative appearance – as well as from the work of Durkheim's student Robert Hertz. These were elaborated by members of the Parisian *Collège de sociologie* and alchemized into a transgressive sociology that added a shot of Nietzschean spirit to the already heady cocktail of Durkheimian symbolic and ritual theory. In the hands of such social thinkers as Georges Bataille and Rogers Caillois, this saw the non-rational, erotic, existential, evil and unconscious deployed in an insistent effort to push back the restrictive limits on human experience imposed by the rationalization of modern life. Despite inauspicious beginnings – the *Collège* folded after scarcely two years – this inter-war curiosity was subsequently tessellated with textual and semiotic understandings of culture within the broader, more rigorous and more significant mosaic of post-structural and post-Marxist thought. We return to this pattern of influence later.

Meanwhile, a very different Durkheim was taking shape within the English speaking world. Barely 300 miles from Paris, in the oak paneled halls of Oxford and Cambridge, Radcliffe-Brown, Evans-Pritchard, and Myer-Fortes took Durkheim to be the pioneering advocate of a new scientific theory of institutions. In this scenario, Durkheim was neither Republican priest nor bohemian prophet, but a rigorous academic whose collectivistic visions order and resolute acknowledgment of the functional demands imposed by intertwined organizations provided the key for robust but rather deterministic interpretations of such exotic puzzles as kinship systems, sorcery, and sacrifice. Pivotal to this view were Durkheim's early and middle period works. While we now see the complexity and ambiguity of these writings (Alexander this volume), it was the social-structural emphasis of *The Division of Labor in Society* ([1893] 1964) (hereafter *Division of Labor*), the functionalist and positivist methodology of *The Rules of Sociological Method* ([1895] 1966) (hereafter *Rules*), the objectivism and determinism of *Suicide* ([1897] 1966) that struck Durkheim's anthropological observers in the 1930s and 1940s. Read in this way, these books provided an intellectual Erecter Set with which the girders, nuts, and bolts of both field observation and armchair-anthropological erudition could be bolted together into more complex and determined articulations, each component playing its role in the stability of an edifice that was at once empirical account and theoretical armature. Only towards the end of this golden age do we see signs of change. The interpretative revisions that informed Evans-Pritchard's *Nuer Religion* (1956) already indicated a move towards a more hermeneutic rather than functionalist understanding of belief systems.

Some three thousand miles to the west, Talcott Parsons was busily converting Durkheim into a pillar of what came eventually to be known as action theory. Less interested at this stage of his career in determining functions than in institutionalizing morality, Parsons saw Durkheim through a Weberian lens as a perceptive theorist of normatively driven human agency and an interpreter of the cultural underpinnings of social life. Parsons ([1937] 1968) drew upon *Elementary Forms* as much as upon the *Division of Labor* in this early effort to demonstrate the centrality of non-rational components in social life and social action. In so doing, his project can be subtly distinguished from the British anthropologists with their interest in gathering objective social facts and explaining social order. Yet when another American, Robert Merton (1968 [1938]), presented his Durkheimian theory that deviance resulted from dynamic tensions between social means and individual ends, he was indebted less to the Durkheim of Parsons, his teacher, than to a Durkheim similar to that of the British anthropologists. This was a figure who highlighted the divisions of social labor and their intersection with social structure in patterns of integration, opportunity, and anomie.

Looking back at the first half of the twentieth century, then, we can see a set of distinctions emerging. These were to become consolidated in the second half as ground rules, or codes, for interpreting and identifying a "real" Durkheim. They marked out a cultural Durkheim (Parsons) from a more structural Durkheim (British anthropology, Merton) and a conservative Durkheim (Third Republic critics) from a radical Durkheim (the *Collège de sociologie*). Arguments for each of these positions have been repeatedly made on the basis of published and unpublished writings, in intellectual histories, and in the details of Durkheim's life. Because we refer to these in the remaining discussion they need only be briefly summarized here. Structural Durkheimianism highlights the submerged morphological forces, legal constraints, and abstract *conscience collective* (collective consciousness/conscience) that narrate the *Division of Labor*, the mechanistic interactions and associations that animate *Suicide*, and the functional determinism and epistemological collectivism suggested by *Rules*. The conservative Durkheim talks about stability, legitimacy, democratic law, and social conformity, not only as empirical realities but also as ideals for the construction of a good society. Radical Durkheimianism points to creativity, effervescence, the need to explode routinization via passionate association and transcendent ritual, and to the ethical imperative to overcome the pathological division of labor with socialism and solidarity. Cultural Durkheimianism takes off from the symbolic classifications, rituals, and discussions of the soul and solidaristic passions that animate the later works, most notably the *Elementary Forms*.

In the second half of the twentieth century, "new" interpretations of Durkheim by both advocates and critics invariably took off from one or more of these positions. We can read this history very much as a case of new wine being poured into old bottles. Although each new argument had distinctive qualities of vintage and intellectual *terroir*, and might have involved a little creative blending, all were made from the same four grape varietals – the same four Durkheims. The fifties and sixties saw a more structural Parsons (1966) give centrality to Durkheim's evolutionary model of social development, moving back to *Division of Labor* and away from *Elementary Forms*. This Durkheim-via-later-Parsons illuminates the transition to modernity in terms of differentiation, value generalization, and growing social system complexity. These shifts in Parsons' reading meant that a structural and conservative Durkheim overshadowed the cultural and radical Durkheim during the mid-century period in the United States. Ironically, this move was taking place just as British social anthropology began to shift towards a more cultural approach to Durkheim. Despite possibilities for convergence, the two interpretative projects crossed like ships in the night – there was no substantial interchange.

Parsons' later understanding formed the basis for modernization theory (e.g. Levy 1952; Smelser 1959, and Eisenstadt 1963) and reached its apotheosis of structural determinism and democratic conservativism in the writings of Niklas Luhmann (1982). Alongside this structural Durkheim there developed an equally cautious cultural one. W. Lloyd Warner ([1959] 1975) treated modern American life as a cosmologically patterned and ritually integrated mass tribe organized around a cult of the dead. It was an approach without great subtlety, but it did at least get the cultural Durkheim onto the agenda as a resource for explaining life in "advanced" societies. A much more sophisticated and more critical extension of Durkheim's later work unfolded under Parsons' influence. Robert Bellah (1972) interpreted America as organized, and challenged, by a tightly integrated civil religion. Edward Shils (1975) illuminated the sacred centers of mass societies, emphasizing how once peripheral groups had become incorporated through education and majestic secular rituals and how ideas of sacrality were pivotal to the legitimacy of core social institutions.

Exciting as this movement was, it had trouble uncoupling the cultural Durkheim from his structural and conservative avatars. The belief that societal evolution led to universalism and value generalization was implicit within the cultural frames developed by Bellah and Shils. So dysfunctions and social exclusion were framed as the relics of tradition or as incomplete institutionalization rather than being imminent to modernity or the binary logic of cultural codes. A retrieval of Durkheim's sustained critique of anomie, perhaps filtered through Merton's reading of the ironies and dysfunctions of the American value system, might have allowed this line of thinking to become a more hard hitting indictment of the present. The necessary connections connecting the periphery to anomie or civil religion to exclusion were never made.

This missed opportunity created an unsurpassed intellectual vulnerability to radical critique. Produced in the afterglow of postwar high modernity, these affirmative readings of structural and cultural Durkheim and their sociological elaborations in empirical research were attacked and discredited, even as they reached their fullest elaboration during the turbulent, contentious decades of the sixties and seventies. For the rebellious intellectuals of that time, as had once been the case for their counterparts in 1920s and 1930s France, Durkheim had become a kind of Goliath against whom various Davids could bid for glory. Or, to switch metaphorical reference, Durkheim now seemed a lumbering anachronism whose proper home was in some Jurassic Park of intellectual dinosaurs.

Blind to the possibility of a radical Durkheim, self-proclaimed conflict theorists read Durkheim through Parsons and then indicted them both. Durkheim became synonymous with theoretical functionalism, with amoral conservatism, with Kantian abstraction and with methodological dead ends. And so it was that, in Charles Tilly's (1981) infamous condemnation, the French founder was declared "useless" for a historical sociology that needed to explore conflict and change. Critical theorists pointed to the manner in which the empirical claims of Durkheimian sociologists often outstripped their theoretical mandate, particularly when themes of social consensus were at play. Railing against "normative functionalism" (in effect an analytic fusion of the cultural, structural and conservative Durkheims), David Lockwood (1964) pointed out that societies seemed to cohere without overarching values, not because of them, and that Durkheim had hopelessly confounded social integration (cultural consensus) and system integration (social order), a criticism that Michael Mann (1970) and Jürgen Habermas (1986) later picked up. Early efforts towards a cultural Durkheimianism were shown to be severely flawed by virtue of their functionalist strain. Steven Lukes (1975) attacked Durkheimian understandings of ritual, suggesting that integrative effects were poorly measured and unevenly distributed and had more to do with cognitive-ideological than affective-moral force. A new and often avowedly anti-Durkheimian approach to ritual as conflict emerged, theorizing a sphere of contestation in which sponsors struggled to engage audiences and establish hegemonic meanings (e.g. Bourdieu 1990: 200–70; Lincoln 1989).

During the same period, and in a remarkably parallel process, the rising tide of "microsociology" condemned a structural Durkheim. Their exclusive focus on everyday life, face-to-face interaction and conversation demanded, in effect, a "collectivist" and "determinist" ancestor to oppose. This Durkheim could be understood for all practical purposes as denying human creativity and agency and as holding positivist certainties about the transparency of social facts that were, at best, sociologically naïve. Even constructively intended efforts, such as Goffman's micro theories of interaction rituals (1967), had the effect of pushing contemporary sociology off its Durkheimian tracks. In Goffman's case, it is yet another story of missed opportunities, at least so far as the cultural Durkheim was concerned. Despite a creative reading of Durkheim as a theorist of embodied face-to-face encounters, and despite insisting from time to time on the sacred nature of the individual, Goffman's work seemed to demonstrate that moral sentiments and social emotions were merely emergent properties of individual level behaviors. "Agency" was restored but at the expense of the moral humanism and cultural complexity that had characterized Durkheim's ritual work. In its place, Goffman and his later Durkheimian followers, such as Collins (1975), posited a mechanistic and often cynical model of human interaction and emotion, one that failed to theorize a cultural realm that could regulate, and not only fall prey to or emerge from, moral calculus, bodily display and emotional need. Nevertheless, this line of work did make fruitful connections between ritual theory and pragmatism, echoes of which can be seen in this volume in the discussions by Collins, Jones, and Bellah on the relationship between behavior, emotion, cognition, and belief.

Microsociology, then, failed to mount a sustained engagement with the cultural Durkheim's theory of ritual action. In the case of critical theory, it was the radical Durkheim who tragically fell by the wayside. The dominance in Anglo-American circles of an anti-cultural Marxism rather than a pro-cultural, Nietzschean critical theory had led to a fatal blind spot in the Left's interpretation of Durkheim's legacy. To understand how these alternative Durkheim traditions have come to be rediscovered, we need to turn back towards France and trace another of Durkheim's posthumous intellectual journeys.

Durkheim's latent force

In the desert there are certain plants whose seeds might lie dormant for decades, awaiting a propitious moment to release their latent energy and make the sands bloom. Even as the conservative and structural Durkheims withered under scorching criticism, the re-growth of cultural and radical Durkheims was underway. Furtive and hardly recognized at first, this intellectual quickening was to represent the full flowering of themes discretely seeded by Durkheim in the *Elementary Forms*. Indeed, the full extent of their connection to that masterwork has only recently become visible. To truly understand Durkheim's legacy for contemporary cultural theory and cultural sociology, it is necessary to step away from our review of Durkheimian sociology as it has been commonly understood and review this largely silent alternative history.

In *Elementary Forms*, Durkheim had surprised even the most long-standing students of his sociology by proclaiming: "There is one region of nature where the formula of idealism applies almost to the letter: This is the social kingdom" (1912: 326 our translation). In society, Durkheim had come to believe, "the idea is the reality." It is only in order to "express our own ideas to ourselves" that we need to "fix them on material things which symbolize them." But here the "part of matter is reduced to a minimum" (1912: 326). Responding to criticism that his earlier sociology had conceptualized an external "physical constraint [as] the most important thing for social life," Durkheim remonstrated, perhaps a little disingenuously, that he had ". . . never considered it more than the material and apparent expression of a profound and interior fact that is entirely ideal: this is moral authority" (1912: 298, note 2). Durkheim's vision in the *Elementary Forms* was of a shared cultural system that is internalized within each individual. It trumps the material base by superimposing upon it a universe of arbitrary but deeply meaningful signs, myths and determinations of action. He wrote:

> The whole social environment appears to us as if inhabited with forces that, in reality, exist only in our consciousness. One knows that the flag, in itself, is nothing but a scrap of cloth for the soldier. Human blood is simply an organic liquid, yet even today we cannot see it flowing without experiencing a violent emotion that its physico-chemical properties cannot explain. From a physical point of view man is nothing more than a system of cells . . . A cancelled postage stamp can be worth a fortune; it is obvious that this value is in no way tied to its natural properties . . . Collective representations very often attribute to the things to which they are attached properties which do not exist in any form or degree. Out of the commonest object they can make a very powerful and very sacred being. Yet, although purely ideal, the powers which have been conferred in this way work as if they were real. They determine the conduct of men with the same inevitability as physical forces. (Durkheim 1912: 325–6)

Durkheim began to develop these new, profoundly cultural ideas during the middle and late 1890s, even as he was completing *Suicide* (1897), the last book of the trilogy that has long formed a central building block for social-structural sociology. He elaborated this new perspective in the courses of public lectures he offered in Paris during the first decade of the twentieth century. There is good evidence to suggest that the Swiss linguist Ferdinand de Saussure followed these Paris lectures, and that in some significant part he built on them to develop his structural linguistics (Alexander 1988b, Collins this volume, Jakobson 1990: 88). In his new science of semiotics, Saussure (1959) suggested that social communication is organized by a system of symbolic signs whose complex internal structure could be likened to a spoken language. Social objects should be seen as signifieds which cannot be separated from cultural signifiers. The symbolic meaning of objects is not objective – not set by their structural location in society or their material facticity or their utility; it is established, rather, by the relation of signifieds to one another inside the broader symbolic system. Reconfiguring in this linguistic manner Durkheim's later sociological ideas, semiotics became one of the dominant intellectual forces of the twentieth century. In the hands of the linguist Roman Jakobson (1990) and the ethnographer Claude Lévi-Strauss (1966), semiotics formed the basis for the "structural" approach in anthropology, whose theories of interwoven and binary cultural codes provided an alternative to the British functionalist legacy. Under structuralism's influence, the literary critic Roland Barthes ([1957] 1973; [1964] 1984; 1975) developed semiotics into a flow-blown theory of social discourse and myth in everyday life, which he called "socio-logic" to distinguish it from the reductionism of a purely institutionally oriented sociology.

It was at this point, from the 1950s to the 1970s, that new forms of cultural social analysis uncovered for the first time the cultural coding of social life. In the French case, this current merged with that of the radical Durkheim. As this had been inflected by Bataille and the *Collège de sociologie*, the path of inheritance was only slightly less disguised than in the case of cultural Durkheim (Riley this volume). The emphasis in this French convergence was on the tensions between system and anti-system in cultural life. Baudrillard, Lyotard, Kristeva, and others elaborated theses whose lineage extended back to a "left sacred" – ideas about dread, productive excess, transgression, death, eroticism, and embodied experience. They pointed in various ways to confrontations between reason and its limits, not only those imposed by the individual, unconscious, and irrational, but by the polluting discourses about evil that shadow every ethical system and by the contradictions and gaps inherent in the act of classification itself. Michel Foucault (e.g. [1961] 1967), of course, was to make this dark counterpoint central to his life's work. He brought discourse back into the heart of social science with his historical investigations into the simultaneously liberating and repressive structures of symbolic thought, and he explained how organizational powers routinized and controlled the expressions of the sacred even as these threatened to escape discourse. Jacques Derrida (1978) developed a systematic method of reading culture that contextualized structures of discourse and opened them up to creative reconfiguration. Even while affirming the binding influence of already existing representational forms, Derrida insisted on their instability and inevitable productive excess at the margins of meaning. For Derrida, transgression was the shadow of the code, just as for Foucault the *cogito* must produce and depend upon the "unthought."

The blooming of this line of French philosophy-cum-social theory paralleled, but also stimulated, the rebirth of the near dormant Anglo-American cultural Durkheim. As notions of discourse, code, and myth were revived in Western intellectual life, it was only a matter of time before the cultural Durkheim's core vocabulary of ritual, symbol, and the sacred was rediscovered. Tied to a more realist, less ideological vision of social life, the cultural Durkheim was decoupled from the structural and conservative Durkheims who had been the dominant incarnation since the 1940s. And so, with the assistance of French structuralism, particularly Lévi-Strauss' writings from the mid-1950s onwards, British and American anthropologists of the 1960s came to break new soil and cultivate their own Durkheimian paddocks. Mary Douglas (1966) demonstrated how symbolic classification creates moral boundaries and powerful forces of purity and pollution, even if her later "grid/group" model of social life was haunted by the ghost of structural Durkheimianism. Victor Turner (1974; [1969] 1977) connected planes of symbolic classification to boundary-bursting ritual processes that were at once radical, communal, resistant, existentially meaningful, and intimate. Unknown to him, this revisited the terrain of the *Collège de sociologie* some thirty years after its demise. Clifford Geertz (1975) insisted, against institutional social science, that ideology, religion, politics, and stratification can be studied as cultural systems, and he produced a series of exemplary interpretative studies of ritual-like performances in secular social life. The resulting fusion of Durkheimian socio-logics with hermeneutic and narrative sensibilities was to open the floodgates in ways that Geertz and other pioneering figures of the 1960s, such as Bellah (Alexander and Sherwood 2002), could scarcely have imagined.

These new intellectual movements created what was eventually hailed as the "cultural turn" in the human sciences. It is hardly an exaggeration to suggest that this change in understanding shifted the very ground for theoretical and empirical analysis across a myriad of disciplines, from philosophy (Rorty 1980; Habermas 1993) and literary studies (Hartman 1987; Brooks 1984) to the social sciences (Hunt 1989; Moscovici 1993). The aftershocks of this earthquake are still being experienced and interpreted today.

For some time, this revolution in the human sciences was speaking "Durkheim" without uttering his name. Foucault hardly mentioned Durkheim, though he widely acknowledged the structural frame. Levi-Strauss claimed his work was anti-Durkheimian, while openly linking it to that of Marcel Mauss, Durkheim's nephew and most revered student, and to their jointly written essay, *Primitive Classification* ([1902] 1963), which adumbrated in a rather constrained manner some of the ideas later to be cut loose in *Elementary Forms* (see Smith 2001: 76–7, 102). Derrida claimed to be refuting Saussure, and indirectly Durkheim, even while he developed a more subtle program that deconstructed his own claim by demonstrating the pervasive influence of sign systems and their ability to elide and transcend individual subjectivities. Turner traced his roots to Durkheim's nemesis, Van Gennep, and scarcely mentions Durkheim even as he systematically incorporates virtually every major theme of Durkheim's later work. Geertz scarcely mentioned Durkheim, and Douglas openly deplored him even though her own teachers in British Anthropology had revered him and her own work represents a profoundly original elaboration of the *Division of Labor* as seen through the more cultural lens of the *Elementary Forms*.

As this brief recounting suggests, the cultural turn owes everything to Durkheim. It built almost entirely upon his legacy, which his direct and indirect disciples distributed over an extraordinary range of disciplines and channeled through an immensity of new kinds of intellectual forms. Why, then, has the debt been such a well kept secret? In some part it reflects the anxiety of influence (Bloom 1975). But much more is involved. The problem, at once scholarly and historical, was that the sociological significance of Durkheim's later, more cultural theory had never been properly understood. Durkheim himself did not do anything to help. Committed to the identity of sociology with natural science, he was inclined, as we suggested earlier, to present his ideas as "writerly," not as changing and developing, but as unified, definitive and coherent. That *Elementary Forms* presented itself primarily as interpretation of symbolism and totemistic ritual in pre-modern life made it even easier for students of modern society to avoid the implications of Durkheim's later symbolic turn. We have already suggested a number of other contingencies that conspired to keep cultural Durkheim on the margins of the gazetteer of twentieth-century cultural theory, when in truth he was the Rome from and to which all roads led. Durkheim's immediate students were themselves divided over his legacy, and the master's premature death, during the First World War, prevented him from ever adjudicating these divisions himself. In the interwar period, as we mentioned at the beginning of this introduction, Durkheimians began to lose control over the reading of their teacher's work. What ensued were the struggles over interpreting and practicing Durkheimian sociology that we have documented here. For much of this time negative views of Durkheim were to predominate. Fear of symbolic contagion led scholars to disguise or misrecognize their debt in ways both intended and unconscious. It is remarkable how often we find the homage to Durkheim refracted into an acknowledgment of the contribution of one or other of his direct or indirect followers, typically Saussure, Mauss or Bataille.

It took new developments in Durkheim scholarship to reveal that these pioneers of the cultural turn were really speaking a Durkheimian prose that was unnoticed because it had become second nature. It is fitting that this comparatively recent discovery was one that their own enthusiasm for the cultural turn did much to excite. The notion that Durkheim's thinking went through phases from materialism to idealism had been noticed first by Parsons in

1937. Yet the insight was so overlaid by Parsons' particular theoretical interest in action theory that it failed in its strictly exegetical task. It was not until the English theorist Steven Lukes' scholarly and panoramic biography, *Émile Durkheim: His Life and Work* (1972), that Durkheim scholars could develop a firm bibliographical hold on the scope of Durkheim's writings from beginning to end. One clear implication of this material was that Durkheim believed himself to have experienced a *coupure* (break) sometime during the later 1890s, at the very time when he was finishing the last of his first three major works (see Fournier this volume, Alexander this volume, and Jones this volume). Following upon Lukes, in 1975 a group of French scholars, led by Philippe Besnard, launched *Les Etudes Durkheimiennes*, which became the vehicle for publishing a series of previously unknown documents demonstrating that, within Durkheim's own research team, there was not only enthusiastic recognition but also intense disagreement about the master's turn toward religion in his later work (Besnard 1979). In 1981, Bernard Lacroix published *Durkheim et le politique*, which highlighted Durkheim's highly ambivalent emotional links to his father's traditional Jewish faith and, while highly speculative, uncovered more historical evidence that a new attitude toward religion emerged in Durkheim's later work. In the second volume of *Theoretical Logic in Sociology* (1982), Alexander demonstrated this shift using internal textual evidence, suggesting, through detailed hermeneutical reconstruction, that Durkheim's theoretical legacy to the social sciences would have to be fundamentally reconceived.[1] While this argument for Durkheim's cultural shift has not, by any means, received universal confirmation within Durkheim scholarship, over the last two decades the language of the early versus the late Durkheim, and the reading of his development as productively shifting to the religious-cum-cultural, does seem to have become increasingly hegemonic, as has a growing awareness of his influence, at once profound and furtive, on both French and Anglophone cultural theory.

The tide began to turn in the 1980s, slowly at first but with gathering speed into the 1990s (e.g. Alexander 1988a; 1988b). Concepts like ritual, symbolism, representation, morality, and solidarity began to appear alongside discussions of discourse, difference, structure, and meaning, and the Durkheimian roots of a newly cultural sociology became not only increasingly evident but increasingly acknowledged, as one scholar after another read with pleasure and astonishment the *Elementary Forms*, as if for the first time. This enthusiasm was tempered by a realism that avoided earlier tendencies to link the cultural Durkheim with conservatism and to separate meaning from organization and power. A new emphasis was given to struggle, contestation, social division, and inequality, now considered within a framework where culture was not simply an instrumental and external environment for action but also a source of motivation that worked through emotions, classification, and collective action. As the "late Durkheim" came to be seen as the source of a major stream in cultural sociology (Alexander 1988b, 2003a; Smith 2001, ch. 5; Alexander and Smith 1996a), an enormous range of new empirical topics came into view that explicitly extended Durkheim's relevance in new and often unanticipated directions. War and violence (Wagner-Pacifici 1986; Smith 1991); race and ethnicity (Jacobs 1996; Rappaport 1997); technology and environmentalism (Alexander and Smith 1996b; Douglas and Wildavsky 1982); money and economic life (Zelizer 1979); democratic transitions (Edles 1988; Chan 1999; Ku 1999) and democratic legitimacy (Alexander 1988c; Rosati 2002); nationalism and collective identity (Tiryakian 1988; Giesen 1998; Spillman 1997); cultural traumas and collective memory (Alexander et al. 2004; Connerton 1989; Eyerman 2001; Giesen 2004; Schwartz 2000); crime and justice (Garland 1990; Smith 1996, 2003) – these are only the most prominent studies bringing Durkheim visibly to the center of the cultural analysis of social process today.

How to read this volume

Although this new, more cultural Durkheim is becoming dominant, the field of interpretation retains its tensions and disagreements. This volume captures both the new hegemony and the continuing debate, providing a window on the scholarship and the theorizing that are Durkheimian sociology today.

Lewis Coser (1992) once suggested that if an introduction systematically catalogues the contents of a volume, it appeals to intellectual laziness. There is a need, however, to sensitize the reader to some common themes and latent debates that might go unnoticed, but which run beneath the textual surfaces of the following chapters. In this way, readers can be provoked and challenged to look more deeply, rather than encouraged to skip the detail and settle for a big picture gloss.

Reviewing the contributions as a whole, we can detect some emphases and interests that would not have been present if this collection had been published thirty years ago. We find an increased attention to the legacy of Durkheim's students, and growing appreciation of the Durkheim school's collective contribution to the formation of a Durkheimian sociology (see chapters by Collins, Fournier, Riley). There is awareness, for example, that Durkheim's *Elementary Forms* was presaged in some respects by Hertz ([1907]1960) as well as by Durkheim's own work with Mauss on *Primitive Classification* (1963 [1903]). This approach replaces the vision of Durkheim as a heroic intellectual surrounded by dependent students with an image in which he is the axis for a system of intellectual exchange. Such a revised model has as its ancillary a stronger focus on the proximate *intellectual* environment in which Durkheim worked (Collins, Fournier, Jones), with this displacing to some extent an earlier scholarly interest in the *political* contexts shaping his ideas.

Ideas of ritual, symbolism and the sacred, of course, are widespread in the collection, and so it is no surprise that the theme of solidarity finds a prominent place, whether coupled to conventional ritual action and strong emotional ties (Bellah, Friedland, Tiryakian) or in a more diffuse institutionalization (Cladis, Grusky). What does seem to be new is the treatment of these themes. In several cases they are elaborated within the context of a sociology of the body. Whether as collective representation, totem, locus of experience or as brute material fact, the body is becoming increasingly central to treatments of Durkheim's cultural sociology (Bellah, Friedland, Riley, Shilling). We mentioned earlier that the idea of Durkheim's thinking undergoing a radical shift during his career has become established in recent years. This volume bears testament to such a claim, even if our contributors differ in fixing the origins and timing of any such shift (Alexander, Collins, Fournier, Jones). Clarifying and debating such points of detail is usually an indicator that a new paradigm has been institutionalized. Finally there seems to be a growing interest in micro- and meso-Durkheimianisms, approaches that conceive face-to-face interactions, social networks, and institutions (Bellah, Collins, Grusky, Jones) as the foundations of social life rather than some over-arching totality known as society.

Conspicuous by their absence are some old debates and themes. Attacks on and defenses of structural functional and conservative Durkheims seem to be passé, although it might well be said that Bauman reworks these themes in a creative and postmodern spirit. Durkheim's contributions to positivism, statistical research methods, and the social fact also fail to attract the attention of our contributors in any substantial way – a telling indicator of the rise of a more hermeneutic and cultural Durkheim during the 1990s.

These presences and absences are notable, yet we would suggest that the more interesting possibilities for contemporary Durkheim scholarship can be found by digging beneath any surface agreement on themes and unearthing instead the divergent theoretical logics just below. Analytically reconstructing these virtual and latent debates provides a window into possible future directions. The first concerns whether analytic and causal primacy should be given to social action or to symbol systems in explaining outcomes such as solidarity, collective action, or even intellectual production. Put in purely late-Durkheimian terms, this issue is all about the relationship between collective representations and ritual behavior. Expressed in the context of major

PHILIP SMITH AND JEFFREY C. ALEXANDER

fault lines within cultural sociology, it is a more local specification of the broader distinction between approaches that draw on the pragmatist and network traditions (Collins 1975, Swidler 1986) and those emerging from semiotics and hermeneutics (Alexander 2003a, Sahlins 1976, Sewell 1980). Whereas the former stress how practical action and patterns of human association give rise to group norms, beliefs and solidarities, the latter perspective looks more strongly to cultural systems as motivating and constraining behavior.

The very existence of this debate testifies to a deep ambiguity in the interpretation of Durkheim's oeuvre. All would agree that Durkheim's later work pointed to the intricate connection between embodied practical actions, on the one hand, and systems of ideas on the other (for a detailed discussion see Shilling this volume). Rituals in his formulation both express and reinforce collective representations and solidaristic emotions. Yet in subsequent scholarship this precarious balance has been decided one way or the other. For some, actions give rise to beliefs. Randall Collins (1975, 1998), for example, has built on Goffman in arguing that solidarity is built up from mutually satisfactory exchanges between individuals. Similarly David Kertzer and others have asserted that rituals generate collective action and collective identity in the absence of prior overarching cultural agreement or any clear understanding of their purpose among practitioners (Kertzer 1989, cf. Schwartz 2000: 64). According to this logic, rituals are a form of practical action that persists without a systematic cultural foundation.

This formulation has the merit of avoiding idealism and reified visions of culture, but can easily tend towards reductionism of one kind or another. For example, it flirts with a kind of biological reductionism wherein intense embodied experiences of a pre-social entity, developed in coordinated actions with others give rise to pro-social emotions that produce culture, identity and solidarity in turn. Here patterns of shared meaning are simply an aggregate of multiple encounters; we have no need for semiotics or for complex theories of ideology to understand what culture is, what it does or why people should want to come together in the first place. As a result, our attention shifts from decoding culture as text to cataloguing interaction settings, gestures, and hard-wired emotional responses. Another form of reductionism emerging from pragmatism is towards rational choice models and exchange, with individuals standing somehow outside of culture and using it strategically to shape paths of ritual and symbolic action. Within this pattern, motivations for action become thin and, indeed, rather un-Durkheimian, for the idea that action is subject to some kind of internalized moral constraint, the residue of a collective conscience, becomes unsustainable. It is entirely symptomatic and instructive that Goffman's own work exhibits both of these reductionist traits. In its quest to anchor a pragmatic reading of Durkheim, it careens endlessly around like a pinball in a machine whose solenoids are (1) assertions that there is an overarching moral order or imperative anchored in the self and in behavioral codes (e.g. the sacred nature of the individual), (2) demonstrations of how individuals reflexively and strategically orient to this moral order, and (3) analogies drawn from ethology that are superimposed on human behavior to reflect upon these strategies and behaviors.

The alternate position is to read Durkheim as a proto-theorist of cultural codes and their practical application. Here, collective representations such as totems, taboos, myths, sacred spaces, and objects, classifications and moral obligations are understood as a meta-text that shapes the concrete practices – the social performances (see below) – of social life. Although reinforced by both ritual and everyday life, these are always in some part prior to concrete action and cannot be reduced to its product. Not only do they constitute an ontologically autonomous "social fact" but they also form the internal reservoir of motivations, emotions, cognitions, and dispositions that bring people together so that they may interact in the first place. Rather than purely textual, or purely instrumental, this reading of Durkheim gestures toward a "cultural pragmatics" (Alexander 2003b; Alexander 2004; Alexander and Mast forthcoming).

What is remarkable about this volume is the way that it documents the number of Durkheim-relevant topics each of these positions can address. In other words, rather than just contending accounts of well chewed over topics like ritual, we find scattered in this text "pragmatist/network" explanations and "idealist" explanations for human evolution, social theory production, social theory content, group identification and social dramas. It might be useful to indicate some of the ways that the contributions to this volume exemplify this fundamental division. We turn first to works which see action leading to meaning. Randall Collins (this volume) claims he will use Durkheim's sociology to explain Durkheim's sociology. In his reading, this means accounting for Durkheim's intellectual product and subsequent readings of this legacy through a network theory of knowledge. For Collins the *Année sociologique* was akin to a social movement whose intellectual vitality and creativity arose from intense exchanges of "idea-emblems" within its network and with other networks with which it intersected at its margins. Intellectual commitments arose as a result of these exchanges, not as a precondition for them. Durkheim and his students didn't write and talk about the sacred because they cared about it – rather they came to care about it because of all that writing and talking activity.

The famous scenes towards the beginning of Stanley Kubrick's film *2001: A Space Odyssey* are entitled "The Dawn of Man." Here our simian ancestors are depicted as struck with awe and terror by a mysterious and sacred obelisk. We see them bang bones and rocks together in a collective frenzy. They gibber, grunt and scream to each other, clearly excited by the percussive and vocal energy. At the close of the sequence an ape throws a femur into the air, and, as it spins, we cut to a shot of a slowly revolving space station. The howling monkey noises are replaced by soothing tones of *The Blue Danube* courtesy of Herbert von Karajan and the Berlin Philharmonic Orchestra. Such is human progress. Kubrick was engaging in myth-making activity with this film. Yet he may have stumbled on some kind of truth in his account of human evolution, for Robert Bellah's chapter brings his striking images to mind. According to Bellah, the "doing" of ritual preceded the possibility for any complex cultural system. Repetition and rhythm involving the sensory and motor systems provided the foundation for trust and intersubjectivity, these in turn leading to synergistic and evolutionary elaborations of the cerebral cortex and the symbol systems that we call culture. Within this perspective, then, we see an argument with a resemblance to Collins', only here meaning is emerging from action over a very *longue durée*. David Grusky and Gabriela Galescu make a similar point with respect to yet another context, that of occupational solidarities and identities. According to them, we need to look at intermediary groups and patterns of association within labor markets, rather than at aggregate classes and ideologies, if we are to understand such ties between work and culture as class consciousness. The resulting call for a "micro-level agenda" that explores "local social organization" is entirely consistent with Collins' understanding that proximate social networks and affiliations are determinate of ideal commitments and beliefs. Robert Alun Jones provides an account of Durkheim's theory production as well as a reading of his theory that is in line with this logic. He argues that understanding ritual as a "positive" social force can be traced to a series of intellectual exchanges and debates on religion that crisscrossed the Channel. Moreover, he sees Durkheim as intellectually indebted to Jamesian pragmatism, albeit in a coded way. According to Jones, "Durkheim insisted that religious experience and practice were far more important than ideas and doctrines, for the reality on which religion depends is not the result of metaphysical speculation but concrete social action" (Jones p. 94 below). This position echoes that of Collins on the interpretation of Durkheim, although it has a vision of theory formation that weights contexts other than face-to-face contact. In this case a textually mediated academic debate over the interpretation of totemism provided the proximate environment within which knowledge was produced.

Somewhat opposed to this position are essays that give priority to cultural systems. Chris Shilling provides a twist on this theme by suggesting that the body – an irreducible *point de départ* for pragmatic and interaction theory – is always already social as well as material. Through an analysis of totemism and the concept of *homo duplex* in Durkheim, Shilling shows that the body is a crucial medium "through which the symbolic order of the clan is reproduced" (p. 215). This cultural system is, however, irreducible to the body or to individual experience. It is this very transcendence that allows humans to escape the material constraint of the individual body and enter into social life as full subjects in the collectivity. Such a theme is further developed in a psychoanalytic direction by Roger Friedland who argues that Durkheim had an understanding of the interplay between the body, libido and symbolic that is in many ways as complex as that of Freud or Lacan. Although there might be an organic nucleus, society spins meanings around this core with such thickness and multi-valency that the body, sexual activity and desire can be more properly understood as expressions an increasingly auto-referential cultural system. Friedland identifies the *Collège de sociologie* as a research tradition that picked up on the potential for synergy between the psychoanalytic and Durkheimian traditions. Alexander Riley also considers this grouping as pivotal. His treatment challenges the assertions of Collins on knowledge formation. While paying due attention to the intellectual, associational and political contexts of Durkheimian thinking, Riley suggests that a more transcendental obsession with ultimate concerns, mystery and annihilation propelled the *Collège de sociologie* on its mission as much as any material and immediate determination. Moreover, although efforts were made to ground ideas in individual experience, the sacred was experienced and analyzed by the group in ways that were already textually and theoretically mediated. Despite the efforts of the group to encounter the sacred in its raw state, it always came to them cooked. That their conceptions of the sacred were mediated by theory and myth rather than by patterns of interpersonal association suggests a much stronger autonomy for culture than Collins would permit.

Edward Tiryakian's contribution to this volume points to the fact that the solidarity that emerged in the United States after September 11 was not simply the result of a collective effervescence resulting from increased face-to-face contact, but rather was founded on a narrative of national tragedy, heroism and vengeance in which sacred symbols were a precondition for mobilization. Tiryakian does not elaborate on the role of the media, but it seems clear from his account that this is a cultural forum that plays a significant role in shaping and amplifying cultural forces even if it acts at a distance. Not only did it report "facts" to distant citizens, it also served as a myth-engine for contemporary America. These myths then enabled the kind of everyday ritual actions that might give rise to solidarity, such as displaying a flag and participating in remembrance activities. The rise of the mass media and its ability to set agendas, propagate symbolic frames, and generate emotional excitement through, for example, media events (Dayan and Katz 1990) presents a significant challenge to the interactionist/pragmatist tradition. It suggests that we can generate emotional energy and solidarity without reliance on face-to-face contact or "real" social networks.

Writing on the Nuer of the Sudan from a broadly structural Durkheimian perspective, Evans-Pritchard (1940) observed processes of group fission and fusion taking place in response to demographic and political shifts. These were accompanied by a re-writing of the genealogy of the clans and their fictive relationships to mythical ancestors. Such post-facto accounts were functional in that they helped to justify emerging social relationships. Taken as a whole, and with a certain pinch of salt, the distinction we have traced here can be understood in a similar way, with contributions attempting to construct what Malinowski once called a "mythical charter." As the camp of the Cultural Durkheim has grown it has become unwieldy and less able to patch up tensions among its members. A new competition has ensued to write the Durkheimian lineage and appropriate its gods. Earlier in this chapter, we identified four understandings of Durkheim. It seems as if a fifth is emerging even as some of the others wither and fade from relevance. The cultural Durkheim is being split into two moieties, the semiotic and the interactional/pragmatic, with each telling stories and constructing histories to lay out symbolic boundaries and to make sense of their current situation.

What makes a reading of the *Cambridge Companion to Durkheim* fascinating is that we can trace this struggle, myth making and fracturing in each essay. It can be detected in efforts to reconstruct Durkheim's "true" intentions, to map out lines of influence and to specify current relevance. Understood in one way, these essays are contributions to a common, solidaristic project of Durkheim scholarship. At the same time, however, they are part of a war of position. To be able to read the dialogue of these centrifugal and centripetal forces into essays that share a common concern with meaning, ritual, emotion and symbolism is to participate in a powerful intellectual drama whose dénouement we must impatiently await.

We can deal with the second latent debate within the *Cambridge Companion to Durkheim* more briefly, since we have already looked at some of this territory. This is a normative dispute, which revolves around the moral evaluation of Durkheimian theory and its relationship to concepts like freedom, emancipation, justice and democracy. The contestation has two interlocking dimensions. Q1: Can Durkheim provide tools for understanding social contestation, inequality and injustice today? Q2: If so, exactly what kind of good society did he advocate? During the twentieth century this dialogue usually took the form of neo-Marxists pointing to the problems of systems theory (Q1) and to Durkheim's political conservatism (Q2), and answering in the negative. Durkheim's supporters usually retorted by elaborations of functionalist theory to account for social "bads" (Q1, e.g. Merton) and by pointing to his Dreyfusard and socialist sympathies (Q2, e.g. Bellah 1972, Gane 1992). As Zygmunt Bauman's essay (this volume) demonstrates, the terms of debate have now shifted, and we have moved beyond the clash of left and right. The subtlety of his transition to a post-Marxist idiom does not prevent Bauman from stepping into the fray with twin barrels blazing. In effect, he recasts the narrative of the Conservative Durkheim in the mould of his distinctive postmodern ethical theory. Bauman reads Durkheim as a modernist legislator hell-bent on establishing repressive control and regulation under the hegemonic sign of "society." His social theories established a fictive ontology that could be deployed against such unruly anti-modern concepts as free will and contingency, replacing them with a mandate for managerial and legislative intervention and the demand that the individual submit to the needs of society.

This argument – that Durkheim is not only useless for understanding inequality, but also the advocate of a repressive philosophy intolerant of chance, difference and cultural vitality – is confronted indirectly in several of the essays. Consider Grusky and Galescu's contribution. They argue that Durkheim has a theory of class and labor inequality that is in many ways superior to those that have emerged from the Marxist and Weberian traditions. Not least, they suggest, this theory is actually more attentive to the categories of lived experience, solidarity, and diverse labor subjectivities than those more rational and objectivist models that have traditionally been advanced in the name of social emancipation. Alexander's interpretative reconstruction of the inner development of Durkheim's early and middle work supports Grusky and Galescu's more empirically oriented argument. Describing Durkheim's ideological position as equivalent to democratic "socialism with a human face," Alexander finds Durkheim engaged in a sustained argument with the Marxists of his own day. His ambition was to conceptualize social control in a manner that was more respectful of autonomy and subjectivity. Durkheim, then, might be read as the founding father of some of the most morally aware and emancipatory social theory of our time. Writing from a more communitarian perspective, Mark Cladis looks to Durkheim's writings and finds there the basis for a social and moral philosophy for our challenging times. According to Cladis, there are profound similarities between Durkheim's position and those of radical cultural critics such as Cornell West. Solidarity, difference, tolerance, justice, and individuality were all central themes for Durkheim; his ambition was not to eliminate these, but rather to encourage a society where they could be mutually reinforcing. Far from encouraging a Brave New World of regulation and conformity, Durkheim was in fact an advocate of moral pluralism and human dignity.

Challenging the repressive hypothesis from a very different angle, Alexander Riley shows how a tradition of libertarian radicalism also emerged from the *Année sociologique*. In its incarnation at the *Collège de sociologie*, this transgressive sociology elaborates the kind of alternative moral universe that Bauman advocates: existentially aware, anti-authoritarian, and supportive of individuality and spontaneity. Further down the track, this tradition of the "left sacred" was to give rise to analytical positions that made room for the marginal, ambivalent and chaotic (Kristeva and Clement 1998; Barthes 1975; Derrida 1978) or documented and critiqued in detail the very processes of regimentation and normative control that Bauman deplores (Foucault 1967, 1991). In a related spirit Roger Friedland locates erotics and desire at the core of Durkheim's understanding of the social contract. In this provocative reading, order is not imposed from above as a dull and authoritarian gardening exercise but rather emerges from the irrepressible eruption of primal libidinal forces. These are channeled into a multiplicity and proliferation of licit and illicit sexualities and are sublimated in turn into religious myth and practice. For Friedland, Durkheim is the master-theorist of such creative excesses and their pro-social consequences rather than the partisan advocate of social rules, social facts, and social norms as tools for optimal regulation and control.

Other new directions

While the contributions to this volume have taken up several of the most important themes for contemporary Durkheimian thought, no single collection could hope to encompass fully a legacy of such scope and depth. Before concluding this introduction, we would like to briefly acknowledge two further areas where Durkheimian sociology is making its presence felt in innovative ways.

The first of these relates to the study of social regulation in the context of deviance, crime, law and punishment. Elaborations of such themes can be found in the *Rules*, the *Division of Labor*, *Suicide* and also lesser known but substantial works such as *Moral Education* (Durkheim 1973) and the essay on *Two Laws of Penal Evolution* (1973). Despite this scattered treatment, Durkheim's thoughts have given birth to research traditions that continue to have energy and force to this day. Most obviously, Durkheim's anomie theory, filtered through Merton (1968) and the Chicago School, has meshed with the agendas in criminology and psychology to generate a body of

cumulative knowledge of a broadly positivist cast that seems ready to generate important middle range theory over the next few years. Although citation
to Durkheim has become increasingly rare or purely ceremonial in this literature, his emphasis on deviance as an objective social fact generated by other
social facts has fed, for example, into the current crop of innovative studies
of neighborhood ecology and social disorganization as well as the continuing
literature on themes of mental health and suicide. A second track into the
study of deviance initiated by Durkheim also looks to be going strong. This
takes its cue from his insistence on deviance as "normal" or functionally
necessary and has resulted in a focus on the recognition and regulation of
outsiders. The interest here, in contrast to the line coming out of anomie
theory, is on social and cultural process as constructing deviance rather than
on objective patterns of offending. Whether openly acknowledged or not,
Durkheim was an influence at the dawn of research on the media and crime,
on moral panics and moral regulation and on labeling theory (see, e.g. Ben
Yehuda 1985; Erikson 1966). More recent work in this genre has thrown
the functionalist supercargo overboard and compensated with extra ballast
from contemporary cultural theory and, indeed, the *Elementary Forms*. This
has enabled analytic attention to be shifted to the contingent ritual, semiotic
and narrative processes that underpin the identification and control of evil
(Thompson 1998) and away from problematic discussions of social stability
and societal needs. The result has been an interdisciplinary literature with
ties to anthropology, cultural studies, the new cultural history, and media
studies, as well as sociology.

Most interesting and promising of all has been a newfound appreciation
of the importance of Durkheim's model for the study not of deviance, but
of criminal justice. His approach runs counter to the dominant trends in
criminological theory and is being increasingly perceived as relevant to the
understanding of both process and outcomes. To understand the significance
of Durkheim's thinking here, it is necessary to realize that within social
theory, law and punishment have been understood primarily as subordinated to bureaucratic rationality or as expressions of a political logic. Michel
Foucault's work has become emblematic precisely because it combines these
traits. For the Foucault (1974) of *Discipline and Punish*, criminal justice
today is a forum in which new forms of power work through order, routine,
and control. These have decisively replaced earlier, more colorful judicial
and punitive activities that involved ritual and symbolism. Culture persists,
but only as a set of dried out, secular codes for the administration of a rationalized power. Likewise, Habermas (1989: 174–9) takes the law to be an
increasingly abstract force within social life that is progressively decoupled
from the inputs of religion or civil society. Although the law has some utopian

potential as a sphere of linguistically and normatively mediated communicative activity (Habermas 1996), Habermas tends to view legal codes as either entirely procedural or as tied to the "colonization of the lifeworld," one of the means through which the impersonal bureaucratic state has come to regulate social life in civil and private spheres. This scenario has its roots in Weber's (1978) understanding of legal history as an evolutionary movement from prophecy towards formal rationalization, with codification and professionalization stripping the administration of criminal justice of substantive value inputs. For Weber the law has become "a rational technical apparatus which is continually transformable in the light of expediential considerations and devoid of all sacredness of content" (1978: 895).

Within this theoretical landscape, Durkheim's position is distinctive precisely because of his insistence that societal evolution has layered administrative complexity onto an emotional and cultural foundation rather than replacing it. To be sure, societal differentiation has seen the collective conscience shift and penal codes change. Yet, however technologically and procedurally mediated, and however "graduated in intensity" (1968: 48), punishment remains for Durkheim an expressive action that has normative inputs, just as even the most rational of legal systems reflects some underlying collective conscience. Durkheimian scholarship on law and justice has traditionally drawn on part 1, and especially chapter 2, of the *Division of Labor* and been concerned with documenting or developing theories of legal evolution, engaging in a comparative and rather abstract analysis of legal systems or working through the implications of the generic assertion that the law reflects morality or the collective conscience (Cotterrell 1999; Luhmann 1985). The rebirth of a cultural Durkheim which we have related here has seen a new form of scholarship emerge that draws inspiration from cultural anthropology and the new cultural history. Equally pivotal has been a shift in textual influences taken from within Durkheim's own oeuvre. Subtle changes in emphasis have emerged with the movement away from the *Division of Labor* and its concern to tie sanctions to morphology and function, towards *Moral Education* where greater attention is given to punishment as performative and demonstrative, and on to the *Elementary Forms*. Here we find the rudiments of a truly semiotic model in which arbitrary religious codes rather than functional needs for solidarity sit at the heart of primitive taboos and ritualized atonements. The resulting literature has been set free to explore more concretely the ways in which culture-structures and cultural process can be central to both the actual practices of social control and the symbolic logics underpinning the formation of law. In this recent Durkheim-inspired scholarship there has been a shift away from abstraction and generality towards more grounded, concrete analyses of criminal justice as ritualized expression, public dramatization and cultural code. It can be treated as a text that is also informed by, but not reducible to, the forms of power, interests and rationality at play in particular settings (Garland 1990). And so the last few years have witnessed an explosion of studies indicating how even today the sacred and profane, ritual and moral boundaries underpin (to mention only some representative studies and topics) the social meanings of punishment technologies (Smith 2003) and organizations such as the police (Reiner 1995); penal processes such as executions (Smith 1996) and reintegrative shaming (Scheff 1990); the formation of legal codes and the concept of the legal subject (Carlsson and Hoff 2000; Hammond 1996); and the legal protections surrounding collective representations such as national constitutions (Hammond 1989) and flags (Welch and Bryan 1996). Far richer in a hermeneutic sense than the Durkheimian legal scholarship that has gone before it, such work promises to refashion our understanding of law and criminal justice in fundamental ways over the next decades, much as the "discovery" of culturally constructed deviance has done since the 1960s.

This recent turn toward the dramaturgy and iconography of legal and penal processes implicitly evokes the other area of recent Durkheim-inspired work we wish to take up here. When David Garland emphasizes the continuing symbolic and affective dimensions of punishment, he often cites its ritual function (Garland 1990: 21ff; n.d.). In doing so, as we have suggested, he evokes the late Durkheim and extends his "religious sociology" into modern life. Yet, in these same late-Durkheimian studies, Garland (1990: 253–68) also conceptualizes modern punishments as "performances."

Is there a difference that matters between conceptualizing individual and collective action as ritual or as performance? That the two terms seem to alternate freely in Garland's analysis is itself revealing. Garland aims to evoke the affective and symbolic (cultural Durkheim) yet to be responsive, as well, to modern social and cultural differentiation (structural Durkheim). For it is indeed a fact that, in complex societies, those who decide upon punishment are separated by office and organization from those who inflict it, and that both of these agents are differentiated from the victims of punishment and the public audience who observes it. These separations have consequences for the analysis of symbolic action: one cannot necessarily predict that the culturally-inspired decision to punish, or the actual application of punishment, will produce on the audience and the victim anything like a ritual effect. Certainly, penal agents write scripts that aim to display the act of punishing in a manner that will powerfully evoke the moral background structures of society. But the distance and impersonality of the punishment process, and the fragmentation of audiences for these punishments, may neutralize or even reverse the agents' intended effects (e.g. Smith 1996).

The increasing, postmodern awareness of such contingencies has stimulated a discernable theoretical movement from ritual to performance studies in recent years. When Durkheim wrote *Elementary Forms*, he provocatively insisted that his analysis of Australian Aborigines could be directly applied to symbolic processes in modern life (see Alexander 1982 and this volume, below). The references in *Elementary Forms* to contemporary symbolic processes – especially book II, chapter 7, "The Origins of the Totemic Principle, or Mana" (e.g. Durkheim 1995: 210–12) – consistently demonstrate homologous ritual effects in simple and complex societies. As we have suggested earlier in this introduction, this Durkheimian provocation triggered an earthquake in twentieth-century social thought that eventually transformed contemporary social science. Yet, to insist on homology between simple and complex societies is both not enough and too much. Certainly modern social action remains symbolic; symbols continue to purify and pollute; and these "religious processes" construct deep solidarities that mark the foundations of social structure. In simple and complex societies, however, these structures and processes unfold in very different ways.

Since Nietzsche in *The Birth of Tragedy* ([1872] 1956), social theorists have tried to capture this difference in terms of an aesthetic model drawn from theatre and drama. Theatre, after all, can create ritual-like experiences, yet it works to evoke such effects in a contrived, ratiocinative way. In the same manner, the "rituals" of modern and postmodern societies – whether formal state occasions (Shils and Young [1956] 1975) or more open-ended and ephemeral media events (Dayan and Katz 1990) – can be seen as social dramas whose effects depend on their ability to achieve an aesthetically powerful theatrical form.

If we return to *Elementary Forms* with these observations in mind, we can discern some brief but significant indications that Durkheim was not himself insensitive to the fact that rituals have a performative dimension. Most broadly, of course, the very idea of rituals indicates attention to place, setting, timing, and interaction, not only to abstract beliefs. This emphasis is a distinctive but not sufficiently remarked upon element of Durkheim's famous definition of church: "A society whose members are united because they *imagine* in the same ways the sacred world and its relationship with the profane world, *and* because they *translate* this shared representation in identical practices" (1912: 60. This and the following quotes from the *Elementary Forms* are our translation). It is necessary, then, not only that people believe in a set of ideas but that they have the ability to enact them. That such translating practices involve an aesthetic dimension is clear from the emphasis Durkheim places on imagination. Beliefs about the sacred and profane involve active fantasy and creativity, not only cognitive assertions about belief. This reference to the creative and artistic element is also evident in Durkheim's insistence, at a later point in *Elementary Forms*, that elementary religious life depends on "figurative representations of the totem" and that the "imagination represents with figures borrowed, with a few exceptions, from either the animal kingdom or vegetable kingdom" (1912: 268, 270). The creative practices that translate the sacred into such a figurative but concrete form can only be theatrical. We are not surprised, then, to see Durkheim writing several pages later that "imagining religious things" is accomplished because a sacred "force can be attached to words spoken, to gestures made" and that "the voice and movements can serve as its vehicle, and, by their mediation it can produce its effects" (1912: 286).

This line of Durkheim's thinking reaches its logical conclusion in his discussion of the positive cult and representative rites. While insisting that "religious thought is something altogether different from a system of fictions," he asserts, at the same time, that "between society, as it is objectively, and the sacred things that represent it symbolically, there is a considerable distance" (1912: 544). This can be overcome only through imaginative and creative effort: "It is necessary for the impressions actually experienced by men and which are the primary materials for this construction, to be interpreted, developed, and transformed until they become unrecognizable. So the world of religious things is . . . a partly imaginary world which for this reason lends itself obediently to the free creations of the spirit" (1912: 545).

Durkheim illustrates this process of practical aesthetic translation, which involves imaginative interpreting, elaborating, and transforming, by reconstructing Spencer and Gillen's account of the Warramunga's Intichiuma ceremony. Implicitly evoking his earlier reference to words spoken and gestures made, to voices and movement, Durkheim suggests that "the rite consists uniquely of remembering the past and in rendering it present, as it were, by means of a true dramatic performance" (1912: 531). His description of the rite continues in a manner that elaborates this understanding.

> The celebrant is in no way considered as an incarnation of the ancestor which he represents, he is an actor playing a role . . . They put into action the mythical history of the ancestor Thallaualla . . . The movement that recurs more frequently consists of a sort of violent rhythmic trembling of the entire body, because the ancestor did this in mythical times to scatter the seeds of life which were inside him. The actors have their skin covered with a down that, as a result of this shaking, becomes detached and flies away. This is a way of representing the flight of the mystical germs and their dispersion through space . . . The place where the ceremony unfolds . . . is a conventional stage. The place where the events took place that are the theme of the rite are represented

by designs. Sometimes these designs are made on the bodies of the actors . . .
In other cases it is in the earth that that the image is traced. On the ground,
previously watered down and covered in red ochre, are traced curved lines
made from a series of white points, which symbolize a river or a mountain.
This is the beginning of scenery . . . These ceremonies . . . are dramas, albeit
plays of a particular kind . . . These dramas are rites.   (1912: 531–4)

Yet, even as he adumbrates contemporary theories of social performance,
Durkheim expresses misgivings about the constructed, contingent, indeed
performative aspects of this ritual event. Despite "the duality of the ancestor
and the celebrant" (1912: 535), Durkheim now insists that representative
rites are successful only if the celebrant actually copies the ancestor's original
actions. Only if "the gestures he makes are those the ancestor made in the
same circumstances," can there be "a sense [that] the hero occupies the stage"
(1912: 535). But it is this "sense" that is at question from a performative
point of view. It depends on actor skillfulness and audience response. Yet
Durkheim concludes, in seeming contradiction of his earlier position, that
the celebrant "does not play the ancestral personage, as an actor would do,"
Rather, "he is that person" (1912: 535).

We can understand this slippage from the contingencies of performance to
the security of ontological ritual if we understand Durkheim's deeper anxiety.
When "certain people are charged with representing ancestors with whom
they have no mythical tie of descent" (1912: 535) he warns, rites can become
"dramatic performances in the literal sense." In fact, this is just what happened in the Emu's Intichiuma ceremony, the single instance that Durkheim
highlights where "it seems as if the theatre of the ceremony is *artificially*
arranged" (1912: 535 italics added). With this pejorative phrasing, it becomes
crystal clear that Durkheim views the theatrical metaphor as threatening his
project of religious sociology. To allow contrivance into ritual theory, he
fears, would allow play and entertainment to undermine the tight, more
authentic connection between symbolic action and *la vie sérieuse*. "We have
already shown that these are closely related to dramatic performances . . .
Not only do they employ the same procedures as true drama, they also chase
after the same goal . . . They make men forget the real world and transport
them to another where their imaginations can be more at ease; they entertain. Sometimes they even have the outward appearance of recreation: we
see the assistants laughing and openly having fun" (1912: 543).

A related danger is that representative rites, and what Durkheim now calls
"the collective recreations," are "so close to each other that one passes from
one genre to the other without loss of continuity" (1912: 543). This situation
can be associated with "the slackening of the tie that attaches to the history

of the tribe the events and personages represented" so that the rites "take on an unreal air and the corresponding ceremonies change their nature. In this way we gradually enter into the domain of pure fantasy and move from commemorative rite to vulgar corroboree, a simple public celebration that has nothing to do with religion any more . . ." (1912: 544). Or to put it bluntly, "when a rite serves no purpose but to entertain it is no longer a rite" (1912: 546).

No doubt Durkheim was also worried that the theatrical analogy would make symbolic actors seem less sincere and, in this way, undermine his democratic-republican argument that social and political authority can, and should, be sustained by deeply meaningful symbolic action and not primarily by coercive forms of structural power or debased populist sentiments. From a normative perspective, of course, distinguishing clearly between instrumental and contrived action, on the one hand, and moral and sincere action, on the other, makes a great deal of sense (e.g. Habermas 1987). From the perspective of empirical analysis, however, there is a danger. Building a firewall between such ideal-types prevents recognizing both as dimensions of every symbolic act. In real life, they are always analytically differentiated yet empirically intertwined. In contrast with the ideal world postulated by normative theory, the aesthetic and the contrived enter into the heart of symbolic action. To conceptualize their interrelation with sacred symbolism and moral concerns is essential if one wishes to theorize the complex and contingent possibilities for creating solidarity in modern symbolic life.

It has taken most of the last century to develop Durkheim's early premonitions about performativity, and it has depended upon leaving behind his rather straight-laced, if normatively understandable, ideological concerns. Even in the recent postwar period, such influential late-Durkheimian thinkers as Shils and Young ([1956] 1975) and Bellah (1970: 168–89) still conceptualized ritual in a way that separated it from the contingencies of complex performance, implicitly suggesting an either/or approach to social action, i.e. that it was instrumental or symbolic, authentic or artificial. Critical theory, whether of Marxist or existential provenance, echoed this dichotomizing tendency in a more pessimistic way.

Yet, during this same period, a new and more complex approach to symbolic action was being developed. Kenneth Burke (1965) suggested that action should be viewed neither as instrumental nor as ritualized but as performative. Drawing upon the Cambridge classicists who had followed up Nietzsche's link between ritual and Greek drama, Burke's "dramaturgical" theory laid out the theatrical elements of social action. Taking a cue from Burke and Durkheim, Erving Goffman (1956) elaborated a pragmatic approach to the staging of face-to-face interaction, and Clifford Geertz

(1973; 1980) developed a more semiotic model of collective performance. Victor Turner (1974) went on to create an impressionistic but highly innovative theory of "social drama," and it was only a matter of time before he teamed up with the dramatist Richard Schechner to declare rituals only theatre by another name (Turner 1982; 1987).

On this basis of this collaboration, Schechner (1976; 1977; 1987; 2002) eventually created "performance studies," the interdisciplinary field that bridges theatre, film, literature, and the social sciences. While the empirical complexities of contemporary social performance, and the sociological concepts for framing them, have only begun to be worked out, it seems that, in his early and ambivalent effort, Durkheim had the basic idea right. Ritual can be understood as performance if the elements that rituals seem "naturally" to combine are analytically broken down. As one line of current thinking suggests, performances are composed of background representations, foregrounded scripts, actors, means of symbolic production, social power, *mise-en-scène*, and audience (see Alexander 2003b, 2003c, forthcoming; Alexander and Mast forthcoming). When these elements are fused – for example, when the "celebrant," or actor, really does seem to be the ancestor he is portraying – then symbolic action has verisimilitude and can take on a ritual-like form. When these various performative elements are not brought together in such a "felicitous" way (Austin 1957), when they are de-fused, performances seem artificial and contrived.

Fused performances are rituals because they are utterly convincing, and Durkheim was right to attribute to such symbolic action the capacity for exercising social authority. De-fused performances fail in their suasive effort, and they are both cause and effect of social conflict and dissent. Critics and audiences laugh at performances that are intended to make them cry; citizen-publics are ironic and dismissive when authorities would have them be attentive and sincere. The further we move away from the comforts and simplicity of smaller and more traditional societies – the very societies upon whose elementary forms Durkheim rested his theoretical case – the harder it is to make rituals stick. Symbolic actions often seem "artificially set up," but not always. This variation is what justifies the continuing relevance of ritual-performance theory today.

The new Durkheim: calling cards and tarot cards

This text does not mark the end of Durkheim, nor even the beginning of an end. Rather, as Churchill might have said, it is the end of the beginning. Classics are hard to understand, and, as we have explained in this introduction, they come to be approached variously in contexts determined by time, place, politics and intellectual history. It is fair to say that it took almost three-quarters of the last century to start to discover what Durkheim, at his best, was really going on about. Once this understanding had been attained, and once the broader historical context had shifted, there ensued a tremendous outpouring of new work. This volume joins other recent edited collections indicating that the center of gravity has decisively shifted from the early and middle Durkheim to the late.[2] We expect it will not be the last. With this new Durkheim securely enthroned, the intellectual agenda has been altered for Durkheim's second hundred years. In Durkheim's first century, the concepts that occupied scholarly debates were structure, function, method, social fact, anomie, suicide, law, socialism, and the division of labor. These are now residual: they were the beginning. We are now at the end of the beginning, and a second set of concepts has come to the fore: ritual, collective representations and discourse, the sacred, solidarity, collective conscience, democracy, and interaction. From these openings there are developing a new set of Durkheimian concerns that are many and various, concerns about performance, justice, regulation, transgression, evil, memory, networks, civil society, morality, punishment, body, practice, difference, emotion, and narrative.

As these lists suggest, the field of themes and correspondences to be worked through is opening upwards, to the kind of productive excess celebrated by Bataille, rather than spiraling downwards to entropy. We are at the end of the beginning rather than the beginning of the end, entering a phase that will witness the construction, not reduction, of complexity from the interplay of these new concepts. We cannot soothsay what talismanic hands will be dealt from these signifiers, or how, in our lifetimes, such collective representations will be played out. The *Cambridge Companion to Durkheim* is not a tarot pack. For all that, it does offer new and diverse accounts of where Durkheim has left his calling card and where he will be visiting next. Perceptive readers will put together their own itineraries.

NOTES

1 We have taken the liberty of reprinting for this volume a revised version of the article in which Alexander summarized this argument.

2 Two collections of essays on Durkheim appeared in English in the early postwar period – an original collection by Wolff (1960) and a compilation of previously published material by Nisbet (1965). Only after these publications, however, did there occur the scholarly renaissance upon which most contemporary Durkheim interpretation rests. In terms of this recent scholarship, the most important ongoing source has been the journal *Durkheimian Studies / Etudes Durkheimiennes*. This pivotal publication first appeared in 1977 in Paris as *Etudes Durkheimiennes*, under the leadership of the late Philippe Besnard. In 1989, Robert Alun

Jones took over as editor, and the journal moved to America. In 1995, the location and editorial board changed hands again, moving to the Oxford Centre for Durkheimian Studies, under the editorial board of W. S. F. Pickering, Kenneth Thompson, William Watts Miller, and Mike Gain. These editors and their associates have engaged in a prolific publishing agenda since the early 1990s that has done much to demonstrate the continuing relevance of Durkheim for social science (e.g. Allen, Pickering, and Watts Miller 1998; Pickering 1999; Pickering and Watts-Miller 1993; for a fuller listing consult the comprehensive bibliography, this volume). These efforts, many of which build upon mini-conferences held at the Oxford Centre, offer independent confirmation of the patterns we find in this volume. There is clearly less interest in writing about Durkheim as a positivist, functionalist, and conservative than in establishing his status as a prescient cultural theorist and democratic moral philosopher. (It is unfortunate that, although quite recent, several of these publications are out of print or are available only as pdf downloads from their publishers.) Aside from England, the other centre of gravity for edited volumes of Durkheim scholarship has been France, where there have been recent collections of original essays (Besnard et al. 1993, Cuin 1997, Borlandi and Cherkaoui 2000), marking the centenaries of *The Division of Labor in Society*, *The Rules of Sociological Method* and *Suicide*. These have been targeted to specific themes rather than to considerations of Durkheim's work in general. Taken as a whole, the recently published French and English volumes emphasize Durkheim scholarship rather than Durkheimian scholarship and Durkheimian sociology. If we were to paint with a broad brush, the emphasis tends to be on the detailed interpretation and understanding of Durkheim rather than opening out his scholarship to wider agendas and landscapes in social and cultural theory. The Cambridge Companion contains works of both stripes. We have included Durkheim scholars engaged in textual and biographical exegesis (the first section of this book) and outsiders who wish to apply, test, and expand Durkheim's ideas in broader theoretical and empirical arenas (the subsequent sections). We see this heterogeneity as a fundamental and necessary characteristic of the ongoing wave of Durkheimian renewal and critique.

REFERENCES

Alexander, Jeffrey. Cultural Pragmatics: Social Performance Between Ritual and Strategy, *Sociological Theory* 22(4): 527–73.
  2003a. *The Meanings of Social Life: A Cultural Sociology*. New York: Oxford University Press.
  2003b. "Towards a New, Macrosociological Theory of Performance." *Theory*, Spring: 3–5.
  2003c. "From the Depths of Despair: Performance, Counter-Performance, and 'September 11.'" *Sociological Theory* 22(1): 88–105.
  2002d. "On the Social Construction of Moral Universals: The 'Holocaust' from War Crime to Trauma Drama." *European Journal of Social Theory* 5 (1): 5–85.
  (ed.) 1988a. *Durkheimian Sociology: Cultural Studies*. New York and Cambridge: Cambridge University Press.

1988b. "Introduction: Durkheimian Sociology and Cultural Studies Today." pp. 1–22 in *Durkheimian Sociology: Cultural Studies*. Edited by Jeffrey C. Alexander. New York and Cambridge: Cambridge University Press.

1988c. "Culture and Political Crisis: Watergate and Durkheimian Sociology." pp. 187–224 in *Durkheimian Sociology: Cultural Studies*. Edited by Jeffrey C. Alexander. New York and Cambridge: Cambridge University Press.

1982. *Theoretical Logic in Sociology*. Vol. 2, *The Antinomies of Classical Thought: Marx and Durkheim*. Berkeley. University of California Press.

Alexander, Jeffrey C., Ron Eyerman, Bernhard Giesen, Neil Smelser and Piotr Sztompka (eds.) 2004. *Cultural Trauma and Collective Identity*. Berkeley and Los Angeles: University of California Press.

Alexander, Jeffrey C. and Jason Mast. n.d. "Cultural Pragmatics: From Text to Performance in Cultural and Sociological Theory" in *The New Performative Turn in Social Science*. Edited by Jeffrey C. Alexander, Jason Mast, and Bernhard Giesen, forthcoming.

Alexander, Jeffrey C. and Steven J. Sherwood. 2002. "'Mythic Gesture': Robert N. Bellah and Cultural Sociology." pp. 1–14 in *Meaning and Modernity: Religion, Polity, and Self*. Edited by Richard Madsen, William M. Sullivan, Ann Swidler, and Steven M. Tipton. Berkeley and Los Angeles: University of California Press.

Alexander, Jeffrey C. and Philip Smith. 1996a. "Durkheim's Religious Revival." *American Journal of Sociology* 102: 585–92.

1996b. "Risk Society as Mythical Discourse." *Zeitschrift für Soziologie* 25: 251–66.

Allen, N. J., W. S. F. Pickering and William Watts Miller (eds.) 1998. *On Durkheim's Elementary Forms of Religious Life*. London: Routledge.

Austin, John L. 1957. *How To Do Things with Words*. Cambridge: Cambridge University Press.

Barthes, Roland. 1975. *S/Z*. London: Jonathan Cape.

[1964] 1984. *Writing Degree Zero and Elements of Semiology*. London: Jonathan Cape.

[1957] 1973. *Mythologies*. St. Albans: Paladin.

Bellah, Robert. 1970. *Beyond Belief*. New York: Harper and Row.

Ben Yehuda, Nachman. 1985. *Deviance and Moral Boundaries*. Chicago: University of Chicago Press.

Besnard, Philippe (ed.) 1983. *The Sociological Domain: The Durkheimians and the Founding of French Sociology*. Cambridge: Cambridge University Press.

1979. "La Formation de l'équipe de l'Année Sociologique." *Review française de sociologie* 20: 7–31.

Besnard, Philippe, Massimo Borlandi and Paul Voigt (eds.) 1993. *Division du Travail et lien Social. La thèse de Durkheim un siècle après*. Paris: Presses Universitaires de France.

Bloom, Harold. 1975. *The Anxiety of Influence*. New York: Oxford University Press.

Borlandi, Massimo and Mohamed Cherkaoui (eds.) 2000. *Le Suicide un siècle après Durkheim*. Paris: Presses Universitaires de France.

Bourdieu, Pierre. 1990. *The Logic of Practice*. Cambridge: Cambridge University Press.

Brook, Peter. 1984. *The Melodramatic Imagination*. New York: Columbia University Press.

Burke, Kenneth. 1965. "Dramatism." *Encyclopedia of the Social Sciences* 7: 445–51.

Carlsson, Bo and David Hoff. 2000. "Dealing with Insolvency and Indebted Individuals in Respect to Law and Morality." *Social and Legal Studies* 9: 293–317.

Chan, Elaine. 1999. "Structural and Symbolic Citizens: Centre Displacement in the 1989 Chinese Student Movement." *International Sociology* 14(3): 337–56.

Collins, Randall. 1998. *The Sociology of Philosophies: A Global Theory of Intellectual Change*. Cambridge, MA: Harvard University Press.

1975. *Conflict Sociology*. New York: Academic Press.

Connerton, Paul. 1989. *How Societies Remember*. Cambridge: Cambridge University Press.

Coser, Lewis A. 1992. "Introduction" in *Maurice Halbwachs: On Collective Memory*. Chicago: University of Chicago Press.

Cotterrell, Roger. 1999. *Émile Durkheim: Law in a Moral Domain*. Stanford: Stanford University Press.

Cuin, Charles-Henry. 1997. *Durkheim d'un siècle a l'autre: lectures actuelles des "Règles de la méthode sociologique"*. Paris: Presses Universitaires de France.

Dayan, Daniel, and Elihu Katz. 1990. *Media Events: The Live Broadcasting of History*. Cambridge: Cambridge University Press.

Derrida, Jacques. 1978. *Writing and Difference*. Chicago: Chicago University Press.

Douglas, Mary. 1966. *Purity and Danger*. London: Routledge and Kegan Paul.

Douglas, Mary and Aaron Wildavsky. 1982. *Risk and Culture*. Berkeley: University of California Press.

Durkheim, Émile. 1973a. "Two Laws of Penal Evolution". *Economy and Society* 2: 285–308.

1973b. *Moral Education*. New York: Free Press.

1912. *Les Formes Elémentaires de la vie religieuse*. Paris: Librairie Félix Alcan.

[1897] 1966. *Suicide*. New York: Free Press.

[1895] 1966. *The Rules of Sociological Method*. New York: Free Press.

[1893] 1964. *The Division of Labor in Society*. New York: Free Press.

Durkheim, Émile and Marcel Mauss. [1903] 1963. *Primitive Classification*. Chicago: University of Chicago Press.

Edles, Laura Desfor. 1998. *Symbol and Ritual in the New Spain: The Transition to Democracy after Franco*. Cambridge: University of Cambridge Press.

Eisenstadt, Schmuel. 1963. *The Political System of Empires*. New York: Free Press.

Erikson, Kai. 1966. *Wayward Puritans*. New York: Wiley.

Evans-Pritchard, E. E. 1940. *The Nuer*. Oxford: Oxford University Press.

1956. *Nuer Religion*. Oxford: Clarendon Press.

Eyerman, Ron. 2001. *Cultural Trauma: Slavery and the Formation of African American Identity*. Cambridge: Cambridge University Press.

Foucault, Michel. [1974] 1991. *Discipline and Punish*. London: Penguin.

[1961] 1967. *Madness and Civilization*. London: Tavistock.

Gane, Mike (ed.) 1992. *The Radical Sociology of Durkheim and Mauss*. London: Routledge.

Garland, David. 1990. *Punishment and Modern Society*. Oxford: Oxford University Press.

n.d. "Penal Excess and Surplus Meaning: Public Torture Lynchings and Twentieth Century America." Manuscript, forthcoming.

Geertz, Clifford. 1980. *Negara: The Theatre State in Nineteenth Century Bali*. Princeton: Princeton University Press.

1973. *The Interpretation of Cultures*. London: Hutchinson.

Giesen, Bernhardt. 2004. *From Triumph to Trauma*. Boulder, CO: Paradigm Publishers.

1998. *Intellectuals and the Nation: Collective Identity in a German Axial Age*. Cambridge: Cambridge University Press.

Goffman, Erving. 1956. *The Presentation of Self in Everyday Life*. Garden City, NY: Anchor Books.

1967. *Interaction Ritual*. Garden City, NY: Anchor Books.

Habermas, Jurgen. 1996. *Between Facts and Norms*. Cambridge, MA: MIT Press.

1993. "Remarks on Discourse Ethics." pp. 19–112 in *Justification and Application*. Cambridge, MA: MIT Press.

1989. *The Theory of Communicative Action*. Vol. 2. Boston: Beacon Press.

Hagstrom, Warren. 1965. *The Scientific Community*. New York: Basic Books.

Hammond, Phillip E. 1996. "Conscience and the Establishment Clause: The Courts Remake the Sacred." *Journal for the Scientific Study of Religion* 35: 365–7.

1989. "Constitutional Faith, Legitimating Myth, Civil Religion." *Law and Social Inquiry* 14: 377–91.

Hartman, Geoffrey. 1987. "The Use and Abuse of Structural Analysis." pp. 129–51 in *The Unremarkable Wordsworth*. London: Methuen.

Hertz, Robert. [1907] 1960. *Death and the Right Hand*. Glencoe, IL: Free Press.

Hunt, Lynn (ed.) 1989. *The New Cultural History*. Berkeley: University of California Press.

Jacobs, Ronald. 1996. "Civil Society and Crisis." *American Journal of Sociology* 101: 1238–72.

Jakobson, Roman. 1990. *On Language*. Cambridge, MA: Harvard University Press.

Kertzer, David. 1989. *Ritual, Politics and Power*. New Haven: Yale University Press.

Kristeva, Julia and Clement, Catherine. 1998. *Féminin et le Sacré*. Paris: Stock.

Ku, Agnes. 1999. *Narratives, Politics and the Public Sphere*. Aldershot: Ashgate.

Lacroix, Bernard. 1981. *Durkheim et la politique*. Paris: Fondation des Sciences politiques and Montréal: Presses de l'Université de Montréal.

Lamont, Michele. 1987. "How to Become a Dominant French Philosopher: The Case of Jacques Derrida." *American Journal of Sociology* 93: 584–622.

Levi-Strauss, Claude. 1966. *The Savage Mind*. London: Weidenfeld and Nicolson.

Levy, Marion. 1952. *The Structure of Society*. Princeton: Princeton University Press.

Lincoln, Bruce. 1989. *Discourse and the Construction of Society*. New York: Oxford University Press.

Lockwood, David. 1964. "Social Integration and System Integration" in *Explorations in Social Change*. Edited by George K. Zollschan and Walter Hirsch. New York.

Luhmann, Niklas. 1985. *Social Theory of Law*. London: Routledge and Kegan Paul.

1982. *The Differentiation of Society*. New York: Columbia University Press.

Lukes, Steven. 1975. "Political Ritual and Social Integration." *Sociology* 9: 289–308.

1977. *Émile Durkheim: His Life and Work*. New York: Harper and Row.

Mann, Michael. 1970. "The Social Cohesion of Liberal Democracy." *American Sociological Review* 35: 423–39.

Merton, Robert. [1938] 1968. "Social Structure and Anomie." pp. 185–214 in *Social Theory and Social Structure*. New York: Free Press.

Moscovici, Serge. 1990 *The Invention of Society*. Cambridge: Polity Press.

Nietzsche, Friedrich. [1872] 1956. *The Birth of Tragedy*. pp. 1–146 in *The Birth of Tragedy and the Genealogy of Morals* by Frederik Nietzsche. New York: Anchor Books.

Nisbet, Robert A. 1965. *Émile Durkheim*. Englewood Cliffs, NJ: Prentice-Hall.

Parsons, Talcott. 1966. *Societies: Evolutionary and Comparative Perspectives*. Englewood Cliffs, NJ: Prentice Hall.

[1937] 1968. *The Structure of Social Action*. New York: Free Press.

Pickering, W. S. F. (ed.) 1999. *Durkheim and Representations*. London: Routledge.

Pickering, W. S. F. and William Watts Miller (eds.) 1993. *Individualism and Human Rights in the Durkheimian Tradition*. Oxford: British Centre for Durkheimian Studies.

Rappaport, Lynn. 1997. *Jews in Germany after the Holocaust: Memory, Identity and Jewish–German Relations*. Cambridge: Cambridge University Press.

Reiner, Robert. 1995. "From Sacred to Profane: The Thirty Years' War of the British Police." *Policing and Society* 5: 121–8.

Rorty, Richard. 1980. *Philosophy and the Mirror of Nature*. Princeton: Princeton University Press.

Rosati, Massimo. 2002. *Solidarietà e sacro*. Rome: Editori Latevza.

Sahlins, Marshall. 1976. *Culture and Practical Reason*. Chicago: University of Chicago Press.

Saussure, Ferdinand de. 1959. *Course in General Linguistics*. New York: McGraw Hill.

Schechner, Richard. 2002. *Performance Studies: An Introduction*. New York: Routledge.

1987. "Victor Turner's Last Adventure." pp. 7–20 in *The Anthropology of Performance* by Victor Turner and Richard Schechner. New York: Performing Arts Journal Press.

1977. *Ritual, Play, and Social Drama*. New York: Seabury Press.

1976. "From Ritual to Theatre and Back." pp. 196–230 in *Ritual, Play, and Performance: Readings in the Social Sciences/Theatre*. Edited by Richard Schechner and Mady Schuman. New York: Seabury Press.

Scheff, Thomas. 1990. "Review Essay: A New Durkheim." *American Journal of Sociology* 96: 741–6.

Schwartz, Barry. 2000. *Abraham Lincoln and the Forge of National Memory*. Chicago: University of Chicago Press.

Sewell, William H. 1980. *Work and Revolution in France*. New York: Cambridge University Press.

Shils, Edward. 1975. *Centre and Periphery: Essays in Macrosociology*. Chicago: University of Chicago Press.

Shils, Edward and Michael Young. [1956] 1975. "The Meaning of the Coronation." pp. 135–54 in *Center and Periphery* by Edward Shils. Chicago: University of Chicago Press.

Smelser, Neil. 1959. *Social Change in the Industrial Revolution*. London: Routledge and Kegan Paul.

Smith, Philip. 2003. "Narrating the Guillotine: Punishment Technology as Myth and Symbol." *Theory, Culture and Society* 20: 27–51.

2001. *Cultural Theory: An Introduction.* New York: Blackwell.

1996. "Executing Executions: Aesthetics, Identity and the Problematic Narratives of Capital Punishment Ritual." *Theory and Society* 25: 235–61.

1991. "Codes and Conflict." *Theory and Society* 20: 103–38.

Spillman, Lyn. 1997. *Nation and Commemoration.* Cambridge: Cambridge University Press.

Swidler, Ann. 1986. "Culture in Action: Symbols and Strategies." *American Sociological Review* 51: 273–86.

Thompson, Kenneth. 1998. *Moral Panics.* London: Routledge.

Tilly, Charles. 1981. "Useless Durkheim." pp. 95–108 in *As Sociology Meets History.* New York: Academic Press.

Tiryakian, Edward. 1988. "From Durkheim to Managua: Revolutions as Religious Revivals." pp. 44–65 in *Durkheimian Sociology: Cultural Studies.* Edited by Jeffrey C. Alexander. New York and Cambridge: Cambridge University Press.

Turner, Victor W. 1987. *The Anthropology of Performance.* New York: Performing Arts Journal Press.

1982. *From Ritual to Theatre: The Human Seriousness of Play.* Baltimore: Performing Arts Journal Press.

1974. *Dramas, Fields and Metaphors.* Ithaca, NY: Cornell University Press.

[1969] 1977. *The Ritual Process.* Ithaca, NY: Cornell University Press.

Wagner-Pacifici, Robin. 1986. *The Moro Morality Play.* Chicago: University of Chicago Press.

Wagner-Pacifici, Robin and Barry Schwartz. 1992. "The Vietnam Veterans Memorial." *American Journal of Sociology* 97: 376–420.

Warner, W. Lloyd. [1959] 1975. *The Living and the Dead.* Greenwich, CT: Greenwood Press.

Weber, Max. 1978. *Economy and Society.* Berkeley: University of California Press.

Welch, Michael and Jennifer Bryan. 1996. "Flag Desecration in American Culture: Offenses against Civil Religion and a Consecrated Symbol of Nationalism." *Crime, Law and Social Change* 26: 77–93.

Wolff, Kurt. 1960. *Emile Durkheim, 1858–1917: A Collection of Essays.* Columbus, OH: Ohio State University Press.

Zelizer, Viviana. 1979. *Morals and Markets.* New York: Columbia University Press.

I
LIFE, CONTEXT, AND IDEAS

2

MARCEL FOURNIER

Durkheim's life and context: something new about Durkheim?

Representation and periodization of Durkheim's life and work

Durkheim (Émile). French Sociologist (Épinal 1858; Paris 1917). Professor of science, education, and social science at Bordeaux (1887) and at La Sorbonne (1902, a position which became the Sociology chair in 1913) and founder of the journal *L'Année sociologique* (1896). He organized the French School of Sociology (with C. Bouglé, M. Halbwachs, L. Levy-Bruhl, and M. Mauss),[1] in an attempt to find a "moral science" in the study of societies and the laws which govern them.

Émile Durkheim's life and work is presented in 22 lines in the *Petit Robert 2* (dictionary of proper names). It contains a summary of his sociological approach (including positivism, the specificity of social facts, a sociology with a naturalist and mechanist character, and the study of "collective representation"), and a list of his books with very short comments (e.g. *The Elementary Forms of Religious Life* (1912), a text that reveals his interest in ethnography). This type of information is significant for those studying Durkheim; particularly those descriptions that place the sociologist and his work *in* France, where he has become – in many ways – a cult object.[2] On one tablet in Bordeaux, where Durkheim taught for many years, it has been written: *"Émile Durkheim, Founder of Sociology."* No more, no less.

A well-known classical sociologist in the English academic world, Émile Durkheim has become the object of a number of commentaries and theoretical interpretations. For instance, 6.3 percent of the 8,353 articles published in the *American Journal of Sociology* and the *American Sociological Review* between 1895 and 1992 quote his texts. This is as many as Weber, the most influential sociologist of the era who was quoted in 6.5 percent of the articles during the same period. As Paul Vogt summarized, "[t]he knowledge of Durkheim and of his books is a full part of the definition of what a sociologist is in America" (1993: 227).

However, only a few books have been dedicated solely to the study of Durkheim's life and world: Alpert (1939a), Clark (1968), LaCapra (1972), and Lukes (1972). Paradoxically, in sociology, theoretical interpretations of the work of the "founding fathers" or of "the classics" appear to be more important than the empirical sociological analysis of life and of society. As in other disciplines, sociology has its own "oral" tradition that is fed by pre-university courses and by introductory texts. In these courses and textbooks, Durkheim has been widely presented as an "organicist," a "functionalist," and a "positivist." As well, the information provided about Durkheim's life and world has generally been restricted to five distinct characteristics: his Jewishness; a teacher of philosophy (lycée); a university professor in education and social science; a leader of a strongly unified group (the journal L'Année sociologique); and a conservative thinker who was initially concerned with the social order and the moral integration of societies. Grand myths surround Durkheim and his life, and as a result he has often been portrayed as Durkheim-the-prophet, Durkheim-the-Regent-of-the-Sorbonne, and Durkheim-Jaurès'-friend-who-never-became-a-socialist, among others.

The only intellectual biography of Durkheim available to date is the magisterial Émile Durkheim: His Life and Work by Steven Lukes (1972), published more than thirty years ago. It emerged from extensive empirical historical research – interviews with many of Durkheim's relatives, archival research, and unpublished sources (letters and manuscripts) – and from a "new" understanding of Durkheim's work. Lukes' objectives were "to help the reader to achieve a historical understanding of (Durkheim's) ideas, and to form critical judgments about their value" (1972: 1). These objectives are explicit in the subtitle of his book: An Historical and Critical Study, and contribute to the book's organization which is, as Lukes admits, "unorthodox." As well, the book is simultaneously chronological and thematic: almost all the chapters are thematic (Theory and Practice of Education, Sociology of Religion, Sociology of Knowledge, etc.) but the book is divided into three parts, one for each period of Durkheim's life: Youth (1858–87), Bordeaux (1887–1902), and Paris (1902–17). Despite the fact that Lukes' text received widespread attention, the bestseller has not yet been translated into French.

Since the publication of Lukes' book, and possibly because it broadened this field of research, there has been an increase in new studies on Durkheim and his disciples. The recent opening up of archives has also given us new data about Durkheim's life and work, and the opportunity for new analyses of the work he produced during the complicated intellectual and social conditions surrounding the emergence of sociology in France. Over the last thirty years, Durkheimian studies have been rapidly increasing; punctuated by the activities of Philippe Besnard (France), W. S. F. Pickering (England), Robert Alun Jones (USA) and Massimo Borlandi (Italy), and the publication of new journals.[3] As well, a "rebirth" of all of Durkheim's texts has occurred in three volumes, edited by Victor Karady (Durkheim 1975).[4] An edition of Durkheim's correspondence with his friends and collaborators (Octave Hamelin, Xavier Léon, Célestin Bouglé, Marcel Mauss, Henri Hubert, François Simiand, and others) has been published (Durkheim 1975, vol. 2; 1979; 1998), and the discoveries of administrative reports (Durkheim 2003), texts (book reviews, courses, oral interventions in academic debates), and notes written by his students have become available. Another manifestation of this rebirth is the multiplication of PhD theses (see, e.g. Leroux 1998, Mergy 2001) and books[5] on Durkheim and his school of thought.

A life is always mysterious and keeps its secret gardens closed. In the case of Durkheim's life there still remains some mystery: for example, his relationship to Judaism, his psychological state, and his political orientation. This paper is limited to some of these topics: his social, religious and cultural background, his personality, his familial and social life, his social network, his relationships to the members of his team, and his political engagement. In the end, a few words about the last days of his relatively short life will be added.[6]

Placing Durkheim's life and career in particular periods is quite simple: (1) he was a philosophy teacher at the Lycée du Puy, de Sens,[7] Saint-Quentin – his nickname was Schopen – and, after a journey in Germany, at the Lycée de Troies (1884–7); (2) he became a chargé de cours and professor of social science and pedagogy at Bordeaux (1887–1904); and (3) he began an appointment in 1902 at the prestigious Sorbonne, suppléant of Ferdinand Buisson (who had been elected to the Chamber of Deputies) for the Science of Education and in 1913 became professor of the Science of Education and Sociology. The "Bordeaux period" seems to have been the most productive. It marked the publication of The Division of Labor in Society (1893) (hereafter Division of Labor), The Rules of Sociological Method (1895) (hereafter The Rules), and Suicide (1897), as well as the 1896 founding of the journal L'Année sociologique and the publication of its first issue two years later.

Doing the same for his work is much more complex. One guiding presumption of Durkheim scholarship over the years has been that "[he] was one of those few philosophers or social scientists who never changed his fundamental ideas" (Nandan 1980: 13). A different and more recent approach focuses more on the discontinuities of his thought. Did a young Durkheim and an old Durkheim exist? Was there a young Durkheim ("Durkheim's first phase") that was more materialist and determinist, and an old Durkheim, the Durkheim of the Elementary Forms of Religious Life (1912) and other later writings, who was more idealistic and benevolent (Alexander 1982: 2)?[8] What are Durkheim's "writings of youth"? Many hypotheses exist. One, supported by Lukes (1972) and Lacroix (1981), states that Durkheim's early texts were written between 1885 and 1887 (as 1887 marked the beginning of Durkheim's career at Bordeaux). For Robert A. Nye (1983), however, it is possible to include *The Rules* (1894) and *Suicide* (1897) in this category as well. Anthony Giddens (1971), Michael J. Hawkins (1980), and Jennifer Mergy (2001) have elaborated another periodization, which seems more precise. They argue that the Young Durkheim's work ranges from 1883[9] or 1885 until 1893 – just before the publication of *The Rules*. During this period, Durkheim published many book reviews, two important analyses in 1888 ("Introduction to the Sociology of the Family" and "Suicide and the Birth Rate: A Study of Social Statistics"), and wrote his two theses, *Quid Secundatus Politicae Scientiae Instituendae Contulerit* (1892) and *Division of Labor* (1893).

Finally, there is a date (1895) or period of transition (1894–6)[10] which also appears to be significant. From 1894 to 1895, Durkheim gave his first lecture at Bordeaux. It was a course on religion, and in 1895, he "achieved a clear view of the essential role played by religion in social life. It was in that year that, for the first time, I found the means of talking about the study of religion sociologically. This was a revelation to me. That course of 1895 marked a dividing line in the development of my thought . . ." (Durkheim 1907; translated by Lukes 1972: 237). For Durkheim, the year 1895, coupled with the reading of the works of Robertson Smith and his school, was a real "Road to Damascus" (Lacroix 1981). Those lectures, and a changed family context (Durkheim's father died in 1896), opened the doors for an objective study of religion to the son of a Rabbi.

Durkheim's social and cultural background or: how to be the son of a Rabbi

On April 15, 1854 in Épinal, a small town (population: 10,000 in 1871) and capital of the department of Vosges in Lorraine, David Émile Durkheim was born. He was the son of a rabbi, Moïse (1805–86), the Chief Rabbi of the Vosges and Haute-Marne and the grandson of a rabbi, Israël David. According to the collective memory of the family, they were "an unbroken line of eight generations of father–son rabbis" (Filloux 1977: 8).[11] And, as Marcel Mauss has stated, it was "a very long line" (Mauss "Note" n.d.: 1).[12]

On August 16, 1837, Moïse Durkheim married Mélanie Isidor (1820–1901) and they had five children. Désiré was born in 1845, and died only a year after his birth. Rosine (1848–1930), Joseph Félix (1849–89),

Cécile (1851–1931) and, finally, Émile, followed. At the time of his birth, his parents were fifty-three and thirty-eight years old, respectively. As the youngest, his mother and sisters most certainly coddled Émile. Thinking about his childhood, he wrote "There is a kind of chronic impatience on the part of one's elders, like a tendency to treat those who are younger as inferiors" (Durkheim [1925] 1963: 163). He also stated that "the family feelings prevent the excess." The Durkheim family was not wealthy but was highly respected at the crossings of culture (or religion) and business. Durkheim's mother, Mélanie, was the daughter of Joseph Marx Isidor, a trader of horses and a man who was considered a distinguished notable. In order to supplement the salary of her husband (only 800 francs a year in 1855) Mélanie opened an embroidery business. The Durkheim family inverted traditional gender roles, as culture was masculine and business was feminine within it. Émile's two sisters, Rosine and Céline, worked with their mother, and Félix, the older son, turned to commerce.

The atmosphere of the household was austere: there was a strict observance of the law, a belief in the cult of the book, and a shared sense of duty. Émile Durkheim was a serious, introverted and very sensitive child, and during much of his life he would never experience pleasure without a sense of remorse (Bouglé 1930a: 28; 1930b: 283). To be Jewish in Épinal was to experience the life of a small, cohesive and marginal group. Durkheim got "the taste of collective life": "nothing is more nice than the collective life, if you got in the habit to do it when you are young," "there is a pleasure to say *we* and not *I*" (Durkheim [1925] 1963: 203).

Durkheim's family did not speak Yiddish at home. To many, his father was viewed as being more "modern" than other rabbis, and in retrospect we can see this in family photographs: through the absence of a beard and the modern nature of his dress (Greenberg 1976: 625). With Félix and Émile, their mother used only their French names. In many ways, they wanted to be French; the family name was pronounced "Durkhem" with a short "e" and not "Durkheim" *à l'allemande*: signs of an open mind and integration, perhaps?

The best and most difficult route to social mobility and integration for a young provincial Jew was education. Émile was destined early to be the next rabbi in the Durkheim family; he learned Hebrew and received religious training,[13] and also attended secular schools. According to a well-known story, he went through a brief "crisis of mysticism" under the influence of an old Catholic teacher in his youth (Davy [1919: 183] 1960: 283; Lukes 1972: 41).[14]

Durkheim was a very good student, with "excellent conduct and remarkable diligence at school," and he was the recipient of an honorable mention at the Concours académique in 1873. He skipped two years and, at the end of his secondary studies, he completed his baccalauréat with ease, distinguishing himself in the Concours général. Academic success gave him the opportunity to pursue his studies. Later, he would frame his decision in these terms: "The Jew tries to go to school and become educated, not because he wants to substitute rational ideas to his collective prejudices but only because he needs to be better armed for struggling" (Durkheim 1897a: 169).[15] Durkheim's father did not disagree with his son's decision to go to Paris in the Fall of 1875 to prepare at the Lycée Louis-le-Grand. It was, after all, one of the best Parisian colleges and he had been there himself when he completed his rabbinical training in Nancy. He had also been encouraged to go to Paris and take courses in sciences and in philosophy, which contributed to his appearance of having a decided taste.[16] He was the studious rabbi devoted to biblical exegesis and Talmudic jurisprudence in the tradition of Lithuanian Judaism (Derczanski 1990: 158)[17] and sensitive to mysticism,[18] but was also open to the scientific study of Judaism. If the successful academic career of his son was treason to a family tradition, it was also the realization of his father's ambition, for in a modern society, the scholar is in a position analogous to the priest or rabbi in a traditional or religious society.

When Émile was finally enrolled in the École Normale, his father wrote a letter to the director requesting that his son be excused from lectures on Saturdays. The request was denied, but Émile stayed at the school and completed his studies with success. There is another, better-known story that suggests that by the time Émile went to the school, he abandoned all Judaist practices (Davy [1919] 1960). During his first year, he read many books on the history of religions (Paoletti 1992) and prepared a conference on the history of Jews in the Roman Empire. In a way, this gesture helped him to confirm his cultural identity and to transform it into a research object. At the exam of *agrégation* in 1882, he came in seventh place, and, according to the comments made by the members of the jury, he came across as a "serious student" who had "committed to ideas." However, they also warned that he should be careful about his tendency to use "abstract and obscure terminology."[19]

A question which has not until recently been dealt with systematically is Durkheim's Jewishness. In Lukes' book, there is no reference at all to the influence of Judaism on his work. Does Durkheim's Jewish background, as an indicator of marginality, explain his interest in sociology (Clark 1968)? Did Durkheim's existence as a Jew contribute "to his intellectual development, specially his understanding of the nature of religion" (Moore 1986: 288)?[20] This last question is a "very tricky one" (Pickering 1994: 11) and is difficult to respond to clearly. Moore's short analysis identifies some research tracks:

"Durkheim's view of religion did not contradict the experience of Jews . . ." (1986: 289); "the Jewish religion is a ritualistic one which places more significance on action or practice than to belief" (1986: 290); "Durkheim's analysis of sacrifice . . . also shows signs of a contemporary Jewish perspective" (1986: 291). Other hypotheses can be applied to Durkheim's work. For instance, some have posited that Durkheimian sociology was the result of his Jewish sensibility and his identification to a familial, tribal, and collectivist group. Still others argue that Durkheim's conceptualization of society corresponds to the Talmudic conception of God (Filloux 1977) or the project of a science of morality translates the Talmudic notion of justice (Schoenfled and Meštrović 1989). Tiryakian (1979) sees a connection between Durkheim's Jewish background and his deep interest in preliterate societies: his interest in the "primitives" is inspired by nostalgia for the primitive community of ancient Israël. Durkheim tried to rediscover his ethnic roots, seeing the Arunta in terms of the Jewish people. (Tiryakian 1979: 111). Pickering argues that "for those who would agree that Durkheim's sociology has been influenced by what he was taught from the Jewish Bible and Talmud, the list of candidates is endless: an unaesthetic approach to life, an emphasis on education, an importance given to ethics, an emphasis on the concept of God as law-maker, and the doctrine of man as homo-duplex. Many of these kinds of arguments are naive (or simply incorrect), and generalizations about Jewishness have to be made with great care" (Pickering 1994: 30–2).

These assertions postulate an essentialist definition of Jewishness that must be criticized. There is not an essential Jewishness, but rather a world of real Jews in France. Strenski (1997) reconstructs the context of social and intellectual relationships and analyzes the world of French-born liberal Jews – a world in which Durkheim was living – and the part of the "Jewish French opinion" to which he was identified. There was a remarkable community of interests between the Durkheimians and the French leaders of the science of Judaism. The carefully documented contextualization provokes reassessments of figures in the history of religion: James Darmesteler, Sylvain Lévi, Louis-Germain Lévi, and Salomon Reinach. Sylvain Lévi, who was a specialist on India and was Mauss' professor at the École pratique, played a prominent role in the development of "methodological ritualism" which the Durkheimians applied to the study not only of religion but also of society.

Durkheim's relationship to Judaism was a complex one. On one hand, he remained within the close-knit Jewish provincial family (Jones 1984: 15), he suffered anti-Semitism and kept his affiliation to the Jewish community. In 1887, he married a Jewess: Louise Dreyfus. It was a "beautiful marriage": their friends said she was the "ideal wife" and a "remarkable partner." As well, she brought more than 100,000 francs to their marriage.

Her father, Henry Dreyfus, was the son of a merchant, a rich Parisian businessman, and founded a prosperous coppersmith's shop with his two brothers (Charle 1974). When the couple moved to Bordeaux, Émile maintained only a few relationships with the leaders of the Jewish community. During the First World War he supported a Jewish organization (the Comité français d'information et d'action auprès des Juifs des Pays Neutres) (Davy [1919] 1960: 193) and he was put on a commission examining the situation of Russian refugees in France. On the other hand, Durkheim's way of life was one of an "assimilated" Jew: he lectured at the University of Bordeaux on Saturday, he didn't go to the synagogue and didn't respect the kosher, and he didn't give his two children, André (1892–1917) and Marie (1888–1953),[21] Hebrew names. As well, he decided not to have his daughter married in the synagogue in 1912 (a decision that caused conflict in his family, resulting in Rosine refusing to assist at the ceremony). However, when he died in 1917, he was buried in the Jewish section of the Montparnasse cemetery. In the right-hand corner of his tombstone there were some Hebrew words (Pickering 1994: 35).

Politics, nationalism, and socialism

Durkheimian theory, which has been linked to and compared with functionalism, has also been contrasted with Marxism and other critical theories. Since Paul Nizan's (1932) *Chiens de garde*, Durkheim has been viewed either as a liberal thinker who transformed French conservative ideas in a systematic sociological theory (Nisbet 1967: 13) or as a conservative theorist of social order who rejected socialism (Coser 1960: 216). Lukes corrected this view, characterizing his position as "strongly reformist and revisionist" (Lukes 1972: 320–1). Recently, under the lens of Filloux, Durkheim has appeared as a socialist thinker who defended a democratic conception of socialism: socialism was at the origin of his sociological vocation and was "its traveling companion" (Filloux 1977: 260). Now, his sociology seems to be more "radical" (Gane 1992) or "critical" than before. However, it is more logically an effort to reconcile the contrary forces of individuality and solidarity and, hence, of individualism and socialism (Stedman Jones 2001: 131). Durkheim has gained the status of a *political* thinker – or more precisely as an analyst of politics – in recent years, one who examines power and the state. Also, he has been presented as a thinker who was searching for a new way to examine the two big contemporary dangers: totalitarianism and anarchism (Lacroix 1981).

Durkheim was marginally involved in "practical" political activity, but did not publish any major works primarily concerned with political analysis

(Giddens 1986: 1). During his lifetime, he was active in politics only twice: first during the "Dreyfus Affair," and again during the First World War. However, he was certainly influenced and perhaps also challenged by three important events and movements: the occupation of Alsace-Lorraine by German troops in the Franco-Prussian War (1870–1), the Third Republic, and the development of a socialist movement in Europe.

When he was a student at the École Normale Supérieure, Durkheim decided, "by vocation and in an environment animated by political and moral will," to dedicate his life to "the study of social questions" (Mauss 1971: 31). In many ways, the context of Durkheim's youth may be characterized by military defeat (the Franco-Prussian war in 1870–1), and since the *Communes* (1871), by a political disunity and instability combined with economic opposition and class conflict. It appears that his experience of French defeat may have contributed to "a strong patriotism, a defensive sense of national decadence and a consequent desire to contribute to the regeneration of France." The task of Durkheim and other intellectuals of his generation consisted of "the revival of France" (Lukes 1972: 42) or, in his own words, to "re-organize" and "remake the country." That was their "mission," and Durkheim appeared to his contemporaries as a prophet and the founder of a new (secular) moral. Once, as they were passing Notre Dame, Durkheim said to his collaborator Célestin Bouglé, "It is from a chair like that that I should have spoken." His objective was to elaborate upon a new republican ideology that was scientifically grounded and to develop a new (positive) science of morals and manners. Morals and pedagogy were the object of many courses at Bordeaux (*L'Évolution Morale*, 1899) and Paris (*Pédagogie et sociologie*, 1902 and *L'Évolution Pédagogique en France* 1904–5). His last project, in 1917, was to write a book on "La Morale." However, only the "introduction" has been published by Mauss (Durkheim 1917). In all of these courses, there were frequent explicit references to the social and economic problems of his time.

The Republican

Durkheim grew up in the political context of the Third Republic (1871–1940), which was established after the war. This Republic has been called the "République des professeurs," because it was associated with the educational reforms of Jules Ferry and the secularization of education. The three key words of the Republican ideology were democracy, secularism, and science (Alpert 1939). When Durkheim was "Normalien," he celebrated the rise of the republican left at the beginning of the Opportunist Republic, and it appears as though Gambetta was his idol (Filloux 1977: 12). Durkheim was sympathetic to the republican and positivist Jules Ferry and his aims of creating a national system of secular education. "To remake it (the country), it must be first educated" (Durkheim 1918: 465).

From the very beginning of his career, education and pedagogy were two of his more fundamental interests. He was appointed at Bordeaux partially because of his republican idealism and his desire to establish a secular morality on science, and was supported by Louis Liard, the director of Higher Education, who had taught there and was active in that city's municipal government. That appointment, after a "study leave" in 1885 in Germany where he visited the Wundt psychology laboratory and studied the state of philosophy and social sciences, was part of the reform of the University and the introduction of new disciplines (mainly the social sciences). Durkheim was originally appointed to Bordeaux in 1887 as professor of social science and pedagogy. Bordeaux's decision depended upon "a number of fortuitous circumstances": the role of Liard, the presence of Espinas, and the openness of a provincial university (Alpert 1937; Karady 1979).

Durkheim's support for the Third Republic was an indicator of his "liberalism" (Richter 1960; Lehman 1993; Seidman 1983), but only in the sense that the theorists of philosophical liberalism influenced him. As well, he stressed the dignity of the individual, of individual rights, free thought, free democratic institutions and the essential liberal values of tolerance and pluralism.

In the early moments of his career, Durkheim read Albert Scheaffle, a German historian and political economist who was a member of the Historical School. Durkheim liked his anti-individualist perspective as it gave great importance to the social – the society as a *sui generis* reality – and he agreed with its opposition to economic liberalism (Jones 1991: 28).

One central question in Durkheim's work was: which came first, the individual or society? This question was also central to French public space. What is democracy? What is the role of the corporation? Do we need social welfare? If we democratize education, how do we reform the school system? Philosophy or politics? At one time, Durkheim had the ambition to do both: pure science on one side and politics on the other. Sociology eventually gave him the opportunity to satisfy his need for both knowledge and action (Halbwachs 1918: 353).

Durkheim's first field of interest within the social sciences was political economy. The critique of the works in this field enticed him to develop his "original perspective": What constitutes national cohesion? What is the role of political authority (Lacroix 1981: 41)? Is social life only a wild struggle for life (Durkheim 1885: 349)? Is there a need for a strong and centralized government? The criticism of utilitarian liberalism and *laissez-faire* economics was central to Durkheim's thought. He didn't support the liberal doctrine of natural rights, and according to him, society was not a forum for exchange but, rather, a system of rights and duties. (Stedman Jones 2001: 49–51). His positions changed over time: from a mistrust of public opinion and the collective action of masses to a fascination for the "creative effervescence," from a more activist notion of citizenship to a critique of direct parliamentary elections. As Hawkins notes,

> His vision of a corporatist society, headed by a strong state whose members were only indirectly elected, and cemented by a commitment to cosmopolitan liberal ideals of universal human rights, goes beyond the confines of liberal democracy, and is in fact difficult to subsume under any of the conventional ideological labels. (Hawkins 1995: 309)

The relation of Durkheim to liberalism is complex and so heavily influenced by his sociology that some can speak of corporatism[22] (which is not incompatible with the republican and democratic traditions) while others can speak of a communitarian defence of liberalism (Cladis 1992).

In France, there was no party equivalent to the English Liberal party. The form of liberal republicanism which emerged in the 1890s was articulated instead to a new political doctrine, "progressisme." The aim of the "République nouvelle" was to form a "common front" against the great enemy, against the great "peril" of revolutionary socialism. This was a period of "esprit nouveau" and "ralliement" around the ideas of good sense, justice, and charity. In many ways, the 1890s can be characterized as a decade of social and political agitation, marked by anarchist attempts (in 1892 and 1894) in Paris, the assassination of the president of the Republic (Sadi Carnot in 1894), the election of the first socialist deputies (1893), significant national breakthroughs from 1889 to 1896, an increase in the membership of the unions,[23] the proliferation of local workers' labour exchanges,[24] and the expansion of the Guesde's Workers' Party from two thousand to ten thousand members (between 1890 and 1893). The "social question" moved to the forefront of national politics, and the Republic moved to the left, attempting to undermine the socialist challenge by incorporating some of the theoretical assumptions and practical programs into the mainstream of a revitalized liberalism (Silverman 1989: 46). The architect of "social republicanism" was Prime Minister Léon Bourgeois, who elaborated a doctrine of organic solidarity as a liberal route to "outbid the socialists." It was an articulation of the principles of liberal individualism and of the communitarian critiques of republican egoism. Bourgeois' book, published in 1896, was entitled *Solidarité*.

The keyword of Young Durkheim's work was *solidarity* and his theoretical perspective was based on the assumption that human societies were altruistic. For him, the pre-eminent character or "nature" of (human) life was *association* (between individuals and groups) and, in his normative reflections, he focused on the associative dimension of macrosocial or political organizations and professional corporations, which were direct relationships between the state and the individual.

The notion of solidarity was so foreign at this period of time that the new discipline of sociology rapidly became the companion of this new ideology. Three years after the publication of *Division of Labor* (1893), Léon Bourgeois gave his manifesto the title *Solidarité*. One of Durkheim's first collaborators, Célestin Bouglé (who was a member of the Radical Party) published a text entitled "La crise du libéralisme" in the journal *Revue de métaphysique et de morale* in 1902. A few years later, he also published a book, *Le Solidarisme* (1907). Solidarism is based on the postulate of interdependence and oriented to the fight against poverty and oppression, and to the defense of greater equality. It was "a third way" between liberalism and collectivism.

The Affair

In 1894, Captain Alfred Dreyfus, an officer on the French General Staff and a Jew, was railroaded: falsely convicted of treason and sentenced to life in prison on Devil's Island. This "Affair" polarized French politics and public opinion. On one side stood the anti-Dreyfus camp; right wing, reactionary, and often anti-Semitic. On the other side stood the more liberal and often socialist pro-Dreyfus camp. From a relatively early date, Durkheim publicly sided with the "Dreyfusards" and took an active role in supporting the movement *Ligue pour la défense des droits de l'homme* [League for the Defence of Human Rights] founded on February 20, 1898 by Senator Ludovic Trarieux. Durkheim became secretary of the Bordeaux branch of the Ligue and, with some difficulty, recruited new members. His convictions were strong enough to convince his former schoolmate Jean Jaurès to throw the full weight of the socialist movement behind the cause of freeing Dreyfus and investigating the military. At the height of the Dreyfus Affair, Durkheim founded (with his colleague Octave Hamelin at Bordeaux) an association of university teachers and students called "La Jeunesse laïque" [literally: "Undenominational Youth"], where he addressed "religion and the freedom of thought" and, later on, "individualism" (Lukes 1972: 358–9). It was during this time that he wrote his still-famous essay "Individualism and the Intellectuals" which was a direct response to the work of Ferdinand Brunetière (1898), a conservative and anti-Dreyfusard scholar,[25] and two other short texts (1899a; 1899b).[26]

Durkheim, who witnessed and suffered from outbreaks of anti-Semitism when he was young, had a "feeling of insecurity" (Pickering 1994: 25) and attempted to avoid being accused of nepotism at the University of Bordeaux (Durkheim 1998: 117). He also attempted to avoid the front stage; he did not sign the "Manifesto of the Intellectuals" published in *L'Aurore* the day after the "J'accuse" of Émile Zola,[27] and he denied having written and asked his students to countersign a letter of congratulations to Zola (Lukes 1972: 333). Many of Durkheim's collaborators at *L'Année sociologique*, including his nephew Marcel Mauss, were with Lucien Herr and Charles Andler on the side of the Dreyfusards.

Durkheim did not launch himself into the Affair for political reasons or because he was Jew, but in the name of moral principle. The Affair has raised, he wrote a few years later, "a serious question of principle" (Durkheim, 1904: 281). Even if there was evidence that anti-Semitic nationalism was central to the right, he interpreted the attack on the Jewish community as the result of a lack of moral unity. He qualified the Affair as "a serious moral perturbation" that resembled a "public flail": "Never (in France) have we have such a moral disorder" (Durkheim 1998: 110). His first priority was to "save our moral patrimony" (Durkheim 1898b: 278). In his response to Ferdinand Brunetière (the Catholic apologist who criticized the individualism of intellectuals as a form of anarchy and accused them of rejecting traditional values in favor of egoistic rationalism), Durkheim clearly distinguished individualism from egoism and emphasized the idea that "individualism is our only collective goal" (Durkheim 1998: 423). By individualism as a moral value, he meant the defence of human dignity, the valorization or "cult of the individual" and the idea of social justice. That is, according to Célestin Bouglé,[28] a "democratic and rationalist individualism" (Bouglé 1905: 588). In other words, no opposition exists between the individual and society, between individualism and solidarity, and between patriotism and humanism. In modern societies, individual differentiation forms the basis of collective integration. The Dreyfus Affair was not only the affair of a single citizen but also of the Republic; not only an affair of one individual but also of humanity (Bouglé 1899 in Mergy 2001: 208).

Being both a Republican and a Dreyfusard appears to have played a major role in the advancement of Durkheim's academic career, and to have facilitated the institutionalization of sociology as an academic discipline. At the beginning of the twentieth century, the Jewish, provincial professor who taught social science and education for many years at Bordeaux had succeeded, moved to Paris, and was associated with the New Sorbonne.

Against Marxism. But what about Socialism?

"Something doesn't go well," wrote Durkheim (Lenoir 1930: 293), looking at the ruins of the century (Lacroix 1981: 33). He was, like other French citizens of the era, afraid. He saw anarchy, the emergence of social movements, and an increased division of opinion. Individualism and egoism were growing up. There was a menace harassing the potential unity of the nation.

It is clear that Durkheim's project (the new discipline of sociology) has been compared and contrasted with and against Marxism. ". . . from *L'Année sociologique* a theory is released that is exactly opposed to a historical materialism that is coarse and simplistic despite its objectivist tendencies. It will make religion, and not the economy, the matrix of social facts" (Durkheim 1998: 71). As early as 1885, Durkheim had seen the potential dangers of "despotic socialism," and criticized the allowance of individuals with "no sphere of action of their own" in the *Division of Labor*. He recognized class conflicts but he did not believe that they were the motor of historical change. As well, he did not view violence as a means for social transformation. His rejection of Marxism was explicit in his review of Labriola's *Essai sur la conception matérialiste de l'histoire*: "The Marxist hypothesis is not only not proven, but it is contrary to the facts which can established" (Durkheim 1897b: 245). That same year, Durkheim also published a review of Gaston Richard's (Durkheim 1897c) book, *Le socialisme et la science sociale* in the *Revue philosophique*. Richard, a former student of Durkheim at Bordeaux, was one of his first collaborators in *L'Année sociologique*.

Durkheim's relationship with Marxism was similar to his relationship with his nephew and close collaborator, Marcel Mauss. Mauss, as a student in 1893 at Bordeaux and two years later at Paris, was a member of the Groupe d'étudiants révolutionnaires, a Marxist group. Mauss published his first book reviews and articles in the journal *Le Devenir social*, in Lagardelle, Sorel. Did his uncle ever attempt to sway his views – especially when he published "Note sur le socialisme" in the *Revue philosophique* in 1893 (Durkheim 1893b)? One of his courses at Bordeaux was Le Socialisme.[29] Interestingly, the first chapter was on Saint-Simon, whom Mauss presented as the founder of both socialism and positivist sociology.

Durkheim's first preoccupation was to study; to objectify socialism as a "social fact of the highest importance" (1928: 38). It was a doctrine, an ideology. According to Durkheim, socialism was not only oriented to economic change, it introduced a higher morality and had the ability to realize more justice (Durkheim 1893b). This realization of justice was also central to Jean Jaurès' definition of socialism. Durkheim insisted that socialism must be compatible with individualism. Therefore, the objective of his first book was to reconcile individualism with socialism. Durkheim was conscious that individualism in modern societies required egalitarianism, a feature that was, in his mind, not about equality of conditions but, rather, equality of opportunity.

Many of Durkheim's collaborators were active in the socialist movement on different levels. Initially they were with the *Groupe d'unité socialiste* which, founded in 1899, was linked to the *Société nouvelle de librairie et d'édition*, a small collective business organized by Luicien Herr and Charles Andler. Its membership included Marcel Mauss, Paul Fauconnet, Louis Gernet, Maurice Halbwachs, Émmanuel Lévy, Henri Hubert, and the brothers Bourgin. The Durkheimians remained on the side of Jaurès and his reformist socialism, and against Guesde's Marxist and revolutionary version of socialism. Later, in 1908, Simiand, Hertz, and Hubert Bourgin founded a new group for reflection and documentation: *le Groupe d'études socialistes*, and published the *Cahiers du socialiste*.

Antagonism or consensus? While Durkheim was not an optimist, he believed that a "sense of solidarity" existed (1928: 376). For many, socialism appeared to be a good alternative. But how can one protect freedom (for the individual *and* for the market)? Equality or inequality? To be individualist or socialist, that is the true dilemma. Is it possible to reconcile individualism and socialism? Durkheim didn't know (Durkheim 1928: 377), but the sociology that he constructed provided him with the solution. Durkheim was looking for a third way between liberalism and socialism, one that also gave a voice to economic groups (corporations).

He sympathized with his friend, the socialist leader Jean Jaurès, but he refused to become a member of the Socialist Party. Many times, he gave his nephew Marcel Mauss advice not to be too active in politics. According to Durkheim, the sociologist is primarily a scholar, one who doesn't have to be sidetracked by the "allure of the crowd" nor play the "political career" (Durkheim 1970: 270). At the very least, the role of the sociologist is, more modestly, as "an advisor and an educator."

Melancholia fin-de-siècle

A new psychology

A new cult of self, the primacy of irrationalism: an expression of the emergence of these new cultural trends in fin-de-siècle France was, in literature and in art, symbolism. This symbolism emerged in reaction to positivism, defended idealism and subjectivism, and gave priority to suggestion and association. The goal of artistic communication was to express the inexpressible and to appeal directly to the inner world of the audience. At the same time, a new body of knowledge was being consolidated and popularized, called the "psychologie nouvelle." This new "science" concerned itself with the exploration of the interior of the human organism as a febrile, mechanistic system of nerves and to the examination of the visual dimensions of the mental operations; often with an emphasis on hypnotism, suggestion, and dream (Silverman 1989: 78–9). Hypnosis held great prestige, and the notion of suggestibility was very attractive. Henri Bergson, Professor of Philosophy at Clermont-Ferrand, was involved in neuropsychiatric research on hypnosis and suggestion. Bergson observed hypnotic sessions, and his *Essai sur les données immédiates de la conscience* (1889) was grounded in large part on the findings of medical clinicians.

The new orientation of psychology in the 1890s was based on the discoveries of two medical pioneers, Dr. Jean-Marie Charcot of Paris and Dr. Hippolyte Bernheim of Nancy, the author of *De la suggestion dans l'état hypnotique et dans l'état de veille* (1884). Charcot was the physician appointed to the Salpêtrière Hospital, the founder of the *Société de psychologie physiologique de Paris* (1885), and president of the first World Congress of Psychology (Paris, 1889) where William James, Durkheim, and Freud were members of the audience (Mucchielli 1998: 196). Dr. Charcot analyzed a series of diseases of the nervous system, called "nervous illnesses," each of which was associated with a set of interior lesions, and he developed a variety of new therapies (for instance, "galvanization" or electric shock therapy, "ferronization" or the ingestion of iron harness; used to treat the different pathologies of the nervous system). The focus of his work eventually shifted to the study of hysteria. His weekly public demonstrations of hysterical hypnosis (which he divided into three phases: lethargy, catalepsy, and somnambulism) at the Salpêtrière were Tout Paris society gatherings. Hypnosis, suggestion, hallucination, split personality, and other "extraordinary phenomena" rapidly moved to the top of intellectual actuality, and the issues surrounding them were not only philosophical (the nature of the mind) but also social and political (in terms of criminal behavior and crowd phenomena). Gustave Le Bon published his book *Psychologie des foules* in 1895. Charcot and his followers established a causal relation between disorders of nervous system and the urban metropolis. In 1890, Charles Richet, a psychologist and a colleague of Charcot, published *Surmenage mental dans la civilisation moderne*, defending a thesis that stated that the expansion of information to be assimilated and the speed of urban life developed the urban dweller's mental sensitivities at the expense of his physical vitality. Surmenage is the overexertion of the nervous system in the context of the new urban conditions of existence in the fin-de-siècle (Silverman 1989: 81).

The syndrome of degeneration

A particular emphasis was put on a condition called neurasthenia, a clinical state of mental hypersensitivity and physical debility, resulting from continuous mental exertion. Neurasthenia was diagnosed medically as "a condition of nervous exhaustion, in which excessive stimulation atrophied the nerves to a point of extreme irritability and physical lassitude" (Silverman 1987: 80). The American physician George Miller Beard first defined neurasthenia in 1880, and he attributed nervous exhaustion to the excessive zeal for the Protestant ethic, and neurasthenia to overwork. His therapy consisted of a combination of rest and electroshock therapy. In France, neurasthenia was linked to the general conditions of modernity, in particular to the agitated pace of urban life. Modern civilization became the source of much social and organic pathology. Dr. Fernand Levillain defended this thesis in a book, *La Neurasthénie*, published in 1891 with an introduction by Charcot. As well, *L'Hygiène du neurasthénique* (1897) by A. Proust and Gilbert Ballet, became the standard medical text on neurasthenia: the symptoms were "weakness," "suggestibility," "lowered resistance," and the like.

"Overtaxation of the nervous system," "refinement of cerebral activities," "our exhausted generation," collective devitalization, and degeneration. All of these symptoms resonated throughout high and low culture, not only in the journal *La Revue des deux mondes* but also in the more popular *L'Illustration*. To many, fin-de-siècle France appeared to be a "nevrosée" collectivity. In the 1880s, Alfred Fouillée began to publish monthly articles in the *Revue des deux mondes* on the new psychology, hypnotism, and suggestion. In 1891, he began writing a series of articles – "Les grandes conclusions de la psychologie moderne" – summarizing the medical debates of the time. One article, published in 1895, was called "Degénérescence." Fouillée's work provided a political dimension to psychiatric discoveries, drawing lessons for republicans from the revelations of irrationalism. Setting up a revision of liberal rationalism, he celebrated suggestibility as a new, unconscious imperative for "the law of solidarity and universal fraternity." In his view, identity is a representation, and the mind itself is a "vessel of the social" (Silverman 1989: 91). Also in 1895, Max Nordau, a practicing physician from Germany and a student of Charcot, published a controversial best seller, entitled *Degeneration*. Nordau viewed decadence as a consequence of mental disorder and the artist was diagnosed as the victim of neuropathology. Valentin Magnan and Paul-Maurice also published on the topic (*Les Dégénérés*) that same year.

B. H. Morel elucidated the syndrome of degeneration as early as 1857, in his *Traité des dégénérescences*. By 1890, this syndrome marked the existence of a simultaneous crisis in the social and biological health of the French nation. Comparisons about the health of the nation were made with Germany, and vital statistics suggested that the nation was in decline: depopulation, low birth rates, alcoholism, crime, suicide, mental illness, prostitution, syphilis, tuberculosis, labor and economic problems (Nye 1990: 235). The state of the French population was alarming, and became the "master-pathology." "Pathologies" and "social" problems emerged as effects of a hereditary degeneration, a widespread degeneracy, or at least as the biological effects of an unhealthy social milieu. French physiologists and medical scientists measured normal and pathological states quantitatively: "normal" states were described as some sort of statistical average (Nye 1990: 244). The "healthy/sick" binary in medicine was replaced by a "normal/abnormal" one.

The "mal de l'infini" and the study of the "social unconsciousness"

In 1888, Durkheim published an article on the relationship between suicide and birth rates, indicating an early interest in finding a "moral" explanation for suicide. Indeed, much of his significant work during the 1890s was concerned with psychology, heredity and pathology. In *Moral Education*, there was a regular lecture series he delivered first at Bordeaux and later at Paris; one that constituted a large account of children's suggestibility (Durkheim 1925). He wrote "Crime and Social Health" in March, 1895 and it was published two months later in the *Revue philosophique*.

"Malaise" and "anxiety": there were often questions concerning psychic problems, mental diseases, and neurasthenia in *Division of Labor* (1893). According to Durkheim, tensions and "agonizing indecision" emerged in society whenever the collective conscience weakens. While Durkheim did not quote Freud, his work, with the introduction of the notion of collective consciousness and the frequent use of metaphors (such as "nervous currents," "waves," and "latent energies"), truly is a collective psychology and an effort to objectify psychic problems: their causes are not only individual but social, not only in the "depths of the soul," but also in the "base of collective life."

Durkheim's analysis was based on an idea of happiness: "Our power for happiness is very restrained," he wrote, quoting the works of physiologists on pain. Harmony, equilibrium, moderation, and "the right environment": these concepts characterized Durkheim's philosophy on life. His argument lent itself to art and aesthetic activities as well: ". . . too great an artistic sensibility is an unhealthy phenomenon which cannot become widespread without danger for society"(Durkheim 1893a: 219). Every society has its own kind of suffering, but in modern societies it is worse: the "wrong," the "evil," becomes larger, and the misfortune ("malheur") is illustrated by the number of suicides; the "real suicides" and the "suicides tristes" which seem to be more frequent in advanced or "civilized" countries.

In *Suicide* (1897), Durkheim (constantly preoccupied with the question of "social disintegration"), analyzed what he saw as the most significant type of suicide in contemporary societies. The egoistic and anomist suicide, what he called after Chateaubriand the "sickness of the infinite," takes different forms: for some, it is the "infinite of the dream," and for others, it is the "infinite of desire." He also identified "currents of collective sadness" which he believed were not pathological if they were not excessive: "We should not believe that unadulterated joy is the normal state of sensibility. Man could not live if he was entirely resistant to sadness." In other words, melancholia, more frequent in modern societies, "is therefore only morbid when it has too central a place in life . . . It is necessary that the taste for joyous expansion be moderated by the opposite taste." To him, it was a question of "measure and harmony," for a society needs both optimism and pessimism. It was also a question of relativism: what is morbid for individuals can be normal for societies. In a footnote, Durkheim used neurasthenia as an example of this: "Neurasthenia is a sickness from the point of view of individual physiology; what would society be without neurasthenics? They evidently have a social role to play" (Durkheim 1897a: 418). To him, it was a characteristic typical of advanced societies, but when it became too strong, collective sadness inevitably turns pathologic and provides space to "discouraging theories" (such as Epicurus and Zeno in the past, and the work of Schopenhauer today). The same can be said for other forms of denial – as seen in anarchism, mysticism, and revolutionary socialism; those who don't necessarily despair but seek to destroy realities (Durkheim 1897a: 426).

Durkheim used the term "hypercivilization" to describe the refinement of the nervous system; that which makes modern peoples "excessively delicate," "more impatient of any sort of discipline," "more accessible both to violent imitation and to exaggerated depression" (Durkheim 1897a: 35–44). The same description holds for neurasthenic individuals. Durkheim treated neurasthenia, this "lesser form of insanity" as social in origin; he offended the proponents of free will among the psychologists and aroused the ire of the alienists with his critique of the psychiatric theories of the "insane suicide" (Nye 1983).

In the first volumes of *L'Année sociologique*, there was an interest in (if not a tolerant reception of) the work of "hygienists" and psychiatrists on social "illnesses." While few discounted the seriousness of the various pathologies (falling birth rates, for example), the journal's collaborators often pointed out the interconnectedness and complexity of social, psychological, and biological phenomena. During the early years, as the index of *L'Année sociologique* details, the issues deemed most important included: crime and criminality, economics, education, punishment and responsibility, religion, women, suicide, and the city. There was also an obvious interest in the family, marriage, kinship, and sexuality (particularly incest and prostitution). As well, two disciplines (anthropology and the history of religions) appeared to be central. New issues grew in importance as a result: belief, cult, god, dogma, church, ritual, fetishism, magic, myth, sacrifice, superstition, taboo, and totems. These characterized the new Durkheimian program: the critical study of the "social unconsciousness" as an objectification of irrationalism.

Durkheim was among the "generation of 1890," that generation of writers and intellectuals who, born within or proximate to the decade of the 1860s, were nurtured in a Republican milieu and were influenced by neo-Lamarckian theory of evolution and heredity. As well, they largely adopted the program of moral and intellectual regeneration of the generation of 1850 – Taine, Renan, and Fustel de Coulanges (Digeon 1959). Durkheim was a "child of his times, rather than the iron-willed rebel he is often made out to be" (Nye 1982: 267) and, in his "milieu" or network, there were psychologists or philosophers who were also interested in psychology and psychiatry: Théophile Ribot (the editor of the *Revue philosophique*), and Pierre Janet (one of his colleagues at the École normale who published *L'Automatisme psychologique*).

Durkheim was culturally and personally predisposed to developing a collective psychology of "a particular type." There are three things about his life that we are certain of: his hyper or "feminine" sensibility, his neurasthenic crisis, and his illness during the last days of his life. His own diagnosis of his mental state consisted of neurasthenia and melancholia. In October 1902, in a letter to his friend (the philosopher Octave Hamelin), Durkheim described his "malaise mental" which was "both psychic and moral." He used the terms "bad state of morale," "lamentable dulling," and "feeling of a certain moral shrinking," to describe his mental maladies. The "crisis" had been more important than he originally thought. Six months later he wrote: "What a winter I've had. The worst is that my depression had never expressed itself in this form . . ." (Lacroix 1981: 138)

The war and the death of Durkheim's son

August 3, 1914: the First World War. Durkheim's nephew, Marcel Mauss, decided to enlist and to go to the front. Eager to be "useful to his country and to the commonwealth" and patriotic, Durkheim – for the second time in his life – played an active political role: he became a member of governmental committees, published an article in the *New York Tribune* (on April 18, 1915) and wrote a number of "documents de propagande" ("Qui a voulu la guerre?" ["Who wanted the war?"] and "L'Allemagne au dessus de tout: la mentalité allemande et la guerre" ["Germany above all: the German mentality and the war"] in 1915, and "Lettres à tous les Français" ["Letters to all French people"] in 1916). The war was a disaster for the Durkheimian school, one punctuated by the deaths of Maxime David, Antoine Bianconi, Jean Reynier, Robert Hertz and, perhaps most significantly, André Durkheim.

In 1916, following the death of his son André, Durkheim was devastated and depressed, withdrawing into a "ferocious silence" and "thinking of the same things day and night." He wrote to his nephew Marcel Mauss:

> I feel detached from all worldly interests. But this also has its joy. It is the joy of the ascetic who feels above everything. It is a severe melancholic joy; and evidently, inasmuch as one can predict the future, such melancholy will be the custom of my life. But I have naturally enough of a propensity . . . I don't know if I ever laughed much, but I'm through with laughing, and my life has totally orientated itself in this direction. You would not believe the impression of happiness this sensation of detachment gives you, due to no longer having any temporal interest. (Durkheim 1998: 508)

The origins of the "mal" seem to be "nervous." Durkheim tried to remain active, and contributed to *La Vie Universitaire à Paris* (1918), was a member of the committee "sur la situation des réfugiés russes," and continued to participate in intellectual and academic conversations (for example, Paul Fauconnet's thesis and the reading of baccalauréat exams). He recovered enough to resume his work on *La Morale*. However, fatigue and nervous spasms plagued him again, and he lost the use of his right hand. In May of 1917, Durkheim confessed: "It is better to die than to live like this." On November 15, 1917, he died at the age of fifty-nine. "The father," said Raoul Bloch to his friend Mauss, "did survive to his distress." In a letter to his friend Henri Hubert, Marcel Mauss wrote, "It is great disaster" (Fournier 1994: 388).

NOTES

Thanks to Candis Steenbergen, PhD candidate at Concordia University, Montreal, for her revision of the English version of our text.
1 The *Petit Robert* 2 also provides space (albeit small) for descriptions of each of Durkheim's collaborators.

2 Durkheim's books have appeared in multiple editions, a journal, *Durkheimian Studies / Études durkheimiennes*, has been created in his name, his correspondence has been published, countless conferences have been organized on his life and works, and a number of anthologies have been published examining and re-examining books that Durkheim wrote a hundred years ago. As well, the *Société des Amis de Durkheim* was founded, and two streets, one in Épinal and now another in Paris near the *Nouvelle Grande Bibiliothèque*, and a college bear his name.

3 For instance, *Études durkheimiennes* (which became *Durkheimian Studies / Études durkheimiennes*), and *Revue d'histoire des sciences humaines* (edited by Laurent Mucchielli).

4 The subtitles of these books published by the Éditions de Minuit, "Le sens commun" collection are: (1) *Éléments d'une théorie sociale*, (2) *Religion, morale et anomie*, and (3) *Fonctions sociales et institutions*. The director of this collection was Pierre Bourdieu. Victor Karady authored many articles on the institutionalization of sociology in France, and was also the editor of three volumes of Marcel Mauss' *Oeuvres* (Mauss 1969).

5 The "pioneers" are T. N. Clark (1968a; 1968b; 1973) and Steven Lukes (1972). During the last two decades, many articles and books have been published in France: J-M. Berthelot (1995), Ph. Besnard (1972a; 1987; 1993), J. C. Filloux (1977), V. Karady (1976; 1979), B. Lacroix (1981), Ph. Steiner (1994), L. Mucchielli (1998), C. Tarot (1999). There are also many special issues of journals (*Revue française de sociologie* 1976, 1979; *L'Année sociologique* 1998; *Revue d'histoire des sciences humaines* 1999) and edited texts (Besnard 1993; Besnard, Borlandi and Vogt 1993; Pickering and Martins 1994; Borlandi and Mucchielli 1995; Cuin 1997). In Anglo-Saxon sociology, there has been a renewal of Durkheimian Studies (Alexander 1994, Cladis 1992, Gane 1992, Giddens 1986, Turner 1993, Meštrović 1988, Pickering 1994, Schmauss 1994, Strenski 1997, etc.).

6 Our new Durkheim biography, *Durkheim, Mauss and Cie* (Fournier, in press) has four objectives: (1) the use of a strict chronology in the analysis of Durkheim's work, (2) a defense of the collective dimension of Durkheim's work ("Durkheim, Mauss and Co"), (3) the introduction of a cultural perspective (cultural background, relation to Judaism, and analysis of Durkheim's personality and way of life in social and cultural context (melancholia *fin-de-siècle*)), (4) and the setting up of a dialogue between his political engagement and his work.

7 In 1995, Neil Gross, a graduate student in sociology at the University of Wisconsin conducting research at the Sorbonne discovered a set of notes, *Cours de philosophie fait au Lycée de Sens*, taken by André Lalande (1867–1962) as a student in Durkheim's course in February 1884. Durkheim was transferred to the Lycée de Saint-Quentin in February 1884. For the remainder of the course, Lalande copied the notes taken the previous year by another of Durkheim's students. The manuscript is available on the world wide web: www.relst.uiue.edu/Durkheim/Texts/1884a/oo.html.

8 Between the "early writings" (1885–1893) and the "later writings," there is, according to Alexander, the "middle period" (1895–7), which is a period of transition. Jerrold Seigel (1987) doesn't take too seriously this idea of a

sudden change – Durkheim has always appreciated the social importance of religion – and suggests a much more gradual process. The date which seems to him more important is not 1895 but 1898: "The moment at which Durkheim reversed himself, giving a religious form to the consciousness and practice that attached modern individuals to the social whole, came in 1898". The occasion was Durkheim's entry into the lists as a defender of Alfred Dreyfus (Seigel 1987: 483–5).

9 In August 1883, Durkheim gave a lecture at the Lycée de Sens, "Le rôle des grands hommes dans l'histoire," which was his first theoretical text (in Durkheim 1975: 1409–17).

10 Durkheim gave his first lecture-course on religion at Bordeaux in 1893–5 and his father died in 1896. Bernard Lacroix presents a socio-psychoanalytical interpretation of this crucial period: before the death of his father the rabbi (Lacroix 1981). According to this interpretation, it should have been impossible for Durkheim to study religion from a positivist and a sociological perspective before the death of his father.

11 The transmission of the rabbinic office has been not only from father to son, but also from the father-in-law to son-in-law.

12 This three-page manuscript was written by Mauss at the beginning of the 1940s in order to defend the "old settlement" of his family in France.

13 According to the testimonial of Durkheim's grandson, Étienne Halphen, Émile Durkheim studied for a time in a rabbinical school (Lukes 1972: 39), but this information is not well documented: where did he get this training? There was not such a rabbinic school near Épinal.

14 Descendants of the Durkheim family know nothing of this story, told by Georges Davy (Pickering 1994: 37).

15 He continues: ". . . it is for him a way of compensating for the disadvantageous situation in which opinion and sometimes the law places him. And as, by itself, science cannot influence a tradition which has kept all its vigor, he superimposes this intellectual life on his customary activity without the former weakening the latter. This is where the complexity of his make up comes from. Primitive in certain aspects, in others cerebral and refined. In this way he combines the advantages of strong discipline which characterizes the small group of the past with the benefits of the intense culture with which our large scale societies are privileged. He has all the intelligence of modern man without sharing his despair" (Durkheim 1897a: 169–70).

16 It appears as though Moïse Durkheim did not complete his studies (Greenberg 1976: 625).

17 According to Derczanski, this tradition, which came from Eastern Europe and found a place in the rabbinic school in Metz, was strongly juridical and stood opposed to every form of messianism and mysticism.

18 In the family, there was a "very precious and very old book which," according to Mauss, contained "some Kabbilistic, mystical comments" (Marcel Mauss, Notes, manuscript, n.d.: 3).

19 The topics of his exams were the relationship between imagination and thinking (in philosophy), and the modern theory of evolution (in the history of philosophy).

20 Steve Fenton took the same position: "Despite his early abandonment of the Jewish faith, the influence of his early life and family origins cannot be lightly dismissed" (Fenton 1984: 15). For an opposing view, see Stjepan C. Meštrović (1988), who thinks that Durkheim's sociology was relatively uninfluenced by Judaism.

21 Marie Durkheim married Jacques Halphen, a rich engineer, and they had three children: Claude (1914), Étienne (1919) and Maurice (1923).

22 In the 1930s, corporatism was associated with fascism. "Is not," asks Svend Ranulf in 1939, a former student of Marcel Mauss, "the rise of fascism an event which, in due logic, Durkheim ought to have welcomed as the salvation from individualism for which he had trying rather gropingly to prepare the way?" Ranulf responds himself, "In due logic, undoubtedly. But there are aspects of fascism which would probably have seemed unacceptable to Durkheim . . ." (Ranulf 1955: 114).

23 Between 1890 and 1895, membership ranged from 5 to 15 percent of the labor force.

24 Under the leadership of Fernand Pelloutier, the local workers initiated a national federation in 1892.

25 Professor at the École Normale Supérieure, historian and critic of literature, Brunetière was the editor of the journal *La Revue des deux mondes*.

26 One of his collaborators, Célestin Bouglé, published a few years later "Individualisme et sociologie" (1905) in the *Revue Bleue*, defending the same thesis as Durkheim.

27 On the first list, there are the name of Durkheim's friends and collaborators: Lucien Herr, Célestin Bouglé, Paul Lapie, François Simiand. The names of Henri Hubert and Paul Fauconnet appear on the second list, and the name of Durkheim, only on the seventh list. Marcel Mauss, who was in England studying at Oxford, signed the petition later (eleventh list) (Winock 1996: 374–390).

28 Agrégé of philosophy and author of a PhD thesis on "Les idées égalitaires," Célestin Bouglé (1869–1927) was a professor of philosophy at Montpellier, and later at Toulouse and Paris.

29 Durkheim's notes have been edited by Marcel Mauss, with an introduction in 1928 (Durkheim 1928).

REFERENCES

Alexander, Jeffrey. C. 1994.
   (ed). 1988. *Durkheimian Sociology: Cultural Studies*. Cambridge: Cambridge University Press.
   1986a. "Rethinking Durkheim's Intellectual Development, I: On 'Marxism' and the Anxiety of Being Understood." *International Sociology* 1: 91–107.
   1986b. "Rethinking Durkheim's Intellectual Development, II: Working Out a Religious Sociology." *International Sociology* 1: 189–201.
   1982. *Theoretical Logic in Sociology*. Vol. 2, *The Antinomies of Classical Thought: Marx and Durkheim*. Berkeley: University of California Press.
Alpert, Harry. [1939] 1961. *Émile Durkheim and his Sociology*. New York: Russell and Russell.

1937. "France's First University Course in Sociology." *American Sociological Review* 2: 311–17.

Bergson, Henri. 1889. *Essai sur les données immédiates de la conscience.*

Berthelot, J.-M. 1995. *1895, Durkheim L'avènement de la sociologie scientifique.* Toulouse: Presses de L'Université Le Mirail.

Besnard, Philippe. 1987. *L'Anomie, ses usages et ses fonctions dans la discipline sociologique depuis Durkheim.* Paris: Presses Universitaires de France.

1979a. "La Formation de l'équipe de *L'Année sociologique*." *Revue française de sociologie* 20: 7–31.

(ed.) 1979b. "Les Durkheimiens." *Revue française de sociologie* 20: 1.

(ed.) 1993. *The Sociological Domain. The Durkheimians and the Founding of the French Sociology,* Cambridge: Cambridge University Press.

Besnard, Philippe, Massimo Borlandi and Paul Vogt, 1993. *Division du travail et lien social. Durkheim cent ans après.* Paris: Presses Universitaires de France.

Borlandi, Massimo and Laurent Muchielli (eds.) 1995. *La Sociologie et sa méthode.* Paris: La Découverte.

Bouglé, Célestin. 1930a. "Émile Durkheim." *Encyclopedia of Social Sciences* 5: 28.

1930b. "L'œuvre sociologique de Durkheim." *Europe* 23: 281–304.

1899. "La tradition française." Conference prononcée à la Mairie de Montpellier: 17 February, cited in Jennifer Mergy. *Nations et nationalismes,* 2001, p. 209.

[1907] 1924. *Le solidarisme.* Paris: Girard.

1905. "Individualisme et sociologie." *Revue bleue* 4 (October): 588.

1902. "La Crise du libéralisme." *Revue de métaphysique et morale* 10: 635–52.

Brunetière, Ferdinand. 1898. "Après le procès." *Revue des deux mondes* 146 (March 15): 428–46.

Charle, Christophe. 1974. "Le beau mariage d'Émile Durkheim." *Actes de la recherche en sciences sociales* 55: 44–9.

Cladis, Mark. 1992. *A Communitarian Defence of Liberalism.* Stanford, CA: Stanford University Press.

Clark, Terry N. 1973. *Prophets and Patrons. The French University and the Emergence of Social Sciences.* Cambridge, MA: Harvard University Press.

1968a. "Émile Durkheim and the Institutionalization of Sociology in the French University System." *European Journal of Sociology* 9: 37–71.

1968b."The Structure and the Function of a Research Center: the Année sociologique." *European Journal of Sociology* 9: 72–91.

Coser, Lewis A. 1960. "Durkheim's Conservatism and its Implication for his Sociological Theory." pp. 211–32 in *Essays on Sociology and Philosophy.* Edited by Kurt H. Wolff. New York: Harper Torchbooks.

Cuin, Charles-Henry. 1997. *Durkheim d'un siècle à L'autre Lectures actuelles des Règles de la méthode Sociologique.* Paris: Presses Universitaires de France.

Dash Moore, Deborah. 1986. "David Émile Durkheim and the Jewish Response to Modernity." *Modern Judaism* (October): 287–300.

Davy, Georges. 1960. "Émile Durkheim." *Revue française de sociologie* 1: 3–24.

1919. "Émile Durkheim: L'homme." *Revue de métaphysique et de morale* 26: 181–98.

Derczanski, Alexandre. 1990. "Note sur la judéité de Durkheim." *Archives des sciences sociales des religions* 69: 157–60.

Digeon, Paul. 1959. *La Crise Allemande de la pensée française, 1870–1914*. Paris: Presses Universitaires de France.

Durkheim, Émile. 2003. *L'Évaluation en comité. Textes et rapports de souscription au Comité des travaux historiques et scientifiques 1903–1917*. Edited by Stéphane Baciocchi and Jennifer Mergy. New York: Durkheim Press and Oxford: Berghahn Press.

1998. *Lettres à Marcel Mauss*. Edited by Philippe Besnard and Marcel Fournier. Paris: Presses Universitaires de France.

1996. *Cours de philosophie fait au Lycéee de Sens*. Bibliothèque de la Sorbonne, manuscript number 2351.

1979. "Lettres de Durkheim, candidat et patron." *Revue française de sociologie* 20 (January–March): 113–18.

1975. *Textes*. 3 vols. Paris: Éditions de Minuit.

[1928] 1971. *Le Socialisme*. Paris: Presses Universitaires de France.

[1925] 1963. *L'Éducation Morale*. Paris: Pressses Universitaires de France.

[1920] 1975. "Introduction à la morale." pp. 313–32 in *Textes*. Vol. 1. Paris: Éditions de Minuit.

[1918] 1975. "La Vie Universitaire à Paris." pp. 453–83 in *Textes*. Vol. 1. Paris: Éditions de Minuit.

1916. *Lettres à tous les Français*. Paris: Comité de publication (1st letter, 5th letter, 10th letter and 11th letter).

[1912] 1968. *Les Formes Élémentaires de la vie religieuse*. Paris: Presses Universitaires de France.

[1907] 1975. "Lettre au Directeur de la *Revue Néo-scolastique*" in *Textes*. Vol. 1. Paris: Éditions de Minuit.

[1904] 1970. "L'Élite Intellectuelle et la démocratie." *Revue bleue*. pp. 279–81 in Émile Durkheim, *La Science Sociale et l'action*. Paris: Presses Universitaires de France.

[1899a] 1975. Contribution to the "Enquête sur la guerre et le militarisme." pp. 160–64 in *Textes*. Vol. 3. Paris: Éditions de Minuit.

[1899b] 1975. Contribution to the "Enquête sur l'antisémitisme publié par H. G. Dagan." pp. 242–57 in *Textes*. Vol. 2. Paris: Éditions de Minuit.

[1898a] 1928. "Représentations individuelles et représentations collectives" in Émile Durkheim, *Sociologie et philosophie*. Paris: Librairie Félix Alcan.

[1898b] 1970. "L'Individualisme et les intellectuels." *Revue bleue*. pp. 261–78 in Émile Durkheim, *La Science Sociale et l'action*. Paris: Presses Universitaires de France.

[1897a] 1969. *Le Suicide: Étude de sociologie*. [Suicide.] Paris: Presses Universitaires de France.

[1897b] 1970. Review of Antonio Labriola, *Essai sur la conception historique de l'histoire*. pp. 245–54 in Émile Durkheim, *La Science Sociale et l'action*. Paris: Presses Universitaires de France.

[1897c] 1970. Review of Gaston Richard, *Le Socialisme et la Science Sociale*. pp. 236–43 in Émile Durkheim, *La Science Sociale et l'action*. Paris: Presses Univesitaires de France.

[1895] 1975. "Crime et santé sociale." pp. 173–80 in *Textes*. Vol. 2. Paris: Éditions de Minuit.

[1894] 1968. *Les Règles de la méthode sociologique.* Paris: Presses Universitaires de France.

[1893a] 1986. *De la division du travail social.* Paris: Presses Universitaires de France.

[1893b] 1970. "Notes sur la définition du socialisme." pp. 226–35 in *La Science Sociale et l'action.* Paris: Presses Universitaires de France.

[1892] 1997. *Quid Secundatus Politicae Scientiae Instituendae Contulerit.* Subsidiary thesis, Bordeaux, Gounouilhou. Translated by W. Watts Miller and Emma Griffiths. Oxford: Durkheim Press.

[1888a] 1975. "Suicide et natalité: Étude de statistique sociale." pp. 216–36 in *Textes.* Vol. 2. Paris: Éditions de Minuit.

[1888b] 1975. "Introduction à la sociologie de la famille." Leçon d'ouverture du Cours de science sociale à la Faculté des lettres de Bordeaux. pp. 9–34 in *Textes.* Vol. 3. Paris: Éditions de Minuit.

[1885] 1975. Review of L. Gumplowicz, *Grundriss der Soziologie.* pp. 344–54 in *Textes.* Vol. 1. Paris: Éditions de Minuit.

[1883] 1975. "Le rôle des grands hommes dans L'histoire." pp. 409–17 in *Textes,* vol. 1, Paris: Éditions de Minuit.

Fenton, Steve. 1984. *Durkheim and Modern Sociology.* Cambridge: Cambridge University Press.

Filloux, Jean-Claude. 1977. *Durkheim et le socialisme.* Geneva: Librairie Droz.

Fournier, Marcel. 1994. *Marcel Mauss.* Paris: Fayard.

n.d. *Durkheim, Mauss and Cie.* Paris: Fayard, forthcoming.

Gane, Mike (ed.) 1992. *The Radical Sociology of Durkheim and Mauss.* London: Routledge.

Giddens, Anthony (ed.) 1986. *Durkheim on Politics and the States.* Cambridge: Polity Press.

1971. "Durkheim's Early Works." pp. 65–81 in *Capitalism and Modern Social Theory.* Cambridge: Cambridge University Press.

Greenberg, Louis M. 1976. "Bergson and Durkheim as Sons and Assimilators: The Early Years." *French Historical Studies* 9: 619–35.

Halbwachs, Maurice. 1918. "La doctrine d'Émile Durkheim." *Revue philosophique* 85: 353–411.

Hawkins, Michael J. 1995. "Durkheim and Republican Citizenship." pp. 12–41 in *Durkheim, Europe and Democracy.* Edited by K. Thompson. Oxford: British Centre for Durkheimian Studies. Published in *Émile Durkheim. Critical Assessments of Leading Sociologists.* Vol. 3. Edited by W. S. F. Pickering. London and New York: Routledge, 2001: 295–316.

1980. "Traditionalism and Organicism in Durkheim's Early Writings, 1885–1893." *Journal of the History of the Behavioral Sciences* 16: 31–44.

Jones, Robert Alun.1993."La Science Positive de la morale en France: les sources allemandes de la Division du travail social." pp. 11–43 in *Division du travail et lien social. La thèse de Durkheim un siècle après.* Edited by Philippe Besnard, Massimo Borlandi and Paul Vogt. Paris: Presses Universitaires de France.

1984. *Émile Durkheim: An Introduction to Four Major Works.* Beverly Hills, CA: Sage.

Karady, Victor. 1979. "Stratégies de réussite et mode de faire-valoir de la sociologie chez les durkheimiens." *Revue française de sociologie* 20 (janvier-mars): 49–83.

1976. "Durkheim, les sciences sociales et l'université." *Revue française de sociologie* 15 (avril-juin): 270.

LaCapra, Dominick. 1972. *Émile Durkheim: Sociologist and Philosopher.* Ithaca, NY: Cornell University Press.

Lacroix, Bernard. 1981. *Durkheim et la politique.* Paris: Fondation des Sciences politiques and Montréal: Presses de l'Université de Montréal.

Le Bon, Gustave. 1895. *Psychologie des foules.* Paris: Librairie Félix Alcan.

Lehman, N. J. 1993. *Deconstructing Durkheim: A Post-Post-Structuralist Critique.* London: Routledge.

Lenoir, Raymond. 1930. "L'oeuvre sociologique d'Émile Durkheim: Souvenirs de Célestin Bouglé, Georges Davy, Marcel Granet, Raymond Lenoir et R. Maublanc." *Europe*: 293–5.

Leroux, Robert. 1998. *Histoire et sociologie en France. De l'histoire-science à la sociologie "durkheimienne."* Paris: Presses Universitaires de France.

Lukes, Steven. 1972. *Émile Durkheim. His Life and Work.* New York: Harper and Row.

Mauss, Marcel. 1971. Introduction in Émile Durkheim, *Le Socialisme* (1928). Paris: Presses Universitaires de France.

1969. *Œuvres.* Paris: Éditions de Minuet. 3 vols.

n.d. Notes, manuscript. Fonds Hubert–Mauss, Archives du Collège de France, Paris.

Mergy, Jennifer. 2001. *Nations et nationalismes: Durkheim et les durkheimiens, De la question de l'Alsace-Lorraine à la Société des Nations.* Thèse de doctorat de science politique, Université de Paris IX Dauphine.

Meštrović, Stjepan G. 1988. *Durkheim and the Reformation of Sociology.* New Jersey: Rowman and Littlefield.

Mucchielli, Laurent. 1998. *La découverte du social. Naissance de la sociologie en France.* Paris: Éditions La Découverte.

Nandan, Yash. 1980. Introduction in *Émile Durkheim, Contributions to L'Année sociologique.* New York: Free Press.

Nisbet, Robert A. 1967. *The Sociological Tradition.* London: Heinemann.

Nizan, Paul. 1932. *Les Chiens de garde.* Paris: Maspero.

Nye, Robert A. 1983. "Hereditary, Pathology and Psychoneurosis in Durkheim's Early Work." *Knowledge and Society: Studies in the Sociology of Culture Past and Present* 4: 102–42.

Paoletti, Giovanni. 1992. "Durkheim à l'École Normale Supérieure: lectures de jeunesse." *Durkheimian Studies* (Fall): 11–17.

Petit Robert 2. 1983. Dictionnaire universel des noms propres. Paris, 7th edn.

Pickering, W. S. F. 1994. "The Enigma of Durkheim's Jewishness." pp. 10–39 in *Debating Durkheim.* Edited by W. S. F. Pickering and H. Martin. London: Routledge.

Pickering, W. S. F. and H. Martin (eds.) 1994. *Debating Durkheim.* London: Routledge.

Ranulf, Svend. 1955. "Methods of Sociology, with an Essay: Remarks for the Epistemology of Sociology." *Acta Jutlandica, Arrskrift for Aarhus Universitet* 27: 114.

Richet, Charles. 1890. *Surmenage mental dans la civilisation moderne.*

Richter, Mark. 1960. "Durkheim's Politics and Political Theory" in *Essays on Sociology and Philosophy*. Edited by Kurt H. Wolff. New York and London: Harper.

Schmauss, Warren. 2001. "Durkheim's Early Views on Philosophy, Hypotheses, and Sociology." *Durkheimian Studies* 7: 9–20.

1994. *Durkheim's Philosophy of Science and Sociology of Knowledge.* Chicago: University of Chicago Press.

Schoenfled, Eugen and Stjepan Meštrović. 1989. "Durkheim's Concept of Justice and its Relationship to Social Solidarity." *Sociological Analysis* 30: 113–21.

Seidman, Steven. 1983. *Liberalism and the Origins of European Social Theory.* Oxford: Blackwell.

Seigel, Jerrold. 1987. "Autonomy and Personality in Durkheim: An Essay on Content and Method." *Journal of the History of Ideas*: 483–507.

Silverman, Debora L. 1989. *Art Nouveau in Fin-de-Siècle France, Politics, Psychology and Style.* Berkeley, CA: University of California Press.

Stedman Jones, Susan. 2001. *Durkheim Reconsidered.* London: Polity Press.

Steiner, Philippe. 1994. *La Sociologie de Durkheim.* Paris: La Découverte.

Strenski, Ivan. 1997. *Durkheim and the Jews of France.* Chicago: University of Chicago Press.

Tarot, Camille. 1999. *De Durkheim à Mauss, L'invention du symbolique.* Paris: La Découverte/MAVSS.

Tiryakian, Edward A. 1979. "L'École Durkheimienne à la recherche de la société perdue: la sociologie naissante et son milieu culturel." *Cahiers internationaux de sociologie* 66: 97–114.

Turner, S. (ed). 1993. *Émile Durkheim: Sociologist and Moralist.* London and New York: Routledge.

Vogt, W. Paul. 1993. "L'Influence de la *Division du travail social* sur la sociologie américaine." pp. 197–215 in *Division sur travail et lien social Durkheim cent ans après.* Edited by Philippe Besnard, Massimo Borlandi, and Paul Vogt. Paris: Presses Universitaires de France.

Winock, Michel. 1996. "Affaire Dreyfus." pp. 370–91 in *Dictionnaire des intellectuels français.* Edited by Jacques Julliard and Michel Winock. Paris: Seuil.

3

Durkheim's squares: types of social pathology and types of suicide

Durkheim was very fond of three-part schemas, perhaps due to his training at the *École Normale Superieure* and in philosophy. His three great works *The Division of Labor* (1893), *Suicide* (1897) and *The Elementary Forms of Religious Life* (1912) are each composed of three "books" (setting aside *The Rules of Sociological Method* (1895), a methodological manifesto, first published in article form). The influence of this ternary rhetoric can be perceived right at the heart of his scientific work. Thus in his first major book, Durkheim identifies three abnormal forms of the division of labor; similarly in *Suicide*, he distinguishes three types of suicide. But this is only an illusion. In both cases Durkheim presents three types but, if one reads properly, he describes four. Beneath the appearance of a triangle there is a square, and this square is logically necessary to Durkheim's reasoning and the coherence of his analysis. These two squares, one for abnormal forms of the division of labor, the other for types of suicide, will be briefly reviewed before returning to the thorny question of their possible relationships.

The triangle/squares

Let us begin with Durkheim's first work, his doctoral thesis which was defended at the age of thirty-four. The principal objective of this book is to show that the division of labor that characterizes modern societies is the bearer of a form of solidarity, organic solidarity, founded on the interdependence of economic and social roles, as opposed to mechanical solidarity typical of primitive societies, where solidarity is the result of the juxtaposition of similar elements, with weakly differentiated social functions. Nevertheless, not everything is rosy in modern societies. Anomalies exist, transitory according to Durkheim, which are among the most common social pathologies. Durkheim identifies three of these. First the "anomic division of labor" resulting from the absence or the lack of rules which assure cooperation between social roles. Second the "forced division of labor" where regulation is present but unjust so there is inequality of opportunity of access to socio-professional occupations and inequity in contracts that fix rewards for services rendered. Finally another "a-normal" form that we propose to call "bureaucratic" which is characterized by an extreme specialization conjoined with weak productivity and poor coordination of functions. A fourth form is in fact added to these three abnormal forms. Even though it deals with the pathology most often evoked as a consequence of the division of labor, Durkheim considers alienation or the absence of significance in "crumbs of work" – to use the expression of Georges Friedmann (1956) – and the reduction of the individual to the role of a machine in two brief pages at the end of the chapter on the anomic division of labor.

It should be noted that even if we have four pathologies of the division of labor, we don't really have a square: anomie and "constraint" are, from one aspect, direct opposites: lack of regulation in one case, regulation to excess in the other. But we don't see how the bureaucratic and the fourth form, which we will call "alienation," oppose each other. In these two cases the division of labor is very marked and in both cases there is a regulating instrument.

In *Suicide* the square is also essential. Not only the construction of the theory but also the empirical demonstrations presuppose it. To obtain the square, we need to add to the three modes of suicide identified by Durkheim (egoism, altruism, and anomie) a fourth type – fatalism. Let us briefly go over the principal characteristics of these types of suicide. Egoistic suicide is the result of a lack of integration of social groups, which provokes too weak an attachment of the individual to his group. This is the most important type of suicide in the eyes of Durkheim and the one to which he devotes most pages, studying the effect of integration of religious life, the family, and political life. Conversely, altruistic suicide is characterized by insufficient individualization which stems from too strong an integration with the group, a situation illustrated by suicide in primitive societies or, in modern societies, the military. Anomic suicide results from a release or absence of norms defining the objectives of action and limiting human desire and ambition. Its central trait is the open-endedness of the objective of a desire that knows no limit. Economic anomie, the counterpart to the ideology of progress at any price, and conjugal or sexual anomie peculiar to bachelors or provoked by the weakening of matrimonial constraint (in married men) by the institution of divorce, are the two illustrations on which Durkheim relies. A fourth type remains. In opposition to anomie, fatalistic suicide can be characterized as the impossibility of internalizing norms which are too constraining or illegitimate.

This fatalistic suicide was relegated by Durkheim to a footnote. The first person to have signaled the existence of fatalistic suicide was Dohrenwend in

1959 but he did not envisage its real scope – he limited fatalism to situations where norms were imposed by an authority external to the group, adhering to Durkheim's allusion to suicide among slaves. If fatalism is today generally recognized as an element of Durkheimian construction and included in good pedagogical presentations of his works (Steiner 1994), we do not witness its significance often enough. In reality its scope of application is at least equivalent to that of anomie, and it is far from being limited, as some exegetes still proclaim, to slaves, to spouses who are too young or to married wives without children – the examples cited by Durkheim – for it is all married women who are defined by excessive constraint and thus fatalism. By the same token regressive anomie and economic crisis are associated with fatalism. Real anomie is the progressive anomie that develops during periods of strong economic expansion. This is the only interpretation that can explain the empirical data that Durkheim used, in particular the effect of the complex interaction between underlying culture, sex, marriage and suicide (Besnard 1973, 1987, 1993b).

Relations between the two squares

Will it help advance our understanding of Durkheimian theory if we match the typology of a-normal forms of the division of labor with those of suicide? The several attempts made at this have not been conclusive. Allardt (1967) was the first to combine the two. But his objective was to distinguish four types of society according to Durkheimian conceptions, rather than to reconstruct the internal logic of these conceptions. This is why he defined two types of unbalanced societies, anomie on the one hand, alienation due to the constraint identified as fatalism on the other, plus two types of balanced societies, altruism coupled with mechanical solidarity, egoism associated with organic solidarity. This taxonomy is based on the intersection of two dimensions. In the first dichotomy the division of labor can be non-differentiated (altruism and anomie) or differentiated (fatalism and egoism). In the second the pressure towards uniformity of collective conscience can be strong (altruism, fatalism) or weak (anomie, egoism). This reconstruction has its merits, but is not sufficient for our purpose. Notably it strays from Durkheimian analysis, for example when considering the division of labor as weakly differentiated in a situation of anomie. But above all, it does not correspond to Durkheim's intentions or to the logic of his analysis at all. In *Suicide*, it is the pathology that interests Durkheim and, far from placing it in certain social states, he discovers it everywhere. More precisely, he investigates the excessive forms of these states and places them at either end of a U-curve, with normal, organic solidarity residing in the hollow of this bend.

For all this, the essential purpose of Allardt was not to relate the a-normal forms of the division of labor (hereafter simply "a-normal forms") to the two types of suicide. This is in direct contrast to the stated objective of Mohamed Cherkaoui (2000) – an objective which was not realized, despite the systematic research involved. The long-standing friendship and respect that I have for this author does not hold me back from critique when this appears necessary. He asserts he will show that "a bi-univocal correlation exists between the types in both taxonomies" (suicides and a-normal forms) (2000: 110). After having reviewed the three types of suicide and the three types of a-normal forms described by Durkheim, Cherkaoui introduced fatalistic suicide, with some hesitation and failing to award it the importance it merited. He discovered a fourth a-normal form "special anomie," mentioned in a footnote by Durkheim. For our part, we have left this aside because it is not clear exactly what the situation is Durkheim is referring to here. Cherkaoui seems no longer at ease because he restricts himself to recopying the few lines that Durkheim devoted to this "special anomie," without adding any commentary or the smallest illustration.

The second time around, Cherkaoui accepts the separation of the two dimensions, integration and regulation, and subdivides them into two variables as follows: interdependence or independence between the social actors and collective sentiments, for integration; existence or absence of institutionalized norms, legitimization and acceptance or not of these norms, for regulation. Essentially, he only retains the first criteria for integration, the combination of the three dichotomizing criteria (+ or −) producing eight types. Here is the table that he constructed. The types of suicide and social pathologies are not included; and it is necessary to explore Cherkaoui's non-systematic commentaries to assign them to the eight combinations.

A : strong tie, or interdependence (+); weak tie, or independence (−)
B : existence of rules or of institutionalized norms (+); absence of institutionalization of these rules (−)
C : legitimacy and acceptance of these norms (+); illegitimacy and refusal (−)

Through their combination we obtain the typology shown in Table 3.1.

It is difficult to understand what this taxonomic game brings to the question that needs to be resolved. Unsurprisingly, constraint is related to fatalism (type 2) and anomie to anomie (type 7). Egoism is saved from bachelorhood by the appearance of a fifth a-normal form, alienation from the fragmentation of work, forgotten until this point (type 8). One can in fact (Besnard 1987: 39; 1993a: 206) bring egoism into the scenario. In both cases, the

Table 3.1

Types	Criteria		
	A	B	C
1	+	+	+
2	+	+	−
3	+	−	+
4	+	−	−
5	−	+	+
6	−	+	−
7	−	−	+
8	−	−	−

antidote is the same: the awareness in the individual that his action is directed toward a goal that evades him.

To make these combinations there is no need to combine three criteria. As soon as we apply them, we have to relate the eight combinations obtained by their crossing with the types of suicide and a-normal forms. And it is there that we fall into arbitrariness. Why should we characterize anomie by independence (weak integration) and fatalism by interdependence (strong integration)? That goes back to assimilating regulation into integration, presented as two autonomous dimensions. Another example, the combination + + + (interdependence, norms, legitimacy) is assigned on the one hand to altruistic suicide, on the other to mechanical solidarity (type 1). Yet one would rather expect to find organic solidarity – excluded from the typology – precisely because it is defined by a strong interdependence between social functions, whereas mechanical solidarity is made up of the juxtaposition of units which are similar but independent. Let us add that the a-normal forms that Durkheim deals with are the pathologies of organic solidarity. In any case we have a sixth form of the division of labor, put in the same bag as altruistic suicide and this incites the writer, by intuitive analogy, to choose mechanical solidarity above organic. The four other combinations of the typology divide themselves into the division of bureaucratic labor (types 5 and 6) and special anomie (types 3 and 4), considered as opposed to each other. This raises two problems: (1) Each of these two a-normal forms corresponds to two distinct locations on the typology; (2) these two a-normal forms are not related to types of suicide and this demonstrates a failure to make the connections Cherkaoui declared at the start of the project.

With this typology that encompasses eight theoretical cases applied to six forms of the division of labor and to four types of suicide, we are far from the objective stated which was to establish a "bi-univocal relationship."

Cherkaoui perceives this, albeit vaguely and talks of a sketch which would merit expanding. But this sketch, besides the arbitrariness mentioned, lies on arguable territory. First of all, is it possible to characterize situations relating to pathology of regulation by the degree of integration and inversion? We have already signaled this problem with regard to anomie and fatalism; but it is more general. The second difficulty arises in considering that the conditions of organic solidarity are totally independent of each other; this concurs with the explicit declarations of Durkheim. It is also a contradiction because Cherkaoui recognized, with regard to integration, that the second element which he calls "sentiment" is derived from the first: if there is no objective interdependence, there is no subjective interdependence. Why is it not the same for regulation? This leads Mohamed Cherkaoui (2000) to describe anomie (type 7) as a situation where institutionalized norms are absent, but where, in spite of their inexistence, they are taken as legitimate!

Durkheim's position on this point is clearly stated in *The Division of Labor* (1893): there are three conditions for the proper functioning of organic solidarity:

- Existence of a system of relations between the "organs" or functions or social roles: we could call this "objective integration" or "interdependence" as Cherkaoui favors.
- The internalized conscience of social actors related to this solidarity or interdependence; this is subjective integration.
- Regulation and the existence of norms which define the manner in which the social functions should interact with each other.

Durkheim stops there in the chapter on the anomic division of labor, but his analysis of the forced division of labor invites the addition of a fourth condition, as the majority of recent commentators have shown (Reynaud 1993, Steiner 1994, Cherkaoui 2000, Paoletti 2002):

- Legitimacy and acceptance of norms.

There is an a-normal form of the division of labor if one of these conditions is not fulfilled. We could confine ourselves to studying which a-normal form corresponds to the lack of which condition. This leaves us with:

- Injustice of norms: forced division of labor which we propose to call "inequality" for the sake of brevity and better correspondence with situations evoked by Durkheim.
- Absence of norms: anomie.
- Absence of subjective integration: alienation.
- Absence of objective integration: bureaucracy.

Table 3.2

	Integration		Regulation	
Division of labor	A	B	C	D
bureaucratic	−			
alienated	+	−		
anomic			−	
unequal			+	−

Only the last correspondence merits a comment. The lack of objective integration is not because there is no division of labor. On the contrary, it is marked. It is the absence of activity that determines the absence of interaction. We will go further by applying two criteria to certain pathologies. Here we are following a recent study by Giovanni Paoletti (2002). We will use his table, having simply changed the names of the a-normal forms. Paoletti distinguishes two primary criteria and two derived criteria, which is logical (hence the "b" and "d" for the derived criteria). But he is wary of combining regulation and integration in the description of types.

Table 3.2 does not require commentary, but it should be noted that the + sign is applied to the first element of integration with regard to alienation. For Cherkaoui, this is "evidence" that interdependence is not present in piece-work. The absence of subjective interdependence is certain, it is indeed the central characteristic of this pathology; but objective interdependence is the primary intent of this exaggerated division of labor. What is true is that technical interdependence of the tasks does not automatically produce moral interdependence (on this point see Friedmann 1956, Pizzorno 1963, Reynaud 1993).

Durkheimian optimism says the opposite. Interaction of the organs usually produces subjective solidarity which gives rise to a regulation of the relations between the social functions. We can therefore adopt this perspective to construct a typology which makes the conditions of organic solidarity interdependent.

Table 3.3 joins the pathologies of the division of labor and the types of suicide under two restrictive conditions. First, egoism corresponds to two a-normal forms; then and above all altruistic suicide disappears. This disappearance is in reality logical. Altruistic suicide and mechanical solidarity are characteristics of societies with a weak division of labor, whereas the a-normal forms signaled by Durkheim are pathologies of the division of labor. Second, the modern examples of altruistic suicide furnished by Durkheim (the military, prisoners) could equally well be seen, perhaps with even more

Table 3.3

Anormal forms and types of suicide	Integration		Regulation	
	A	B	C	D
bureaucracy, egoism	−	−	−	−
alienation, egoism	+	−	−	−
anomie, anomie	+	+	−	−
inequality, fatalism	+	+	+	−

Table 3.4

Pathologies and types of suicide	Integration		Regulation	
	A	B	C	D
bureaucracy, egoism	−	−	+	?
alienation, egoism	+	−	+	−
anomie, anomie	?	?	−	?
inequality, fatalism	?	?	+	−

accuracy, as coming under the umbrella of fatalistic suicide. Finally, the curvilinear relationship between integration and suicide is not established on a solid empirical basis, whereas this is well established in the case of regulation with its two poles of anomie and fatalism. Fatalism is necessary to Durkheim's demonstration, in contrast to altruism.[1]

Despite its formal coherence, the typology at which we have arrived is not satisfactory. It does not conform to Durkheim's descriptions in that it obliges us to characterize the situations in two dimensions at once, integration and regulation. It is arbitrary to see an absence of norms in bureaucracy and alienation, even though, according to Durkheim, a regulatory organ exists in these situations. So we fall again into the same arbitrariness for which we reproached Cherkaoui. Thus the only remaining solution is to match the uncertainties with a question mark, as in Table 3.4.

We can see that all these taxonomic games do not advance us much towards the understanding of Durkheimian theory. The attempt to relate the pathologies of the division of labor and the types of suicide is deceptive. Thus, putting the two anomies in alignment does not enlighten us to the meaning of the concept. Anomie in the *Division of Labor*, a simple and temporary deficiency in regulation, is quite different from that of *Suicide* which is at a chronic stage and "for all this normal" in industrial societies. Neither does this study of the correspondence between the two typologies permit us to establish the symmetries amongst the opposing types. Fatalism is not the exact opposite of anomie: there one touches on one of the principal difficulties of the interpretation of *Suicide*, a book left open by reason of its incompleteness (Besnard 1973).

NOTES

This chapter was translated by Philippa Smith in consultation with its author.
1 One could add a supplementary line to this table: + + + + which corresponds to normal organic solidarity, but our aim concerns a-normal forms. Let us add that the exclusion of altruism also permits us to relate three types of suicide to three types of a-normal forms if we accept the hypothesis that challenges the autonomy of alienation in piece-work with regard to anomie, keeping to the same text as Durkheim (as in Reynaud, 1993: 300). It is true that it would be a bit paradoxical to take Durkheim word for word in his first work and at the same time betray his words in his others.

REFERENCES

Allardt, Erik. 1967. "Durkheim e la sociologia politica." *Rassegna italiana di sociologia* 8: 47–66.

Besnard, Philippe. 1993a. "Les pathologies des sociétés modernes." pp. 197–211 in *Division du travail et lien social. La thèse de Durkheim un siècle après*. Edited by Philippe Besnard, Massimo Borlandi, and Paul Vogt. Paris: Presse Universitaires de France.

1993b. "Anomie and Fatalism in Durkheim's Theory of Regulation." pp. 169–90 in *Émile Durkheim: Sociologist and Moralist*. Edited by Stephen Turner. London: Routledge.

1987. *L'Anomie*. Paris: Presses Universitaires de France.

1973. "Durkheim et les femmes ou *Le Suicide* inachevé." *Revue française de Sociologie* 14: 27–61.

Cherkaoui, Mohamed. 2000. "Suicides et formes anormales de la division du travail." pp. 109–23 in *Le Suicide un siècle après Durkheim*. Edited by Massimo Borlandi and Mohamed Cherkaoui. Paris: Presses Universitaires de France.

Dohrenwend, Bruce Philip. 1959. "Egoism, Altruism, Anomie, and Fatalism: A Conceptual Analysis of Durkheim's Types." *American Sociological Review* 24: 466–72.

Durkheim, Émile. 1912. *Les Formes élémentaires de la vie religieuse. Le système totémique en Australie*. Paris: Librairie Félix Alcan.

1897. *Le Suicide. Étude de sociologie*. Paris: Librairie Félix Alcan.

1895. *Les Règles de la méthode sociologique*. Paris: Librairie Félix Alcan.

1893. *De la division du travail social*. Paris: Librairie Félix Alcan.

Friedmann, Georges. 1956. *Le Travail en miettes*. Paris: Gallimard.

Paoletti, Giovanni. 2002. "Il quadrato di Durkheim; la definizione del legame sociale ei suoi critici." pp. 235–261 in *Émile Durkheim. Contributi a una rilettura critica*. Edited by M. Rosati and A. Santambrogio. Rome: Meltemi.

Pizzorno Alessandro. 1963. "Lecture actuelle de Durkheim." *Archives européennes de Sociologie* 4 (1): 1–36.

Reynaud, Jean-Daniel. 1993. "La formation des règles sociales." pp. 295–317, in *Division du travail et lien social. La thèse de Durkheim un siècle après*. Edited by Philippe Besnard, Massimo Borlandi, and Paul Vogt. Paris: Presses Universitaires de France.

Steiner, Philippe. 1994. *La Sociologie de Durkheim*. Paris: La Découverte.

4

ROBERT ALUN JONES

Practices and presuppositions: some questions about Durkheim and *Les Formes élémentaires de la vie religieuse*

According to an old saw, the problem of understanding a classic text is above all one of knowing how to ask the right questions. This small piece of wisdom is enormously attractive to the scholar approaching *Les Formes élémentaires de la vie religieuse* (1912) (hereafter *Les Formes élémentaires*) – a work that advances two outrageously ambitious theories and at least a dozen subsidiary hypotheses, and whose interpretive possibilities sometimes seem endlessly bewildering. The caution here, of course, is that what is or is not a good question must ultimately be settled, not by the text itself, but by the interests and purposes of the scholarly community. Good questions, in other words, will be those that lead to answers – or perhaps to other and better questions – that are interesting and useful *to us*. This caveat entered, I begin by asking what seems to be a good question – i.e. What did Durkheim *himself* consider the most important and distinctive aspects of his classic work? My assumption here is that the effort to answer this question will lead to other questions – some better, some worse – and of course to other answers as well.

On February 4, 1913 – as if anticipating my initial question – Durkheim spoke at a meeting of the *Société francaise de philosophie*, defending the "two principal ideas" that "dominate" *Les Formes élémentaires*. The first was what he called the "dynamogenic quality of religion" – i.e. its power to provide, not a speculative source of knowledge, but a real source of action. The man who is with his god, Durkheim emphasized, has "a certain confidence, an ardor for life, an enthusiasm that he does not experience in ordinary times. He has more power to resist the hardships of existence; he is capable of greater things and proves it by his conduct." But these effects can be realized only in so far as the god is represented in the mind, "with an energy sufficient for the representation that expresses them to be efficacious." The gods must be "believed in, and believed in with a collective faith," for "the faith of each can be strong only if it is partaken of by all" (Durkheim 1913b: 4–5, 6).

80

The second idea – closely related to the first – was the "duality of human nature." Every religion contains an idea that corresponds to the distinction between body and soul, flesh and spirit, sometimes expressed more philosophically in the Cartesian and Kantian distinctions between sensations and concepts, or sensible appetites and moral actions. More than a distinction, however, this idea expresses a profound opposition – our concepts "do violence to" our sensations, our moral actions "offend" our instincts and inclinations: "No matter what we should do," Durkheim complained (1913b: 8), "we can never be completely in accord with ourselves, for we can follow one of our two natures only if the other thereby suffers. We are thus condemned to life perpetually divided against ourselves." But if Durkheim had no solution, he at least had an explanation. Cartesian metaphysics and the Kantian antinomies merely translate the more primitive distinction and opposition between the sacred and the profane; and all are dependent upon social causes. Again, society cannot exist without penetrating individual minds, and cannot penetrate individual minds without elevating the individual above himself. The individual is thus comprised of two different "beings" – the first derived from and expressing our physical organism, the second derived from and expressing society. It is inevitable that these two beings should oppose one another, for the first is reflected in those sensations and appetites for which the individual demands satisfaction, while the second gives rise to reason and moral action, without which society is literally impossible. Metaphorically, therefore, the gods (i.e. society) depend upon men (i.e. individuals) for their existence, just as men (individuals) depend upon the gods (society) for the best attributes of themselves; and once this is recognized, Durkheim concluded, the task of the science of religions becomes clear – i.e. to explain the nature and origin of the forces upon which our social actions rely.

In intellectual history, such open declarations by an author of what really matters in his work are rare, and this one leads almost inevitably to a second question – i.e. At what point in the development of Durkheim's sociological thought did these ideas first emerge? They are certainly not reflected in the earliest evidence we have of Durkheim's thought – i.e. André Lalande's detailed notes of Durkheim's lectures on philosophy delivered at the *Lycée de Sens* (1883–4) – which suggest that Durkheim had yet to develop any sociological sensibilities whatever.[1] Durkheim's earliest writings on religion – e.g. his reviews of Herbert Spencer's *Ecclesiastical Institutions* (1885) and Jean-Marie Guyau's *L'Irréligion de l'avenir* (1887) – contain intimations of ideas later found in *Les Formes élémentaires* – e.g. his anti-intellectualist belief that Tylor's animistic hypothesis of 1871 was mistaken; that the idea of God is a "minor accident" that both "hides and expresses" more fundamental social realities; that religion is less a matter of speculative belief than one of habit and custom, and that while science will gradually replace this speculative function, religion will endure as a regulative "social discipline." It would be a mistake, however, to exaggerate the significance of these early reviews, which contain no mention of totemism and, indeed, might reasonably be described as "pre-ethnographic." Most important, while Durkheim's early understanding of religion was certainly "sociological," this should be taken in the rather stark, Kantian sense of obligation and constraint – i.e. religion is repeatedly conjoined with law and morality as one of the three great regulative institutions of society, and its more positive, "dynamogenic" qualities are nowhere in evidence.

This same emphasis is carried on throughout *De la division du travail social* (1893), which is still indifferent to ethnography, where totemism is mentioned only *en passant*, and where Durkheim continues to use a vocabulary of duty, obligation, and constraint – e.g. religion forces the individual into practices "that are irksome to him and sacrifices, whether great or small, which cost him something. He must give from his possessions the offerings which he is constrained to present to the divinity. He must take from his work or leisure time the necessary moments for the performance of rites. He must impose upon himself every kind of privation that is commanded of him, and even renounce life itself if the gods so decree. The religious life," Durkheim insisted, "is made up entirely of abnegation and altruism" (Durkheim [1893] 1984: 49). At the same time, Durkheim seems to have viewed religious beliefs and sentiments as largely epiphenomenal, lacking in independent explanatory power – e.g. referring to Fustel's *La Cité antique* (1864), he complained that "having postulated the religious idea, without tracing its derivation from anything," Fustel had "deduced from it the social arrangements which he noted, whilst, on the contrary, it is these arrangements that explain the power and nature of the religious idea" (Durkheim [1893] 1984: 130).[2]

In *Les Règles de la méthode sociologique* (1895) (*Les Règles*), of course, constraint is "the characteristic trait of every social fact." The individual finds himself "in the presence of a force which dominates him and to which he must bow." To induce the individual to submit to this force, it is sufficient "to make him aware of his natural state of dependence and inferiority. Through religion," Durkheim added, "he represents this state to himself by the senses or symbolically," while through science, "he arrives at an adequate and precise notion of it" (Durkheim [1895] 1982: 143). In sum, it is easy to agree with Steven Lukes, who long ago characterized Durkheim's earliest writings on religion as "largely formal and rather *simpliste*" (Lukes 1972: 240).

At this point, it has become customary to mention the lecture course on religion that Durkheim taught at Bordeaux (1894–5); for while no record of its content has survived, its significance was attested to by Durkheim himself twelve years later – i.e. "it was not until 1895," Durkheim recalled in 1907:

> that I achieved a clear view of the essential role played by religion in social life. It was in that year that, for the first time, I found the means of tackling the study of religion sociologically. This was a revelation to me. That course of 1895 marked a dividing line in the development of my thought, to such an extent that all my previous researches had to be taken up afresh in order to be made to harmonize with these new insights . . . [This reorientation] was entirely due to the studies of religious history which I had just undertaken, and notably to the reading of the works of Robertson Smith and his school.
>
> (Durkheim 1913a: 326)[3]

Unfortunately, Durkheim never disclosed the precise nature of this revelation, and in fact, there is no indication whatever, in anything written by Durkheim in the years immediately after 1895, that he had seriously embraced the arguments of Smith's *Religion of the Semites* (1889).[4] In *Le Suicide* (1897), we instead see the influence of Frazer's *Golden Bough* (1890), for the central idea of Frazer's work – i.e. the myth of a "man–god" sacrificed so that his spirit might be passed on unimpaired to his successor – epitomized the altruistic suicide that Durkheim found among primitive peoples (Durkheim [1897] 1951: 218, 220). In his first edition (1890), Frazer had attributed this idea to the influence of his friend, Robertson Smith; but in the second edition (1900), this influence was explicitly denied. Indeed, in Frazer's work this "central idea" had been wrenched from its more powerful, sociological context – i.e. Smith's description of "the mystic unity of life in the religious community," which "is liable to wear out, and must be revived and strengthened from time to time" (Smith [1894] 1972: 405–6; also see Jones 1984: 49). Of this more sociological conception – the model on which Durkheim's interpretation of the Australian evidence would be constructed just a few years later – not a trace appeared in *Le Suicide*.

Durkheim's early contributions to *L'Année sociologique* continued to reflect this largely negative, Frazerian emphasis. In his essay on incest (1898a), for example, Durkheim seems at last to have appreciated the significance of totemism; but even after reviewing the substantial literature that had grown up around it, Durkheim's understanding of totemism seems to have relied more heavily on Frazer's *Totemism* (1887), insisting that it was but a single instance of a far greater institution that lay at the basis of all religions – i.e. the idea of taboo. Durkheim's understanding of taboo – also derived from Frazer – became the foundation for his classic distinction between the sacred and profane; but Durkheim's language continued to be dominated by reference to rules, duties, prohibitions, obligations, interdictions, sanctions, and constraints. Of the "dynamogenic quality of religion" and the "duality of human nature," not a single trace appears (Durkheim [1898a] 1963: 71–2, 77–8).

By the time we reach Durkheim's 1899 essay on the definition of religious phenomena, however, scholars who have traced the development of Durkheim's ideas about religion have begun to disagree. Steven Lukes, for example, has described it as "a first, rather groping attempt to see religion as a social phenomenon," contrasting it with Durkheim's later, "more nuanced and complex" sociology of religion (1972: 240). W. S. F. Pickering has disagreed, insisting that the essay "was written as a result of the new insights that [Durkheim] had gained from reading Robertson Smith," and that "the judgment of Lukes that the essay is of little consequence is a hasty one" (Pickering 1984: 72). But Lukes was right. Religious phenomena, Durkheim insisted, are characterized above all by "obligatory beliefs," where "obligatory" was emphasized to distinguish religion from science (voluntary beliefs), and "beliefs" to distinguish religion from law and morality (obligatory behavior) (Durkheim [1899] 1975: 92–3). The suspicion that Durkheim had not yet taken the measure of Smith's Semites is encouraged by the fact that, for Smith, it was precisely the "fixed and obligatory" character of ancient ritual that distinguished it from "variable and discretionary" mythological beliefs derived from ritual – i.e. the famous "ritual theory of myth" (Durkheim [1899] 1975: 99 n25). And this suspicion is encouraged still further by the fact that, in 1899, Durkheim was still unable to find a clear distinction between religion and magic, despite Smith's earlier – and powerfully sociological – insistence that the difference was isomorphic with that between social and individual, public and private, conscience and self-interest, etc. (Durkheim [1899] 1975: 99 n24; also see Smith [1894] 1972: 55).

By 1902, however, Durkheim would regret that so much of the ethnographic literature had focused on the "negative" elements of totemism (e.g. taboos, abstentions, interdictions, etc.), rather than the "positive" aspects of the cult (e.g. prestations, communal sacrifices, feasts, dances, etc.), particularly in light of the fact that these more positive features were the more primitive. And by 1906–7, when he offered a second lecture-course on religion at the Sorbonne, Durkheim spoke of religion as the symbolic representation of a force that elevates the individual above himself, strengthening the life within him (see Durkheim 1907: 103–8). During these years, therefore, Durkheim's account of religious phenomena seems to have changed dramatically, from an emphasis on obligation and constraint to a focus on its "dynamogenic quality" and the "duality of human nature." This, in turn, raises a third question – i.e. what was Durkheim *doing* when he shifted his emphasis from the negative to the more positive aspects of religious beliefs and practices?[5] And the answer to this question requires a deeper grasp of the intellectual context within which *Les Formes élémentaires* was conceived.

Frazer's initial understanding of totemism was reflected in his *Totemism* (1887) and the first edition of *The Golden Bough* (1890). The first, written under the guidance of Robertson Smith,[6] was largely a descriptive summary of what was already known about the phenomenon, although Frazer noted in closing "the tendency of totemism to preserve certain species of plants and animals must have largely influenced the organic life of the countries where it has prevailed" (Frazer 1887: 95–6). The second, which owed far more to the animistic hypothesis of E. B. Tylor,[7] advanced the first of Frazer's three theories of totemism – i.e. for the protection of his "life" or "soul," the primitive man temporarily or permanently deposits his soul in an animal or plant, which explains the man's reference for the animal, his objection to killing it, the animal's reciprocal kindness to and protection of the man, and the general notion that the man and his totem animal are kinsmen by descent (Frazer 1890, vol. 2: 337–58).

Early in 1897, as he was completing his *Pausanias* and starting to consider a second edition of *The Golden Bough*, Frazer received a letter from his friend, the anthropologist Lorimer Fison. Enclosed was a second letter that Fison himself had recently received from the ethnographer Baldwin Spencer, which mentioned *en passant* that members of the Arunta tribe of central Australia "ate their own totems" in a solemn ceremony known as the *intichiuma* (Ackerman 1987: 154). However incidental Spencer's remark (it was contained in a postscript), it raised the possibility of confirming Smith's theory of a primitive, totemic sacrament in which the god and his worshippers shared a common, joyful meal, thus reaffirming their mystical bond of kinship and solidarity. The difficulty for Smith's theory had been that the sole concrete example of such a totemic sacrament was one reported by St. Nilus, of pre-Islamic nomads sacrificing and consuming a camel; and when further examples were not forthcoming, Frazer himself had become increasingly skeptical. In his eulogy for Smith in 1894, therefore, Frazer had praised Smith for being the first to recognize that mystical, communion sacrifices are found outside of Christianity, in heathen and even savage religions; but on the related question of a primitive, totemic sacrifice, Frazer had stated simply that "the evidence thus far does not enable us to pronounce decisively" (Frazer [1894] 1920: 206).

Intrigued by the postscript, Frazer and Spencer soon established a mutually beneficial correspondence. Frazer not only helped Spencer and his collaborator, F. J. Gillen, find a publisher (Macmillan) for their work, *The Native Tribes of Central Australia* (1899), but he also read the proofs and thus shortened their time to publication. On September 15, 1898, having reviewed the second proof of *Native Tribes*, Frazer wrote to Spencer and proposing his second theory of totemism – i.e. "a system expressly devised for the purpose of procuring a plentiful supply of food, water, sunshine, wood, etc." All the desirable things in nature were put in classes, Frazer suggested, and each was assigned to a specific group of people charged with securing the multiplication of the members of that particular class. Each group would then quite naturally have identified with the species of animal, plant, etc., assigned to them, because by doing so, they would know all the secrets of that species – e.g. what they eat, how they mate and multiply, how they might be caught, etc. – and this would help the group to do its job (Marett and Penniman 1932: 24–5). Finally, Frazer suggested that Spencer's observations of the *intichiuma* ceremonies had at last confirmed the theory of Robertson Smith: "The ceremonial eating of the totem by the men of the totem," Frazer wrote, "seems to me a true totem sacrament (the first well-authenticated example of such a sacrament that has come to light, I believe), the object of which is to identify the man with his totem by imparting to him the life and qualities of the totem animal" (Marett and Penniman 1932: 26–7).[8]

But Frazer and Spencer were not entirely on the same page. The latter's descriptions of the *intichiuma* undoubtedly contained their element of rational premeditation; but as Robert Ackerman has pointed out, these were always embedded in dense ritual context, while Frazer's *Homo economicus aboriginalis* had a propensity for economic planning that would have made him at home in the Fabian Society (Ackerman 1987: 156). Still, when Spencer wrote back to Frazer on October 20, he offered qualified support for Frazer's new theory, adding that it was consistent with his growing suspicion that "the religious aspect of the totem [i.e. the prohibition against killing and eating a representative of the totemic species] is the more ancient, and that the now existing social aspect [i.e. clan exogamy] has been tacked on at a later period" (Marett and Penniman 1932: 31). Frazer concurred, writing back to Spencer on November 28 to add that, "if we define religion as the propitiation of natural and supernatural powers, and magic as the coercion of them, magic has everywhere preceded religion" (Marett and Penniman 1932: 41.) This would become the basis of Frazer's famous evolutionary distinction between magic, religion, and science – i.e. as experience teaches men that they can't *compel* the higher powers to comply with their wishes, they condescend to *entreat* them; and still later, as men begin to understand that even their entreaties are in vain, they again resort to compulsion – albeit this time in the narrower, more disciplined methods of science. On December 14, 1898, at a meeting of the Royal Anthropological Institute hastily arranged by Frazer, Spencer presented the observations. Frazer then followed his correspondent to the podium, expressing his general agreement – adding that he had drawn the same inference from the Australian facts the previous September. It was this rationalist, utilitarian theory of totemism that Frazer elaborated in "The Origin of Totemism" (1899a), "Some Ceremonies of the Central Australian Tribes" (1899b) and, of course, the second edition of *The Golden Bough* (1900).

In general, the second edition was simply a stronger, more aggressive restatement of the main themes of the first. The subtitle – reflecting Frazer's more formal, evolutionary distinction – was changed from "A Study in Comparative Religion" to "A Study of Magic and Religion." And if the 1890 edition had avoided the sensitive question of the status of Judaism and Christianity, the edition of 1900 dropped all pretense, offending both Jews and Christians by arguing that Purim – and therefore the Passion narrative based upon Purim – reflected the same seasonal pattern of other Near Eastern fertility rituals, and that Jesus "was *really* (and therefore, in Frazer's reductionist analysis, *only*) a member of that group of dying and reviving gods that included . . . Attis, Adonis, and Osiris" (Ackerman 1987: 169). The book's controversial reputation probably increased sales, and the response of popular audiences was favorable; but among Frazer's professional colleagues, the response was negative. A. C. Haddon was embarrassed by it, and Moses Gaster, an eminent folklorist as well as a Sephardic rabbi, attacked Frazer's "ridiculous" Purim fantasy. While Frazer would remain the favorite anthropologist of the lay public, many of those closest to him and most knowledgeable in the field would become, and henceforth remain, his opponents (Ackerman 1987: 169–72).

The most important of these opponents was R. R. Marett, who had come to Oxford as an undergraduate in 1884, been attracted to Tylor's evolutionary anthropology, won a fellowship at Exeter College in 1891, and eventually stayed on for life. One of Marett's undergraduate acquaintances had been F. C. S. Schiller, who had gone to teach in the United States and become a friend and philosophical disciple of William James. In 1897, Schiller returned to Oxford, where he became the leading British exponent of Jamesian pragmatism and later secretary of the Oxford Philosophical Society. Marett was president of this Society, to which he presented the only published version of his essay on "Origin and Validity in Ethics" (1902) – a synthesis of evolutionary utilitarianism and Jamesian psychology.[9] In the Fall of 1899 – just before the meeting of the British Association for the Advancement of Science – Marett's Oxford colleague, the classical archaeologist John Myers, asked him to write something "really startling" to enliven the anthropological session.

The result was "Pre-Animistic Religion" (1900), in which Marett suggested, *pace* Tylor, that animism was not the earliest form of religion, but had rather been preceded by some common yet highly specific feeling or emotion whose elements were admiration, wonder, and above all a sense of awe. Where this emotion outstripped the power of rational explanation, Marett argued, there arises an impulse to objectify and even personify this mysterious feeling for the supernatural; and in the will, there arises a corresponding impulse to make this feeling innocuous or even propitious, through constraint, communion, or conciliation. Marett could agree with Frazer that totemism was largely an effort to control forces of nature rather than conciliate them; but he disagreed in arguing that, in practice, magic and religion were not mutually exclusive, but frequently overlapped. The primitive need for an explanation of the mysterious element in these practices was satisfied by the conception of an affinity between the spirits of animals and their human clients, as well as the elevation of animals into sacred objects. Totemism, in short, was the rationalization of a more primitive, pre-animistic notion of the supernatural forces. Finally, Marett dismissed the associationist psychology that had guided Tylor and Frazer as well, insisting that students of primitive religion place less emphasis on "ideal constructions" and more on "that steadfast groundwork of specific emotion whereby man is able to feel the supernatural precisely at the point at which his thought breaks down" (Marett 1900: 22–32).

Four years later, Marett turned his critical attention more directly to Frazer, attacking his evolutionary distinction between magic, religion, and science. Why, Marett asked, does Frazer believe that magic is something utterly different from religion, its negative pre-condition, whose failure is religion's opportunity? Briefly, Marett answered, because "sympathetic magic" seemed to him a simple extension of the laws of associationist psychology. But "no psychologist worth seriously considering," Marett objected, still believes that association is a sufficient explanation for reasoning and thought, for the association of ideas depends on continuity of interest, while the construction of new thought not only reproduces, but actually transforms what is old. Marett's critique of Frazer's associationist theory of magic thus seems to have been drawn from James' *Principles of Psychology* (1890), and his own account of primitive magic seems to have owed at least an equal debt to James' famous essay on "The Will to Believe" (1896). In magic, Marett observed, the rational subject must "positively acquiesce" in the state of mind accompanying the symbolic practice, while simultaneously recognizing that it is irrational. This requires a kind of faith, a "will to believe," which is in some sense self-justifying – i.e. psychologically, it "really works," and is therefore efficacious.

Magic is thus "a more or less clearly recognized pretending, which at the same time is believed to project itself into an ulterior effect" (Marett [1904] 1909: 50–1). In the exercise of magic, the savage recognizes that the "cause" produces its "effect" not *mechanically* (e.g. as a spear is thrown, hits, and kills its target), but *mysteriously* (e.g. as a projection of will or psychic force); and from the standpoint of the victim over whom it is exercised, magic is experienced as a kind of "rapport" or "mysteriously enforced assent." No less than a religious transaction, that between a magician and his victim is "an affair between persons," an exertion of will that finds its way to another will, and dominates it. But how does the savage understand the nature of this mysterious force? This is precisely what R. H. Codrington had described in *The Melanesians* (1891) – i.e. *mana* is the power that does the work, and the object of the beliefs and practices that constitute Melanesian religion is to obtain and control *mana*. Moreover, because *mana* is both non-intrinsic and contagious, it easily passes from the magician himself to other things, which in turn become personified and deified; and from here, it is but a short step to the belief that these other things (e.g. animals, plants, etc.) have "wills" that might also be constrained (Marett [1904] 1909: 67–84).

Across the Channel, Durkheim watched these developments with considerable interest. First, and most immediately, Frazer had denied the universality of totemism and its long-undisputed connection with exogamy, even as Durkheim had firmly committed himself to both just one year earlier. Second, Frazer had suggested that some of society's most powerful interdictions had been rationally and purposefully constructed following an earlier period of permissiveness. That the origin of such interdictions lay in the "collective unconscious," and that primitive societies could hardly be characterized as "permissive," had been among Durkheim's central arguments since the early 1890s. Third, and perhaps most alarmingly, Frazer had suggested that the essential function of totemism was to provide for economic needs, and that this was also its sufficient explanation. The fifth chapter of *Les Règles*, of course, had been written to oppose such "teleological" confusions of the function of a social fact with its cause, and to insist that needs and desires, while they might hasten or retard social development, cannot themselves "create" social facts at all.

In "Sur le totémisme" (1902), Durkheim set about cobbling together his response to Spencer and Gillen's *Native Tribes* and the second edition of *The Golden Bough*. The point here is not that Durkheim had changed his mind in some fundamental way, or that his new emphasis on "the positive aspects of the cult" was "discontinuous" with his earlier preoccupation with taboo;

rather, Durkheim now had a different problem – i.e. to resurrect totemism as a religious institution in the face of Frazer's argument that it was purely a magical, economic phenomenon, and to reconnect totemism's "religious" and "social" elements despite Frazer's insistence that exogamy was a later, derivative institution. In effect, Durkheim was like a carpenter who, having completed one job that required one set of tools, has turned to another that demand a quite different set.

Some of the tools Durkheim used were new, as in the case of Marett's anthropological adaptation of Jamesian psychology; but as so often with "classic texts" like *Les Formes élémentaires*, some were quite old and conventional, having been used for other purposes by an earlier generation of anthropologists. Durkheim thus began by reminding his readers that before Spencer and Gillen, the coexistence of totemism and exogamy had been "proven in an innumerable multitude of cases," and that if Frazer's second theory of totemism were to be taken seriously, the beliefs and practices of the Arunta should be susceptible to no alternative interpretation. But "[i]nstead of a perfectly pure model of the totemic regime," Durkheim then asked, "could not Arunta totemism be, on the contrary, a subsequent and perverted form?" The location of the Arunta at the very center of the continent, Durkheim admitted, implies that they have had less contact with advanced civilizations than their coastal counterparts; but "the social system of inferior societies," he added, "is . . . capable of evolving and transforming itself by means other than the influence of more civilized peoples." In fact, "many reasons" – e.g. their greater sense of unity, their forms of political organization, the relative refinement of their matrimonial relations, etc. – led Durkheim "quite legitimately to think that the Arunta have behind them a long historical past, and that they are among the most advanced of Australian peoples" (Durkheim 1902: 89–90).

Such an appeal to evolution was among the oldest rhetorical strategies of Victorian anthropology. In effect, Durkheim thus placed Spencer and Gillen's "facts" in a new narrative context, transforming and even reversing their meaning and significance. In his 1898 presentation to the Royal Anthropological Institute, for example, Spencer had described the Arunta as divided into two exogamic "moieties" (Durkheim used the term "phratries"), adding that – because representatives of each totemic clan are included in both – marriage is permitted between members of the same clan. To restore the connection between totemism and exogamy, Durkheim had only to argue that the "phratrie" had been the original form of the clan which, in the course of its subsequent evolution, had been segmented into secondary clans with representatives in each phratrie. If we assume this, Durkheim observed, "then there was at least a moment when marriage was forbidden between members of the same totemic society; and thus it is not true that, among the Arunta, the totem has always been without influence on marriage nor, above all, that totemism generally implies endogamy" (Durkheim 1902: 92).

The problem here, as Durkheim recognized, was that the Arunta "traditions" described a distant past in which the Arunta practiced clan endogamy, as well as a subsequent, less-distant past in which – as the consequence of a self-conscious social reform – clans were organized into two exogamous phratries (see Spencer and Gillen 1898: 276–7). But here Durkheim simply appealed to Smith's ritual theory of myth, arguing that these traditions are "systems of representations invented in large part by the popular imagination in order to somehow render existing practices intelligible to the mind" (Durkheim 1902: 96). Durkheim's real reason for dismissing Spencer's argument, of course, was that it was ill-fitted to his more conservative, uniformitarian conception of the relationship between social institutions and merely political reforms – i.e. the phratrie "plays too large a role in their religious life, is too closely associated with the totemic cult, constitutes too vital an element of their social organization to be some sort of adventitious institution, introduced tardily and externally into their social system" (Durkheim 1902: 96).

But how, then, did exogamy – once the rule of both clan and phratry – cease being the rule of the first while remaining the rule of the second? In other words, how did parts of each clan come to be represented in both phratries, thus permitting clan endogamy? Durkheim's answer – again a rather ad hoc appeal to the more traditional view of totemism held by McLennan, Smith, and the early Frazer – was that the Arunta had once practiced matrilineal descent combined with patrilocal habitation, a precarious arrangement which required children to live with their fathers only to be separated from them to join their mothers on religious and social occasions. This inherently unstable institution eventually gave way, in a veritable "revolution," to patrilineal descent, which in turn required each phratry to cede one of its clans to the other in order to integrate children within the phratry of their fathers (Durkheim 1902: 98–112).[10]

This "revolution" postulated by Durkheim to account for certain anomalous features of the *social* aspect of Arunta totemism was then extended to account for its equally anomalous *religious* features. The current toleration with respect to the eating of the totem, for example, could be conveniently explained as the consequence of the weakening of the structure of Arunta society, itself a consequence of the shift from matrilineal to patrilineal descent. Here Durkheim appealed to precisely the *same* principle appealed to by Frazer – i.e. the consubstantiality of clan member and totem – to support precisely the *opposite* argument – i.e. that men could not possibly have killed and eaten their totems in an earlier, more stable social order; and the traditions that described the clan's ancestors as eating their totems with impunity, like those which described them as practicing endogamy, were dealt with through an appeal to the ritual theory of myth – in this case, as the mythological elaboration of that part of the *intichiuma* in which a portion of the totem was ceremonially consumed by each member of the clan. This ceremony, Durkheim insisted, was indeed the totemic sacrament postulated by Robertson Smith – not in the magical sense proposed by Frazer – but in the genuinely mystical and religious sense intended by Smith himself (Durkheim 1902: 112–15).

It remained, of course, to explain the efficacy of this rite. In his 1906–7 lecture-course on religion at the Sorbonne, Durkheim thus insisted that we go beneath the mere symbols of totemism to its underlying "principle." The diversity of things that serve as totems, Durkheim continued, suggests strongly that their sacred quality lies, not in some material attribute, but rather in their common participation in something that is neither material nor perceptible – i.e. in an anonymous, impersonal force (*une force anonyme et impersonnelle*). This force – exemplified in the Melanesian *mana* – was of course the object of Marett's hypothesized "pre-animistic" religion which, in 1904, had become the foundation of his attack on the associationist psychology that underlay Frazer's theory of magic. The totem, Durkheim agreed with Marett, is only the sensible form under which the primitive man represents this anonymous, impersonal force to himself; and thus to explain totemism we must explain the origin of this force.

What are its characteristic features? On the one hand, Durkheim emphasized, it is external, existing outside of the individual, imposing duties, obligations, and rules of conduct upon him, and constraining his behavior; but on the other hand, Durkheim also appealed to his recently discovered "positive cult" – i.e. this is *une force secourable*, one that elevates the individual above himself, maintaining and strengthening the life within him. Durkheim now saw totemism on the model of Smith's ancient Semites, "in which the habitual temper of the worshippers is one of joyous confidence in their god, untroubled by any habitual sense of human guilt, and resting of the firm conviction that they and the deity they adore are good friends, who understand each other perfectly, and are united by bonds not easily broken" (Smith [1894] 1972: 255). "The believer who feels in harmony with his god," Durkheim observed, using the words and phrases similar to those that would mark his 1913 address before the *Société française de philosophie*, "draws from this belief a new strength, and faces the difficulties of life with greater energy." This "activité vivifiante" occurs primarily (though not exclusively) in those situations where the clan has recently been gathered together, or where the group has a particularly strong sense of its own existence; for indeed, only society has the capacity, not only to regulate and constrain our behavior from the outside, but also to act within us, in such a way as to lift us above ourselves – in short, to make us stronger (Durkheim 1907: 103–8).

The argument that this "dynamogenic" quality of religion had been suggested to Durkheim through pragmatist sources is strengthened by the etiology of the phrase itself. It was first used by the French psychologist Charles Féré, a student of Charcot and later collaborator with Binet who, in *Sensation et mouvement* (1887) described some experiments that attracted the interest of James. Féré was interested in the effect of sensory stimuli on muscular activity, and arranged a series of experiments in which a "self-registering dynamometer" – i.e. a device for measuring mechanical force – was used to measure the strength of the muscular contractions of a subject's hand under a variety of different stimuli. Ordinarily, James reported in *Principles of Psychology* (1890), the maximum strength remained relatively constant from day to day; but if the subject received a "sensorial impression" simultaneously with the contraction, the strength of the contraction typically increased – a reinforcing effect that quickly received the name of "dynamogeny." James was particularly impressed by the large variety of stimuli – e.g. heat, cold, pricking, itching, faradic (discontinuous) stimulation of the skin, lights of particular colors, musical notes proportional to their loudness and height, odors and tastes, etc. – all seem to have this "dynamogenic" quality whereby the subject was unconsciously, and quite literally, "made stronger" (James 1890: 379–80).

For James – as for Durkheim – these experiments had obvious significance for our understanding of religion phenomena. In the eighth lecture of *The Varieties of Religious Experience* (1902) – the first of three dealing specifically with the psychology of religious conversion – James described the young St. Augustine as a classic example of what he called a "discordant personality" or "divided self." The story is familiar to every reader of the *Confessions* (c. 400) – e.g. Augustine's Christian mother and pagan father, his physical migrations from Carthage to Rome and Milan, his intellectual migrations from Manicheanism to skepticism to neo-Platonism, which left his "inner self . . . a house divided against itself," and finally the famous, decisive event in the garden at Milan, where he heard the child's voice say "*Sume, lege*" (take and read) and, opening the Bible at random, read the passage that seemed divinely sent to relieve his spiritual conflict (St. Augustine 400: 170, 177–8). "There could be no more perfect description of the divided will," James observed, "when the higher wishes lack just that last acuteness, that touch of explosive intensity, of *dynamogenic quality* (to use the slang of the psychologists), that enables them to burst their shell, and make irruption efficaciously into life and quell the lower tendencies forever" (James 1902: 145; emphasis added). Even if such conversion experiences can be explained naturalistically, James went on to argue, we should assess them pragmatically, in terms of what he called their "value" or "fruits for life" (James 1902: 191).

There can be little doubt that this was Durkheim's source. In *Les Formes élémentaires*, after describing these "impressions of joy, of interior peace, of serenity, of enthusiasm which are, for the believer, an experimental proof of his beliefs," he went on to refer specifically to *The Varieties of Religious Experience*, adding that "[t]ogether with a recent apologist of the faith, we admit that these religious beliefs rest upon a specific experience whose demonstrative value is, in one sense, not one bit inferior to that of scientific experiments, though different from them. We, too, think that 'a tree is known by its fruits,' and that fertility is the best proof of what the roots are worth" (Durkheim [1912] 1915: 465). Not that Durkheim was in any serious sense a pragmatist – on the contrary, his lecture course on pragmatism at the Sorbonne (1913–14) was designed to distance himself – and his students – from the pragmatists, and especially from James. But like the pragmatists – and especially Dewey – Durkheim insisted that religious experience and practice were far more important than ideas and doctrines, for the reality on which religion depends is not the result of metaphysical speculation but concrete social action. Because all societies need periodic reaffirmations of their collective sentiments, Durkheim was also convinced that there was something "eternal" in religion, destined to outlive the particular symbols – e.g. totemic, Christian, or whatever – in which it had previously been embodied (Durkheim [1912] 1915: 465).[11]

In sum, the Durkheim who had early on cast his lot with a precarious Third Republic sought a normative vocabulary that would encourage the citizen's submission to and integration within something real, big, and strong – society understood on the model of the Mosaic dispensation; and like Freud, he found this in Frazer's powerfully metaphorical concept of taboo. But the Durkheim who endured the Dreyfus Affair – like the carpenter putting down one set of tools for another – sought a language that would do justice to the human capacity for the embracement of ideals, for mystical self-transcendence, for the Good as well as Duty, to the notion of society understood in terms of the Pauline conception of Gospel as well as Law; and belatedly, he cobbled this vocabulary together from the fragments of Robertson Smith's theory of a primitive totemic sacrament, as well as Marett's strong reading of Codrington and James.

This description of "what Durkheim was *doing*," of course, leaves unanswered the question of whether his explanation of totemism was *true*.

But again, this question leads to another: what do we mean by "true"? Consciously or otherwise, most sociologists cleave to a "correspondence" theory of truth – i.e. they believe that propositions are true because they accurately represent some reality independent of mind. By this criterion, Durkheim's theory of totemism – by contrast with Frazer's – would be "true" in so far as Durkheim presented his readers with an accurate representation of the beliefs and practices of Australian aborigines. But here we face immediate and serious difficulties. The problem isn't simply that the Australian "facts" were at variance with Durkheim's description, although its empirical deficiencies were noted immediately by Baldwin Spencer, as they would be subsequently by Goldenweiser, van Gennep, Evans-Pritchard, Stanner, and others.[12] The more fundamental difficulty is that, for the last half-century, few philosophical conceptions have been subject to a more withering and sustained assault than those of "accurate representation" and "mind-independent reality" (see, e.g. Kuhn 1993: 330; Putnam 1990: 28; Davidson 1990: 305; and Rorty 1996). Even if one still clings to a correspondence theory of truth (which I do not), there remains a problem acknowledged by one of its most steadfast defenders – i.e. that if social facts are "real," they are so in a sense different from the "brute facts" of the physical world which (unlike social facts) exist independently of custom, habit, or agreement (see Searle 1995).

But what is particularly interesting – and what makes the Victorian anthropological obsession with totemism from McLennan to Freud particularly edifying – is that it might not have been "real" even in this more limited, Searlean sense. As early as 1896, Franz Boas had already suggested that the apparent universality of totemism disguised the fact that it had developed from different sources in different social and cultural contexts (Boas [1896] 1940: 274–5). By 1910, Boas' student A. A. Goldenweiser had observed that an analysis of the various features of totemism demonstrated that they were essentially independent of each other – historically, psychologically, or both (Goldenweiser 1910: 183). In 1916, responding to Freud as well as Durkheim, Boas insisted that the alleged "unity" of totemic phenomena existed only subjectively, in the minds of evolutionary anthropologists, a "remodeling of activities, thoughts, and emotions under the stress of a dominant idea" (Boas 1916: 321–2). And in 1962, of course, Claude Lévi-Strauss would describe the entire, *fin-de-siècle* vogue of totemism as an effort to create the sense of a concrete, objective institution which – utterly primitive and at great evolutionary distance – might reassure us of the superiority of our own, more civilized beliefs and practices (Lévi-Strauss [1962] 1964: 1–2). Even in the qualified sense suggested by Searle, therefore, it is difficult to make the case that totemism is – or ever was – a "mind-independent reality."

Retrospectively, the anthropological obsession with totemism – in free fall even as the classic works of Durkheim and Freud appeared – evokes only the smug condescension of those certain that they would not have committed the same blunders. But the problem isn't that the sentences of *The Golden Bough*, or *Les Formes élémentaires*, or *Totem und tabu* don't "accurately represent" the "mind-independent reality" of Australian totemism. The problem is that this is simply the wrong question to ask. Instead, we should ask less about the pursuit of truth, which is allegedly absolute and eternal, than about the justification of belief, which is transitory because it is relative to specific audiences. Again, we should ask less about objectivity, in the sense of how things are independently of our language, than about intersubjectivity, or the processes whereby we reach consensus on the descriptions that might best serve our interests and purposes. And again, we should ask less about beliefs as representations of reality than as tools to be used in concrete social practices – including the practice of science (see Rorty 1994, 1999).

A frequent objection to this proposal is that the commitment to truth as correspondence to a mind-independent reality is a presupposition of the practice of science itself, and that by dismissing it, we undermine those institutions that have traditionally protected this practice (see Searle 1992). But as Richard Rorty has recently argued, a practice "presupposes" a belief only if dropping the belief constitutes a good reason for altering the practice; and while certain social practices obviously presuppose certain "empirical" beliefs – e.g. the funding of medical research clearly presupposes the belief that diseases are caused by bacteria and viruses rather than by demonic possession – it is not equally clear that the practice of science presupposes the more "philosophical" belief in "truth as correspondence to a mind-independent reality." This is because we have achieved a reasonable degree of intersubjective consensus on what counts for and against the belief in demonic possession, but very little on what counts for or against the correspondence theory of truth; and this is why our social practices depend so little on our philosophical beliefs, and most people do without them altogether – as, indeed, the phrase "merely philosophical" implies (Rorty 1996: 22).

But if the significance of philosophy to social science has thus been exaggerated, that of history has not. By asking questions about Durkheim and *Les Formes élémentaires*, for example, we have been led to the argument that the practice of social science can get along quite well without epistemological presuppositions, and it is arguable that it could get along even better if social scientists would stop looking for them.[13] The phallogocentric distinction between disciplines that are "hard" and "soft," for example, would probably disappear. Chemists and biologists, to whom philosophical presuppositions are unknown, would cease being the role-models for anthropologists and historians; and English professors would no longer have to justify their promotions in terms of the "contribution to knowledge" made by their latest books on Milton, Austen, or Eliot. Finally, sociologists might stop asking themselves whether they are following strict scientific procedures and start asking whether they have any suggestions to make about how our lives, or our institutions, might be improved.

NOTES

1 A complete set of the *Sens* lectures (in French) is available on the Internet at www.relst.uiuc.edu/durkheim/Texts/1884a/oo.html. A summary of their content (in English) is also accessible at www.relst.uiuc.edu/durkheim/Texts/1884a/tr.abst.html. A complete English translation is in progress. I have devoted a complete chapter to the lectures in Jones 1999: 112–71.
2 On the relationship between Fustel and Durkheim, see Jones 1990.
3 In 1905–7, the Catholic philosophy journal *Revue néo-scolastique* published a series of articles by the Belgian priest Simon Deploige attacking Durkheim's elevation of "society" to a power superior to that of the individual. Durkheim responded in a series of letters to the editor, and it is from these that this now famous passage is taken. Deploige's articles were subsequently published as *Le Conflit de la morale et la sociologie* (1911). Durkheim's hostile review of that work in *L'Année sociologique* contains a similar reference to "all that we owe to Robertson Smith and to the works of the ethnographers of England and America" (1913a: 326).
4 Pickering (1984: 62, 70) thus began his account of the relationship with the observation that "no one knows for sure what elements of Robertson Smith were of such revelatory importance to Durkheim," and concluded with the comment that "the enigma remains."
5 For the historiographical justification of asking this particular question, see Skinner 1969.
6 As a co-editor of the *Encyclopedia Britannica*, Smith had enlisted Frazer to write the articles on "Taboo" and "Totemism" for the 23rd volume (to be published in 1888). In typical Frazerian fashion, however, the length of the second soon swelled until the publisher felt compelled to issue it separately as a short volume in 1887 – the abridged version appearing a year later in the *Britannica* itself.
7 As John Burrow succinctly put it, Frazer "wrote anthropology like Tylor, not like Robertson Smith" (1966: 241 n2).
8 Frazer's embracement of Smith's theory of a primitive totemic sacrament was hardly unqualified. In the second edition of *The Golden Bough* (1900), responding to the suggestion of Hubert and Mauss (1899: 4) that Frazer's theory of sacrifice was simply a "theological exaggeration of Smith's doctrine," Frazer insisted (wrongly) that he had never assented to Smith's theory, nor had Smith assented to his. "What we have found," Frazer observed, "is not religion, but that which was first the predecessor, and afterwards the hated rival of religion; I mean magic" (1900: 202).

9 Later, when James visited England, Marett would come to know him quite well, and James would give his approval to the position Marett reached in *The Threshold of Religion* (1909).

10 The argument presented by Durkheim here is identical to that presented in "La Prohibition de l'inceste et ses origines" (1898b).

11 On Durkheim's writings on education, see Jones 1999: 45–111.

12 Having just read "Sur le totémisme," Spencer wrote to Frazer that "[Durkheim's] whole article is full of misconceptions" (Marett and Penniman 1932: 84–5; see also Goldenweiser 1915; van Gennep 1920; Evans-Pritchard 1965: 64–7; and Stanner 1967).

13 My hopes for social science here are merely a subset of those expressed by Richard Rorty for the future of the university itself (1996: 27).

REFERENCES

Ackerman, Robert. 1987. *J. G. Frazer: His Life and Work*. Cambridge: Cambridge University Press.

Augustine, St. [400] 1961. *The Confessions*. Harmondsworth, Middlesex: Penguin.

Boas, Franz. 1916. "The Origin of Totemism." *American Anthropologist* 18: 319–26.

[1896] 1940. "The Limitations of the Comparative Method of Anthropology." pp. 270–80 in *Race, Language, and Culture*. Edited by Franz Boas. New York: The Free Press.

Burrow, John W. 1966. *Evolution and Society: A Study in Victorian Social Theory*. Cambridge: Cambridge University Press.

Codrington, Robert Henry. 1891. *The Melanesians: Studies in Their Anthropology and Folk-Lore*. Oxford: Clarendon Press.

Davidson, Donald. 1990. "The Structure and Content of Truth." *Journal of Philosophy* 87: 279–328.

Durkheim, Émile. 1913a. "Deploige, Simon. Le Conflit de la morale et de la sociologie." *L'Année sociologique* 12: 326–8.

[1913b] 1984. "Contribution to Discussion of: The Problem of Religion and the Duality of Human Nature." pp. 1–62 in *Knowledge and Society: Studies in the Sociology of Culture, Past and Present*. Edited by Henrika Kuklick and Elizabeth Long. Greenwich, CT: JAI Press, Inc.

[1912] 1915. *The Elementary Forms of the Religious Life*. New York and London: The Free Press.

1907. "Cours d'Émile Durkheim à la Sorbonne." *Revue de philosophie* 5: 92–114, 7: 528–39, and 12: 620–638.

[1902] 1985. "On Totemism." *History of Sociology* 5: 79–121.

[1899] 1975. "Concerning the Definition of Religious Phenomena." pp. 74–99 in *Durkheim on Religion: A Selection of Readings with Bibliographies*. Edited by W. S. F. Pickering. London and Boston: Routledge and Kegan Paul.

[1898a] 1963. *Incest: The Nature and Origin of the Taboo*. New York: Lyle Stuart.

[1898b]. "La Prohibition de l'inceste et ses origines." *L'Année sociologique* 1: 1–70.

[1897] 1951. *Suicide: A Study in Sociology*. Glencoe, IL: The Free Press of Glencoe.

[1895] 1982. "The Rules of Sociological Method." pp. 29–163 in *The Rules of Sociological Method and Selected Texts on Sociology and its Method*. Edited by Steven Lukes. London and Basingstoke: Macmillan.

[1893] 1984. *The Division of Labor in Society*. New York: The Free Press.

Evans-Pritchard, E. E. 1965. *Theories of Primitive Religion*. Oxford: Oxford University Press.

Féré, Charles. 1887. *Sensation et mouvement*. Paris: Librairie Félix Alcan.

Frazer, James George. 1900. *The Golden Bough: A Study in Magic and Religion*. London: Macmillan.

[1894] 1920. "William Robertson Smith." pp. 194–209 in *Sir Roger de Coverly and Other Literary Pieces*. Edited by James George Frazer. London: Macmillan.

1890. *The Golden Bough: A Study in Comparative Religion*. 2 vols. London: Macmillan.

1887. *Totemism*. Edinburgh: Adam and Charles Black.

Freud, Sigmund. [1913] 1950. *Totem and Taboo: Some Points of Agreement between the Mental Lives of Savages and Neurotics*. New York and London: W. W. Norton.

Goldenweiser, Alexander A. 1915. "Review of Emile Durkheim: Les Formes Élémentaires de la vie religieuse." *The American Anthropologist* 17: 719–35.

1910. "Totemism: An Analytical Study." *Journal of American Folk-Lore* 23: 179–293.

Hubert, Henri, and Marcel Mauss. [1899] 1964. *Sacrifice: Its Nature and Functions*. Chicago: University of Chicago Press.

James, William. 1984. "Robertson Smith and James Frazer on Religion: Two traditions in British Social Anthropology." pp. 31–58 in *Functionalism Historicized: Essays on British Social Anthropology*. Edited by George W. Stocking, Jr. Wisconsin: University of Wisconsin Press.

[1902] 1958. *The Varieties of Religious Experience: A Study in Human Nature*. New York: New American Library.

[1896] 1956. "The Will to Believe." pp. 1–31 in *The Will to Believe and Other Essays in Popular Philosophy*. Edited by William James. New York: Dover.

[1890] 1918. *The Principles of Psychology*. New York: Dover Publications.

Jones, Robert Alun. 1999. *The Development of Durkheim's Social Realism*. Cambridge: Cambridge University Press.

1990. "Durkheim and *La Cité antique*: An Essay on the Origins of Durkheim's Sociology of Religion." *Quaderni di sociologia*, January.

Jones, Robert Alun, and W. Paul Vogt. 1984. "Durkheim's Defense of Les Formes élémentaires de la vie religieuse." In Henrika Kuklick and Elizabeth Long. Eds., *Knowledge and Society: Studies in the Sociology of Culture, Past and Present*, pp. 45–62. Greenwich, CT: JAI Press.

Kuhn, Thomas S. 1993. "Afterwords" in *World Changes: Thomas Kuhn and the Nature of Science*. Edited by Paul Horwich. Cambridge, MA: MIT Press.

Lévi-Strauss, Claude. [1962] 1964. *Totemism*. Boston, MA: Beacon Press.

Lukes, Steven. [1972] 1988. *Émile Durkheim: His Life and Work: A Historical and Critical Study*. London: Penguin Books (Peregrine edition).

Marett, Robert Ranulph and Thomas K. Penniman (eds.) 1932. *Spencer's Scientific Correspondence with Sir J. G. Frazer and Others*. Oxford: Clarendon.

Marett, Robert Ranulph. [1904] 1909. "From Spell to Prayer." pp. 33–84 in *The Threshold of Religion*. Edited by Robert Ranulph Marett. London: Methuen and Co.

[1900] 1909. "Pre-Animistic Religion." pp. 1–32 in *The Threshold of Religion*. Edited by Robert Ranulph Marett. London: Methuen and Co.

Pickering, W. S. F. 1984. *Durkheim's Sociology of Religion: Themes and Theories*. London, Boston, and Melbourne: Routledge.

Putnam, Hilary. 1990. *Realism with a Human Face*. Cambridge, MA: Harvard University Press.

Rorty, Richard. 1996. "Does Academic Freedom Have Philosophical Presuppositions?" pp. 21–42 in *The Future of Academic Freedom*. Edited by Lewis Menand. Chicago: University of Chicago Press.

[1994] 1999. "Truth Without Correspondence to Reality." pp. 23–46 in *Philosophy and Social Hope*. Edited by Richard Rorty. Harmondsworth, Middlesex: Penguin.

Searle, John. 1995. *The Construction of Social Reality*. New York: Free Press.

1992. "Rationality and Realism: What Is at Stake?" *Daedalus* 122: 55–84.

Skinner, Quentin. 1969. "Meaning and Understanding in the History of Ideas." *History and Theory* 8: 3–53.

Smith, William Robertson. [1894] 1972. *Lectures on the Religion of the Semites: The Fundamental Institutions*. New York: Schocken.

Spencer, Baldwin and F. J. Gillen. [1899] 1968. *The Native Tribes of Central Australia*. New York: Dover.

1898. "Some Remarks on Totemism as Applied to Australian Tribes." *Journal of the Royal Anthropological Institute of Great Britain and Ireland* 28: 275–80.

Stanner, W. E. H. 1967. "Reflections on Durkheim and Aboriginal Religion." pp. 217–40 in *Social Organization: Essays Presented to Raymond Firth*. Edited by Maurice Freedman. Chicago: Aldine.

Tylor, Edward Burnett. [1871] 1920. *Primitive Culture: Researches into the Development of Mythology, Philosophy, Religion, Language, Art, and Custom*. London: John Murray.

Van Gennep, Arnold. 1920. *L'État actuel du problème totémique*. Paris.

5

RANDALL COLLINS

The Durkheimian movement in France and in world sociology

Émile Durkheim was not merely an individual, but the head, simultaneously symbolic and real, of a social movement. Of all the "great sociologists" who make up the canon of founders of the discipline, Durkheim's work was most thoroughly a collective production. This is so in every sense recognized by present-day sociologists. We are inclined to see any individual as a product of social conditions who responds to problems set by his or her historical milieu with the tools then at hand; yet we often set sharp limits to such sociologizing in the case of our particular intellectual heroes. Our feeling of respect raises them to the status of uniquely creative individuals, a sacred realm from which we, in turn, receive a sense of participation in something more important than ourselves. It is an unfinished task to explain why we feel more elevated in worshipping a heroized individual than in showing respect for the accomplishments of a social movement: why the collective symbol is generally an individual even where we have the ability to recognize the collectivity itself. In the case of some putative sociological founders, such as Karl Marx, the name of the emblem swallows up even known co-authors, like Friedrich Engels, who were often as much animator and originator as collaborator (Carver 1983; Rigby 1992). The intellectual world, as much as politics or religion, needs a sociology of the construction of emblems.

In the case of the Durkheimians, we see a second level of collective production of ideas beyond the baseline influence of historical and personal milieux. The Durkheimians began as a movement highly aware of their collaborative task; narrowly it focused on producing the *Année sociologique*, and more broadly on building a scientific sociology. The enterprise was replete with collective activity, ranging from overt co-authorship, to extensive direction and editorial revision, the planning of lines of intellectual attack, the apportioning out of tasks, compiling of results, along with deliberate recruiting of members, and strategic decisions as to whose work to publicize as part of the sociological enterprise and what to exclude. The purpose of the *Année sociologique* was to display what the world of scholarship had to offer collectively that could be shaped into a new science; the Durkheimians saw themselves as the inner circle of a wide ring of proto-sociologists, whose contributions they would collaboratively theorize into clear and general principles of the new sociological science. Within the inner ring, there was an explicit ethos of shared tasks and mutually supportive contributions. In these collaborations, it is not easy to separate the intellectual origins of particular conceptions and assign them as the exclusive property of one or another figure. The conventional practice of intellectual history, as consisting in assigning credit to particular individuals and charting who influenced whom, is particularly inappropriate in the case of the Durkheimians. Even if we were to play the influence-game to the hilt, we would find the links of transmission from one thought to another reverberated through a densely interacting group of collaborators; an honest score-card of contributions would have to set alongside each name a string of minute fractions. Given that some scholars work relatively more individually or collectively than others, the Durkheimians' intellectual accomplishments are one of the strongest examples of how a consciously organized intellectual movement generates sustained creative advance.

And more. The Durkheimians challenge us to push onward to a third level of the social production of intellectual life. Durkheim himself, drawing on his earlier collaboration with Marcel Mauss on *Primitive Classification* (1903), (and he in turn on his collaboration on primitive religion with Henri Hubert (1899), and on the stimulus of the French and German neo-Kantians and the movement of comparative ethnography of religion) formulated in *The Elementary Forms of Religious Life* (1912) an explicit theory of the social formation of the categories of thought. It is a step in this lineage of ideas to recognize that not only general categories are socially constructed, but that the thinking that any particular individual does at any particular moment is also constructed; this social construction of thoughts is most visible in the case of intellectuals, whose significant social milieu is the network of other intellectuals with whom they interact.

On this level, the individual re-emerges in sociological analysis, not in the naïve sense of hero-thinker whose unique contributions are to be totted up in the way sports fans obsess over record books, but the individual as located in specific social groupings where concepts circulate and intellectual projects are formed so as to attract the support of some and repel the conceptions of others within the political alignments of an intellectual field. As I have argued elsewhere (Collins 1998), there is a sociology of thinking as ongoing process of making coalitions in the mind, bringing together ideas charged with the sense of membership in particular intellectual groups. In this process, idea-emblems become charged with emotional energy, with fluctuating portions of that moral force of which the Durkheimians were supremely conscious; and the individuals at the center of networks which circulate these idea-emblems become the most intensely energized by their project. Thus become constituted those immensely hard-working individuals, who consciously take on the direction of a project, fired with intellectual vision of what can be created, individuals like Émile Durkheim himself. The sociology of ideas, which on the second level discussed above dissolves individuals into a social movement, on this third level can now show how particular individuals are apportioned their parts of a collective attention space; and how the ideas which circulate collectively also find most forceful expression through a particular individual or small number of centrally located individuals. The relationship between Émile Durkheim and Marcel Mauss, a somewhat reluctant recruit who nevertheless evolves into his mentor's alter ego, is rich in illustrations of the details of how intellectual social movements allocate and energize individuals to play their parts.

Against the essentialist scholarship of intellectual hero-worship, we need to remind ourselves that the great Durkheim was not born to theorize an emerging sociology, but more nearly the other way around; a period of educational reform set the opportunity to construct a new academic discipline, and favored that movement which could generate the most programmatic enthusiasm; in the intellectual politics of the time, the strongest coalition was that which developed the most generalizing and at the same time empirically synthesizing theory. We should use the historical Durkheim, whose works we read in the light of later generations of elaborators and critics, as a peephole through which to peer back into the years when these ideas and these intellectual energies were being shaped. We are aided by multiple such peepholes, since the Durkheimian movement is so visible early on, bringing into focus what is generally vague, or half-deliberately hidden, in the case of other "seminal" thinkers. My project is to provide a Durkheimian analysis of Durkheim, and thus necessarily of the entire Durkheimian movement.

The originating networks

Social movements usually start with a shift in institutional bases, and that is the case with what eventually was to crystallize into the Durkheimian sociology movement. In fact it develops from a concatenation of such networks; social movements typically come in cascades, as the energies and accumulated techniques of earlier movements spin off new movements with new aims. The growth of the Durkheimian movement gives an excellent opportunity to see how a set of movements give not only mutual support, but also tensions and distractions that shape the content of each specific branch.

First came the movement for reform of the French educational system. In broadest scale, this was a movement going on all over the Western world in the late nineteenth century; the German research university, invented early in the century, had given the intellectual lead to Germany, through the superiority of its scientific laboratories and research seminars through which professors made their careers by being rewarded for new discoveries. In England, the USA, Scandinavia, Italy, and elsewhere, there were reform movements from the 1860s or 1870s onward, typically to replace religiously based education with the new German university model. In France under the Second Empire, the political alliance of state and Catholic church posed a powerful obstacle; Renan and Taine acquired reputations as leading intellectuals by touting German-style secular scholarship and calling for reform to catch up with Germany. Defeat in the Franco-Prussian war of 1870–1 and the rise of the Third Republic gave special impetus to the combination of French nationalism, republicanism, and catching up with Germany through educational reform. After much struggle with conservatives, republicans finally won control of both the Chamber of Deputies and the Senate in 1879; the leading advocate of secular education, Jules Ferry, became Minister of public instruction. His efforts to remove the Jesuits from control of secondary education led to the fall of the government, with Ferry emerging as chief executive twice between 1880 and 1883, and establishing for the first time in France free and compulsory public elementary schooling. Full-scale reform was launched in 1884, when reformers gained sufficient control to take on the task of replacing Catholic secondary and primary education; since a main resource of the reformers was the centralized and hierarchic structure of French education, this involved reform of the university faculties as well (Weisz 1983; Fabiani 1988). The *École Normale Supérieure* (ENS) was the teacher-training school for *lycée* [secondary school] teachers, as well as for university teachers in the subjects in the *faculté des lettres*. Thus the ENS cohort around 1880 should be expected to take positions of leadership in the reforms. It does indeed; as we see, the élan of this movement energized various ancillary projects, and from this cohort came not only Durkheim but Henri Bergson, and the leading socialist, Jean Jaurès. Other students who would seize the opportunities for building new disciplines included Alfred Binet and Pierre Janet in psychology and Lucien Lévy-Bruhl in anthropology.

Durkheim began his career by being recruited into the educational reform movement (sources for the following: Lukes 1973, Fournier 1994, Besnard 1983; and the letters and notes in Durkheim 1998). He was a student at the ENS during 1879–82, the very years that Jules Ferry reached power. And he followed, quite literally, in the career footsteps of two of the leading reformers, Louis Liard and Ferdinand Buisson. Both were protégés of Ferry, who chose them as his key administrative directors as he gradually gained control over administrative personnel at the department of public instruction (Weisz 1983: 118–25). Liard had come out of the ENS in the early days of struggle for the Republic and in 1874 became professor of philosophy at Bordeaux; in 1884, he was picked to be director of higher education and set in motion the republican program for reform of the universities. Liard in turn chose Durkheim, an 1882 graduate of the ENS, to go to Germany to investigate the secrets of the research university from inside. Upon his return, in 1887 Durkheim stepped into Liard's old position at Bordeaux, a promotion from his previous positions as provincial lycée teacher. Buisson was Liard's counterpart as director of primary education from 1879–96; in 1896 he got a chair of "science de l'éducation" at the Sorbonne; it was this chair that Durkheim acquired in 1902, through Liard's support, after Buisson resigned upon election to the chamber of deputies representing the Radical Socialist party. Where the footprints diverged was in the intellectual content. Liard and Buisson were educational reformers pure and simple, administrators and politicians; whereas Durkheim struggled to redefine their chairs: in 1896, getting the Bordeaux chair retitled "science sociale"; and in 1913, the Sorbonne chair as "science de l'éducation et sociologie."

Durkheim, we might note, spent most of his life in the provinces; educated in Epinal through age seventeen, he had only his school years in Paris; then he taught at a series of provincial lycées. During his fifteen years at Bordeaux he produced almost all of his important works, and launched the projects that were finished after he moved to Paris. But although he was away from the center, he was shaped by it as a career goal; he was launched as an agent of the reform movement struggling to capture control of the educational system, and his intellectual activities were moves to bring him back to Paris. This meant more than personal ambition; Paris was the magnetic center of attention in intellectual space; to establish a new kind of position there would take innovation at the highest level of intellectual standards.

The opportunity to reform the educational system was an opportunity to create new disciplines. This was a stimulus to major intellectual creativity, for a new field needed to stake out a distinctive terrain, legitimated by a program statement of general conceptions and charting a pathway to important future discoveries. For this reason the founding generation of any new field is necessarily at its most theoretical, and thus its "great thinkers" are found there. In this generation there were moves to found not only sociology, but psychology, anthropology, criminology, geography, statistics, political or administrative science, comparative studies of religion, and still other possible scholarly identities and configurations. To be sure, disciplines were being established in other countries' academic systems as well, and one might ask why this was not simply a matter of importing psychology, for example, from the German laboratories which were springing up from the 1870s onwards; or establishing a university base for the non-academic sociology which had been publicized in writings of Comte, Spencer, Schaeffle, and others. We should take pains to avoid the retrospective fallacy, as if there were a single possible straight line of development from these early points to the fully institutionalized disciplines of the twentieth-century academic world. In the late nineteenth century, there were a multitude of competing positions on how to study the world of human activities; it was not at all clear whether these should be part of the biological sciences, or the lineup of political ideologies, or connected to law and public administration (as for instance economics was to become in French universities), or part of the general education taught in the secondary schools; or whether there would be a distinction between sociology and anthropology, or between sociology and social work. The general prestige of the German research universities did not mean that imitators would simply copy the newest German developments. These were also in transition, maneuvering with local circumstances; for example, German psychology laboratories were established in philosophy departments, and the struggle to make them independent did not come until around 1910 (Kusch 1995). Local politics of the French academic system ensured that it would not simply reproduce the German model, however important it was as a stimulus.

Durkheim, as an agent of the reform movement in higher education, was from the beginning of his career explicitly concerned with the shape of new disciplines. The search for a distinctive turf led him to formulate the character of sociology as dealing with "social facts," the *sui generis* character of patterns of social interaction, constraining the individual from without. This was a demarcation vis-à-vis psychology, the most successful of the rival new social disciplines. The danger of sociology being absorbed into the biological or economic fields pressed Durkheim to further distinctions. This was no mere exercise in taxonomy, since Durkheim was attempting to make his field impressive by showing that important explanatory generalizations would flow from this distinctive approach; thus the Durkheimian movement acquired an identity as it showed how the economy rests upon a precontractual base, and emerges from ritual forms of exchange. Durkheim's formulation of the distinctiveness of sociology followed from the major concerns of his ENS teacher, Émile Boutroux, whose philosophy stressed the distinctive methods of each science, irreducible to any other. Articulating the forms or logic of each area of knowledge was a principal neo-Kantian concern, and Boutroux (who had studied with Zeller at Heidelberg before coming to the ENS) acted as a French branch of the neo-Kantian movement. This had arisen in the German universities from the 1860s and remained dominant until after 1900, under the lead of Zeller, Lange, Cohen, Windelband, Dilthey, and others; it had successfully reclaimed a place for philosophy in the age of the specialized research sciences by staking out the meta-territory of adjudicating the knowledge claims of the various fields. (The argument over the distinctive character of *Naturwissenschaft* and *Geisteswissenschaft* was the most famous of such topics.) Thus the differentiation of disciplines in the German universities had created the analytical tools – the neo-Kantian conception of the distinctive logic of fields of inquiry – which a French intellectual movement could use to seek out yet further disciplines still to be established. When Durkheim visited Germany to study its leading developments, the universities he chose were Berlin (the site of the great Humboldtian innovation), Leipzig (where Wundt had established his psychology laboratory less than ten years earlier), and Marburg (the acknowledged headquarters of the neo-Kantian movement). We should note, too, that neo-Kantian tools were widely available, but that different uses could be made of them in different organizational settings; Weber presented his own sociological methodology in strongly neo-Kantian terms, but very much as an interpretive science, part of the *Geisteswissenschaften*, whereas Durkheim used the tools to formulate sociology as a distinctive natural science.

Besides the educational reform movement and the resulting rival movements to establish new disciplines, there were political movements calling out the loyalties and enthusiasms of French academics. Socialism elicited sympathies among administrators and teachers; their positions in the centrally organized educational system gave them a strong identification with the prestige of government service, and kept them independent of both capitalists' and workers' material interests. Although many had altruistic concerns for the workers, their socialism was generally of the top-down kind (exceptionally, Jaurès did go on to become the leader of the workers' party), and typically found expression in the Radical Socialist party, which eventually (after the rise of a more revolutionary left) became a party of the center. Sociology in the 1880s often had a connection with socialist ideology; the organic analogies of Schaeffle's sociology, like Tönnies' critique of the shift from *Gemeinschaft* to capitalist *Gesellschaft*, favored a more organic society of the future. Durkheim had socialist sympathies early in his career, and Mauss and others of the early movement moved between moderate socialism and more radical versions; Mauss was involved in the foundation of the publication *L'Humanité* in 1904 which would later evolve into the communist paper.

The Dreyfus affair was the organizing event for a temporary confluence on the plane of political action of all the movements from which Durkheimian sociology was formed. Durkheim and his colleagues were militant Dreyfusards. The specific issue of the injustice done to Captain Dreyfus was magnified during 1898–1900 into a showdown between conservative and liberal forces struggling over control of French institutions; it was fought out especially intensely in the academic world, where it became the symbolic battleground between educational reformers – just then fighting out the last phase of the take-over of Catholic schools – and their opponents. In the academic world, the conflict lined up the secularizers, scientists, and professional educators, against the spiritualist philosophers and the class elites in the schools of law and medicine. The very conception of the "intellectual," as the high-culture person, living for ideas and dedicated to *engagé* politics, was an identity constructed in the coalition which became publicly visible in the Dreyfusards (Charle 1990). The political boundaries of the coalition help explain why Durkheim allied his sociology with science, whereas Weber in Germany could ally it with the equivalent of the spiritualists. The outcome of the Dreyfus affair ushered in a republican Radical administration with strong anti-clerical principles (separation of church and state was carried through in 1905), and was directly responsible for Durkheim finally acquiring a chair in Paris.

Nevertheless, there was tension between the several movements which were the matrix of the Durkheimian movement. That movement was centrally focused on establishing sociology as a distinctive discipline with an impressive scientific program. Its members considered this program as a contribution to social peace, the resolution of class conflict, and the forming of the French nation under egalitarian republican ideals; but these were to be applications of the scientific knowledge it was creating. Too much concern for immediate political action, in Durkheim's view, was a distraction from the necessary scholarly work. Thus Durkheim was continually reining in his nephew Mauss, scolding him for spending too much time on political activities, and indirectly trying to discourage the political enthusiasms of the others. The Dreyfusard movement was a momentary passion which could be indulged because it had relatively short-term aims. As Durkheimian sociology crystallized, socialism became a more apparent rival, since it carried an intellectual ideology, but one which brought down the level of abstraction which made sociology a science. Sociology was to be a general science of all society, not merely an ideology in the service of bringing about socialism in contemporary circumstances. And the worker-oriented brand of socialism, with its emphasis on class conflict, was another warning beacon to be steered away from; sociology was finding its distinctive turf as the science of social solidarity, and conflict would thus be studied as a failure in the mechanisms of solidarity.

Finally, on the terrain of the movement to establish academic sociology, there were submovements, rivals over just how the intellectual program was to be shaped, and who would be the intellectual leaders (and by the same token, occupants of its chairs). Here Durkheim's program was shaped by oppositions quite nearby; his movement's niche must be not assimilated to a rival's position. Thus the school of research led by Le Play, investigating family life and household economy especially in rural regions, established since the 1850s (and based on Le Play's research opportunities as professor in the School of Mines) was kept at a distance, as occupying too narrow a niche; the Durkheimians would find the most general, abstract conception of social life on which to stake out their research program. Most immediately there was Alfred Espinas, already at Bordeaux since 1881 as professor of philosophy and Dean of the faculty; relations were cordial at first, but soured as Durkheim began to formulate a position distinctive from Espinas' studies of animal societies and of the evolution of technology. A rival, full-scale movement was René Worms' International Institute of Sociology, which he founded in the late 1890s. This was the rival strategy – international collaboration in periodic conferences – but its eclecticism left no lasting impression on theoretical conceptions, and its lack of a base in the French educational system fated it to ephemerality.[1]

The strongest intellectual success was Gabriel Tarde, moving along a very different career trajectory; trained as a lawyer, he was chief of the statistical service at the ministry of justice; the regularity of statistical patterns of crime from year to year and region to region provided an object of theoretical explanation in *The Laws of Imitation* (1890), which won him a public reputation as the leading French social scientist. But Tarde remained an isolated individual without a academic base or following; the chair awarded him at the Collège de France in 1901 was in modern philosophy, assimilating his position to existing academic identities rather than fostering a new one. Tarde influenced Durkheim through the dynamics of opposition by further refining his niche; Durkheim's early work relied on comparisons of legal codes as an empirical index, and in research for *Suicide* (1897) he drew on Tarde's own statistical bureau. The effort to distinguish his own position from Tarde's sharpened Durkheim's criticism of psychological explanations, and pushed him to an alternative conception of punishment as an exemplary ritual upholding the social norms rather than influencing individual criminals. Still other rivals appeared from the ranks of Parisian intellectuals; when a chair in "philosophie sociale" was proposed for the Collège de France in 1897, Durkheim lost the competition to Jean Izoulet, a lycée teacher and author of a work on the modern city. But Izoulet lacked a movement for founding a sociological school, and his chair resulted in no lasting impression. Let us emphasize again: we are interested in Durkheim's career, not simply because he is our hero whom we are rooting on to victory; but because this was the movement that found the niche in intellectual space where a generalizing, explanatory sociology could be established. What is significant about the politics of the fin-de-siècle French intellectual scene is that it produced such a program which promoted sociology in a generalizing form which could be exported to the rest of the world.

Among the resources for this movement was a personal network of recruitment. This began with Durkheim's family, when his nephew was sent to live with him while doing his university studies at Bordeaux in 1890–3 – just at the beginning of Durkheim formulating a distinctive brand of sociology. When Mauss moved to Paris for further studies and eventually employment, his uncle used him as confidant, research assistant, and reporter on the Parisian intellectual scene. Mauss was not entirely willing to be used in this way, and Durkheim's letters reveal how he made use of family pressures to keep him loyal; the letters are a mixture of advice, instruction, scolding, but always framed by affectionate greetings to Marcel ("Je t'embrasse") and to other cousins who lived with him. The entire family network was invoked as a circle of solidarity to keep Marcel in line. Mauss became the agent through whom Durkheim carried out recruitment among the Paris in-groups. The recruitment base was the range of movements we have surveyed: recent ENS graduates enthusiastic for educational reform; other young researchers (historians, religious specialists) aware of prospective restructuring of academic disciplines, which could open up new career positions at the center; socialists; Dreyfusards. If Jews were prominent in the Durkheimian movement, it was because they were especially likely to be secularists; opportunities for assimilation and social mobility in the new Republic attracted them to the reform movement successfully wresting control of a government administration and public educational from conservative Catholic domination.

A social movement builds upon a material resource base. The equivalent of a "social movement organization" for the Durkheimians was most obviously the *Année sociologique*, but this too emerged for a larger constellation of movements in the publishing world. The publisher Felix Alcan made his niche since the early 1880s by backing the new social sciences. He published the major works of Durkheim and the Durkheimians (much in the same way that the existentialist movement of the 1930s and 1940s was promoted by the publishing program of Gallimard); just prior to agreeing with Durkheim to publish the *Année sociologique*, he had launched the *Année psychologique* (in 1895), in effect betting on another new field on the strength of a previous success – the editor, Binet, had been appointed to direct a psychology laboratory at the Sorbonne in 1892. Durkheim initially rode the back of the new movement in psychology; the *Revue philosophique*, edited by Ribot, published his earliest reviews and his important papers (including an advance version of *Rules of the Sociological Method*) until the launching of the *Année sociologique*; despite Durkheim's criticism of psychological explanations he kept up good relations with the editor. After the *Revue de métaphysique et de morale* was founded in 1893, devoting a section of reviews called "*L'Année sociologique*," Durkheim recruited its key participants Bouglé, Lapie and Simiand to his discipline-building enterprise.

It was the *Année sociologique*, above all, which crystallized the Durkheimian movement (Besnard 1979; 1983). In addition to Mauss' circle of friends Paul Fauconnet, Henri Hubert, and Albert Milhaud, the early movement included Francois Simiand, Emmanuel Lévy, Paul Lapie, Célestin Bouglé, and Gaston Richard; later would come Robert Hertz, Maurice Halbwachs, and others. The most regular of these became known as the Durkheimian *équipe*, although the term overstates the hierarchic as opposed to participatory character of this movement. (Bouglé jokingly referred to it as "le clan tabou-totem"; Durkheim 1998: 15.) The *Année sociologique* was a place to publish programmatic statements and major pieces of research; as well as a highly self-conscious collective activity, with something of the character of a socialist intellectual enterprise. Every aspect of the *Année sociologique* emphasized group identity, and generated the enthusiasm and creative energy of the participants, not merely to promote Durkheim, but to build the program of sociology in its own right.

A unique characteristic of the *Année sociologique* was its emphasis upon building general theory through empirical comparison and synthesis. Its aim was to review world literature in the social sciences, and on that basis to develop a general theory. This was no conventional review journal; articles were reviewed as well as books. All reviews were to be analytical; as Durkheim wrote to Mauss, it was a waste of paper to review a book only to say that it was bad.[2] Preference was given to empirical works that could be usefully theorized, over theories and philosophical treatments lacking the analytical punch of the Durkheimians. This massive review served two purposes. One was to demonstrate that sociology was not merely amateur speculation or political ideology, but had a strong empirical base; if this did not yet exist in France and in regular academic institutions, the *Année sociologique* could show that the materials of historians, criminologists, ethnographers, and religious scholars provided a potential which required only a theorizing movement to bring out. And the very activity of bringing all this material together forced the Durkheimians to operate at a high level of generality; the comparative method was the intellectual equivalent of the organic solidarity which Durkheim had theorized was the basis of unity within an advanced division of labor. The *Année sociologique* in the years between the beginning of collaborative work in 1896, and the final volume of the pre-war series in 1909–12 comprised the Durkheimian movement at its height. Its importance can be seen by comparison with the second series in the mid-1920s: by now the effort to review and synthesize world sociology had been dropped; it was merely a place for the Durkheimians to publish their own work, as an established, successful movement, but lacking the ambitious goals of the early period.

We are now in a position to pass in review the main phases of the intellectual development of Durkheimian sociology. In the first phase, Durkheim becomes ambitious for sociology, riding the energy of the movements for educational reform and disciplinary innovation; using materials similar to existing sociologists like Spencer and Schaeffle, he conceives of society as an organism, differentiating over the course of evolution. To distinguish sociology clearly from the rival new discipline of psychology, he takes pains to critique utilitarian conceptions of social cooperation. Bolstered by his socialist sympathies, he begins to formulate the distinctive Durkheimian proofs for the collective basis of individual action in his arguments for the priority, both analytical and historical, of precontractual solidarity over deliberate contracts for economic exchange, and thereby undercuts the tradition of "social contract" theory as inadequate basis for sociology. Durkheim does not merely assert the organic analogy, in the manner of his predecessors; he refines it into an explanatory theory of the conditions which produce stronger and weaker degrees of group solidarity. Identifying with the scientific movement, he collects empirical indicators and attempts comparative tests; in *The Division of Labor*, the causal influence of social morphology, indexed by population size and density, is related to strength of collective sentiments, indexed by the punitiveness of laws and their degree of consideration for individuality. In the atmosphere of declericalization, Durkheim is happy to find a way of accounting for the changing history of religious conceptions; but it is not merely the debunking project of the political opponents of religion, but an effort to show that both the primitive gods and the ethical God of the monotheists are stages of the collective conscience. Answering a common conservative charge against secular reformers. Durkheim shows that the history of social forms evolves successive stages of morality; a secular society will not be left without morality, but indeed is evolving one of superior inclusiveness and humanitarianism.

In the mid-1890s, Durkheim located another source of research data, which would distinguish the scientific brand of sociology still more clearly from the evolutionary comparisons which had been the stock in trade of previous sociologists. Now he focuses on the contemporary workings of the legal system. The *Rules of the Sociological Method* is not only a statement of abstract principles, explicitly carving out a sociological domain as the treatment of social facts as things; it also is a demonstration of the innovative insights provided by sociology in the domain of criminology. Critiquing both biological and psychological models of criminal behavior, Durkheim shows that in punishment social constraints make themselves most palpable; hence his famous argument that punishments are constructed to remind society of itself, and that even a society of saints would evolve its own standards by which imperfections would be punished. Hard on the heels of this work comes *Suicide* (1897), in its time the most highly theorized use of government statistics. Feeling his program has not yet been accepted, Durkheim is not content with his previous demonstrations of the priority of social over the individual, but hammers home the lesson from yet another angle. Suicides are worthy of attention because of what they reveal about their opposite. The taking of one's life reveals by contrast the conditions under which life is meaningful; thus a demonstration of the social configurations of suicides is another proof of how social morphology affects human consciousness, both in its collective and individual forms. In these works he crystallizes the stance that was to be the hallmark of the Durkheimian school: breaking through and even reversing commonsense conceptions by formulations which appear paradoxical and yet reveal the powerfully constraining substratum of social life.

Yet despite the dramatic quality of these intellectual performances, and their high water mark in marshalling a variety of empirical evidence to establish a social scientific theory, Durkheim was passed over for the chair at the Collège de France in 1897. His letters of this period show depression, even momentary disillusionment with the whole project of sociology, which he feels is making no impression on the public, in the face of lesser rivals (Durkheim to Mauss, July 1897; in Durkheim 1998: 75–9). By this time, however, the *Année sociologique* project is under way, and its momentum takes over. The growing centrality of religion in Durkheimian theory during this period comes as much from his collaborators as from Durkheim himself. The drift may be explained as a process of feeling out scholarly niches until the movement flows into the one that finally gives the group public visibility and intellectual success. The weakness of Durkheim's emphasis on social morphology was that Durkheim's position was too close to that of numerous social geographers, biologists, and demographers. For example, the statistician Adolphe Coste in the 1890s was also publishing "une sociologie objective" describing stages of social evolution which have corresponding stages of "ideological facts," with the determining factors indexed by population density (on this now forgotten work, see Sorokin 1928: 359–70; it should be noted that Durkheim's very earliest publications, in 1885–6, were reviews of Coste, Spencer, and Schaeffle). Durkheim's use of crime and other public statistics was overshadowed by Tarde.

The comparative study of religion, magic, and myth, however, provided fertile material; it was very much in the public eye, with the popularity of works like Frazer's *Golden Bough* (1890), and appealed to a cosmopolitan audience welcoming alternatives to institutional Christianity; it was under-theorized, with most arguments speculating on psychological laws or on remote origins rather than the significance of religion as a general social phenomenon. To be sure, the work of William Robertson Smith (notably *The Religion of the Semites*, 1889) which held that religion was primarily a social practice rather than a body of abstract ideas, was received by Durkheim as highly congruent with a sociological approach. But Robertson Smith, for all his influence in launching Frazer's career at Cambridge in the 1880s, was a professor of Arabic, less concerned with a general theory of religion than with specific interpretations of Middle Eastern monotheist traditions. Robertson Smith was shaped by other sorts of intellectual oppositions; his main opponents were conservative Christian theologians who prosecuted him as a heretic. Religion ideally fitted the Durkheimians' project because it was a place where social interaction – the local social morphology of the group assembled in rites of worship, magic, and other religious practices – could be studied in its relation to social constraint, moral sentiment, and ideas; religion revealed the connection between social action and collective representations, thus opening the way to a theory of symbolism. Comparative religion, in sum, was sociologically under-theorized, as well as rich in directions for research by scholars armed with sociological conceptions; it opened up career niches not only in religious studies, but in what would become social and symbolic anthropology, and eventually in the study of such modern secular phenomena as rituals and symbolism in their own right. With the formulation of a Durkheimian sociology of religion, the long-run success of the movement was assured. It would be in the light of Durkheimian religious sociology that his earlier works would be saved from oblivion and given attention for their key analytical insights.

This Durkheimian sociology of religion was a genuinely collective formulation. Durkheim began to work on the area in the mid-1890s, but it was Mauss and an early recruit, his historically-trained friend Henri Hubert, who first demonstrated the power of sociological analysis in their work on sacrifice (1899), generalizing the pioneering work of Robertson Smith. By the early 1900s, one might almost say, the torch had been passed to Hubert and Mauss, especially in their work on magic (1902–3) which brings out strongly the concentration and distribution of socially contagious emotions which differentiate individuals by social status, thus opening a distinctively Durkheimian approach to individualism, as well as to stratification. Magic, too, shows the social process of charging up objects with collective significance. This gives new depth to Durkheim's theme of the precontractual basis of exchange, for now the origins of money can be shown in the circulation of objects carrying social prestige in the form of reputation for magical potency (Mauss 1914; 1934). The publication of Durkheim's masterwork, *The Elementary Forms of Religious Life*, in 1912 was a summary of what the movement had done over the past fifteen years. The work of his years in Paris, from 1902 onwards, was a consolidation. His life work had been done in the struggle to get a highly visible position at the center; once there, he struck out in no new directions. But the chair at the Sorbonne was not merely for Durkheim himself, but for Durkheim as the "tabou-totem" of the movement; and that movement now was flowing triumphantly on its momentum.

The retreat of the Durkheimian movement in inter-war France

Social movements cannot stay mobilized forever, and thus in a sense it was inevitable that the Durkheimians would undergo a decline in élan. But the situation in French intellectual life from the end of the First World War through the 1940s was not so much the routinization of a movement through successful institutionalization; nor again was it the disappearance of a defeated movement, like the fate of so many others. The Durkheimians underwent a falling off in intellectual ambition, away from the program to develop sociology as the generalizing science of social phenomena, to a much more limited and traditional position in the intellectual field. Externally, they had some successes in academic policy and in French national politics, but these turned into liabilities as the intellectual generation of the 1930s and 1940s came to publicly scorn the Durkheimians as a biased and outdated sect.

A superficial interpretation has it that the Durkheimians declined because their promising younger members – Robert Hertz, Maxime David, Antoine Bianconi, Jean Reynier – were killed in the First World War. The underlying assumption is particularistic and unsociological. The more important issue is why the movement was not able to recruit new members in the 1920s at the rate it had sustained before the war; above all there was a decline in the number of recruits from the elite ENS which had sustained the original take-off (Heilbron 1985; this is the source for much of the information presented in this section). The difficulty of the movement was that it institutionalized but in a fashion that left it marginal in the academic world and forced to make compromising alliances that diluted its message; this reduced both its accomplishments and its visibility, and put an end to the period of anticipation while the movement was looking forward to a glorious position in the reformed academic system of the future.

Sociology was institutionalized in France but just barely. There were four chairs which included sociology in their title (though usually in conjunction with something else): Durkheim's old chair at Bordeaux; a new chair at Strasbourg (i.e. a university recaptured from Germany), created for Maurice Halbwachs in 1919; and two at the Sorbonne, Durkheim's old chair, and another founded in 1908 and held by Célestin Bouglé more or less continuously until 1939 (see Heilbron 1985: 205 for the many changes in titles and ranks of these chairs). The chairs were in the "faculté des lettres," and thus cut off from the "faculté de droit" which housed economics and trained most students in social science.

Throughout the French educational system, sociology was taught mainly to philosophy students; and aside from the places where the four sociology chairs existed, it was taught by philosophers as part of the philosophical curriculum. This was not necessarily a weak position to be in; philosophy students were the largest group in the "faculté des lettres" (since philosophy remained the capstone of the secondary school education) and they remained the breeding ground for most of the elite intellectuals outside of the natural sciences, as indeed continued to be the case through the late twentieth century – giving French intellectual life a more philosophical orientation than elsewhere in the world. And sociology in the 1920s was riding high within philosophy, considered very modern and especially important in educational and social contributions. Mauss, inheriting the mantle of Durkheim, declared in 1923 that sociology was destined to replace philosophy, since it would give a scientific account of the categories of knowledge as well as of morality (Mauss 1923; quoted in Heilbron 1985: 216). This was the Durkheimian program at its most ambitious (for a current revival, see Anne Rawls forthcoming).

But what the philosophy students and teachers saw was more narrowly traditional. Durkheimian sociology was becoming regarded as a species of idealist philosophy. It was simultaneously an antidote to materialism and thus to extreme leftism and class conflict; as well as a reasoned, secular alternative to religious teachings, a lively alternative since the French school system at the lower levels of instruction had only recently been wrested from church control. Durkheimian sociology extolled the collective nature of the system of values and ideals which give meaning to individual lives. This was a shift in emphasis from the original Durkheimian program of social morphology, to examine how patterns of social interaction generate emotions (moral sentiments) which sustain symbols and shape individual motivations. There has been much scholarly discussion of whether Durkheim himself in his later works shifted towards an idealist position.[3] Yet one may say that *Elementary Forms* is the strongest contribution to understanding the interactional patterns – social rituals – which flexibly and situationally generate moral values and symbolic meanings. As Durkheim himself underlines, without repeated performance of the rituals, the beliefs fade away. What seems clear is that the Durkheimian movement in the situation after Durkheim's death strongly moved towards this interpretation of sociology. Especially instrumental was Bouglé. Under his influence sociology was taught for a while around 1920 to teachers preparing for the elementary schools, and became an optional subject at the lycées in 1923. Bouglé eventually rose to the position of director of the ENS during 1935–40. His institutional prominence, and that of the other Durkheimians who occupied positions in academic teaching and administration, led this part of the movement to soften the original emphasis on scientific research in a comparative mode; sociology was presented as moral teaching, of the preeminence of the group over individual selfishness, of respect for collective institutions, and above all as French national patriotism.

The academically most influential sociologists were caught up in administration of the national educational system. In the highly centralized French system, secondary school teaching was a typical career pattern even for those eventually attaining higher professorships, and the most prestigious careers went through school inspectorships and administrators of nation-wide examinations. To the extent that writing counted, it was not so much research but publication of textbooks and editions of classic texts (Fabiani 1988). The scientific and scholarly aims of the Durkheimians survived better in persons who found their material base outside the teaching enterprise, in the specialized research institutes. Here the more productive Durkheimians continued to work: Mauss, Simiand, Granet, Hubert, in the 4th and 5th sections of the EPHE, the Ecole des langues orientales, the Institut d'ethnologie, the Collège de France.[4] But these positions did not train regular students who could sustain a research program; and they softened the focus of the sociological program so that it became less theoretical, less generalizing, more focused upon the erudition of a particular area of factual knowledge. The research-based sociologists were well aware that the program had become diluted in the hands of Bouglé and the academic administrators, and they objected to the shift towards idealism and narrowly construed moralism and French patriotism, even opposing the various moves to introduce sociology into primary and secondary curricula. The two groups split as well on political affiliations: the academics generally upheld the program of the Radical Party, which is to say the middle-road, militantly secular Republicans whose primary base was civil servants and teachers; the Durkheimian researchers tended to be socialists and internationalists.

In the public eye, it was the nationalist and spiritualist image of the Durkheimians that predominated. Thus in the 1930s, the new generation of younger intellectuals regarded the Durkheimians as representing just that fanatical patriotism that brought about the carnage of the world war and impeded any solution to current domestic and international conflicts. With the new vogue of German thinking – phenomenology, existentialism, the Hegelian revival – the Durkheimians' apparent anti-Germanism was seen as dogmatic and antiquated. In 1932, Paul Nizan, in a generational manifesto *Les Chiens de garde* [The Watch-dogs] sardonically depicted the death toll at Verdun as proud victories for Boutroux, Bergson and Durkheim. In a more substantive vein, Jean-Paul Sartre would set off his own brand of existentialism by repudiating the Durkheimian principle of the social as a reality *sui generis*: ". . . la sociologie de Durkheim est morte: les faits sociaux ne sont pas des choses . . . ils renvoient à l'être par qui les significations viennent au monde, a l'homme . . ." (Sartre 1947: 136; quoted in Heilbron 1985). Politically and intellectually, the Durkheimians were not only out of vogue, they were pilloried for being what was at fault with the old thinking of the nationalist Third Republic.

In part this was the result of the failure of French sociology to win a strong independent base for teaching and research; the promising beginnings of the program as the mutual development of theory and empirical research came apart into vapid generalizations drenched in nationalism, and in another direction specialized erudition no longer identified with the unity of a sociological theory. Worse yet, the moments of political success for the Durkheimian nationalists cost them dearly in the slightly longer run. In the 1920s, Radical Party deputies would quote Durkheim from the floor of the Chamber of Deputies. The upshot was much the same as in a previous abortive launching of French social theory. François Guizot, whose analytical histories in the 1820s had been the height of institutional history-writing and the source for both Marx and Tocqueville, found his scholarly reputation swallowed up by hatred of his policies as a leading official of the Orleanist monarchy of the 1830s and 40s (Siedentop 1997). Too much partisan political success, it seems, is fatal for the reputation of an intellectual program which aspires to universality.

The Durkheimian movement outside France

The future growth of the Durkheimian movement would thus have to come from outside France if from anywhere. Only by finding bases elsewhere would Durkheimian sociology survive as an identity which eventually could be revived in France. In the medium run this survival was insured by the academic system of the USA, which institutionalized sociology as an independent department at the turn of the twentieth century, and expanded its positions enormously with the continued expansion both in numbers of universities and in enrollments throughout most of the century. And since American universities, unlike the French, combined teaching and research positions, career patterns promoted a certain amount of research in the Durkheimian scientific theoretical program. In contrast to France, where sociology was made an academic discipline primarily by the Durkheimian movement with its unified theoretical program, sociology in the USA was academized from an array of intellectual and social movements. These included scholarship imported by sojourners to and émigrés from Germany; indigenous movements such as symbolic interactionism deriving from pragmatism in American philosophy; the popular movement of evolutionism; and a number of activist movements in social welfare and other community reforms. Thus the Durkheimian theory/research program was only a small piece of the intellectual landscape of American sociologists. Although it was one of the most theoretically coherent and the most ambitious in its goals for the discipline, its superiority in these respects was not much recognized until the 1930s and 1940s, when it became publicized and developed in a distinctive manner by the structural-functionalist movement of Talcott Parsons and Robert Merton. This in turn set the task for Durkheimian sociologists after the 1960s: to ensure that the Durkheimian program, as a core program for sociological science, would not go down with the fading popularity of functionalism.

Let us return briefly to survey the spread of the Durkheimian movement earlier in the century. There are scattered followers of Durkheim among the intellectuals of southern and eastern Europe. One of the founders of the national reform movement in Turkey was Gökalp, a sociology professor who wrote explicitly in a Durkheimian vein (Mann 2005: 121). The Young Turks were just such a secularizing, nationalist, and republican movement as the milieu in which the Durkheimians arose in France. The Durkheimian doctrine of national solidarity as a secular religion, expressed initially as a general scientific insight, was perfectly adapted for export into nation-building contexts where it could be expressed in particularistic terms. This was of course to jettison its universalistic discovery-making aims as a theoretical research program. Nationalist sociologists might contribute something to political movements and individual careers, but at the cost of undermining sociology's scholarly potential, and given nationalist excesses, its moral reputation as well.

What saved the Durkheimian research program was a meshing of scholarly networks which took place in the 1920s and 1930s. British social anthropologists, just then institutionalizing as a research discipline, made contacts with Durkheimians, and began to adopt the Durkheimian program as a key part of their own research movement (Goody 1995). Institutionally, British anthropology began in the 1880s and 1890s as what might be called cultural anthropology, concerned above all with the origins and stages of development of religion. Its empirical resources were classical texts, supplemented by archeological excavations, missionaries' and travelers' accounts. Its early practitioners came from fields such as classical languages and geographical exploration, and its leaders such as James Frazer at Cambridge and Edward Tylor at Oxford promoted a movement that although widely known in public readership rested upon marginal specializations within classical literary studies and positions in museums and libraries. The professional anthropologist who deliberately goes to the field to study a society with theoretical considerations in mind was just making an appearance in the early twentieth century; and what systematic work there was tended to be carried out by museum-oriented ethnographers cataloguing material artifacts (as in the USA), or on the other hand in the service of biological theories of race which concentrated attention on bodily measurements.

The individual most successful at uniting sustained observation with concern for social theory was Bronislaw Malinowski, who returned in the early 1920s from many years' research in the Trobriand Islands – he had been trapped there during the world war – to set up a research seminar at the London School of Economics. Malinowski's militant new program was to break with the literary, textual, and comparison-gathering style of the students of religious origins, mythology and magic; a society was to be studied as a whole, as a group of people interacting through an ensemble of institutions by which their lives were sustained, and their beliefs were to be understood in the context of their way of life. Malinowski's program had an affinity with the Durkheimians' concern for systematic explanation in terms of social morphology, although Malinowski himself was not very favorably disposed to the Durkheimians. He stood alone as the world's most accomplished field ethnographer, a reputation that came as Malinowski's books confronted Freudian ideas – just then in their first burst of public popularity – with exotic field data, and fashioned novel explanations for fundamental issues of family, sexuality, and magic. Nevertheless, he facilitated the blending of the Durkheimian movement into what became known as the British school of social anthropology. This came about in part because his own work was taken up by Mauss: Malinowski's *Argonauts of the Western Pacific* (1922) provided the materials on the kula ring exchange which provided the center piece for Mauss' most famous work, *The Gift* (1925). Blending also came about because Malinowski's seminar became the center of a social movement.

In the late 1920s and early 1930s Malinowski's LSE seminar attracted a group of converts to the new program of holistic understanding of the functioning of a society on the basis of lengthy acquaintance in the field. Exemplary work that established the new standard for fieldwork was carried out in the 1930s in British colonial Africa by Malinowski's students Edward Evans-Pritchard and Meyer Fortes. The functionalist program acquired theoretical importance on the basis of demonstrations of how African kinship systems meshed with political and economic organization; religion became viewed no longer as a set of beliefs surviving from earlier stages and casting light on origins, but instead as a form of action carried out among the exigencies of social life. In Evans-Pritchard's famous analysis, *Witchcraft, Oracles, and Magic among the Azande* (1937), the Azande oracle represented neither superstition nor archaic mentality but workable practices for negotiating the uncertainties and social conflicts of tribal life. Evans-Pritchard acquired a chair of anthropology at Oxford, Fortes at Cambridge. In the absence of sociology, which smacked of low-brow welfare reformism and thus did not fare well in the upper-class British academic atmosphere, anthropology acquired the prestige of constructing a theoretical science of society.

The structural-functionalist movement emerged from a combination of the Malinowski seminar, with a connection with the Durkheimians established by way of A. R. Radcliffe-Brown. Starting as a Cambridge student from Frazer's circle, Radcliffe-Brown's career was formed in the opportunities of the British empire; he did field work in the Andaman Islands of the Indian ocean nearly contemporary with Malinowski's Trobriand Islands work, and after getting chairs first in South Africa and then at Sydney, went on to extensive field studies in Australia. In 1924 he was drawn into correspondence with Mauss and became converted to the merits of the Durkheimian program, especially the functions of social ritual. Making explicit one of the implications of Durkheim's analysis of piacular rites, Radcliffe-Brown formulated a famous statement of the function of funerals as integrating the group after the loss of a member. Radcliffe-Brown (1937) produced the most explicit statements of the structural-functionalist program of social anthropology. Because he was most distant of all the field researchers from Malinowski's influence at the LSE seminar (and indeed an early fieldwork rival of Malinowski, and thus motivated to seek out a position that would give him a distinctive reputation), he was freer to adopt Durkheimian theory, which was far more systematic than Malinowski's eclectic stance; and this put him in a position to take over leadership of the new movement of holistic field ethnographers by articulating his work with theirs in an ambitious theoretical program. When Radcliffe-Brown acquired a chair at Oxford in 1937 – the occasion for publication of his major theoretical statement – the movement was consolidated by control of the major academic bases and a commanding position in the intellectual focus of attention.[5]

From here we may trace two pathways back into sociology. This could not happen at the time in Britain where sociology was institutionally marginal; one possible route was that the Durkheimian/social anthropological hybrid could be imported into American universities, where sociology was prospering. The other route was that the social anthropologists would expand their scope of application from tribal to modern societies; this led to a sociology of rituals and eventually to a strongly micro-sociological extension of the Durkheimian tradition. This latter route we will consider below with W. Lloyd Warner and Erving Goffman. The former route was taken by Talcott Parsons; in the late 1920s he was a young economics instructor at Harvard, sojourning in the time-honored fashion in European universities, and in 1932–3 was a visiting member of the Malinowski seminar at LSE. Exploiting institutional opportunities at his home university, where Harvard was just establishing a new sociology department, Parsons saw that sociology could claim the highest level of intellectual standards befitting America's most prestigious university, by emphasizing its qualities as the generalizing science of the social world. The Malinowski seminar brought him into contact with the Durkheimian current now flowing in British anthropology, which Parsons as an American academic (rather than a British anthropologist) recognized could be generalized beyond the special circumstances of tribal societies. Thus Parsons was responsible for leading a movement of "back to Durkheim" seen through the eyes of the structural-functionalists. There were other inputs into Parsons' program – sojourning at Heidelberg had brought him into contact with the remnants of the Weber circle; and at Harvard he was part of an interdisciplinary circle of admirers of Pareto's system of social-cum-economic-cum-ideological cycles (Camic 1991). But the Durkheimian inputs were what gave the grandest scope for sociology; the work of Weber and Pareto would appeal to an economist seeking institutional and cultural depths going beyond the technical analysis of markets, but Weber's neo-Kantianism was interpretive and anti-scientific, and Pareto's system although aggressively positivist was also considered dangerously close to rightist ideology. Parsons' programmatic statement *The Structure of Social Action* (1937) may be read as a claim for the analytical importance and indeed centrality of sociology as the generalizing social science; its analytical core is in its chapters on Durkheim.

By contrast, Pitirim Sorokin, Parsons' rival in Harvard's new sociology department, in his 1928 work *Contemporary Sociological Theories*, devotes seventeen pages (of 760 total) to Durkheim, whom he puts in a "sociologistic school" along with the now mostly forgotten names of De Roberty, Espinas, lzoulet, Draghicesco, and Cooley. Pareto gets twenty-five pages in what Sorokin calls the "mechanistic school" of social physics; Weber gets nine pages lumped in with "psycho-sociologistic theories of religion . . . and other cultural phenomena." Marx and Engels get twenty-three pages in the chapter on "Sociologistic school: economic branch." These are dwarfed by Sorokin's attention to geographical-determinist, anthropo-racial, biosocial/demographic, and psychological schools, which together get some 480 pages. The comparison between Sorokin's and Parsons' treatments nicely illustrates the problem of an intellectual movement as providing a focus of attention in a diffuse attention space. The same intellectual figures are visible to both, and would have been generally known among specialists. But Sorokin gives only the impression of erudite eclecticism, in which nothing builds toward any very clear direction of theoretical advance.

Parsons simplifies the attention space, radically pruning and obliquely dismissing just the sort of schools to which Sorokin gives most attention. Durkheim becomes especially valuable for sustained analysis because his argument for social phenomena as *sui generis* provides a weapon against biological reductionism, so prominent in Sorokin's survey. Side-stepping the debates between individual and super-organic which had been a staple of theoretical discussion, Parsons uses contemporary philosophical sophistication about levels of symbol systems (drawing on themes both of Husserlian phenomenology and Russellian mathematical logic) to argue that these are analytical choices rather than ontological realities, and that treating the realm of social phenomena as distinctive in its own right opens up a fruitful field of analysis. The fruitfulness of this approach, Parsons hammers home, is shown by Durkheim's program. He singles out as the analytical key the issue that he labels "the Hobbesian problem of order"; Durkheim's demonstration that individuals pursuing self-interest cannot establish stable social cooperation, either political or economic; and thus not only the state but the market itself, the epitome of self-interested individual exchange, must rest upon precontractual solidarity. This move underscores Parsons' exit from economics into sociology. This also gives a center around which to organize the rest of Durkheim's sociology; the comparative studies of legal systems as indicators of the repressiveness of the collective conscience at different levels of the division of labor; the ritualistic enactment of criminal punishments as serving to uphold consciousness of social norms rather than as affecting the individual criminal; the demonstration that conditions for social solidarity determine propensity to suicide; the character of religion as reflecting group structure and expressing membership and moral solidarity: these are the empirical program for scientifically demonstrating the mechanisms of pre-contractual solidarity. Weber, Pareto (and Parsons' token economist, Alfred Marshall) are brought in to bolster the argument by theoretical convergence, in Weber's case giving specific content to the religious solidarity which provides the underpinnings for modern capitalism.

Parsons thus gave renewed prestige and prominence to the Durkheimian theoretical program as the clearest vision of sociology's fundamental problems and of their most fruitful line of solution. Where the Durkheimians tended towards comparative statics (except in Durkheim's own early work on mechanical and organic solidarity), and the British social anthropologists even more explicitly and polemically cut themselves off from what they regarded as speculation on historical origins, Parsons showed how the most sophisticated concerns of analytical sociology – the sources and mechanisms of non-utilitarian social solidarity – could provide a theory of change. In Parsons' later works, he would model this partly on Weber's comparative sociology of the world religions, partly on a theory of institutional differentiation generalized from Durkheim's comparison of low and high levels of the division of labor. A theoretical research program shows its strength by the problems which it opens up while guaranteeing the importance of contributions to their solution. With a prominent institutional base at Harvard, equipped with sophisticated theoretical tools, and energized by the proud identity of carrying forward the classics of modern sociology, the movement around Parsons turned out a generation of leading sociologists. Besides Parsons himself, his many prominent students included Robert Merton, who gave a theoretical core to the Columbia department, one of the early bastions of empirical research in American sociology. Here Durkheimian sociology was elaborated into a theory of deviance (as various types of anomie induced by social structure); while the comparative methodology of the study of suicide was touted in the 1950s as exemplar for the multivariate analysis of now-burgeoning survey research.

The very success of the Durkheimian program in its structural-functionalist garb led to its next moment of crisis and decline. In the 1960s, there was a massive increase in numbers of sociologists, as American universities rapidly proliferated and student demand mushroomed. Functionalism was attacked by several rival research programs. From one side came several branches of militant micro-sociology: a renewed symbolic interactionism, originally based in the Chicago department which had long rivaled Columbia and Chicago, and now diffused to the new high-prestige center of sociology at Berkeley and thence to the new universities of the West coast and elsewhere; a movement calling itself "ethnomethodology" born of a fusion of Husserlian phenomenology with a research program of detailed observations of everyday life; a renewed individual actor theory initially grounded in small group research and calling itself exchange theory, later allying with economics under the rubric of rational choice. On the macro level, functionalism became a foil for several versions of conflict theory, including both ideologically militant Marxism adopted by the rebellious student movement, and in a more detached vein, neo-Weberian historical comparative sociology now interpreted as a more complex version of multi-dimensional social struggle. Weber, at mid-century generally considered the intellectual property of the functionalists, now was reshaped as an intellectual resource for those seeking a more defensible and less dogmatic path forward from the insights of Marx. The functionalist research program lost its attractiveness for the new generation of sociologists; in part subjected to glib and even scurrilous attacks as a bastion of conservatism, as oblivious to social conflict, stratification, and social change; in part abandoned by theoretically oriented researchers who found the functionalist approach to these favorite topics clumsy, constraining, or even tautological.[6]

Analytically, a key weakness came from Parsons' adoption of the British social anthropologists' strategy: that a society ought to be treated as a closed system, in which its several institutions function in tandem. This had opened up a fruitful field of studies, above all in relatively simple tribal societies, where one could show how kinship, religion, economic conditions and practices – and be it noted, patterns of political conflict as well – all mutually reinforced and reproduced one another. It was even possible to show self-equilibrating processes, by which a disturbance in one part could set causal loops in motion which tended to restore the pre-existing pattern. From the point of view of Parsonian scholars, the conception of a bounded, self-integrating society also made it possible to ferret out a unique cultural pattern which constituted its value-system and symbolic blue-print and thus to do justice to the particularity of societies, and to their unique historical pathways; a marriage of Durkheim, the British social anthropologists, and Weber opened the possibility of finding the local equivalents of the Protestant ethic which gave each part of the world its distinctive character.

Among other research strategies contributing to the downfall of the functionalist program, came the propensity of late twentieth century macro-historical scholars to take bounded social units as ephemeral constructions, at best local nodes shaped by larger dynamics of economic world-systems, geopolitical conflicts, and overlapping networks. Researchers also now preferred to begin with interest groups as their unit of analysis, starting with economic classes, racial/ethnic groups, genders and sexual preference groups, professional or organizational factions, and going on to developing explanations in terms of their oppositions and oppressions, resources, and opportunities. The analytical weakness of this conflict-oriented analysis, from the Durkheimian viewpoint, is precisely the Hobbesian problem of order: how could such interest groups themselves be constituted as stable clusters of social action, instead of fragmented in an individualistic war of all against all? Whence, indeed, the relative stability of the larger institutional order which provides such groups the flow of material and cultural resources which enable them to mobilize? And how can one account for the very process and tactics of domination and conflict, such that moral appeals and cultural understandings are key weapons in conflict, bringing waves of sympathetic allies, or delegitimating those groups whose actions are seen as too extreme or beyond the tacit rules of conflict?

The latter twentieth century found ways to draw on Durkheimian insights in answering these questions, while maintaining the focus on domination and conflict, and without reverting to the holistic conception of the functionally integrated society. In effect, the solution has been to move in the direction of a micro-Durkheimianism. The issue is posed: how does any group acquire solidarity so that it can engage in social action? The Durkheimians provided the mechanisms: performance of social ritual, which generates membership symbols, moral beliefs, collective effervescence and emotional strength; and patterns of social morphology, which determine what kinds of symbols, emotions, and membership boundaries are formed. Here we need to retrace our steps, back to the British social anthropologists, and from these to the networks which flowed from these into sociology. The theory of rituals, laid out by Durkheim in *Elementary Forms* as an explanation of aboriginal religion (and which Durkheim applied also to political rituals around sacred objects such as flags), was cast in a functionalist form in works such as Radcliffe-Brown's analysis of funeral ritual. Two important steps followed towards a ritualism of social conflict: demonstrating that rituals operate not only in tribal but in complex modern societies; and that rituals and symbols are themselves stratifying and conflict-mobilizing, demarcating ranks and lines of opposition.

W. Lloyd Warner, a pupil of Radcliffe-Brown who had begun by studying tribal organization in tropical Australia, promoted both steps by organizing an in-depth field study of a Massachusetts city referred to as "Yankee City" (Warner and Lunt 1941). In effect, Warner found it to be organized into a hierarchy of tribes in the form of social classes. Classes have their own rituals and sources of symbolic solidarity, ranging from recounting kinship ties, through distinctive church membership, clubs and entertainments, dances and dinner parties, even distinctive burial grounds. Symbolic practices not only unify groups within but fortify barriers to those without. Furthermore these collective understandings are shared across groups to just the extent that they confront one another as higher and lower, as privileged and unprivileged; the focus on acquiring the cultural understandings of the dominant group becomes all the more acute when families try to move upward across the line, a maneuver that requires not only material entrée but symbolic acceptance. (The implication is there is less incentive for those at the top of a hierarchy to understand the culture of those below them.) Although it was not sufficiently appreciated at the time, Warner gave a model of how pockets of group solidarity can be mutually antagonistic, yet make up a stable macro-social order; that it is sufficient to have a Durkheimian solution to the Hobbesian problem of order at the micro level, while the macro level can be as blatantly oppressive as any Marxian analysis might consider.

Warner (1959) went on to show that collective symbols as well, ostensibly representing the entire community, are generally controlled by a particular class; thus memorial parades and commemorations for the war dead or for patriotic ancestors were the province of the old-line upper class, allowing participation of lower-ranking groups only under sufferance. To approach the sacred objects at the center of a community is allowed only at the price of making obeisance to its class hierarchy. We see here another aspect of the power of Durkheimian rituals; to adopt a Goffmanian way of speaking, they are where the action is, exerting a magnetic attraction over whoever would like to be part of the collective effervescence and enclosed in its world of symbols. Social membership is not all-or-none but is enacted through degrees of closeness, and it is the varying distances which individuals stand from the attention-getting rites which generates a hierarchy of prestige. Read in this fashion, prestige hierarchies are not primordial or analytically transcendent; social prestige is a particular condition of Durkheimian collective conscience, and if it is a weapon of class domination, it becomes so to just the extent that a class monopolizes the enactment of the rituals filling the community's attention space.[7]

Warner's student and research assistant, Erving Goffman, took these Durkheimian insights to a still more micro level of analysis. Warner had moved to Chicago in the late 1940s, where Goffman was one of his first students. Goffman began his career by combining ritual analysis (he had been introduced to this as an undergraduate at Toronto under another British anthropologist) with the Chicago tradition of ethnographies of deviance and occupational back spaces, and with the Chicago symbolic interactionist concern for fluid situational action. These ingredients (along with a interest in popular Freudianism), led Goffman to formulate a distinctive, hybrid topic: the ritualism of everyday life. Goffman's earliest publication (1951) was in

Warner's vein, on "Symbols of class status," but he soon moved toward exploring the purely analytical aspects of the realm of everyday interaction – what Anne Rawls later (1987) would call "the interaction order *sui generis.*" Goffman shifted the unit of analysis down far beneath the order of group solidarities and identities as conventionally known; strands of personal relationship among individuals, and even ephemeral encounters, all have their social reality which is sustained only insofar as participants enact them ritually. Thus the banal gestures of politeness – greetings, goodbyes, keeping up a flow of small talk, handshakes, calling someone by their title or their personal name – operate the same way as the religious rituals which Durkheim analyzed as the center of group solidarity among participants in the worship.

Goffman picked apart several orders of enacted social membership. Some of these are rituals which establish ranking via the minutiae of precedence and control of the idealized aspects of the situation. This type of ritual gives a micro-situational basis to the stratified social order. Here Goffman opened the way to an explanation of differences in class cultures based on the habitual interactions of those who give orders or take orders, those who may be called the "frontstage class culture" of the higher social classes and the "backstage class culture" of the lower classes (Collins 1975). This aspect of Goffman gave impetus to the concern in the 1980s for the micro-foundations of macro-sociology.

On a more individualized level are rituals which enact an inter-personal tie such as a love affair, a friendship, a family obligation, or just the relationship of casual acquaintance among social equals; Goffman is suggesting that it is the ongoing repetition of such rituals, meaningless in themselves, which keeps up strands of solidarity in an individualized modern society. Here one gets, too, a Durkheimian theory of the modern self. Going beyond the symbolic interactionist theory which regards selves as structured by internalizing the viewpoint of the other, Goffman argues that selves are constituted not so much by looking inwards from the viewpoint of imagined others – an enterprise that Goffman suggests on the basis of micro-situational observations is far from easy or accurate – as by the success or failure of interaction rituals to keep up a flow of symbolic tokens in whatever is the conventional coin of the realm. Goffman allows for a world of micro-interactions that can be full of misunderstandings and deceptions, but that nevertheless produces situational solidarity because it is the carrying out of ritual forms that keeps interaction orderly. Politeness does not have to be sincere, it only has to be mutually sustained. The same goes for modes of interaction filled by sentimentality, gushy enthusiasm, heartiness, or intimate revelations; none of these necessarily express the inner feelings of individuals; they need only be present as a shared social activity – keeping a ritual going enough to sustain a relationship. Goffman provides a micro-sociology capable of giving a refined theory of social selves in all their situational variations, even while according selves no ultimate ontological reality or analytical priority.

Concluding his most explicit application of Durkheimian theory, "In this paper I have suggested that Durkheimian notions about primitive religion can be translated into concepts of deference and demeanor, and that these concepts help us to grasp some aspects of urban secular living," Goffman (1956) declaimed: "Many gods have been done away with, but the individual himself stubbornly remains a deity of considerable importance. He walks with some dignity and is the recipient of many little offerings." If a society of low institutional differentiation and high interactional density manifests itself symbolically in the worship of supernatural gods, the modern (for that matter, "postmodern") world of ultra-differentiated spheres, fleeting encounters and privatized individuality manifests itself in the cult of the individual self. Goffman thus even suggests Durkheimian tools for analysis of the phenomenon of "political correctness" that emerged after his death.

On a level yet more micro, Goffman points to the fleeting interaction, the situation itself, as the most fundamental form of membership. Taking Durkheim's construction of social reality through collective symbolism down to the level of the smallest unit of "the social," Goffman holds that situations are little social systems, with their own requirements for order; which is to say (putting this so as to shed the functionalist overtones) the reality of a situation is not simply given; it comes off only to the extent that it is enacted, and that can only be done by meeting the obdurate requirements of interaction ritual. The situation itself must be collectively presented, taken as real; a fruitful way to follow this up, we are now finding, is to research in ultra-micro detail the focus of mutual attention, the degree of entrainment of bodily gestures, sounds, rhythms, and emotions (for elaboration, see Collins 2004a). In this vein, Richard Hilbert (1992) has suggested that the project of ethnomethodological research is to study the Durkheimian collective conscience as an ongoing local production, examining the taken-for-granted practices which beneath the surface of conscious awareness make possible the sense of normalcy, and thus the sense that there is indeed a social world "out there." It is "out there" indeed, in Durkheim's sense of social facts taken as things; but in this micro-transformation of the Durkheimian tradition, it is the micro-situational interaction which is the constraining and most thoroughly collective experience, while the larger social institutions are real only to the extent that chains of micro-situational interaction rituals continue to sustain them. Once again we see solidarity is local and micro, indeed hard to escape at the interactional level: whereas the macro level can be full of splits, oppositions, latent and overt conflicts. In this view, Durkheimian analysis works best as micro-sociology, while its contribution to macro-sociology is not to establish by fiat the existence of a functionally integrated social order, but to show how local pockets of solidarity string together a stratified and conflictual ensemble.

Exemplary of the contemporary tendency to elaborate Durkheimian themes on the micro level is the work of Thomas Scheff (1990). Using ultra-refined empirical tools including video and audio recordings of natural interaction studied in split-second detail, Scheff provides evidence that people take interactional solidarity as the baseline of normalcy: a situation of intact social bonds manifested in bodily and emotional micro-coordination is attracting and energizing; subjectively it generates a feeling of pride in a socially attuned self. The attraction of social attunement or micro-solidarity is demonstrated by contrast with its opposite; when attunement fails there is the feeling of shame. Individuals act situationally to avoid shame; this is the motivation for cognitive conformity, even to the extent of distorting one's perceptions to fit strong group pressure, as Scheff shows in a reinterpretation of the famous Asch experiments. Using video recordings of couples' quarrels, Scheff gives evidence that shame which cannot be repaired turns into anger; unexpressed anger, in turn, recycles in micro-interactional gestures which continue to violate solidarity and thus repeatedly generate still more shame. Scheff's work continues the Durkheimian program of mutually supporting theoretical and empirical work, which is to say scientific sociology at its best. It demonstrates, too, that the Durkheimian mechanism of solidarity operates through bodily interactions at a fine-grained level, beneath normal conscious reflection, shaping flows of collective emotion which then become apportioned to individual selves. It stresses an insight of the later Durkheimian movement, that solidarity is locally produced, and varies with the degree of success and failure of what I would call micro-interactional rituals. And it shows that a theory of solidarity, far from being oblivious to social conflict, gives us a refined mechanism by which to understand just how conflict is mobilized in the very emotions which come from the breakdown of solidarity. Here too contemporary Durkheimian research promises a path towards a sociology general enough to encompass all the variants of human social life.

The Durkheimian underground in France and its re-emergence

I have sketched a history in which the Durkheimian movement mobilized during the reforms of the French educational system at the turn of the twentieth century; became weakly institutionalized in France after the world war, and thus leaned heavily on political and intellectual alliances which cost it

scholarly respectability by the 1930s and 1940s; survived by migrating intellectually across the Channel to provide a theoretical core for British social
anthropology, and migrating again across the Atlantic as the analytical main-
stay of the school of structural-functionalism; after the collapse of the functionalist program in the 1960s, reviving once again as a micro-sociology
of interaction rituals and the dynamics of emotional solidarity, while ced-
ing macro-sociology to conflict-oriented approaches. This simplified account
leaves out the paths by which Durkheimian tradition re-established itself in
France.

For the intellectual networks from the generation of Durkheim to the generation of Mauss and Halbwachs did not end there. Among Mauss' pupils
was Claude Lévi-Strauss; his reputation-establishing work, *The Elementary
Structures of Kinship* (1949) extended Mauss' model of gift exchange into
a theory of kinship in state-less tribal societies as the formation of alliances
through the exchange of women. As in the kula ring, such gifts bring a stream
of obligations in their train, the different forms of which Lévi-Strauss worked
out as the structural patterning of entire societies through their kinship system. His subsequent work in the 1950s and 60s on symbols and myths echoed
Durkheimian analysis of primitive classification; for a while Lévi-Strauss
tried to work out a systematic connection between social morphology (the
campsite, the divisions of kinship) and social symbolism (art, language, myth)
as manifestations of a common underlying structure (notably in *Structural
Anthropology* 1958) before narrowing his focus to the structure of oppositions recognizable in an ensemble of myths. Lévi-Strauss rarely mentioned
Durkheim, now long out of favor in French intellectual life; but he did write
(1968) a preface to a posthumous collection of Mauss' papers extolling the
latter's importance for French anthropology.

In the 1950s, the focus of French intellectual politics had changed again.
Sartre and the existentialists, who dismissed the Durkheimians, became in
turn the foil for the structuralist movement, shifting emphasis from the
personal and individual to impersonal semiotic codes. There are echoes
of the Durkheimians here as well. Ferdinand de Saussure, working qui-
etly in Geneva in the early years of the century at a linguistics that would
break from psychological and historical theories of word change, drew on
Durkheim in formulating the distinction between *parole* and *langue* as a
separation between individual practice and language as a system of collective representations (Saussure [1915] 1966; Jameson 1972). By a roundabout pathway, passing through connections with the Russian formalist
movement in literary analysis and migrations ending in Paris in the 1950s,
Saussurian linguistics became regarded retroactively as one of the classics
of the structuralist movement; thus in the structuralists there was a good

deal of Durkheimianism, but unrecognized as such. For scholars caught up in the prestige of the structuralist movement and its further transformations into deconstructionist and postmodernist theories, the movement emblems – Saussure, Lévi-Strauss. Bakhtin, Husserl, Lacan – fill the horizon and block out other streams like the Durkheimians, which were just as important in setting the trajectory toward analysis of a social system of symbolic representations. This too teaches us something: there is room for only a limited number of sacred objects defining the solidarity of intellectual groups; some are necessarily squeezed out to make room for others.

Nevertheless Durkheim became re-established as an emblem in France within a narrower specialty. By the 1960s, sociology was developing a secure base as the French universities went through a big expansion from elite to mass enrollments. Durkheim became the topic of respectful scholarship, as well as a theoretical resource. As a sign of the times, based on one of the first research institutes established distinctly for sociology, Pierre Bourdieu and his group devoted one of their earliest publications to popular uses of photography; in an explicitly Durkheimian vein, they analyze it as a ritual of family solidarity on ceremonial occasions like weddings and visits (Bourdieu et al. [1965] 1990). In French sociology as in sociology programs elsewhere in the world, the hybrid canon of Durkheim with Marx and Weber that we see in the works of the Bourdieu school, now balanced off what had earlier been perceived as one-sidedness and political bias of the Durkheimians. The Durkheimian movement as a distinct entity was a thing of the past; its blending with a broader community of professional sociologists has ensured its survival as a sacred memory, a symbol of us all.

NOTES

1 Durkheim to Mauss, June 18, 1894: ". . . ce qui m'éloigne de cette revue c'est la réputation de farceur qu'a Worms, et que surtout je ne puis collaborer à une revue dont le directeur n'a aucun titre scientifique" (Durkheim 1998: 35–6). Worms had just founded in 1893 the *Revue internationale de sociologie*.

2 Letter of November 1897 (Durkheim 1998: 87): "Reste le point le plus important. Il faut dégager notre critique des procédés ordinaires; notre but n'est pas de distribuer des éloges et des blâmes, des bons et des mauvais points, mais de chercher dans les livres le résidu qui en peut titre gardé . . . Il me parait inutile de perdre une page à dire qu'un livre est mauvais."

3 Alexander (1982) interprets Durkheim's interest in religion in the late 1890s as a break in his theoretical program, from a materialist concern with social morphology and economic phenomena, to idealism, giving priority to meanings and moral norms. I would judge that Alexander is led astray by attempting to fit Durkheim into a somewhat idiosyncratic usage of the concepts of "materialism"

and "idealism," in which the former means not only the causal priority of material conditions but self-interested materialist motives (in the Marxian sense), while
the latter is in effect a residual category of all "ideal" factors including morality,
emotions, ideals, and ideational conceptions. But Durkheim, even in his earliest
focus on the social morphology of population density, emphasized the solidarity
inherent in social interaction, and tried to demonstrate that selfish and narrowly
material interests were derivative; while in his latter focus on religion, Durkheim
was demonstrating how the emotional processes of human bodies assembled for
religious ceremonies determine the various kinds and degrees of moral rules and
membership symbols which are given significance. Durkheim never abandoned his
concern for social morphology; he refined it to the level of the micro-morphology
of the group interaction, and brings out explicitly the emotional nature of this
interaction; the "ideal" sphere is something which can be explained, rather than
having explanatory priority. Thus *Elementary Forms* is simultaneously a theory
of social rituals and an explanation of the social categories of the understanding (in an explicitly Kantian sense) as reflections of the social morphology of the
group. Alexander goes astray, too, in reading too much of Talcott Parsons' "volun-
tarism" back into Durkheim, thereby obscuring the way in which the Durkheimians
treated phenomena of the will as apportionments of collective emotional energy.
(This is brought out most clearly in Hubert and Mauss' theory of magic (1902–3),
which they present as the prototype of the power of collective emotions which
animate individuals.) Alexander admits that the alleged break from "materialism"
to "idealism" was never perceived by the Durkheimians, who maintained their
program was the same throughout.

4 An exception was Halbwachs, who held a chair at the rather marginal, and indeed
formerly German, university at Strasbourg until getting one of the Sorbonne chairs
in 1935. Of all the Durkheimians, Halbwachs continued most directly in the original research program (such as his further studies of suicides), perhaps because he
alone maintained an academic research base.

5 Upon his retirement in 1946 Radcliffe-Brown was succeeded by Evans-Pritchard.

6 It proved possible to rescue Parsonian functionalism, or at least to preserve its
analytical sophistication, in the form of a neo-functionalism; thus Alexander (1982)
drops Pareto from the canon and substitutes Marx, going on to point out the
continued validity of a multi-level analytical conception in which material and
cultural, individual and collective conditions all find their place, as against the
incompleteness and analytical blinders of one-sided and reductionist viewpoints.
This position held a respectable niche in the theoretical landscape as of the late
twentieth century; but it has not recaptured the élan that functionalism once had
as an intellectual movement; it is a branch of the Durkheimian tree, but shaped by
several generations of grafting rather far from the trunk.

7 Intellectual developments often occur in parallels, and an equivalent move was
made in Britain, by Evans-Pritchard's student Mary Douglas (1970), and by the
educational sociologist Basil Bernstein (1971–5), who applied anthropological
techniques to modern societies, and analyzed stratification as symbolic boundaries
and antagonisms. Bernstein's work parallels Goffman's micro-sociology, in showing how differences in social class speech patterns operate as class membership
codes.

REFERENCES

Alexander, Jeffrey C. 1982. *Theoretical Logic in Sociology*. Vol. 2, *The Antinomies of Classical Thought: Marx and Durkheim*. Berkeley, CA: University of California Press.

Bernstein, Basil. 1971–5. *Class Codes and Control*. London: Routledge.

Besnard, Philippe. 1979. "La formation de l'équipe de *L'Année sociologique.*" *Revue française de sociologie* 20: 7–31.

Besnard, Philippe (ed.) 1983. *The Sociological Domain: The Durkheimians and the Founding of French Sociology*. Cambridge: Cambridge University Press.

Bourdieu, Pierre, Luc Boltanski, Robert Castel, Jean-Claude Chamboredon and Dominique Schnapper. [1965] 1990. *Un art moyen*. Paris: Éditions de Minuit.

Camic, Charles. 1991. Introduction to *Talcott Parsons, The Early Essays*. Edited by Charles Camic. Chicago: University of Chicago Press.

Carver, Terrell. 1983. *Marx and Engels: the Intellectual Relationship*. Brighton: Harvester Press.

Charle, Christophe. 1990. *Naissance des "intellectuels," 1880–1900*. Paris: Les Éditions de Minuit.

Collins, Randall. 2004. *Interaction Ritual Chains*. Princeton University Press.

1998. *The Sociology of Philosophies: A Global Theory of Intellectual Change*. Cambridge, MA: Harvard University Press.

1975. *Conflict Sociology*. New York: Academic Press.

Douglas, Mary. 1970. *Natural Symbols*. London: Routledge.

Durkheim, Émile. 1998. *Lettres à Marcel Mauss*. Présentées par Philippe Besnard et Marcel Fournier. Paris: Presses Universitaires de France.

1968. *Journal sociologique*. Paris: Presses Universitaires de France.

1912. *Les Formes élémentaires de la vie religieuse. Le système totémique en Australie*. Paris: Librairie Félix Alcan.

Durkheim, Émile and Marcel Mauss. [1903] 1963. *Primitive Classification*. Edited and translated by Rodney Needham. Chicago: University of Chicago Press.

Fabiani, Jean-Louis. 1988. *Les Philosophes de la République*. Paris: Éditions de Minuit.

Fournier, Marcel. 1994. *Marcel Mauss*. Paris: Fayard.

Goffman, Erving. 1956. "The Nature of Deference and Demeanor." *American Anthropologist* 58: 473–99.

1951. "Symbols of Class Status." *British Journal of Sociology* 2: 204–304.

Goody, Jack. 1995. *The Expansive Moment. Anthropology in Britain and Africa 1918–1970*. Cambridge: Cambridge University Press.

Heilbron, Johan. 1985. "Les métamorphoses du Durkheimisme, 1920–1940." *Revue francaise de sociologie* 26: 203–37.

Hilbert, Richard. 1992. *The Classical Roots of Ethnomethodology: Durkheim, Weber and Garfinkel*. Chapel Hill, NC: University of North Carolina Press.

Hubert, Henri, and Marcel Mauss. 1902–1903. "Esquisse d'une théorie générale de la magie." *L'Année sociologique* 7. Translation 1975. *A General Theory of Magic*. New York: W. W. Norton.

1899. "Essai sur la nature et la fonction de la sacrifice." *L'Année sociologique* 2.

Jameson, Fredric. 1972. *The Prison House of Language*. Princeton, NJ: Princeton University Press.

Kusch, Martin. 1995. *Psychologism*. London: Routledge.

Lévi-Strauss, Claude. 1968. "Introduction a l'œuvre de Marcel Mauss" in *Marcel Mauss, Sociologie et anthropologie*. Paris: Presses Universitaires de France.

Lukes, Steven. 1973. *Émile Durkheim: His Life and Work*. London: Allen Lane.

Mann, Michael. 2005. *The Dark Side of Democracy*. Cambridge: Cambridge University Press.

Mauss, Marcel. 1934. "Intervention à la suite d'une communication de François Simiand, 'La monnaie, réalité sociale.'" *Année sociologique* série D. English translation in Randall Collins (ed.) 1994. *Four Sociological Traditions: Selected Readings*. New York: Oxford University Press.

[1923] 1969. "Mentalité primitive et participation." pp. 126–7 in *Oeuvres*. Vol. 3. Paris: Les Éditions de Minuit.

1914. "Les origines de la notion de monnaie." *Anthropologie* 25. Reprinted in *Marcel Mauss, Œuvres*. Vol. 1. Paris: Éditions de Minuit, 1969. English translation in Randall Collins (ed.) 1994. *Four Sociological Traditions: Selected Readings*. New York: Oxford University Press.

Nizan, Paul. [1976] 1932. *Les chiens de garde*. Paris: Maspero.

Radcliffe-Brown, A. R. 1937. *A Natural Science of Society*. Oxford University Press.

Rawls, Anne Warfield. 1987. "The Interaction Order Sui Generis: Goffman's Contribution to Social Theory." *Sociological Theory* 5: 136–49.

n.d. *Durkheimian Epistemology*. Cambridge University Press, forthcoming.

Rigby, Stephen H. 1992. *Engels and the Formation of Marxism*. Manchester University Press.

Sartre, Jean-Paul. 1947. *Situations: I*. Paris: Gallimard.

Saussure, Ferdinand de. [1915] 1966. *Course in General Linguistics*. New York: McGraw-Hill.

Scheff, Thomas. 1990. *Microsociology, Discourse, Emotion and Social Structure*. Chicago: University of Chicago Press.

Siedentop, Larry. [1828] 1997. Introduction to *The History of Civilization in Europe* by Francois Guizot. Harmondsworth: Penguin Books.

Sorokin, Pitirim. 1928. *Contemporary Sociological Theories*. NY: Harper and Row.

Warner, W. Lloyd. 1959. *The Living and the Dead*. New Haven, CT: Yale University Press.

Warner, W. Lloyd and Paul S. Lunt. 1941. *The Social Life of a Modern Community*. New Haven, CT: Yale University Press.

Weisz, George. 1983. *The Emergence of Modern Universities in France 1863–1914*. Princeton, NJ: Princeton University Press.

6

JEFFREY C. ALEXANDER

The inner development of Durkheim's sociological theory: from early writings to maturity

On one thing most of Durkheim's readers, past and present, have always agreed: he, like Marx, emphasizes social structure. Durkheim helped to create classical sociology because he located social forces "outside" the individual actor. But from this point on, theoretical agreement ends. The problem for Durkheim and his interpreters, just as for Marx and his interlocutors, is what does structure mean? How does structure hold individuals within its limits? Of what are these limits composed? If structure exists, somehow, outside of the individual, can it act only in opposition to freedom?

The problematics of Durkheim interpretation, then, are precisely the ones around which Marxist inquiry has always revolved. The fundamental question has been how Durkheim stipulates the relation between structured and free action. People keep reading Durkheim, and arguing about him, to find out whether the determinateness of social structures must involve the sacrifice of autonomy and, conversely, whether insisting on human agency entails denying external control. How generations have understood Durkheim – and answered these theoretical questions through such interpretive understanding – has fundamentally shaped the pattern of sociological discourse. Debates over the meaning and path of Durkheim's work are, inevitably, arguments about the most basic directions of sociological explanation and more general social thought.

Is there a fundamental conflict between Durkheimian and more materialist forms of sociology, whether Marxist, Weberian, organizational, or behaviorist? Many have contended there is not, and they have found not only occasional passages but large sections of Durkheim's work to prove it. The present essay will engage in a meticulous reconstruction of Durkheim's theoretical development, from his earliest writings to his maturity. This hermeneutic effort will demonstrate that these interpreters are mistaken. We will see that Durkheim reached his theoretical maturity after a prolonged, if confused, flirtation with materialist forms of structural theory, and eventually a fierce struggle against them.

Durkheim's early writings: ideological consistency and theoretical change

Durkheim came to his intellectual vocation in the late 1870s and 1880s, in the crucible of the formation of the Third Republic in France. From the very beginning of his identification as a sociologist – which Mauss dates from 1881 – he linked his intellectual vocation to certain normative or ideological goals: first, French society must be changed so that it could become stable; second, this stability could be achieved only if there were justice, particularly justice in economic distribution; third, the increased state organization necessary to create justice should never occur at the expense of individual freedom. Durkheim described these goals as socialism, but he insisted, to use contemporary terms, that this be socialism with a human face. These normative commitments to humanism and justice remained constant throughout the course of his life. The problem, for Durkheim, was the translation of these goals into a theoretical and empirical perspective. It is precisely here that the changes in Durkheim's sociology occurred.

From the beginning, Durkheim was convinced that the achievement of democratic socialism depended upon avoiding the kind of instrumentally rationalistic theory of social structure proposed by English utilitarians and Marxist socialists. Such reductionist and instrumental approaches, Durkheim believed, could describe the reformist state only as an external and coercive force vis-à-vis individual will (Durkheim [1888] 1975: 379). Quoting approvingly from Schaeffle, the German socialist of the chair, Durkheim (1886: 77) insists that the concept of socialism "could be unburdened of all contradictions" only if "the fundamental principles of Marx's theory are renounced" (Durkheim [1888] 1975: 387).[1]

Yet in the years between the publication of Durkheim's first essay reviews, in 1885, and the appearance of his first major work, *The Division of Labor in Society* (hereafter *Division of Labor*), in 1893, Durkheim proved unable to transform this general analytic conviction into a viable and precise sociological theory. Although the full story of Durkheim's earliest writings cannot be recounted here, the fundamental lines of his frustrating early development can briefly be presented.[2] In the eight-year period that defines Durkheim's early writings – a period that covers sixteen essays and two major monographs – one can discern an ambivalent yet nonetheless distinctive theoretical evolution *away* from his normative ambition of creating social structures with a human face.

In the earliest of these writings, Durkheim emphasized the importance of "sympathetic instincts" inherent in every human being. Since these natural sentiments led to associations, Durkheim (e.g. 1887a: 309) thought he had discovered a way that moral order could be social and individual at the same time. Yet eventually he rejected this solution as too precarious. Such independently motivated individuals, he came to believe, would develop no sense of the social whole outside of their own selves. Even if they were enmeshed in society, they would not be conscious of any subjective connection (e.g. Durkheim 1885: 453; [1885] 1978: 114). As an alternative to this vision, Durkheim considered the position that morality was in some way external to the individual and could, therefore, more powerfully control him. Yet even as he elaborated this new position, he worried about the status of the individual in such a scheme, and to resolve this worry he postulated that such a moral order could grow out of the individual action itself. Following Wundt, he portrayed the individual as permeable and "anti-substantialist," so order could be internal and external at the same time (Durkheim 1887b: 128). Yet this flirtation with Wundt turned out to be brief, for, once again, Durkheim (1886: 76) concluded that if individual volition were so predominant a force, the social order was bound to be unstable.[3]

Because he did not yet understand the process by which social order could be outside the isolated individual and still be subjective, or "inside," at the same time, Durkheim was compelled at this early point to turn to the notion that structure could be stable only if it were external in an ontological sense. He turned, in other words, back to an instrumental, quasi-materialist position. Even in his earlier work he had often evoked, in a hesitant and ambivalent way, a model of the actor as an adaptive and rationalizing force (e.g. Durkheim 1886: 60–9). This model now became explicit: the adaptive actor was endowed with egoistic motives and portrayed as responding primarily to external conditions. What has happened, ironically, is that Durkheim has retreated to the very instrumental position he had, at the beginning of his career, so criticized in Marx. He has laid the groundwork for a vision of state and society which was as mechanical and coercive as what he has supposed to be Marx's own.

What is extraordinary is that Durkheim himself seemed to feel that exactly the opposite was true. In his opening lectures at Bordeaux in 1888 and 1889, during which he first developed this more instrumentalist perspective, and in his 1892 Latin dissertation when he first systematized it, Durkheim asserted that this instrumental transformation would, in fact, allow him finally to reconcile individual freedom and social order. The trick was his empirical focus on the division of labor. Like the classical economists whom he had earlier criticized, at this point in his development Durkheim ([1888] 1978: 207) believed that the division of labor was a neat device for reconciling free choice with the collective ordering of individual interests. With this new understanding of modern life, he announced in the preface to *Division of Labor* ([1893] 1964: 37), the "apparent antinomy" between individual autonomy and social determinism has been resolved: social solidarity is to be transformed in a manner beneficial to both individual and society, and this will occur because of "the steadily growing development of the division of labor."[4]

In fact, of course, these hopes were illusory. Durkheim's earliest premonitions were correct: He could not sustain his commitment to individual subjectivity if social structure were to be given a purely external and material cast. In Book 1 of *Division of Labor*, Durkheim ([1893] 1964: 127) begins by embracing labor division in an extremely individualistic way. "It is in the nature of special tasks," he writes, "to escape the action of the collective conscience." The contract itself, according to this logic, becomes the prototypical form of cooperation and aggregation. Since "society is made up of a system of differentiated parts which mutually complement each other" ([1893] 1964: 151, translation altered), it is only natural to assume that "the involvement of one party results either from the involvement assumed by the other, or from some service already rendered by the latter" ([1893] 1964: 124, translation altered). But as Durkheim's argument develops, he very quickly sees through the individualistic quality of such reasoning. As he does so, he emphasizes the non-contractual, supra-individual controls which are necessary if the freedom inherent in labor division is to be balanced by stability and collective control. In the course of the remainder of Book I, Durkheim vacillates between describing these collective elements as normative and non-rational, or as state-directed and instrumentally coercive.

Durkheim's normative version of non-contractual social control is best known, and the notion of the diffusion of the collective conscience in modern society is certainly a significant point in Durkheim's fifth chapter ([1893] 1964: 147–73). What is much less widely recognized, however, is that alongside this exposition of the normative dimension there also exists in Durkheim's first book a strongly instrumentalist approach to social order. The restitutive law that creates the *non-contractual* regulation of contract is portrayed by Durkheim ([1893] 1964: 11) as "only a means" ("*C'est seulement un moyen*"), and he insists ([1893] 1964: 112) that "these prescriptions do not correspond to any sentiment in us." Modern law becomes a purely rational and coercive vehicle, and the modern regulating state merely "the essential cog in the machine" ([1893] 1964: 113).

In the second Book of *Division of Labor*, this *instrumental* perspective on collective order emerges with full force: labor division becomes the product not of free and rational choice or the normatively regulated pursuit of interest, but the result of "the struggle for existence" ("*la lutte pour la vie*") (Durkheim [1893] 1964: 226) – a struggle that is itself determined by changes in ecological volume and density and, ultimately, by unequal control over scarce resources. By Book 3, the results of this shifting theoretical logic are clear: Durkheim is forced to recognize, and eventually to give causal primacy to, unequal material conditions and to the purely coercive state. Because of the "great inequality of the external conditions of the struggle" ("*la lutte*") ([1893] 1964: 370 n. 26), the modern worker is subject to the "forced division of labor," an order that operates with unstoppable mechanical force. If Durkheim had begun *Division of Labor* with an empirical emphasis on individualism that belied his emerging, if somewhat anomalous, theoretical determinism, he had concluded it with an explanation of order that seemed emphatically to confirm it.

> If one class of society is obliged, in order to live, to take any price for its services, while another can abstain from such action thanks to resources at its disposal which, however, are not necessarily due to any social superiority, the second has an unjust advantage over the first at law.
>
> (Durkheim [1893] 1964: 384)

Durkheim's middle period: dissatisfaction, misinterpretation, and radical revision

Despite the fact that Durkheim trumpeted the results of *Division of Labor* as demonstrating the empirical power of his new science, there is good reason to believe that, consciously or unconsciously, he felt enormous dissatisfaction with what he had wrought in his first great work. First, of course, there is the great discrepancy between his theoretical development in *Division of Labor* and the goals he had set out eight years before. He had started out to provide an alternative to the Marxian understanding of socialist industrial society; he had concluded, in the third Book of *Division of Labor*, by offering a model of capitalism that differed from Marx only in its inability to describe fully the class origins of the material inequality it described (see, e.g. O'Connor 1980).[5] Second, there is evidence for this dissatisfaction in the ambiguous and contradictory quality of *Division of Labor* itself. If Durkheim had concluded with an instrumental and coercive understanding of modern social order, he had certainly given ample evidence elsewhere in the work, particularly in the individualistic and normative passages in Book 1, that he still valued more subjective and voluntaristic understandings, even if he could not successfully articulate them.

Powerful additional evidence of Durkheim's theoretical dissatisfaction can be found in two little-known essays that he published in 1893, in the very shadow of *Division of Labor*. In the first, a review of Gaston Richard's *Essai sur l'origine de l'idée de droit* ([1897] 1978b), Durkheim argues against the notion that the simple calculus of interest, structured by a powerful state, can teach humanity to follow a more just path. It is, he writes (1893b: 292), only "completely interior sentiments" that can be relied on, for "it is inside the conscience and not outside, it is in the sympathetic and altruistic disposition and not in the sentiments of interest that it is necessary to go look for the solution." Later that year, in his "*Note sur la définition du socialisme,*" Durkheim makes this challenge to the latter books of *Division of Labor* even more forcefully. The problem of capitalism, he writes (1893a: 510), does *not* derive from its failure to provide "material contiguity." That it did so derive, as we have seen, had been a central argument in *Division of Labor* (Book 3). Durkheim now professes, however, that businesses may well have material relations with one another, "acting and reacting" among themselves. Workers, too, may pursue their interests alongside of their fellows. He now suggests, however, that problems of industrial society arise because such material contiguities do not, in and of themselves, guarantee that businesses or workers "have ends which are common to them," do not ensure that they can actually form among themselves any "moral community." It is the moral community, he now insists, that must be the object of socialist change, not the economic redistribution and reorganization he had identified in *Division of Labor*. One must understand, he insists, that "a revolution could not occur without a profound moral transformation," and that the famous "social question" of Marxist socialism is not economic but moral.

These essays, in fact, presaged long-term shifts in Durkheim's theory of social structure, shifts that Durkheim himself (with a single brief exception to be discussed below) never admitted as having occurred at all. In the following year, in an essay that would become the first chapter of *Rules of Sociological Method* (hereafter *Rules*), Durkheim ([1895] 1938) laid out an affective and normative understanding of the roots of social life that systematically called into question the instrumental theory of interaction, volume, and density that had informed Book 2 of *Division of Labor*.[6]

Durkheim begins innocuously enough, claiming in his preface ([1895] 1938: ix) that he wishes only "to expound the results of our work in applied sociology," yet in the very first paragraph he reveals that this is hardly the case. "When I execute my contracts," Durkheim writes ([1895] 1938: 1), "I perform duties which . . . conform to my own sentiments and I feel their reality subjectively." The social order that contracts represent, apparently, need not be based primarily on the external sanctions of state-supported law. Durkheim proceeds in the following pages to define sociological facts in a startlingly subjective way. They are, he writes ([1895] 1938: 2), "ways of acting, thinking, and feeling," a phrase that he often reduces (p. 9) to the short-hand "beliefs and practices" ("*les croyances et les pratiques*").

Durkheim still insists that social facts be grounded in a substratum, but he ([1895] 1938: 3) now defines this organizational base as "religious denominations, political, literary, and occupational associations." The "actions and reactions" that create social organization – and which in Book 2 of *Division of Labor* were ecological and economic – are here completely emotionalized. They refer to the "special energy" that is created when individual consciences interact, and their product is "collective sentiment" ([1895] 1938: 9). Collective facts, Durkheim now insists, consist only of more or less crystallized emotion. In periods of pure association, this emotion is still close to the primordial "liquid" form, and the significant collective facts are volatile phenomena like "transitory outbursts" and "great movements of enthusiasm" ([1895] 1938: 4). Eventually, however, emotion acquires a certain "rigidity"; it develops "a body, a tangible form" that is more sharply differentiated from the individual psyches that first produced it ([1895] 1938: 7). Social order, in sum, is simply "currents of opinion" more or less solidified, currents that reflect the state of the collective "soul" or "spirit" (*"l'âme collective"*) at different times ([1895] 1938: 8).[7]

In his lectures on socialism in 1895–6, Durkheim used his new perspective to elaborate his remarks in the 1893 *"Note"* about socialism as a voluntary and subjective moral system. He now insists ([1895–6] 1958: 204) that the crucial reforms suggested in Book 3 of *Division of Labor*, political reorganization and economic redistribution, will be ineffective unless the "state of our morality" is also reformed. The problem of order is posed here as one of renewed symbolic or moral authority.

> What is needed if social order is to reign is that the mass of men be content with their lot. But what is needed for them to be content, is not that they have more or less but that they be convinced that they have no right to more. And for this, it is absolutely essential that there be an authority whose superiority they acknowledge and which tells them what is right.
>
> (Durkheim [1895–6] 1958: 200)

In *Suicide*, published the following year, this new insistence on solidarity and affectivity as the source of collective order is applied to a wide range of modern social institutions. If the object of *Suicide* is the social fact which Durkheim calls "suicidogenic currents," the status of this supra-individual fact is the inverse of the economic or political "facts" that Durkheim had early emphasized. Durkheim ([1897] 1951: 299) defines suicidogenic currents as composed of a "collective force of a definite amount of energy." They reflect a social substratum which is itself composed of "beliefs and practices" ([1897] 1951: 170) and they form a society that Durkheim ([1897] 1951: 310) describes as only in the last analysis having "a physical existence."

In the same year that *Suicide* was written, indeed, by the time that monograph had appeared in print, Durkheim was embarked on a radically new, more explicitly cultural, or "spiritualized" elaboration of this subjective mode of theorizing. I will discuss this development later in this chapter. Before doing so, the extratheoretical sources of Durkheim's intellectual shift must be closely examined, for it is only in this fuller context that the true ramifications of Durkheim's development can clearly be understood.

I have followed thus far an internalist approach to Durkheim's development, demonstrating that it was explicitly theoretical dissatisfaction that was the trigger to the upheaval in Durkheim's work. Indeed, no major social or personal event could have created such a rapid disavowal, for the intellectual changes began almost simultaneously with the publication of *Division of Labor* itself. At this point, however, I would like to suggest that Durkheim's profound intellectual misgivings made him particularly sensitive to change in his social and cultural environment. France was changing in a way that could only have intensified Durkheim's theoretical dissatisfaction.

The early 1890s marked the renewal of Marxism in French society. This was stimulated in part by increased class conflict in the political and economic realms, as indicated, for example, by the election in 1893 of fifty socialists – by no means all of the Marxian variety – to the French parliament and by the great upsurge in strikes and worker protests that characterized this period.[8] These social developments were certainly not primarily stimulated by Marxian ideology, but they constituted, nonetheless, important reasons for the growing attention that French intellectuals paid to Marxist theory.[9] Leading journals like the *Revue de métaphysique et de morale* and the *Revue philosophique*, where Durkheim had published most of his important early work, now published ongoing discussions of socialist theory and reviewed numerous works by Marx and Engels and their followers. The first exclusively sociological journal in France, the *Revue internationale de sociologie*, also devoted considerable space to articles on socialism and Marx, and in the first issue of the *Annales de l'institut international de sociologie*, historical materialism became the focus of a number of the authors. This new enthusiasm for Marxism spread even to Durkheim's inner circle. "Some of the most brilliant among his own students," writes Durkheim's nephew and collaborator, Marcel Mauss ([1928] 1958: 2–3), "were converted to socialism, especially Marxism." Mauss adds that "in one 'Social Study' circle some examined *Capital* as they elsewhere considered Spinoza."

This contextual knowledge helps us to reconstruct, hypothetically to be sure, Durkheim's predicament in the early 1890s. He had just concluded his first major work, a treatment that evidently he had already begun to regret and apparently had already begun to revise. Moreover, he was in the midst of the revival in popularity of a system of thought, Marxism, that seemed closely to resemble the one he had just publicly proclaimed, not only in its ideological commitment to socialism and science but, more importantly, in its analytical theory and its empirical analysis of modern society. One might imagine that Durkheim wished very badly to distinguish his new ideas from those of Marxism. At the same time, he would not wish to indicate that these new ideas differed in any way from those he had previously held. Durkheim's predicament, in other words, was far from being purely an imagined one.

In the very midst of Durkheim's theoretical shift away from the instrumentalism of *Division of Labor*, he was confronted with what could only have been an enormously frustrating realization: his French audience viewed him as a confirmed materialist very much in the Marxist mode, if not a Marxist himself! Almost without exception, the reviews that Durkheim received in the four years following publication of *Division of Labor* represented his subsequent writing – as he himself had asked for it to be read – merely as the extension of that first work.[10] The reviewers were in universal agreement, moreover, that *Division of Labor* had itself been one-sidedly materialist in its orientation. In the first and probably most important review, Brunschvieg and Halévy (1894) wrote that, even if Durkheim refused to accept all the consequences of his position, *Division of Labor* was, at the end of the day, "mechanical and material" in its causal analysis. Reading *Division* into the later *Rules*, they argued (1894: 565–7), in the face of Durkheim's very explicit theorizing, that his proposed method excluded all psychological elements from society. And in a series of concluding arguments that must have been especially grating to Durkheim, they offered suggestions that Durkheim himself had actually already taken up. Social laws, they write (1894: 571), should be studied in terms of the spontaneous interaction of the individuals whose spirit gives them life. Only in this way could these so-called laws be seen for what they really are, namely, common ideas and sentiments.

The same perspective on Durkheim's sociology is expressed in the 1896 issue of the same review. Charles Andler finds the determinism and fatalism of Durkheim's sociological analysis to be antithetical to the democratic culture he is trying to create. In concluding, he accuses Durkheim of the "Marxist error."

The "conditions of economic production" are an example where Durkheim's theory could no doubt be better applied [than to society as a whole], without, however, still being completely relevant. Monsieur Durkheim generalizes the economic "thingism" [*"le choisisme"*] of Marx while making from it a "thingism" that is specifically sociological. In doing so, he generalizes the Marxist error. (1896: 252 n.r).

And in a review published in Germany in 1897 by Paul Barth, a follower of Dilthey, Durkheim had evidence that this materialist misinterpretation had spread beyond the border of France alone. Barth's *Die Philosophie der Geschichte als Soziologie* discusses Durkheim's work in his chapter entitled "The Economic Conception of History." He attacks Durkheim for being, like Spencer, "an almost superstitious worshiper of the contract" and he argues (Barth [1897] 1922: 612) that, in his early works at least, Durkheim views morality as a "hindrance to economic progress" and as "unfavorable to the autonomy of the individual."[11]

As if to confirm this materialist evaluation by his non-Marxist critics, Durkheim was hailed in 1895 by Sorel, the major Marxist intellectual in France, as a kindred spirit. In the lead article of the first issue of the Marxist journal, *Le Devenir*, Sorel (1895: 16–17) applauds *Rules* for its anti-psychological emphasis on coercion and constraint. Neatly summing up the prevailing perspective on *Rules* as in complete continuity with *Division of Labor*, he notes (1895: 1) that Durkheim had "just brought together in a small volume of very modest style, what is essential in his doctrine." As for the earlier *Division of Labor*, Sorel (1895: 23) calls it an exposition of "great beauty" and makes a direct parallel between it and the theory of Marx. "With Durkheim," he writes, "we are placed on the ground of real science, and we see the importance of struggle *[la lutte]*." But Durkheim seems to hesitate, Sorel regretfully notes, before taking the final step toward a fully materialist history. In order to define the conditions of existence more specifically, "he would have to place himself on the ground of Marxist philosophy" (1895: 177). If Durkheim could borrow from Marxism the conception of classes, "I would be the first," Sorel affirms (1895: 180), "to acclaim him my master," for he is the "only French sociologist who possesses a sufficient philosophical preparation and well developed critical spirit to be able to perceive in historical change scientific laws and the material conditions of becoming." Durkheim could only have read Sorel's essay with chagrin.

Insofar as they referred to Durkheim's *Division of Labor*, these reviews must be read as legitimate readings and criticisms of key elements of his work, and they must have brought home to Durkheim with unassailable force certain vital implications of his first theoretical work. As such, they could only have reinforced his growing conviction that radical theoretical renovation was necessary. The intensity of Durkheim's feelings on this issue are revealed, ironically perhaps, by the vehemence with which he rejected these critical claims. For Durkheim protests too much, never acknowledging even their partial validity. Indeed, he carried a bitter resentment against such criticisms throughout the rest of his life. In his Preface to the first edition of *Rules*, in 1895, he ([1895] 1938: xxxiv) protests against "what critics have called our 'positivism,'" objecting that although his method "will perhaps be judged crude and will possibly be termed 'materialistic,' it is actually nothing of the kind." Soon after (Durkheim 1896: 20), he responded to Andler's review by writing to the editor that "I regret absolutely the ideas that are attributed to me." He insists that Andler "has been able to attribute them to me only by taking advantage of several isolated words, while I had myself taken greater care to put the reader on guard against such an abuse." In a private letter the following year that refers to the German review by Barth, Durkheim writes to his follower Célèstin Bouglé that he had "never dreamt of saying that one could do sociology without any psychological background, or that sociology is anything other than a form of psychology" (in Lukes 1972: 234 n.35).

Durkheim's frustration could only have been increased by the realization that these critical responses to his work failed completely to recognize the enormous changes that he himself had introduced in *Rules* – changes that were intended to circumvent the very errors of which he now stood accused. But Durkheim himself had never acknowledged that a break existed. Is it any wonder that his reviewers simply took him at his word? They could see in *Rules* only the formalization of the method of *Division of Labor*. "On the very points on which we had expressed ourselves most explicitly," Durkheim ([1895] 1938: xli) writes in exasperation in his preface to the second edition of *Rules* in 1901, "views were freely attributed to us which had nothing in common with our own; and opponents held that they were refuting us in refuting these mistaken ideas." The critics, he wrote ([1895] 1938: liii), "claimed that we are explaining social phenomena by constraint." But this, he insists rather lamely, "was far from our intention – in fact, it had never even occurred to us that it could have been so interpreted, so much is it contrary to our entire method."

Such disingenuousness can be explained only by Durkheim's anxiety about being misunderstood. For he now found himself in a true quandary. He had realized, consciously or not, that the theory that informed so much of *Division of Labor* was a drastic mistake. Yet his positivist faith in scientific objectivity, his intellectual pride in the integrity of his theorizing, and perhaps also his lack of critical self-consciousness – all of these factors prevented Durkheim from acknowledging in the mid-1890s that he was, in fact, embarked upon a drastic theoretical revision. To his understandable but, nonetheless, illegitimate indignation, no one seemed aware of this fateful turn, neither his antagonistic critics nor his faithful students. If his new path were to be recognized – if his divergence from the theory of Marxian socialism were ever to be recognized for what it was – his innovation would have to be asserted in a much more emphatic and radical way.

The transition to the later writings: "revelation" and anti-materialist reconstruction

At a later and more secure point in his intellectual career, Durkheim talked about the "revelation" that had allowed him to resolve this quandary. "It was not until 1895," he wrote in the 1907 letter (Durkheim 1907) protesting another polemical review, "that I achieved a clear sense of the essential role played by religion in social life."

> It was in that year that, for the first time, I found the means of tackling the study of religion sociologically. This was a revelation to me. That course of 1895 marks a dividing line in the development of my thought, to such an extent that all my previous researches had to be taken up afresh in order to be made to harmonize with these new insights . . . [This reorientation] was entirely due to the studies of religious history which I have just undertaken, and notably to the reading of the works of Robertson Smith and his school.
>
> (Durkheim 1907: 612–14)[12]

Durkheim refers here to the course on religion that he first offered at Bordeaux in the school year 1894–5, a course in which he encountered the new historical approach to religion. Smith's work was revolutionary because it linked the theological ideas of the great religions to religious practice and ritual association, and it argued that this interaction is what gave to symbols their sacred power.[13] Knowledge of Smith's work was evidently crucial for Durkheim, allowing him to transform the scheme of affective and moral interaction of his middle period work into a more comprehensive understanding that linked the power of solidarity to the sacred ideational forces he called collective representations.

Until recently, few analysts were aware of this formative break in Durkheim's development, and those who have noted it have almost always taken this encounter with Smith as being revolutionary in itself, as constituting an "epistemological break" *sui generis*.[14] In view of the preceding discussion, however, it is clear that this encounter must be seen in the context of Durkheim's ongoing development: it offered him an escape from the quandary he faced. Durkheim felt compelled to find a way of making his subjectification of social order at once more explicit and more refined. It was only within this context that he gave his course on religion and encountered the new anthropological writings of Smith and his followers. Durkheim could have been so attracted to Smith only because he himself had already embarked on a similar path. Moreover, while Smith shared with Durkheim an emphasis on the human practice, or association, that underlined any commitment to ideal beliefs, Smith applied this thinking about the relation between beliefs and practices only to religious activity, not to social action itself. Why, then, does Durkheim's public statement insist that his encounter with Smith initiated a much more radical break, one that forced him completely to rethink all his previous work? Because, quite simply, Durkheim had never publicly admitted, and may himself never consciously have been aware, that his own writing had already taken a dramatic turn with the earlier publication of *Rules*. Nonetheless, Durkheim did not, in fact, really abandon all of his pre-1895 sociology. Indeed, it was the momentum created by his earlier shift that led him to find in the anthropology of religion the more subjectivist vocabulary he so urgently sought. The subjective model of association was already in place in early 1899. When he encounters religion later that year, or in 1895, there is more of a convergence than a radical break. Rather than a call to start anew, Durkheim must have seen in Smith's writing on religion a means of finally completing a renewal already well underway. He read this theory of religion in a way that meshed perfectly with his own developing theory of association.

Durkheim now understood how society could be determinate, organized, and subjective at the same time: collective order would be accepted because it was held to be sacred. It would be revered and sanctified in the very same moment that it would be obeyed. Although Durkheim's systematic understanding of the religious nature of society did not appear until 1897, he had already begun to express this intuition in 1896, and in the final Book of *Suicide* we find him arguing that legal and moral precepts are the "sacrosanct" form of living sentiments. After making this point, in fact, he makes a footnoted assertion that strikingly reveals the polemical animus that is behind this new religious reference:

> We do not expect to be reproached further, after this explanation, with wishing to substitute the exterior for the interior in sociology. We start from the exterior because it alone is immediately given, but only to reach the interior. Doubtless the procedure is complicated; but there is no other unless one would risk having his research apply to his personal feeling concerning the order of facts under investigation, instead of to this factual order itself.
>
> (Durkheim [1897] 1951: 315 n.12)

Two years later, in the conclusion to his first attempt to describe religious representations as the center of secular order, he makes precisely the same point. "Nothing is wider of the mark," he writes, "than the accusation of materialism which has been leveled against us." Quite the contrary, he argues ([1898] 1974: 34), "from the point of view of our position, if one is to call the distinctive property of the individual representational life spirituality, one should say that social life is defined by its hyperspirituality." And perhaps most revealing, in the 1902 preface to the second edition of *Division of*

Labor, he announced ([1893] 1964: 4) that his earlier explanation had been "incomplete." "If it is true," he writes, "that social functions spontaneously seek to adapt themselves to one another, provided they are regularly in relationship, nevertheless this mode of adaptation becomes a rule of conduct only if the group consecrates it with its authority." The strain of mechanistic functionalism in *Division of Labor* has here been publicly disavowed.

With the spiritualization of his understanding of order, Durkheim could, therefore, finally fulfill his thwarted theoretical and ideological ambition. In doing so, moreover, he can meet head on the threat of misinterpretation produced by the increasingly polarized intellectual and political climate of the day. It seems only fitting that, as soon as his new understanding has been articulated, Durkheim should return to the problem of mechanistic Marxism, the theoretical tradition against which he had tried initially to direct his work and with which he felt he had so mistakenly been identified. In the very first year that his explicitly "religious," or cultural sociology appeared, Durkheim initiated debate with two of the leading Marxists of the day.

One of these, Paul Lafargue, the son-in-law of Marx himself, was engaged only indirectly (see Vogt 1976). Lafargue had reviewed a book on Marxist socialism by Gaston Richard, at the time a member of Durkheim's circle and the author of the book on law that had earlier been the occasion of Durkheim's first break with *Division of Labor*. Lafargue denounced Richard's work on socialism as anti-Marxist and idealist. Durkheim chose to reply to Lafargue with a review of his own. For the most part, this review consisted of a complimentary summary of Richard's sharp rejection of Marx's ideas. Toward the end of the review, however, Durkheim took Lafargue directly to task. "We . . . find at once surprising and regrettable," he wrote ([1897] 1978b: 135), "the attacks to which he [Richard] has been subject on the part of the authorized representatives of socialist doctrine." After this rebuke, Durkheim stresses that his own position on socialism is similar to Richard's. Socialism has no validity as a scientific theory, he writes. It must, rather, be viewed as a collective representation: "Socialism is, above all, the way in which certain strata of society which have been tested by collective suffering represent the latter to themselves" ([1897] 1978b: 137). The popularity or persuasiveness of socialism must not be viewed, in other words, as evidence for the validity of Marx's theory about the coercive and external nature of social order. To the contrary, socialism itself was a "religious" force; its power, therefore, only demonstrated the role of symbolic representation in social life. Socialism could be understood, Durkheim concludes, only by penetrating the underlying moral reality that produced it. It was Durkheim's new ability to define socialism specifically as a "representation" that evidently gave him the confidence to make the challenge to Marx much more direct.

More important, however, is Durkheim's challenge to Antonio Labriola in a review that directly engages Marxism as a theoretical system. Labriola's *Essay on the Materialist Conception of History* had just been translated into French, and Georges Sorel, in an introduction to the work, had hailed its publication as a "landmark in the history of socialism" (Labriola 1897: 19). Labriola was one of the premier Marxist philosophers of his time – and Antonio Gramsci's teacher – and he presented his master's theory in anything but a vulgar light. In making his review, therefore, Durkheim could publicly confront the major alternative to the nascent sociological theory of his middle-period work. He could finally respond to the gauntlet Sorel had thrown down two years before.

Durkheim organized his response to illuminate the differences between his theory and Marx's at the most general level. After a balanced presentation of Labriola's argument, he approvingly discusses the anti-individualist position of historical materialism. Rather than focusing on pure ideas, or on isolated individuals, historical materialism focuses on a much more fundamental level, on "the artificial milieu which the work of associated men has created of whole cloth and then superimposed on nature" (Durkheim [1897] 1978a: 126). Durkheim insists ([1897] 1978a: 127), however, that this kind of collective emphasis is not exclusive to Marx. What is peculiar is that Marx's collectivist theory emphasizes the primacy of material factors. "Just as it seems true to us," Durkheim writes ([1897] 1978a: 128), "that causes of social phenomena must be sought outside individual representations, it seems to that same degree false that they can be reduced, in the final analysis, to the state of industrial technology, and that the economic factor is the mainspring of progress." Durkheim then demonstrates this Marxist error by discussing his own newly discovered view of the importance of religion. In opposition to historical materialism, he claims that "historians tend more and more to meet in the confirmation that religion is the most primitive of all social phenomena." "Everything," he insists ([1897] 1978a: 129–30), "is religious in principle." Is it not probable, he asks, "that the economy depends on religion much more than the second on the first?"

Durkheim's interpreters have often mistakenly read his religious theory as a kind of deracinated materialism. Others, when they have recognized the seriousness of the break, usually insist on seeing in the theory that results from it an alternative that subsumes Marx's by being much more multidimensional in scope. This 1897 confrontation with Marxism demonstrates that both views are incorrect.[15]

The "spiritual" program of Durkheim's later cultural sociology

Despite an emerging interpretive consensus that a turn toward religion does mark Durkheim's later writings, its vast theoretical implications have never been fully appreciated. It is scarcely realized that, after 1896, Durkheim felt compelled to revise every strand of his sociological theory. While detailed archival records of his pedagogy were apparently destroyed by the Nazis, judging from the last set available it seems clear that Durkheim introduced alterations into his long-standing lecture notes to reflect his new understanding of the role that ritual, sacred authority, and representation played in secular life.

Durkheim's society became a hierarchy of institutions that were composed of crystallized emotions, not material forms. At the top were sacred symbols of culture, the themes of individualism that provided the most universalistic imperatives of modern social life. At the bottom were two spheres of particularist spirit, the family and occupational group. The state and legal orders mediated between these institutions and general culture through representations that had a more transcendent nature. Education was another institution that provided a universalizing spiritual force; as such, it provided the background for any effective functioning of law and government policies. In this scheme, the coercive aspects of order are eliminated. Economics, for example, was either moralized as a form of cultural particularism or relegated to the position of a residual category – an instrumental, individualist, and profane fact that simply could not be explained.

At the heart of this later religious sociology was Durkheim's journal, *L'Année sociologique*. It is important to connect this act of professional entrepreneurialism to a theoretical program. Durkheim created the journal as an intellectual vehicle only after he had achieved his symbolic breakthrough in the years 1895–7. Although many of his students implicitly demurred, he himself fully intended to make *L'Année* into a statement of his religious model of social order. "This year, as well as last," he wrote ([1899] 1960: 350) in his Preface to the *L'Année*'s second issue, "our analyses are headed by those concerning the sociology of religion." He acknowledges that "the according of the first rank to this sort of phenomenon has produced some astonishment," but he defends this decision on grounds that clearly derive from his recent theoretical insights.[16] "It is these [religious] phenomena," he writes ([1899] 1960: 350), "which are the germ from which all others – or at least almost all others – are derived."

> Religion contains in itself from the very beginning, even if an indistinct state, all the elements which in dissociating themselves from it, articulating themselves, and combining with one another in a thousand ways, have given rise to the

various manifestations of collective life . . . One cannot understand our perception of the world, our philosophical conceptions of the soul, or immortality,
or life, if one does not know the religious beliefs which are their primordial
forms.   ([1899] 1960: 35–51)

L'Année would concentrate on demonstrating exactly these historical connections and, by implication, Durkheim's analytic points as well. Durkheim
concludes this defense of his organizational format by emphasizing that religion is important not only from an historical perspective; it is equally crucial
in terms of the general theoretical framework it provides. "A great number of problems change their aspects completely," he writes, "as soon as
their connections with the sociology of religion are recognized." He concludes by insisting that "our efforts must therefore be aimed at tracing these
connections."

With the single exception of the brief reply to a critic which I have noted
above, Durkheim never admitted the extent to which his encounter with religion had transformed his sociology. Indeed, he never admitted to any radical
break in his work at all. He never disclaimed the instrumental presuppositions of *Division of Labor*, nor did he ever acknowledge that *Rules* was
not a codification of the theory employed in that earlier work but, instead, a
blueprint of things to come. Nor, needless to say, was the religious encounter
that transformed his later writing ever accorded its due.

This silence about the true inner development of his work is certainly a
major reason for the gross misinterpretation to which Durkheim's work has
been subject, not just among contemporary critics but among observers in his
own time and even among his own students. Like all great social theorists,
Durkheim desperately wanted to present his work as a consistent whole.
To do anything else, to acknowledge, for example, that an encounter with
religion could cause major theoretical upheaval, would imply that his tower-
ing oeuvre was not completely "scientific," that it was not, in other words,
derived simply from acute insight into the structures of the empirical world.
"What caused the failure of Saint-Simonianism," he wrote in his lectures
on socialism ([1895–6] 1958: 240), was that "Saint-Simon and his disciples
wanted to get the most from the least, the superior from the inferior, moral
rule from economic matter." Only too late had Saint-Simon realized that self-
interest "was no longer enough," that "without charity, mutual obligation,
and philanthropy, the social order – and still more the human order – was
impossible" ([1895–6] 1958: 185). Durkheim was determined that this mistake would not happen to him. What Saint-Simon had realized only at the end
of his life, Durkheim had been able to understand while there was still enough
time left to change his theoretical direction in a drastic and fundamental

way. Durkheim had learned that to create social order without sacrificing autonomy, men must "feel a positive bond among them" ([1895–6] 1958: 185), and the model of this bond, he had discovered, must be the communion of religious life.

From his first day as a sociologist, it had been one of Durkheim's principal ambitions to create a humanistic alternative to instrumental Marxism. Only after his breakthrough to a symbolic conception of social structure, however, did he feel ready to create a theoretical alternative that could match its generality and scope. This new theory, he insisted, was just as collective, but, because it was also resolutely anti-instrumental, it would avoid the problem of coercion that seemed to correspond to the Marxist understanding of social control. Durkheim finally had differentiated his own theory from Marx's in a conclusive way. That in doing so he had created a theory whose subjectivity was as exaggerated as the objectivism he despised did not dissuade him. He was in flight from *Division of Labor*, with all the intellectual and social consequences it had implied.

NOTES

1 It is an undecided historical question whether or not Durkheim actually knew Marx's own work. Although there is some evidence that he did, he was surely responding more immediately to the mechanical Marxism of the German and French "Marxists" of the First International. Whether his criticism, therefore, can be considered a valid response to Marx's original theory depends on what one considers the relation to be between Marx and his immediate followers. In my view, Durkheim's understanding of Marxism as a mechanistic theory was essentially correct, although this judgment is not relevant to the argument of the present essay, which concerns only Durkheim's understanding of Marx and Marxism. For an extensive comparison of Marx's actual theory with Durkheim's, see Alexander 1982.
2 The interpretation presented here is developed in a much more elaborate manner, with ample quotations from the primary texts, in Alexander 1982.
3 It is interesting to recall that Wundt also had a profound influence on the social behaviorism of George Herbert Mead. Mead took over the same "anti-substantialist" understanding of the individual that so attracted Durkheim, and for the same reason: only with this conception could order be both collective and subjective at the same time. The subsequent misrepresentation of Mead's thought as a form of "substantialist" individualism – by Herbert Blumer and others in the American symbolic interactionist community – has obscured this commonality between the two thinkers. Although Durkheim rejected Wundt's understanding in these early writings, he returned to it, in a more sophisticated way, in the later work I will discuss below.
4 The preceding analysis of the gradual but nonetheless distinctive shift from moral individualism to moral collectivism and, finally, to instrumental collectivism in the course of Durkheim's early writings suggests that interpreters have been wrong

to stress the internal consistency of this period and its continuity with the rest of Durkheim's work (e.g. Giddens 1970, Wallwork 1972: 27–46, Filloux 1977: 23–34). Such an insistence on the continuity of Durkheim's early writings makes it virtually impossible to understand his emerging perspective on the importance of the division of labor and, even more importantly, his eventual dissatisfaction with this position.

5 The changing and contradictory nature of Durkheim's argument in *Division of Labor* has not been recognized by most of his interpreters. This has occurred in part because of an understandable yet unfortunate tendency to defer to Durkheim's own perspective on the work's contents. In discussing Book 2, for example, critics have accepted Durkheim's claim that he is measuring not simply demographic but also moral density. Pope (1973) views Durkheim's emphasis on population expansion and exchange as simply another example of the "social realist" approach to morality that dominates the entire work. This perspective, however, collapses the problem of individualist-versus-collectivist reasoning with the problem of action, failing to distinguish the radically different approaches to the social that are possible even when a collectivist, social realist position is accepted. Though much more nuanced and generally more accurate than Pope's account, Lukes' (1972: 154, 169) discussion similarly fails to distinguish the tremendous differences between moral and material density in Book 2. In his discussion, Lukes (1972: 168–72) often simply reproduces the vagueness and the contradictory quality of the Durkheimian original. While he accuses Durkheim of technological determinism and of being inconclusive about the basic details of the social change he describes (1972: 164), these charges are never systematically documented. One reason for this failure is Lukes' argument for the close continuity of *Division of Labor* with Durkheim's earlier writings. In fact, Lukes views the whole sequence of Durkheim's writings from 1885 to 1893 as clarification and specification rather than as involving the development of contradictory theoretical logics. Filloux (1977: 74–8) adopts much the same sanguine posture. Giddens has gone so far as to argue not only for the internal continuity of *Division of Labor* but for its centrality in Durkheim's corpus as a whole. The work provided, Giddens writes (1971: 190), "a definitive perspective upon the emergence of the modern form of society which Durkheim never abandoned and which constitutes the lasting ground of all his later works." Even the critics who have emphasized discontinuity in *Division of Labor* have insisted that there exists within this work a developmental and logically coherent movement toward "better theory." Nisbet (1965: 36–47), for example, argues that a normative perspective on social order gradually overshadows an earlier instrumental one. Earlier, Parsons (1937: 308–24) had argued for much the same position, claiming that Book 2, Chapter 7 – the chapter I have identified as a point where Durkheim turned toward a troublesome instrumentalism – represented the emergence of a more satisfactory normative perspective. While Durkheim's French interpreters have been much more willing to recognize the economistic and even Marxist elements of *Division of Labor* (e.g. Aimard 1962: 217–18, Cuvillier 1948: 83, Kagan 1938, passim), they have, almost without exception, merely turned the error of English and American critics on its head: the instrumental perspective on order, they have argued, was consistent and continuous throughout Durkheim's 1893 work.

6 The essays that became *Rules* were first published in 1894 in the *Revue philosophique*. For a fuller explication of the contradictory tendencies in *Rules*, see Alexander (1997).

7 "L'âme" is translated as "mind" throughout *Rules* – and in Durkheim's other work as well – but it seems more appropriate in light of the emerging direction of Durkheim's theorizing to translate it more literally as "soul" or "spirit."

8 For discussion of this political development and its relation to new and more normative developments in Durkheim's work, see Tiryakian (1978: 233–4).

9 This portrait of the impact of Marxian and socialist ideas on French intellectual circles draws upon Vogt (1976) and Llobera (1978), although I disagree substantially with the interpretations these authors give.

10 The sole exception that I have been able to locate to these negative reviews is an essay written by Paul Lapie (1895: 309–10), "L'Année sociologique, 1894." Lapie saw very clearly the subjective, normative basis that Durkheim gave to social facts in the essays that became *Rules*, and he applauded him for it. Later, as director of primary education in France, Lapie introduced Durkheimian sociology into the required national curriculum. This movement toward subjectivity may have pleased Lapie because he shared Durkheim's opinion that scientifically based Republican ethics were essential to the survival of French democracy.

11 This attack from a scholar so closely associated with Dilthey, the philosophical creator of the anti-positivistic method of hermeneutics, suggests how such widespread distortions played havoc with modern sociology's sense of itself. Durkheim's mature program can be regarded as one of the most powerful macro-hermeneutics of modern society. Yet Weberians and others who uphold the hermeneutic approach, like Lukes (1982: 11–15), have attacked Durkheim's positivism as antithetical to Dilthey's interpretive and humanistic principles. It is true, of course, that Durkheim himself remained formally committed to objectivist methods, failing to comprehend the interpretive methods that fundamentally if still implicitly informed his later work, much less to appreciate their scientific validity.

12 I have made a few alterations here from Lukes' translation (1972: 237), the most important of which is that in the original Durkheim employs the verb "*marquer*" in the present tense, whereas Lukes translates it in the past tense, as "marked." The literal translation gives a more vivid sense of the fact that Durkheim feels as if the revelation about the role of religion which he is recounting some ten years subsequent to the event is still, in fact, occurring.

13 The work that had the most impact on Durkheim was Smith's "Lectures on the Religion of the Semites," written in 1887. For the complex process of transmission between Smith's work and Durkheim, see Jones, chapter 4 in this volume.

14 Those who emphasize the continuity of Durkheim's work, of course, ignore this break. As for those who make the opposite mistake – taking the encounter with Smith's work as constituting, in itself, an epistemological break – see, for example, Beidelman (1974), who overemphasizes Smith's effect on Durkheim primarily because he is not aware of the movement of Durkheim's thought before he encountered Smith's work. Lukes (1972: 238–9) is guilty of the same exaggeration when he tries to demonstrate the impact of Smith simply by comparing his religious theory with Durkheim's earlier writing on the narrow topic of religion itself, ignoring

the considerable shifts that had taken place in Durkheim's general social theory in the immediately preceding years. While Filloux's (1977: 91–2) assessment is more cautious on this point, he moves too far over to the other side by claiming that Durkheim knew "in principle that all is religious" as early as 1886 and 1887, and that Smith merely gave him a better understanding of how this social permeation of religion could come about. Filloux, in other words, inverts an interpretation like Giddens', asserting that Durkheim's work consistently emphasizes religion from beginning to end.

15 Perhaps the major failure of interpretation of this crucial phase in Durkheim's theoretical development rests with the widespread inclination of writers to describe the issue he was grappling with as exactly parallel to the Marxian concern with base versus superstructure. Thus, Émile Benoit-Smullyan (1948: 511) writes about the crucial relationship for Durkheim of "material substratum" and "collective representation." Pope (1973) talks about whether or not "material foundations" still play a significant role. Giddens (1977: 290) tries to indicate the continuing impact, and therefore anti-idealist reference, of social institutions on ideas in Durkheim's sociology of religion. This same dichotomy is the principal organizing rubric for Lukes' (1972: 237–44, 450–84) thinking about the shift in Durkheim's theory initiated by religion, as it is for La Capra (1972: 245–91), Marks (1974), Gouldner (1958), and Aron (1970: 53–79). These interpreters take different positions on whether or not a shift did occur, but the error is the same no matter what their conclusion. For the issue in this confrontation with religion is not whether or not the material base will be dominant. This issue had already been decided by Durkheim in 1894. The issue rather is what will be the nature of the normative order to which Durkheim is already committed. Many interpreters, of course, have simply failed to appreciate the significance of this early encounter with religion altogether. In his influential earlier work on Durkheim, Parsons (1937: 409), for example, viewed Durkheim's religious understanding as coming into play only with the publication of *The Elementary Forms of Religious Life*. (It is testimony to the sensitivity of this early interpretation that Parsons was able to describe the transition to subjectivity in Durkheim's middle writings despite the fact that he was not aware of the early significance of religion.) Yet, even among those who have seen the importance of this encounter, none have adequately assessed its enormous impact on Durkheim's later theory of society. Lukes (1972), for example, who was one of the first to highlight this crucial biographical fact, basically considers this religious breakthrough as a separate line of analysis culminating in *Elementary Forms*, and he integrates it hardly at all with Durkheim's writing on education, politics, and other institutions. The only important exceptions, to my knowledge, are Gianfranco Poggi (1971: 252–4, and passim) and Lacroix (1977). Poggi's analysis, however, is mainly programmatic, failing to link the new importance of religion to any decisive break in Durkheim's work. Lacroix's work has two problems, from my perspective. First, although he firmly exposed "*la coupure*" that Durkheim's religious revelation created in his theoretical development, he tries to tie this religion-inspired shift too closely to the middle-period work. Any definitive resolution of this question, of course, would have to depend on firmer historical evidence, which is by all accounts nonexistent. At this point, however, it seems evident that Durkheim's theory underwent two shifts after the publication of *Division of Labor*, not one. The first, which begins even as the

latter work is published – in the 1893 *"Note"* and socialism review cited above – reorganizes his schema in a subjective manner without any particular reference to collective representations or religion. The second phase, which is barely visible in the lectures of 1895 and which does not become explicit until 1897, brings "spiritual" considerations into the center of this newly subjectified theory. Only the second development, it would seem, can be linked to the "revelation" of 1895. The second problem with Lacroix's analysis is that it does not expose the "religious dimension" of Durkheim's later institutional theory in a systematic way. Bellah's interpretation (1974) takes some initial steps in the direction in which such an analysis would have to go. For a full exploration of the manner in which Durkheim's entire body of post-1896 writing is reorganized around the religious model, see Alexander 1982.

16 Evidently this "astonishment" was not limited to Durkheim's critics. Paul Lapie, the reviewer turned follower who had earlier applauded the subjective turn of Durkheim's *Rules*, complained in an 1897 letter to Célestin Bouglé, one of Durkheim's collaborators on *L'Année*, that "Durkheim explains everything, at this time, by religion; the interdiction against marriages between relatives is a religious affair, the punishment is a religious phenomenon, all is religious" (quoted in Lacroix 1977: 213 n.2).

REFERENCES

Aimard, Guy. 1962. *Durkheim et la science économique*. Paris: Presses Universitaires de France.

Alexander, Jeffrey C. 1997. "Les Règles secrètes de Durkheim." pp. 191–202 in *Durkheim d'un siècle a l'autre: Les Lectures actuelles des règles de la méthode sociologique*. Edited by E. H. Cuin. Paris: Presses Universitaires de France.

1982. *The Antinomies of Classical Thought: Marx and Durkheim*. Berkeley and Los Angeles: University of California Press.

Andler, Charles. 1896. "Sociologie et démocratie." *Revue de métaphysique et de morale* 4: 243–56.

Aron, Raymond. 1970. *Main Currents of Sociological Thought*, vol. 2. New York: Doubleday Anchor.

Barth, Paul. [1897] 1922. *Die Philosophie der Geschichte als Soziologie*. Leipzig: O. R. Reisland.

Beidelman, T. O. 1974. *W. Robertson Smith and the Sociological Study of Religion*. Chicago: University of Chicago Press.

Bellah, Robert N. 1974. Introduction to *Émile Durkheim on Morality and Society*. Edited by Robert N. Bellah. Chicago: University of Chicago Press.

Benoit-Smullyan, Émile. 1948. "The Sociologism of Durkheim and His School." pp. 499–537 in *An Introduction to the History of Sociology*. Edited by H. E. Barnes. Chicago: University of Chicago Press.

Brunschvieg, L. and E. Halévy. 1894. "L'Année philosophique, 1893." *Revue de métaphysique et de morale* 2: 564–90.

Cuvillier, A. 1948. "Durkheim et Marx." *Cahiers internationaux de sociologie* 4: 75–97.

Durkheim, Émile. 1907. Letter to the Director. *Revue néo-scolastique* 14: 612–14.

[1899] 1960. "Preface to *L'Année sociologique* 2." pp. 347–52 in *Émile Durkheim et al. on Sociology and Philosophy*. Edited by Kurt Wolff. New York: Harper and Row.

[1898] 1974. "Individual and Collective Representations" in *Sociology and Philosophy*. New York: Free Press.

[1897] 1978b. "Review of Gaston Richard, *Le Socialisme et la science sociale*." pp. 131–8 in *Émile Durkheim on Institutional Analysis*. Edited by Mark Traugott. Chicago: University of Chicago Press.

[1897] 1978a. "Review of Antonio Labriola, *Essai sur la conception matérialiste de l'histoire*." pp. 123–30 in *Émile Durkheim on Institutional Analysis*. Edited by Mark Traugott. Chicago: University of Chicago Press.

[1897] 1951. *Suicide*. New York: Free Press.

1896. Letter to the Editor. *Revue de métaphysique et de morale* 4: 20. (Special supplement of July 4.)

[1895–6] 1958. *Socialism and Saint-Simon*. Yellow Springs, OH: Antioch.

[1895] 1938. *Rules of Sociological Method*. New York: Free Press.

[1893] 1964. *The Division of Labor in Society*. New York: Free Press.

1893a. "Note sur la définition du socialisme." *Revue philosophique* 34: 506–12.

1893b. "Richard, G., *Essai sur l'origine de l'idée de droit*." *Revue philosophique* 34: 290–96.

1907.

[1888] 1978. "Introduction to the Sociology of the Family." pp. 205–28 in *Émile Durkheim on Institutional Analysis*. Edited by Mark Traugott. Chicago: University of Chicago Press.

[1888] 1975. "Le Programme économique de M. Schaeffle." pp. 3–7 in *Émile Durkheim: Textes*. Paris: Editions de Minuit.

1887a. "Guyau, *L'Irréligion de l'avenir. Etude de sociologie*." *Revue philosophique* 23: 299–311.

1887b. "La Science positive de la morale en Allemagne." Part 3. *Revue philosophique* 24: 113–142.

1886. "Les Etudes de science sociale." *Revue philosophique* 22: 61–80.

[1885] 1978. "Review of Schaeffle, *Bau und Leben des Sozialen Korpers: Erster Band*." pp. 93–114 in *Émile Durkheim on Institutional Analysis*. Edited by Mark Traugott. Chicago: University of Chicago Press.

1885. "A Fouillée, La Propriété sociale et la démocratie." *Revue philosophique* 19: 446–53.

Filloux, Jean-Claude. 1977. *Durkheim et le socialisme*. Geneva: Librairie Droz.

Giddens, Anthony. 1977. "The Individual in the Writing of Émile Durkheim." pp. 273–91 in *Studies in Social and Political Theory*. Edited by Anthony Giddens. New York: Basic Books.

1971. *Capitalism and Modern Social Theory*. London: Cambridge University Press.

1970. "Durkheim as a Review Critic." *Sociological Review* 18: 171–96.

Gouldner, Alvin W. (ed.) 1958. Introduction to *Socialism and Saint-Simon: Émile Durkheim*. Yellow Springs, OH: Antioch.

Kagan, George. 1938. "Durkheim et Marx." *Revue d'histoire économique et sociale* 24: 233–44.

Labriola, Antonio. 1897. *Essai sur la conception matérialiste de l'histoire*. Paris: V. Giard and E. Brière.

La Capra, Dominick. 1972. *Émile Durkheim: Sociologist and Philosopher*. Ithaca, NY: Cornell University Press.

Lacroix, Bernard. 1977. *Durkheim et la question politique*. Paris: PUF.

Lapie, Paul. 1895. "L'Année sociologique, 1894." *Revue de métaphysique et morale* 3: 309–39.

Llobera, Joseph R. 1978. "Durkheim, The Durkheimians, and their Collective Misrepresentation of Marx." Paper presented at the Ninth World Congress of Sociology, Uppsala, Sweden.

Lukes, Steven. 1982. Introduction to *Durkheim: The Rules of Sociological Method and Selected Texts on Sociology and Its Method*. Edited by Steven Lukes. New York: Free Press.

1972. *Émile Durkheim: His Life and Work*. New York: Harper and Row.

Marks, Stephen R. 1974. "Durkheim's Theory of Anomie." *American Journal of Sociology* 80: 329–63.

Mauss, Marcel. [1928] 1958. "Introduction to the First Edition." pp. 1–4 in *Socialism and Saint-Simon* by Émile Durkheim. Yellow Springs, OH: Antioch.

Nisbet, Robert A. 1965. Introduction *Émile Durkheim*. Edited by Robert A. Nisbet. Englewood Cliffs, NJ: Prentice-Hall.

O'Connor, James. 1980. "The Division of Labor in Society." *The Insurgent Sociologist* 10: 60–8.

Parsons, Talcott. 1937. *The Structure of Social Action*. New York: Free Press.

Poggi, Gianfranco. 1971. "The Place of Religion in Durkheim's Theory of Institutions." *European Journal of Sociology* 12: 229–60.

Pope, Whitney. 1973. "Classic on Classic: Parsons' Interpretation of Durkheim." *American Sociological Review* 38: 399–415.

Sorel, George. 1895. "Les Théories de M. Durkheim." *Le Devenir* 1: 1–25, 148–80.

Tiryakian, Edward A. 1978. "Émile Durkheim" in *A History of Sociological Analysis*. Edited by T. B. Bottomore and Robert A. Nisbet. New York: Basic Books.

Traugott, Mark (ed.) 1978. *Émile Durkheim on Institutional Analysis*. Chicago: University of Chicago Press.

Vogt, W. Paul. 1976. "The Confrontation of Socialists and Sociologists in Pre-War France, 1890–1914." *Proceedings of the Western Society for French History* 4: 313–20.

Wallwork, Ernest. 1972. *Émile Durkheim: Morality and Milieu*. Cambridge: Harvard University Press.

7

KAREN E. FIELDS

What difference does translation make? *Les Formes élémentaires de la vie religieuse* in French and English

> Is there a man, learned or unlearned, who will not, when he takes the volume into his hands, and perceives that what he reads does not suit his settled tastes, break out immediately into violent language, and call me a forger and a profane person for having the audacity to add anything to the ancient books, or to make any changes or corrections therein?
>
> St. Jerome (*ca.* 342–420 AD; as quoted in Glassman 1981: 15)

Applied to translation, the phrase "X said" is more remarkable than appears at first glance. It certainly is useful, as just now to quote St. Jerome's exasperated depiction of the translator's work. Even so, to use it is to ignore a half-truth, for the phrase cannot mean what it says. The patron saint of translators composed his one-liner in Latin, while the English words on which I must rely to read it belong to the translator. So "X said" is no more than a shorthand. And as a shorthand, moreover, "X said" obscures what it abbreviates. Two statements of disparate origin, not one, inhabit every translation: what X said and what X has been made to say.[1] Those two statements are forever distinct and variously related. As the first translator, in 1915, of Durkheim's 1912 masterpiece, *Les Formes élémentaires de la vie religieuse* (hereafter *Elementary Forms*), Joseph Ward Swain invented many statements of the second, made-to-say kind.[2] Re-translating *Elementary Forms* in 1995, so did I. My own statements, like Swain's, bear different kinds and qualities of relationship to the original.[3] I propose to explore some of the relationships that matter when English is the language in which *Elementary Forms* is to be read.

I begin with circumstantial relationships, so called to highlight time and purpose. Next come active relationships that constitute the translator's work of devising equivalents. Finally, I examine interpretive relationships. Some are so noticeably consequential – *représentation* and *conscience* – that italics often announce their presence. Others could be announced that way: *moral*, *idéal*, and even *social*; for different reasons, *élémentaire* and *simple*; and finally, were it practical, sometimes French for "it" and "the." Along the way, I examine certain challenges to translation from English to English, so to speak – as well as from French to French. In *Les Étapes de la pensée sociologique*, for example, Raymond Aron (1967: 64) pronounced himself so ill-equipped to enter into Durkheim's thought that he deliberately chose to quote extensively instead of paraphrasing.

Texts and circumstances

Begin with purpose. Talcott Parsons made translations for his theoretical study *The Structure of Social Action* (1937). Each of the resulting texts – what he makes Durkheim say – has its proper context in Parsons' overall interpretation. The same applies to English renderings of the French commentators Raymond Aron and Claude Lévi-Strauss. The context changes, however, when W. S. F. Pickering and Jacqueline Redding select passages for their valuable collection *Durkheim on Religion* ([1975] 1994),[4] and when Mark S. Cladis and Carol Cosman delete passages for their abridgement, *Elementary Forms* (2001).[5] Like Parsons' quotations, these shortened versions stand in part-to-whole relationships with the original. Unlike Parsons' quotations, however, their purpose is not primarily to interpret but to make a French text accessible to English-speaking readers. Even so, they cannot help but embody interpretation in the made-to-say sense, like Parsons', and, just as significantly, in a made-*not-to*-say sense as well. Examples taken from these varied sources will bring out relationships between different translating and different purposes.

Now consider time. Eighty years separate the two full translations. Swain's was published only three years after the French translation, and was the first of Durkheim's books to appear in English (Pickering [1975] 1994: 4). Presumably, Durkheim oversaw what became in English *The Elementary Forms of the Religious Life* (1915), and made the decision to drop its subtitle, *Le Système totémique d'Australie.*[6] Swain's pioneering shaped my own work, but I benefited as well from aids he did not have: critiques and specialized readings (like Parsons') that came later, as well as field applications by anthropologists – Lloyd Warner, Claude Lévi-Strauss, E. E. Evans-Pritchard, Bronislaw Malinowski, and others. Such works changed the original, in a sense, by clarifying it. Evans-Pritchard's classic *Witchcraft, Oracles, and Magic Among the Azande* (1937) dramatically exhibited the belief-expressing rites and rite-explaining beliefs of *Elementary Forms*.

Time marks readers as well. Audiences eighty years ago responded differently from audiences now to Durkheim's project of studying religion in general through its "simplest and most primitive" forms. The intervening history has primed some of today's readers against that very project, so defined, joining them to some of Durkheim's contemporaries, who were primed against it by their own history. To us, it seems essential to passionately rebut the supposed simplicity of the peoples he studied. Back then, passionate reactions assumed it. In 1916, T. S. Eliot reviewed an academic blast against *Elementary Forms* by C. J. Webb (1916), an Oxonian defender of "the rights of 'individual' religion," the personality of God, and individual immortality (p. 115). The heat was on: against the "collective" notions of Durkheim and his school; and against the very idea that study of the stone-tool-using peoples of Aboriginal Australia might yield valid generalizations about religious life, anywhere. Parsons ([1937] 1968: 417) could have been referring to Webb when he mentioned "religious circles" whose "instantaneous indignation" met the man who "start[ed] out to vindicate the permanence of religion against those who would dissolve it into illusion [and] emerg[ed] with an even more objectionably 'materialistic' view than those he criticize[d]." Raymond Aron described reaction in France to its initial publication as *violent*. And, addressing his own generation, he quoted Durkheim against Durkheim: "Does a science of religion according to which men worship society safeguard its object or make it disappear?" (Aron 1967: 51).

We may wonder, therefore, what Swain felt, South Dakota-born Episcopalian that he was, as he reflected upon every single word – the translator's duty (Gale 2004).[7] A broadside by his contemporary, the French Protestant Gaston Richard (an ex-Durkheimian), inveighed against *Elementary Forms* for displacing William James' "interior God" ("subliminal 'I'") in favor of collectivity. "Society exterior to man," Richard exclaimed (1923 in Pickering [1975] 1994: 244), "of which a horde of black Australians, the Blackfellows, are deemed to be the best example!" Seen one way, Durkheim had spectacularly affirmed a fundamental truth – that humankind is one. Seen otherwise, he had abraded prevailing common sense that justified not only religious missions to *peuples inférieurs* but also armed *missions civilisatrices*.

In *Elementary Forms*, the cyclical time of repetitive events provides the frame within which religion's object emerges as real.[8] But Durkheim's route to religion in its "simplest and most primitive form" passed via the invidiously linear time of the evolutionist idiom. He needed *élémentaire* and *simple* for methodological reasons (Durkheim 1995: 3ff); but *inférieur* and *primitif* traveled with them like barnacles on a boat. Read today, Durkheim's evolutionist idiom tends to recast his universalism as its opposite. Swain's custom of literal translation abets that. When Durkheim writes, "les religions même les plus inférieures" (1912: 440), Swain gives us "even the *most inferior* religions" (1915: 347), not "the lowest" of standard evolutionary parlance. In that way, literalness moves Durkheim toward Lucien Lévy-Bruhl's *Les*

Fonctions Mentales des peuples inférieurs (1910) – even though he differed with it (see Durkheim 1913 in Pickering [1975] 1994: 169–73, 165 note 64). The revealing English title of Lévy-Bruhl's book was *How Natives Think*. Supposing Durkheim regarded the evolutionist pairs simple/complex and lower/higher as interchangeable, and they often seem to be, I thought "simplest" would render his meaning more faithfully; but, wrongly, I failed to mark my hermeneutic addition. I will return to that problem.[9]

With the same general effect as "most inferior," Swain almost always chose "confuse" for *confondre* and its French cognates. That choice often connotes a rational incapacity that enables Richard's horde of "Blackfellows" to say, "I am a Kangaroo," and intend an empirical equation.[10] But since one meaning of *confondre* is "to amalgamate" or "to meld," "fusion" is often better than "confusion," unless the context itself clarifies. Here, for example, Lévi-Strauss (translated by Rodney Needham) says that "[e]very sacrifice implies a solidarity of nature between officiant, god, and the thing sacrificed . . . Thus the idea of sacrifice also bears within it the germ of a confusion with the animal . . ." (1962: 3). The confusion at issue not an empirical one. Again: Swain's translating "obscure consciences" as "obscure minds" (Durkheim 1915: 219) seems unexceptionable until we ask whether Durkheim would have answered the question "Obscure to whom?" by saying, "The 'native,' himself, *évidemment*." After reading the environing paragraph's clues, and consulting the dictionary to see if *obscur* is sensitive to perspective (it can be), I thought he would not have, and therefore added "to us" – this time, supplying a note (Durkheim 1995: 193n). Because Durkheim's evolutionist idiom was his route toward a destination of far greater interest than the befuddled colonial "native," allegedly unaware that a thing cannot be itself and something else, those attentions seemed to me requisite. It falls to the re-translator to open the way for today's reader to arrive at that destination too.

In Swain's day, however, literalness was thought equivalent to accuracy, and readers expected to hear not only foreign words but foreign structures "through" their own language. The Bible translator Eugene Glassman (an Urdu specialist) recounts the appreciation once prevalent among seminarians for the 1901 American Standard Version of the Bible: It sounded authentic to them, and, better still, it exercised their Greek syntax (1981: 48). Swain's *Elementary Forms* often exercises one's French syntax and vocabulary, alike: "[T]he mental habits it [totemism] implies prevented men from seeing reality as their senses show it to them; but as they show it, it has the grave inconvenience of allowing of no explanation" (Durkheim 1915: 269). Here, literalness yielded not only "inconvenience" for *inconvénient*, instead of "drawback," but also a structurally French sentence densely forested with half-translated "it's." Swain's other encounters with false cognates are too numerous to list. Suffice it to mention only one that is often noticed, his constant use of "assistant" for *assistant*, because it provides a capsule lesson about change in English itself. The 1901 *Century Dictionary* gives Swain's usage first (p. 348).[11]

The workaday reality of meeting deadlines is another port through which time enters Swain's translation. He finished his English *Elementary Forms* three years after its French publication and, a year later, defended his doctoral dissertation at Columbia University: *Hellenistic Influences on Christian Asceticism*. Not surprisingly, despite its many merits, Swain's work on *Elementary Forms* bears many marks of haste. He allowed the English version to read less well than its French predecessor, leading an anonymous reviewer in 1918 to judge it "good but of less literary finish than the original" (p. 158). In addition, Swain occasionally skipped passages, including this remarkable one: "Now they [religious representations] cannot weaken without the sacred beings' losing their reality, because the sacred beings exist only in and through their representations" (Durkheim 1995: 349).[12] Given the implications of that statement, I pondered its deletion, for another like it is deleted as well. Was that an ordinary slip, or a discreet bit of graffiti on Durkheim's wall? To be a translator is not necessarily to be without opinions.

Swain did indeed bury a pivotal three sentences, at book II, chapter 7.4, through utterly wrong translation:

> Rien ne vient de rien. Les impressions qu'éveille en nous le monde physique ne sauraient, par définition, rien contenir qui dépasse ce monde. Avec du sensible, on ne peut faire que du sensible; avec de l'étendu, on ne peut faire de l'inétendu.
> (Durkheim 1912: 321–2)

I imagine no wayward impulse here, but believe Swain was simply stumped by this monster, as deadlines pressed. And since translators strive to avoid (obvious) obscurity, he chose to abandon his customary literalness and, with it, his customary accuracy:

> Nothing is worth [*vaut* replacing *vient*] nothing. The impressions produced in us by the physical world can, by definition, contain nothing that surpasses this world. Out of the visible [for *sensible*], only the visible can be made; out of that which is heard [*entendu* replacing *étendu*] we cannot make something not heard.
> (Durkheim 1915: 256)

The monster is the pair *étendu/inétendu*. Sixty years later, Pickering and Redding ([1975] 1994) offered "vast" and "minute." No. As we will see, that pair probably held no obscurity at all for those of Durkheim's original French audience who had attended a *lycée*.

Translating Durkheim

Devising equivalents

I use the word "devise" to underline the translator's work, for while the original controls that work, it cannot dictate. Consider first Durkheim's celebrated definition of religion:

> Une religion est un système solidaire de croyances et de pratiques relatives à des choses sacrées, c'est à dire séparées, interdites, croyances et pratiques qui unissent en une même communauté morale, appelée Eglise, tous ceux qui y adherent. (Durkheim 1912: 65)

"Durkheim said" often introduces this English sentence of Swain's:

> A religion is a unified system of beliefs and practices relative to sacred things, that is to say, things set apart and forbidden – beliefs and practices which unite into one single moral community called a Church, all those who adhere to them. (Durkheim 1915: 62)

But "Durkheim said" could equally well introduce Talcott Parsons' sentence, which is accurate too, yet different:

> A religion is "an integrated [*solidaire*] system of beliefs and practices relative to sacred things, that is separate and taboo, which unite in one moral community called a church all those who adhere to it." (Parsons [1937] 1968: 412)[13]

Notice that Parsons' equivalents for *séparées* and *solidaire* differ from Swain's, and that he acknowledges room for doubt about "integrated" for *solidaire*. Other published renderings differ on the same points: "integral" and "separated," by the anthropologist A. A. Goldenweiser (1915 in Pickering [1975] 1994: 211), and "interdependent" and "apart," by Aron's translators (1967: 48). Each conveys a somewhat different meaning; none betrays Durkheim's own; all stand alongside Swain's and Parsons' translations in the same relation to the original. "*Integrated* system" for *système solidaire* no doubt appealed to Parsons, a grand theorist of "system integration." Nevertheless, on the question which might be closest to Durkheim's intention, the French sentence remains agnostic. It is the translator's turn.

Sometimes, the cause of translators' divergence is not the openness of the original but an obscurity that tends to close it. Thus, while discussing the problem of defining religion, Durkheim seems to contrast *philosophes* and *érudits* (philosophers and learned people), with what purport is unclear: "[L]e problème reste entier et le grand service qu'a rendu la philosophie est d'empêcher qu'il n'ait été proscrit par les érudits" (Durkheim 1912: 6). Here is Swain: "The problem remains intact, and the great service of philosophy is to have prevented its being suppressed by the disdain of scholars" (Durkheim 1915: 17). Here is Redding: "[T]he problem itself has not been forgotten,

KAREN E. FIELDS

thanks to the philosophers who grappled with it when other scholars ignored it" (Durkheim [1975] 1994: 105). My own solution is not the whiggish end of an evolutionary ascent toward the real meaning: "[T]he problem of definition remains; and philosophy's great service has been to prevent it from being settled once and for all by the disdain of savants" (Durkheim 1995: 4). Cosman's solution is similar: "[T]he problem of defining religion remains; and philosophy's great service has been to prevent it from being settled by the disdain of specialists" (Durkheim 2001: 6). Diverse solutions mark the translator's activity.

Moreover, that activity sometimes reveals the translator's sensibility when the original suggests the author's own but holds it out of reach. Durkheim used the lovely verb *plâner* to describe the posture of humanity's earliest gods, but what did he mean? The context is that he has quoted the Latin maxim *Primus in orbe timor fecit deos* ("First in the world, fear made the Gods") for the purpose of refuting it. Humanity's first gods were near at hand, kindly protectors, he tells us, not remote gods who *plânent*. Does he mean they "soar high above," as Swain said (Durkheim 1915: 255), do they "look down from on high" as Redding wrote (Durkheim [1975] 1994: 133), or, as Cosman (Durkheim 2001: 169) and I (Durkheim 1995: 225) thought, do they "loom"? We cannot know where Durkheim's own sensibility led him. The four different translators chose differently between simple remoteness, august curiosity, and menace.

A translation is thus a product and a process. As a product, it cannot help but appear to be what it cannot possibly be: the text itself, though in a different language. Certainly, the writer's craft can foster that appearance whether by giving the author idiomatic language or by making him sound foreign. Thus, a recent Kant translation by Guyer and Wood (1998) labored to provide a reading experience as close as possible to that of his first German readers, complete with strange typography. Still, the road to English is paved with the translator's judgments (Stern 1999: 138). Whatever the appearance, a text cannot move by itself; it must be rebuilt. As a process, then, every translation is a reconstruction, and every translator works like an artisan, not a medium. That is why we hear Parsons *and* Durkheim on what a *système solidaire* is, and also why even a short French sentence rarely yields identical short English sentences by different translators. In sum, while the reservations to be had about "correcting" are obvious, St. Jerome's talk of adding and changing describes reasonably well what translators, not mediums, do.

Swain sometimes let his own activity show through brilliantly non-literal renderings. His "thoroughgoing idiocy" (Durkheim 1915: 203) for Durkheim's *absurdité foncière* (1912: 250) fully captures Durkheim's tone in attacking the notion that a "primitive" thinks like a child. He again captures Durkheim's tone in his question, at the very end of book I, chapter 2: "What sort of science is it whose principal discovery is that the subject of which it treats does not exist?" It suits the French: "Qu'est-ce qu'une science dont la principale découverte consisterait à faire évanouir l'objet même dont elle traite?" With this outrageously rhetorical question, Durkheim floodlights what has gone before: religion so defined as to make its essential elements objectively observable by any and everyone, hence accessible to *science positive* (excluding God, the supernatural, miracles, and the like). Now, after having demolished naturist and animist theories, both afoul of his criterion, Durkheim's question fires the *coup de grâce*. Swain faithfully renders its meaning, nuance, atmosphere, and even attitude. Notice the hissing "s's" that launch the English sentence.

Or does he? Swain ignores Durkheim's *consisterait*, a conditional that reiterates doubt (previously expressed) that the theories being attacked could properly be called "science" at all. "What sort of science *would it be?*" is closer to his idea than "What sort of science *is* it?" Besides, the French does not invite "does not exist," either. *Faire évanouir* means "to make [something] disappear" or "vanish into thin air," like a ghost (*Le Petit Robert* 1992).[14] Arguably, the difference wrought by both changes is not large. Still, ponder Swain's "does not exist" in conjunction with "What sort of science *is* it?" The phrase "does not exist" surely carried resonance of its own – and, in some measure, Swain's own – into hot debates of the day about the meaning and future of religion. The translator's interpretation has many possible points of entry.

When the Kant specialist W. H. Werkmeister wrote, "[A]ny translation is *ipso facto* an interpretation," he was stating both an irremediable fact about the enterprise and an admonition about the translator's proper place. To succeed, he continued, it was necessary – but not enough – for a translator to know both languages sufficiently well to render a text accurately ("finer nuances and overtones" included). Beyond that, the translator must understand the author's point of view sufficiently well to understand "what the author has to say in defending his point of view" – that is, to recognize the author's destination in a work, and the steps the author believes necessary to reach it (Werkmeister 1982: 133). Those matters are not up to the translator. In the choice of destination and of arguments to get there, it is the author's turn.

Before proceeding, then, let me disclose my understanding of Durkheim's steps and destination. Like *Suicide*, where social causation is ascribed to seemingly individual acts, *Elementary Forms* is argued using the very sort of case that would seem most unfavorable to it.[15] Durkheim chooses totemic beliefs and rites, with their *confusions* of human and non-human realms, to show not only that a science of religion can and must treat religion as being about something real, but also that religion expresses "fundamental and permanent" traits of all humankind. To reach his destination, he needs socially constructed knowledge and socially constructed reality. Therefore, like the famous statistics of *Suicide*, the ethnographic passages of *Elementary Forms* are important in exposition as well as in discovery, and, besides, they are laden with suggestions for empirical work.[16]

One such passage (book II, chapter 7.3) displays a rite in which Warramunga men of the Uluuru phratry are celebrating their kinship and their common descent from a mythical giant snake, Wollunqua. In a review essay about *Elementary Forms*, Jeffrey Alexander and Philip Smith singled out the following quotation, drawn by Durkheim from the British ethnographers Sir Baldwin Spencer and Francis James Gillen (1904: 231):

> Tandis que les feux, faisant ressortir violemment la blancheur des gommiers sur le fond des ténèbres environnants, les Uluuru s'agenouillèrent les uns derrière les autres à côté du tumulus, puis ils en firent le tour en se soulevant de terre, d'un mouvement d'ensemble, les deux mains appuyées sur les cuisses, pour s'agenouiller à nouveau un peu plus loin, et ainsi de suite. En même temps, ils penchaient leurs corps tantôt à droite, tantôt à gauche poussant tous à la fois, à chacun de ces mouvements, un cri retentissant, véritable hurlement, *Yrssh! Yrrsh! Yrrsh!*   (as quoted in Smith and Alexander 1996: 589)

The centrality of this passage can be inferred from its placement: at the climactic midpoint of a chapter that synthesizes key arguments of the preceding 342 pages; immediately before a discussion probing the nature of abstract thought (book II, chapter 7.4); and immediately after a description (book II, chapter 7.2) of *effervescences collectives* during the French Revolution, so powerfully transforming that they could make a *bourgeois* into a *bourreau* (executioner). Durkheim's juxtaposition of Australian *effervescences* with French ones provoked Aron (1967: 58) to mention those "two curious and characteristic passages." But he apparently missed, or dismissed, the high-wire performance to come: the claim that the human capacity for logic is present in the fusions (*confusions*) of disparate realms that the rite accomplishes. Swain worked to render Durkheim's you-are-there vividness:

> While fires were lighted on all sides, making the whiteness of the gum trees stand out sharply against the surrounding darkness, the Uluuru knelt down one behind the other beside the mound, then rising from the ground they went around it, with a movement in unison, their hands resting upon their thighs,

then a little further on they knelt down again, and so on. At the same time, they swayed their bodies, now to the right and now to the left, while uttering at each movement a piercing cry, a veritable yell, *Yrssh! Yrssh! Yrssh!*

(Durkheim 1915: 248–9)

I took a few more liberties than Swain did:

With fires flickering on all sides, bringing out starkly the whiteness of the gum trees against the surrounding night, the Uluuru knelt in single file beside the mound, rising in unison with both hands on their thighs, kneeling again a little farther along, and so on. At the same time, they moved their bodies left and then right, at each movement letting out an echoing scream – actually a howl – at the top of their voices, *Yrssh! Yrssh! Yrssh!*   (Durkheim 1995: 219)

Smith and Alexander (1996: 589) correctly observe that neither of these English reconstructions "quite captures the urgent yet supple rhythm of Durkheim's own writing." Something is inevitably lost in translation, but the two partial translations capture nothing. They delete the passage.

By designating "ethnographic material" as a rubric for what may safely be omitted, both imply a shared interpretive judgment that Durkheim's ethnography is tangential to what he had to say. To obtain excerpts of about 65 pages for *Durkheim on Religion*, Pickering explained ([1975] 1994: 7 and in his *Durkheim's Sociology of Religion* 1984: xxiv), he selected religion only, excluding ethnography and sociology of knowledge, and including nothing from book III, where those subjects are intertwined.[17] Cladis, on the other hand, set out to obtain an *Elementary Forms* three-fourths the length of the original – by including the "main arguments" and "topical issues such as the role of women in religion," but excluding "digressions, redundant examples, endnotes referring to dated controversies and ethnographic material. . . ." (Durkheim 2001: xxxvi).[18]

It is a short step from omitting Durkheim's ethnography at will to handling that evidence as if it was theoretically inert. But is it? According to Parsons, the "narrowly technical empirical material" served as "the vehicle for unusually far-reaching theoretical reasoning." He called *Elementary Forms* a brilliantly-realized "crucial experiment, the intensive study of a limited body of facts, those of Australian totemism" (Parsons [1937] 1968: 411). A contrasting view faults precisely that limited body of facts as a basis for theorizing – essentially one continent and indeed, according to many a bird's-eye summary, essentially one people, the Arunta. If the evidence goes unread, these and similar judgments cannot be evaluated. In fact, the Warramunga, Durkheim's subject just now, figure alongside more than twenty Australian peoples. I believe the comparisons he was able to make (for example, in regard to their varied theories of descent) sharpened his notion of collective representations.[19] Having chosen his route and destination, Durkheim presented the ethnography with care. So to discount it is to seize the author's turn. The point of re-translating an old book is not to perpetuate given understandings of it, but to offer a new audience the wherewithal to read and learn from it for themselves.

To delete ethnography at will, furthermore, is to miss not only Durkheim the scientist, reading his evidence, but also Durkheim the translator, writing it up. Thanks to a French scholar, Jean de Lannoy (1992), we have a detailed analysis of Durkheim's style. He helps us see *Elementary Forms* in its native distinctiveness rather than as a calvary for translators or a frustration to sociological interpreters.[20] In the course of exhibiting Durkheim's systematic use of the rhetorical techniques available to him, de Lannoy singles out the passage just quoted: "Nowhere else is Durkheim's care in the construction of his text more apparent" (1992: 73–5, my translation). There, he translated "almost literally" but "selectively," de Lannoy tells us, correcting the ethnographers' style when he found it *un peu répétitif.* And he alternately used contraction and expansion to intensify the effects. For instance, when Spencer and Gillen say, "stand out in strong contrast," he makes them say *ressortir violemment,* and for "the white trunks of gum trees," they say *la blancheur des gommiers.* Meanwhile, "the darkness beyond" lengthens and rhythmically deepens into *le fond des ténèbres environnants.* Finally, he invented the pounding cadence *Yrrsh! Yrrsh! Yrrsh!* (de Lannoy 1992: 74). The interpretive context of Durkheim's own translation is specific: his forthcoming arguments about thought built amid the frenzy of painted men.

The chapter ends with a hard-to-translate last word on the relationship between religion's *confusions* and science's clear and distinct ideas. Lévi-Strauss, who quoted the passage at length in *Totemism,* called it "Durkheim at his best" ([1962] 1963: 96). The final sentence reads this way: "Elle [la pensée religieuse] emploie, par suite, les mécanismes logiques avec une sorte de gaucherie, mais elle n'en ignore aucun (Durkheim 1912: 342)." Because the verb *ignorer* means both "not to know" and "to pay no attention," something is about to be lost in translation. Swain's rendering loses "not to know": "[I]t [religious thought] consequently employs logical mechanisms with a certain awkwardness, but it ignores none of them" (Durkheim 1915: 272). My own loses "pay no attention": "As a result, it employs logical mechanisms with a certain gaucheness, but none of them are unknown to it" (Durkheim 1995: 241). Rodney Needham's loses the same meaning I do: "[I]t . . . employs logical mechanisms with a kind of awkwardness, but it is ignorant of none of them" ([1962] 1963: 96). Cladis and Cosman (Durkheim 2001) delete the sentence and the nine lines that precede it. Redding neatly tucks in both senses of *ignorer:* "[I]t uses logical mechanisms in a clumsy way, but it does not overlook any of them" (Durkheim [1975] 1994: 144).

Thus far, we have examined problems of equivalence as solved by various translators: non-literal yet faithful rendering; different yet literal and faithful renderings of the same passage; literal rendering with literary re-arrangement; and deletion. Let us turn now to literal renderings that betray the author's meaning by mishandling structural differences between English and French. The need to interpret small words like "the" and "it" is easily overlooked. Examine, from that standpoint, the second "the" in Swain's title, *The Elementary Forms of the Religious Life* for *Les Formes élémentaires de la vie religieuse*. Although *la* can be translated as "the," it cannot always be translated. Thus, *C'est la vie!* means "That's life!" not "That's the life!" Analogously, "religious life" is not the same as "*the* religious life," which has misleading connotations: monasteries and religious virtuosi; beliefs and practices restricted to a separate sphere uniquely their own; and the inward spirituality that C. J. Webb (1916) and Gaston Richard (1923) so passionately affirmed. Most everyday conceptions of "religion" include all of them, but they are not the subject of *Elementary Forms*. I re-titled the book accordingly (see Durkheim 1995: lxi).

The word "it" poses other problems. In this medical analogy, Durkheim's gendered pronouns *il* and *elle* indicate what goes with what:

> Pour bien comprendre un délire et pour pouvoir lui appliquer le traitement le plus approprié, le médecin a besoin de savoir quel en a été le point de départ. Or cet événement est d'autant plus facile à discerner qu'on peut observer ce délire à une période plus proche de ses débuts. Au contraire, plus on laisse à la maladie de se développer, plus il se dérobe à l'observation; c'est que, chemin faisant, toute sorte d'interprétations sont intervenues qui tendent à refouler dans l'inconscient l'état originel et à le remplacer par d'autres à travers lesquels il est parfois malaisé de retrouver le premier. (Durkheim 1912: 10)

Swain loses the thread of what is advancing (the illness) and what is receding (its point of departure), because he renders *il* and *elle* simply as "it":

> In order to understand a hallucination perfectly, and give it its most appropriate treatment, a physician must know its original point of departure. Now this event is proportionately easier to find if he can observe it [what?] near its beginnings. The longer the disease is allowed to develop, the more it [what?] evades observation; that is because all sorts of interpretations have intervened as it [what?] advanced, which tend to force the original state into the background, and across which it is sometimes difficult to find the initial one.
> (Durkheim 1915: 19)

If "Durkheim said" is attached to this mangled English, he is likely to be thought a confused and careless writer.

Look back a moment at *délire*, the illness. A controversy in the journal *Durkheimian Studies* about its proper translation accented the reader's possible misunderstanding. On one view, the trouble with "delirium," for *délire*, was its specifically pathological connotation, as in the drunk's *delirium tremens*. Therefore, "delusion" might keep better faith with Durkheim's insistence on religion's foundation in the real, while keeping his position distinct, in the reader's mind, from Freud's or Marx's.[21] By his own choice of language, however, Durkheim was fighting fire with fire on that very terrain. My view, accordingly, was that whatever damage is done by "delirium" cannot be undone by "delusion." I thought it a better strategy to use a relatively dis-used term, "delirium," thereby slowing the reader down for a moment's reflection on what has been said.

Let me conclude this exploration of equivalence with a more delicate predicament. What should the translator do when a holy/profane dichotomy suddenly appears? In book I, chapter I, Durkheim establishes the sacred/profane dichotomy as the fundamental characteristic of religious phenomena, but he uses holy/profane repeatedly in book II, chapter 2 and again in book III, chapter 2. Faced with this seeming lapse, Swain made repairs by sometimes (though not always) translating *saint* as "sacred" rather than as "holy." Should he have taken that liberty?

Perhaps Swain felt free to do so, because Durkheim had fixed *sacré* very clearly in his definition of religion – things "set apart and forbidden." Ordinarily, we call things "holy" if extra-ordinary properties are held to be inherent in them, and we understand special treatment to be a consequence of those properties. Parsons' "separate and taboo," lacking a verb, leans toward that idea. But Durkheim reversed the order, making sacredness the consequence of rites, of ritual doing that creates what it signifies.[22] Book III, chapter I, is replete with examples and opens this way: "What distinguishes [sacred beings] is a discontinuity between them and profane beings . . . *A whole complex of rites seeks to bring about that separation, which is essential*" (Durkheim 1995: 303, my emphasis). By the end of book III, chapter 2, the reader (of a complete edition) has encountered three species of lice serving as sacred objects, and even sacred excrement (Durkheim 1995: 230 note 43, 334, 336).

Since this distinction is quite clear (*saint* is absent from book III, chapter I) what accounts for Durkheim's shifting between the two pairs elsewhere? Possibly, ordinary usage competed with the technical term. *Saint* and *sacré* are sometimes (but not always) interchangeable in French, as in English; but they diverge as well, just as "holy" and "sacred" do. Compare "sacred cow" and "holy cow." Who says "the Sacred Bible?" Durkheim's shifting may reflect the very power of ordinary usage. My hunch is that those parts of *Elementary Forms* in which he shifts may have been written before he arrived at the sacred/profane dichotomy as the definition of religion.[23] Be that as it may, the *saint/sacré* distinction I propose is devilishly hard to keep hold of, because its two perspectives are combined and in motion: Imagine the emperor with and without his clothes, all at once; or the emperor as emperor and as something else at the same time. Freeze that motion, as Parsons does in the following, and Durkheim's witty illustrations of lice and excrement promptly misfire: "Sacred things are things set apart by a peculiar attitude of respect which is expressed in various ways" (Parsons [1937] 1968: 411).

To conclude: I think Swain was wrong to repair Durkheim's departures from the specialized meanings with which he creatively re-equipped old words. If there is a principle of keeping faith with an author, it covers fault-lines and inconstancies too. My hermeneutic addition of "simplest," without annotation, was wrong for that reason. But there is also a principle of keeping faith with the reader, who cannot know what is indicated by the shifting terms "holy" and "sacred." Correcting silently, and intermittently, Swain betrayed both author and reader.

Translating familiar words

Any translation is an interpretation, as Werkmeister said and as we have abundantly seen. The reverse is not true, however: An interpretation is not a translation. That reality stands out when familiar appearance masks the foreignness of words like *conscience, représentation, idéal,* and *moral.* Just to demonstrate that foreignness requires many words of interpretation. Meanwhile, the translator's work is to devise an equivalent and be brief about it. Thus, Swain usually renders *conscience,* which means both "consciousness" and "conscience," simply as "mind." His choice is accurate, and yet, according to a convention that has developed since, it is inadequate. Following that convention, Pickering and Redding claim that both *conscience* and *représentation* "defy translation," and italicize both ([1975] 1994: ix). For reinforcement in confronting the hermeneutical dragons so identified, they recommend Steven Lukes' *Durkheim: His Life and Work* (1972). There, five interpretive pages examine those two terms alone – which remain in italics for the next 555 pages. This specific solution to a specific problem of translation has the grave inconvenience that it cannot be a general solution to the general problem of translation.

It may be Parsons who instigated this practice and its narrow focus. Two generations ago, he recommended leaving *conscience* untranslated, to avoid the "interpretive bias" he detected in the tendency to ignore "conscience" in favor of its cognitive counterpart, "consciousness."[24] Lost thereby was the close relationship he saw between *conscience collective* and the idea of "common moral values in relation to action" (Parsons [1937] 1968: 309 note 3). Parsons' point about the normative side of *conscience collective* is well taken: Durkheim coined the term in *The Division of Labor in Society* ([1893] 1984), whose subject is indeed imperative norms that govern behavior. Still, if *conscience* is to be left untranslated to forestall interpretive bias against its "moral" content in Durkheim's writing, then *moral* deserves scrutiny of its own. For example, would "moral" in Parsons' sense be left undisturbed if, as Robert Nisbet (1974: 187) has said, *moral* and *social* were "virtually interchangeable" from Montesquieu's day to Durkheim's?

Consider in that light a sentence Swain mishandles by not scrutinizing *moral*. "Morales et en même temps efficaces," Durkheim says, about social forces acting upon individuals. By using "moral," which in English typically has the meaning Parsons intends, Swain begets a false contrast: "moral and *at the same time* efficacious" (Durkheim 1915: 239). Such a contrast is not normally to be expected from the author of a book about imperative norms. Redding's "moral as well as effective" (Durkheim [1975] 1994: 127) brings out the problem more clearly. I tried "moral yet mighty" (Durkheim 1995: 210) and Cosman, "moral and forceful" (Durkheim 2001: 156). None work; the problem is "moral." To release the false contrast, something must replace "moral" to suit *moral* in the sense the *Petit Robert* (1992) lists fifth: "pertaining to the spirit, to thought (as opposed to material and physical)."

With that definition in hand, we more easily follow when Durkheim calls the soul after death *une puissance morale*, "a moral power" (Durkheim 1995: 404), and when, pinpointing the *efficacité morale* of sacrificial rites, he gives us *assistants* whose shed blood is "the soul seen from outside" (Durkheim 1995: 262). Try this elegant formulation: "L'efficacité morale du rite, qui est réelle, a fait croire à son efficacité physique, qui est imaginaire . . ." (Durkheim 1912: 513). A very similar sentence contains the word "ideal."[25] So the *moral* we now have stands at a distance from Parsons' "common moral values in relation to action." It seems more closely related to "consciousness" than to "conscience" – but notice, once again, that French packages the same range of meanings in the word *moral*. And so, we may suppose they are together as well when he speaks of language as *la conscience des consciences* (Durkheim 1995: 445). "We often lie to one another unintentionally," wrote Durkheim, because "we all use the same words without giving them the same meanings" (Durkheim 1995: 437). So now, a question: Which *moral* did Durkheim mean in the phrase Parsons translated as "one moral community called a church?"

The soul as a "moral power" appears in book II, chapter 8, "La Notion d'âme," "The Idea of Soul." Swain mistakenly rendered that title as "The Idea of *the* Soul" – another "the" too many. When Durkheim means *the* soul as an inward, individual possession, he says so; and that contrasts with "soul" without "the," a generic substance or essence thought of as partly independent of individuals. The word *moral*, in the *Petit Robert*'s fifth sense, seems to fit both. Working through book II, chapter 8 with that correction, I was led, by a roundabout route described elsewhere (Fields 1996: 198–200), back to the pair *étendu/inétendu*. In that chapter, Durkheim suggests that soul (as generic essence) serves as a theoretical idea by which the Australians account for descent and, thereby, for social continuity through time. In that way, he is able to show what is real about the Warramungas' collective memory and collective representation of their ancestor, the snake. Soul, whether generic or individual, is opposed to body. It is real, but without extension. The Warramunga people's shared resemblance to Wollunqua – and to one another – depended neither on the biology of procreation nor on that of appearance: they painted it on and acted it out.

Real but without extension, that resemblance could be felt inwardly and visibly made, all at the same time. So the pair *étendu/inétendu* invoked Descartes' famous pair *res extensa / res cogitans* – extended thing/thinking thing, or body/soul.[26] Though it was a mystery to Swain, and to Redding later on, for Durkheim's original audience, the reference undoubtedly lay in plain sight.[27] Here, then, is my rendering of the monster that stopped Swain:

> Nothing comes out of nothing. The sensations the world evokes in us cannot, by definition, contain anything that goes beyond that world. From something tangible, one can only make something tangible; from extended substance one cannot make unextended substance. (Durkheim 1995: 226)

In short, we have something imagined, yet real, that is added to physical things or to people. What is added possesses the objectivity of things but not their materiality. The words *moral, idéal, spirituel, social* – and of course *sacré* – stand together on the soul (mind) side of this Durkheimian terrain, where their meanings take on shapes unlike those of their English counterparts. Obviously, *conscience* and *représentation* stand with them. How should they be translated?

Anxious about these bugbears of Durkheim translation as I began my work, I sought advice from my colleague, the late Lewis R. Beck, a philosopher. He told me that the heavy weather surrounding *représentation* and its kindred verbs resulted from bad Kant translation. "All you need," he said, is "the idea of something present to the mind," and he made a graceful two-handed gesture around his head. For the verb forms of *se représenter*, "*present* to the mind," "conceive," "imagine," "picture," and the like, were all *fine*. I took his advice. Literal rendering of the verb *se représenter* yields "represent to oneself," a result that can be quite misleading. When I first read Swain's rendering, in which religion is "a system of ideas with which the individuals represent to themselves the society of which they are members" (Durkheim 1915: 257), I imagined people making emblems. But a "*system* of ideas" is precisely what an emblem cannot be. "Imagine" made sense.

Se représenter can also mean "remember" or "recall." That sense yields "representative or commemorative rites" (book III, chapter 4) – like those of the Warramunga people that recall their common history and common descent. The non-reflexive form, *représenter*, means "stand for," in line with our typical use of the noun "representation" as well. That meaning gives us their snake-like movements. But beware: everyday English usage gives us neither the performance nor the commemoration, with Wollunqua as centerpiece, that this example of *représentation* puts before us. Notice that the Warramunga make their time immemorial present – to the senses and to the mind – by enacting it in a rite that creates what it signifies. A final trait of *représentation* (in common with *conscience*) is its ambiguity as between a capacity of the mind and the mind's content, a process and a product, thinking and something thought of, and in the end, therefore, mind itself both within and outside individuals.

Armed with this much, the reader can meet Durkheim halfway when he uses the term *représentation* in the passage Swain accidentally dropped (above, p. 164): "the sacred beings exist only in and through their representations," and in the footnote where he adds: "In a philosophical sense, the same is true of anything, for things exist only through representation. But as I have shown . . . this proposition is doubly true of religious forces, because there is nothing in the makeup of things that corresponds to sacredness" (Durkheim 1995: 349 note 55). With that statement about sacredness, we arrive at a *collective* representation, and at workings of the *collective* consciousness (or conscience). Sacredness cannot be sacredness if present to only one mind, a single *conscience*. Such was the predicament of Freud's cases, described in *Totem and Taboo* (1913); and, as Origen noticed almost two millennia ago, an analogous predicament inheres in every attempt to recount someone else's mystical experience (Ashton 2003). What distinguishes sacredness is that the faithful all witness it together; they witness it as inherent in things around them. Accordingly, they do not form a "group mind," the captive of collectivity; instead, they have and inhabit the same real world. In conclusion, then, if asked what Durkheim meant by the phrase "a moral community called a Church," one might answer, "an imagined community," one whose ties that bind also define a world.

"Something is always lost in translation," says the adage. But St. Jerome's ancient description of the translator's work stands as a reminder that something is also, quite literally, gained: adding, changing, and even correcting, as he bluntly insisted, the work of an artisan. His Latin-speaking audience wanted to read the Bible in their own language, but its books had to be rebuilt on linguistic terrain foreign to them. Not only did vocabulary, grammar, and syntax have to be reconstructed, but so, too, did the rhetorical and stylistic conventions the original authors used. Now, as then, that reconstruction cannot even begin without interpretation, and the inevitable end result of all such reconstruction is divergence, of one kind and another, between what X said and what X is made to say. Now, as then, furthermore, the translator's work is easily mis-imagined as a kind of mediumship, to be judged false or faithful by simple reference to the original. But we have seen that the original cannot dictate as to a medium. In any case, it is never a medium who brings the message – and, as Jerome's annoyance makes plain, not always a silent audience who receives it.

NOTES

Thanks to Moussa Bagate, Barbara J. Fields, Terry F. Godlove, and, most of all, to Egon Bittner, who is still my teacher.
1 I borrow this formulation from Werkmeister (1982).
2 Hereafter referred to as Durkheim 1915.
3 Hereafter referred to as Durkheim 1995.
4 Hereafter referred to individually, as Pickering or Redding (Durkheim [1975] 1994), according to their respective functions.
5 Hereafter referred to individually, as Cladis or Cosman (Durkheim 2001), according to their respective functions.
6 "A Study in Religious Sociology" initially replaced the French subtitle but was later dropped. I followed suit (Durkheim 1995).
7 After translating *Elementary Forms*, Swain published a monograph on early Christianity and four books on European history.
8 For a quite different interpretation, see Pickering (1984: 102ff).
9 Compare Cosman's translation (Durkheim 2001: 143, 229) where the hermeneutic additions discussed in this section are adopted but not annotated. The passages in question are not included in Pickering's ([1975] 1994) *Durkheim on Religion*.
10 Durkheim repeatedly said otherwise (see, e.g. Durkheim 1995: 191). Also, see Lévi-Strauss' comment about "to be," in *Totemism* ([1962] 1963: 93) and his view (pp. 1–3) that the nineteenth-century fascination with totemism reflected an urge to draw strong distinctions between Europe's mental habits and those of peoples elsewhere.

KAREN E. FIELDS

11 On the other hand, the *Century Dictionary* lists "assistance" meaning "spectators" as "obsolete or in conscious imitation of the French" (1901: 348).

12 Others appear in my translation (Durkheim 1995: 351 note 64, 446, and elsewhere); all are marked.

13 Note that Parsons envisages adherence to "it," the system.

14 *Le Petit Robert* (1992) is my main reference throughout.

15 See Aron (1967: 27) who mentions this feature of *Suicide* but ignores it in *Elementary Forms*.

16 I claim them in my own historical study (Fields 1985) of millenarian beliefs whose corresponding rites, such as talking in tongues, have in some times and places proved effective against political power.

17 But Durkheim deployed his sociology of knowledge throughout *Elementary Forms*, a book about "religious life." As early as 1899, he expressly refused to say simply "religion," full stop. See "On the Definition of Religious Phenomena," in *Durkheim on Religion* (Pickering [1975] 1994: 74).

18 The abridgement cuts about 150 pages and 1,050 notes.

19 Durkheim's exploration of descent – in book II, chapter 8 – can be applied to races, a singularly durable collective representation in American life (see Fields 1996, 2001, 2002).

20 See, e.g. Pickering and Redding ([1975] 1994: ix) and Lukes (1972: 31–6). See, also, Aron (1967: 27) who in passing identifies Durkheim's argument by elimination in *Suicide* as the trademark of a "good *normalien*" – that is, a product of the École Normale Supérieure, the *crème de la crème* of higher education in France.

21 See Lutzky (1997: 15–19) and the rejoinders by Pickering and Redding (1997). I responded the following year (Fields 1998). See also Pickering's (1984: 136) discussion of Durkheim's phrase "a delirium that is well founded."

22 I draw this formulation from Jay (1992: 1–16).

23 See, e.g. Durkheim's 1899 piece, "Concerning the Definition of Religious Phenomena" (in Pickering [1975] 1994: 74–99), which has no sacred/profane dichotomy.

24 For a perceptive account of *conscience* in its multiple meanings, see Bohannan (1960).

25 "[B]ien que purement idéals, les pouvoirs qui lui sont ainsi conférés agissent comme s'ils étaient réels; ils déterminent la conduite de l'homme avec la même nécessité que les forces physiques" (Durkheim 1912: 399).

26 I here correct my mistake (Durkheim 1995: 226) in presenting that pair as *res extensa/res inextensa*.

27 This is not to say Descartes would have countenanced this permutation of his thought.

REFERENCES

Aron, Raymond. 1967. *Main Currents of Sociological Thought II*. Translated by Richard Howard and Helen Weaver. New York: Doubleday.

Ashton, John. 2003. "The Religious Experience of Jesus." The 2002–3 William James Lecture. *Harvard Divinity Bulletin*, Fall/Winter 2003: 17.

Bohannan, Paul. 1960. "*Conscience Collective* and Culture." pp. 77–96 in *Émile Durkheim, 1858–1917*. Edited by Kurt H. Wolff. Columbus, OH: Ohio State University Press.

The Century Dictionary and Cyclopedia. 1901. New York: Century.

de Lannoy, Jean. 1992. "Le Style de *Les Formes Élémentaires de la vie religieuse* d'Émile Durkheim." *Durkheimian Studies* 2: 61–78.

Durkheim, Émile. 2001. *The Elementary Forms of Religious Life.* Edited and with an introduction by Mark S. Cladis. Translated by Carol Cosman. Oxford: Oxford University Press.

1995. *The Elementary Forms of Religious Life.* Translated and with an introduction by Karen E. Fields. New York: Free Press.

1918. Unsigned Review of *The Elementary Forms of the Religious Life: A Study in Religious Sociology.* Translated by J. W. Swain (London: George Allen and Unwin, *The Monist* 28, 158–9.)

[1915] 1964. *The Elementary Forms of the Religious Life.* Translated by Joseph Ward Swain. New York: Free Press.

1912. *Les Formes élémentaires de la vie religieuse: le système totémique en Australie.* Paris: Alcan.

[1893] 1984. *The Division of Labor in Society.* Translated by W. D. Halls. New York: Macmillan.

Eliot, T. Stearns. 1916. "Review of C. J. Webb, *Group Theories of Religion and the Religion of the Individual.*" *International Journal of Ethics* 27: 115–17.

Fields, Karen E. 2002. "Individuality and the Intellectuals: An Imaginary Conversation between Emile Durkheim and W. E. B. Du Bois." *Theory and Society* 31: 435–62.

2001. "Witchcraft and Racecraft: Invisible Ontology in Its Sensible Manifestations." pp. 283–319 in *Witchcraft Dialogs: Anthropological and Philosophical Exchanges.* Edited by George Bond and Diane Ciekawy. Athens, OH: Ohio University Press.

1998. "More on Translating *Délire.*" *Durkheimian Studies* 4: 30–31.

1996. "Durkheim and the Idea of Soul." *Theory and Society* 25: 193–203.

1985. *Revival and Rebellion in Colonial Central Africa.* Princeton, NJ: Princeton University Press.

The Gale Group. 2004. "Joseph Ward Swain, 1891–1971." *Contemporary Authors Online.* Available at http://galenet.galegroup.com/servlet/LitRC?vrsn.

Glassman, Eugene H. 1981. *The Translation Debate: What Makes a Bible Translation Good?* Downers Grove, IL: InterVarsity Press.

Goldenweiser, A. A. 1915. "Review: *Les Formes élémentaires de la vie religieuse.*" In *Durkheim on Religion.* Edited by W. S. F. Pickering. Translations by Jacqueline Redding. ([1975] 1994). Atlanta, GA: Scholars Press.

Jay, Nancy. 1992. *Throughout Your Generations Forever: Sacrifice, Religion, and Paternity.* Chicago: University of Chicago Press.

Kant, Immanuel. 1998. *Critique of Pure Reason.* Translated and edited by Paul Guyer and Allen W. Wood. Cambridge: Cambridge University Press.

Lévi-Strauss, Claude. [1962] 1963. *Totemism.* Translated by Rodney Needham. Boston, MA: Beacon Press.

Lukes, Steven. 1972. *Durkheim: His Life and Work.* New York: Harper and Row.

Lutzky, Helen. 1997. "*Délire*: Delirium or Delusion?" *Durkheimian Studies,* 3: 15–19.

Nisbet, Robert. 1974. *The Sociology of Émile Durkheim.* New York: Oxford University Press.

Parsons, Talcott. [1937] 1968. *The Structure of Social Action*. New York: Free Press.

Le Petit Robert: *Dictionnaire de la langue française*. 1992. Paris: Dictionnaires Le Robert.

Pickering, W. S. F. 1984. *Durkheim's Sociology of Religion: Themes and Theories*. London: Routledge and Kegan Paul.

—— ed. [1975] 1994. *Durkheim on Religion*. Translations by Jacqueline Redding. Atlanta, GA: Scholars Press.

Pickering, W. S. F. and Jacqueline Redding. 1997. Rejoinders to Helen Lutzky "*Délire*: Delirium or Delusion?" *Durkheimian Studies* 3: 16–19.

Richard, Gaston. 1923. "Dogmatic Atheism in the Sociology of Religion." pp. 228–76 in *Durkheim on Religion*. Edited by W. S. F. Pickering. Translations by Jacqueline Redding. ([1975] 1994). Atlanta, GA: Scholars Press.

Smith, Philip, and Jeffrey C. Alexander. 1996. "Review Essay: Durkheim's Religious Revival." *American Journal of Sociology* 102(2): 585–92.

Spencer, Baldwin and Francis James Gillen. 1904. *Northern Tribes of Central Australia*. London: Macmillan.

Stern, Robert. 1999. Review of *Critique of Pure Reason*, by Immanuel Kant. Translated and edited by Paul Guyer and Allen W. Wood (Cambridge: Cambridge University Press, 1998) in *Kantian Review* 3: 137–40.

Webb, C. J. 1916. *Group Theories of Religion and the Religion of the Individual*. London: Allen and Unwin.

Werkmeister, W. H. 1982. "What Did Kant Say and What Has He Been Made to Say?" pp. 133–45 in *Interpreting Kant*. Edited by Moltke S. Gram. Iowa City: University of Iowa Press.

II
SYMBOLS, RITUALS, AND BODIES

8

ROBERT N. BELLAH

Durkheim and ritual

Although this chapter will begin with Émile Durkheim's ([1912] 1995) *The Elementary Forms of Religious Life (Elementary Forms)*, I will focus on the place of ritual in the Durkheimian tradition, rather than add to the already enormous amount of explication of that book and the place of ritual in it.[1] Even so, because of the vast influence of Durkheim on several disciplines, my treatment will be highly selective. I will focus on the ways in which ritual continues to be central for the understanding not only of religion, but of society.

There is probably no better place to begin a discussion of the place of ritual in the thought of Émile Durkheim than with a famous passage in his *Elementary Forms*:

> Life in Australian [Aboriginal] societies alternates between two different phases. In one phase, the population is scattered in small groups that attend to their occupations independently. Each family lives to itself, hunting, fishing – in short, striving by all possible means to get the food it requires. In the other phase, by contrast, the population comes together, concentrating itself at specified places for a period that varies from several days to several months. This concentration takes place when a clan or a portion of the tribe . . . conducts a religious ceremony.
>
> These two phases stand in the sharpest possible contrast. The first phase, in which economic activity predominates, is generally of rather low intensity. Gathering seeds or plants necessary for food, hunting, and fishing are not occupations that can stir truly strong passions. The dispersed state in which the society finds itself makes life monotonous, slack, and humdrum. Everything changes when a [ceremony] takes place . . . Once the individuals are gathered together a sort of electricity is generated from their closeness and quickly launches them into an extraordinary height of exaltation . . . Probably because a collective emotion cannot be expressed collectively without some order that permits harmony and unison of movement, [their] gestures and cries tend to fall into rhythm and regularity, and from there into songs and dances . . .
>
> (Durkheim [1912] 1995: 216–18)

Thus Durkheim makes his critical distinction between profane time, which is "monotonous, slack and humdrum," and sacred time, which he characterizes as "collective effervescence." Sacred time is devoted primarily to ritual. Further, the community that ritual creates is at the center of Durkheim's definition of religion: "A religion is a unified system of beliefs and practices relative to sacred things, that is to say, things set apart and forbidden – beliefs and practices which unite into one single moral community called a Church, all those who adhere to them" (Durkheim [1912] 1995: 44).[2]

Although Durkheim speaks of "beliefs and practices" and organizes his work in three books, the first introductory, the second and much the longest on beliefs, and the third on ritual practices, it would not be right to assume that Durkheim privileges beliefs over practices. We learn from what is perhaps the key chapter of the whole book, book II, chapter 5, entitled "Origin of These Beliefs," that ritual is prior to belief and gives rise to it:

> Collective representations . . . presuppose that consciousnesses are acting and reacting on each other; they result from actions and reactions that are possible only with the help of tangible intermediaries. Thus the function of the intermediaries is not merely to reveal the mental state associated with them; they also contribute to its making. The individual minds can meet and commune only if they come outside themselves, but they do this only by means of movement. It is the homogeneity of these movements that makes the group aware of itself and that, in consequence, makes it be. Once this homogeneity has been established and these movements have taken a definite form and been stereotyped, they serve to symbolize the corresponding representations. But these movements symbolize those representations only because they have helped to form them.
> (Durkheim [1912] 1995: 232)[3]

Collective representations – beliefs – are essential in the process through which society becomes aware of itself, but they arise from and express the homogeneous physical movements that constitute the ritual, not the other way around. Thus Durkheim does not authorize a "symbolic interpretation" of ritual that attempts to read off symbolic meaning from observed events. Rather he would interpret the "emblems," as he calls them, the bullroarers or other ritual implements engraved with abstract totemic designs, in terms of the ritual actions within which they are used. Meaning arises from this totality, not as an interpretation of it.

Mary Douglas, whose work will be discussed further below, offers the idea of the exemplar as a way of avoiding the distinction between the real and the symbolic. She cites Godfrey Lienhardt's work on Dinka ritual as "a model of cognition based on repeated enactment of exemplars," which does not point beyond itself "symbolically":

A Dinka rite mimes a wish, the miming articulates an intention. The community
that has killed and eaten together the sacrificial ox has enacted some of its
complex intentions about itself. It would be absurd to say that their ritual has
represented a communion meal, when they have just eaten one. Their wish
for community to be possessed by divinity is realized (not represented) in the
trance of their priests whom the spirit does possess. The quivering flesh of the
dying victim is not symbolizing something other than itself, it is an example of
the same quivering in the flesh of the person in trance. The community is not
depicting something but giving itself a sample of its idea of true community.
Against this sample it measures its own achievement of the ideal. The sacrifice
is a self-referencing enactment. In structuring the community's self-perception
it structures its future behavior: as Goodman says, the version of the world
that has been adopted itself affects the world.   (Douglas 1992: 249–51)[4]

Thus with respect to the Durkheimian understanding of ritual it is social
enactment that is primary. A world of symbolic meanings can and does arise
from such enactments, a world with many implications for the rest of social
life, but the ritual enactment retains its primacy and cannot be reduced to
the symbols that derive from it.

Since ritual, for Durkheim, is primarily about the sacred in a sense in which
the religious and the social are almost interchangeable, subsequent work on
ritual under his influence has not moved far beyond him by placing ritual at
the core of any kind of social interaction whatsoever. While on the one hand
this might be seen as broadening the idea of ritual to include "secular ritual,"
the same development might be seen as disclosing an element of the sacred,
and thus of the religious, at the very basis of social action of any kind.
Recent work of Randall Collins represents this development most clearly.
In *The Sociology of Philosophies: A Global Theory of Intellectual Change*
(1998), Collins combines Durkheim and Goffman to define the basic social
event as, in Goffman's (1967) phrase, an interaction ritual.[5] At the most
fundamental level interaction rituals involve:

1. a group of at least two people physically assembled;
2. who focus attention on the same object or action, and each becomes
   aware that the other is maintaining this focus;
3. who share a common mood or emotion.

In this process of ritual interaction the members of the group, through their
shared experience, feel a sense of membership, however fleeting, with a sense
of boundary between those sharing the experience and all those outside it;
they feel some sense of moral obligation to each other, which is symbolized
by whatever they focused on during the interaction; and, finally, they are
charged with what Collins calls emotional energy but which he identifies

with what Durkheim called moral force. Since, according to Collins (1998: 22–4), all of social life consists of strings of such ritual interactions, then ritual becomes the most fundamental category for the understanding of social action. Collins then makes another move that has, I believe, the greatest significance:

> Language itself is the product of a pervasive natural ritual. The rudimentary act of speaking involves the ingredients listed at the outset of this chapter: group assembly, mutual focus, common sentiment; as a result, words are collective representations, loaded with moral significance. (Collins 1998: 47)

Ritual and the origin of language

This observation of Collins, in turn, suggests a digression into the present evolutionary understanding of the origin of language. The origin of language was for long a taboo subject because it opened the door to unrestrained speculation. The question remains and probably will always remain, speculative, but advances in neurophysiology on the one hand and Paleolithic archeology on the other have opened the door to much more disciplined forms of speculation such as that of Terrence Deacon in his book *The Symbolic Species: The Co-Evolution of Language and the Brain* (1997). Deacon is a biological anthropologist and neuroscientist and is trying to understand the emergence of language among our ancestral hominids whose brains were not organized for language use, although, as we know, our nearest primate relatives can, with the most enormous effort and external training, be taught at least a rudimentary use of words. But, as Deacon puts it, "The first hominids to use symbolic communication were entirely on their own, with very little in the way of external supports. How then, could they have succeeded with their chimpanzee-like brains in achieving this difficult result? . . . In a word, the answer is ritual" (1997: 402).

Deacon makes the case for the parallel between teaching symbolic communication to chimpanzees and the origin of language in ritual as follows:

> Indeed, ritual is still a central component of symbolic "education" in modern societies, though we are seldom aware of its modern role because of the subtle way it is woven into the fabric of society. The problem for symbolic discovery is to shift attention from the concrete to the abstract; from separate indexical links between signs and objects to an organized set of relations between signs. In order to bring the logic of [sign–sign] relations to the fore, a high degree of redundancy is important. This was demonstrated in the experiments with the chimpanzees . . . It was found that getting them to repeat by rote a large number of errorless trials in combining lexigrams enabled them to make the transition

from explicit and concrete sign–object associations to implicit sign–sign associations. Repetition of the same set of actions with the same set of objects over and over again in a ritual performance is often used for a similar purpose in modern human societies. Repetition can render the individual details of some performance automatic and minimally conscious, while at the same time the emotional intensity induced by group participation can help focus attention on other aspects of the object and actions involved. In a ritual frenzy, one can be induced to see everyday activities and objects in a very different light.

(Deacon 1997: 402–3)[6]

But if repetition and redundancy are always, as we shall see, important in ritual, what was the evolutionary push that made the transition from indexical to symbolic signs essential, and therefore the ritual mechanism so indispensable? Deacon describes the situation at the period of this critical transition:

The near synchrony in human prehistory of the first increase of brain size, the first appearance of stone tools for hunting and butchery, and a considerable reduction in sexual dimorphism is not a coincidence. These changes are interdependent. All are symptoms of a fundamental restructuring of the hominid adaptation, which resulted in a significant change in feeding ecology, a radical change in social structure, and an unprecedented (indeed, revolutionary) change in representational abilities. The very first symbols ever thought, or acted out, or uttered on the face of the earth grew out of this socio-ecological dilemma, and so they may not have been very much like speech. They also probably required considerable complexity of social organization to bring the unprepared brains of these apes to comprehend fully what they meant . . . Symbolic culture was a response to a reproductive problem that only symbols could solve: the imperative of representing a social contract.

(Deacon 1997: 401)

Ritual is common in the animal world, including among the primates. But non-human ritual is always indexical, not symbolic; that is, it points to present realities, not to future contingencies. The primary focus of animal ritual is on issues of great importance and uncertainty: sex and aggression. Through ritual actions animals represent to each other their readiness or unreadiness for sexual contact or for combat. Through the ritual "dance" an unwilling partner may be "persuaded" to engage in sexual intercourse, or an originally combative opponent may be persuaded to offer signs of submission. Such ritual behaviors help to make possible these inherently difficult transactions.

The "reproductive problem" to which Deacon suggests symbolism was the solution, however, required more than assuring a present response; it required assurance of future actions – it required promises. At the point where efficient adaptation to the environment made cross-gender pair bonding necessary, with its division of labor between the provision of meat and care of infants, the stability of what was now necessarily "marriage" required more than non-symbolic ritual:

> Sexual or mating displays are incapable of referring to what might be, or should be. This information can only be given expression symbolically. The pair bonding in the human lineage is essentially a promise, or rather a set of promises that must be made public. These not only determine what behaviors are probable in the future, but more important, they implicitly determine which future behaviors are allowed and not allowed; that is, which are defined as cheating and may result in retaliation. (Deacon 1997: 399)

Another advantage of symbolic ritual as against purely non-human animal ritual is that it gives rise not to ad hoc relationships, but to a whole system of relationships:

> Ritualized support is also essential to ensure that all members of the group understand the newly established contract and will behave accordingly. As in peacemaking, demonstrating that these relationships exist and providing some way of marking them for future reference so that they can be invoked and enforced demand the explicit presentation of supportive indices, not just from reproductive partners but from all significant kin and group members . . .
>
> Marriage and puberty rituals serve this function in most human societies . . . The symbol construction that occurs in these ceremonies is not just a matter of demonstrating certain symbolic relationships, but actually involves the use of individuals and actions as symbol tokens. Social roles are redefined and individuals are explicitly assigned to them. A wife, a husband, a warrior, a father-in-law, an elder – all are symbolic roles, not reproductive roles, and as such are defined with respect to a complete system of alternative or complementary symbolic roles. Unlike social status in other species, which is a more-or-less relationship in potential flux, symbolic status is categorical. As with all symbolic relationships, social roles are defined in the context of a logically complete system of potential transformations; and because of this, all members of a social group (as well as any potential others from the outside) are assigned an implicit symbolic relationship when any one member changes status. (Deacon 1997: 406)[7]

And Deacon points out that, over the last million years, although language undoubtedly developed toward more self-sufficient vocal symbol systems, whose very power was the degree to which they could become context-free, nonetheless, "symbols are still extensively tied to ritual-like cultural practices and paraphernalia. Though speech is capable of conveying many forms of information independent of any objective supports, in practice there are often extensive physical and social contextual supports that affect what is communicated" (1997: 407).

Deacon's argument runs remarkably parallel to that of Goffman, Collins, and of course Durkheim. The point is that symbolism (including centrally language), social solidarity based on a moral order, and individual motivation to conform, all depend on ritual. But Deacon, as we have seen, has indicated that the very first emergence of symbolism "may not have been very much like speech." There is reason to believe that full linguisticality, language as, with all its diversity, all known human cultures have had it, is relatively recent, perhaps no older than the species *Homo sapiens sapiens*, that is 120,000 years old (Nichols 1998). But symbol-using hominids have been around for at least a million years. Can we say anything about what kind of proto-language such hominids might have used? Perhaps we can in a way that will further illuminate the nature of ritual.

Ritual and the origin of music

While in the last decade or two a number of valuable books concerned with the origins of language have been published, it was not until the year 2000 that an important volume entitled *The Origins of Music* appeared. A number of articles in this edited volume by Wallin, Merker, and Brown begin to indicate what the "ritual" that Deacon suggests provided the context for the origin of language might have been like: namely, it involved music. The ethnomusicologist Bruno Nettle, in discussing features of music found in all cultures, writes: "It is important to consider also certain universals that do not involve musical sound or style. I mentioned the importance of music in ritual, and, as it were, in addressing the supernatural. This seems to me to be truly a universal, shared by all known societies, however different the sound" (2000: 468). He draws from this the conclusion that the "earliest human music was somehow associated with ritual" (Nettle 2000: 472). But "music" in most cultures involves more than what can simply be heard, as our current usage of the word implies. As Walter Freeman puts it, "Music involves not just the auditory system but the somatosensory and motor systems as well, reflecting its strong associations with dance, the rhythmic tapping, stepping, clapping, and chanting that accompany and indeed produce music" (2000: 412). And Ellen Dissanayake writes, "I suggest that in their origins, movement and music were inseparable, as they are today in premodern societies and in children . . . I consider it essential that we incorporate movement (or kinesics) with song as integral to our thinking about the evolutionary origin of music" (2000: 397).

While the contributors to *The Origins of Music* are not of one mind about the social function of music that gave it its evolutionary value, several of them emphasize the role of music in the creation of social solidarity. As Freeman puts it, "Here [in music] in its purest form is a human technology for crossing the solipsistic gulf. It is wordless [not necessarily, R. B.], illogical, deeply emotional, and selfless in its actualization of transient and then lasting harmony between individuals . . . It constructs the sense of trust and predictability in each member of the community on which social interactions are based" (2000: 420). Dissanayake, who locates music fundamentally in the mother–infant relationship in the human species with its much longer period of infant dependence on adult care, compared to any other species, writes:

> I suggest that the biologically endowed sensitivities and competencies of mother–infant interaction were found by evolving human groups to be emotionally affecting and functionally effective when used and when further shaped and elaborated in culturally created ceremonial rituals where they served a similar purpose – to attune or synchronize, emotionally conjoin, and enculturate the participants. These unifying and pleasurable features (maintained in children's play) made up a sort of behavioral reservoir from which human cultures could appropriate appealing and compelling components for communal ceremonial rituals that similarly promoted affiliation and congruence in adult social life. (Dissanayake 2000: 401)

Finally Freeman, unlike Deacon, brings us back to Durkheim when he quotes a passage from *Elementary Forms*:

> Émile Durkheim described the socializing process as the use of ". . . totemic emblems by clans to express and communicate collective representations," which begins where the individual feels he *is* the totem and evolves beliefs that he will become the totem or that his ancestors are in the totem. Religious rites and ceremonies lead to "collective mental states of extreme emotional intensity, in which representation is still undifferentiated from the movements and actions which make the communion toward which it tends a reality to the group. Their participation in it is *so effectively lived* that it is not yet properly imagined." (Freeman 2000: 419)

Dissanayake emphasizes the socializing and enculturating aspects of the quasi-ritual interactions between mother and infant, interactions that actually create the psychological, social and cultural capacity of children to become full participants in society. While we might think of these "socializing" or even "normalizing" functions of ritual as Durkheimian, we should not forget that Durkheim believed that through experiences of collective effervescence, not only was society reaffirmed, but new, sometimes radically new, social innovations were made possible. Freeman puts this insight into the language of contemporary neurobiology:

> I conclude that music and dance originated through biological evolution of brain chemistry, which interacted with the cultural evolution of behavior. This led to the development of chemical and behavioral technology for inducing altered states of consciousness. The role of trance states was particularly important for breaking down preexisting habit and beliefs. That meltdown appears to be necessary for personality changes leading to the formation of social groups by cooperative action leading to trust. Bonding is not simply a release of a neurochemical in an altered state. It is the social action of dancing and singing together that induces new forms of behavior, owing to the malleability that can come through the altered state. It is reasonable to suppose that musical skills played a major role early in the evolution of human intellect, because they made possible formation of human societies as a prerequisite for the transmission of acquired knowledge across generations. (Freeman 2000: 422)

Having seen how much light this new work on the origins of music has shed on questions of the place of ritual in human evolution, let us finally return to the question raised by Deacon about the fact that early symbol use "may not have been very much like speech," but was probably some kind of proto-language. Steven Brown (2000) starts from the point that, though language and music today are clearly different in that their primary locations in the brain are different, nonetheless, even in terms of brain physiology, there is a great deal of overlap between them. He then suggests that language and music form a continuum rather than an absolute dichotomy, with language in the sense of sound as referential meaning at one end, and music in the sense of sound as emotive meaning at the other. What is interesting is the range of things in between, with verbal song at the mid-point (verbal song is the commonest form of music worldwide). Moving toward language as referential meaning from the mid-point we have poetic discourse, *recitativo*, and heightened speech. Moving toward music as emotive meaning from the mid-point we have "word painting," *Leitmotifs*, and musical narration (Brown 2000: 275). From this existing continuum, from features of their overlapping location in brain physiology, and from parsimony in explanation, Brown argues that rather than music and language evolving separately, or emerging one from the other, the likeliest account is that both developed from something that was simultaneously proto-language and proto-music and that he calls "musilanguage" (2000: 277). If we postulate that musilanguage was also enacted, that is, involved meaningful gesture as well as sound, then we can see ritual as a primary evolutionary example of musilanguage and note that even today ritual is apt to be a kind of musilanguage: however sophisticated its verbal, musical, and gestural components have become, they are still deeply implicated with each other.

The nature of ritual

Having considered the roots of ritual and its most fundamental human functions, we will now consider somewhat more closely the basic features of ritual. The most important book on ritual in recent years is Roy Rappaport's *Ritual and Religion in the Making of Humanity* (1999),[8] a book immersed in the Durkheimian anthropological tradition. Rappaport's first, and highly condensed, definition of ritual is "the performance of more or less invariant sequences of formal acts and utterances not entirely encoded by the performers" (1999: 24). Rappaport's stress on "invariant sequences of formal acts and utterances" brings us back to features of musilanguage that may have been essential in the transformation of meaningless sound sequences into highly condensed, in the sense of undifferentiated, but still referentially/emotively meaningful, sound events. A key aspect of these transitional events is redundancy, essential in helping humans move from indexical to symbolic meaning. According to Bruce Richman, musical redundancy is communicated in three forms: (1) repetition, (2) formulaicness, that is "the storehouse of preexisting formulas, riffs, themes, motifs and rhythms," and (3) expectancy "of exactly what is going to come next and fill the upcoming temporal slot" (2000: 304). In the redundancy created by expectancy, the most important element is tempo, the rhythm that may be created by drumming, the stamping of feet, or other means. It is noteworthy that humans are the only primates with the ability to keep time to an external timekeeper, such as the beating of a drum (Brown, Merker, and Wallin 2000: 12). This ability to "keep together in time" (McNeill 1995) is probably one of several biological developments that have evolved synchronously with the development of culture, but one of great importance for the ritual roots of society.[9] In any case it is closely related to the "more or less invariant sequences of formal acts and utterances" that are central to Rappaport's definition of ritual.

From his very condensed original definition of ritual Rappaport draws implications, which he spends the rest of a rather long book developing. For our purposes, the most important implications have to do with the creation of social conventions, a moral order, a sense of the sacred, and a relationship to the cosmos, including beliefs about what lies behind the empirical cosmos (1999: 27). Rappaport, like most other writers on ritual, is aware of the wide variety of actions that can be classified under this term. One defining feature of ritual for him is performance (1999: 37). In his usage of this potentially ambiguous term, performance carries the sense of what is called in the philosophy of language performative speech: something is not simply described or symbolized, but done, enacted. This gets back to Deacon's point about promises or Freeman's emphasis on trust. The sheer act of participating in serious rituals entails a commitment with respect to future action, at the very least solidarity with one's fellow communicants. Thus, as Rappaport uses the term, it would explicitly not be the same as participating in a dramatic "performance," where the actor sheds the "role" as soon as the performance is over, and the audience, however moved, goes away knowing it was "only a play."[10] On the contrary, serious ritual performance has the capacity to transform not only the role but the personality of the participant, as in rites of passage (van Gennep [1908] 1960). The fundamental relationship between saying and doing Rappaport sees as establishing "convention in ritual" and the "social contract and morality that inhere in it." This is the ground, he argues, for "taking ritual to be humanity's basic social act" (Rappaport 1999: 107).

Talal Asad (1993) in an important critique of anthropological theories of ritual as "symbolic action," that is, action whose meaning can simply be read off by the anthropological observer, emphasizes instead the older Christian meaning of ritual as discipline. In this he would seem, in part, to be paralleling Rappaport's distinction between dramatic performance, which is expressive of meaning but has no moral consequence, and ritual as performative in the sense of a fundamental change of disposition on the part of the participant. Asad writes:

> [T]he idea of the sacraments as metaphorical representations inhabits an entirely different world from the one that gives sense to Hugh of St. Victor's theology: "Sacraments," he stated, "are known to have been instituted for three reasons: on account of humiliation, on account of instruction, on account of exercise." According to this latter conception, the sacraments are not the representation of cultural metaphors; they are parts of a Christian program for creating in its performers, by means of regulated practice, the "mental and moral dispositions" appropriate to Christians.   (Asad 1993: 78)

It is precisely the element of discipline or external constraint that Radcliffe-Brown, as quoted by Rappaport, sees in the ritual dances of the Andaman Islanders:

> The Andaman dance, then, is a complete activity of the whole community in which every able-bodied adult takes part, and is also an activity to which, so far as the dancer is concerned, the whole personality is involved, by the intervention of all the muscles of the body, by the concentration of attention required, and by its action on the personal sentiments. In the dance the individual submits

to the action upon him of the community; he is constrained by the immediate effect of rhythm, as well as by custom, to join in, and he is required to conform in his own actions and movements to the needs of the common activity. The surrender of the individual to this constraint or obligation is not felt as painful, but on the contrary as highly pleasurable.

(Rappaport 1999: 221, quoting A. R. Radcliffe-Brown [1922] 1964: 251–2)[11]

Although ritual is deeply involved with what Marcel Mauss ([1935] 1973: 70–88) called "techniques of the body," it also at the same time involves a complex set of meanings, which cannot simply be read off from the ritual but must be understood in the context of the whole form of life of the ritual participants. One of Rappaport's most interesting ideas is his typology of three levels of meaning that are normally involved in ritual (1999: 70–4). *Low-order meaning* is grounded in distinction (a dog is not a cat) and is virtually the same as what is meant by information in information theory. Low-order meaning answers the question "what is it?" but it doesn't have much to say about the question "what does it all mean?" *Middle-order meaning* does not so much distinguish as connect: its concern is with similarities, analogies, emotional resonances and its chief form is metaphor (the fog comes on little cat feet). Art and poetry operate primarily at this level and it is very important for ritual, in which the focus on techniques of the body in no way excludes symbolic meanings. Since ritual depends heavily on exact repetition, it cannot convey much information – it doesn't tell one anything new – but it does link realms of experience and feeling that have perhaps become disconnected in the routine affairs of daily life. *High-order meaning* "is grounded in identity or unity, the radical identification or unification of self with other" (Rappaport 1999: 71). Such meaning, the immediate experience of what has been called "unitive consciousness" (Maslow 1962), can come in mystical experience, but, according to Rappaport, the most frequent context for such an experience is ritual. Here he links back to Durkheim's famous definition of ritual – it is in the effervescence of ritual that the individual concerns of daily life are transcended and society is born.

The world of daily life – economics, politics – is inevitably dependent on information, on making the right distinctions. Rational action theory assumes that all we need is information, in this technical sense of the term. But Rappaport, with Durkheim, argues that if rational action were all there is, there would be no solidarity, no morality, no society and no humanity. The Hobbesian world of all against all is not a human world. Only ritual pulls us out of our egoistic pursuit of our own interests and creates the possibility of a social world. As this highly condensed résumé of Rappaport's argument suggests, there is reason to wonder about the future of ritual in our kind of society. Technological and economic progress is based on the enormous proliferation of information, but information is in a zero/sum relation to meaning. Undermining middle- and high-order meaning is not just a threat to ritual and religion, if Rappaport is right, but to society and humanity as well.

Both Rappaport in the last pages of his book and Durkheim in the Conclusion of *Elementary Forms* refer to the difficulty yet necessity of ritual performance in the contemporary world. Rappaport refers to the "skepticism and cynicism" with regard to such matters today and Durkheim refers to the "moral cold" which he already experienced as current in his day. Both have some optimism that, as has happened before, new resources for ritual meaning and moral solidarity could emerge once again in modern society. Neither of them, to my knowledge, explicitly discussed the subject of anti-ritualism. They seem to imply that modernity entails a gradual erosion of the sacred as expressed in ritual rather than an active opposition to it. Mary Douglas has helped the discussion by making anti-ritual an explicit topic of analysis.

Ritual in the work of Mary Douglas

Mary Douglas is, I believe, the most interesting living Durkheimian. Her work is voluminous and she has frequently returned to the subject of ritual. In the necessarily brief space I can devote to her, I would like to concentrate on her early, but very influential, book, *Natural Symbols: Explorations in Cosmology* ([1970] 1982). The whole book can be seen as centrally concerned with the threat to ritual in contemporary life, the source and meaning of anti-ritualism, and the possibility of countering it. Her point of departure is an incisive analysis of the destructive consequences of the Vatican II reform that led to the abandonment of Friday abstinence, that is, the prohibition of eating meat on Fridays. For what she calls the "Bog Irish," that is, working-class Irish living in London, that prohibition was central to their understanding of themselves and their world. She tries to understand how middle-class reformers could so totally fail to understand the meaning of this ritual prohibition.

She begins her effort to understand ritual and anti-ritual tendencies in modern life with some interesting observations of Basil Bernstein's about London families in the mid-twentieth century and uses them to construct a general theory of the relation between social control and symbolic codes. Bernstein noted that there were two rather different forms of family in his sample and that these two forms differed by class. Working-class families used what he called positional control systems and restricted speech codes and middle-class families used personal control systems and elaborated speech codes.

Because the word "restricted" is invidious in a way I think neither Bernstein nor Douglas intends, I will henceforth speak of "condensed" rather than "restricted" speech codes in contrast to elaborated ones, and will make this terminological change even when quoting them.

Douglas describes the condensed speech code that is generated in the positional family:

> The child in this family is controlled by the continual building up of a sense of social pattern: of ascribed role categories. If he asks 'Why must I do this?' the answer is in terms of relative position. Because I said so (hierarchy). Because you're a boy (sex role). Because children always do (age status). Because you're the oldest (seniority). As he grows, his experience flows into a grid of role categories; right and wrong are learnt in terms of given structure; he himself is seen only in relation to that structure.   (Douglas [1970] 1982: 24)

Douglas notes that this pattern can be found in some aristocratic as well as working-class families. She then describes the other form:

> By contrast, in the family system which Professor Bernstein calls personal a fixed pattern of roles is not celebrated, but rather the autonomy and unique value of the individual. When the child asks a question the mother feels bound to answer it by as full an explanation as she knows. The curiosity of the child is used to increase his verbal control, to elucidate causal relations, to teach him to assess the consequences of his acts. Above all his behaviour is made sensitive to the personal feelings of others, by inspecting his own feelings. Why can't I do it? Because your father's feeling worried; because I've got a headache. How would you like it if you were a dog?   (Douglas [1970] 1982: 26)

Douglas quotes Bernstein to the effect that in the middle-class family the child is being regulated by the feelings of the regulator: "'Daddy will be pleased, hurt, disappointed, angry, ecstatic if you go on doing this' . . . Control is effected through either the verbal manipulation of feelings or through the establishment of reasons which link the child to his acts" ([1970] 1982: 26).

Douglas sums up the middle-class pattern in a way that should give us pause: "In this way the child is freed from a system of rigid positions, but made a prisoner of a system of feelings and abstract principles" ([1970] 1982: 27). I'm sure that I speak for most of us when I say that "we" think the personal form and the elaborated code are surely preferable to the positional form and the condensed code, to a considerable degree because the personal form and the elaborated code would seem to foster in the child just the individual initiative that we have come to value so highly. Yet Douglas, well before anyone was talking about Foucault, is suggesting that the personal form of control is still control, and perhaps, in its own way, as coercive as the positional form.

But I would draw a further conclusion. No one ever starts with the elaborated code. All children begin with positional control and the condensed language code because personal control and the elaborated code require skills that no newborn has. The relation between mother and child, or perhaps we should better say between parent and child, is necessarily positional, because highly asymmetrical: an infant needs to be held, cared for, talked to or sung to, but cannot be addressed with elaborate appeals to feelings or ideas, at least not for quite a while. In fact, interaction with an infant looks suspiciously like ritual. Linguists have discovered that in all cultures parents speak to infants in something they call "motherese" (see, e.g. Pinker 1994: 39–41) a kind of simplified, highly repetitive, sing-song, partly nonsense, kind of language, one that communicates feeling rather than information. Each language has its own version of motherese, to be sure, but the basic characteristics seem to be quite universal. Non-verbal communication with an infant is probably even more important. Erik Erikson (1968) suggested that the "greeting ceremonial" between mother and child, marking the beginning of the infant's day, is the root of all subsequent ritualization.

Infants become human because of habitual, non-discursive, verbal and non-verbal interaction with adults, which is, in Basil Bernstein's terms, necessarily positional in control and condensed in speech code. Dissanayake puts it well when, as we have seen above, she says the function of this kind of interaction is to "attune or synchronize, emotionally conjoin, and enculturate the participants" (2000: 401) or, we could say, to position them, to give them an identity relative to others, to provide them a social location. And that is what ritual is basically doing. Not only in infants, but in the infancy of the species, as we have seen, there is reason to believe that language itself developed out of ritual, differentiated out of an initial fusion with music, "musilanguage" (Brown 2000), the motherese of the species so to speak.

If, as I have argued, positional control and condensed code are basic to our humanity and cannot be dispensed with, why did we develop personal control and the elaborated code in the first place? Mary Douglas ([1970] 1982) has two answers to this. One has to do with how strong social solidarity is in any given society. A society with clear boundaries and well-defined roles is positional by definition, and will almost certainly have a well-developed ritual system involving a condensed speech code, while societies with loose boundaries and not very well-defined roles require that people relate to each other on a more or less ad hoc basis, negotiating each encounter as they go along, with little taken for granted, and thus will be personal in control and elaborated in speech. She is at pains to argue that there is no overall historical tendency to go from condensed to elaborated – that is, tribal people cannot be presumed to have strong solidarity and well developed rituals because we have instances such as the pygmies of central Africa who are both loosely bounded and largely free of ritual. Be that as it may, her primary interest is in contemporary society and the way in which the division of labor, which is for her the second source of personal control and elaborated code, differentially impacts working-class and middle-class families:

> It is essential to realize that the elaborated code is a product of the division of labour. The more highly differentiated the social system, the more specialised the decision-making roles – then the more the pressure for explicit channels of communication concerning a wide range of policies and their consequences. The demands of the industrial system are pressing hard now upon education to produce more and more verbally articulate people who will be promoted to entrepreneurial roles. By inference the [condensed] code will be found where these pressures are weakest [that is to say among people whose jobs are both routine and require little verbal facility].　　　(Douglas [1970] 1982: 21)

Although Douglas finds the social basis for positional control and condensed code in some modern professions, the military for example, most of the professions that increasingly dominate the higher echelons of our occupational world require people well versed in personal control and elaborated speech. The symbolic analysts, as Robert Reich characterizes our top professionals, are critical by their very job description. Douglas characterizes them as follows:

> Here are the people who live by using elaborated speech to review and revise existing categories of thought. To challenge received ideas is their very bread and butter. They (or should I say we?) practise a professional detachment toward any given pattern of experience. The more boldly and comprehensively they apply their minds to rethinking, the better their chances of professional success. Thus the value of their radical habit of thought is socially confirmed, and reinforced. For with the rise to professional eminence comes the geographical and social mobility that detaches them from their original community. With such validation, they are likely to raise their children in the habit of intellectual challenge and not to impose a positional control pattern.
> 　　　　　　　　　　　　　　　　　　　　　　　　　(Douglas [1970] 1982: 31)

Indeed, she goes on to say, they are likely to prefer personal forms of control and to focus on feelings rather than rules in child-rearing. As a result, "ideas about morality and the self get detached from the social structure" ([1970] 1982: 31). It is not that children raised in such a milieu lack ethical ideas; sensitivity to the feelings of others can arouse strong ethical passions when others are observed to be suffering. The problem is that without some positional sense of social membership and without strong condensed symbols, ethical sensitivities may simply dissipate into good intentions without leading to sustained moral commitments.

Douglas is very even-handed in her sense that we need both modes of relating. She affirms "the duty of everyone to preserve their vision from the constraints of the [condensed] code when judging any social situation . . . [W]e must recognise that the value of particular social forms can only be judged objectively by the analytic power of the elaborated code" ([1970] 1982: 166). She is well aware that condensed codes in the context of positional authority can be both authoritarian and unjust. "Do it because I said so," is an example of condensed code that carries the implication of some, perhaps quite unpleasant, non-verbal sanction that will follow if the recipient of the command rejects it. Except under conditions of extreme emergency, an elaborated request for reasons is justified. Similarly the condensed statement "Little girls don't do that" is open to challenge with respect to the whole taken–for-granted definition of gender. These are the kinds of reflection, which lead "us" to presume that personal control and elaborated code are always preferable to the alternative.

Yet Douglas warns us against precisely that conclusion:

> There is no person whose life does not need to unfold in a coherent symbolic system. The less organized the way of life, the less articulated the symbolic system may be. But social responsibility is no substitute for symbolic forms and indeed depends upon them. When ritualism is openly despised the philanthropic impulse is in danger of defeating itself. For it is an illusion to suppose that there can be organisation without symbolic expression . . . Those who despise ritual, even at its most magical, are cherishing in the name of reason a very irrational concept of communication.   (Douglas [1970] 1982: 50)

So where does Douglas leave "us," including her? She is not asking us, as some converts to various forms of fundamentalism are, to abandon our personal and elaborated selves and jump back into the positional box. No, she is asking us with all our critical rationality to see that we need both forms of control and both codes. She writes:

> In the long run, the argument of this book is that the elaborated code challenges its users to turn round on themselves and inspect their values, to reject some of them, and to resolve to cherish positional forms of control and communication wherever these are available . . . No one would deliberately choose the elaborated code and the personal control system who is aware of the seeds of alienation it contains.   (Douglas [1970] 1982: 157)

Whether, even in the most secular society where the elaborated code and personal control systems predominate, ritual can really be abandoned remains to be seen.

Ritual in various spheres of life

Our society does not understand ritual very well and for many of us even the term is pejorative; further, the great religious rituals that in almost all earlier societies carried what Rappaport (1999) calls high-order meaning have been privatized so that they act, not for society as a whole, but only for the particular groups of believers who celebrate them. The ambiguous term secularization might be used to describe not only the alleged decline of religion, but the decline of ritual as well. But, although some forms of ritual have become less evident, or retreated from the public sphere, it is also true that even in contemporary society we remain surrounded by ritual in a myriad of forms. It might even be argued that ritual is to be found everywhere that humans live together if we look in the right places, although where those places are may be very different from one society to the next. In this connection I would like to pursue a bit further the idea of interaction ritual as developed by Goffman and Collins.

Like so much else in the study of ritual the idea of interaction ritual can be found in germ in Durkheim's *Elementary Forms*:

> [The] stimulating action of society is not felt in exceptional circumstances alone. There is virtually no instant of our lives in which a certain rush of energy fails to come to us from outside ourselves. In all kinds of acts that express the understanding, esteem, and affection of his neighbor, there is a lift that the man who does his duty feels, usually without being aware of it. But that lift sustains him; the feeling society has for him uplifts the feeling he has for himself. Because he is in moral harmony with his neighbor, he gains new confidence, courage, and boldness in action – quite like the man of faith who believes he feels the eyes of his god turned benevolently toward him. Thus is produced what amounts to a perpetual uplift of our moral being.
>
> (Durkheim [1912] 1995: 213)

Goffman (1967) made the point that any social interaction, even between two persons, inevitably has a ritual dimension involving stylized elements of both speech and gesture. Collins (1998) has built on Goffman's work to argue that the basic social fact is the local interaction ritual, and that individuals cannot be said to have a higher degree of reality than the interaction in which they engage since they are in fact constituted in and through the interaction. Goffman (1967) saw deference as one indispensable element in interaction ritual. In hierarchical societies the ritual enactment of shared moral understandings expresses a sacred hierarchical order and the place of the interacting partners in it. In our society where the moral order emphasizes equality, even though hierarchy is inevitably present, there is a special effort to protect the sacredness of the individual person, no matter how disparate the status of the individuals involved. Even in a relatively fleeting encounter, then, the basic elements of ritual can be discerned: the synchronizing rhythm of conversational speech and gesture and the affirmation of social solidarity that they imply, regardless of the content of the conversation, and, if only by implication, the recognition of the sacredness, either of the code governing the interaction, the individuals interacting, or both.

Even in mundane daily life, ritual is not only a matter of occasional meeting and parting; it is very much part of the periodicity of life. Eating together may well be one of our oldest rituals, since humans are the only primates who regularly share food (Isaac 1978). Margaret Visser (1992) has made the case for the centrality of what she calls "rituals of dinner," because eating together is just the sort of occasion that makes ritual necessary. She writes:

> Table manners are social agreements; they are devised precisely because violence could so easily erupt at dinner. Eating is aggressive by nature and the implements required for it could quickly become weapons; table manners are, most basically, a system of taboos designed to ensure that violence remains out of the question. But intimations of greed and rage keep breaking in: many mealtime superstitions, for example, point to the imminent death of one of the guests. Eating is performed by the individual, in his or her most personal interest; eating in company, however, necessarily places the individual face to face with the group. It is the group that insists on table manners; "they" will not accept a refusal to conform. The individual's "personal interest" lies therefore not only in ensuring his or her bodily survival, but also in pleasing, placating, and not frightening or disgusting the other diners.   (Visser 1992: xii–xiii)

Although Visser underlines the elements of personal interest and group pressure, which are always involved in ritual, one would need to add that the "ritual of dinner," in the sense of "breaking bread together," implicitly, and often explicitly, has a religious dimension, as when there is a blessing before or after the meal, or, as in some Asian societies, a token offering to the ancestors precedes the meal.

Periodicity is characteristic of ritual of a wide variety of types ranging from the most secular, or even trivial, to the most solemn and religious. Academic life is highly ritualized and the school year is marked by numerous ritual events. Sporting events, both professional and collegiate have become highly ritualized in modern societies, and follow different seasonal patterns depending on the sport. A full discussion of the senses in which sporting events can be interpreted as rituals would exceed the bounds of this chapter. Suffice it to say that the absence or weakness of the performative dimension in Rappaport's (1999) sense make sporting events, like concerts, operas, plays or movies seen in theaters, problematic as ritual events in the full sense of the word. If involvement with a team becomes a major life concern, or even gives rise to "fan cults" in some cases, this might move such sporting events more fully into the ritual category. Political life also gives rise to various periodicities, including national holidays, elections, inaugurations, and so forth (the nation-state as a sacred object will be considered further below). Religious ritual has a strong tendency toward periodicity – Judaism, Christianity, and Islam require weekly worship – and yearly liturgical calendars are widespread. Economic transactions, as Durkheim pointed out, are the least likely to be ritualized, being highly utilitarian in character. Nonetheless, economic exchange in pre-modern societies is often accompanied by ritual, and a full analysis of economic life in our own society would probably discover more than a few ritual elements.

William McNeill in his important book *Keeping Together in Time: Dance and Drill in Human History* (1995) deals with many issues relevant to the concerns of this chapter, but he begins with military drill, not something students of ritual would usually start with. The two places where what McNeill calls "muscular bonding" have been most central have been, in his analysis, religion and the military (1995: 1–11). Learning that from McNeill, I was not entirely surprised to discover that not only was Colin Powell raised an Episcopalian, but that his service as an altar boy prepared him psychologically for a career in the army. The proximity of Episcopal liturgy and military life, while making a certain amount of sense, was not something I would spontaneously have imagined. McNeill does a great deal to clarify this otherwise somewhat disconcerting conjuncture. His starting point is frankly autobiographical: how did it happen that as a draftee in 1941, while enduring basic training in a camp on the barren plains of Texas, he actually enjoyed the hours spent in close-order drill? His answer in his admittedly somewhat speculative history of keeping together in time (after all who bothered much to write about such things) is that "moving our muscles rhythmically and giving voice consolidate group solidarity by altering human feelings" (McNeill 1995: viii).

Virtually all small communities of which we have knowledge, whether tribal or peasant, have been united on significant occasions by community-wide singing and dancing, usually more or less explicitly religious in content. (McNeill points out that what we today usually mean by "dancing," namely paired cross-gender performances with some degree of sexual intent, is, when viewed historically, aberrant to the point of being pathological [1995: 65]).

McNeill notes that in complex societies divided by social class muscular bonding may be the medium through which discontented and oppressed groups can gain the solidarity necessary for challenging the existing social order, using early prophetism in Israel as an example. He puts in perspective something that has often been noticed, namely that the liturgical movements of the more advantaged members of society are apt be relatively sedate, whereas those of the dispossessed can become energetic to the point of inducing trance (McNeill 1995: 86–90).

Close-order drill, McNeill's starting point, turns out to have emerged in only a few rather special circumstances, although dancing in preparation for or celebration after military exploits is widespread in simple societies. Here again there are ambiguities. Intensive drill in the Greek phalanx or trireme provided the social cohesion and sense of self-respect that reinforced citizenship in the ancient *polis*, but in early modern Europe its meaning was more ambiguous, sometimes reinforcing citizenship, sometimes absolutism. McNeill gives the interesting example of the strongly-bonded citizen armies of the French Revolution that then turned out to be manipulable elements in the establishment of Napoleon's autocracy (1995: 113–36). His comments on the use of rhythmic motion, derived in part from military drill but in part from calisthenics, in the creation of modern nationalism, culminating in Hitler's mass demonstrations (inspired in part by the mass socialist parades on May Day, which in turn were inspired in part by Corpus Christi celebrations), are very suggestive (1995: 147–8). But if such sinister uses of keeping together in time are always possible, all forms of nationalism have drawn on similar techniques.

Benedict Anderson, in his valuable analysis of modern nationalism (1991), describes what he calls unisonance, which is another form of keeping together in time:

[T]here is a special kind of contemporaneous community which language alone suggests – above all in the form of poetry and songs. Take national anthems, for example, sung on national holidays. No matter how banal the words and mediocre the tunes, there is in this singing an experience of simultaneity. At precisely such moments, people wholly unknown to each other utter the same verses to the same melody. The image: unisonance. Singing the Marseillaise, Waltzing Matilda, and Indonesia Raya provide occasions for unisonality, for the echoed physical realization of the imagined community. (So does listening to [and maybe silently chiming in with] the recitation of ceremonial poetry, such as sections of *The Book of Common Prayer*.) How selfless this unisonance feels! If we are aware that others are singing these songs precisely when and as we are, we have no idea who they may be, or even where, out of earshot, they are singing. Nothing connects us all but imagined sound. (Anderson 1991: 145)

Through the prevalence of television, rituals today can be shared by millions within and even beyond the nation state. I think of two instances: one where ritual worked effectively and one where it collapsed. I am old enough to remember well the November afternoon in 1963 when John F. Kennedy was shot in Dallas, Texas. For the following three days millions were glued to their television screens as a ritual drama of great complexity unfolded. The rituals were both national and religious. They involved the casket lying in state in the Rotunda of the United States Capitol, and then being taken by procession to the railway station, from which it was transported by train to Boston for a Catholic funeral mass presided over by the Cardinal Archbishop of Boston. The sudden loss of a head of state is apt to be traumatic in any society. The three days of ritual following Kennedy's death did seem to help make it possible to return to some kind of normal life after such a catastrophe.

In democratic societies, elections are ritual events, even if minimally religious ones. The very fact that millions of people go to the polls on one day and that there is great national attention to the outcome guarantees a high order of emotional intensity to such an event. Since television, elections have gathered very large audiences to await the outcome and the ritual concession and acceptance speeches that follow. But in the United States federal election of 2000, nothing seemed to go right. The television media made two wrong calls as to who won the election and then had to admit that the election in Florida, on which the Electoral College vote hung, was too close to call. What followed was anything but effective ritual. Almost every key actor in the events after the election failed to follow the appropriate ritual script – indeed things reached the point where it wasn't clear what the script was. The resolution of the election by a partisan vote of the Supreme Court of the United States, which has no role to play in elections according to the American Constitution, was the final failure of ritual closure. A failed electoral ritual produced a winner with severely damaged legitimacy.[12]

Conclusion

In conclusion, with the help of a couple of examples, I would like to suggest that any adequate account of ritual would need to situate ritual and anti-ritual in a long-term historical perspective. Already in *Natural Symbols* Mary Douglas ([1970] 1982), though starting with anti-ritual tendencies in the Vatican II reforms, gives her reflections a deeper historical background by frequent reference to the Protestant Reformation and even earlier renewal movements that had anti-ritual tendencies. She also points out that the extirpation of ritual is never complete, that the Protestants in depriving the Eucharist of its deep ritual meaning by reducing it to a mere commemoration at the same time made the Bible into a sort of ritual talisman. The doctrine of the "Word alone," though it had major consequences for the religious and social life of Northern Europeans ever since the Reformation, nonetheless gave rise to its own forms of re-ritualization.

But the perseverance of ritual in changing forms as well as the periodic anti-ritual challenges to it would require a historical study that would take us far beyond the confines of this chapter. Here I can only allude to a couple of studies that contribute to this important project. One is a study of the early history of the Vedic/Hindu tradition that has survived for over 3,000 years. The other is Mary Douglas' recent work ([1993] 2001; 2001) on ancient Israel.

In his *Reflections on Resemblance, Ritual, and Religion*, Brian K. Smith (1989) presents what I believe is a basically Durkheimian history of the development of ritual in India.[13] Although he does not cite Durkheim, he does draw significantly from Marcel Mauss and from Mauss' student, Louis Dumont. Smith makes the point that it is ritual action and not its symbolic interpretation that does the work of unifying the fragmented:

> For the Vedic priests and metaphysicians, ritual activity does not "symbolize" or "dramatize" reality; it constructs, integrates, and constitutes the real. Ritual forms the naturally formless, it connects the inherently disconnected, and it heals the ontological disease of unreconstructed nature, the state toward which all created things and beings naturally tend. (Smith 1989: 51)

Interestingly enough, Smith, writing before Rappaport's (1999) book was published, organizes his argument around three levels of meaning that are parallel to Rappaport's low-, middle-, and high-order levels. Smith argues that Vedic ritual works primarily with the middle level of resemblance, analogy, and metaphor, making connections between the cosmos, society and the individual, connections that position the participants in relation to one another, the Gods, and the natural world. Here we are clearly seeing the Bernstein/Douglas condensed code and positional control at work. Smith sees ritual as operating between two opposite poles, either of which would make ritual action impossible, poles that can be equated, I would argue, with Rappaport's low- and high-order meaning, but defined by Smith as radical difference and radical identity (1989: 51–2). The pole of radical difference is a form of low-order meaning that could be interpreted in contemporary terms as an extreme nominalistic atomism, a kind of *tabula rasa* from which scientific observation and investigation can begin (although however much the philosophy of science prefers reductionism, analogy seems always to sneak in by the back door). At this level operationally defined propositions replace metaphor and the world of ritual is (apparently) abolished. The pole of radical identity, a form of high-order meaning, implies a fusion of self and world that actually appears in the history of Indian religion, but is always antithetical to ritual and its differentiations, although in the end mystical union can no more absolutely do without metaphor and its accompanying ritual than can science.

Smith suggests two significant kinds of change in the history of Indian ritual, both of which are involved in the development of what has come to be called Hinduism, though, according to Smith, Hinduism never abandoned its Vedic core. One of these changes involves the development of a non-dualistic metaphysics and the practice of mystical union, first in the Upanishads and then in the (from the point of view of Hinduism) heretical religions of Buddhism and Jainism. From about the sixth century BC the figure of the renouncer appeared both within and beside the Hindu tradition. The renouncer, typically a religious intellectual who has withdrawn to the forest, stands outside the ritual system and the society it constantly reproduces, most notably outside the caste system, though ultimately, as Louis Dumont ([1960] 1980) has argued, the renouncer and the society renounced in fact form a complementarity. The anti-ritualism of the renouncer is illustrated quite early, according to Smith, in the Mundaka Upanishad which, "as part of a critique of ritualism in light of the new emphasis on mystical knowledge alone, declares sacrifices to be 'leaky vessels,' unfit for the true voyage – the attainment of liberation from *karma*" (1989: 106). At its most radical, the quest for high-order meaning through mystical union obliterates the world of ritual, though in the long run it gives ritual a new meaning. Self-liberation is a kind of "sacrifice" of the self, thus keeping the ritual metaphor (Smith 1989: 173, 209), but the path of self-liberation in both Vedanta Hinduism and Buddhism soon developed its own ritual complex.

The other great change, which occurred at approximately the same period, is the domestication of Vedic ritual. Early Vedic ritual of highly elaborated sacrifice focused on royal and aristocratic lineages and was an expression of the political power of the lineage. With the rise of centralized monarchies these great rituals fell into disuse, but what had been minor domestic rituals under the old system took on a new centrality. It was domestic sacrifice, carried out by the householder and his wife in the home, that became the core of Hindu practice and the place where Vedic ritual survived until today (Smith 1989: 195–9).

Even this very inadequate summary of Smith's complex and subtle argument suggests two important points about ritual: (1) Ritual can take many, sometimes highly diverse, forms; ritual and society tend to change in relation to each other. (2) Ritual under a variety of circumstances gives rise to anti-ritual movements that can have significant consequences for the history of religion, though the elimination of ritual is not one of them.

Mary Douglas ([1993] 2001; 2001), drawing on the work of many others, has recently pointed out developments in the history of ritual in ancient Israel that are to some degree parallel to the Indian developments. The prophetic movement from the eighth to the sixth centuries BC in Israel was often quite critical of ritual. It did not, as in the case of India, offer mystical contemplation as an alternative. Rather it was ethical demand that was said to be more acceptable to God than ritual – righteousness, rather than sacrifice – a view summed up in Psalm 51, 16–17: "For thou hast no delight in sacrifice; were I to give a burnt offering, thou wouldst not be pleased. The sacrifice acceptable to God is a broken spirit; a broken and contrite heart, O God, thou wilt not despise." The Hebrew prophet was not in the Indian sense a renouncer – we might even coin the term "denouncer" as a counter-term for the Hebrew prophets – but, as the passage from the Psalms suggests, the external sacrifice, as in the case of India, has become an internal one. However different the two examples, we can discern, in Bernstein/Douglas terms, a personal rather than a positional note in both cases. What these examples suggest is that anti-ritual movements of religious renewal begin long before the Protestant Reformation, at least as early as the axial age, the first millennium BC.

The other change in ancient Israel was the domestication of ritual, related to a number of social changes. The late pre-exilic effort to centralize the sacrificial ritual in the temple in Jerusalem meant that sacrifice could no longer be performed in local areas. With the exile, the sacrificial system broke down completely, although it was revived, perhaps in truncated form, during the Persian Period and later, finally collapsing with the destruction of the second temple by the Romans in AD 70. During all this period the ritual system was by no means abandoned and has survived until today at the level of the local congregation and the household, particularly in connection with issues of ritual purity. Similar and different sorts of changes could be traced in all the religions that have survived over long periods of time in greatly changing social conditions. And if ritual has survived in all of the great religious traditions, in spite of periodic anti-ritual movements of great intensity, it survives in ostensibly secular contexts as well, as the work of Goffman and Collins cited above indicates.

The present moment, with its tendency to privilege information, that is low-order meaning, above middle- and high-order meaning, is not a propitious one for ritual or even for the understanding of it. Nevertheless, I have argued, in the spirit of Durkheim and in agreement with Rappaport, that ritual is "humanity's basic social act," a position that, though contestable, has a great deal of evidence in its favor.

NOTES

This chapter has a considerable overlap with, though significant differences from, my chapter "The Ritual Roots of Society and Culture," in Michelle Dillon, ed., *Handbook for the Sociology of Religion* (New York: Cambridge University Press, 2003).

1 For a recent discussion see N. J. Allen, W. S. F. Pickering, and W. Watts Miller (1998).

2 In the original, the entire definition is in italics (Durkheim 1968: 65).

3 Anne Warfield Rawls has usefully emphasized what she calls "concrete practices," that is actual bodily movements, as the basis of Durkheim's theory of ritual. It was her article, "Durkheim's Treatment of Practice: Concrete Practice vs. Representation as the Foundation of Reason" (2001) that called this passage to my attention.

4 I should note that though, on occasion, Douglas has criticized Clifford Geertz for being "idealistic" in discussing culture independent of its embeddedness in society, in this instance she uses Geertz to reinforce her argument about exemplification, citing his book *Negara: The Theater State in Nineteenth Century Bali* (1980).

5 Goffman, like Collins, is explicit in recognizing his debt to Durkheim.

6 In spite of the Durkheimian echoes of this passage, Deacon makes no reference to Durkheim, nor to Goffman or Collins. The strength of disciplinary boundaries seems to have necessitated independent discovery, though we cannot rule out the influence of unconscious diffusion of ideas.

7 For a somewhat different attempt to find ritual at the basis of kinship in the very earliest human society see N. J. Allen (1998).

8 Keith Hart in his preface to this posthumously published book invokes Émile Durkheim's *Elementary Forms of Religious Life* and holds that Rappaport's book is "comparable in scope to his great predecessor's work," (1999: xiv) a judgment with which I agree.

9 On the coevolution of mind and culture see Clifford Geertz, "The Growth of Culture and the Evolution of Mind" (1973a).

10 Victor Turner has usefully emphasized the relation between ritual and dramatic performance, and the boundary between them is indeed fuzzy. See particularly part ii of his *On the Edge of the Bush: Anthropology as Experience* (1985).

11 Asad emphasizes the painful aspect of ritual discipline, but he focuses particularly on the sacrament of penance. See "Pain and Truth in Medieval Christian Ritual," in Asad (1993).

12 Clifford Geertz brilliantly describes a failed ritual of much more modest scale in his "Ritual and Social Change: A Javanese Example" (1973b). The events of September 11, 2001 may have given George W. Bush a legitimacy that he had not previously had, but that in no way invalidates the argument that the presidential election of 2000 was a failed ritual.

13 In his subsequent book, *Classifying the Universe: The Ancient Indian Varna System and the Origins of Caste* (1994) Smith draws explicitly and extensively, if critically, from Durkheim with respect to the social basis of classification in the Indian tradition.

REFERENCES

Allen, N. J. 1998. "Effervescence and the Origins of Human Society." pp. 149–161 in *On Durkheim's Elementary Forms*. Edited by N. J. Allen, W. S. F. Pickering and W. Watts Miller. London: Routledge.

Allen, N. J., W. S. F. Pickering and W. Watts Miller. 1998. *On Durkheim's Elementary Forms of Religious Life*. London: Routledge.

Anderson, Benedict. [1983] 1991. *Imagined Communities: Reflections on the Origin and Spread of Nationalism*. Revised edition. London: Verso.

Asad, Talal. 1993. *Genealogies of Religion: Discipline and Reasons of Power in Christianity and Islam*. Baltimore, MD: Johns Hopkins.

Brown, Steven. 2000. "The 'Musilanguage' Model of Music Evolution." pp. 271–91 in *The Origins of Music*. Edited by Nils Wallin, Björn Merker and Steven Brown. Cambridge, MA: MIT Press.

Brown, Steven, Björn Merker, and Nils Wallin. 2000. "An Introduction to Evolutionary Musicology." pp. 3–21 in *The Origins of Music*. Edited by Nils Wallin, Björn Merker and Steven Brown. Cambridge, MA: MIT Press.

Collins, Randall. 1998. *The Sociology of Philosophies: A Global Theory of Intellectual Change*. Cambridge, MA: Harvard University Press.

Deacon, Terrence. 1997. *The Symbolic Species: The Co-Evolution of Language and the Brain*. New York: Norton.

Dissanayake, Ellen. 2000. "Antecedents of the Temporal Arts in Early Mother-Infant Interaction." pp. 387–404 in *The Origins of Music*. Edited by Nils Wallin, Björn Merker and Steven Brown. Cambridge, MA: MIT Press.

Douglas, Mary. 2001. *Leviticus as Literature*. Oxford: Oxford University Press.

[1993] 2001. *In the Wilderness: the Doctrine of Defilement in the Book of Numbers*. Oxford: Oxford University Press.

1992. "Rightness of Categories." pp. 239–71 in *How Classification Works: Nelson Goodman among the Social Scientists*. Edited by Mary Douglas and David Hull. Edinburgh: Edinburgh University Press.

[1970] 1982. *Natural Symbols: Explorations in Cosmology*. New York: Pantheon Books.

Dumont, Louis. 1960. "World Renunciation in Indian Religions." *Contributions to Indian Sociology* 4, 1960: 33–62. Reprinted in Louis Dumont, *Homo Hierarchicus: The Caste System and Its Implications*, Complete Revised English edition. Chicago: University of Chicago Press, 1980: 267–86.

Durkheim, Émile. 1968. *Les Formes Élémentaires de la vie religieuse*. Paris: Presses Universitaires de France.

[1912] 1995. *The Elementary Forms of Religious Life*. Edited and translated by Karen E. Fields. New York: Free Press.

Erikson, Erik H. 1968. "The Development of Ritualization." pp. 711–33 in *The Religious Situation 1968*. Edited by Donald R. Cutler. Boston, MA: Beacon Press.

Freeman, Walter. 2000. "A Neurobiological Role of Music in Social Bonding." pp. 411–22 in *The Origins of Music*. Edited by Nils Wallin, Björn Merker and Steven Brown. Cambridge, MA: MIT Press.

Geertz, Clifford. 1973a. "The Growth of Culture and the Evolution of Mind." pp. 55–83 in *The Interpretation of Cultures*. New York: Basic Books.

1973b. "Ritual and Social Change: A Javanese Example." pp. 142–69 in *The Interpretation of Cultures*. New York: Basic Books,

1980. *Negara: The Theater State in Nineteenth-Century Bali*. Princeton, NJ: Princeton University Press.

Goffman, Erving. 1967. *Interaction Ritual*. New York: Doubleday.

Isaac, Glynn. 1978. "The Food Sharing Behavior of Proto-Human Hominids." *Scientific American* 238: 90–108.

Maslow, Abraham. 1962. *Toward a Psychology of Being*. Princeton, NJ: Van Nostrand.

Mauss, Marcel. [1935] 1973. "Techniques of the Body." *Economy and Society* 2: 70–88.

McNeill, William H. 1995. *Keeping Together in Time: Dance and Drill in Human History*. Cambridge, MA: Harvard University Press.

Nettle, Bruno. 2000. "An Ethnomusicologist Contemplates Universals in Musical Sound and Musical Culture." pp. 463–72 in *The Origins of Music*. Edited by Nils Wallin, Björn Merker and Steven Brown. Cambridge, MA: MIT Press.

Nichols, Johanna. 1998. "The Origin and Dispersal of Languages: Linguistic Evidence." pp. 127–70 in *The Origin and Diversification of Language*. Edited by Nina J. Jablonski and Leslie C. Aiello. San Francisco: Memoirs of the California Academy of Sciences, Number 24.

Pinker, Steven. 1994. *The Language Instinct*. New York: William Morrow.

Radcliffe-Brown, A. R. [1922] 1964. *The Andaman Islanders*. Glencoe, IL: The Free Press.

Rappaport, Roy A. 1999. *Ritual and Religion in the Making of Humanity*. Cambridge: Cambridge University Press.

Rawls, Anne Warfield. 2001. "Durkheim's Treatment of Practice: Concrete Practice vs. Representation as the Foundation of Reason." *Journal of Classical Sociology* 1: 33–68.

Richman, Bruce. 2000. "How Music Fixed 'Nonsense' into Significant Formulas: On Rhythm, Repetition, and Meaning." pp. 301–12 in *The Origins of Music*. Edited Nils Wallin, Björn Merker and Steven Brown. Cambridge, MA: MIT Press.

Smith, Brian K. 1989. *Reflections on Resemblance, Ritual, and Religion*. Oxford: Oxford University Press.

1994. *Classifying the Universe: The Ancient Indian Varna System and the Origins of Caste*. New York: Oxford University Press.

Turner, Victor W. 1985. *On the Edge of the Bush: Anthropology as Experience*. Tucson, AZ: University of Arizona Press.

van Gennep, Arnold. [1908] 1960. *The Rites of Passage*. Chicago: University of Chicago Press.

Visser, Margaret. 1992. *Rituals of Dinner: The Origins, Evolution, Eccentricities, and Meaning of Table Manners*. New York: Penguin.

Wallin, Nils, Björn Merker and Steven Brown. 2000. *The Origins of Music*. Cambridge, MA: MIT Press.

9

CHRIS SHILLING

Embodiment, emotions, and the foundations of social order: Durkheim's enduring contribution

Since the early 1980s there has been a remarkable growth in sociological studies of the body and in interdisciplinary work which has sought to resensitize social thought to the corporeal foundations of social action (Shilling 2005). Two broad theoretical perspectives have tended to dominate these analyses. On the one hand, certain writers have identified the governmental management of the body as setting key parameters to the overarching *external environment* in which social action occurs. Bryan Turner ([1984] 1996), for example, draws on Thomas Hobbes' and Talcott Parsons' concerns with the "problem of order" in order to identify the reproduction and regulation of populations through time and space, the restraint of desire, and the representation of bodies, as four key issues that face all societies. On the other hand, analysts have identified the body as central to the *internal environment* of social action. Arthur Frank (1991: 43), for example, examines the opportunities and constraints of action as given by the "problems of bodies themselves." Such action-oriented studies typically develop by being attentive to "the body's own experience of its embodiment" and by drawing on interactionist, phenomenological, and existentialist resources provided by such figures as Georg Simmel and Maurice Merleau-Ponty (Csordas 1994; Frank 1991: 48; Leder 1990).

These two broad approaches focus on a subject that has historically been something of an "absent presence" within the discipline (Shilling 1993). What I mean by this is that the body has rarely been the object of sustained sociological interest in its own right, even if it emerged as a significant social phenomenon in major studies of, for example, the metropolis, the division of labor, and rationalization. Nevertheless, these approaches remain indisputably related to the sociologies of order and of action that have long characterized the sociological heritage (Dawe 1970). The focus on bodies as providing the "core problems" confronted by the external environment in which action occurs views human physicality as an object ordered by society. Bodies are essentially a structural problem. The interest in the body as central to the internal environment of social action, in contrast, highlights how human behavior involves subjects who engage sensorially and emotionally (as well as cognitively) with their social world. Embodiment is here viewed as integral to, and sometimes coterminous with, social action.

In this context, it should come as no surprise that classical sociological writings have been utilized by contemporary theorists of the body. Parsons' reinterpretation of the Hobbesian "problem of order" and Weber's examination of religious ethics and social action, for example, feature prominently in their work. Perplexingly, however, there has been a relative neglect of Émile Durkheim's contribution to this area. Only a few body theorists have taken his work seriously (see, e.g. Falk 1994; Janssen and Verheggen 1997; Mellor and Shilling 1997; Shilling 2005), while Durkheim scholars have generally overlooked his significance for analyzing the centrality of the emotional body to social collectivities (but see Gane 1983; Meštrović 1993). This is a serious lacuna as it is possible to derive from Durkheim's writings a theory of the physical, emotionally expressive and experiencing body as a crucial multi-dimensional *medium* for the constitution of society. Bodies possess this status for Durkheim for three reasons. They are a major *source* of those symbols through which individuals recognize themselves as belonging to a society. They constitute a major *location* for these symbols (that are also incorporated into what Marcel Mauss ([1934] 1973) referred to as the *habitus* and shape the gestures, habits, and affects of individuals). Finally, they possess social potentialities which provide the *means* by which individuals transcend their egoistic selves and become energetically attached to the symbolic order of society. This approach allows us to appreciate the significance of the body for varied theoretical concerns as it avoids analytically conflating the body with either the structural exercise of control or the individual exercise of free social action.

This chapter develops via an explication of what I shall refer to as the *paradox of the body* which lies at the center of Durkheim's theory of society. Durkheim's ([1914] 1973) writings on *Homo duplex* argued that humans are born as individual bodies with the capacity to sense their environment in a rudimentary manner, and with asocial and egoistic impulses that can never be eradicated entirely even within the most integrated social order. Durkheim also suggests, however, that the embodied nature of humans provides individuals with the capacity and the need to transcend their natural, individuated state, and to join with others possessed of shared ideas and moral ideals. The paradox contained within this analysis is that individuals must deny part of what is essential to their bodily selves in order to enter into the symbolic order of society, yet *need* this social order if they are both to survive and flourish.

I begin by focusing on the role of the body in Durkheim's theory of totemism, a theory which demonstrates how society is expressed through collective representations or a *symbolic order* (the signs, myths, ideas, and beliefs characteristic of the *conscience collective* of the group). I then interrogate Durkheim's view of the relationship between human nature, collective effervescence, and this symbolic order of society. This relationship is not only key to his theory of totemism, but informs his view of the processes elementary to the constitution of *all* social life, and also illustrates how the emotions form a link between individual bodies and the social body. While the main aim of this chapter is to examine the theory of the body that can be derived from Durkheim's work, it is not possible to appreciate fully the significance of his writing without examining how it formed the context for, and anticipates, much recent analysis in this area. For this reason, the latter stages of discussion provide a brief engagement with the scope and intent of some of this work. This shows that Durkheim's writings established an enduring frame of inquiry, which has often gone unacknowledged, and also contain a latent potential for theorizing the body in new and exciting directions.

Totemism and the social body

Conventional interpretations of Durkheim have tended to minimize the importance of the body, and its relevance to collective forces and social currents, to his conception of society (see, e.g. Lukes 1973: 36). It has been suggested recently, however, that these interpretations suffer from an overly cognitivist reading of Durkheim's work; a reading associated variously with a neglect of the Schopenhauerian elements in his writings, or a tendency to dismiss his concerns with collective effervescence by associating them with the debasement of logical thought implied by crowd psychology (Meštrović 1993; Richman 1995; Shilling and Mellor 2001). Whatever the reasons for this "disembodied" presentation of Durkheim, such a reading becomes increasingly difficult to sustain in relation to his theory of totemism (Durkheim [1912] 1995). Durkheim ([1912] 1995: 92–3) studied totemism as a central part of his last major study because he believed its primitive religious form provided a clear illustration of the processes elementary to the construction of religion, to collective representations and, indeed, to *all* societies. These processes implicate the individual body, which is inescapably anchored in the natural world, as a critical medium through which the symbolic order of society, or the social body, is constructed.

Totemism is a mode of ritual religious practice which has at its center the symbolic equation of a clan or tribe with an animal, plant or other object most frequently found in its place of ceremonial meeting. Totemism unites individuals around a system of symbols (which organize thought) and an associated system of norms and prohibitions (which organize ritual action) and is ultimately explicable, according to Durkheim, as a result of the social group's worship of itself. As Durkheim ([1912] 1995: 208) argues, the symbol of the totem "is the symbol of both the god and society," and the god of the clan is "the clan itself . . . transfigured and imagined in the physical form of the plant or animal that serves as totem." At the center of this process of idealization *of* the clan *by* the clan lies the human body and its capacities for an effervescent attachment to the symbolic order through which society is expressed.

Durkheim ([1895] 1982) may have viewed the social as distinct from the natural, but he also saw the body as a natural medium through which the symbolic order of a clan or tribe is forged. Durkheim's view of the body as a *source* of the social is exemplified in his view that certain natural properties of the human body provide a basis for symbolizing what is sacred to the social group; that which is "set apart" and "forbidden" from the mundane world of daily existence yet which is central to the group's understanding of itself. While Durkheim refers to the natural body as profane, he also argues that the totemic prohibitions and imperatives surrounding the body's hair, sideburns, foreskin, fat, etc., "are sufficient to prove the existence in men of something that keeps the profane at a distance and has religious efficacy" (Durkheim [1912] 1995: 138). Far from belonging exclusively to the profane world of nature, then, the body "conceals in its depth a sacred principle that erupts onto the surface in particular circumstances" (Durkheim [1912] 1995: 138). Manifest via cutting, scarification, tattooing, painting or other forms of decoration, these eruptions affirm the communion of individuals in a shared moral whole ([1912] 1995: 138, 233). Blood is of particular importance here as a source of symbolism for life, and constitutes "a sacred liquid that is reserved exclusively for pious use" ([1912] 1995: 125).

If the body is a source of the symbolism through which social life is expressed, it is also a medium for the constitution of society by virtue of its status as a primary *location* for this symbolism. Indeed, Durkheim ([1912] 1995: 114) argues that the image-imprinted-on-flesh "is in fact, and by far, the most important" mode of representation that exists within totemic societies. It is because totemic bodies "share in a common life, [that] they are often led, almost instinctively, to paint themselves or to imprint images on their bodies that remind them of their common life" (Durkheim [1912] 1995: 233). Tattooing, "the most direct and expressive means by which the communion of minds can be affirmed," is an important example of this "instinct" and occurs within clans or tribes "apart from any reflection or calculation" (Durkheim [1912] 1995: 233–4).

Finally, the body also provides the *means* by which individuals are able to inhabit, and are positively attached to, totemic life. Durkheim associated the body with emotional properties which meant that the very act of bodily congregation was "an exceptionally powerful stimulant," while common bodily actions and gestures possessed the power to spark passionate, contagious emotions within people ([1912] 1995: 217; see also Barbalet 1994). Thus, social assembly and interaction can, at their height, generate "a sort of electricity" which launches people to an "extraordinary" state of "exaltation," while even mundane social life is associated with a pervasive stimulation of energy within individuals; an energy that is harnessed and directed through the rituals common to group life ([1912] 1995: 213, 217). Durkheim refers to these emotions as forms of "collective effervescence," a term he used to capture the idea of social force at its birth, and it is the power of this effervescence that allows individuals to be incorporated into the collective moral life of the tribe or clan. This is because collective effervescence induces changes in individuals' internal bodily states which have the *potential to substitute the world immediately available to our perceptions for another, moral world in which people can interact on the basis of shared understandings* (Durkheim [1914] 1973). The emotional capacities of individuals are collectively stimulated and structured through various rituals that "fix" them to those symbols that are central to people's identity and understanding. As Durkheim ([1912] 1995: 221]) argues, "The symbol thus takes the place of the thing, and the emotions aroused are transferred to the symbol. It is the symbol that is loved, feared and respected." It is through this transfer of energy that the *inner lives* of individuals are structured in accordance with collective symbols, and that a group becomes conscious of itself, and is bound together, as a moral community (Durkheim [1912] 1995: 221–3, 239; Gane 1983: 4). In addition to the body being a source of collective symbolism, and generally having the emblem of its clan imprinted on it, then, it also emotionally and sensorially internalizes and expresses the moral symbols of the collectivity to which it belongs.

The body's importance as a medium through which the symbolic order of the clan is reproduced is highlighted by Durkheim's ([1912] 1995: 401) account of totemic funeral rites. Durkheim argues that these funeral rites are characterized by intense emotions because the transformation of the totemically imprinted, or enculturated, body of the individual into a corpse represents a threat to the life of the group. As Hertz ([1906] 1960: 77) notes, death "destroys the social being grafted upon the physical individual" (cited in Jannsen and Verheggen 1997: 303). As the tribe is threatened by this death, funeral rites involve a *collective obligation* to mourn; a mourning that is not generally "the spontaneous expression of individual emotions," but results from the moral pressure on individuals to "bring their feelings into harmony with the situation" (Durkheim [1912] 1995: 403). Mourners are obliged to engage in recuperative rites involving "harsh abstinences and cruel sacrifices" in which the collective participation of the clan soon gives rise to collectively felt emotions. Each person "is pulled along by every other, and something like a panic of sadness occurs" (Durkheim [1912] 1995: 403–4). Rites demand "that one think of the deceased in a melancholy way" and may even require one to "beat, bruise, lacerate, and burn oneself" (Durkheim [1912] 1995: 402). The contagious quality of "bodies in emotion," indeed, is such that "people in mourning are so carried away in torturing themselves that they sometimes do not survive their wounds" (Durkheim [1912] 1995: 402). If mourning involves confronting the damage that a death does to the clan, however, it also involves a repairing of that damage. The "excess of energy" occasioned by funeral rites eventually leads to "a sensation of renewed strength, which counteracts the original enfeeblement . . . it begins again to hope and live" (Durkheim [1912] 1995: 405). The totemic clan is protected and social normality returns.

Having emphasized the importance of the body as a medium through which social life is structured, Durkheim makes it clear that totemism is more than the sum of its individual bodies. Society in general, indeed, has as its precondition the capacity of individuals to *transcend* their natural bodily dispositions; a transcendence involving a "recasting" of our partial animal nature in line with the symbolic order of society which is then able to take on *a logic and a life of its own* (Durkheim [1912] 1995: 62). Thus, the totemic images and the associated categories and concepts of thought common to the clan are irreducible to the human body and to the natural world (Durkheim [1912] 1995: 118). The sensory impressions of individuals may form a basis for these representations, but cannot provide a broader framework for logical thought as they are "made up of vague and fluctuating images" that are "found to have elements in common" (Durkheim [1912] 1995: 147). Social life is expressed through a vast array of collective symbols, most of which cannot be traced directly to the body but to the morphology of the social group, and these result in a "whole world of feelings, ideas, and images that follow their own laws," none of which is "directly commanded and necessitated by the state of the underlying reality" (Durkheim [1912] 1995: 426). Nevertheless, those symbols which are generated from the body are associated with a special intensity. This is because Durkheim recognizes that without the body there can be no life and no society (Janssen and Verheggen 1997). As Durkheim ([1912] 1995: 211) argued, in order for *any* society to exist, the life of the group must "enter into" individuals and become "organized within" them.

Homo duplex

Durkheim studied totemism for sociological purposes. He was concerned to ascertain and reveal processes elementary to the constitution of *all* religions and societies; yet, the emphasis he placed on the positive and negative significance of the body was neglected by the majority of his contemporaries (Durkheim [1914] 1973). A notable exception to this can be found in the work of Durkheim's close colleague, Marcel Mauss ([1934] 1973) on "techniques of the body." Nevertheless, recent presentations of Durkheim as a theorist of supra-individual social facts, who has little to say of interest to the embodied constitution of social orders, repeat this neglect of his concern with bodily passions and collective forces. This is despite the fact that Durkheim's 1914 essay on the constitutional duality of human nature developed the principles of explanation informing his analysis of embodiment, and was written explicitly in order to clarify the explanatory structure of his larger 1912 study on the elementary forms of religious and social life. This 1914 essay highlights the relevance of the body as a medium for the constitution of all societies, and also enables us to illustrate its relevance to Durkheim's earlier studies.

Individual bodies

Durkheim's ([1914] 1973) essay on *Homo duplex* focuses on the costs borne by the individual as a result of the body being a medium for the constitution of social life. These costs are associated with the pain experienced by individuals when they transcend the asocial, immanent aspects of their bodily being and occupy the social pole of their *Homo duplex* nature. Durkheim begins by noting that humans have, in every age, been aware of the duality of their nature and have traditionally expressed this duality through the idea that they possess a this-worldly, profane, physically limiting body, and a transcendent, sacred soul invested with "a dignity that has always been denied the body" and which "inspires those feelings that are everywhere reserved for that which is divine" (Durkheim [1914] 1973: 151). Instead of dismissing these beliefs, Durkheim suggests that they signify something real about the tension between our individual and social existence: the reality that humans are both egoistic and moral beings.

Humans possess an *individual* bodily being constituted by their drives, appetites and sensory impressions which "are necessarily egoistic: they have our individuality and it alone as their object. When we satisfy our hunger, our thirst and so on, without bringing any other tendency into play, it is ourselves, and ourselves alone that we satisfy" (Durkheim [1912] 1995: 151).

The mere presence of asocial, egoistic bodies would be "as lacking in mutually recognizable identity as so many potatoes in a sack," with neither reason
nor identity nor community, and would hold little interest for sociologists
(Fields 1995: lvi). With nothing but a collection of "individual bodies," there
"is no language and no kinship; there are age differences but no generations;
there are sex differences but no genders" (Fields 1995: lvi). What *is* of sociological interest, however, is when the individual, egoistic pole of *Homo
duplex* is made increasingly subordinate to its social and moral characteristics: when the individual body becomes attached to, and partly transformed
within, the social body.

These processes are associated with a relative emancipation from the senses
and the acquisition of a common moral sensitivity associated with a capacity
for "thinking and acting conceptually" which is general to the community
in which individuals live and is translated into common "rules of conduct"
(Durkheim [1912] 1995: 275, 151). The *Homo duplex* character of humans,
however, means that we can never be "completely in accord with ourselves
for we cannot follow one of our two natures without causing the other to
suffer" (Durkheim [1914] 1973: 154). We do not, in other words, offer our
bodies voluntarily as a social medium. Instead, our sensuous nature attaches
us "to the profane world with every fibre of our flesh" while the social
world painfully clashes "with our instincts" (Durkheim [1912] 1995: 316).
We can only pursue moral ends, which have as their object the collectivity, by
offending "the instincts and the penchants that are the most deeply rooted
in our bodies. There is not a moral act that does not imply a sacrifice"
(Durkheim [1914] 1973: 152). The very possibility of society, indeed, depends
on physical, emotional, and psychical pain.

This pain is not just associated with the denial of instinct, but with the
fact that the symbolic order of society "can never succeed in mastering our
sensations and in translating them completely into intelligible terms. They
take on a conceptual form only by losing that which is most concrete in
them, that which causes them to speak to our sensory being and to involve it
in action" (Durkheim [1914] 1973: 153). Despite this partial loss of the individual within the symbolic order, society "requires us to make ourselves its
servants" and "subjects us to all sorts of restraints, privations, and sacrifices"
which "are contrary to our inclinations and to our most basic instincts" yet
"without which social life would be impossible" (Durkheim [1912] 1995:
209).

Durkheim ([1912] 1995: 321) argues that society manifests an "inherent
asceticism" that readies us for the need to "overcome our instincts" and lifts
us above our egoistic bodily selves, yet this is not simply a negative constraint
on the individual. The absorption of individuals into the symbolic order of

society also enables humans to fulfill their social and moral capacities by *liberating* the agent from the enslavement they suffer from the asocial pole of their *Homo duplex* nature (Durkheim [1912] 1995: 151). Society equips individuals with *new* abilities which make them better able to survive and prosper: it "uplifts" individuals and brings them to "maturity" (Durkheim [1912] 1995: 211). The embodied individual may be internally divided, but is enhanced, as well as deprived, by the symbolic order of society.

Social symbols, social bodies

The positive integration of individual bodies into the symbolic order of society is greatly facilitated by the fact that embodied agents need society to survive as much as society needs individuals to exist. To begin with, the symbolic order imparts a dignity, a sacredness, and a recognition on the part of the individual that they possess the capacity to exercise agency. As Durkheim ([1912] 1995: 229) argues, society conceives the individual "as being endowed with a *sui generis* character that insulates and shields him from all reckless infringement – in other words, that imposes respect." Indeed, "man could not have arrived at the idea of himself as a force in charge of the body in which it resides without introducing concepts borrowed from social life into the idea he had of himself" (Durkheim [1912] 1995: 370). The collective notion that the individual is sacred also provides the basis for the "cult of the individual" that Durkheim ([1893] 1984) suggests should come to characterize the *conscience collective* of societies possessed of a highly developed and "normal" division of labor.

The symbolic order does not simply facilitate a recognition on the part of the individual that they can exercise agency, but increases massively their capacity for effecting change. This is because common social symbols are the result of an "immense cooperation" and a "multitude of different minds," and reflect a store of knowledge that possess a "very special intellectuality that is infinitely richer and more complex than that of the individual . . . distilled in them" (Durkheim [1912] 1995:15). Rather than limiting the options and choices open to agents, then, the symbolic order of society provides us with a means of "liberating ourselves from physical forces" (Durkheim [1912] 1995: 12, 274). This is because gaining an understanding the social and natural world requires individuals to place some distance between themselves and their immediate sense impressions, and the symbolic order of society facilitates this process (Durkheim [1912] 1995: 159). Durkheim, indeed, makes a distinction between two forms of consciousness. Individual consciousness merely expresses our "organism and the objects to which they are most directly related" (Durkheim [1914] 1973: 159). Social consciousness, in contrast, makes possible rational activity and thought, possesses a stability that is resistant to the variations and oscillations of an individual's sense impressions, and energizes individuals to act with a conviction which comes from a collective force. The collective capacity to express thought in symbols can be seen historically as having provided humans with an immense evolutionary advantage by allowing them to communicate more easily, to plan ahead and to codify information, and to specify more accurately relations of cause and effect (Durkheim [1914] 1973: 160; [1912] 1995: 435–6; see also Elias 1991).

If the symbolic order can impart dignity to the individual, allow people to benefit from the advantages of a common life, and provide for a better understanding and control of the environment, this has to do with its relationship to *natural* as well as social reality. The society from which representations emanate may be a "specific reality" but "it is not an empire within an empire: it is part of nature and nature's highest expression. The social realm is a natural realm that differs from others only in its greater complexity . . . This is why notions worked out on the model of social things can help us think about other sorts of things" (Durkheim [1912] 1995: 17). If society is an artifice "it is an artifice that closely follows nature and strives to come ever closer to nature" (Durkheim [1912] 1995: 17). Instead of being in complete opposition to the embodied nature of humans, then, society represents a *fulfillment* of much of that nature. Collective symbols, in short, enhance an individual's knowledge, allow them to feel "more at ease" in the world, and leave them "with a justified impression of greater liberty" (Durkheim [1912] 1995: 274).

The suggestion that human nature may not only be enhanced by but may come to *need* this symbolic means of attachment to social life is nowhere clearer than in Durkheim's study of suicide. Durkheim suggests that the rupture of individuals from social life could prove fatal: two of the major forms of suicide "spring from society's insufficient presence in individuals" (Durkheim [1897] 1952: 258). Anomic suicide is characterized by "unregulated emotions" that are "adjusted neither to one another nor to the conditions they are supposed to meet; they must therefore conflict with one another most painfully" (Durkheim [1897] 1952: 285). Passions can find no object to satisfy them; they exhaust themselves in frustration at the limits of society and lapse into "a sort of melancholy" having become lost in "the infinity of desires" (Durkheim [1897] 1952: 286–8). Egoistic suicide, in contrast, is associated with a loss of meaning and purpose rather than an excess of desire. It results from an "excessive individualism" in which "the individual ego asserts itself to excess in the face of the social ego and at its expense" and thereby loses the support of that collective energy that attaches an individual to something greater than themselves (Durkheim [1897] 1952: 209–11). Life seems empty and "the bond attaching man to life relaxes because that attaching him to society is itself slack" (Durkheim [1897] 1952: 214–15). The individual is no longer protected by the "sacred canopy" of transcendental meaning once provided by society (Berger [1967] 1990): "All that remains is an artificial combination of illusory images, a phantasmagoria vanishing at the least reflection . . . Thus we are bereft of reasons for existence" (Durkheim [1897] 1952: 213). Society and the symbolic order through which it is expressed is not ultimately antagonistic to human nature, just one element of it. It represents a "higher existence" that its members cannot do without (Durkheim [1897] 1952: 213).

Durkheim's insistence that the health of an embodied individual is not simply dependent on biological factors, but requires for its well-being that it be able to exercise its social capacities within a wider social whole to which it belongs, brings together social considerations and the fate of the body. His analysis has been supported by more recent studies. Kushner's (1989) study of suicide, for example, suggests that adverse social conditions can affect moods such as depression by changing levels of serotonin metabolism. This biocultural study combines the concerns of sociological studies such as Durkheim's with a biochemistry of mood, suggesting that changes in individuals' relationship with society can make them more vulnerable to contemplating and committing suicide (see also Freund 1990).

Effervescent action

The attachment of individual bodies to the symbolic order of society is dependent, as we have seen in the case of totemism, on the collective effervescence associated with group assembly and interaction. Collective symbols are only able to acquire and retain their efficacy in the minds and sentiments of individuals because they have attached to them the energies associated with what people experience as sacred to group life. The collective effervescence linked with the experience of the sacred is so powerful, indeed, that Durkheim ([1912] 1995: 44) argues that there can be no society without a sense of the sacred: the sacred energizes the symbolic order of society and motivates people to act in relation to the moral norms of that order. Rituals were central to the organization and direction of these processes in primitive times, but processes of initiation and education remain vital within modernity and the ritual "effect of culture" is still directed towards developing the altruistic over the egoistic aspects of our nature (Durkheim 1961: 222). "Above all" writes Durkheim, children have to be given the clearest idea of the social group they belong to; an idea which must be given "enough color, form and life to stimulate action" (Durkheim 1961: 228–9). Re-emphasizing the importance of an embodied rather than a purely intellectual attachment to society, Durkheim insists that this representation "must have something emotional; it must have the characteristic of a sentiment more than of a conception" (Durkheim 1961: 229).

The significance of this effervescent attachment to the symbolic order of society is twofold. First, it is contagious, flowing between people like an "oil slick" and facilitating what Comte (1853, vol. II: 190) referred to as the fetishism of investing ideals and images with great powers. Second, it stimulates effervescent action which is of utmost importance for individuals and societies. Durkheim provides us with various examples of this form of action. The general stimulation of energies during the French Revolution of 1789, for example, produced both sublime and savage moments, superhuman heroism and bloody barbarism, as ordinary individuals became transformed into new, more extreme beings (Durkheim [1912] 1995: 213). Effervescent actions also transformed a range of profane phenomena into sacred things which *strengthened* revolutionary society. Despite the avowedly anti-religious character of the Revolution, notions of Fatherland, Liberty and Reason assumed a sacred quality. This resulted in a new religion "with its own dogma, symbols, altars and feast days," which exerted a solidifying impact on the new society (Durkheim [1912] 1995: 216).

Effervescent action can even result in self-sacrifice. In the case of the soldier struggling to defend a country's flag on the battlefield, Durkheim suggests that "the soldier who dies for his flag dies for his country." This sacrifice of life for the sake of the symbol, often after heroic attempts to keep the flag or territory claimed by the flag from the hands of enemies, can only be explained because the flag has become charged with the emotional power of the collective life of the country (Durkheim [1912] 1995: 222). The effervescent power that has been invested in the flag is such that Durkheim talks of the flag *itself* sometimes causing action. The individual has the sense and the representation of something sacred residing outside their self which takes them beyond that self into a life which is extraordinary (Durkheim [1912] 1995: 222–3).

If the extraordinary energies occasioned by group life demonstrate how the emotionally charged body serves as a medium through which the symbolic order of society is constructed and expressed, the limitations of this body also provide a medium through which this order may dissolve. This is because individual bodies are unable to maintain the energy symbols were imparted with during collective gatherings. Group life injects a vital significance into collective symbols, but when social life becomes slack these representations begin to lose the energy that gave rise to them and the reality they incarnated.

They need to be revitalized in the sacred energies of the crowd as a way of replenishing "the energy they lose in the ordinary course of events" or will become "worn away with the passage of time" (Durkheim [1912] 1995: 217, 342). This is why Durkheim ([1912] 1995: 403) argues that society "exerts moral pressure on its members" during funeral rites and other occasions of collective crisis in order to produce an emotional state among the group which "reflects the circumstances it is then going through." If society permitted individuals to remain indifferent to the deaths and crises that threaten to diminish it, "it would be proclaiming that it does not hold its rightful place in their hearts. Indeed, it would deny itself" (Durkheim [1912] 1995: 403).

Durkheim's ([1912] 1995: 404) analysis of scapegoating also illustrates how the symbolic order of society affirms its power by encouraging people to search for an "outsider," not attached to the sacred symbols and rites of the group, to blame for great misfortune or loss and "on whom the collective sorrow and anger can be discharged" (see also Girard 1972; Lukes 1973: 345). This analysis reflects Durkheim's argument that the sacred can be either benevolent, life-giving and associated with order and the stimulation of feelings of love and gratitude, or violent, death-bringing and associated with disorder and feelings of fear and horror (Durkheim [1912] 1995: 412; see also Hertz [1906] 1960).

The essential ambivalence of the effervescent actions generated by the sacred is a theme that was illustrated by the mass ceremonies, rituals and genocidal destruction characteristic of Nazism prior to and during the Second World War. Theweleit (1977), for example, examines how the extraordinary symbolism of German fascism was mirrored in a sacralization of the "armoured" male body of the soldier, and the pure body of the mother, and a demonization and scapegoating of the "Red Flood" of communism which was associated with bodily dissolution and fears of moral decay. The intense emotions generated by this virulent manifestation of the sacred were evident in the barbaric acts of violence perpetrated on individuals in and outside of the community who were associated with this threat. Richman (1995) has suggested that the rise of Nazism made Durkheim's contribution increasingly difficult to appreciate or develop, yet Durkheim's colleagues, members of the Collège de Sociologie, and certain contemporary social theorists concerned with the embodied and emotional foundations of human being, illustrate the continued value of his work. Thus, Mauss ([1936] 1992) notes that Durkheim's theories can apply to Nuremberg rallies as much as liberal-democratic forms of the "cult of man," while Bataille ([1938] 1988) uses them to support his philosophy of "excess."

More recently, the notion of effervescent action has been employed by theorists concerned to chart social and cultural changes in the modern era. Maffesoli is one of several writers to have been heavily influenced by Durkheim. Maffesoli's (1996) account of neo-tribes theorizes the break-up of mass culture into a proliferation of "affinity"-based groups with over-lapping memberships. These tribal groups emerge from the opportunities provided by custom to engage in fleeting physical contacts and Dionysiac outbursts which connect them to "collective frameworks of memory" and the lived tides of experience (Maffesoli 1996: 25). Whereas social contracts provide a basis on which people can interact, Maffesoli's tribes provide an opportunity for people to "keep warm" together. Maffesoli focuses on the socially integrating effects of the sacred, but other writers have exploited the ambivalence Durkheim associates with the sacred and have concentrated on the violent, shocking, and exclusionary consequences of effervescent actions; a step which locates Durkheim's work firmly within the province of conflict sociology (Collins 1975). This concern with the destructive effects of effer-vescent solidarities and action has been developed in a sustained manner by Meštrović. In his study of what he refers to as "the Balkanization of the West," Meštrović (1994) uses contemporary wars and conflicts to illustrate the ineffectiveness of rational dialogue, and the resurgence of a virulent, violent human sensuality.

It is Tiryakian's (1995) discussion of the "velvet revolutions" of 1989 in East Europe, however, that perhaps comes closest to Durkheim's own appre-ciation of the ambivalent effects of effervescent action in relation to social orders. Tiryakian draws on the concept "collective effervescence" to illumi-nate the contagious spread of ideas of democratic reform and popular rebel-lion amongst the former Communist countries of Eastern Europe. Tiryakian (1995: 276) notes the rapidity of the collapse of these regimes, triggered by a series of effervescent mass demonstrations and the spontaneous revivifica-tion of previously dormant collective symbols. More broadly, Tiryakian is interested in the unpredictability of social change; an unpredictability that cannot be accounted for easily in many sociological accounts of how social transformations arise and develop. In Durkheim's concept of collective effer-vescence, however, he finds a vision of the emotional dynamics of social life that can illuminate some of the vast social changes that have marked the recent history of Eastern Europe.

Embodiment and the cult of the individual

Durkheim's 1914 essay on the constitutional duality of human nature makes it clear that he did not confine his analysis of the body as a medium for the constitution of society to totemic clans. Nevertheless, it is worth considering whether the distinction he drew between mechanical and organic forms of solidarity (a distinction which has been drawn on frequently by his contemporary interpreters) has important consequences for the status of distinctively modern forms of embodiment. Durkheim's conception of mechanical and organic solidarities echoed Tönnies' ([1887] 1957) use of *Gemeinschaft* and *Gesellschaft* to distinguish between the principles of organization characteristic of pre-modern and modern societies. Tönnies argued that the transition between these two types of society was the outcome of two forms of *embodied will* (Levine 1995: 203). While *Gemeinschaft* was based on the expression of instinct, habit and emotional spontaneity, *Gesellschaft* was a contractually based arrangement founded upon a more deliberative, calculating, and rational type of will. The physical and emotional body appears to fade from view in this conception of the transition to modern society, and this raises the question of whether there has been a decline in the body's importance as a source of and location for *social* symbolism, and a corresponding fall in its significance as a means through which individuals became attached to the symbolic order of modern society. This issue can be approached via the work of Mauss and the writings of those who have focused on the status of the body in modernity.

Mauss' ([1934] 1973: 71–2) analysis of body techniques built on Durkheim's work by exploring how social techniques that are both traditional and effective to a society become ingrained through apprenticeship into the capacities and habits of the body. Mauss reemphasizes the body's importance to modern societies by suggesting that that "there is perhaps no natural way for the adult" to manage his or her body, and that "each society has," and *has* to have, "its own special habits" pertaining to the body. These techniques amount to a social *habitus* and are transmitted by initiation and education and acquired by a process of imitation. They involve just about all aspects of human behavior, include techniques of standing, walking, squatting, infant care, etc., and remain vital to modern societies. This is because their transmission involves an "education in composure" congruent with the needs of an increasingly specialized and rationalized society (Mauss [1934] 1973: 86). Once acquired, techniques of the body inhibit "disorderly movements" and allow for "a coordinated response of coordinated movements setting off in the direction of a chosen goal" that is fundamental to rational action (Mauss [1934] 1973: 86).

Mauss is concerned with differentiation between societies, while the more recent work of Pierre Bourdieu develops this interest in how the embodied habitus is differentiated *within* modern societies. Bourdieu (1984) argues that an individual's social class location structures their bodily dispositions, and is manifest in patterns of taste, and in the processes of recognition involved in the accumulation and transmission of social, cultural and economic capital.

The experience and expression of the body is a manifestation of class which helps "fit" people to their social positions and assists in the reproduction of relationships of domination and subordination (Bourdieu 1981; 1986). The body serves not simply as a source of and location for symbolism, but carries social inequalities deep into the very core of an individual's bodily experience and expression (Bourdieu 1984: 217–18). The body thus remains integral to an understanding of modern societies.

Elias' ([1939] 2000) explorations of the relationship between large-scale historical changes and the minutiae of individual behavior places the concerns of Mauss and Bourdieu in a broader historical context, and focuses on trends towards *individualization* as much as it does on class and status differences in embodied identities. Elias examines the processes whereby the passions which used historically to manifest themselves instantaneously in actions, and result in a daily life marked by physical violence and volatility, are increasingly monitored and regulated by the individual within the modern age. The advancing social division of labor, monopolies of violence and taxation, and the struggle for distinction in daily life, exert a gradual yet unremitting effect on individual bodily experience and expression. The cultivation of controlled appearance, self-restraint, and foresight become essential qualities for individual survival and prosperity in modernity, in contrast to the frequent need for aggressive self-defense in many medieval societies. The relative civilization of the body that results from these processes is reflected in children's education and constitutes an essential counterpart to the growth of a more peaceable society in which individuals feel a growing degree of empathy and identification with each other. Far from the body's social importance diminishing in modern society, it remains an essential means by which individuals come to possess the habits, controls, and capacities enabling them to survive and prosper.

We may have traveled some distance from Durkheim, but I want to suggest that Bourdieu's concerns with the class-based *habitus* can be seen as a reflection of the fate of the body within an "abnormal" form of the division of labor (in which people are fated to their social position by birth rather than being matched to a role on the basis of their talents). Elias' interest in the increasing individualism of the body, furthermore, returns us to the substantive concerns of Durkheim, albeit via a radically different methodological route, and I shall now focus on the relevance of Durkheim's own concerns with the development of individualism (and the development of these concerns within the Durkheimian tradition) to contemporary theories of the body.

Durkheim ([1893] 1984: 122) initially argued that the development of a moral individualism within organic solidarity (in which the "dignity" or "cult of the individual" appears as a normative counterpart of modern society) does *not* have society as its object: we are not bound to society by this cult but "to ourselves." He also charted a decline in the scope of those sentiments and beliefs common to individuals in a highly differentiated society, and expressed concern about the continued strength of the sacred in modernity. The development of individualism has been a prominent theme in contemporary studies of embodiment which suggest that the decline of overarching meaning systems in modernity has been accompanied by the appropriation of the body by individuals as a sign of their own distinctive self-identity (Giddens 1991). However, Durkheim's deliberations on the "cult of the individual," and his abandonment of the distinction between mechanical and organic solidarity after *The Division of Labour* (1893), progress in a manner which suggests that such individualized alterations of the body possess a highly generalized symbolic importance. Durkheim suggests that the "cult of the individual" remains dependent on the symbolic order of society and addresses itself not to the particular, isolated individual, "but to the human person wherever it is to be found, and in whatever form it is embodied" (Durkheim [1898] 1973: 48). The "cult of the individual," then, and an associated respect for the great variety apparent in contemporary body modifications, can be interpreted as "the glorification not of the self but of the individual in general" (Durkheim [1898] 1973: 48–9). It is this "sympathy for all that is human," associated with what Durkheim refers to as a "religion of the individual," that "binds us all to each other," prompting individuals to "reach outside" themselves in looking to others as a means of adding "to the energy" they possess (Durkheim [1898] 1973: 48–9, 53; [1912] 1995: 427).

Durkheim's comments on the "cult of the individual" suggest that the body may continue to act as a source of, and a location for, a symbolism that is essentially social. This may be expressed through the proliferation of styles of fashion, dress and deportment, or by increasing spectacular interventions *into* the body made possible by advances in medical and transplant surgery, sports science, *in vitro* fertilization and recent developments in cybertechnology (Featherstone and Burrows 1995; Shilling 2005). While widely different from the bodily interventions characteristic of Durkheim's lifetime, they provide an illustration of his argument that it is the development of societal specialization that allows for the possibility of individualism. The analysis of this moral order which affords dignity to the individual has been most developed, however, within the writings of Erving Goffman (1983; 1977; 1969). Goffman is widely acknowledged as applying Durkheim's legacy to the sphere of everyday interaction (Collins 1988: 43), and does much to illustrate the continued relevance of his writings on the body.

The interaction order and the moral body

The great suggestiveness of Goffman's work lies in the fact that it can be viewed as formally elaborating on the bodily processes by which the "dignity" or the "cult of the individual" is maintained, yet as informally betraying the partiality of this cult in its present, in what Durkheim might refer to as "abnormal," form. What I mean by this is that while Goffman's (1983) analysis of the "interaction order" details the ritual conditions surrounding the everyday physical encounters through which individuals acquire individual identities that are made "sacred," he also provides numerous examples of discrimination and inequality in relation to this order, and of the chronic manipulation of this order by self-seeking individuals. These features of his work suggest that "the individual" is not a universal category which denotes what *all* people have in common, but applies to those people and social groups defined as worthy in relation to the *partial* symbolic rules, or "vocabularies of bodily idiom" closely associated with this order.

The "interaction order" refers to the domain of face-to-face relations (of bodily co-presence) wherever these take place and includes within its scope the physical and emotional features of interaction. Goffman (1983) conceived of the "interaction order" as an analytically separable domain of social life, which led to the production of symbolic meanings that imposed moral obligations on both individuals and institutions (Rawls 1987). Three elements of the "interaction order" are of particular importance for our concerns. First, Goffman considers the daily rituals and rules governing interaction as reflected in what he refers to as "shared vocabularies of body idiom" (Goffman 1963: 35). Body idiom is a conventionalized form of non-verbal communication which is by far the most important component of behavior in public. It is used by Goffman (1963: 33) in a broad sense to refer to "dress, bearing, movements and position, sound level, physical gestures such as waving or saluting, facial decorations, and broad emotional expressions," and represents an updating of Durkheim's concern with symbolic order and imprinting of tribal signs on the body. Second, the "interaction order" is the arena in which individuals gain a moral identity as a full member of society. The shared expectations surrounding encounters, associated with the norms of body idiom, possess an importance and moral weight because people are confronted with the necessity of establishing relations with others, in order to construct a morally respectable social self. In contrast to tribal societies, the individual management of encounters, rather than the collective structuring of gatherings, plays a more important role in the development of identity within modernity. Third, individuals remain vulnerable within the "interaction order"; interaction occurs within arenas which expose people, physically and mentally, to others (Goffman 1983: 4; 1977: 329). These conditions mean that if people transgress the trust and norms that underpin the "interaction order," their identity can quickly become tainted (Goffman 1968: 12). Viewed as morally culpable, their behavior is considered "evidence of weakness, inferiority, low status, moral guilt, and other unenviable attributes" (Goffman 1956: 266). The "interaction order" is, then, a deeply moral domain in which the construction of a social self is regarded as "a sacred thing" (Goffman 1969).

If the body is deeply implicated in the generation of social understanding and identity within the interaction order, it is also a means for the attachment of individuals to this order. Adherence to interactional rules via controlled expressions, movements and carefully reciprocated communications of the body allows people to present an acceptable social self, to acquire status, and to feel "at ease" while intervening in daily life. The disruption of the interaction order, in contrast, can lead to an intense emotional embarrassment associated with the "feeling of a gap between the socially legitimate body and the body which one has and is" (Connerton 1989). If a person breaks with the bodily norms associated with interaction, and perceives themselves to be risking a discredited social self, common physiological changes include "constrictions of the diaphragm," a feeling of "wobbliness," "dryness of the mouth," and "tenseness of the muscles" and manifest themselves in "blushing, fumbling, stuttering," "quavering speech," "sweating" and "hesitating or vacillating movement" (Goffman 1956: 264–5). While Durkheim focuses on the general rush of energy which accompanies gatherings and the diminution of effervescent feeling associated with a slack social life, Goffman undertakes what may be seen as a complementary examination of embarrassment as *a major* ordering emotion. The experience and expression of embarrassment, following a breach of the bodily norms, casts "a shadow of sustained uneasiness upon the participants, transforming the entire encounter into an incident itself." Embarrassment, like a negative form of effervescent energy, is contagious and spreads "in ever widening circles of discomfiture" to the point when the individual is discredited, stigmatized, and may flee, destroying the social order of the encounter (Goffman 1956: 264–7).

Thus far, Goffman provides us with a focus on how interactional order is a moral order constituted through the medium of the body. There are important parallels here with Durkheim's interest in the relationship between the body and the symbolic order of society even if there is a distinction to be drawn between Goffman's focus on the details of interactional encounters and Durkheim's concern with collective gatherings. Both view the body as a medium for the constitution of something greater than itself. Both view the embodied individual as being accorded a moral respect and dignity within modern societies characterized by an advanced division of labor, and both associate this with a sacralization of the self. Durkheim admits that the "cult of the individual" will develop fully only after "abnormal" forms of the division of labor have disappeared and moral norms have caught up with the rapid economic and social dislocations that characterized modernity. Goffman, in contrast, possesses a less historically informed conception of the "sacred individual" within the "interaction order," yet acknowledges the inequalities embedded within the bodily norms associated with this order and can illuminate a Durkheimian concern with what may be referred to as "abnormal" forms of the "cult of the individual" (Goffman 1983; Shilling 1999). Here, there is the sense of a serious threat to the idea that there may exist a sacred, social order that bestows dignity on individuals in general.

The shared vocabularies of body idiom central to interaction provide individuals with categories which not only enable them to label others but to grade them *hierarchically* and to engage in *discrimination*. Goffman examines how bodily norms stigmatize certain peoples by labeling certain of their physical attributes as deeply discrediting. This stigmatization makes it highly difficult for affected individuals to enter into "normal" interaction and, therefore, to acquire a socially acceptable moral identity. It can effectively remove them from society in that individuals stand alone as "a discredited person facing an unaccepting world" (Goffman 1968: 12–13, 31). Goffman's analysis of stigma displays a particular interest in the problems of the disabled because of the difficulties they have in being accepted as full members of society. Nevertheless, the term has far wider applicability in illustrating how individuals are not accorded equal respect or dignity within the "interaction order." As Goffman (1963: 14–15) notes, a stigma is a *relationship* between attribute and stereotype and can include tribal stigmas of "race, nation and religion" which are received by others as signifying "an undesired differentness" and a negative departure from normative expectations. If physical disability and bodily markers of "racial" difference may exclude individuals from full, normal status within the interaction order, so too may their sex. Goffman argues that men "often treat women as faulted actors with respect to 'normal' capacity for various forms of physical exertion"; an attitude which involves a "steering" of women's behavior and which excludes that reciprocity which is an essential part of the "interaction order" (Bartky 1988). The vocabularies of bodily idiom, or symbolic order, which enter into the process whereby individuals are made "sacred" is, then, beginning to look less like the universal human signified by Durkheim's "cult of the individual" and a little more like a resource through which the dominant reaffirm their standing over the dominated.

The distinction between the "cult of the individual" and the symbolic norms associated with discrimination and inequality helps illuminate one of the major tensions which have interested classical and contemporary theorists of the body. This concerns whether the contemporary individual preoccupation with the body reflects essentially positive or negative developments in society. Writings concerned with body cultivation as a relatively positive expression of individualism associate this development with a lifestyle politics in which individuals have appropriated a greater responsibility for their identity, health and broader environment (Giddens 1991). However, the Durkheimian tradition of which Goffman is a part also provides us with a basis on which to analyze the body's implication in social inequalities. Much of the reason for this has to do with the pervasiveness of the social symbols and norms that impinge upon people's embodied identity. The vocabularies of body idiom used by people to classify others are also used for the purposes of self-classification. If a person's bodily appearance and management categorizes them as an "outsider" by others, Goffman argues (1963) that they will generally internalize that label and incorporate it into what becomes experienced as a "spoiled" self-identity. As Goffman argues (1963), our virtual social identity (the view and experience we have of our self-identity) tends to approximate to our social identity (the identity that others bestow on us). This is evident in the work of those concerned with "race," gender and social difference who view bodily norms as a "mask" placed by one group on another.

Frantz Fanon's classic 1952 analysis of the relationship between the construction of blackness and colonialism examines how the symbolic framing of the body can constitute an oppressive "second skin." Fanon discusses how the white male colonial gaze helps inform an interaction order in which black people are equated with, and reduced to, their bodies. Blackness becomes the essence of what the self is; an essence seen through a "white mask" and filled with negative connotations which promote shame and self-contempt. Talking about his own experiences, Fanon notes how the white "generalized other" reflected his bodily being back to him so that "My blackness was there, dark and unarguable. And it tormented me, disturbed me, angered me" (Fanon [1952] 1999: 261). Consciousness of the body becomes "solely a negating activity" which fills the body's space with uncertainty, with a "third-person consciousness" which makes even the process of reaching for a pack of cigarettes and a box of matches an activity full of awkwardness (Fanon [1952] 1999: 258). Notable here is Fanon's suggestion that colonization involves the ruled becoming emotionally attached to symbols that *diminish* them as individuals.

Tseëlon (1995) makes a similar point when arguing that from an early age women have much pressure placed on their appearance and have constantly to wrestle with a body idiom which reflects male notions of a female essence. Goffman (1977: 320–9) himself recognized the operation of a "courtesy-courtship" system in the West in which women are called upon to be constantly "on stage" and are "somewhat vulnerable in a chronic way to being hassled." Social responses to the process of ageing provide us with another area in which dominant vocabularies of body idiom can be seen as exclusionary. Featherstone and Hepworth (1988), for example, argue that old age is frequently experienced as if it were a mask which veiled the real identity of the individual. People in their seventies and eighties may struggle to be "young at heart," but are masked in an old skin which evokes negative reactions from individuals immersed in a consumer culture which values the simple attribute of youth, and have to struggle against internalizing the feeling of worthlessness.

These examples provide us with an "abnormal" form of the "cult of the individual." Social symbols, or norms of bodily idiom, value only one type of individuality, and constitute for many an oppressive mask which reduces the life chances of individuals by constructing a view of them as "not quite human" (Goffman 1963: 15). Mary Douglas' (1966; 1970) anthropological theory of the body as a classification system serves to summarize the conclusions of these diverse studies. Following Durkheim, Douglas portrays the body as both a symbol and a metaphor for social cohesion, differentiation, and conflict. During times of social crisis, Douglas argues that there is likely to be a more widespread concern with the maintenance and purity of bodily boundaries. In light of her analysis, it is no accident that the body should have become an intensified object of concern at the same time that global processes are threatening to destabilize national boundaries (Robertson 1992). From individual attempts to tan or lighten the skin in order to approximate more closely to prevailing notions of health and beauty, to political concerns to ensure the exclusion of "alien" bodies from the Mexican borders of California and from the European Union, the body has become a significant symbolic motif for our times. What Durkheim continues to add to our understanding of these developments, however, is the suggestion that these symbols stimulate, and have attached to them, *collective* moral sentiments which are experienced within the very core of an individual's identity.

These understandings and sensations of exclusion and conflict are not confined to stigmatized groups, furthermore, but can be seen as imprinted on

and seeping through the bodies of those favored by dominant vocabularies of body idiom (Mellor and Shilling 1997). Sennett's (1994) analysis of
the white middle class' fear of social engagement and its pursuit of safety
and comfort, for example, is evident in its promotion of the "hard body"
which prizes the appearance of power and control as one way of coping
with the social differentiation and crime associated with urban America.
This hard body is no longer actually necessary for privileged groups in the
world of high technology industry, but provides a corporeal and psychological shield against other social groups. This shield is associated with
contemporary concerns with "fitness," where "working out" became a
"balletic imitation of true work," and an "internal environmentalism" of
health consciousness characterized by an obsession with the purity of what
is allowed within the body's boundaries (Ehrenreich 1990: 233–4; Bourdieu
1984).

   These body disciplines may reflect the middle class's desire for "definition";
signifying a self-containment and a separation from other social groups
(Ehrenreich 1990: 236). Opposition to the socially transgressive delights of
smoking, heavy drinking and "junk food" (which joins health and fitness
concerns to "moral" issues) can also be seen as a form of distinction in relation to the lower classes (with whom such things become associated). These
body disciplines may be an expression of and help reinforce social difference,
yet there is, in Marcuse's (1962) terms, always a danger of the body being
dominated by a "performance principle" which results in "surplus repression." There is no sacred "loss of self" in an inclusive symbolic order here,
and no sensual satisfaction akin to Wilhelm Reich's implicit concern with
an effervescent release of self in multidimensional relationships with other
humans (Robinson 1969).

   Bodies remain, in each of these examples, a source of and a location for
social symbols; yet, these symbols do not encompass a universal individual
nor do they exhibit respect for individual differences. Instead, they are reflec-
tive of broader power differences, the domination of one group by another,
and the existence of an "abnormal" form of the cult of the individual in
which certain differences are prized over others.

Concluding comments

Durkheim's analysis of the processes by which embodied individuals are
incorporated into social orders accords a significant influence to the impact
social life exerts on the body, yet also attributes considerable import to bodily experience and to the body as a positive social resource. As such, his

work continues to provide us with a provocative alternative to those contemporary deliberations on the body that have exerted most influence in the area.

Recent theories which conceive of the body in terms of the external environment of action have the advantage of highlighting how the economic, social, and cultural contexts in which social action occurs have to deal with the irreducible weight of human bodies; a weight that cannot be captured by conventional understandings of the structures that constrain human behavior. Nevertheless, this approach is unable to consider in any detail how individuals may be emotionally integrated into the symbolic norms, or ruptured from these norms in a manner conducive to social change. Analyzing the body in terms of the internal environment of action, in contrast, provides a useful corrective to theories based on the view that action can be defined or investigated apart from people's physically structured frailties, desires, and capacities. Rational choice theory, for example, tends to assume that actors cognitively establish goals before acting (and thereby propose that the normal state of the body is lethargy) and that the body as a permanently available instrument of action (that is autonomous vis-à-vis other people and the environment). It also tends to reduce the body to a mere medium of self-expression and thereby underestimates the importance of human frailty, the unintended and unexpected events of life, and the impact of collectivities on the body (Joas 1983; 1996). Theorists of bodily action and experience, however, themselves often neglect the issue of how society is internalized into, effects the actions of, and may assist in realizing the embodied potentialities of individuals.

Durkheim's determination to place *Homo duplex* at the center of his theory of society manages to harness the issues reflected in contemporary concerns with the body to those associated with current concerns with emotions; areas which have too frequently been separated by artificial subdisciplinary boundaries. It also has the advantage of neither conceptualizing the body as the exclusive property of the individual, nor of perceiving its relevance purely from the viewpoint of society (an approach which often dissolves the facticity of the body into ethereal "images" or "discourses" or the performative demands of a sexual "matrix"). Social structures, institutions and rituals may constrain individuals to act in particular ways rather than others, but they also provide individuals with the resources through which they may fulfill their embodied potentialities. Similarly, the body may provide the vehicle through which individuals are able to exercise social agency, by acting in relationship to the perspectives and behaviors of others, yet it is also characterized by both significantly pre-societal passions and needs and by an openness to the influence of society. Durkheim takes the potentially banal observation that those who participate in the symbolic order of any society are embodied beings, and places it at the center of a sophisticated theory of society.

REFERENCES

Barbalet, Jack. 1994. "Ritual Emotion and Body Work: A Note on the Uses of Durkheim" in *Social Perspectives on Emotion*. Vol. 2. Edited by William Wentworth and John Ryan. Greenwich, CT: JAI Press.

Bartky, Sandra. 1988. "Foucault, Feminism and Patriarchal Power." pp. 61–86 in *Feminism and Foucault: Reflections on Resistance*. Edited by Irene Diamond and Lee Quinby. Boston, MA: Northeastern University Press.

Bataille, Georges. [1938] 1988. "The Sorcerer's Apprentice," in Hollier, D. *The College of Sociology 1937–1939*. Minnesota: University of Minnesota Press.

Berger, Peter. [1967] 1990. *The Sacred Canopy*. New York: Anchor Books.

Bourdieu, Pierre. 1986. "The Forms of Capital." pp. 241–58 in *Handbook of Theory and Research for the Sociology of Education*. Edited by John G. Richardson. New York: Greenwood Press.

    1984. *Distinction. A Social Critique of the Judgment of Taste*. London: Routledge.

    1981. "Men and Machines." pp. 304–17 in *Advances in Social Theory and Methodology*. Edited by K. Knorr-Cetina and A. V. Cicourel. London: Routledge.

Brubacker, Roger. 1985. "Rethinking Classical Theory." *Theory and Society* 14: 745–75.

Collins, Randall. 1988. "Theoretical Continuities in Goffman's Work." pp. 41–63 in *Erving Goffman: Exploring the Interaction Order*. Edited by Paul Drew and Anthony Wootton. Cambridge: Polity.

    1975. *Conflict Sociology*. New York: Academic Press.

Comte, A. 1853. *The Positive Philosophy of Auguste Comte*, vols. 1 and 2. Translated by Harriet Martineau, London: John Chapman.

Connerton, Paul. 1989. *How Societies Remember*. Cambridge: Cambridge University Press.

Csordas, Thomas J. (ed.) 1994. *Embodiment and Experience: The Existential Ground of Culture and Self*. Cambridge: Cambridge University Press.

Dawe, A. 1970. "The Two Sociologies." *British Journal of Sociology* 21: 207–18.

Douglas, Mary. 1970. *Natural Symbols: Explorations in Cosmology*. London: The Cresset Press.

    1966. *Purity and Danger. An Analysis of Concepts of Pollution and Taboo*. London: Routledge and Kegan Paul.

Durkheim, Émile. [1914] 1973. "The Dualism of Human Nature and its Social Conditions." pp. 149–66 in *Émile Durkheim: On Morality and Society*. Edited by Robert N. Bellah. Chicago: University of Chicago Press.

    [1912] 1995. *The Elementary Forms of Religious Life*. Edited and translated by Karen E. Fields. New York: Free Press.

    [1898] 1973. "Individualism and the Intellectuals." pp. 43–57 in *Émile Durkheim: On Morality and Society*. Edited by Robert N. Bellah. Chicago: University of Chicago Press.

1961. *Moral Education. A Study in the Theory and Application of the Sociology of Education.* New York: Free Press.

[1897] 1952. *Suicide.* London: Routledge.

[1895] 1982. *The Rules of Sociological Method.* London: Macmillan.

[1893] 1984. *The Division of Labour in Society.* London: Macmillan.

Ehrenreich, Barbara. 1990. *The Fear of Falling: The Inner Life of the Middle Class.* New York: Harper Perennial.

Elias, Norbert. [1939] 2000. *The Civilizing Process.* Translated by Edmund Jephcott. Oxford: Blackwell.

1991. *The Symbol Theory.* London: Sage.

Falk, Pasi. 1994. *The Consuming Body.* London: Sage.

Fanon, Frantz. [1952] 1999. "The Fact of Blackness." pp. 257–66 in *Theories of Race and Racism: A Reader.* Edited by Les Back and John Solomos. London: Routledge.

Featherstone, Mike (ed.) 2000. *Body Modification.* London: Sage.

Featherstone, Mike and Roger Burrows. 1995. "Cultures of Technological Embodiment: An Introduction." *Body and Society* 1: 1–20.

Featherstone, Mike and Mike Hepworth. 1988. "Ageing and Old Age: Reflections on the Postmodern Life-Course." pp. 143–57 in *Becoming and Being Old: Sociological Approaches to Later Life.* Edited by Bill Bytheway, Teresa Keit, Patricia Allatt and Alan Byrman. London: Sage.

Fields, Karen. 1995. "Translator's Introduction: Religion as an Eminently Social Thing" to *The Elementary Forms of Religious Life*, by Émile Durkheim. New York: Free Press.

Frank, Arthur. 1991. "For a Sociology of the Body: An Analytical Review." pp. 36–102 in *The Body: Social Process and Cultural Theory.* Edited by Mike Featherstone, Mike Hepworth and Bryan S. Turner. London: Sage.

Freund, Peter. 1990. "The Expressive Body: A Common Ground for the Sociology of Emotions and Health and Illness." *Sociology of Health and Illness* 12: 454–77.

Gane, Mike. 1983. "Durkheim: The *Sacred* Language." *Economy and Society* 12: 1–47.

Giddens, Anthony. 1991. *Modernity and Self-Identity.* Cambridge: Polity.

Girard, René. 1972. *Violence and the Sacred.* Translated by Patrick Gregory. Baltimore, MD: Johns Hopkins University Press.

Goffman, Erving. 1983. "The Interaction Order." *American Sociological Review* 48: 1–17.

1977. "The Arrangement Between the Sexes." *Theory and Society* 4: 301–31.

1969. *The Presentation of Self in Everyday Life.* Harmondsworth: Penguin.

1968. *Stigma: Notes on the Management of Spoiled Identity.* Harmondsworth: Penguin.

1963. *Behavior in Public Places. Notes on the Social Organization of Gatherings.* New York: The Free Press.

1956. "Embarrassment and Social Organization." *American Journal of Sociology* 62: 264–71.

Halbwachs, Maurice. [1941/52] 1992. *On Collective Memory.* Edited, translated and with an introduction by Lewis A. Coser. Chicago: University of Chicago Press.

Hertz, Robert. [1906] (1960). *Death and the Right Hand.* Glencoe, IL: The Free Press.

Janssen, Jacques and Theo Verheggen. 1997. "The Double Center of Gravity in Durkheim's Symbol Theory: Bringing the Symbolism of the Body Back In." *Sociological Theory* 15: 294–306.

Joas, Hans. 1983. "The Intersubjective Constitution of the Body-Image." *Human Studies* 6: 197–204.

1996. *The Creativity of Action*. Cambridge: Polity.

Kushner, 1989. *Self Destruction in the Promised Land: A Psychocultural Biology of American Suicide*. New Brunswick, NJ: Rutgers University Press.

Leder, Drew. 1990. *The Absent Body*. Chicago: Chicago University Press.

Levine, Donald. 1995. *Visions of the Sociological Tradition*. Chicago: University of Chicago Press.

Lukes, Steven. 1973. *Émile Durkheim: His Life and Work*. London: Allen Lane.

Maffesoli, M. 1996. *The Time of the Tribes*. London: Sage.

1935 [1973]. "Techniques of the Body." *Economy and Society* 2: 70–88.

Marcuse, Herbert. 1962. *Eros and Civilization. A Philosophical Inquiry into Freud*. New York: Random House.

Mauss, Marcel. 1934 [1973]. "Letter to S. Ranulph" in *The Radical Sociology of Durkheim and Mauss*. Edited by Mike Gane. London: Routledge.

Mellor, Philip A. and Chris Shilling. 1997. *Re-Forming the Body: Religion, Community and Modernity*. London: Sage.

Meštrović, Stjepan G. 1994. *The Balkanization of the West. The Confluence of Postmodernity and Postcommunism*. London: Routledge.

1993. *The Barbarian Temperament. Toward a Postmodern Critical Theory*. London: Routledge.

1996. *Postemotional Society*. London: Sage.

Rawls, Anne Warfield. 1987. "The Interaction Order Sui Generis: Goffman's Contribution to Social Theory." *Sociological Theory* 5: 136–49.

Richman, Michele. 1995 "The Sacred Group: A Durkheimian Perspective on the Collège de Sociologie 1937–1939." pp. 58–76 in *Bataille: Writing the Sacred*. Edited by Carol Bailey Gill. London: Routledge.

Robertson, Roland. 1992. *Globalization, Social Theory and Global Culture*. London: Sage.

Robinson, Paul. 1969. *The Sexual Radicals: Wilhelm Reich, Geza Roheim, Herbert Marcuse*. London: Temple Smith.

Sennett, Richard. 1994. *Flesh and Stone. The Body and the City in Western Civilization*. London: Faber and Faber.

Shilling, Chris. 2005. *The Body in Culture, Technology and Society*. London: Sage.

2001. "The Embodied Foundations of Social Theory." pp. 439–57 in *Handbook of Social Theory*. Edited by George Ritzer and Barry Smart. London: Sage.

1999. "Towards an Embodied Understanding of the Structure/Agency Relationship." *British Journal of Sociology* 50: 543–62.

1997. "Emotions, Embodiment and the Sensation of Society." *The Sociological Review* 450: 195–219.

[1993] 2003. *The Body and Social Theory*. London: Sage.

Shilling, Chris and Philip A. Mellor. 2001. *The Sociological Ambition: Elementary Forms of Social and Moral Life*. London: Sage.

Theweleit, Klaus. [1987] 1977. *Male Fantasies*. Vol. 1, *Women, Floods, Bodies, History*. Minneapolis, MN: University of Minneapolis Press.

Tiryakian, Edward A. 1995. "Collective Effervescence, Social Change and Charisma: Durkheim, Weber and 1989." *International Sociology* 10: 269–81.

Tönnies, F. [1887] 1957. *Community and Association*. Michigan: Michigan State University Press.

Tseëlon, Efrat. 1995. *Masque of Femininity: The Presentation of Woman in Everyday Life*. London: Sage.

Turner, Bryan S. [1984] 1996. *The Body and Society*. Oxford: Blackwell.

10

ROGER FRIEDLAND

Drag kings at the totem Ball: the erotics of collective representation in Émile Durkheim and Sigmund Freud

Politics has a sex because sex is our first politics, our first agency, our first subjection. Over the long sweep of history, collective representation, the capacity to stand for the collectivity, to speak in its name, has been gendered. Men have historically dominated the public sphere, their bodies massed, displayed, and sacrificed as the primary medium and content of collective representation. Women are absent, off-stage, or more recently, play minor parts. If the public sphere, and the collective body conjured into symbol there, is male, it presumably has a penis; but the fact is that its sex, its erotic energies, have gone largely un-theorized. If we are to understand the logic of collective representation we must align its symbolization with its sex.

In this chapter, I wish to explore the sexuality of collective representation as achieved in ancient rituals as interpreted by Émile Durkheim and Sigmund Freud, the founders of sociology and psychoanalysis respectively. In *The Elementary Forms of Religious Life* ([1912] 1995) (hereafter *Elementary Forms)* and *Totem and Taboo* ([1913] 1946), both studied the "totemism" of the aboriginal tribes of Australia which they argued was the simplest and hence the earliest religion. For both, collective representation was the creation of a collective body through the individual bodies of men. While scholarship has accumulated requiring revision of the empirical materials upon which they based their theories, their theories are still studied and taught without reference to it, as modalities of thinking, as our own totemic representations.

For Durkheim, the human body is the essential site, medium, and language of collective representation. Collective representation operates through sym-bolic incorporation, through ritual processes of embodiment. The leader, he writes, is "a group incarnated" (1995: 212). As against those who locate culture at the level of discourse, as a sign-system, Durkheim insists on its bodily practice, not as unconscious *habitus*, but as a conscious ritual. Col-lective representation derives its energy from the massing of human bodies; it inscribes the social on and in the flesh. Durkheim's is not a theory grounded in cognition, as in Lévi-Strauss who sought the taxonomic regularities of mythic culture in the structure of the mind, nor the new cognitivists who search for the mental universals of conceptual order, nor the cognitivized incorporation at the center of Bourdieu's theory of *habitus* (Bourdieu 1990; Widick 2003).

While Durkheim was empirically conscious of the sexuality of collective representation, that sex remained undeveloped analytically, theoretically unconscious. In contrast, Freud, who studied the same totemic representation would shock his peers by making its sexuality an explicit object of concern, but in the process would operate out of his own theoretical unconscious, the liberal, contractarian theories of his day, reducing the social to its sources within dyadic pairs. Durkheim and Freud are normally treated as mutually exclusive, wholly other, mutually profaning. I read them together through the totem to provoke a rethinking of the relation between the social and the sexual. Freud read and cited Durkheim's *Elementary Forms*. As far as we know Durkheim never read Freud's *Totem and Taboo*, at least he never cited it or anything else Freud wrote. It's a pity. Sexualizing Durkheim and socializing Freud may open new ways to figure the social and its effervescent energies.

Elementary forms

In *Elementary Forms*, Durkheim did not simply locate the social origins of religious rites, he located the ritual origins of society. These collectivities were bounded, unified, and set in motion through totemic ritual. Each clan has its own totem, a unique species of animal or plant with which it understands itself as having a kinship, as being an ancestor. The clan members each regard the totem as sacred.

The totem, Durkheim argues, is the tangible form of an intangible "substance" (1995: 191), "an anonymous and impersonal force" that diffuses through the universe. "By that principle," Durkheim writes: "are maintained the lives of the clan's people, the lives of the animals or plants of the totemic species, the lives of all things that are classified under the totem and participate in its nature" (1995: 206).

The totem is a collective representation, both name and emblem, a physical representation that is the exclusive property of the group that claims kinship with it. They, and they alone, can wear its image and be buried beneath it. Each clan member carries the name of the totem. To name is not to label, but to identify in the sense that naming not only produces the identity of the named subject, but is "part of the being" (Durkheim 1995: 114). That capacity to name has social origins. Unlike Lévi-Strauss who will argue that the social is first classified through the properties of nature, Durkheim and Mauss argue that nature is hierarchically classified through the experience of the social, which is itself natural (Durkheim and Mauss 1963; Martin 2000).

But for Durkheim, not only is the totem a symbol – not a simple sign, a throwing together, as the etymology suggests – of divergent orders, the natural and the social, but the representation of the first is productive of the second. It appropriately touches the flesh of those who are produced as a collectivity. Totemic naming is a performative action that touches the flesh and makes it collective, or rather makes the collectivity by touching the flesh. "For the primitive," Durkheim writes (1995: 134), "the name is not simply a word, a mere combination of sounds; it is part of the being and, indeed, an essential part." The word is part of the thing, metonym, not metaphor.

Clan members imprint the totem on their flesh. The emblem is embodied through gashes, paints, tattoos, which are worn whenever the clan comes together. Durkheim's account gives primacy to writing, not speech, a material image, not a spoken word, a writing authoring and authorizing the self. He thus anticipates Michel de Certeau's "scriptural economy," his understanding that "there is no law that is not inscribed on bodies," that the law "engraves itself on parchment made from the skin of its subjects." De Certeau will claim that "[b]ooks are only metaphors of the body" (1984: 140).

The strictest taboos pertain to the totemic representation, not to the species themselves. By giving primacy to the name, he anticipates Jacques Lacan's semiotic psychoanalytic theory, in which the child becomes a subject by his entry into an authoritative language of kinship names, a language "unconscious in structure," whose logic governs subjectivity and sexual combination. A child, Lacan argues, enters this language through the portal of "the name of the father," through symbolic order, not biological parentage, the biological father's authority, the "paternal function," likewise being constituted by this language (Lacan [1966] 1977: 65–8). For Durkheim that writing into the skin marks and mimes our dependence on its language, our perpetual and overwhelming debt.

Totemic representation is written in blood. Just as Christians drink the blood of Christ and the Israelites were sprinkled with blood of the covenant by Moses at Sinai, so, too, in totemic rituals, the men of the Arunta draw the sacred emblem of their totem on ground soaked in blood. When Arunta boys are initiated, the totemic image is subincised in their flesh, the blood collected and later used in rituals. Among the Binbinga, the blood on the knife used to write a boy into collective membership must be licked clean by the initiate. Adult members will open their veins, sprinkling the novitiate with their blood. The most sacred blood is that which flows from the penis during circumcision (Durkheim 1995: 137).

Representation is more powerful than reference, totemic symbol than totemic species. The representation of the totem, its drawing or figure, is more sacred than the totemic species itself, a relation homologous to the division Lacan will institute between the phallus and the penis (Lacan 1977). The totem is first written on the individual body when that body is made a symbol of the collectivity, when that individual body is initiated, hailed as a subject, transformed into a representative of the group (Durkheim 1995: 116). The initiated individuals are now part of the totem and the totem part of them. Individual males can only align their individual bodies with the representation of the collectivity when they are able to represent the collectivity. Becoming a man is identical to becoming a member of the collectivity, becoming a member being identical with being allowed to mass with the other men around and through the totem. Acceding to this totemic language is an accession to the law, a politico-linguistic practice, by which an individual becomes a subject, a full individual by being incorporated into the collectivity.

In Durkheim's account, the social organization of the clan does not explain the totemic system. Social unity derives not from an observed social morphology, from how people exist materially on the land, but from a system of symbols that places them in relation to each other by the way it places them in relation to the species of nature. In the societies Durkheim is studying, totemic descent is predominantly inherited through the mother's line, matrilineally, while residence is organized through the father's house, patrilocally (Durkheim 1995: 104, 131, 185). This means that residential groups are composed of peoples who worship different totems. It is not through the sharing of a common physical space of sociality, but only through an imagined kinship with a common totem, a name and emblem that periodically brings the clan members together in ritual, that the clan takes form (Durkheim 1995: 234).

Durkheim's theory of collective representation is based on trinitarian architecture: collectivity, symbol, and an energy mediating the two. The totem, the god, is a symbol of society, because, Durkheim argues, the experience of society is the basis for the experience of God, the experience of the collectivity being the anonymous power that outlives us, one to which we bend without regard to our personal benefit or cost, one that penetrates our very being, that is in us, but not of us (Durkheim 1995: 213–14).

Totemic rites are the occasion for the collective experience of the collectivity, for the experience of its energies, its "indefinite powers and anonymous forces" (1995: 201–2). Durkheim calls this energy "effervescence" (1995: 213), something that suggests champagne or Alka-Seltzer, by which he means a contagious experience that depends upon contagion, the experience of which, he argues, is at the origin of the sacred and moral authority in general. The force of massing in collective rites, synchronous aggregation and movement around a symbol, is the source of the energies upon which the sacred depends. Collective rites register in people's bodies, take intense physical forms – men howl, move wildly about, have sexual relations with women that are normally forbidden, exhaust themselves.

"They bring about such an intense hyper-excitement of physical and mental life as a whole," Durkheim writes, "that they cannot be borne for very long. The celebrant who takes the leading role eventually falls exhausted to the ground" (1995: 218). "[I]t is the nature of moral forces expressed merely by images that they cannot affect the human mind with any forcefulness without putting it outside itself, and plunging it into a state describable as 'ecstatic' . . . [A] very intense social life always does a sort of violence to the individual's body and mind and disrupts their normal functioning. This is why it can last only a limited time" (1995: 228).

Unlike Levi-Strauss' structuralism, Durkheim's taxonomic order is energized, set in motion, through desire, a passionate debt, an irresistible seduction, a proliferating gift which can never be repaid. Effervescent aggregation performs, expresses, mimes, indeed, is, the enabling powers of collective life, upon which not only does the finest within us depend, but from which we derive our meaning and our material existence, indeed which enables us to be. It is from this energy, transported within us, that not only religion, but all authority, is composed. Moral authority, an authority for which we have respect, whether of a person, a text, a practice, has the same origins as religion (Durkheim 1995: 215). Authority derives not from reasoned consent or self-interested contract, but "because a certain psychic energy intrinsic to the idea we have of that person bends our will and turns it in the direction indicated" (Durkheim 1995: 209). Swift and sure bodily punishments should thus be understood as special markings, signs that command respect, indicators that collective representation and its commands are to be obeyed instantly. These sanctions are signs of their sanctity as much as they are instruments by which to assure reasoned compliance. The countless acts of obedience are not simple behavioral information indicating that dissidence is dangerous, but they, too, function to maintain the intensity of that "psychic energy." The threat of punishment is less important to maintaining compliance than the "mental representation" it signifies and solidifies. The violence heaped upon offenders of the law, of the prohibitions marking and protecting the most sacred things, is of the same symbolic economy as that which draws the group together and makes it one, the energy of collective effervescence. Violence signifies the effervescence which is its source. Neither punishment nor gift can be assimilated to a law.

For Durkheim God is a representation of moral authority within us, something which we understand is in us, but not of us (1995: 213). The process involves an unconscious transference, an external sociality is experienced internally through its intense physical and emotional effects. The complex sources of these effects elude mental representation, eludes thought, and are projected on to some simple object like a totem or flag, to which the emotional energies of intense sociality attach themselves (1995: 221, 230).

As opposed to those, like Lévi-Strauss and the followers of the "linguistic turn," who will later argue that the social is based on the model of language, Durkheim not only argues that the taxonomic order of language is derived from the experience of the social, but that the social does not have its own language, indeed must exceed language. Society must speak, or more precisely write, indirectly, must translate. Durkheim prides himself on having discovered the gap between the sacred and the profane, which he unfortunately locates institutionally in the division between religious and economic life, thereby barring the way to joining his theoretical framework to the enchanted symbolism – the fetishism of commodities, the transrationality of property, the spectacle of consumption – likewise animating capitalism.

However, the *Elementary Forms* unveils an equally profound gap between the social and its representations. The sacred translates into symbols, symbols that both contain and constitute our social energies. Yet these energies, these forces, exceed their representations. "[I]t is in the nature of religious forces," Durkheim writes, "to be incapable of full individualization" (1995: 203). Society translates itself behind our backs, unconsciously. For Durkheim the job of the social analyst is to capture this translation and then to show how the dream, the fiction, is a productive part of the reality. Durkheim is arguing that a sociologist interprets social interpretation, there being no outside its text, here a nature story. Unlike Lévi-Strauss who will locate the unconscious mental character of collective representation as taxonomic codes of language, codes founded on the transposition of attributes of natural objects, things "good to think with" (Lévi-Strauss 1963: 18), Durkheim locates it in the non-representable, excessive experience of the social.

Like Ferdinand de Saussure, who attended his lectures (Alexander 1988: 4), Durkheim argues that language makes thought possible, not the other way around. But by refusing psychology, Durkheim also opens the way to the logic of Jacques Derrida's deconstruction, to a self which can never be self-present to its signs, signs in which the self is always already inscribed, in short, to *différance* (Derrida 1992). However, Durkheim points to a social, hermeneutical phenomenology of the flesh as its ground, quite unlike Derrida, who builds religion's two sources – the experience of faith and the sacred – from a structure of bodily experience which is not experienced, an experience mediated through bodily metaphors without flesh (Derrida [1996] 1998). The desire of presence would be to be, to have, a body, to be both subject and object, to be present in one's body, for the body not to be set apart as a sign of one's self.

In the empirical materials, Durkheim repeatedly emphasizes the human body's role in social signification, in the generation not only of collective representation but of the collectivity represented. Human body and totem reference each other, participate in each other's nature, they are co-substantial. Totemic representation is a ritual poesis. Durkheim's human body is not just Bourdieu's classificatory "writing pad," but a desirous, energized, existential phenomenological basis of social authority. Durkheim thus echoes the work of Friedrich Nietzsche for whom concept is metaphor, in that we can never have access to the essence of things, only their metaphors, metaphors grounded in the bodily experience of pleasure and pain (Kofman [1983] 1993: 6–22). For Durkheim, authority not only has a body but must be embodied. It does not, indeed cannot, operate through the mind alone. Neither rationality, the balance sheet of interested compliance and dissent, nor categorical cognition, are sufficient. Simply registering a totemic image is not enough to "affect the human mind with any forcefulness" (1995: 228). Moral force depends in its origins on "delirium," "ecstasy," "violence to the individual's body and mind."

Contrary to the certainty that science makes religion increasingly untenable, to the Kantian separation of reason and faith, Durkheim argues that religion made science possible, because it enabled us to understand that humans and the natural world were made of the same "essence," that the same forces regulated both our behavior and those of the natural world (1995: 238). The logic of collective representation makes us consubstantial with the world through the ways in which men are consubstantial with each other. Durkheim locates the very origin of conceptual and causal thought in this embodied experience of oneness. The understanding of internal ties between external objects originates in our ability to "join together what the senses put asunder," the conceptualization of "internal connections" between things being derived from our experience of the internal connection between men, "a hyperexcitation of intellectual forces," driven by our "natural taste for unrestrained assimilations" (1995: 239, 241). Our capacity for rationality, our ability to presuppose cause and effect in the world, depends on this original collective representation, that versus Hume, science does not derive from sense perception alone, and versus Kant, cause and effect, the connection of one thing to another, the ability to "establish relationships between things that make them appear to us as functions of one another and as vibrating sympathetically in accordance with an internal law this is rooted in their nature" (1995: 239) need not presume *a priori*'s in the nature of our consciousness, but rather derive them from the sociological *a priori* of social representation itself.

There is no epistemological gap between religion and science. "Today as in the past, to explain is to show how a thing participates in one or several other things" (Durkheim 1995: 240). Science, like religion, operates through assimilations and divisions which cannot be derived from sense perception alone. This would be Heidegger's (1977) point in his notion of the "ground plan," one taken up as well in Foucault's *Order of Things* ([1966] 1970). For Durkheim, however, there is a fire at the birth of thought. "Creating a whole world of ideals, through which the world of sensed realities seemed transfigured, would require a hyperexcitation of intellectual forces that is possible only in and through society." Reason has socially sensuous origins.

That the totem is a symbol of the collectivity does not mean then that it is merely an expression of the collectivity, a cultural reflection of its social existence, of its density, its bounded interactions. The symbol rather is integral to the formation of the collectivity. Through the totemic symbol, unique and exclusive, individuals engage in a communication that ends "in a communion – that is, in a fusion of all the individual feelings into a common one" (Durkheim 1995: 231). "The appearance of this resultant [the symbol] notifies individuals that they are in unison and brings home to them their moral unity. It is by shouting the same cry, saying the same words and performing the same action in regard to the same object that they arrive at and experience agreement" (1995: 232). The symbol of the collectivity is necessary to produce collective consciousness, consciousness that they are a collectivity.

The clan member experiences a kinship with the totem, he "participates in its nature," is composed of the same substance. The clan member and the totem, the person and the animal, the body and the symbol, are consubstantial. The clan member is the symbol made flesh, an embodied symbol. And it is through their flesh, their bodies, that the individuals perform the collective symbol into a collectivity, by massing their bodies, moving in unison around and with the symbol (Durkheim 1995: 232).

In totemic rites, collective consciousness requires that the body itself become a symbol, an instance of the collective body, by "participating" in the symbol by which it knows itself, by a physical fusion of body and symbol. The collectivity is a collective body, a group of individual bodies which periodically experience themselves as one body. The experience of collectivity derives from the common movement, from ritual interaction with the totemic object. Common bodily movement, Durkheim asserts, symbolizes the totemic representation "only because they have helped to form them.

Without symbols . . . social feelings could have only an unstable existence" (1995: 232).

The alchemistry of the social has a circular circuit. An interaction generates an energy, which registers inside us, an energy imperfectly translated into symbolic form, a form which is nonetheless necessary to set the interaction and its energies into motion. This shuttling back and forth between representation and reality, as Durkheim recognizes, is an exclusively male mimesis. The unremarked fact in Durkheim's tale is that the collectivity is a fusion of naked men (Durkheim 1995: 310). It is men, and men alone, moving, massing, touching, screaming, in that moment of ritual ecstasy, of delirium, overturning every convention. If the clan members are of the same substance of the totem, then the totemic ritual must be a performance of that consubstantiality, not just of each man with that of his totem, but more importantly for the social constitution, with each other. The energy of the totemic principle is homosocial, bonding between men.

Durkheim made the daring argument that the same energies animating the crowds who made the French Revolution powered the totemic rites of the aboriginals, that the same energy, or effervescence, made collective representation possible in both cases. He thereby recognized the relation between the sexualized delirium of the totemic rite and the violence of the revolutionary crowd. Durkheim thus refuses to distinguish between the moral authority of sovereigns and saints, assimilating aboriginal totemic rite to the passions of the French Revolution. He thus suggests not the restricted project of a sociology of religion, but the more capacious project of a religious sociology, one that will be taken up by the *Collège de Sociologie* in 1937–9 (Falasca-Zamponi 2001; Richman 2002).

Collective representation is a massing of bodies. As Elias Canetti (1973: 32) would point out with respect to the crowds of modern mass politics, their essential attribute was a desire to grow, a love of density (highest at the moment of "discharge" into an open crowd). What struck Canetti about the crowd was its physicality, its making many bodies into one, by suspending men's natural aversion to physical contact with other men, "the repugnance to being touched." In the modern crowd, what men feared now becomes what they most desire (1973: 15–16). Just as Durkheim derived the sacred, and the signification of shared consubstantiality of totem and clan, from the effervescent massing of male bodies, Canetti argued that the energies derived from tactility among men in common movement in the dense crowds of modern politics were the template for all demands of equality (1973: 32–4), a theme that would later be taken up by Tambiah (1996).

How might the sex of that ecstasy figure into the constitution of the social? Why is it that the self-same revolutionary crowds which Durkheim understood as an all-male chorus, whose virile ecstasies produced the rights of man, Gustav LeBon and others saw as corrosive, irrational, feminine forces tending towards decomposition (Falasca-Zamponi 1997)? How can it be that the energies of the rites of collective representation are interpreted as both masculine and feminine? Is it simply a matter of political positionality, that those who discern their social necessity and revolutionary productivity are comfortable with their maleness, while those who fear their disruptive potential conjure them as feminine forces?

   This shuttling back and forth between representation and reality is an exclusively male mimesis. Even though the totem is passed through their line, women were forbidden from participating in these sacred rites, forbidden from taking the totem on to their skins, even from witnessing it through their eyes (Durkheim 1995: 125, 132, 384). Is the exclusion of women from collective representation due simply to the logic of masculine domination, to their status as socially fissiparous objects of desire?

   Effervescence is associated with violation. In Durkheim's account the communion of men around the symbol leads to a sudden dissolution of individual and even collective male property rights in particular women, individual men who are men by their property rights to particular women (1995: 218–19). In signifying and generating the energies of the social in the violation of its codes, Durkheim anticipates not only anthropologists, like Edmund Leach (1985) who pointed that the sacrality of founding patriarchs and sovereigns, like Abraham and David, is marked by their ability to violate sexual laws of incest and endogamy, but political theorists like Carl Schmitt ([1932] 1996) who locate sovereign authority in the political decision on the "exception," an authority which cannot be assimilated to the law to determine a collective enemy and to suspend the law, and what Jacques Derrida ([1990] 2002) would subsequently refer to as the mystical basis of state authority, an originary violence that can never be subordinated to or derived from the law. The way in which Durkheim implicates bodily violation in the sacred and renders it socially productive puts him in stark contrast to his American interpreters who would confine the sacred to civic ritual, rendering it abstract, depriving it of its inherent transgressive and thus transformative possibilities (Bellah 1967; Shils 1975).

   While Schmitt and Derrida emphasize an originary, extra-legal violence in collective representation, Durkheim points to the procreative, life-giving powers of the totem. The totem with which men identify their bodies is a fantastic bi-sexual organ, not just playing the role of phallic propagation, of inseminating powerful seed between the loins of maidens, but placing whole embryos there, man and woman in one organ, the woman reduced to an incubator, a warm hotel room. The totemic myths locate the first ancestors as unborn, Adamically arriving in this universe from outside the wombs of women. The first Arunta ancestors, the Alcheringa, are known as the "uncreated ones" (Durkheim 1995: 250). Wherever these incarnations of the totemic principle alight, their bodies took form as rocks, trees, or water holes. It is here that the *churingas*, pieces of wood or stone with images of the totem engraved upon them, are stored, sacred places, safe havens, refuges where conflicts are proscribed. The *churinga* is believed to have extraordinary powers, to heal, to secure fertility, to make strong those who are kin with the species represented, and to make weak and enfeeble their enemies. These sites contain the embryos of babies which enter the women of the appropriate marriage class through the hip (1995: 253–4). Totemic discourse thus gives the men extra-uterine, feminine powers, as though the totem's passage through the womb, through the female line, brought the female function along with it, lodging it there in the symbolic logic of the totem. Ancestors can throw the *churinga*, a stone with an image on it, into the body of a woman where it takes human form.

If the totem can penetrate the female body with such procreative powers, is the totemic ritual powered simply by male identification with the totem, or does this massing carry another logic, that of penetration, of not simply being the totem, but of having and being had by the totem? Durkheim makes clear that society is constituted through common submission, in the taking inside something which is in us, but not of us. "For society, that unique source of all that is sacred, is not satisfied to move us from outside and to affect us transitorily, it organizes itself lastingly within us" (1995: 266).

The reproduction of the sacred totem is a masculine fertilization, an all-male sexual act. In *Intichiuma* ceremonies, the men of the Arunta and other clans take responsibility for assuring the reproduction of the totemic species. At the ancestral abodes, they inseminate the world with dust, sand, seeds, sparks from those sites, often mixed with their own blood (Durkheim 1995: 330–7). Spencer and Gillen report that the chief of the Wonkgongaru, ancestors of a fish, enters a water hole, allowing the blood to flow from a puncture in his scrotum (1904: 336). For this rite to assure the totem's reproduction, the men must typically eat just a little of the totem's substance (1904: 338–41). The taboo is violated, the totem taken inside. "There is no positive rite," Durkheim writes, "that does not fundamentally constitute a veritable sacrilege" (1995: 342). But it is not here a sacrificial death at the heart of life. The ancestors ate regularly of the totem; they cannot, they do not, explain why. The Unmatjera believe that if a man were to eat too much during this rite, "he would swell up and die" (Spencer and Gillen 1904: 324). A man impregnates and is impregnated. Spencer and Gillen report that in every tribe they studied, young men endured a subincision of their penises, slitting it open from the base to its tip, in parallel with the "rite of cutting open the vagina . . . practiced upon the young women" (1904: 133). Like the totem, the initiate is a man-woman, separate totems for men and women being a relatively rare and a later development (Durkheim 1995: 166–8).

If individual women give birth to individual bodies, groups of men procreate collective bodies. The first is heterosexual across the boundaries of social groups; the second is homosocial. The woman takes inside a man's seed. What do the men take inside? Other men. Durkheim tells us that during moments of collective effervescence, when the collectivity takes physical form as a mass of men, the individual is filled with the collective, is no longer an individual self, but an embodiment of the collectivity. If the collectivity represented is a company of men, surely the energies that bind it must somehow derive from passionate affinity, a desire for and the pleasures of union with members of one's same sex. And if women are excluded from these rites, might a more dangerous boundary transgression than sexual exclusivity of marriage, incest taboos or exogamy be the inhibited aim energizing these dangerous rites? Might that have something to do with the strict prohibition against eating the totemic animal, a prohibition that only the most sacred men, long ago, could accomplish without harm? Might it also have something to do with the absolute boundary between the sacred and the profane?

Totem and tattoo: the tabooed Freud

Durkheim never made sexuality part of the theoretical constitution of the social. Freud, on the other hand, pointed to the sexual, and indeed the homoerotic, origins of political authority. Within the sociological community, Freud is largely a tabooed ancestor, an undergraduate pleasure. Freud, like Durkheim, studied totemism, sought to locate the origins of the group, publishing *Totem and Taboo* in 1913, one year after the publication of Durkheim's study. Freud, the psychoanalyst, like Durkheim the sociologist, translates collective dreams, representations that imperfectly convert social experience into symbols, whose manifest content is always inadequate relative to the thoughts and feelings condensed, displaced, or refracted within them.

Freud argues that totemism and exogamy appear together, two of the strongest and earliest taboos, two forbidden forms of having: one cannot eat the totemic animal, nor have sexual relations with the women of one's own clan. Taboos do not derive from divine prohibition, nor are they justified. They have no known origin. They are punished automatically by "an inner, automatic arrangement." Freud, like Durkheim, works with an electric body.

Tabooed objects radiate a "dangerous power," are "charged," an electricity transmitted by touch (1946: 27–31). "This power is inherent in all persons who are more or less prominent, such as kings, priests, and the newly born; in all exceptional physical states, such as menstruation, puberty, and birth; in everything sinister, like illness and death, and in everything connected with these conditions by virtue or contagion or dissemination" (1946: 31). Freud calls that energy libido, the energy of desire, an energy that binds the subject to the object world, an energy that can be redirected, or displaced, from its original object, concealed and occluded, but never lost ([1905] 2000: 83). It is an elementary economics.

Freud, too, argues that primitive religion contains the secret, not just of religion, but of modern authority. Just as Durkheim's totemic representations contain this energy, so do Freud's representatives of the collectivity – the kings and priests, "bearers of that mysterious and dangerous magic power which communicates itself by contact, like an electric charge, bringing death and destruction to any one not protected by a similar charge" (1946: 56). When the king touches intentionally, it heals; but when he is touched, it destroys. Arching between sovereign and subject, the energy is munificent; turned about, it blows the circuit box.

The taboos surrounding the powerful, which guard their approach through protocol, sequester them in sacred sites, give them great powers, yet hedge in their freedom with a dense web of etiquette originate, Freud argues, in the unconscious hostility, nay the murderous urges, their subjects harbor towards them. Our attitude towards the powerful is ambivalent – both veneration and hatred, love and a sense of persecution. Through taboo, we protect both them and ourselves from the aggression within us. Like Durkheim's sacred, taboo's current is alternating, the original meaning of the word being both holy and unclean (Freud 1946: 88–9).

Freud reads totemic ritual as symptom, an expression of a shared unconscious wish. The psychic economy governing taboos is similar to that which he observed in his obsessive neurotic patients who cannot explain why they forbid themselves from touching certain things because they believe that the power within them is contagious, that violation of the prohibition will lead inexorably to punishment, and therefore engage in all manner of rituals of purification and penance. In the case of obsessional neurosis, some desire is repressed, kept out of awareness, and although unavailable, nonetheless makes its presence felt. It is this desire, Freud argues, that powers the prohibition, prohibition proportional to the inadmissible desire (1946: 44).

For Freud the certainty of punishment prevents us from realizing that we, too, have desires to do what has been forbidden (1946: 46, 94). For Durkheim, in contrast, the swiftness and severity of punishment is an indicator of the social sacrality of that which had been violated, reflecting not the heterosexual pleasure individually denied, but the homosocial pleasures enabling social authority. Potential individual bodily pains are commensurate to the collective bodily pleasures generating that sacrality. Durkheim refuses the atomic individual of contractarian liberalism, locating the basis of the social in the group, while Freud, for all his irrational, divided eroticization of social relations, ultimately organizes that erotic logic through dyadic relations grounded in individuals competing over sexual objects, even if those individuals and the logic of that competition is socio-legal in nature.

The two taboos – against eating the totem and incestuous intercourse with the women, both daughters and mothers, of one's family – parallel what Freud finds in his neurotic patients, namely an ambivalent desire to kill the father and to have sexual relations with the mother, the Oedipal complex. The Oedipal myth, in which a son unknowingly slays his father and sleeps with his mother, reveals, Freud argues, the unrealized and unrealizable desires of the unconscious, unspeakable murderous wishes that all sons carry toward their fathers as a result of their rivalrous love for their mothers, a rage born out of a frustrated desire to possess her exclusively.

The Oedipal complex is resolved ontogenetically through identification with the father, taking his prohibitive powers inside as conscience, or superego, renouncing the desire to possess the mother. In normal human development, the son resolves his desire to have the mother by choosing to be his father. Object choices are replaced by identifications, having the mother by being the father. If, for Durkheim, the totem is a symbol of masculine society, for Freud, it is a symbol of the primal father, a figure with whom the sons of each generation identify, a representation with which they align their bodies, as they enter into manhood, assume their role as representatives of the collectivity.

If Durkheim started with the simplest societies to find the elementary structures of our own religious thought, Freud went to the elemental and most common psychic disorders, assuming that the development of each individual recapitulates the history of the species. Little children, for example, believe that their wishes, their thoughts, have enormous power in the world, a conception identical to that which organizes magic, magic being akin to the play of children (1946: 109–10), a suspension of the distance separating the world of imagination from the world of objects. This belief in magic, "forcing the laws of psychic life upon the reality of things" (1946: 119), corresponded, Freud contended, to the first stage of individual development, in which sexual impulses are not directed to the external object world, but towards the self, the ego. Freud first identified this autoeroticism as narcissism in his psychoanalytic biography of Leonardo da Vinci ([1910] 1964).

The magical, animistic thought of primitive peoples, Freud argued, reflected this infantile "sexualization" of thought. In the neurotic, who responds to the reality of thought, not of experience, one can see the earliest forms of society, where thinking had yet to be desiccated of desire, the renunciation of the "pleasure principle" necessary to science.

Our individual psychic structure, Freud argued, contains the deposits of collective history, inherited "psychic dispositions," the contents of an unconscious "mass psyche" (1946: 204). Likewise in his studies of dreams, Freud points to common dreams which cannot be the product of individual experience (Roth 1987: 142). In *Totem and Taboo* Freud locates that historical moment that has left its deposit as a "piece of inherited psychic property" (1946: 43). The totemic taboo, he suggests, reflects an actual historical memory, a moment when men did what they desired. The Darwinian theory upon which he drew at that time argued that pre-historical men traveled in hordes, each led by a dominant man who kept all the women of his horde as his own. Freud also relied on the theories of William Robertson Smith (1846–94), a scholar of the Old Testament, who had done work based on a traveler's account of the totemism of the ancient tribes of the Sinai desert (Smith 1969). Smith described how the group would tie up a camel on an altar of stones, circumambulating the tethered dromedary, until the leader drove in the first knife, his followers drinking the blood spurting out, after which they would all hack "off pieces of the quivering flesh and devouring them raw with such wild haste, that in the short interval between the rise of the day star . . . and the disappearance of its rays before the rising sun, the entire camel, body and bones, skin, blood and entrails is wholly devoured" (Smith 1969: 338). Smith, who influenced Durkheim as well, argued that these totemic rites, in which the members worshipped and actually consumed an animal they considered to be their ancient ancestor, was a means by which humans partook of the divine and thereby sacralized the social group, functioning to sustain its solidarity.

Identification precedes object choice as an affective modality, being before having (Roth 1987). Freud argues that the proscribed totem is a projective substitute for the father, the ego ideal, here akin to children who identify with, yet project their hostility towards, and consequent fear of, their fathers on to animals (1946: 166–7). Through the ceremonial eating of the totem, the members of the clan affirm their consubstantiality, their being of the same substance or kinship, with each other and with the deity (1946: 178). The totemic ritual is then not only a performance of identity with the father; it is also, Freud contends, a violent assimilation, a having, not a being.

There is, Freud contends, a bloody moment in our history that accounts for this totemic sacrifice, a "great event with which culture began" (1946: 187).

The democracy of brothers has murderous origins. This great sociological bedtime story goes like this:

> One day the expelled brothers joined forces, slew and ate the father, and thus put an end to the father horde. Together they dared and accomplished what would have remained impossible for them singly . . . Of course these canni-balistic savages ate their victim. The violent primal father had surely been the envied and feared model for each of the brothers. Now they accomplished their identification with him by devouring him and each acquired a part of his strength. The totem feast, which is perhaps mankind's first celebration, would be the repetition and commemoration of this memorable, criminal act with which so many things began, social organization, moral restrictions and religion.
> (Freud 1946: 183)

The totemic sacrifice represents the sons' victory over patriarchal power, or in later interpretations when the facticity of the event was suspended, their vanquishing of a perennial desire, not an historical act, to destroy the father, or the father's place. No wonder, Freud argued, the totemic sacrifice, the periodic sacrifice of the most sacred animal, indeed its eating, was always accomplished together, never alone; no wonder it was obligatory. All had to take responsibility for this murder.

The killed animal is first mourned and then celebrated, reflecting the sons' love of the father, an absent father who can now be safely loved, incorporated through identification in the form of the superego. Freud writes portentously, "The dead now became stronger than the living had been." As in Durkheim's treatment of the social, this paternal corpse lives on inside of us, but is not of us. Christianity's success, Freud argues, derives from its supreme atonement for this murderous desire, this original sin, the son becoming a god, the children identifying themselves with him by ritual consumption of his body and blood (1946: 198–9). The social has criminal origins, scenes bloodied by forbidden love and death.

The wish to be like the father, to be omnipotent, does not die with the father, but rather grows, becoming "an ideal . . . having as a content the fullness of power and the freedom from restriction of the conquered pri-mal father, as well as the willingness to subject themselves to him" (Freud 1946: 191–2). This father ideal is the basis of the gods and "godlike kings who transfer the patriarchal system to the state" (1946: 193). Sacrifice to the gods replaces totemic sacrifice. And to the state, instead of sacrificing totemic animals, we now sacrifice human kind. "It must be said that the revenge of the deposed and reinstated father has been very cruel; it culminated in the dominance of authority" (1946: 193). Generalized authority origi-nates in ambivalent death wishes against patriarchal power. As in Durkheim, the structure of religious representation is the same as that of the modern state.

Sociality has a sexual organization. Freud links exogamy and totemism, totemism being the first definition of the social group within which sexual intercourse was denied. Freud pairs the prohibition of killing the totemic animal with the prohibition of incestuous relations within the family (1946: 185). He argues that "the exogamy connected with the totem . . . makes it impossible for the man to have sexual union with all the women of his own group, with a number of females, therefore, who are not consanguineously related to him, by treating all these women like blood relations" (1946: 9). He cites Durkheim, who points out that according to totemic law, a son would be of the same totemic blood as that of his mother and sisters (1946: 156, 163). However Freud changes Durkheim's causal logic. Unlike Freud, Durkheim, in his *Incest: The Nature and Origin of Taboo* ([1897] 1963), derived incest taboos not from profane heterosexual competition for the father's women, but from a sexually unmarked revulsion at profane contact with the substance of one's totem. In Durkheim's account there is no foregone heteroerotic desire by the sons for their mothers or sisters. Referring to a "repression of incest," Durkheim argued that the clan men experienced a "religious horror" at sexual contact with the menstrual blood, with their own substance. It is sexual revulsion at the social same, not social revulsion at the sexual other.

In the societies upon which Freud is building his argument, the totem is, as he himself recognizes, inherited matrilineally, while families are formed patrilocally (1946: 158). Matrilineal inheritance sets up a strange sociological flaw in Freud's argument. The totemic rite is of matrilineal kin, not patrilocal family (1946: 175). In such cases it manages the consubstantiality of the sons with their mothers, not their fathers. The totemic taboo prevents sons from having sexual relations with the substance of their mothers, not their fathers. Although he recognizes this (1946: 158), Freud insists on making the totem into a paternal symbol:

> If the totem animal is the father, then the two taboo rules which constitute its nucleus, – not to kill the totem animal and not to use a woman belonging to the same totem for sexual purposes, – agree in content with the two crimes of Oedipus. (Freud 1946: 171)

In fact, when sons eat their totem, they are eating the substance of their mother's line, not their father's. Freud has the sons eating the mother's totem, although he has remade him into a man, a "female" father substitute. The relationship between son and father is refigured as an oral relation between son and mother, a consumption which Freud describes, in *Group Psychology and the Analysis of the Ego*, as the first ambivalent identification, in which food is both assimilated and destroyed as an external object, "a devouring affection" (Freud 1959: 47). The annual totemic sacrifice is an object-cathexis, a having of the father, not a being of the father. The cultural logic of the totemic sacrifice repudiates the Oedipal resolution in which paternal identification displaces maternal object-love. In this rite, the father is ritually allowed to become an object of the son's desire, identification symbolically realized through consumption (1946: 191), sacrifice making the introjection material.

There is, Freud surmises, a phylogenetic moment that is consonant with this unspeakable desire to have the father, or to be had by him. The desire to kill the father, Freud tells us, originates in a paternal proscription of his sons' intra-clan heterosexual relations. While we now effortlessly make the exogamous jump, in Freud's mythic text there is still an active pre-exogamous moment, unsettling for the sexuality of that paternal place. In both *Totem and Taboo* and the later *Group Psychology and the Analysis of the Ego* ([1921] 1959), paternal proscription of sexual relations with the women of the clan passes to exogamy through homoerotic bonding. Freud locates the origins of the sons' collective organization, their ability to challenge the father's sexual monopoly, in "the homo-sexual feelings and activities which probably manifested themselves during the time of their banishment" (1946: 186; 1959: 72). The father's imposition of heterosexual austerities on his sons pushes them into mutual erotic identification, "into group psychology." After killing the primal father, the sons agree that all the clan's women would be denied them.

In *Totem and Taboo* Freud made homoerotics into a substitution for heteroerotics, one standing at the origin of the first social contract, the sons' renunciation of the women of the clan as sensuous objects, and their conversion into sexual property to be exchanged exogamously. If exogamous heterosexuality is an original consequence of social organization, endogamous homosexuality is its original source, the erotic face of its "mystical foundation" in Derridean terms. Freud never wavered on this foundational basis of modern social organization. Indeed, in *Group Psychology and the Analysis of the Ego* Freud makes heterosexual desire into an enemy of social organization, whereas "desexualized, sublimated homosexual love for other, which springs from work in common" is a "civilizing factor" (1959: 44; see also [1905] 2000). There "is no room for woman as a sexual object," he writes, in the "great artificial groups" of society (1959: 94). The implication, of course, is that there is a place for men as sexual objects. "It seems certain," he writes, "that homosexual love is far more compatible with group ties, even when it takes the shape of uninhibited sexual impulsion . . ." (1959: 95).

If in his mythico-history, Freud makes the homoerotics of the brother clan the mediation between the primal horde and exogamous patriarchy, in his clinical studies he makes homoerotics integral to the formation of the male individual ego, to masculine identification, and to the psychic operation of authority more generally. Freud begins his *Three Essays on the Theory of Sexuality* with a discussion of "sexual aberrations," pride of place among these given to the "invert," he (or she) who is deviant with respect to their sexual object. The relation between sexual instinct and sexual object, he argues, is contingent, "merely soldered together" (Freud [1905] 2000: 14). That we make people of the opposite sex our exclusive object choices is not then a fact of nature, but of culture, a "fumbling" libidinal trajectory. In his psychoanalytic biography of Leonardo da Vinci ([1910] 1964), published three years before *Totem and Taboo*, Freud declares "everyone, even the most normal person, is capable of making a homosexual object-choice, and has done so at some time in his life, and either still adheres to it in his unconscious or else protects himself against it by vigorous counter-attitudes."[1] For Freud symptoms are substitutes, or "transcriptions," of repressed desires, the "negative of perversions" (2000: 31). He makes the extraordinary generalization: "The unconscious mental life of all neurotics (without exception) shows inverted impulses, fixation of their libido upon persons of their own sex" (2000: 32). Civilization, a skein of neurotic symptoms, thus has a homoerotic constitution.

In the normative resolution of the Oedipal complex, a boy's inability to have the mother as a sexual object is resolved through his ability to be the father, forbidden heterosexual desire retained and resolved through gender identification. But paternal identification also transmutes a homosexual object-choice, one that is at the heart of sociality. Just like the totemic clan the individual subject is formed through bodily representation. In *Ego and the Id*, Freud argues that the self – the ego – is first figured through an imagined body, a sexed morphological imaginary ([1923] 1960: 16). The imagined body in whose bounded image ego formation takes place during the "mirror stage" has a sex. The male self is both formed and sexed as a resolution of an inhabitation of the bodily form of paternal authority, an outside which is in us, but not of us, but the condition for our being. As Judith Butler has pointed out, this homoerotic loss initiates the ego as a perceptual object, as a container for reflexively turned, unavowable erotic desire and sadistic rage at its loss and uninhabitability (Butler 1997: 132–50). That desire is both refused and retained in a melancholic gender identification, an ungrievable loss (1997: 132–50). Men want to have the femininity they can never be and want to be the masculinity they can never have. The habitable space of gender is grounded in an uninhabitable space of sex. Paternal identification solves not one, but two problems in this sexual economy.

Group formation likewise operates through paternal identification, which, like his murder, is enabled through homoerotic solidarity among the sons. Immediately after explaining in *Group Psychology* that the introjected paternal object is a substitute for the libidinal object tie with the woman (1959: 50), Freud launches into the genesis of male homosexuality, the boy's failure to give up the mother as a cathected object, the "negative" Oedipal complex, the transformation of the male ego on the model of the female. Boy becomes girl mirroring the way in which Freud has the man, through the matrilineal totem, becoming woman. Group formation is quintessentially masculine, yet involves men being womanly.

In analyzing the paternal identification process at its heart, Freud stages two scenes of group formation: the primal horde and the hypnotist's gaze. In the other scene in which Freud conjures the group – hypnosis – he declares that this dyad is identical with group formation, group formation with two members (1959: 59). The hypnotic is uncanny, "something old and familiar that has undergone repression" and returns in unfamiliar guise. That something, Freud asserts, is the source of the taboo, a mysterious power. It is the performative power of the father's gaze, through which the ego comes into existence and through which it can be destroyed. The authority of the group, like that of the hypnotist, is an erotic penetration by the father, a cathected object brought inside. Hypnosis works when the son allows himself to be penetrated, when a man becomes womanly, when he responds to the command to "sleep," to withdraw all interest from the object world around him.

Rereading Freud's originary myth, the sons' rage then is not just over sensuous access to sisters and mother, who would be of the same substance according to totemic inheritance, but over another pain, the forbidden desire to be the sensuous object of the father's gaze, the desire to be the mother which is simultaneously a desire to be had by the father. Identification with the father then is also a homoerotic tie, a desire to have, resolved by a constriction to be, an internalization of another masculine bodily representation.

The sex of collective representation

Moral authority, Durkheim writes, derives its power through psychic properties, mythologized because "the influence of society ... moves along channels that are too obscure and circuitous, and uses psychic mechanisms that are too complex, to be easily traced to the source" (1995: 210–11). Durkheim pointed to the pleasures of masculine assembly, whether in the corporate group or the totemic rite, as the energy animating collective representation, both its force and its formation. Through effervescent assembly, man comes into "relations with extraordinary powers that excite him to the point of frenzy" (Durkheim 1995: 220). He also argued that it was only through such energized aggregation that men became aware of their status as *homo duplex*, both individual and social, "the twofold nature in which he participates" (1995: 221). The totem, "the visible body of the god," is thus an unconscious projection, the "body" of an unrecognized "Other," a collective body that has penetrated into oneself, powered by a force of desire, something "set apart and forbidden" (1995: 44, 223).

Does psychoanalytic theory point to other "obscure channels" for moral authority? Both Durkheim and Freud give primacy to representation over referent, to images, to "psychic realities," to the semiotic over the somatic. Both also, however, make somatics into a constituent of semiosis. Both operate through the medium of an unconscious process, the unspeakable impersonal anonymous force of masculine society on the one hand, and the unfulfilled and unfulfillable wish to be the father on the other.

And yet one cannot simply be folded one into the other. Freud starts with the sexual interests of individuals as determined by sons' relations to female bodies as instruments of pleasure, the social being a misrecognized generalization of patriarchal authority. Durkheim, in contrast, starts with the sociality of a wider kin network, making interest, utility, and calculation, a subsidiary form. Freud's theory thus fuses bourgeois individualism and sexuality, not just the properties of sex, but to sex as property. He gives primacy to sexual possession, to possession of the other as an object, to pleasure as possession, to objects as the condition of an always alienated subjectivity.

Freud reads the totem through the shared experience of ambivalent renunciation, its social productivity being a medium to accommodate Oedipal guilt, transposed and generalized as authority. Freud thus starts – as do the liberal economists – with a distributive problem, with freedom foregone, sexual opportunity costs. Durkheim, in contrast, starts with a production function, an enabling, an empowerment, the totem's producing the social as the social produces man, men sacrificing themselves to the totem as they produce the social. Totemic ritual mimes the human making of society and societal making of man (1995: 348–54). Without effervescent assembly, he writes, collective representation would "eventually disappear into the unconscious" (1995: 349). For Durkheim, the symbolic logic of totemic representation lies in the reciprocal dependence of individual man and collective society, whereas in Freud, it lies in the ambivalent love of the father.

Both Freud and Durkheim make homosocial energy the basis of solidarity in complex groups. However Freud locates the origin of the social in a

ROGER FRIEDLAND

renunciation of heterosexual desire, while Durkheim makes its homoerotic expression a source of the social. Freud is here the individual instrumental, sexual Hobbesian, while it is Durkheim who makes the social, indeed the moral, derive from collective passion, "delirium" and "ecstasy" (1995: 228). If Freud locates the origin of the social in an original instrumental, contractual suppression of male heterosexual desire, Durkheim locates it rather in a recurrent expression of homosocial desire. If Durkheim's hermeneutic key to the totem is our unconscious debt as individuals to the social, Freud's is man's unconscious internal aggression to the patriarch.

Freud derives the experience of consubstantiality of totem and man from a fleshy family, from the mother–child bond and the son's deferred identification with the father. Durkheim, in contrast, derives consubstantiality from the experience of a wider social, a representation of embodied oneness with other men. Freud's is an imaginary resolution to a scarce heterosexual economy, while Durkheim's is an imaginary expression of a fulfilled homosocial congress. In point of fact, Freud's clinical theory of individual development is more consistent with Durkheim's account of totemism than is his own historical mythology. And Durkheim, in turn, points to the truth, and indeed a liberatory aspect, of Freud's homoerotic theory. For what in Freud is a feminizing, violent subordination to masculine hierarchy, is, in Durkheim, a masculinizing, non-violent, non-hierarchical assimilation. Freud eroticizes power; Durkheim does not.

Both Durkheim and Freud make somatics into a constituent of semiosis, an immanent relation between individual and collective bodies, as metaphor, mechanics, and energetics of collective representation. We can align these two symbolic orders through the logic of incorporation, through society's "two bodies" – actually four – of individual and collective bodily representation and representative, of individual and collective subjects and their flesh. It is stunning, by its obviousness, that individual bodies arrive *ex machina* in Durkheim's account, an account not only without women, but without human babies, an infancy at the very center of psychoanalytic theory.[2] Yet it is the utter dependence of the individual on the society, its language and law, and the child on its parents, that constitutes their parallel and reciprocal sociality. Durkheim shows how the totemic clan is represented through the individual body of an animal or plant written into the individual male body, bodies the energy of whose massing both animates and represents the collectivity. If ironically Durkheim specifies the homoerotic logic of totemic identification, it is Freud who provides a psychological mechanism – unconscious bodily identification – by which that body might be incorporated into the self. The totem of the clan, being a higher order of social organization than the natal family, can then be read as an occupation of the place of the

260

father recapitulating the sons' identification with the person of the father in the family. In structuralist terms, there is no contradiction between the two. The anti-reductivist sociological hostility to psychoanalysis is only tenable if it is assumed that the individual is not already a social formation. The subject of psychoanalysis is itself a social construction, a polity inside the skin, built on the image of an other's body. In psychoanalytic theory, individuals inhabit two collective bodies, their own and that of the larger society. Both collective and individual bodies are bounded, set in motion as reflexive subjects, through an internalized authority, a sovereign within. For a boy, the ideal of authority is typically represented by the father. The father enters this mechanism as symbol, as an authoritative ideal, an ideal of authority, not the person, but the place, of patriarchy. It is not surprising, then, that Freud introduces a collective subject – the collectivity that is an authoritative symbol – to this eroticized individual subject-making mechanism. Freud makes the loss of the ideal of a "country" a substitute for a lost person as well as itself a basis of melancholia, the loss of a collective symbolic object setting in motion the experience of ego loss (Freud 1960). Melancholia is a response to the loss of an ideal, of an individual or a collective subject, the one able to substitute for the other. This suggests that the two bodily egos, individual and collective, can each be a medium through which the other operates psychologically; that perceived threats to the individual subject, failures of the masculine self, can be acted out on a collective register, as efforts to masculinize the collectivity; and that perceived threats to the collective subject, incapacities of collective or national agency, might be countered and redressed through attempted reconstructions of the sexualized masculine self (Friedland 2002). The transom of subject-formation – from individual to collective – works both ways.

Mindful of its ethnocentric, anachronistic dangers, I argue that psychoanalytic theory suggests other "psychic mechanisms" and the sexual truth of Durkheim's collective representation, the pleasurable, yet forbidden, energies that power totemic projection.[3] Through the erotic logic of ambivalent identification and the embodied formation of the ego, it provides a mechanism by which social externality is internalized, a psychic structure critical to the operation of the social of which it is already a product. It suggests that for men a homoerotic charge animates the authority relation. There is thus a reason why friends and enemies of the mass, the crowd in the street, can both celebrate and denigrate it by identifying it as masculine and feminine, because it is both masculine and feminine. The gender of authority relations does not neatly align with its sexuality. There is a homoerotic secret to the division that inaugurates authority, a division that makes it both thrilling and shameful, necessary and difficult, independent of its instrumental effects, its ability to coordinate and produce the good things of life. The pure sacred is impure.

Normally the sons wear the totem, have it imprinted in the skin, written on their bodies – they are the father, or more precisely the paternal place – but they also occasionally take the totem into themselves, devour it: they have the father, and thereby assure the reproduction of the totemic species, which is the clan. The clan brothers eat the totem, become womanly, and here, in this moment of homoerotic identification, authority is born. Authority is a strange fusion of being and having, founded on an admixture of love and hatred, a pleasurable fear, precisely the combination of fascination and fear that Rudolph Otto would identify with the Holy (Otto [1917] 1958).[4] Not just deferred heterosexual pleasure, then, but disavowed homoerotic pleasure as well, is part of the constitution, part of the force of internalized authority. It follows that exclusion of women from collective representation is driven not simply negatively by heterosexual interest in male powers, but positively by desires for homosocial pleasures. Lévi-Strauss' exchange of women as the currency of social cohesion, the use of women to prevent murder among men of different clans, becomes then a secondary moment. In the totemic rite, there is an accelerated exchange of women, the right to have superseded by the anterior property right as manifested as the right to give, to make a gift, if not to exchange. Freud's argument implies that this giving carries another charge, a mediated sexual exchange between men, which accords with its transgressive occurrence during the homosocial totemic rite, sexual congress with forbidden women substituting for that between men.

Sexualizing Durkheim's social

Durkheim intimated the sexualization of the social, effervescence as an eroti-cized sociality. If Durkheim did not theoretically engage the erotics of the sacred which he recognized empirically, some of his Parisian successors did. Founded in 1937 in the face of what they perceived as the enervated quality of parliamentary democracy, the stunning rise of fascism and the prospect of yet another European war, the short-lived *Collège de Sociologie* drew off Durkheim and Mauss' insistence that the effervescent sacred energized the social and its indeterminate transformations (Richman 2002). Durkheim's collaborator Marcel Mauss' non-utilitarian treatment of the moral and sacred qualities of the gift and of sacrifice, was also formative (Wolin 2004). The intellectual leaders of the *Collège* – Georges Bataille, Roger Caillois and Michel Leiris – sought those evanescent collective states of emotional violence out of which the fascists were building new virile national bodies, hoping to locate the social powers out of which liberating, oppositional forces might be fashioned. They too sought a new collective virility dimmed by parliamentary democracy and capitalist instrumentality. Indeed Durkheim and the *Collège* would be accused, by its positive valuation of an irrational solidarity, of having prepared the intellectual ground for fascism (Falasca-Zamponi 2001; Wolin 2004).

Declaring himself "ferociously religious," in the augural issue of his and Pierre Klossowki's *Acéphale* (June, 1936) presaging the formation of the *Collège*, Bataille wrote:

> What we are starting is a war . . . The world to which we have belonged offers nothing to love outside of each individual insufficiency: its existence is limited to utility. A world that cannot be loved to the point of death – in the same way that a man loved a woman – represents only self-interest and the obligation to work . . . Existence is not only an agitated void, it is a dance that forces one to dance with fanaticism.   (Bataille [1936] 1996c: 179)

What was required was a "sacred sociology," one that saw the sacred as "determining the social structure," that understood, quoting Kierkegaard, that politics would one day "show itself to be a religious movement" (Falasca-Zamponi 2001). Kierkegaard, analyzing Abraham's binding of his son for sacrifice, had pointed to the incommunicability of faith, its irreducibility to ethics, its "madness" ([1843] 1986). The *Collège* drew on the duality Durkheim had located inside the sacred itself: the pure sacred, understood as "guardians of physical and moral order, as well as dispensers of life, health, and all the qualities that men value," and the impure sacred, "evil and impure powers, bringers of disorder, causes of death and sickness, instigators of sacrilege" (Durkheim 1995: 412; see Riley, this volume). Because Durkheim assumed the sacred objectified shared feelings of collective solidarity or threatened social dissolution and disorganization, of collective life and death, there was an "ambiguity of the sacred," such that the pure could contaminate and the impure sanctify (1995: 412–15).

If Durkheim emphasized the pure sacred, identified with the totemic rite, the *Collège*, and Bataille in particular, re-centered the effervescent social in the impure sacred, in transgression, in a "left" sacred opposing the instrumental powers of the "right" sacred, a move that would suffuse much of post-structuralist theory after the war. This was different than Jeffrey Alexander's well-taken call to culturalize evil as a socially productive valuation, as opposed to the absence of the good (Alexander 2003). Durkheim, Bataille claimed, had only been able to define the sacred negatively vis-à-vis the profane, identifying it with a particular form of sociality. Bataille claimed to identify the sacred positively as the "heterogeneous," those forces which cannot be assimilated to a homogenous domain of commensurable objects – excessive, unproductive, unconscious – mobs, waste, madmen, dreams, corpses, and indeed the "force of a leader" ([1933] 1996b: 143). Bataille was impressed by fascism. "Just like early Islam, fascism represents the constitution of a total heterogeneous power whose manifest origin is to be found in the prevailing effervescence" (1996b: 153). It was only through heterogeneous forces that society could find a reason for being; Durkheim's unities of sociality were insufficient to produce "the pure *having to be*" ([1933] 1996b: 147). Collective authority depended on divine madness.

For Bataille, the logic of the sacred was to give oneself, to open oneself out, to move beyond instrumental calculability. Bataille drew on the sacrificial paradigm and the way it transformed the persons sacrificing:

> Such an action would be characterized by the fact that it would have the power to liberate heterogeneous elements and to break the habitual homogeneity of the individual, in the same way that vomiting would be opposed to its opposite, the communal eating of food. Sacrifice considered in its essential phase would only be the rejection of what had been appropriated by a person or by a group. Because everything that is rejected from the human cycle is altered in an altogether troubling way, the sacred things that intervene at the end of the operation – the victim struck down in a pool of blood, the severed finger or ear, the torn-out eye – do not appreciably differ from vomited food. Repugnance is only one of the forms of stupor caused by a horrifying eruption, by the disgorging of a force that threatens to consume. The one who sacrifices is free – free to indulge in a similar disgorging, free, continuously identifying with the victim, to vomit his own being just as he has vomited a piece of himself or a bull, in other words free to throw himself suddenly *outside of himself*, like a gall or an aissaouah. (Bataille 1996e: 70)

Here was a communicative irrationality.

For Bataille, the sacred's first moment was located in that impure sacred, in our attraction to what most repulses, particularly to death, to the violated body and the corpse. Bataille read Freud ([1933] 1996b: 160). In *Beyond the Pleasure Principle*, published in 1920, Freud posited pleasure as a diminution of excitation, asserting the existence of an instinct to cancel this excitation, a cancellation whose logical end was death.[5] "[T]he aim of all life," Freud declared, "is death." Bataille likely appropriated Freud's theory to radicalize the self-transcendence of Durkheim's effervescent assembly. Bataille thus located the end of social being in unproductive expenditure, *dépense*, not saving, investment or production, in the accumulation of power or wealth, which, he argued, are derivative from and subordinate to such expenditure (Bataille [1933] 1996a; see also [1967] 1988).

The sacred, he argued, is constituted through loss, through expenditure, the sovereign operation. Activities like sacrifice, war, spectacle, communal feasts, and sexuality without "genital finality" were occasions affording such expenditure. The bourgeoisie's hatred of expenditure combined with religion's decline had opened the way to fascist militarism, its effervescence, the masses' love of the leader, the purity of its sadism. "The affective flow that united [the leader] . . . with his followers . . . is a function of the common consciousness of increasingly *violent* and excessive energies and powers that accumulate in the person of the leader and through him become widely available" (Bataille [1933] 1996b: 143). As Richard Wolin (2004) shows, Bataille esteemed Mussolini's fascism, was drawn to fascist practices, sharing their disdain for parliamentary representation and their valorization of collective violence, seeking at one point to develop a left fascism, faced with the evident failure of the proletarian revolution. This, of course, included an appreciation of war. War, Caillois, Bataille's co-founder of the *Collège*, declared, was the modern equivalent of the festival, an occasion affording the excess necessary to revitalize the social order (Caillois 1939, cited in Falasca-Zamponi 2001). Bataille, too, celebrated collective violence, and war, as a social practice beyond calculation, capable of accessing the sacred, lifting humans beyond the status of mere things, expenditure. Durkheim's socially procreative erotics had become an aesthetics of violence, collective life made primordially through death.

In Bataille's address to last meeting of the *Collège* in July 1939, after Hitler had already absorbed Austria and Czechoslovakia, when the French socialists were divided on the necessity of war, and the Hitler–Stalin pact was just a month away, he dared to speak, still, of sexual love as a model of social formation. "Love expresses a need for sacrifice: each unity must lose itself in some other, which exceeds it" (Bataille [1939] 1996d: 250). The sacred derived from expenditure of man's substance, out of man's "need to expend a vital excess," out of a loss of oneself, this loss implying therefore the creation of a "laceration," "rip," or "wound." Like Freud, Bataille discerns the prospect of death inscribed in the very logic of love. It was out of this common desire for loss, for access to the sacred, to love excessively, Bataille argued, that social being was composed.

The implication was clear; the proliferation of sacrificial destruction, like eroticism unhinged from the "durable organization" of conjugality, was to flee this dilemma into "a measureless annihilation in a violent expenditure." "Just as eroticism slides without difficulty toward the orgy, sacrifice, becoming an end in itself, lays claim to universal value, beyond the narrowness of the community" (1996d: 252). Hitler was at the door. Bataille spoke in the same month that Adolph Eichmann was appointed head of the Nazi's Prague office of emigration. The sacrifices had just begun.

Had the theoretical annihilation of the human as the foundation of the social prepared the way? Bataille's legacy has become administrative. It is the refusal to assimilate the death camp to a sacrificial logic that animates the Italian philosopher, Giorgio Agamben's critique of Bataille, for having failed to understand that the life, and hence its sacrifice, in which he grounds the sacred, and thus the sovereign, is, in fact, the outside inside of the state, the originary exclusion upon which both sovereignty and the state, particularly the modern state, is founded ([1995] 1998). Agamben refuses to derive sovereign power as a secularization of religion, locating it rather in a space created "prior" to that between religion and law, a space of exile and death that is neither political *bios* nor familial *zoe* (1998: 74, 90, 110). The content of sovereign power derives from an originary exclusion of what he calls bare life from both law and religion, which he condenses in the figure of *homo sacer*, the man who can be killed without it being a homicide and whose killing can never qualify as a sacrifice (1998: 83). It is this life, caught in the sovereign ban, declared outside the law and thus vulnerable to death, that is, he argues, the original sacred life and the referent of the sovereign decision. Bare life is "the earthly foundation of the state's legitimacy and sovereignty" (1998: 127). There is a link then between citizenship grounded in birth and the death camp. The ability to politicize *zoe* is the foundational sovereign right, the right to decide what life is worth living. Agamben not only makes life-taking, rather than life-making, the sovereign foundation, he makes sado-masochism its central erotic axis.

For all his reversals, Bataille propounded a restricted sexual economy. He sought the heterogeneous in a new erotic cartography. In the image for *Acéphale* the headless male figure has a skull at his groin, its mouth located where the absent penis would have been located. In his fiction and his essays, Bataille liked to put the body's organs in anomalous, and thus repulsive, places. But in point of fact, the *Collège de Sociologie* was committed to a heterogeneous virility, relentlessly masculinist and heterosexual in theoretical orientation, a virility diminished by the individuating forces of democracy and capitalism. Although anal eroticism, as a paradigmatic form of unprocreative erotics, peppered Bataille's essays and fiction – see for example, "The Solar Anus," or "The Story of the Eye," – the homoerotic had no role, let alone a privileged one, in his theoretical construction of the sacred.

Yet that homoeroticism was central to Nazism's rise. Bataille wrote on fascism just as Hitler was preparing the murderous destruction of the homosexual Ernst Rohm's SA, itself dominated by gay men. It is arguable that homoeroticism, an expenditure without biological product, might be integral to production of the sacred, the heterogeneity inside homogeneity, a central part of the "accursed share," necessary to the production of a social body. One of Bataille's favorite examples was the Aztec sacrifice, which, he argued, negated the human as thing, as use-value, the "accursed share, destined for violent consumption" (1988: 59). "This was the price," he writes, "men paid to escape their downfall and remove the weight introduced in them by the avarice and cold calculation of the real order" (1988: 61).

What Bataille likely did not know is that the sacrificial Aztec rite is grounded in a birth story of a nation and a god, a birth story where the boundary between male and female is ritually transgressed. The god Huitzilopochtli emerges from the female body of Coatlicue, impregnated by divine semen in the form of feathers, just as his enemies ascend the Mount of the Serpent, enemies led by Coyolxauhqui, a woman warrior (Moctezuma 1987: 50). A new collective body is born as Huitzilopochtli decapitates Coyolxauhqui with a serpent of fire, her body rolling down the mountain, falling into pieces (Carrasco 1987: 134–5). This founding moment of gendered violence was built into the Templo Mayor, replicating the mountain where Huitzilopochtli was born, with an oval stone carving of the dismembered body of that woman warrior, Coyolxauhqui (Carrasco 1987: 135). Warriors were brought here, sacrificed at the Temple's top, their bodies thrown down the steps, dismembered, eaten. Men, in their subordination to the Mexica, in their subjugation, become women, following the fleshy disassemblage, the deconstruction, of Coyolxauhqui, the woman warrior. And when the sacrificial victims fell to the bottom of the stairs, they would be cut apart to be consumed by Aztec men, men becoming one with the men they have transformed into women (see also Carrasco 1999: 205–6).

The argument that there is often a homoerotic constitution to the sacred, and indeed to authority more generally, does not depend on ethnocentric psychoanalytic projection, on my apparently unnatural mating of Durkheim and Freud. The ethological, ethnographic, religious, and political record provides ample evidence, which exceed the limits of this chapter.

Beyond social theory's anti-climax

Durkheim did not theorize the erotics of the sacred because of the way in which he corporealized *homo duplex*, identifying the profane, non-social ego with the pleasures of the body, and the sacred social with the non-corporeal soul and the sacrifice of those pleasures, indeed, the infliction of pains up to and including sacrificial death (see Durkheim 1995: 315–32; Shilling, this volume). "The ideal beings to which cults are addressed are not alone in demanding of their servants a certain contempt for pain; society, too, is possible only at that price" (1995: 321). However, *homo duplex*, in totemic rite

at least, is not homologous with corporeality and spirituality, with individual pleasure and collectively imposed pain. It does however seem to align
with the individuated heterosexual exchange of women between clans and
the de-individuated homosexual massing of men within the clan. If sacred
authority has a homoerotic constitution, if this is the impure sacred core of
sovereign representation, then Bataille was wrong to argue that the sacred
derives from the desire for loss. Rather it derives from the desire to lose
the loss of paternal love. Could it be that the impassible divide between
sacred and profane is partially grounded in the social organization of this
sexuality, that the establishment of a collective domain outside the heterosexual family also generates and depends upon a separate domain of homoerotic pleasure and imagination? Is it possible that the establishment of the
state is itself a sexual act, a double separation of two sexes, woman and
man, heterosexual and homosexual, that the state not only has a sex, but is
a sex?

It is not just Durkheim's installation as a totemic ancestor of post-
structuralist varieties of cultural sociology that is at stake here. Contained
within Durkheim's masterpiece is a call to make sociology of religion once
again the discipline's central task, not as the study of the mechanics and
regularities of an institutional sphere that still eludes theoretical definitions
not inflected with theology, but the task of a religious sociology, the interpretation and explanation of the sacred in its constitutive role in the social.
Thinking Durkheimian sociology and Freudian psychoanalysis together, as
already intimated by the *Collège de Sociologie*, implies that this engagement
with the sacred will involve not only an embodied, but a newly sexualized,
social theory.[6] Theorists like Michael Taussig and Elaine Scarry have shown
the socially productive powers of bodily techniques, precisely because they
exceed language, pushing us towards metonymy and humanism respectively.
In the case of the first, Taussig argues that magic's "implosive viscerality," its
use of movement of indeterminate objects across the bodily frontier mimes,
both concealing and reproducing, the sacred, "public" secret of "reality as
really made up" (Taussig 1998: 234). In the case of the second, bodily pain,
because it cannot be translated into words, is used to substantiate unsubstan-
tiable social truths through torture and war (Scarry 1985).[7] Pierre Bourdieu
(2001) and Michel Foucault (1990) have prepared the sexual ground, by
showing the ways in which sexuality is socially constituted.[8] But it is time
to move beyond reading the sexual through social categories, as an eroticization of domination, to try also to read the social through the sexual, to
grasp the ways in which sexual, desiring bodies, imaginary identifications,
and erotic energies, animate the formation of particular institutional practices and configurations. As Widick has pointed out (2003), Bourdieu himself

increasingly moved towards the psychoanalytic in his later work, equating his *illusio* with libido ([1994] 1998: 76), and then in *Pascalian Meditations* ([1997] 2000: 166), calling up Freud himself in order to understand "[t]he initial form of *illusio* is investment in the domestic space, the site of a complex process of socialization of the sexual and sexualization of the social." Bourdieu called for the combination of sociology and, by implication, a psychoanalytic psychology, to accomplish this task. This is not to suggest that psychoanalysis is sufficient for understanding social life (Roth 1987). However, the humans who inhabit sociological accounts – lacking in fantasy, unconsciousness, erotic passion, and thirst for the social gift – are patently inadequate to the world around us.

Sexual desire, and indeed sex itself, now stalks the sociological house. Its theoretical embrace will require us to grapple with feminist and queer theory not as a recognition of difference, but as a pathway into the erotic constitution of the social, to sexuality not as an attribute of persons, nor as immanent in textual formations, but as an institutional problem (Seidman 1997; Grosz 1995). The sex of social theory is at stake, the intimate relation between biology and cosmogony, individual and social bodies, pleasure and power. This theoretical task is of political moment, for around the world we face an often-violent politicization of religion, intense, often effervescent, collective identifications with God where sexual pleasure, the sexual meanings of manhood and womanhood, are at the center of the storm (Friedland 2002; Juergensmeyer 2000).

NOTES

I am indebted to Jeffrey Alexander and Phil Smith for coaxing this out of me and their daring to publish it. I am particularly grateful to William Robert, Steven Seidman, and Richard Widick who critically read this chapter. As always I am grateful to friends, colleagues and students who have pointed the way, among whom are Tom Carlson, Elisabeth Weber, Finbarr Curtis, Simonetta Falasca-Zamponi, Richard Hecht, David White, and Christine Thomas.

1 It is from Da Vinci's reference to Eros as the "preserver of all living things," that Freud will adopt the term as his own to denote sexual instincts (1964: 17).
2 I am indebted to Richard Widick for bringing this home to me.
3 The dangers of presentist anachronism is no more or less grave for psychoanalytic theory than for social theory more generally. Indeed sometimes the degrees of invisibility don't seem that different.
4 Freud would argue that strong fear, the extreme fear of the paranoid, could always be linked back to repressed homosexual fantasies (Freud [1911] 1996). The paranoid, Freud declares, translates love of an external male object into hatred of that object, justifying that hatred by a sense of persecution. There is a psychic economy of paranoia in the constitution of authority.
5 Caillois drew explicitly on this text. See Hollier 1988: xvi.

6 In writing about sexuality in this way, I am mindful of the argument that sexuality is a historically specific discursive formation, a transformation of bodies, desire and pleasures into a unitary anatomical politics, that organizes hetero-homosexuality as well as gender (Foucault 1978). I treat desire as an invested erotic relation to other bodies, including one's own, sexuality being the practice of that relation.

7 Indeed, in the magic of the Waldemar Bogoras, Taussig points out "[t]he greatest trick of course was . . . to change one's sex, thanks to help from the spirits, a change that could well eventuate at least in the case of a man, in his taking male lovers or becoming married to a man. Such 'soft men,' as they were called, were feared for their magic more than unchanged men or women" (1998: 228).

8 Bourdieu's study, *Masculine Domination*, inadvertently sets up this problem by arguing on the one hand, that normal heterosexual male desire is an "eroticized domination" (2001: 21), while on the other hand positing "love" as a "miraculous truce in which domination seems dominated" (2001: 110). The latter becomes a "secular substitute for God." The implication is that there is an eroticized domination in religious imagination.

REFERENCES

Agamben, Giorgio. [1995] 1998. *Homo Sacer: Sovereign Power and Bare Life*. Translated by Daniel Heller-Roazen. Stanford, CA: Stanford University Press.

Alexander, Jeffrey C. 2003. "A Cultural Sociology of Evil." pp. 109–20 in *The Meanings of Social Life: A Cultural Sociology*. Oxford: Oxford University Press.

1988. "Introduction" in *Durkheimian Sociology: Cultural Studies*. New York: Cambridge University Press.

Bataille, Georges. [1967] 1988. *The Accursed Share*. Vol. 1. Translated by Robert Hurley. New York: Zone.

[1933] 1996a. "The Notion of Expenditure." pp. 116–29 in *Visions of Excess: Selected Writings, 1917–1939*. Edited and translated by Allan Stoekl. Minneapolis: University of Minnesota Press.

[1933] 1996b. "The Psychological Structure of Fascism." pp. 137–60 in *Visions of Excess: Selected Writings, 1917–1939*. Edited and translated by Allan Stoekl. Minneapolis: University of Minnesota Press.

[1936] 1996c. "The Sacred Conspiracy." pp. 178–81 in *Visions of Excess: Selected Writings, 1917–1939*. Edited and translated by Allan Stoekl. Minneapolis: University of Minnesota Press.

[1939] 1996d. "The Collège of Sociology." pp. 246–53 *Visions of Excess: Selected Writings, 1917–1939*. Edited and translated by Allan Stoekl. Minneapolis: University of Minnesota Press.

[1930] 1996e. "Sacrificial Mutilation and the Severed Ear of Vincent Van Gogh." pp. 61–72 in *Visions of Excess: Selected Writings, 1917–1939*. Edited and translated by Allan Stoekl. Minneapolis: University of Minnesota Press.

Bellah, Robert. 1967. "Civil Religion in America." *Daedalus* 96: 1–21.

Bourdieu, Pierre. [1998] 2001. *Masculine Domination*. Translated by Richard Nice. Stanford, CA: Stanford University Press.

[1997] 2000. *Pascalian Meditations*. Trans. Richard Nice. Stanford, CA: Stanford University Press.

[1994] 1998 *Practical Reason*. Stanford, CA: Stanford University Press.

Bourdieu, Pierre. 1990. *The Logic of Practice*. Stanford: Stanford University Press.

Butler, Judith. 1997. *The Psychic Life of Power: Theories in Subjection*. Stanford, CA: Stanford University Press.

Caillois, Roger. 1939. *L'homme et le Sacré*. Paris: Edition Leroux.

Canetti, Elias. 1973. *Crowds and Power*. Harmondsworth: Penguin.

Carrasco, David. 1999. *City of Sacrifice: The Aztec Empire and the Role of Violence in Civilization*. Boston, MA: Beacon Press.

1987. "Myth, Cosmic Terror, and the Templo Mayor." pp. 124–62 in *The Great Temple of Tenochtitlan: Centre and Periphery in the Aztec World*. Edited by Johanna Broda, David Carrasco and Eduardo Matos Moctezuma. Berkeley, CA: University of California Press.

De Certeau, Michel. 1984. *The Practice of Everyday Life*. Berkeley, CA: University of California Press.

Derrida, Jacques. [1996] 2002. "Faith and Knowledge: The Sources of 'Religion' at the Limits of Reason Alone." pp. 40–101 in *Acts of Religion*. Edited by Gil Anidjar. New York: Routledge.

1992. ". . . That Dangerous Supplement . . ." pp. 76–109 in *Acts of Literature*. Edited by Derek Attridge. New York: Routledge.

[1990] 2002. "Force of Law: The 'Mystical Foundation of Authority.'" pp. 228–98 in *Acts of Religion*. Edited by Gil Anidjar. New York: Routledge.

Durkheim, Émile. [1912] 1995. *The Elementary Forms of Religious Life*. Edited and translated by Karen E. Fields. New York: The Free Press.

[1897] 1963. *Incest: The Nature and Origin of the Taboo*. Translated by Edward Sagarin. New York: Lyle Stuart.

Durkheim, Émile and Marcel Mauss. [1903] 1963. *Primitive Classification*. Translated by Rodney Needham. Chicago: University of Chicago Press.

Falasca-Zamponi, Simonetta. 2001. "Politics as Sacred: The *Collège de Sociologie*." Paper presented at Cultural Turn III, "Profane and Sacred," February 1998, University of California, Santa Barbara.

1997. *Fascist Spectacle: The Aesthetics of Power in Mussolini's Italy*. Berkeley, CA: University of California Press.

Foucault, Michel. 1990. *The Use of Pleasure: The History of Sexuality*. Vol. 2. Translated by Robert Hurley. New York: Vintage

1978. *The History of Sexuality: An Introduction*. New York: Pantheon.

[1966] 1970. *The Order of Things: An Archaeology of the Human Sciences*. New York: Vintage.

Freud, Sigmund [1923] 1960. *Ego and the Id*. Translated by Joan Riviere. New York: W. W. Norton.

[1921] 1959. *Group Psychology and the Analysis of the Ego*. Translated by James Strachey. New York: W. W. Norton.

[1920] 1989. *Beyond the Pleasure Principle*. Translated by James Strachey. New York: W. W. Norton.

[1913] 1946. *Totem and Taboo*. Translated by Abraham A. Brill. New York: Vintage.

[1911] 1996. "Psychoanalytic Notes on an Autobiographical Account of a Case of Paranoia (Dementia Paranoides)" in *Three Case Histories: The "Wolf Man," the "Rat Man," and the Psychotic Dr. Schreber*. New York: Touchstone.

[1910] 1964. *Leonard da Vinci and a Memory of His Childhood*. New York: W. W. Norton.

[1905] 2000. *Three Essays on the Theory of Sexuality*. Translated by James Strachey. New York: Basic

Friedland, Roger. 2002. "Money, Sex and God: The Erotic Logic of Religious Nationalism." *Sociological Theory* 20: 381–425.

Grosz, Elizabeth. 1995. *Space, Time and Perversion*. New York: Routledge.

Heidegger, Martin. 1977. "The Age of the World Picture" in *The Question Concerning Technology and Other Essays*. Translated by William Lovitt. New York: Harper Torchbooks.

Hollier, Denis. 1988. *The College of Sociology (1937–1939)*. Translated by Betsy Wing. Minneapolis: University of Minnesota Press.

Juergensmeyer, Mark. 2000. *Terror in the Mind of God: The Global Rise of Religious Violence*. Berkeley, CA: University of California Press.

Kierkegaard, Søren. [1843] 1986. *Fear and Trembling* New York: Penguin.

Kofman, Sarah. [1983] 1993. *Nietzsche and Metaphor*. Translated by Duncan Large. Stanford, CA: Stanford University Press.

Lacan, Jacques. 1977. "The Signification of the Phallus." pp. 281–91 in *Écrits: A Selection*. Translated by Alan Sheridan. New York: W. W. Norton.

[1966] 1977. "The Function and Field of Speech and Language in Psychoanalysis." pp. 30–113 in *Écrits: A Selection*. Translated by Alan Sheridan. New York: W. W. Norton.

Leach, Edmund. 1985. "Why Did Moses have a Sister?" pp. 7–33 in Edmund Leach and D. Alan Aycock, *Structuralist Interpretation of Biblical Myth*. Cambridge: Cambridge University Press.

Levi-Strauss, Claude. 1963. *Structural Anthropology*. Translated by Claire Jacobson and Brooke Grundfest Schoepf. New York: Basic Books.

Martin, John Levi. 2000. "What Do Animals Do All Day? The Division of Labor, Class Bodies, and Totemic Thinking in the Popular Imagination." *Poetics* 27: 195–231.

Moctezuma, Eduardo Matos. 1987. "The Templo Mayor of Tenochtitlan: History and Interpretation." pp. 15–60 in *The Great Temple of Tenochtitlan: Centre and Periphery in the Aztec World*. Edited by Johanna Broda, David Carrasco, and Eduardo Matos Moctezuma. Berkeley, CA: University of California Press.

Otto, Rudolf. [1917] 1958. *The Idea of the Holy*. Translated by J. Harvey. London: Oxford University Press.

Richman, Michèle. 2002. *Sacred Revolutions: Durkheim and the Collège de Sociologie*. Minneapolis: University of Minnesota Press.

Roth, M. 1987. *Psychoanalysis as History: Negation and Freedom in Freud*. Ithaca, NY: Cornell University Press.

Scarry, Elaine. 1985. *The Body In Pain: The Making and Unmaking of the World*. New York: Oxford University Press.

Schmitt, Carl. [1932] 1996. *The Concept of the Political*. Translated by George Schwab. Chicago: University of Chicago Press.

Seidman, Steven. 1997. *Difference Troubles: Queering Social Theory and Sexual Politics*. Cambridge: Cambridge University Press.

Shils, Edward. 1975. *Centre and Periphery: Essays in Macrosociology*. Chicago: University of Chicago Press.

Smith, William Robertson. 1969. *Lectures on the Religion of the Semites: The Fundamental Institutions*. New York: KTAV Publishing House.

Spencer, Baldwin and Francis J. Gillen. 1904. *The Northern Tribes of Central Australia*. London: Macmillan and Co.

Tambiah, Stanley. 1996. *Leveling Crowds: Ethnonationalist Conflicts and Collective Violence in South Asia*. Berkeley, CA: University of California Press.

Taussig, Michael. 1998. "Viscerality, Faith, and Skepticism: Another Theory of Magic." pp. 221–56 in *In Near Ruins: Cultural Theory at the End of the Century*. Edited by Nicholas Dirks. Minneapolis: University of Minnesota Press.

1992. "Maleficium: State Fetishism." pp. 111–48 in *The Nervous System*. New York: Routledge.

Widick, Richard. 2003. "Flesh and the Free Market: On Taking Bourdieu to the Options Exchange." *Theory and Society*, forthcoming.

Wolin, Richard. 2004. *The Seduction of Unreason: The Intellectual Romance with Fascism from Nietzsche to Postmodernism*. Princeton, NJ: Princeton University Press.

II

ALEXANDER T. RILEY

"Renegade Durkheimianism" and the transgressive left sacred

Émile Durkheim's *The Elementary Forms of the Religious Life* ([1912] 1991) (hereafter *Elementary Forms*) is considered by many the conclusive statement on religion of the Durkheimian school. In fact, this is rather a simplification of a more complicated intellectual history. A more careful evaluation of the examinations of religious phenomena by the members of the Durkheimian team demonstrates some intriguing theoretical distinctions that give rise to broader differences in intellectual position-taking and helps explain serious differences in the trajectory of influence of the Durkheimian school on subsequent generations of intellectuals. These differences stem largely from the description of the nature of the sacred in the Durkheimian tradition.

The sacred is of course the key to the Durkheimian definition of religion. In *Elementary Forms*, Durkheim proceeds in typical fashion toward a working definition of this difficult category by eliminating competing definitions, only offering his own after all others examined have been effectively annihilated. Religion, he argues, can only adequately and inclusively be characterized as ideas and rites oriented toward the setting aside and protection of *sacred* things. But in what manner can we as social scientists classify sacred things and distinguish them from things non-sacred? One might suggest that sacred things can be defined merely as those things set aside and protected in any given society. But this is clearly a circular definition. In any society, Durkheim asserts, there are things sacred and things profane. The profane he is content to leave with a negative definition: that which is *not* sacred. But it will not do to take the same route with respect to the definition of the sacred (i.e. the non-profane), as this is the substantive category upon which his entire theory of religion is based. The sacred inspires respect, but why? What is it about sacred things that so inspire us and that allow us to distinguish them from profane things? And is this awe-inspiring capacity monolithic and identical in all sacred things?

It is in struggling toward a definition of sacredness that things become very interesting indeed in the Durkheimian tradition. For we discover that, while the sacred/profane polarity is one of the central conceptual tools of the Durkheimian sociology of religion, it is not the only set of key oppositions Durkheim makes use of in sociologically classifying religious experience, rite and representation. The sacred is in fact not only the holy or consecrated, but it can also be the accursed, "something devoted to a divinity for destruction, and hence criminal, impious, wicked, infamous" (Pickering 1984: 124). Durkheim argues that the sacred, in addition to being opposed in a binary relationship to the profane, is itself comprised of two opposing binary poles: on the one hand, the pure, beneficent powers and forces that maintain physical and moral order, life and health, and, on the other, those that are impure, evil and produce disorder, sacrilege, disease, and death (Durkheim 1991: 681–2). These two types would be developed in the early Durkheimian school as pure, beneficent, or right sacred and impure, trangressive, or left sacred. As W. S. F. Pickering has noted, the sociological richness of the concept can be seen by tracing the term to its Latin derivation *sacer*, which contains both of the seemingly contradictory meanings. The French *sacré* likewise can mean both, and is frequently used in both senses (*la musique sacrée*, holy or sacred music, and *un sacré menteur*, a damned or accursed liar), whereas the English "sacred" has in practice lost the second meaning, a fact which by itself perhaps explains a good deal of English-language misreading of the Durkheimian treatment of this issue.

Like the sacred/profane distinction, that between the two varieties of sacredness, the right or pure sacred and the left or impure sacred, is also derived from Robertson Smith, but Durkheim and his colleagues developed it as a theoretical tool to a considerably greater extent. The nature of the relationship between pure and impure sacred is complex, for the two are in many ways not clearly distinguishable. Durkheim points out that in fact a pure sacred object or power frequently becomes impure while remaining sacred (i.e. without simply becoming profane) and vice versa through a modification of "exterior circumstances." For example, in certain societies, a corpse moves as a result of a specific ritual process from the status of an impure sacred object inspiring dread and the possibility of evil contagion to that of a venerated sacred object that is even ingested by surviving family or clan members as a boon and a protection against evil (Durkheim 1991: 684). But are pure and impure sacred two distinct states or manifestations of a single kind of power, never present in any empirical site at the same moment, or rather two seemingly contradictory yet actually complementary and mutually dependent facets of any empirical sacred object or force? Durkheim is not clear on this point. He seems to want at once to separate them empirically, while acknowledging the potential of the one to become the other, and to recognize the acute difficulty of actually making a neat distinction between the reverence associated with the pure sacred and the fear and horror linked to the impure. Are not, he asks, truly intense experiences of the pure sacred characterized by some degree of what can be called fear or dread, and does not a certain reverence attach itself to the horror we feel in the face of the most intensely impure sacred objects? (Durkheim 1991: 683–4).[1]

Given this ambiguity in the nature of the sacred, some intriguing dilemmas present themselves in drawing conclusions about the role of the sacred in social life. Durkheim argued that ritual practices could be divided into negative or ascetic rites, which are designed to prevent the mingling of profane and sacred worlds and consist entirely of abstentions and interdictions, and positive rites, which are the actual practices that bring the worshipper into contact with the sacred and are ultimately at the heart of religious ritual since only they contain their reason for existence in themselves (Durkheim 1991: 509–11, 551). It is the positive rites, the most important historical example of which is the institution of sacrifice, that provide the setting for the most essential element of religious phenomena, according to Durkheim. This is the sentiment of collective effervescence that is generated in those moments of ritual worship of the sacred. But which form of the sacred, pure or impure, is enacted by positive rites? The answer would seem to be straightforward: it must be the pure sacred, as this is the life-celebrating and beneficent force. Durkheim certainly suggests that this must be the case:

> Thus far from being ignorant of actual society and making a false abstraction of it, religion is the image of society; it reflects society in all its aspects, even the most vulgar and repulsive. Everything is found here and if, most often, it is the case that good is superior to evil, life superior to death, the forces of light superior to the forces of darkness, it is because reality is not otherwise. For if the relationship between these contradictory forces were reversed, life would be impossible.
> (Durkheim 1991: 700)

However, there is a clear distinction in the manner in which the notion is theorized by Durkheim, on the one hand, and by his three closest colleagues who also worked on religious topics, on the other. This distinction has to do with rather different emphases with respect to Robertson Smith's distinction between the pure and the impure sacred. In Durkheim, the emphasis is on the pure sacred, the sacred as positive rite and negative interdiction, i.e. the sacred as the *moral*. Though he acknowledges the impure sacred and the ambiguity of its relationship to the pure sacred, his concentration, both in his *chef-d'oeuvre* on religion and in his practical discussions of the role of the sacred in contemporary secular France, is clearly on the latter. In fact, a very difficult question concerning the origin of the impure sacred emerges from Durkheim's argument. The sacred is ultimately generated by the social itself, he argues, as a means for its constant reinvigoration. But why should society create a force, the impure sacred, that bodes ill for it, even threatens it with destruction? No clear answer is suggested in Durkheim's analysis (Pickering 1984: 129; Arppe 1995: 214).

The real Durkheimian engagement with the left or impure sacred took place not in the *Elementary Forms* or in any other work of Durkheim himself, but rather in the work of his protégés Marcel Mauss, Henri Hubert, and Robert Hertz. The more or less simple reduction in Durkheim of the sacred to the social as moral bond is more problematic in their work. There is a concerted effort on the part of the three junior colleagues, in contrast to Durkheim, to attend to "the accursed part of the sacred," to acknowledge in its full theoretical and practical complexity this notion that is

> at the same time the foundational principle of the system and a part of the system that needs explanation. [For] As a synonym for communal force, it is the condition of possibility of social symbols; thus, its meaning cannot be exhausted in its own symbolic representation. (Arppe 1995: 210)

It is this attention to "the problem of evil" in the social that ultimately separates the two treatments of the sacred and of the social more generally. What precisely is the role played by the impure sacred in the generative processes of collective effervescence and revitalization that are so important in the Durkheimian sociology of religion? Clearly, some part of this sensitivity to the "other half" of the sacred in the trio Mauss/Hubert/Hertz comes from their great immersion as students in Indian religious history and structure, as there is a much greater treatment of these themes here than in the greater (Judeo-Christian) and lesser (i.e. primitive) religious traditions known better to Durkheim. Indeed, the groups that have emphasized aspects of the impure sacred in Brahmanic religion and its historical descendents have played a considerably larger role in the development of their religious systems than have analogous groups in Judaism and Christianity. For example, Gnosticism in Christianity and Tantricism in Hinduism and Buddhism each developed notions of the religious adept who, having reached a certain stage of spiritual development or relationship with the deity, is at least in certain cases no longer bound by particular moral strictures and can often increase his spiritual understanding by deliberately transgressing moral rules. Tantra however has played a significant role in historical Hinduism and Buddhism, while the historically emergent emphasis on the pure sacred in Christianity led to the total crushing of Gnosticism in the first centuries of the Church's establishment.

The distinction is however something deeper than just a difference of empirical area of specialization. As Pickering has noted, Durkheim extends

the sacred/profane opposition in such a way as to link to the former collective representations, the realm of the ideal in general, and the collectivity
or society, while the profane encompasses individual representations, the
corporal or material realm, and the individual (Pickering 1984: 120). He
famously distinguishes magic and religion on this axis, although Mauss and
Hubert argued rather the contrary in their study of magic. Indeed, in this
and other collective work they undertook, Mauss and Hubert endeavored
to elaborate a concept that they believed broader and more inclusive than
that of the sacred to understand in sociological terms the origin and power
of religious rites and beliefs. According to Mauss,

> We detected at [magic's] foundation, as at the foundation of religion, a vast com-
> mon notion that we called by a name borrowed from Melaneso-Polynesian,
> that of mana. This idea is perhaps more general than that of the sacred. Since
> then, Durkheim has tried to deduce it logically from the notion of the sacred.
> We were never sure he was right, and I continue still to speak of the magico-
> religious base. (Mauss 1979: 218)

While Durkheim indicated a distinction between, on the one hand, the
series church/pure sacred/collective well-being and that of magic/impure
sacred/collective ill-being, he left the latter largely unexplored, while Mauss
and Hubert theorized it in much greater detail. In his introduction to
the French translation of Chantepie de la Saussaye's *Manuel d'histoire
des religions*, Hubert (1904) presents a qualified but vigorous criticism of
Durkheim's theory of religion and the sacred, aiming at Durkheim's concentration on religious facts attached to a Church and to the pure sacred
exclusively. He criticizes the Durkheimian emphasis on "the formation of
doctrines and churches," as this is a reduction of "the total history of the
religious life," which must include religious practice in societies without
established churches or fixed systems of belief (Hubert 1904: xxii).[2] Hubert
was quite concerned that the history of religion not be reduced to the history
of "church religions" (e.g. Christianity, Buddhism, Islam) to the exclusion of
"religions of the people" (e.g. Roman, Greek and Assyrian religion) (1904:
xxi).[3] He also uses a telling comparison in indicating the mutual participation of magic and religion in a greater whole for which the social study of
religious phenomena must account:

> Magic indeed resembles religion in its modes of action and its notions; they
> intermingle often even to the point of indistinguishability; magical facts are in
> sum religious facts; but it is the case that *magic forms with religion a more
> general class wherein they sometimes oppose one another, as for example crime
> and law oppose one another.* (Hubert 1904: xxiv, emphasis added)

Durkheim had of course discussed the sociological necessity of crime in his *Rules of Sociological Method*, demonstrating its importance for an understanding of the phenomenon of normal societies and moral action, but stopping well short of considering it an equal participant in a "more general class" with legal, moral action. Hubert's intent here, as in the argument in the essay co-written with Mauss on magic, is to emphasize the sociological illegitimacy of favoring religion over magic, or the pure over the impure sacred, simply because of an *a priori* moral project. Further on, Hubert (1904: xlvi–xlvii) is still more explicit that the notion of the sacred "appears under two different aspects, depending on whether we consider it in magic or in religion." In the latter case, the sacred takes on the face of interdictions and taboos; in the former, it is "willful sacrilege."

The later work of Mauss too was in many ways an elaboration of these early insights that distinguished the Hubert-Mauss model from that of Durkheim. This can be seen perhaps most clearly in Mauss' work on the notion of the gift. In his endeavor to establish an understanding of reciprocal gift-giving as a "total social fact," as a phenomenon that reveals the dense intertwining of social realms as diverse as the juridical, economic, religious and aesthetic, which even "in certain cases involve[s] the totality of society and its institutions" (1950: 204, 274), Mauss borrows a Maori term, *hau* (or "spirit of things"), to attempt to define the power gift objects have to compel givers and receivers to "give, receive, render" (1950: 205). As Lévi-Strauss notes disapprovingly in his preface to the volume in which Mauss' essay was reprinted,[4] Mauss uses the notion of *hau* here in much the same way the notion of *mana* had been used in the earlier essay on magic. Mauss quotes a Maori sage, Tamati Ranaipiri, to demonstrate the nature of the spiritual power inherent in the given object itself that provides a "moral and religious reason" (Mauss 1950: 153) for the imperative to give, receive and render the same, which he then summarizes as follows:

> It is clear that in Maori law, the legal bond, the bond by things, is a bond of souls, for the thing itself has a soul. From which it follows that to present something to someone is to present something to oneself . . . [F]or, to accept something from someone is to accept something of his spiritual essence, of his soul; the retention of this thing would be dangerous . . . Finally, this thing given is not an inert thing. Animated, often individualized, it tends to return to what Hertz called its "hearth of origin." (Mauss 1950: 160–1)[5]

Ironically, Lévi-Strauss' criticism of Mauss is fundamentally that the latter refused the sort of reduction of the impetus or force behind the phenomenon of gift-exchange to the social (in the form of its unconscious symbolic logic) that would have been characteristic of a more pure Durkheimian solution.

Instead, Lévi-Strauss argues, Mauss has fallen victim to the familiar trap of the ethnographer who comes to accept as explanation the mystifications of the populations he is studying (Lévi-Strauss 1950: xxxviii). The *hau*, he argues,

> is not the explanation behind exchange: it is the conscious form under which men of a determined society, where the problem had a particular importance, understood *an unconscious necessity* the reason for which is elsewhere.
>
> (Lévi-Strauss 1950: xxxix)

Lévi-Strauss, in his attempt to reduce the sense of both *mana* and *hau* to the universal and timeless unconscious mental structures that are the foundation of his own theoretical model,[6] rejects as simply anti-scientific the untidy "notions of sentiment, of fatality, of chance and the arbitrary" that Mauss invokes (Lévi-Strauss 1950: xlv). Mauss' "error" then, here as in the case of *mana*, is to refuse to reduce either the motive power behind the obligation to give and receive gifts or the power behind magical efficacy and belief to some ultimately structuralist social necessity for order, be it logical or moral (in Lévi-Strauss' criticism, it is primarily the former; in Durkheim's theory of the sacred, it is the latter). In fact, in both cases, Mauss' intention is explicitly inclusive (1950: 164–9);[7] he refuses to consider as fundamental to the explanation of religious phenomena a concept that includes only those ideas and practices that are at bottom moral, or logically essential to the productive order of the social system, and that exclude ideas and practices that elude the moral categories and can even be destructive of social order. For Mauss, this inclusivity is necessary in the case of magic, in order to account for its deliberately anti-moral elements and, in the case of gift-giving, in order to account for agonistic gift-giving, such as that exemplified in the Kwakiutl *potlatch*, which is, far from the sort of non-agonistic gift-return cycle evident elsewhere (the kind perhaps more amenable to explanation by Lévi-Strauss), rather a form of virtual warfare (Mauss 1950: 269–70).

Nearly the entirety of Hertz's published work deals extensively with the pure/impure sacred distinction, but nothing does so more clearly than his essay on social rituals surrounding death. Here, Hertz examined the ways in which primitive societies symbolically deal with the liminal experience of death. Funeral rites in the Indonesian societies he examined consist of two separate burials, one occurring soon after death and the second only some significant time later. The corpse itself moves through two classificatory stages during this process, beginning as an impure sacred object and becoming pure sacred with the final burial rites. Hertz has been read here and in his other work as using the sacred/profane dichotomy as a simple equivalent of the pure/impure sacred one (see Evans-Pritchard 1960; Parkin 1996), and indeed he does explicitly note "a natural affinity and almost an equivalence between the profane and the impure" in his article on religious symbolism and the preference for the right hand (Hertz 1960: 95). Yet the language he uses in both these essays and particularly in the essay on death indicates clearly that he is discussing the distinction between impure and pure sacred statuses. The newly deceased is an object of "horror and dread," his relatives "impure and accursed" during the time they are denied normal membership in the society prior to the final burial ceremony (Hertz 1960: 37, 50). More, it is clear he is talking about the impure sacred and not the profane if we follow Durkheim's formula for equating the latter with the non-social, as all of the aspects of the deceased and his relatives discussed are thoroughly social in their effects and remedies. In the final analysis, Hertz's work uncovers the myriad ways in which the impure sacred emerges within the social bond, creating liminal spaces through which social actors move and exerting a power that is ultimately generative at the core of the social bond.

The theoretical importance of the left/impure sacred for understanding the Durkheimian project and its legacy is significant. Indeed, the notion of the impure sacred raises the question of how to account for the concept of evil within the discourse of sociological theory. Durkheim reconciles himself to the existence of the impure sacred by placing it in a clearly inferior position vis-à-vis the pure sacred, but this move is not justified by any argument. Mauss, Hubert, and Hertz endeavor to provide a solution to this problem, and in doing so they do more than make a contribution to a narrow specialist's question in the sociology of religion. They open up a path toward a kind of renegade Durkheimian mode of political and cultural intervention that would have an important and very interesting influence in subsequent intellectual generations. For although the personal political directions taken by the three younger Durkheimians were not grossly dissimilar to that of Durkheim,[8] who was the very embodiment of the reformist and secularist socialist of the Nouvelle Sorbonne so despised by the French religious right of the era (Bompaire-Evesque 1988),[9] their engagement with the impure/left sacred arguably provided an intellectual discourse that others did use to take up very different positions in the fields of culture and politics. In some sense, we can even derive two different basic intellectual political positions from the emphases on the two different kinds of sacred. In brief, the concentration on the pure sacred yields an intellectual politics that is, like that of Durkheim himself, classically progressive and rationalist, in which the realms of science and politics are kept separate and the existential concerns of the thinker him/herself are bracketed from his/her political project, while an emphasis on the impure sacred tends to lead to an intellectual politics that is more based in emotional force (collective effervescence in pure form) and transgression, wherein the line separating scientific knowledge and politics is significantly less clear and the existential situation of the theorist takes on a great deal more importance.

Allan Stoekl (1992) has suggested (by way of Roland Barthes) that the modern French intellectual can be best understood as caught between two oppositional categories, the "writer" and the "author"; the first is concerned with representation and communication via argumentation of a rational tenor, while the second is engaged in "the not necessarily rational force of writing or language itself" (Stoekl 1992: 7). In these two forms, the French intellectual has taken up the seemingly contradictory political tasks of acting both as representative and theoretician of the state and as critical dissident, and the stylistic and political conflict in these two models of intellectual identity is at the heart of the French situation. Durkheim, according to Stoekl's argument, occupies a foundational place in this narrative, as he was the first modern French intellectual to clearly pose the opposition in its essential form, which is in fact concerned with the intellectual's relation to the sacred. In Durkheim's treatment of the totem as at once "(re)instituting act and . . . representation" (Stoekl 1992: 8), that is, as both rational and pre-rational expression of the social bond, he is laying down the terms of the task of the twentieth-century French intellectuals who followed him: namely, the struggle to reconcile the two within oneself, and within the terms of the category of the sacred. In the French context, both writers and authors envision a key political role for the intellectual (quite more important than, for example, the political role of the intellectual in the USA), but the tenor of that role changes significantly hinging on this question that is for Stoekl ultimately stylistic. Stoekl is correct in noting the distinction, but incorrect in believing it merely stylistic. It actually hinges on the substantive question of which half of the sacred is taken up as the focus of an intellectual project.

The intellectual and political salience of the impure/left sacred arguably was augmented by specific changes in the French intellectual world in the interwar years. The decline in influence of institutional Durkheimian thought was serious in the wake of the Great War, owing not least to the death of many members of the Durkheimian school in the war (see Besnard 1983: 34–5; Mauss 1969: 473–99; Clark 1973: 209), but the Durkheimian interest in the impure sacred was picked up in certain intellectual circles that were in reaction against the perceived radical secularism of the Third Republic and its concomitant failures on several crucial domestic and international issues. In fact, the war itself, and the several near-disasters it brought the French prior to the victory at the Marne in September 1914, not to mention its consequences in the loss of nearly an entire generation of young men, were seen by many as a direct effect of the failure of the Republican secular ethic to properly maintain France's power position vis-à-vis the other central continental power, Germany. The wave of flight from secular Republican liberalism during this period was led in many respects by Catholics, and this was a period of intense conversion and return to the Catholic faith on the part of a significant number of intellectuals (see Gugelot 1998). But even those who remained unfriendly to the Church and to other traditional religious paths often reacted violently against the Republic, its secular liberal ethics and morality and its representative intellectuals. For many of these interwar intellectuals, the alternatives to that lifeless and suffocating Republic, with its purported excesses of democracy, science and reason, consisted of various efforts to tie together the spirit animating three emergent forces in French society: the modernist avant-garde (which, in its fascination with African and other primitive art and culture, became engaged in criticisms both of Western progressivist aesthetics and the French colonial political project); the anti-democratic movements of communism and/or fascism (which saw in the rising powers of Fascist Italy and Soviet Russia the virile successors to the tired old democratic republic); and a renewed mystical religious sense separated from and in fact often hostile to the Church.

The particular role played by the French reception of Nietzsche is of great importance in understanding the motivations and directions of this inter- and post-war intellectual pursuit of the impure sacred. Much scholarly work has demonstrated the ways in which, beginning in the early 1900s, Nietzschean thought became a tool for French thinkers of this period looking to move beyond both the secular rationalist and the traditional religious alternatives to morality and meaning. Nietzsche's proposed means for self-overcoming and the heroic embrace of tragedy were adopted initially almost exclusively by poets, artists, and generally peripheral cultural figures, but soon the ideas began to be engaged by intellectuals in more culturally central locations. Even at least one figure in the respectable ENS/Sorbonne group surrounding Durkheim can be explicitly shown to have held a great interest in Nietzsche. This was Hertz, who wrote at great length in intellectual correspondence about his debt to the German thinker (Riley 1999).

But Hertz was killed in the Great War in 1915, so he played no real direct personal role in translating the interest in the impure sacred to the younger generation of thinkers who were reading Durkheim and Nietzsche while seeking radical personal and political alternatives to the stifling conformities of the Third Republic. Mauss, who pursued a frenetic teaching schedule at three different institutions (the *École Pratique*, the *Institut d'Ethnologie*, and the *Collège de France*) during the interwar period, instead became the central intellectual influence for these neo-Durkheimian researchers of the impure sacred. His students were not the philosophy and history *agrégés* and *normaliens* who had been attracted to Durkheim's work twenty-five or thirty years earlier, but a much more heterogeneous and volatile mix of orientalists, ethnologists, artists and writers. Johan Heilbron described vividly the circle of young intellectuals who would become Mauss' heirs and their position vis-à-vis the rest of the university world:

> they were rather *outsiders* in the university world; Maussian ethnology was not, in their eyes, a continuation of Durkheimian sociology, but something "new," tied to exoticism, to the world of art, or simply to archaeological studies, to the history of religion or to Oriental languages. For them, Durkheim had been "a severe professor, cold, rather rigid, truly the head of a school, while Mauss was a completely different kind of man: he was warm, expansive, he radiated."
> (Heilbron 1985: 230, emphasis in original)[10]

An important group of Mauss' students and followers in the 1920s and 1930s were attracted by all three of the emergent cultural movements discussed above (i.e. the modernist avant-garde, anti-democratic radical politics and anti-Catholic mysticism), and they saw in Maussian thought, and more broadly in the Durkheimian interest in the impure sacred, a consistent way of integrating the three into a lived practice as intellectuals.

Georges Bataille discovered Mauss' work in the fall of 1925 (through the influence of his friend and former schoolmate at the *École des Chartes*, Alfred Métraux), and a number of other similar thinkers, including Roger Caillois and Michel Leiris, were also attracted during this period (Armel 1997: 219; see also Clifford 1988; Surya 1987: 181).[11] These three (Bataille, Caillois and Leiris) shared a primary engagement and interest in avant-garde literary and artistic circles of the period. All were involved to a considerable degree in André Breton's surrealist group, though each broke with Breton eventually. Bataille emerges as the central figure, at least in organizational terms, of the several associations and groups in which the three participated collectively in the 1930s that attempted to put into practice their reading of the Durkheimian engagement with the impure sacred.

The most important of these neo-Durkheimian groups dedicated to the interrogation of the impure sacred was the group formed by Bataille in early 1937, the *Collège de Sociologie*. Bataille had been the founder or co-founder of a number of earlier intellectual groups that were conceived as efforts to found a new kind of intellectual project at once politically radical, aesthetically avant-garde and existentially constitutive of the kind of effervescence spoken of by the Durkheimians. One of these groups, *Acéphale*, was a kind of secret society Bataille organized with Pierre Klossowski, Jean Wahl, Jules Monnerot and several others in 1936. *Acéphale* (literally, "headless" or "leaderless") published a review that appeared a total of four times between

June 1936 and June 1939, and in this way was perhaps not completely unlike many other intellectual associations of the period, but its central purpose was as a transgressive, subversive group of marginal adepts who attempted to recreate and reinvoke the power of the sacred and of the mythic as effervescent, quasi-religious elements outside the official political arena. Bataille and the others involved saw the group as a collective space within which a new way of enacting an intellectual identity could be pursued, a new way consistent with the basic insights of the Durkheimian tradition, albeit mingled with the avant-garde aesthetic and revolutionary political goals that had emerged in the cultural landscape of France after the First World War. The group attracted a wild and sometimes dark reputation for its interest in the extreme faces of such collective effervescence and experience of the sacred. There was even a rumor circulating among some of those close to the group that they intended at one point to carry out a human sacrifice, using a member of the group (Bataille himself perhaps, or his lover and fellow traveler Colette Peignot who was already ill with the tuberculosis that would end her life in November 1938), in order to re-enact the foundational myth necessary to make of the sacrificed a "founder-hero" and of the group a new religion. This rumor remained only a rumor (see Felgine 1994: 139–40).

The *Collège* was in some ways an extension of *Acéphale*, an application of the same principles of intellectual action to an expanded and more public arena. The express goal of the *Collège* was the creation of a *sacred sociology*, which was defined as an enterprise that would at one and the same time analyze and describe the sacred in its effervescent role in the social *and* endeavor to construct direct experiences of the sacred for the participants of the group and, by extension, for other members of society. These two tasks were seen as inseparable by the group. In pure theoretical terms, it was the radical separation between the sociologist as subject and the social, or the other, as object that was put in question by the *Collège*. Jean Jamin (1980: 14) restates the key question posed by the *Collège* thus: "How and under what conditions can a subject position other subjects as objects of knowledge?" In responding in a fashion that denied the separation between sociological analysis of the sacred and the existential quest for the same, the *Collège* attempted to assert an identity as a

> moral community . . . militant, interventionist . . . that not only gave life to the concepts and methods of official sociology represented by Mauss – in transferring them from the exotic to the everyday, from the distant to the near, nearly to the self (Bataille, Leiris) – but also made each of its members into travelers of social experiences. They became the voyagers and the actors of a sociological experiment. (Jamin 1980: 12)

Taking as their starting point the same recognition made by the Durkheimians of the dual character of the sacred, the members of the *Collège* followed and expanded on Mauss, Hubert, and Hertz in their concentration on the left or impure sacred and in their understanding of the proper manner in which to engage the sacred themselves. For them, the quest for a community both intellectual and affective at the same time was a powerful motivating force. It is difficult to generalize about the work of the individuals involved as they were such an idiosyncratic group, but there are nonetheless powerful lines of common interest and orientation connecting them.

Bataille maintained an interest in religious subjects and the idea of the sacred from an early age, when he embraced a mystical Catholicism in his early twenties that informed his first publication, a paean to the Notre Dame cathedral at Reims that had been one of the many French cultural treasures bombed by the Germans during the First World War. Even upon losing his Catholic faith a few short years later, he continued an existential inquiry into the problems of the sacred, sexuality and death that lasted throughout his life. All of his major works are examinations of these problems from a perspective that is greatly indebted to two sources often considered by intellectual historians as utterly oppositional: Durkheimian sociology and German existentialism, and especially Nietzsche. The unifying theme in his work is itself something of a meeting point of these two influences, although terminologically it is clearly Maussian in origin. In analyzing the social and the individual's participation in it, Bataille took as central the notion of expenditure, i.e. of the offering, free giving, or destroying of some capacity, force or good. Mauss' discussion of the gift was essential to Bataille's conception, and he tied his understanding of gift-giving and expenditure even more explicitly to the sacred.

For Bataille, the crucial moments in social life are those in which society expresses itself by ritual offering or destruction of *la part maudite*, the accursed share, in the moments that produce effervescence and power through a total and excessive expenditure of energy, even to the point of death. Sacrifice, war, *potlatch*, games, festivals, mystical fervor and possession, sexual orgies and perversions are all modes in which this kind of expenditure is carried out. This is obviously a discussion that turns traditional sociological and philosophical treatments of production and society, which take production as primary and expenditure as dependent upon it, on their heads. Bataille was among the group who attended, in the 1930s, the lectures at the *École Pratique des Hautes Etudes* by Alexandre Kojève on Hegel,[12] where he learned of a way to read Hegel as a radical and proto-existentialist critic of the systematizing Marxists and others who saw production and work as the keys to human society. From Kojève's Hegel, who took great pains to demonstrate "the unreasonable origins of reason" (Descombes 1980: 14), Bataille took as basic the *desire* of man that, like animal desire, can be satiated only in destruction, in action that radically annihilates the object desired. He also followed Kojève in the conception of the philosopher's ultimate concern as not simply the world or society but as necessarily *himself* and his own experience prior to everything else.

The culminating point of this position in the published work is perhaps Bataille's *La part maudite* (1949), in which he demonstrates in an explicitly historical and sociological manner the centrality of this idea of excess and the necessity of its perpetual regeneration and violent expenditure in society. Here, he invokes historical references ranging from Aztec human sacrifice to primitive *potlatch*, Tibetan Lamaism and the modern West in order to extend the point made by Mauss in his essay on the gift and in his other treatments of the *fait social total*. Bataille demonstrates how the analysis of *general* economy in society (as opposed to *limited* economy, that which restricts itself to production and labor) reveals the essential role played by excess and expenditure, and how this new understanding of economy enables an understanding of the centrality of the sacred (see especially Bataille 1949: 113–14). For the sacred, in its transgressive, impure guise, is one of the central ways in which this expenditure of excess is carried out.

In other discussions of eroticism, violence and death, he echoes this point. The transgressive moment, he argues, "does not deny the taboo but transcends it and completes it" (Bataille 1986: 63); that is, an understanding of the sacred in purely right sacred terms overlooks the very necessity of the left sacred for the completion of the sacred experience. In Bataille's view, the sacred is the experience of "the greatest anguish, the anguish in the face of death . . . in order to transcend it beyond death and ruination" (Bataille 1986: 87), and this experience is possible only when taboos and restrictions representing protection from things and realms that can produce death are transgressed. Thus, sexual taboos are burst asunder and the participants experience the transcendent moment in which the fear of death and decay that is intimately entwined in the sexual act (for "in the long or short run, reproduction demands the death of the parents who produced their young only to give fuller rein to the forces of annihilation" (Bataille 1986: 61)) is overcome, however briefly. Similarly, Bataille sees as the primary element in sacrifice not the offering to the god but rather the transgression, in a violent act of collective murder, of death taboos in the interest of thereby experiencing collectively the effervescent moment in which all perceive "the continuity of all existence with which the victim is now one" (Bataille 1986: 22).

In all this, Bataille takes as given the Durkheimian starting point of the sociality of the sacred and of effervescence, but he adds the compelling response of existentialism, which is that such phenomena cannot be studied from afar by the philosopher or sociologist but that they fundamentally implicate and involve him/her. He makes very clear the point that Mauss, Hubert, and Hertz suggested in their own projects, which is that the problem of the sacred is first and foremost a *personal* problem and that any scientific treatment of it cannot escape this fact.

Caillois was the only one of the three central *Collège de Sociologie* members who studied with Mauss as a student rather than following his courses as an *auditeur libre*. While a student at the *École Normale Supérieure* (from which he would graduate with an *agrégation* in grammar), Caillois was already attending Mauss' post-graduate seminars at the *École Pratique* and he took a diploma from its section in religious sciences in the same year he obtained his *agrégation* (1936), working closely with Mauss and Georges Dumézil on myth and later publishing a thesis on "Les Démons de midi" (Fournier 1994: 708). But his connection to a certain unorthodox Durkheimianism extended further back even than these studies; while a *lycée* student in Reims in the early 1920s, one of his philosophy professors was none other than Marcel Déat, the renegade *L'Année sociologique* collaborator and friend of Célestin Bouglé who turned to the radical right and French national socialism in the 1930s (Felgine 1994: 31). Caillois wrote several book-length studies on precisely the central themes explored by the Durkheimian religion group. *Le myth et l'homme* (1938) and *L'homme et le sacré* (1939) were greatly indebted to Mauss and to Durkheim, and also to Marcel Granet and Georges Dumézil. Though Mauss made some stern criticisms of the work on myth, finding the discussion of literature as modern myth too mired in "irrationalism" and "a vague sentimentality" (Mauss letter to Callois 1938), it cannot be denied that Caillois' position on the foundational character that mythical thought has for social knowledge generally is fundamentally Durkheimian. The book on the sacred is still more obviously Durkheimian, or more precisely Maussian, in spirit, with a great number of references to the work of the religion cluster. In many ways, it reads something like the "textbook" on the sacred that Mauss himself was the best suited to write but never did (see Felgine 1994: 205–6). It also clearly shows the progression in the emphasis given to the sacred as transgression, that is, the impure sacred, as opposed to the sacred as respect that we noted in Mauss, Hubert and Hertz. Caillois included as well a discussion of sexuality and the sacred that presaged Bataille's later work on eroticism as one of the central fields in which the impure sacred manifests itself.

Leiris' most important contribution to the *Collège* in substantive terms was a paper on "Le Sacré dans la vie quotidienne" that he delivered in January 1938. In this paper, he demonstrated a concern for the sacred that was perhaps still more reflexive than even that of his comrades in the *Collège*. Leiris made completely explicit the connection between the ethnographer's concern with the sacred and his/her own participation in it by engaging in an analysis of the construction of the sacred in his own childhood and the ways in which that sacred structure lived on in his adult life. We find in Leiris' personal geography of the sacred the same distinction between left and right, impure and pure sacred, or in Caillois' terms, sacred of transgression and sacred of respect; his father's top hat and revolver are examples of the latter, the bathroom and a nearby racecourse exemplify the former (Leiris 1988: 24–31).

The brevity of this central contribution to the *Collège* should not deceive us, for the publication of Leiris' notebooks in preparation for the subject demonstrate a deep and lasting concern for the subject of the sacred (Leiris 1994). More, as is the case with Bataille and Caillois, much of his work beyond the explicit connection to the *Collège* was also engaged with the sacred as an object of central existential importance in his own life. He continued the autobiographical investigation of the sacred he had begun in the *Collège* after its collapse with a work in 1939 dedicated to Bataille (*L'Age d'homme*), and then a series of books that comprise his masterwork, *La Règle du jeu*. In these works, the connection between the Durkheimian concern with the sacred and the ethnographic project, on the one hand, and the surrealist concern with literature as a profound form of self-examination, on the other, is explored in depth. In the detailed exploration of his own sacred landscape via examination of dreams, childhood memories and transgressive or limit experiences of debauchery, he hoped to create a true *littérature engagée*, in which the writer becomes *l'homme total*, "one for whom real and imaginary are one and the same" (Boyer 1974: 10), precisely in exploring the one individual in whom he can see the totality: himself. *L'Afrique fantôme* had been among the first, tentative sketchings of this quasi-scientific literature in which the methods of the ethnographer (the keeping of a "field journal" and note cards, a certain distancing from the object under investigation) are put to use on the ethnographer himself (Boyer 1974: 40–1).

The members of the *Collège* were attempting to find a point of connection between the insights provided by this new social science into the nature and reality of human existence and the deep and personal existential yearnings gnawing internally at many intellectuals at this crucial moment in European cultural history, i.e. the moment of the West's full entry into a modernity characterized most centrally by the disappearance of traditional cultural responses to deep questions of personal meaning and identity and the failure to locate adequate replacements for this lost symbolic treasury. In them, and arguably also in the younger members of the Durkheimian religion group, we see the struggle between their commitment to the goals of objective social science and their desire to put this science and other intellectual currents at the service of their own existential quest, but Hertz, Hubert, and Mauss managed yet to keep the combatants separated, if only with great difficulty and with more than occasional mutual intrusions. The members of the *Collège* are more willing for a number of reasons to allow these two realms, kept separated in any case only with considerable difficulty, to intermingle freely. This difference perhaps explains some of the clear distinctions in the projects of the *Collège* and those of Hertz and Mauss while attesting at the same time to the parallel dilemmas they faced and the reasons they could use the same Durkheimian body of thought as a tool in facing them. The *Collège* coupled a Durkheimian recognition of the place of the sacred in collective life and in the perpetual renewal of the community through collective effervescence in ritualistic ecstasy with a Nietzschean tweaking of the entire edifice so as to turn the ritualistic idea of the sacred into a celebration of the transgressive moment *per se*.

The *Collège*, forgotten by institutionally-centered intellectual history and, until very recently, all but completely unknown to the history of the social sciences in France, was nonetheless a significant presence in Parisian intellectual circles of the 1930s. Along with the three central members, participants in the group included Pierre Klossowski, Anatole Lewitsky (another ethnologist and student of Mauss), Jules Monnerot, Jean Wahl, Jean Paulhan, and Denis de Rougemont, while Kojève, Jean-Paul Sartre, Claude Lévi-Strauss, Julien Benda, Pierre Drieu la Rochelle and Walter Benjamin all attended at one time or another, though more infrequently (Bataille 1985: xxi; Fournier 1994: 707). The group was very short-lived, but its agenda with respect to the impure/left sacred was taken up by a number of important later thinkers often associated with poststructuralism and postmodernism. We can even see a certain parallel in the two groups of thinkers in the two political/cultural crises in which they emerged and participated: the *Collège* and the democratic crisis brought on by the failure of the Popular Front and the fascist threat in the 1930s, the poststructuralists and the tumult of May 1968.

Michel Foucault was perhaps the most important of these later thinkers in pursuit of the impure sacred. The sacred was an important conceptual theme for Foucault in much of his work. He had an abiding interest in the work of Bataille,[13] which he described as producing a space in which "transgression prescribes not only the sole manner of discovering the sacred in its unmediated substance, but also a way of recomposing its empty form, its absence, through which it becomes all the more scintillating" (Foucault 1977: 30). He argued that sexuality and other subjects he explored in his work (e.g. madness and death) become tied up with the Nietzschean death of God and the very possibility of the emergence of literature itself in so far as they constitute experiences that defy language to speak of them and that are nonetheless spoken of, thereby enacting a violence on both language and the transgressive experience itself that Foucault read sympathetically:

> On the day that sexuality began to speak and to be spoken, language no longer served as a veil for the infinite; and in the thickness it acquired on that day, we now experience the absence of God, our death, limits, and their transgression. But perhaps it is also a source of light for those who have liberated their thought from all forms of dialectical language, as it became for Bataille, on more than one occasion, when he experienced the loss of his language in the dead of night.
>
> (Foucault 1977: 51)

If the sacred is for Bataille desecrated and simultaneously remade in excessive festivals of orgiastic violence and sexuality, for Foucault it is in the act of writing itself that the connection to the sacred as transgression is created and maintained.

In his history of madness and the birth of the asylum in western Europe, Foucault argues that it is the confusion of madness with "unreason" (*déraison*) that threatens to eliminate completely the possibility of perhaps our last remaining access to the sacred through the experience of the "mad" work of art (Foucault 1973: 288). "Unreason" is seen as a realm of knowledge that offers insights not provided by other kinds of knowledge, and scientific knowledge, far from providing any possibilities for social rejuvenation, is described as actively responsible in its psychological guises for the misrecognition and subsequent destruction of this knowledge. This engagement with the left or transgressive sacred as a radical form of knowledge and experience of the social was not merely a fleeting phenomenon for Foucault. In *The Order of Things* (1970), he discusses the possibility of the death of Man as a mutation in the fabric of knowledge that might release us from the totalizing singularity of identity. Foucault speculates upon this "explo[sion of] man's face in laughter" (1970: 385) in light of the artistic projects of Mallarmé, Artaud, Roussel and others who worked in the region bordering transgression and the sacred "where death prowls, where thought is extinguished, where the promise of the origin interminably recedes" (1970: 383), and he finds that the "counter-sciences" of psychoanalysis, ethnology, and linguistics (at least in their structuralist forms) undertake the very dissolution of Man and the turn to the dark being of Language that provided the ground for the transgressions of the poets.

Foucault was at least as scandalous as Bataille in his willingness to discuss even the most disturbing manifestations of the left sacred. From the transgressive, "mad" artist, he turned to the transgressive power of yet another type of dangerous individual who lurks in the borderland between the moral and transgressive and "establishes the ambiguity of the lawful and the unlawful" through his/her words and deeds (Foucault, ed. 1975: 206). He argues that the aesthetic experience that constitutes an encounter with the left sacred might go beyond the creation of a work of art to include even acts considered by a horrified citizenry vile and criminal, like those of Pierre Rivière, the young man in provincial France who murdered several members of his own family in the 1830s and subsequently wrote in a mémoir of the otherworldly imperatives that compelled him to do so. Later still, in his work on normalization and discipline (see, e.g. Foucault 1978; 1979), he examined specific contemporary Western social spaces in which contact with the sacred is increasingly structurally denied. Again scientific discourses are seen as responsible for creating as categories of deviance certain realms of knowledge and practice (e.g. deviant sexualities) that for Foucault offer potential possibilities for transgressive knowledges and "pleasures" (Foucault 1978: 157). Political regimes of both the liberal capitalist and communist models endeavor to close off experience of the transgressive sacred and Foucault condemns both with equal fervor on this ground. The sole political position-taking Foucault celebrates is that which embraces the escape of normativity in the kind of transgressive, dangerous "political spirituality" of e.g. the Iranian Revolution of 1979.

Evidence of influence from Durkheimian roots that point to a particular mobilization of the left or impure sacred can also be seen in the work of Jacques Derrida. A connection to Mauss is directly observable, as Derrida wrote a long essay devoted in large part to a commentary on Mauss' essay on the gift (Derrida 1991). But beyond this, we can locate in his overall philosophical project clear connections to the later Durkheimian interest in the impure sacred. At the core of Derrida's work is a preoccupation with the aspect of Western metaphysics that requires certain foundational binary categories that are actually undone by certain crucial concepts that can invoke both poles of a contradictory binary and that demonstrate the ultimate instability of seemingly firmly constructed philosophical systems of reasoning. He has examined in great detail the role played in foundational texts and writers of the Western philosophical tradition by these unstable concepts and categories in order to unveil the holes in binary thought generally that they represent, and to criticize what he sees as a systematic classification of writing as somehow more radically separated from real metaphysical presence than is speech (see especially Derrida 1976; 1982: 1–27). Examples are the word *pharmakon* (which can mean both "poison" and "remedy") in Plato (Derrida 1981), *supplément* (which, Derrida argued, means both "addition to" and "replacement of," with reference to writing's relationship to speech) in Rousseau (Derrida 1976: 141–64) and *gift* (which, as Mauss (1969: 46) himself had pointed out, descends from a Germanic root that has the dual meaning of "offering" and "poison," the former preserved in modern English "gift," the latter in modern German "gift").

Derrida's therapeutic project was to offer a new, radical kind of thought and writing that undoes this rigidity precisely by refusing the binary categories, exposing their limitations and reveling in transgression of the hierarchical rules of traditional thought. His own method of deconstruction aims to do precisely this, and in several works he has noted the efforts of others he sees as exemplary in this regard. In a reading similar to that of Foucault, Derrida (1978: 266) sees in Bataille's work a radical effort at "a sovereign form of writing" that embraces "the poetic or the ecstatic," which is defined by Bataille as "that *in every discourse* which can open itself up to the absolute loss of its sense, to the (non-) base of the sacred, of nonmeaning" (Derrida 1978: 261, emphasis in original). Derrida interpreted the "theater of cruelty" of Artaud, which excluded from its ranks "all non-sacred theater," as analogous to his own efforts (Derrida 1978: 243). Jean-Michel Heimonet (1987) has carefully demonstrated the direct links between the treatment of the sacred in modern poetry by members of the *Collège de Sociologie* (Bataille, Caillois, and Jules Monnerot) and Derrida's theory of *différance*. Leiris, Caillois, and Bataille were determined in their efforts to attach the Durkheimian theory they had encountered in Mauss' work to what they and others (especially the various members of the Surrealist movement) saw as a contemporary crisis in literature that was in their view linked, like the political and broader cultural crises of inter-war France, to the disappearance of myth and the sacred (see, e.g. Rieusset 1983: 67–123).

Like Foucault and Derrida, Jean Baudrillard utilized the category of the impure sacred, specifically in analyzing forms of knowledge and exchange that have often been discounted by other observers as examples of false consciousness or cultural domination. Although his early work bears the imprint of a neo-Marxism influenced by Henri Lefebvre, by the mid-1970s, Baudrillard had formulated a powerful critique of the foundational assumptions of critical social theory that was informed by the political events of May 1968 and owed a heavy theoretical debt to Maussian ethnology and the Durkheimian engagement with the impure sacred. He began a vigorous attack on the idea of a social order fundamentally based on the existence of a "mass" with a rational will and a teleological place in history. It is the historical notion of the "the masses" or the "social" as a foundational tenet of the discipline of sociology that he argued has denied the validity of the experience of surplus, sacrifice, and the sacred (Baudrillard 1983: 79). Sociology, in Baudrillard's reading, has always understood society as a utilitarian network of relations with use value as the driving force behind it. This understanding has led to the classification of the "masses" as alienated or mystified in so far as they forsake rational communication and commerce. But he argued it is precisely in spectacle[14] and in revelry in apparent meaninglessness that the sacred is experienced by the silent majorities. The "masses" explode the Enlightenment vision of the social completely in refusing "progressive" political mobilization for the modern festival of a soccer match (Baudrillard 1983: 12). These festivals are in some sense the contemporary equivalent of Mauss' agonistic potlatch and Bataille's Aztec sacrifices.

Through lengthy analyses of the historical failures of social scientific and political movements predicated upon the outmoded productivist paradigm and a genealogical examination of death as a form of social relation in Western societies that recalls Hertz in its essentials, Baudrillard offered a radical thesis regarding the dilemmas faced by contemporary Western capitalist societies and the possible means of responding to them. As a result of our entry into a modern period characterized by the total victory of productivism, we have removed much of the world from our cycle of exchange, i.e. we have expelled some actors (most importantly, the dead) from our circle of social relations, and we thus now experience a frustrated and anxiety-ridden state of existence as a result of the destruction of the more complete system of exchange characteristic of many primitive societies wherein all excess, symbolic and material, is consumed in festival or ritual sacrifice rather than being accumulated. In short, Baudrillard pointed to the *potlatch* and to the experience of the left sacred examined by Mauss, Hertz, Bataille, and Caillois to demonstrate the failures of our own modern paradigm of exchange and social relation. He explored a number of what he considered radical responses to the crushing strictures of the modern productivist paradigm of exchange: our cultural fascination with violent death, especially in auto accidents, which partakes of some of the same symbolic significance as is experienced in ritual sacrifice; the obscure work on anagrammatic poetry by Ferdinand de Saussure, which is, per Baudrillard, an attempt to work through a poetics in which, as in *potlatch*, all excess is destroyed rather than accumulated for further deciphering or signification;[15] and political terrorism, which, in so far as it consists of a "radical denial of negotiation" (Baudrillard 1993: 37) constitutes a turning of the principle of domination, which is normally the State's unique power to refuse the counter-gift and thereby to deny the recipient's opportunity for symbolic return, back against the State itself, a move that holds out the possibility for the collapse of the State.

Baudrillard gave more nuance to his contemporary theory of the left sacred with his concept of seduction. Paralleling the move to "liberate" sex with the move to "liberate" labor, he opposed the productivist paradigm again by positing a radical form of exchange (seduction) that "takes the form of an uninterrupted ritual exchange where seducer and seduced constantly raise the stakes in a game that never ends" (Baudrillard 1990: 22). Seduction is dangerous and violent. It refuses the banality of bodies and the orgasm for the play of secrets and challenges. Baudrillard reappropriated Huizinga's (1950) notion of play as a fundamental mode of interaction and combined it with his interpretation of the sacred as foundational mode of experience of the social. What emerges is at bottom agonistic and outside (and transgressive) of reason and law. The points of comparison with Mauss' notion of gift-giving and *potlatch* are obvious. Baudrillard (1990: 33) argues for a mode of social relations predicated not upon any foundational rational, wealth-maximizing agents but rather upon ludic wearers of "symbolic veils," which is more fundamental than any form of exchange based upon the centrality of production. The choice of specific terminology and examples here (e.g. his analyses of courtship play and pornography, the latter of which is in his view not seductive) is often provocatively weighted toward the language of gender and sex, but it is clear that he intended his analysis to apply to social relations *generally* and not merely to relations of sexual pursuit or attraction. It is thus, notwithstanding Baudrillard's extended polemic against the "social," a *general* social theory with strong ties to a neo-Durkheimian form of engagement with the impure sacred that is advanced here and that is at the heart of his work.

This interest in the impure sacred and the transgressive cultural and political perspective it enabled has thus survived the demise of the Durkheimian school that gave it birth and relocated itself in a number of subsequent theoretical projects including those of several of the most significant post-structuralist thinkers. A number of interesting points suggest themselves in the way of a conclusion. First, the significant turn in many theoretical circles to the body in recent years has arguably been enabled by this concentration on the impure sacred. The institutionalized Durkheimian tradition (and indeed much of mainstream social theory outside the Durkheimian tradition as well) has largely taken from Durkheim's own focus on the pure sacred the latent idealism that accompanies it; mind/body, or ideal/material, is another of those binary oppositions that can be included along with the others suggested or explicitly formulated in Durkheim's theory of religion. It is largely in the circles that have inherited the Maussian/Hubertian/Hertzian attention to the impure sacred that the body has been more explicitly integrated into the theoretical project. Themes of sexuality and erotic transgression have been of central concern in the analysis of the impure sacred from the work of Mauss et al. through Bataille to Foucault and Baudrillard.

A second telling point here has to do with the expansion in the application of the concept of the sacred inherent in a focus on the impure sacred. In Durkheim's analysis, it seems taken for granted that a certain secularization of the sacred is inevitable, even if some core function provided by the sacred must be preserved for the social body. He speaks, in other words, as a representative of the modern secular intellectual class, convinced that the "primitive" varieties of the sacred are on their way out but still troubled (in a way, we should be sure to recognize, that many of Durkheim's more anti-clerical colleagues certainly were not) by his realization that the social fabric depends on the sacred glue for its coherence. As such, the political program that emerges from his emphasis on the pure sacred rather overemphasizes the abstract, disembodied aspects of the sacred. Insofar as his project is motivated by his own personal need for a solution to the problem of the sacred, the solution proffered is geared to a society of essentially secularized intellectuals like himself. The focus on the impure sacred also betrays a personal, existential interest in the sacred, which inevitably has political consequences, but hardly the same ones as the focus on the pure sacred. Here, the formulation of a definition of the sacred expressly rejects a model of the social as consisting of rational, secularized proto-intellectuals. Precisely because the model of the intellectual represented by Durkheim and his secular *Sorbonnard* colleagues had been subjected to rigorous criticism in the generation following them, the new engagement with the sacred explicitly built this criticism into its formulation of an invigorated notion of the sacred for modern society. Thus one finds in the effort to concentrate on the impure sacred a rejection of the split between intellectuals and masses (a split Durkheim attempts to reconcile by incorporating the latter category into the former) that is implicitly present in Durkheim's analysis. Instead, one finds here an effort to formulate a more holistic theory of the sacred not limited by the hyper-rationalized perspective of the optimistic positivist intellectual of the pre-First World War period, a theory informed by the failures of many twentieth-century political projects that over-rationalization and the denial of the "dark side" of social life that accompanies it must be corrected by a broader recognition of the very deep, and sometimes troubling, roots of the sacred.

NOTES

1 Interestingly, Durkheim provides pork as an example of an ambiguous sacred phenomenon for "certain Semitic peoples," which is forbidden but in which case it is not clear *why* it is so, that is, if it is pure or impure sacred. We know that Durkheim, as he acknowledged himself, suffered terribly on the first occasions on which he ate pork after formally renouncing the dietary habits enforced by

orthodox Judaism (see also his remarks on this topic in his review of Guyau's *L'Irreligion de l'avenir* (1975: 161), where he writes "The Christian who, for the first time, takes his meals normally on Good Friday, the Jew who, for the first time, eats pork, both experience a remorse that is impossible to distinguish from moral remorse").

2 More, he argues here, there are no religious phenomena that are not ultimately "composite," that is, there are no purely religious or purely magical phenomena.

3 See also François Isambert (in Besnard 1983: 160): "At the frontier of folklore and sociology: Hubert, Hertz and Czarnowski, founders of a sociology of folk religion."

4 It had first appeared in the second series of the *Année sociologique* in 1924–5.

5 Mauss cites Hertz as the latter had collected a large amount of information concerning the *hau* for his unfinished thesis on sin and expiation and Mauss had come into possession of his notes and papers at the death of Durkheim in 1917; his uncle had received them from Hertz's wife in 1915 on Hertz's death (see Mauss 1950: 159 footnote 1). Numerous commentators (including Raymond Firth and Marshall Sahlins) have taken Mauss to task for quoting Ranaipiri out of context and thereby perhaps subtly changing the meaning of the quotation (see Godelier 1999: 16).

6 Lévi-Strauss' (1950) introduction to the collected volume of Mauss' essays is of course more than a simple introduction, as has long been recognized; it is a very skilled effort to mold Mauss into a precursor to the very structuralist theorizing of which Lévi-Strauss had been an important innovator in the late 1940s and early 1950s.

7 For example, he notes the relation of the seemingly fundamentally political economic institution of gift-giving and religious obligation in the form of sacrifice.

8 There are distinctions, especially between Durkheim and Hertz, which I have argued elsewhere (Riley 2000) are clearly quite significant and even prescient of the still greater differences between e.g. Durkheim and the *Collège de Sociologie*, but taking up that case at length here would take us away from the topic at hand.

9 Arthur Mitzman (1973: 111–12) characterizes Durkheim's politics as akin to those of the "conservative socialists of the chair" in German academia during the same period (e.g. Gustav Schmoller, Adolf Wagner) in order to distinguish his position from the more alienated and Nietzschean positions of figures like Tönnies and Michels.

10 The quotation marks within the excerpt mark where Heilbron is quoting from remarks he gathered in interviews with Mauss' students.

11 Bataille, unlike Leiris and Caillois, may not have actually attended Mauss' courses, though he distinguishes the supposed increased attention to the importance of transgression in Mauss' "oral teaching" as opposed to in his written work (Bataille 1986: 65).

12 Some of these lectures, given between 1933 and 1939, were transcribed and published by the surrealist Raymond Queneau in 1947 as *Introduction à la lecture de Hegel*. The Kojève seminar was, like the course of Mauss, a fascinating site in which intellectuals from radically different milieux and with radically different concerns came together to engage what was seen as one of the

most exciting minds of the period. Among the other seminar participants were Jean-Paul Sartre, Maurice Merleau-Ponty, André Breton, Raymond Aron, Jacques Lacan, and Bataille's comrade in *Acéphale* and the *Collège de Sociologie*, Pierre Klossowski (Boschetti 1988: 66; Surya 1987: 196).

13 In addition to an essay on Bataille (published in the review Bataille had founded in 1946) for a special issue on his death (Foucault [1963] 1977), Foucault assisted in the publication of Bataille's *Oeuvres complètes* (1973) and wrote the introduction. David Macey (1993: 16) indicates an interesting familial connection between Foucault's family and Bataille's: Foucault's father, who was a physician, operated on Jean Piel, who was related by marriage to both André Masson (who was also affiliated with numerous Bataille projects) and Bataille (Piel, Masson and Bataille married three sisters), and Masson had given Foucault's father one of his drawings.

14 Baudrillard borrowed this term from Situationism, but he significantly modified its original Marxist implications. While the Surrealist Guy Debord defined the spectacle as "the existing order's uninterrupted discourse about itself . . . the self portrait of power in the epoch of its totalitarian management of the conditions of existence" (Debord 1983: paragraph 24) and thereby construed the spectacle as a powerful contributor to the mystification and alienation of the masses, Baudrillard saw in this revelry the excess and irrationality of modern capitalism as the best approximation of a contemporary experience of the sacred.

15 Baudrillard saw goods and words as functional equals here. The anagrammatic poem is the symbolic extermination of language itself and of the very notion of value, just as the destruction of goods in potlatch exterminates value for the primitive. It is comparable to the symbolic calling forth of the gods by the primitive, solely "in order to put them to death" (Baudrillard 1993: 209).

REFERENCES

Armel, Aliette. 1997. *Michel Leiris*. Paris: Fayard.

Arppe, Tiina. 1995. "Émile Durkheim et *la part maudite* du sacré." *Société* 48: 209–18.

Bataille, Georges. 1986. *Erotism: Death and Sensuality*. Translated by Mary Dalwood. San Francisco: City Lights Books.

1985. *Visions of Excess*. Edited by Allan Stoekl. Minneapolis: University of Minnesota Press.

1973. *Oeuvres completes*. Paris: Gallimard.

1949. *La Part maudite*. Paris: Éditions de Minuit.

Baudrillard, Jean. 1993. *Symbolic Exchange and Death*. Translated by Iain Hamilton. London: Sage.

1990. *Seduction*. New York: St. Martin's Press.

1983. *In the Shadows of the Silent Majorities . . . or the End of the Social, and other essays*. Translated by Paul Foss, Paul Patton and John Johnston. New York: Semiotexte.

Besnard, Philippe, ed. 1983. *The Sociological Domain: The Durkheimians and the Founding of French Sociology*. Cambridge and Paris: Cambridge University Press and Editions de la Maison des Sciences de l'Homme.

Bompaire-Evesque, Claire-Françoise. 1988. *Un Débat sur l'université au temps de la Troisième Republique: la lutte contre la nouvelle Sorbonne*. Paris: Aux Amateurs de Livres.

Boschetti, Anna. 1998. *The Intellectual Enterprise: Sartre et Les Temps Modernes*. Evanston, IL: Northwestern University Press.

Boyer, Alain-Michel. 1974. *Michel Leiris*. Paris: Éditions Universitaires.

Clark, Terry N. 1973. *Prophets and Patrons: The French University and the Emergence of the Social Sciences*. Cambridge, MA: Harvard University Press.

Clifford, James. 1988. *The Predicament of Culture: Twentieth-Century Ethnography, Literature and Art*. Cambridge, MA: Harvard University Press.

Debord, Guy. 1983. *Society of the Spectacle*. Detroit: Black and Red.

Derrida, Jacques. 1991. *Donner le temps*. Paris: Galilée.

   1982. "Différance." pp. 1–27 in *Margins of Philosophy*. Translated by Alan Bass. Chicago: University of Chicago Press.

   1981. "Plato's Pharmacy." pp. 61–171 in *Dissemination*. Translated by Barbara Johnson. Chicago: University of Chicago Press.

   1978. "From Restricted to General Economy: A Hegelianism without Reserve." pp. 251–77 in *Writing and Difference*. Translated by Alan Bass. Chicago: University of Chicago Press.

   1976. *Of Grammatology*. Translated by Gayatri Chakravorty Spivak. Baltimore, MD: Johns Hopkins University Press.

Descombes, Vincent. 1980. *Modern French Philosophy*. Cambridge: Cambridge University Press.

Dosse, François. 1992. *Histoire du structuralisme, II: Le chant du cygne, 1967 à nos jours*. Paris: Éditions la Découverte.

Durkheim, Émile. 1975. *Textes*. Vol. 2, *Religion, morale, anomie*. Paris: Éditions de Minuit.

   [1912] 1991. *Les Formes élémentaires de la vie religieuse*. Paris: Librarie Général Française.

Evans-Pritchard, E. E. 1960. Introduction to *Death and The Right Hand* by Robert Hertz. Glencoe, IL: Free Press.

Felgine, Odile. 1994. *Roger Caillois*. Paris: Stock.

Foucault, Michel. 1979. *Discipline and Punish*. Translated by Alan Sheridan. New York: Vintage.

   1978. *The History of Sexuality*, vol 1. Translated by Robert Hurley. New York: Pantheon.

   ed. 1975. *I, Pierre Rivière, Having Slaughtered my Mother, my Sister, and my Brother* . . . Translated by Frank Jellinek. New York: Pantheon.

   1973. *Madness and Civilization*. Translated by Richard Howard. New York: Vintage.

   1970. *The Order of Things*. New York: Vintage.

   [1963] 1977. "A Preface to Transgression" in *Language, Counter-Memory, Practice: Selected Essays and Interviews by Michel Foucault*. Edited by Donald Bouchard. Ithaca: Cornell University Press. Reprinted and translated from the original published in *Critique*, 1963: 751–70.

Fournier, Marcel. 1994. *Marcel Mauss*. Paris: Fayard.

Godelier, Maurice. 1999. *The Enigma of the Gift*. Translated by Nora Scott. London: Polity Press.

Gugelot, Frédéric. 1998. *La Conversion des intellectuels au catholicisme en France, 1885–1935*. Paris: CNRS Éditions.

Heilbron, Johan. 1985. "Les métamorphoses du Durkheimisme, 1920–1940." *Revue française de sociologie* 26: 203–37.

Heimonet, Jean-Michel. 1987. *Politiques de l'écriture, Bataille/Derrida: Le sens du sacré dans la pensée française du surréalisme à nos jours*. Chapel Hill: University of North Carolina Department of Romance Languages.

Hertz, Robert. 1960. *Death and the Right Hand*. Translated by Rod and Claudia Needham. Introduced by E. E. Evans-Pritchard Glencoe, IL: Free Press.

Hubert, Henri. 1904. "Introduction to Pierre-Daniël Chantepie de la Saussaye" in *Manuel d'histoire des religions*. Translated by Henri Hubert et al. Paris: Armand Colin.

Huizinga, Johan. 1950. *Homo Ludens: A Study of the Play Element in Man*. Boston, MA: Beacon Press.

Isambert, François. 1983. "At the Frontier of Folklore and Sociology: Hubert, Hertz and Czarnowski, Founders of a Sociology of Folk Religion" in *The Sociological Domain: The Durkheimians and the Founding of French Sociology* by Philippe Besnard. Cambridge: Cambridge University Press and Paris: Éditions de la Maison des Sciences de l'Homme.

Jamin, Jean. 1980. "Un sacré collège, ou les apprentis sorciers de la sociologie." *Cahiers internationaux de sociologie* 68: 5–30.

Leiris, Michel. 1988. "The Sacred in Everyday Life." pp. 24–31 in *The College of Sociology, 1937–1939*. Edited by Denis Hollier. Minneapolis: University of Minnesota Press.

    1994. *L'Homme sans honneur, notes pour le sacré dans la vie quotidienne*. Edited by Jean Jamin. Paris: Jean Michel Place.

Lévi-Strauss, Claude. 1950. "Introduction à l'oeuvre de Marcel Mauss." pp. ix–lii in *Marcel Mauss, Sociologie et anthropologie*. Paris: Éditions de Minuit.

Macey, David. 1993. *The Lives of Michel Foucault*. London: Hutchinson.

Mauss, Marcel. 1979. "L'oeuvre de Marcel Mauss par lui-même," reprinted in *Revue française de sociologie* 20: 214–18.

    1969. *Oeuvres*. Vol. 3, *Cohésion sociale et divisions de la sociologie*. Paris: Éditions de Minuit.

    1950. "Essai sur le don. Forme et raison de l'échange dans les sociétés archaïques," reprinted in *Marcel Mauss, Sociologie et anthropologie*. Paris: Éditions de Minuit.

Mauss, Marcel to Roger Caillois, unpublished letter. 1938. 22 June. Fonds Hubert/Mauss, Archives of the *Collège de France* in Paris.

Mitzman, Arthur. 1973. *Sociology and Estrangement*. New York: Knopf.

Parkin, Robert. 1996. *The Dark Side of Humanity: The Work of Robert Hertz and its Legacy*. Amsterdam: Harwood Academic Publishers.

Pickering, W. S. F. 1984. *Durkheim's Sociology of Religion: Themes and Theories*. London: Routledge.

Rieusset, Isabelle. 1983. Fonction et signification du myth dans le *Collège de sociologie*. PhD thesis, Université de Paris VII.

Riley, Alexander. 2000. In Pursuit of the Sacred: The Durkheimian Sociologists of Religion and Their Paths Toward the Construction of the Modern Intellectual. PhD thesis, University of California, San Diego.

1999. "Whence Durkheim's Nietzschean Grandchildren? A Closer Look at Robert Hertz's Place in the Durkheimian Genealogy." *Archives européennes de sociologie/European Journal of Sociology* 40: 302–30.

Stoekl, Allan. 1992. *Agonies of the Intellectual: Commitment, Subjectivity, and the Performative in the Twentieth-Century French Tradition*. Lincoln: University of Nebraska Press.

Surya, Michel. 1987. *Georges Bataille: La Mort à l'oeuvre*. Paris: Librarie Seguier.

III

SOLIDARITY, DIFFERENCE, AND MORALITY

12

EDWARD A. TIRYAKIAN

Durkheim, solidarity, and September 11

I

Jeffrey Alexander (1987) has vigorously defended the centrality of the classics in the social sciences in opposition to a more "natural science" optic regarding the progress of a scientific discipline. It is part of the training of sociologists to internalize the classics (Alexander 1987: 20) as much as they internalize the methods and rules of evidence required to established empirical facts, which are the "stuff" of the natural sciences. The classics, thus, provide frames for finding, sensing, and mapping the major dimensions of the social order (Wrong 1994).

To add to Alexander's discussion, I suggest that we see a two-way interaction between the classics and our contemporary situation. On the one hand, the classics are heuristic in sensitizing us to a broader view and a broader search of social structures and patterns in our contemporary social world. They provide us with a "perspective" which may be otherwise missing simply because we may be so immersed in our situation as to be, in a certain sense, myopic of broader operative features. On the other hand, our contemporary situation may bring to light elements or dimensions that undergird the classic text, helping to understand (that is, to stand under) the text; ultimately, to bring out features of the text that may have remained obscure. Thus, to bring out a new understanding of our contemporary situation, to make sense of what might be otherwise an unwieldy set of data, and to make new sense of an accepted text is really a dialectical process of theorizing, from the past to the present and from the present to the past.

These remarks may be exemplified by taking as an ingress a well-trodden classic of Durkheim, *The Division of Labor in Society*. It was his doctoral dissertation, which unlike almost any doctoral dissertation that comes to mind, went through several editions in his lifetime and beyond,[1] and English translations have been widely available since 1933.[2] Further, to mark its centennial in the preceding decade, collective works appeared on both sides of the Atlantic (Besnard et al. 1993; Tiryakian 1994a).

In standard theory courses, students (at least in theory) become well-versed in certain themes which justify the classical status of this text: (1) That *The Division of Labor* was a devastating critique of utilitarian thought in arguing for the social embeddedness of economic institutions (Durkheim's refutation of Herbert Spencer's liberal individualism). (2) That the work provides a broad frame for the evolution of society from "simple, segmented" society organized by kin-based clans to increasingly more complex, more differentiated societies functionally integrated, i.e. made cohesive, by the division of labor that is at its most complex form in the modern industrial order. (3) That Durkheim made an ingenious use of the legal code to examine shifting proportions or the relative weight of restitutive (or civil) law that regulates relations between individual actors and criminal law where the offense is against the State, which stands for the entire collectivity.[3] (4) That Durkheim's functional analysis of modern society as an evolving, adaptive totality is tempered by a jarring analysis of the pathologies of the industrial order, making *anomie* a problematic condition of modernity. Durkheim sought a structural remedy for a structural malaise, namely the renovation of professional associations, something akin to craft unions but in a more corporatist image than the British trade union. (5) That Durkheim made use of a major conceptual dichotomy: mechanical and organic solidarity which is one of many such dichotomous pairings in classical sociology, along with *Gemeinschaft* and *Gesellschaft*,[4] capitalist and socialist, primary and secondary groups, "I" and "me," and so on.

"Mechanical" for Durkheim is the condition typical of early, segmentary, relatively homogeneous society when sentiments and beliefs are shared in common, where individuation is minimal, and collective thinking is maximal. "Organic" is the condition that becomes prevalent with demographic increases in the population producing a more differentiated population that becomes interdependent with an increase in the division of labor. Functional instead of kin relations become salient in establishing social cohesion via thick layers of functional interdependence, and for Durkheim, the modern division of labor tends to become a moral force in providing for social cohesion and allowing individualism to flourish, since our individuality is given so many options in the modern occupational structure. Other themes might be adduced but it would not serve the purpose of this essay to draw them out.

It is the last-named theme above that retains attention. As the editors of one of the commemorative works laconically stated it, "the notions of 'mechanical solidarity' and 'organic solidarity' are undoubtedly what one retains of

The Division of Labor in Society when one has forgotten everything else (or when one has learned little from it)" (Besnard et al. 1993: 3). The objective of this essay is to take this very old familiar pair of concepts and apply it to a totally new setting, that of post-September 11. My argument here is that "mechanical" and "organic solidarity" have had and continue to have new manifestations in America and globally. I also wish to take what happened, or rather some of the consequences of the aftermath of September 11,[5] to link us back to Durkheim's societal setting, something which exegetes of classics frequently neglect. In sum, it is the *actuality* of the classic that I hope will emerge from this study. That seems to me the way to make students feel that a classic text is, in keeping with this volume's title, a *companion*.

II

If Durkheim never defines "solidarity" (Besnard et al. 1993: 3), this should not be construed as an intentional theoretical disregard on his part. The question of solidarity was close to his preoccupations both as a sociologist and as an active member of French society during his whole lifetime. It went well beyond his explicit treatment of "mechanical" and "organic solidarity" even if he discarded this pair of concepts after the dissertation. The preoccupation with "solidarity" can be discerned in his two following substantive studies, *Suicide* ([1897] 1930) and *The Elementary Forms of the Religious Life* ([1912] 1995; hereafter, *Elementary Forms*). While displaying his sociological virtuosity of analysis, close to the surface of each Durkheim is pointing to the significance of the social ties of solidarity, in giving meaning to the life of social actors, in renovating and providing a foyer for social ideals and values. At the core of his message is this: solidarity, our attachment and ties to others,[6] is the founding, the source of morality (Miller 1996: 150; Jones 2001: 97).

If we bring together Durkheim's discussion of "organic solidarity" as an aspect of modernity with his discussion of types of suicide, we can draw as an inference what sort of solidarity he saw early in his career as desirable for individuals and for modern society. It is a rich network of social ties, beyond the kinship network, that are freely entered into and developed by social actors; such social ties are both pleasurable and are also sources of obligations voluntarily accepted. The relations I have with my co-workers [to invoke Benedict Anderson (1991), with not only my fellow workers here-and-now but also with my "imagined community"] are, in Durkheim's treatment of *Suicide*, anchors without which individuals may drift into the *néant* of egoistic or anomic suicide. To be sure, the social ties, in the form of normative demands of the group for its survival, even at the expense of the individual actor, may be more *chains* than anchor. This extreme form of solidarity has its pathological instance in "altruistic" suicide: the latter might be viewed as prototypical of the small tight-knit group of "mechanical solidarity."[7]

Solidarity is equally an important underlying aspect of his later *magnum opus, Elementary Forms*. Recall that in his definitional gambit of the phenomenon, he underscores not only the twin components of the sacred (beliefs and practices set apart) but also that these are constitutive of *"one single moral community called a Church, all those who adhere to them."* To make sure the reader does not miss the emphasis, Durkheim adds in the next breath, "The second element thus holds a place in my definition that is no less essential than the first. In showing that the idea of religion is inseparable from the idea of a Church, it conveys the notion that religion must be an eminently collective thing" (Durkheim 1995: 44).

If a major aspect of his monumental study is, broadly speaking, to establish the sociology of knowledge by an in-depth analysis of primitive totemism, the concern with the real social world of the modern present is never far away. In the concluding chapter he evokes the collective enthusiasm of the French Revolution and anticipates "hours of creative effervescence during which new ideals will again spring forth" (Durkheim 1995: 429). His following discussion arguing for a new symbiosis of religion and science – with the authority of science as unquestioned, to be sure – situates him as an advocate of a sociologically enriched "Project of the Enlightenment."[8] One can read *Elementary Forms* as a sociological critique of reason, and it is that. For the present discussion, solidarity is an important part of that critique. The cognitive development of mankind, ratiocination, thinking and acting morally – all these aspects of a higher, impersonal life that can be attained by individuals and which Kant, *the* philosopher of the Enlightenment had grasped – could not take place without solidarity. Or as Durkheim stated it,

> Collective thought is possible only through the coming together of individuals ... The realm of impersonal aims and truths cannot be realized except through the collaboration of individual wills and sensibilities.   (1995: 447)

While *Elementary Forms* is undoubtedly a seminal work, in the context of discussing solidarity I do not read it as anything final. Turning to religion as a social phenomenon intimately connected to the deep structures of society, Durkheim was pointing to the incompleteness of "organic solidarity" in the occupational sphere in providing for the moral integration of modern society. Even if the "pathologies" of the modern division of labor were substantially reduced – for example, by minimizing social inequalities that prevent some from participating in the labor market to the fuller extent of their ability – would this suffice? Durkheim, sociologist and moralist, was looking for broader bases than professional and occupational associations, which after all are still in the realm of the profane, however that *profane* is enriched beyond the interests of the market place. The religious life tapped at aspects of the *sacred*, especially beliefs and rituals (see the essay of Robert Bellah in this volume and his earlier excellent overview of Durkheim (Bellah 1973)) which, when free of coercion, bind together an entire society.

The question that remains when one finishes *Elementary Forms* is: can the moments of "collective effervescence" regenerative of societal solidarity occur in the modern world, and under what circumstances? For a believer in democracy like Durkheim, it might well be the historic night of August 4, 1789 when the National Constituent Assembly eliminated feudal privileges, paving the way for the egalitarian ideals of the Rights of Man.[9] It would *not* have been, for Durkheim, Berlin in February 1933 and the burning of the Reichstag, but in retrospect, modernity gives no assurance as to which form effervescence might take. In the few years that remained to Durkheim after *Elementary Forms*, there was an unexpected "happening" that relates to and even completes his quest for solidarity albeit he did not write a monograph about it. But before presenting it, *and relating this to "September 11,"* we need to contextualize Durkheim's treatment of solidarity.

III

However much we see today Durkheim as a "theorist" of society, which indeed he was, we need to keep in mind that he was very much a social actor of turn-of-century France, interested in questions and problems of his day, as any contemporary sociologist might well be, however the settings may differ. Durkheim was not the only one who made much of the question of solidarity; other prominent figures addressed the very same theme, so much so that it might almost be considered the key social philosophy of the Third Republic in the 1890s and first decade of the new century. Moreover, it has continued to have appeal in France today.[10]

Around the turn of the last century, the political figure (head of the centrist left Radical-Socialist Party), and future Nobel Peace Prize winner Léon Bourgeois articulated the idea of solidarity as social justice in economic exchanges, without which violence and frustration ensue. The same year as the publication of Durkheim's revised edition of *The Division of Labor*, Bourgeois mentioned in his preface to the third edition that "solidarity" had become tantamount to "fraternity" in the republican discourse (Bourgeois 1902: 6). Cognizant of the need to rise above political cleavages and acrimony between liberal economists and socialists, Bourgeois saw the appeal to solidarity as establishing common social bonds between contentious factions. He proposed that solidarity

> is the study of the exact causes, of the conditions and the limits of this solidarity, which only can give the measure of the rights and obligations of each towards all and of all towards each, and which will assure the scientific and moral conclusions of the social problem. (Bourgeois 1902: 15)

The above might well be taken as a mission statement for Durkheim's mature conception of sociology. And it is hard to say that it is not Durkheim writing some pages later:

> Let us not be surprised if at present all our institutions, all legislation is questioned. The moral and social malaise from which we suffer is but the clash between certain political, economic and social institutions and the moral ideas that the progress of human thought have slowly transformed.
> (Bourgeois 1902: 77)

As social philosophy, then, solidarism[11] sought a union of morality and the social sciences in refashioning the social world, an extension of the democratic ideas of the Enlightenment. At the prestigious *École des Hautes Etudes Sociales* during the academic year 1901–1902 Bourgeois and Dean of the Faculty Alfred Croiset organized a series of colloquia in Paris on the theme of solidarity, with a volume of proceedings appearing a few years later (Bourgeois and Croiset 1907). The speakers were a distinguished group of public figures, including Durkheim's teacher and influential philosopher Émile Boutroux, Ferdinand Buisson at the University of Paris (whose chair Durkheim occupied in 1906 when Buisson became a cabinet minister), Xavier Léon (director of the *Revue de Métaphysique et de Morale* in which Durkheim published some key essays) and other intellectual notables.

For whatever reason, Durkheim does not appear to have given a colloquium on the topic, since he was not in the list of volume contributors. Yet the volume has clear reference to sociology. Croiset in his preface indicated that solidarity "is a socialist idea drawn from the nineteenth century which takes society, the collectivity . . . as a special object of study . . . that becomes sociology" (Bourgeois and Croiset 1907: viii). And in his presentation, Alphonse Darlu (who had taught Marcel Proust in his philosophy course at the *Lycée Condorcet*) pointed out that as the guiding principle of contemporary philosophy "the idea of solidarity is a social idea, one can even say a sociological one" (Bourgeois and Croiset 1907: 129).

While approving that solidarity is a new, positive ethical doctrine that encourages social activism, Darlu went on to question those strict sociologists *like Espinas and Durkheim* who take society to be an end in itself (Bourgeois and Croiset 1907: 129n, my emphasis). Darlu, Bourgeois, and the others in this volume took their distance from an overdetermination of morality by sociology, at least in their upholding of the individual as both a social agent and as an autonomous moral agent. Still, there was a lot of consensual overlap between them and Durkheim, especially if one were to compare these to either liberal economic individualism, on the one hand, or the Marxist collectivism, on the other.

In the background of the salient discourse of solidarity, I would propose, were some harsh social realities of France, some peculiar to the country, some shared with other advanced industrial societies. However prosperous and affluent France had become at century's end with industrialization, the image of *La Belle Époque* that we may gather from movies about the period or a hurried look at the exuberant art of Impressionism and post-Impressionism is misleading. There were severe political and cultural strains and widening socioeconomic inequalities:

> At the beginning of the twentieth century, France seemed not only divided, but threatened with internal conflicts, some of which had already erupted. It was at the same time a prosperous country . . . but also [one] of the excluded.
>
> (Félix 1991: 166)

> Whatever else it was, the *Belle Epoque* was a fine time for ferments, flare-ups, disorders, rampages, riots, turbulence, tumults, barricades, and bloodshed.
>
> (Weber 1986: 128)

In retrospect, the most patent but not sole social conflict of the period was the trial in the 1890s of a Jewish military captain accused and convicted of passing defense secrets to Germany. The ensuing "Dreyfus affair" rocked France and pointed to various fault lines, with massive street demonstrations and ultimate polarization that brought to a head simmering boils between various social factions. Many of the military high command had Catholic loyalties that clashed with the republican regime's anticlerical outlook (especially regarding control over education), while republicans were nervous that another military coup might take place like the aborted one by General Boulanger in the preceding decade.[12] Ultimately, Dreyfus was shown to have been framed and was finally released; although his vindication was a triumph for the civilian republican regime and particularly for the academic intellectuals of the left, the political scars were not healed for the remaining years of the Third Republic.[13]

However gripping and ultimately a triumph for liberal democracy was the Dreyfus affair, there were other serious cleavages in the social fabric. If Durkheim talked about *anarchy* in the same breath as *anomie* in the preface to the second edition (1997: xxxiii), it was a reflection of the real presence in France and other countries such as Spain and Russia of anarchism as a movement of individual terrorist acts, a cult of violence. The cult appealed to avant-garde artists – much as it seemingly does today to "punk" and other artists – and in its more extreme forms translated into assassinations of heads of state, including President Carnot of France and President McKinley of the United States.[14]

Anarchism/anomie fed on severe economic malaise, ranging from a variety of financial scandals and stock swindles, to serious discontent in the working class and marginalized agricultural producers; class divisions hardened with the syndicalist movement and following violent strikes, the formation of the militant *Confédération Générale du Travail* (CGT) in 1895, and subsequently the launching of the Socialist Party in 1905 headed by Jean Jaurès (Félix 1991: 165). The latter had cordial ties with Durkheim as a fellow *Normalien* and as a fellow militant on behalf of exonerating Dreyfus.

Internal conflicts and growing external conflicts with Germany[15] were very much part of the pre-war scene in France. French political life reflected this, with a polarization between those favoring taking a hard line against Germany and those seeking accommodation in order to attend to internal social (especially labor) problems. Ultimately, what came to dominate the scene were the war clouds. In July 1914 Jaurès got the Socialist Party to accept staging a general strike against war and sought a repeal of the military draft; two weeks later he was assassinated by a young fanatic who felt Jaurès was a traitor, playing in the hands of Germany (Favier 1987: 1025). This and the war on France declared by Germany at the beginning of August marked a new type of solidarity, one that was not analyzed in *The Division of Labor*, but one which Durkheim was to experience along with his fellow citizens: *national solidarity*. I draw attention to it not only because it is an additional dimension of the concept of solidarity in relation to Durkheim's France but also because the circumstances of its manifestation in 1914 have some interesting structural similarities with the post September 11 United States.

IV

The assassination on July 31, 1914, of Jean Jaurès was followed by Germany's declaration of war on France the following Monday.[16] The twin attacks produced an unprecedented wave of solidarity that adds an important chapter to Durkheim's analysis of social integration. On Tuesday morning, August 4, the public funeral of Jaurès drew a large, emotional, bipartisan crowd. The secretary of the CGT, Léon Jouhaux, who shortly before advocated opposition to war and the three-year draft, announced he was in total support of resisting the aggressors; the president of the Chamber of Deputies declared that foes and friends alike of Jaurès had been struck by the assassination: there were no longer foes in France, only Frenchmen "ready to make sacrifices for the holiest of causes: the salvation of civilization" (Félix 1991: 10). And the grand climax of that day was a presidential message read to the hushed Chamber of Deputies that afternoon; a message that read in part:

> France represents again today before the world freedom, justice and reason . . . She will be heroically defended by all her sons for whom in front of the enemy nothing will break the *sacred union*. (Félix 1991: 171)[17]

A "collective effervescence" ensued, in the Chamber and in the country in general. In the Chamber, after the message closing with "Lift up your hearts and vive la France!" the legislators in a heightened state of emotion fell into each other's arms, including two on opposite sides of the bench who had not spoken to each other in over forty years (Félix 1991: 171). Across the country the center of republican France was joined in the *union sacrée* with the marginals of the periphery: pacifists, revolutionary syndicalists, farmers, and even the staunch foe of the regime, priests, 5,000 of whom were killed in the First World War out of 45,000 drafted (Félix 1991: 174). Durkheim had, of course, not anticipated the conditions that gave rise to *national solidarity*, nor in the brief time that remained to him did he have the leisure and the occasion to theorize this extraordinary and rare form of solidarity. Durkheim himself, like all his countrymen, whether of the left, the center, or the right, religious or secular, experienced national solidarity. Too old to volunteer, he used his talents as an intellectual to assist the war effort in writing pieces destined to influence a yet neutral America as to where lay the aggression behind the greatest bloodshed in history (Durkheim 1915; Durkheim and Denis 1915).

V

Fast forward to September 2001. Less than a year before, the United States had engaged in one of the most acrimonious presidential elections recorded, with just about half of the voters feeling they had been cheated by a judicial but not judicious decision of the Supreme Court. The outgoing administration, despite notable domestic achievements, had been tainted by ethical and other breaches of conduct. The racial gulf between whites and blacks, despite all the socioeconomic improvement of African-Americans stemming from the civil rights movement, was still patent. Republicans and Democrats sought to wrest control of the other chamber, one hanging on to the House, the other with the help of a defection having barely gained control of the

Senate. And after what seemed in retrospect the good times of the 1990s, the country (along with the world economy) was in an economic downturn with significant layoffs in employment. I bring this out to suggest that, structurally speaking, *the United States on the eve of September 11 was similar to the situation of France in 1914.* The startling attack on the World Trade Center and the Pentagon produced, to be sure, enormous damages, physical and psychological. But, for the purpose of this paper, it also produced a massive national solidarity. The president of the United States, George W. Bush, became transfigured from a minority president to a wartime leader with the highest public opinion support recorded in American poll history. The theme of national unity from the start was recurrent in speeches made by the White House, similar to the messages of Poincaré to the Chamber of Deputies and to his countrymen. The following are illustrative:[18]

> This is a day when all Americans from every walk of life unite in our resolve for justice and peace.   (September 11, 2001, address to the Nation)

> Today, we feel what Franklin Roosevelt called the warm courage of national unity. This is a unity of every faith, and every background.
> (September 14, 2001, remarks at National Day of Prayer and Remembrance)

> All of America was touched on the evening of the tragedy to see Republicans and Democrats joined together on the steps of this Capitol, singing "God Bless America."   (September 20, 2001, address to a joint session of Congress)

And just as the president of the Chamber of Deputies in 1914 appealed to national unity for the holiest of causes, the salvation of civilization, such "civilization," previously tarnished by academic controversies around *multiculturalism* (Taylor and Gutman 1994; Jopke and Lukes 1999), was extolled as that separating good from evil, the just from evildoers:

> Civilized people around the world denounce the evildoers who devised and executed these terrible attacks.
> (September 13, 2001, Proclamation of a National Day of Prayer and Remembrance)

> This is not, however, just America's fight . . . This is the world's fight. This is civilization's fight. This is the fight of all who believe in progress and pluralism, tolerance and freedom. . . . The civilized world is rallying to America's side.
> (September 20, 2001, Address to a joint session of Congress)[19]

In the aftermath of September 11, President Bush may be taken as a "collective representation," to use Durkheimian terminology, of American sentiments of national solidarity combined with the desire for resistance and retaliation to perceived wanton aggression. The solidarity was enhanced by nationwide sharing of heroes – the firefighters and police who gave their lives to rescue lives at "ground zero" in New York City – and by symbols of oneness: the ubiquitous display of the American flag, the singing of "God bless America," and so on.[20]

National solidarity, however, is insufficient to broaden our conceptual horizon. In recognition of the profound interlacing of the world from various processes of globalization, it is relevant to view "September 11" as having generated *global solidarity*. Because of television, to paraphrase Gitlin (1980), literally "the whole world was watching" when the second plane, United flight 175, rammed into the second World Trade Center tower. The devastating attack on a pillar of modernity did produce on a global basis an unprecedented feeling of horror and sympathy. When President Bush proclaimed on September 13 that the following day be a National Day of Prayer and Remembrance and asked the American people to mark the day at noontime with memorial services, he did not anticipate that this would be observed in other countries, Western and non-Western. Remarking on this outpouring of solidarity, he later told Congress:

> I want to thank the world for its outpouring of support. America will never forget the sounds of our National Anthem playing at Buckingham Palace, on the streets of Paris, and at Berlin's Brandenburg Gate. We will not forget South Korean children gathering to pray outside our embassy in Seoul, or the prayers of sympathy offered at a mosque in Cairo . . .
>
> (September 20, 2001, Address to a joint session of Congress)

Of course, in the same address, the President not only humbly acknowledged his country receiving global solidarity, he also forcefully requested it:

> Every nation, in every region, now has a decision to make. Either you are with us, or you are with terrorists. From this day forward, any nation that continues to harbor or support terrorism will be regarded by the United States as a hostile regime.

VI

"September 11" offers supplementary materials for the pertinence of "mechanical" and "organic" not as static but as dynamic concepts of modernity. Recall that in *The Division of Labor* (book 1, chapter 2) Durkheim broaches the discussion of mechanical solidarity by discussing the strong collective feelings generated in reaction to a crime:

As for the social character of the reaction, this derives from the social nature of the sentiments offended. Because these are to be found in every individual consciousness the wrong done arouses among all who witness it or who know of its existence the same indignation. All are affected by it; consequently everyone stiffens himself against the attack. (Durkheim 1997: 57)

One can venture that far from "mechanical solidarity" being peculiar to pre-modern, pre-industrial society,[21] it was certainly reactivated in the United States during and after September 11. All segments of the population, all regions of the country felt the attack on the World Trade Center and on the Pentagon was an attack against the American people, a crime of violence which made all segments realize what they shared as Americans. The American flag became a renewed symbol of collective identity, displayed in churches, on lapels, on cars; the pledge of allegiance to it, which had been contested by some organizations, reentered the public sphere. This renewed mechanical solidarity was carried out very much in a religious framework that underlies Durkheim's *Elementary Forms*: beliefs and rituals reaffirming the sacredness of the collectivity (and the presidential addresses are replete with religious imagery, including invoking a "crusade" against the criminal terrorists in the world).

Of course, there is a dark side to mechanical solidarity. For in highlighting what the collectivity has in common with each other in the way of beliefs and practices, it may set up compartments that lead to the exclusion of those who are deemed outsiders. For many years, the United States had had violent confrontations outside its borders with Arabic/Islamic nations (notably Libya, Sudan, Iraq, Iran) and the theme of an Islamic "jihad" against the West had gained currency (Barber 1996; Huntington 1996). The attack on the United States and the pointing of fingers to an Islamic-inspired terrorist organization could easily have provoked a mass vengeance on the Arab-Islamic population in the United States. A heightened emphasis of being a "we" can generate an equally strong vilification of a "they" as outsiders, perhaps even more so in a Puritan culture which tends to differentiate between "saints" and the "wretched." The actions of the government toward the Muslim-Arab population in the United States have been equivocal. On the one hand, there has been by both the public and the private sector (especially the churches) professions, actions of inclusion toward Islam as a "peaceful" religion that is a valued part of American religious pluralism.[22] On the other hand, government surveillance of persons of Arabic names and descent, including students in the United States from Arabic countries has been widely reported.

Finally, one other dimension of September 11 that merits attention is an *enhanced organic solidarity*. It may be seen as global solidarity at the micro level. Let me cite from personal experience. Shortly after September 11, I received e-mails from sociologists I know around the world, from such countries as France, Germany, Macedonia, Italy, Japan, and China, among others. They were spontaneously expressing messages of condolence, sympathy, and solidarity with our entire nation, and they saw me as a nexus to the American people because we were fellow sociologists. I have checked with colleagues in other disciplines and found that the same phenomenon has happened to them, namely, spontaneous messages of support and sympathy from their counterparts around the world. I don't know whether Durkheim in August 1914 received telegrams from American sociologists when France was overrun by Germany. I am sure he would have seen these messages as an important extension of his concept of organic solidarity as a reflection of globalization, and Durkheim would surely have been interested in making a comparative study of these e-mails of solidarity as important new "social facts" of our advanced modernity.

NOTES

1 The second edition (1902), published nearly ten years after the initial defense and therefore after two other classical treatises (*Suicide* and *Rules of the Sociological Method*), has the most important additions, notably a new introduction advocating the modernization of corporatism.
2 The George Simpson translation of 1933 did yeoman's duty for half a century, being replaced by Halls' translation of 1984, currently in paperback edition (Durkheim 1997).
3 Given Durkheim's argument that one cannot get directly at social bonds or social relationships, his invoking an objective social fact like the corpus of the legal code and changes over time in it was a pioneering effort in developing social indicators (Land 2000).
4 Durkheim in the course of his fellowship study of German social scientists had come across Tönnies and published in 1889 a review of *Gemeinschaft und Gesellschaft* that had appeared two years earlier. The review gives the reader a good view of the treatise, and faults the author for an undocumented bias shown towards the small-scale, traditional society of the *Gemeinschaft* kind. Durkheim closes by affirming that modern complex society is also "organic" but that a book examining the evolution of *Gesellschaft* through laws and customs would be necessary to demonstrate this (Durkheim 1975: 390). Neither the review nor the treatise itself used the term "solidarity."
5 Consequences of a world historical event such as "September 11" continue to unfold in the historical process. In this instance, the counteractions of the American government together with the domestic and international repercussions of the terrorist attack on New York and Washington, will continue to unfold for an indefinite period. This is accentuated by a declared "war on terrorism" having no territorial boundary. However, the implicit time frame for this essay is narrower: my focus is the reactions to the September 11 morning attacks from that fateful

morning to the beginning of the American bombardment of Taliban Afghanistan a month later. Following Van Gennep (1960) and Victor Turner (1962), this was essentially a "liminal period," in this case, between "normalcy" and "wartime."

6 Sociologically, "others," following Comte, would be not only those of our generation but also those of previous and future generations.

7 Although Durkheim's own treatment of "altruistic suicide" suggests it is predominantly associated with archaic or pre-modern forms of organization, this does not mean such suicides have disappeared from the contemporary scene. I have discussed this in reference to the plethora of "suicide-bombers" (Tiryakian 2002).

8 I follow Holub's (1991: 136) discussion of Habermas taking that "project," identical with the project of modernity, as both promoting the rationalization of the spheres of science and morality (and also of art) and releasing "the creative potentials of each of these domains." The "Project of the Enlightenment" as seeking an accumulation of positive knowledge in the spheres of science, religion and the aesthetic to provide a richer and more fully rational organization of the "life-world" is a key theme in Habermas (1989), one which agrees with my reading of Durkheim's ultimate endeavor in *Elementary Forms* ([1912] 1995).

9 See the poignant passage in the Conclusion of *Elementary Forms* (1995: 429f). Alternatively, Durkheim might have evoked the solidarity generated at the spectacular mass funeral procession to the Pantheon of Victor Hugo, poet, national hero and icon of democratic republicanism, in 1885; or perhaps, to the effervescence aroused in the confrontations between the Dreyfusards and the anti-Dreyfusards in Paris in the late 1890s at the time of the retrial of Captain Dreyfus. More modern settings of collective effervescence that would have drawn Durkheim's sociological attention as sites of possible progressive renewal of collective ideals and aspirations could well include, appropriately enough, the Solidarnosc movement in Gdansk and elsewhere in Poland in 1980–1, and, in his own Sorbonne backyard, the student movement of May 1968. Since Durkheim gave year-long courses on "pragmatism" and "socialism" in response to students' interest in these movements, one can envision Durkheim giving a course on the student movement in the wake of 1968.

10 Since 1997, solidarity has entered into official governmental recognition as a cabinet position in the important *Ministère de l'Emploi et de la Solidarité*, charged among other tasks with caring for the unemployed and with fighting racial and ethnic discrimination.

11 In the mainstream of social democratic thought, I would argue that solidarism, which may sound quaint to contemporary ears, is very proximate to Amitai Etzioni's (2000) communitarianism and Anthony Giddens' (1998) Third Way.

12 It might be noted that three-quarters of a century after Boulanger another military coup in France was narrowly averted at the end of the Algerian War when De Gaulle came out of retirement in time to lead the country out of the morass of the Fourth Republic and into a more modernized Fifth Repbulic.

13 Hubert Bourgin, an alumnus of the prestigious École Normale Supérieure and who in his younger years had been a member of the *Année sociologique* team, bitterly complained in his memoirs of the politicization of French higher education, especially at the hands of "philosophers of anarchy." He does, however, provide an intimate and respectful look at Durkheim (Bourgin 1938).

14 For a succinct discussion, see "anarchism," *Encyclopedia Britannica Online.* <http:search.eb.com/bol/topic?eu = 127633 and sctn = 6>.

15 The conflict with Germany was twofold: conservatives in France were bent on restoring the "lost territories" of Alsace and Lorraine which Germany had taken as an outcome of its victorious war in 1870, and a new German imperialism sought claims to Morocco, which France considered under its sphere of influence.

16 For a detailed chronology of the ante bellum period and thereafter, see Favier (1987).

17 In his presidential memoirs, Poincaré relates the pregnant phrase *union sacrée* to the ancient Greeks opting to die together in indissoluble friendship to defend the Temple of Delphi (1927: 541).

18 All the following may be located at http://web.archive.org/web/20010911-20011201*/www.whitehouse.gov/.

19 Recognition of solidarity may have an instrumental as well as an expressive side. Asking others to make sacrifices because we are together may be in some instances to promote *my* rather than *our* ends.

20 I have discussed elsewhere (Tiryakian 2004) related aspects of September 11 in terms of Durkheim's *Elementary Forms.*

21 Elsewhere (Tiryakian 1994b) I have alluded to the lure of mechanical solidarity in modern society at various levels, for example in invoking ethnic, racial or gender solidarity.

22 It is interesting to note two months after September 11 the US Postal service issued a 33-cent stamp commemorating in Arabic calligraphy the Islamic Eid festivals in honor of Ramadan. American bombardment of the Taliban in Afghanistan was not suspended during Ramadan, however.

REFERENCES

Alexander, Jeffrey C. 1987. "The Centrality of the Classics." pp. 11–57 in *Social Theory Today.* Edited by Anthony Giddens and Jonathan H. Turner. Stanford, CA: Stanford University Press.

Barber, Benjamin R. 1996. *Jihad vs. McWorld. How Globalism and Tribalism are Reshaping the World.* New York: Times Books.

Bellah, Robert N. 1973. Introduction to *Émile Durkheim: On Morality and Society.* Chicago: University of Chicago Press. Heritage of Sociology series.

Besnard, Philippe, Massimo Borlandi and Paul Vogt (eds.) 1993. *Division du travail et lien social. La thèse de Durkheim un siècle après.* Paris: Presses Universitaires de France.

Bourgeois, Léon. 1902. *Solidarité.* 3rd edition. Paris: Librairie Armand Colin.

Bourgeois, Léon and Alfred Croiset (eds.) 1907. *Essai d'une philosophie de la Solidarité.* 2nd edn. Paris: Félix Alcan.

Bourgin, Hubert. 1938. *De Jaurès à Léon Blum. L'École Normale et la Politique.* Paris: Arthème Fayard.

Daniel-Rops, Henri. [1963] 1966. *A Fight for God 1870–1939.* Translated by John Warrington. London: J. M. Dent and Sons; New York: E. P. Dutton.

Durkheim, Émile. 1915. *"Germany Above All:" German Mentality and War.* Paris: Armand Colin.

[1912] 1995. *The Elementary Forms of Religious Life*. Edited and translated by Karen E. Fields. New York: Free Press.

[1897] 1930. *Le Suicide. Étude de Sociologie*. Nouvelle Édition. Paris: Félix Alcan.

[1893] 1997. *The Division of Labor in Society*. Translated by W. D. Halls and with an introduction by Lewis Coser. New York: Free Press.

[1889] 1975. "Communauté et Société selon Tönnies." pp. 383–90 in *Durkheim, Textes*. Vol 1. Edited by Victor Karady. Paris: Éditions de Minuit.

Durkheim, Émile and E. Denis. 1915. *Who Wanted War? The Origins of the War According to Diplomatic Documents*. Translated by A. M. Wilson-Garinei. Paris: Armand Colin.

Etzioni, Amitai. 2000. *The Third Way to a Good Society*. London: Demos.

Favier, Jean, et al. 1987. *Chronique de la France et des Français*. Paris: Larousse/Editions Jacques Legrand.

Félix, Christian. 1991. *Alsace-Lorraine et Union Sacrée*. Ecully, France: Horvath.

Giddens, Anthony. 1998. *The Third Way: The Renewal of Social Democracy*. Cambridge: Polity Press and Malden, MA: Blackwell Publishers.

Gitlin, Todd. 1980. *The Whole World is Watching: Mass Media in the Making and Unmaking of the New Left*. Berkeley, CA: University of California Press.

Habermas, Jürgen. [1981] 1989. *The Theory of Communicative Action*. Vol. 2, *Lifeworld and System: A Critique of Functionalist Reason*. Translated by Thomas McCarthy. Boston: Beacon Press.

Holub, Robert C. 1991. *Jürgen Habermas: Critic in the Public Sphere*. London and New York: Routledge.

Huntington, Samuel P. 1996. *The Clash of Civilizations and the Remaking of World Order*. New York: Simon and Schuster.

Jones, Susan Stedman. 2001. *Durkheim Reconsidered*. Malden, MA: Blackwell.

Joppke, Christian and Steven Lukes. 1999. *Multicultural Questions*. Oxford: Oxford University Press.

Land, Kenneth C. 2000. "Social Indicators." pp. 2682–90 in *Encyclopedia of Sociology*, revised edition. Edited by Edgar F. Borgatta and Rhonda V. Montgomery. New York: Macmillan.

Miller, W. Watts. 1996. *Durkheim, Morals and Modernity*. Montreal and Kingston: McGill-Queen's University Press.

Poincaré, Raymond. 1927. *Au service de la France*. Vol. 5, *L'Union Sacrée 1914*. Paris: Plon.

Taylor, Charles and Amy Gutman (eds.) 1994. *Multiculturalism*. Princeton: Princeton University Press.

Tiryakian, Edward A. 2004. "Three Levels of Teaching Durkheim," in *Teaching Durkheim on Religion*. Edited by Terry F. Godlove. New York: Oxford University Press.

1994b. "Revisiting Sociology's First Classic: *The Division of Labor in Society* and its Actuality," *Sociological Forum*, 9: 3–16.

(ed.) 1994a. "The 100th Anniversary of Durkheim's Division of Labor in Society." *Sociological Forum* 9.

Turner, Victor W. 1962. "Three Symbols of Passage in Ndembu Circumcision Ritual." pp. 124–73 in *Essays on the Rituals of Social Relations*. Edited by Max Gluckman. Manchester: Mancheser University Press.

Van Gennep, Arnold. [1909] 1960. *The Rites of Passage*. London: Routledge.

Weber, Eugen. 1986. *France, Fin de Siècle*. Cambridge, MA: Harvard University Press and London: Belknap.
  1959. *The Nationalist Revival in France, 1905–1914*. Berkeley, CA: University of California Press.
Wrong, Dennis H. 1994. *The Problem of Order: What Unites and Divides Society*. New York: Free Press.

13

DAVID B. GRUSKY AND GABRIELA GALESCU

Is Durkheim a class analyst?

The study of social class remains deeply connected to a classical tradition featuring the scholarship of Marx (e.g. [1894] 1964) and Weber (e.g. [1922] 1968). Indeed, when a new class scheme is proposed or an existing one elaborated, a common rhetorical strategy among its proponents is to justify that revision as some truer expression of classical ideas about the structure of inequality. This fascination with the classical tradition is of course realized in a highly selective way, with the scholarship of Marx and Weber typically featured; that of Sorokin, Parsons, and Warner treated as secondary; and that of Durkheim dismissed or ignored. The purpose of our chapter is to show that important insights about contemporary class structure can be gleaned from a fresh rereading of Durkheim's account of occupational associations (see Parkin 1992: 1; Pearce 1989: 1; Müller 1993: 106; cf. Lee 1995; Fenton 1980; Lehmann 1995). We hope to convince even the most jaded skeptics of exegesis that Durkheim is well worth revisiting, that his account is more prescient than typically has been appreciated, and that it can accordingly provide the foundation for a new class analysis that is tailor-made for contemporary research purposes.

The work of Durkheim has not figured prominently in any of the four waves of class analysis that can be identified over the last half-century. The first wave, which emerged in the immediate postwar period, drew on Weber and Sorokin for the purpose of discrediting Marxian class models and advancing gradational interpretations of inequality (e.g. prestige scales).[1] In some variants of this tradition, the rise of a consensual occupational hierarchy was interpreted in functionalist terms (e.g. Parsons 1954), but such functionalist gloss didn't draw on the work of Durkheim save in the most general of ways. The second wave of class models, presumably triggered by the oppositional cultural forces of the 1960s and 1970s, involved a resurgence of neo-Marxism in which categorical models of class came to the fore and supplanted the previously dominant gradational scales. The great virtue of such categorical models, so it was contended, was that they allowed for accounts of collective action, revolutions, and other macro-level outcomes in which inter-class relations and conflict became privileged independent variables. In the third wave of class analysis, the latter macro-level agenda gradually fell out of favor (see Holton and Turner 1989), but categorical class models of both Marxian and Weberian provenance continued to be applied for the more modest academic enterprise of explaining micro-level variability in individual-level outcomes (e.g. voting behavior, consumption practices, attitudes). This is the period (i.e. 1980–90) in which categorical class models, once regarded as faintly suspect, came gradually to be institutionalized within academia and harnessed for the purpose of mainstream quantitative research. By the mid-1990s, even this more modest variant of class analysis began to be called into question, with postmodernists arguing that big-class schemes cannot satisfactorily explain individual-level behavior and are therefore unable to deliver on the micro-level agenda. These critics continue to contend that attitudes and behaviors increasingly arise from a "complex mosaic of taste subcultures" that are quite unrelated to class membership (Pakulski and Waters 1996a: 157) and that the concept of social class is therefore an intellectual dead-end misrepresenting the "basic fissures that define the contours of social life" (Kingston 2000: 210–12; also, Hall 2001; Pakulski and Waters 1996b, 1996c; Lee and Turner 1996; Clark 1996; Joyce 1995; Kingston 1994; Clark and Lipset 2001, 1991; Pahl 1989).

This stylized history is of interest because the scholarship of Durkheim is so thoroughly absent from it. To be sure, the first three waves of class analysis were in active engagement with the classical tradition, yet Marx and Weber were represented as dominant within this tradition whereas Durkheim was quite spectacularly ignored. By contrast, fourth-wave postmodernists have moved to the view that classical scholarship is no longer applicable to a new post-class world, thus providing an even more extreme counterpoint to the position that we offer here. We seek, then, to return to the classical heritage but also draw more explicitly on Durkheim than class analysts usually have. We will show that contemporary scholarship became vulnerable to fourth-wave postmodernist critique because it was obsessed with the "big class" formulations of Marx and Weber and was accordingly resistant to Durkheim's fundamental insight that the site of production is structured around rather smaller functional niches (i.e. occupations). This emphasis on local occupational organization, had it been incorporated into class models, would have inoculated class analysis against much postmodernist criticism.[2]

If class analysts have largely ignored Durkheim, it might be supposed that scholars of Durkheim stepped into the breach and attended more closely to the implications of his scholarship for theories of class. Although some of the older commentary on *The Division of Labor* (hereafter *Division of Labor*) does of course address issues of class, the main objective of such commentary was either to represent Durkheimian class analysis as primitive and undeveloped or to use it to discredit Marxian models of class (e.g. Bottomore 1981; Tiryakian 1975; Dahrendorf 1959: 48–51; Zeitlin 1968). In either case, this line of commentary falls short of developing Durkheim's work into a more comprehensive model of class, a task that we take on here.[3] At the same time, contemporary exegesis focuses increasingly on *The Elementary Forms of Religious Life*, providing as it does the requisite classical source for the cultural turn in sociology (see Smith and Alexander 1996; Meštrović 1992). In our own analysis, we will return to the *Division of Labor* as an important starting point, while also appreciating and exploiting the cultural side of Durkheim.[4] We will follow Durkheim's lead in recognizing that technical positions in the division of labor can be transformed into socially meaningful groups with their own distinctive cultures.

We attempt, therefore, to develop an exegesis that can be used to motivate a new neo-Durkheimian class model, the main feature of which is the simple insight that class-like organization emerges at a more detailed level than is conventionally appreciated. That is, rather than abandoning the site of production and emphasizing "postmodern" sources of attitudes and behavior (e.g. race, gender, lifestyles), one should recognize that the labor market is well organized and explanatorily powerful at the micro-level of occupations. The great virtue of disaggregating is that the nominal categories of conventional class analysis can be replaced by *gemeinschaftlich* groupings that are embedded in the very fabric of society and are thereby meaningful not merely to sociologists but to the lay public as well (see Grusky and Sørensen 1998, 2001; Grusky and Weeden 2002, 2001; Grusky, Weeden, and Sørensen 2000). By contrast, scholars working within a nominalist big-class tradition seek to construct class categories that reflect social processes, forces, or distinctions (e.g. authority, rent-extraction, property) that are regarded as *analytically* fundamental, even though the categories implied by such approaches may be only shallowly institutionalized. In some cases, a theory of history is grafted onto such nominalist models, thus generating the side-claim that currently latent (but analytically fundamental) class categories may ultimately come to be appreciated by actors, serve as bases for collective action, or become institutionalized groupings that bargain collectively on behalf of their members. It is high time, we think, to attend to the empirically more viable task of characterizing such structure at the site of production as can *currently* be found.[5]

We will show that a micro-class model of this sort was anticipated by Durkheim. In our earlier expositions of this model, our intellectual debt to Durkheim was duly acknowledged, but the relationship between his scholarship and a micro-class approach was not elaborated in any detail (e.g. Grusky and Sørensen 1998, 2001; Grusky and Weeden 2002, 2001; Grusky, Weeden, and Sørensen 2000). This chapter now takes on such a task. We will proceed by discussing (a) how Durkheim developed, rather unwittingly, a class analysis grounded in the technical division of labor, (b) how this class analytic approach might be modified to address developments that Durkheim did not fully anticipate, and (c) how the resulting approach, while arguably an advance over conventional forms of class analysis, nonetheless leaves important problems unresolved.

Durkheim and the class structure: a selective exegesis

We begin, then, by considering how Durkheim approached issues of class and occupation, relying not only on his famous preface to the *Division of Labor* but also on related commentary in *Suicide* (1897) and elsewhere (see, esp., Hawkins 1994 for a comprehensive treatment). In the secondary literature on such matters, it is often noted with some disapproval that Durkheim treated class conflict as a purely transitory feature of early industrialism, thereby "ignoring . . . the [enduring] implications of class cleavages" (Zeitlin 1968: 235; also, see Lockwood 1992: 78; Bottomore 1981). As is well known, Durkheim indeed argued that class conflict in the early industrial period would ultimately dissipate because (a) the growth of state and occupational regulation should impose moral control on the conflict of interests (i.e. the "institutionalization" of conflict), and (b) the rise of achievement-based mobility should legitimate inequalities of outcome by making them increasingly attributable to differential talent, capacities, and investments rather than differential opportunities (i.e. the rise of "equal opportunity"). In light of current developments, it is not altogether clear that such emphases within the work of Durkheim should still be regarded as an outright defect, foreshadowing as they do important developments in the transition to advanced industrialism. The twin forces of normative regulation and meritocratic allocation have, in fact, been featured in much subsequent discussion about the "institutionalization" of class conflict (e.g. Dahrendorf 1959), even though the early work of Durkheim has not always been accorded a properly deferential place in this commentary.

This institutionalization of conflict has motivated contemporary class theorists to de-emphasize macro-level theories of history (see Holton and Turner 1989) and to reorient class analysis to the simpler task of explaining micro-level behavior in the present day (e.g. voting behavior, lifestyles). The obvious question that then arises is whether the class categories devised by Marx and others for macro-level purposes are also optimal for this more limited micro-level explanatory agenda (Grusky and Weeden 2001). For the most part, scholars of contemporary class relations have concluded that they are not, leading to all manner of attempts to increase the explanatory power of class models by introducing further distinctions within the category of labor. The main failing, however, of such efforts is that the posited categories have been only shallowly institutionalized, with scholars seeking to defend their competing schemes with all imaginable criteria save the seemingly obvious one that the posited categories should have some institutional veracity.

In this context, the scholarship of Durkheim is again instructive, as it refocuses attention on the types of intermediary groups that have emerged in past labor markets and will likely characterize future ones. This is to suggest, then, that Durkheim contributed to class analysis on two fronts, simultaneously providing (a) a negative macro-level story about the social forces (e.g. institutionalization of conflict) that render big classes unviable in the long run, and (b) a positive micro-level story about the "small classes" (i.e. *gemeinschaftlich* occupations) that are destined to emerge at the site of production and shape individual values, life chances, and lifestyles. The latter micro-level story, which is typically dismissed as irrelevant to class analysis, is the focus of our commentary here. We feature this story because small classes can be shown to take on properties that class analysts have conventionally (but mistakenly) ascribed to big classes.

In laying out this micro-level story, it has to be conceded that Durkheim is (famously) silent on the proximate mechanisms by which occupational associations will emerge, as he simply presumes, by functionalist fiat, that outcomes that putatively serve system ends will ultimately win out. This approach leads Durkheim to equate "the normal, the ideal, and the about-to-happen" (Lukes 1973: 177). By contrast, Marx and most neo-Marxians put forward analyses that are mechanism-rich, relying on such forces as exploitation, opposed interests, and conflict as proximate sources bringing about the postulated end-states. In some of his writings, Durkheim does hint at proximate mechanisms, but for the most part he is correctly taken to task for failing to "proceed to an investigation of causes" (Bottomore 1981: 911). It is nonetheless worth asking whether the end state that Durkheim describes captures some of the developmental tendencies within contemporary systems of inequality.

How, then, might one characterize Durkheim's view of the "normal, ideal, and about-to-happen" (Lukes 1973: 177)? We take on this question below by describing the three forms of micro-level organization that, according to Durkheim, are destined to emerge at the site of production.

The rise of occupational associations

The *Division of Labor* is most instructively read as an extended discourse on the level (i.e. class or "micro-class") at which the site of production will come to be organized.[6] When class analysts summarize this work, they typically emphasize the argument that big classes are purely transitory and will fade away as "normal" forms of adaptation emerge (i.e. the "negative macro-level story"), while the predicted rise of social organization at the local occupational level (i.e. the "positive micro-level story") is disregarded or viewed as irrelevant. By contrast, we think that the micro-level story in Durkheim is worth considering more carefully, not merely because local organization can take on class-like properties (as argued below), but also because it can crowd out or substitute for class formation of a more aggregate sort. Indeed, Durkheim argued that occupational associations are destined to become the main organizational form "intercalated between the state and the individual" ([1893] 1960: 28), supplanting both Marxian classes and other forms of intermediary organization (e.g. the family). Although Durkheim emphasized the informal ties and bonds that were cultivated in occupational associations, he also laid out a variety of formal functions that such associations were likely to assume, including (a) establishing and administering a system of occupational ethics, (b) resolving conflicts among members and with other associations, and (c) serving as elemental representative bodies in political governance (see Durkheim [1893] 1960: 26–7; also, see Durkheim [1897] 1970a: 372–82). The foregoing functions are best carried out at the local level because an "activity can be efficaciously regulated only by a group intimate enough with it to know its functioning [and] feel all its needs" (Durkheim [1893] 1960: 5).

These associations find their historical precedent in medieval guilds and bear some resemblance to the professional and craft associations that are now so ubiquitous. For Durkheim, it is revealing that occupational associations have a long history that extends well into ancient times, with early forms evidently appearing "as soon as there are trades" (Durkheim [1893] 1960: 7). If occupational associations have surfaced throughout recent history, Durkheim reasoned that they must have a "timeless authenticity" (Parkin 1992: 77) suggestive of important underlying functions. Among these functions, Durkheim particularly stressed that occupations can rein in excessive ambition and aspirations, if only by inducing workers to calibrate their aspirations for remuneration to the occupational norm rather than some less attainable standard. The egoism unleashed by the breakdown of the traditional social order can therefore be contained by subjecting workers to a new form of extra-individual authority at the occupational level (Durkheim [1893] 1960: 10). By implication, the macro-level and micro-level stories in *Division of Labor* are closely linked, with the declining fortunes of big classes reflecting, in part, the institutionalization of occupations and the consequent legitimation of inequalities that both (a) undermine the unity of the working class, and (b) convince workers to regard occupational differences in remuneration (including those between big classes) as appropriate and acceptable. If there is a class-analytic theory of history in Durkheim, it is clearly one that emphasizes the role of occupations in justifying inequality, making it palatable, and hence undermining the more spectacular theories of history that Marx and various neo-Marxians have advanced.

The "localization" of the collective conscience

The rise of occupational associations is also relevant to the "problem of order" and Durkheim's putative solution to it.[7] As traditional forms of organization wither away, there has been much concern in sociology (see Parsons 1967, 1968) that the forces of differentiation and specialization might prove to be maladaptive, leading to excessive egoism, unrestrained individual action, and a diminished commitment to collective ends. This concern has, in turn, set off a search for countervailing processes that might contain or at least offset these individuating forces. When Durkheim is invoked in this literature, he is frequently credited with recognizing that the modern collective conscience has been transformed to encompass increasingly abstract and generalized sentiments, especially those stressing the dignity of individuals (i.e. the "cult of the individual") and their right to pursue freely opportunities unhampered by circumstances of birth (i.e. "equal opportunity"). In content, these beliefs may be deeply individualistic (Durkheim [1893] 1960: 172), but they are nonetheless shared across individuals and, as such, constitute the modern-day collective conscience.

The latter story remains, however, partial and incomplete without a parallel discussion of the rise of occupation-specific beliefs and how these also operate to suppress egoism, bind workers to an extra-individual community, and thereby counteract the forces of individuation (Durkheim [1893] 1960: 2, 4–5, 10; Pope and Johnson 1983: 682–84; also, see Hawkins (1994) for a review of other relevant pieces). To be sure, Durkheim appreciated that modern occupations will not develop the total, all-encompassing morality of traditional social systems (see Pope and Johnson 1983: 684; Hawkins 1994: 464), yet he was still impressed with how "imperative" ([1893] 1960: 227) the rules of occupational morality have been in the past and would likely come to be in the future. This new form of solidarity of course links individuals to local subgroupings (i.e. occupations) rather than the larger society itself; and, consequently, the modern tendency is to move toward "moral polymorphism," where this refers to the rise of multiple, occupation-specific "centers of moral life" (Durkheim 1958: 7; also, see Durkheim 1993). At the level of values, the Durkheimian solution thus references not only the integrative effects of highly abstract system-wide sentiments, but also the "mechanical solidarity" that persists as more concrete and specialized sentiments are ratcheted down and re-express themselves within occupational groupings (see Parsons 1968: 339).[8]

This line of argument has of course been carried forward by subsequent generations of French sociologists. For example, Bouglé ([1927] 1971) treated the Indian caste system as an extreme case of "moral polymorphism" in which the occupational communities are organized in deeply hierarchical terms, are especially well-protected against "polluting" interaction (e.g. intermarriage), and are self-reproducing to an unusual degree (i.e. hereditary closure). Although the Indian case represents, for Bouglé, the purest form of the caste system, it is but a "unique dilation of universal tendencies" (Bouglé [1926] 1971: 28) that generate profound occupational differentiation in all societies. Likewise, Halbwachs (e.g. [1945] 1992) argued that occupations tend to breed distinctive traditions and forms of consciousness, with his examples of such polymorphism often drawing on detailed occupations (e.g. general, legislator, judge) as well as big classes (also, see Halbwachs 1958; Coser 1992: 18–20). The Durkheimian imagery of "moral polymorphism" emerges yet more clearly in the (comparatively) recent work of Bourdieu. In his influential *Distinction*, Bourdieu (1984: 101) characterized the *habitus* and the distinctive lifestyles it generates in terms of quite detailed occupations (e.g. professors, nurses), albeit with the proviso that such occupations provide only imperfect signals of "homogeneous conditions of existence."

The practical implication of this Durkheimian formulation is that detailed occupations, more so than big classes, become the main site at which distinctive attitudes and styles of life are generated. As Durkheim puts it, occupations have their own cultures comprising "certain ideas, certain usages, and certain ways of seeing things" ([1911] 1956: 68), and workers participate in them as naturally and inevitably as they "breathe the air" around them ([1905] 1970b: 286, translated in Watts Miller 1996: 125). These specialized cultures arise because (a) the forces of self-selection operate to bring similar workers into the same occupation (Durkheim [1893] 1960: 229), (b) the resulting social interaction with co-workers tends to reinforce and elaborate these shared tastes and sentiments (Durkheim [1893] 1960: 228–9, 361), and (c) the incumbents of occupations have common interests that may be pursued, in part, by aligning themselves with their occupation and pursuing collective ends (Durkheim [1893] 1960: 212–13). If communities of practice indeed become localized in this fashion, then the conventional micro-level objective of explaining class outcomes of all kinds (i.e. attitudes, behaviors, lifestyles) is best pursued at the local occupational level. In effect, Durkheim is describing a unification of class and *Stand* that, according to Weber ([1922] 1968), occurs only rarely in the context of conventional aggregate classes.

Occupations and organic solidarity

The Durkheimian solution to the problem of order comes in two parts, the first involving the emergence of occupation-specific sentiments that generate mechanical solidarity (as described above), and the second involving the rise of occupational interdependencies that generate organic solidarity. We turn to a consideration of the second part of the story and its implications for class analysis. As before, we shall find that detailed occupations play a central role in the Durkheimian vision, but now as the elementary units of interdependence (i.e. "organic solidarity) rather than as repositories of shared moral sentiments (i.e. "mechanical solidarity").

The natural starting point here is the long-standing concern (e.g. Smith [1776] 1991; Comte [1830] 1988) that the forces of occupational specialization and differentiation may be alienating because they render work increasingly routine and repetitive. By way of response, Durkheim ([1893] 1960) suggests that such alienating effects can be countered when workers are in "constant relations with neighboring functions" (p. 372), thereby sensitizing them to their larger role within the division of labor and convincing them that their "actions have an aim beyond themselves" (pp. 372–3). In this sense, extreme specialization need not be intrinsically alienating, as individuals will come to recognize and appreciate their contribution to the collective enterprise, no matter how humble, repetitive, or mundane that contribution happens to be.[9] It bears emphasizing that Durkheim again has local organization working to undermine aggregate class formation; that is, constant contact with "neighboring functions" (p. 372) allows workers to appreciate interdependencies and to infuse their own work with some larger meaning, thus undermining any competing Marxian interpretation of work as exploitative and alienating. In the language of class analysis, Durkheim clearly has workers attending to the "relational features" of intermediary groupings, yet the relations of interest are those of visible cooperation and coordination at the micro-level rather than hidden exploitation at the macro-level.

For Durkheim, organic solidarity is also normatively expressed through the rise of occupational regulation that institutionalizes industrial conflict, most notably that between labor and capital. As before, the claim here is that occupational groupings will be the main impetus and carriers of normative regulation, since they are close enough to the activity being administered to "know its functioning, feel all its needs, and [understand its] variations" (Durkheim [1893] 1960: 5). It follows that occupational associations will increasingly devise codes of conduct and specify the terms under which labor is divided. In early industrial systems, such regulation is either lacking altogether (i.e. the "anomic division of labor") or is enforced without full consent of all parties (i.e. the "forced division of labor"), and conflict therefore remains unchecked and revolutionary ideologies become appealing. As the division of labor advances, Durkheim expects regulation to develop spontaneously through social intercourse and to become embodied in formal industrial law, with the initial appeal of socialist and other revolutionary programs accordingly undermined. The resulting normative regulation may again be seen as a form of micro-level organization that works to impede class development at the macro-level.

Was Durkheim right?

It is useful at this point to consider whether the Durkheimian story about the rise of local organization has any contemporary relevance. Although class analysts routinely consider whether Marxian and Weberian formulations have been "borne out," the class analytic arguments of Durkheim have not typically been put to similar test. To the contrary, the *Division of Labor* is usually regarded as a quaint piece of disciplinary "prehistory" (Barnes 1995: 170), and class analysts have accordingly felt no real need to engage with it.

This fixation with Marx, Weber, and their followers is not especially sensible given the course of recent history. In many ways, the labor market has become increasingly "Durkheimianized," not merely because industrial conflict at the macro-class level has come to be regulated and contained, but also because occupational groupings have emerged as the elementary building blocks of modern and postmodern labor markets. As Treiman (1977) notes, contemporary workers routinely represent their career aspirations in occupational terms, while professional and vocational schools are organized to train workers for occupationally-defined skills, and employers construct and advertise jobs in terms of corresponding occupational designations (also, see Parsons 1954; Wilensky 1966). This "occupationalization" of the labor market has been fueled by (a) a long-term growth in the size of the professional sector (with its characteristically strong occupational associations), (b) the rise of new quasi-professional occupations and associations built around emerging abstract skills in the division of labor, (c) the growing application of such devices as licensing, registration, and certification for the purposes of effecting (partial) closure around occupational boundaries, and (d) the strengthening of local labor unions (e.g. the American Federation of Teachers) as more encompassing visions of the labor movement unravel and "sectional self-interest . . . becomes the order of the day" (Marshall et al. 1988: 7; also, Visser 1988: 167).[10] These considerations led Krause (1971: 87) to conclude long ago that "there has historically been more occupation-specific consciousness and action than cross-occupational combination" (also, see Freidson 1994, 75–91; Van Maanen and Barley 1984: 331–3; Dahrendorf 1959). Indeed, when the history of guilds, unions and related production-based associations is reevaluated from the long view, it becomes clear that true classwide organization emerged for only a brief historical moment and that postmodern forms are reverting back to localism and sectionalism. The foregoing interpretation is consistent with the Durkheimian formula that micro-level organization crowds out and substitutes for class formation of a more aggregate sort.

This is not to suggest, of course, that the site of production has evolved entirely as Durkheim envisaged. As we see it, Durkheim was remarkably prescient in discerning the occupationalizing forces at work, but he clearly overstated the power of these forces and the consequent speed with which they might possibly play out. The Durkheimian formula is especially vulnerable on the three counts reviewed below.

Multifunctionalism and competing associational forms

In most of his relevant essays, Durkheim has occupational associations taking on a wide variety of functions, such as (a) regulating the labor market through norms governing pay, working conditions, and inter-occupational relations, (b) providing a *gemeinschaftlich* setting in which workers can "lead the same moral life together" (Durkheim [1893] 1960: 15), and (c) serving as an "essential organ of public life" charged with electing parliamentary delegates (Durkheim [1893] 1960: 27). Relative to these expectations, contemporary occupational associations might well seem poorly developed, especially with respect to the political functions served. There is, to be sure, much political action at the detailed occupational level (see e.g. Abbott 1988), but nowhere have occupations achieved the central, direct, and formal role in political governance that Durkheim outlined. Rather, occupations are typically consigned to the role of lobbying the state for highly specialized benefits, most notably the right to train and certify members and to otherwise establish control over the supply of labor. Even in this limited domain, occupational associations continue to compete with alternative associational forms, including most obviously labor unions. As Durkheim anticipated, the conflict between labor and capital has indeed been tamed and contained, but this has occurred as much by institutionalizing large unions as by replacing them with occupational associations or local craft unions. The resulting web of associational forms is inconsistent with the Durkheimian imagery of all-purpose associations that divide the workforce into mutually exclusive groups, squeeze out all competing organization, and accordingly become the *sole* intermediary between the individual and the state.[11]

Incomplete occupationalization

In some sectors of the class structure, occupational associations have simply failed to emerge, either because they have been overrun by competing forms (e.g. unions) or because social organization of all forms has proven unviable. For example, occupationalization has not yet taken hold in the lower manual sector, presumably due to low skill levels, limited investments in training, and relatively rapid changes in manufacturing process. It is unclear whether these poorly organized sectors will remain unorganized, will ultimately develop strategies allowing for some form of closure and occupationalization, or will continue to decline in size and eventually wither away. Although skill upgrading works to diminish the proportion of the workforce in poorly organized sectors, this process has of course played out only fitfully and may have reached its limit (e.g. Spenner 1995).[12] The contemporary class structure is best viewed, then, as a complex patchwork of moral communities and realist occupations interspersed with large regions of purely nominal categories in which occupationalization has yet to play out, if ever it will.[13]

Cross-national variation

There is also much cross-national variation in the extent to which the labor market has become occupationalized (see table 13.1; also, see Grusky and Weeden 2001: 210; Grusky and Sørensen 1998: 1220–2). The German labor market, for example, is built directly on institutionalized occupational groupings and may therefore be seen as an especially successful realization of the Durkheimian formula.[14] As scholars have long stressed, Germany has well-developed systems of vocational training and apprenticeship, both of which serve to encourage occupation-specific investments and promote professional commitment and craftsmanship (e.g. Blossfeld 1992). In systems of this sort, workers must invest in a single trade early in their careers, and the correspondingly high costs of retraining produce relatively closed occupational groupings. The case of Japan reveals, to the contrary, the extent to which local structuration can be institutionally suppressed. The standard

Table 13.1 *Countries classified by type and amount of class structuration*

	Disaggregate structuration	
Aggregate structuration	*High*	*Low*
High	Germany	Sweden
Low	U.S.	Japan

characterization of Japan emphasizes such distinguishing features as an educational curriculum that is generalist in orientation rather than functionally differentiated, a vocational training system that cultivates firm-specific "nenko skills" (Dore 1973) through teamwork and continuous job rotation, an organizational commitment to lifetime employment that further strengthens firm-specific ties at the expense of more purely occupational ones, and a weakly developed system of enterprise unions that cuts across functional specializations and hence eliminates any residual craft-based loyalties (Ishida 1993; Cole 1979; Dore 1973). This conjunction of forces thus produces a "post-occupational system" that some commentators (e.g. Casey 1995) might well regard as prototypically postmodern. Finally, the Swedish case is equally problematic for Durkheim, not merely because occupational solidarities have been suppressed through "active labor market" programs (Esping-Andersen 1988: 47–53), but also because aggregate classes have become corporate actors in ways that Durkheim explicitly ruled out as developmentally abnormal. Arguably, Sweden provides the textbook case of class formation of the aggregate variety, given that craft unionism and guild organization have long been supplanted by classwide forms of collective bargaining. It follows that "abnormal" organizational forms have, at least in Sweden, had rather more staying power than Durkheim allowed.

The occupationalizing forces that Durkheim emphasizes have therefore been suppressed in some countries and sectors of the labor force. The main question that emerges is whether these zones of resistance (a) will ultimately be overcome by the forces for occupationalization, (b) will live on in current form as testimony to the diversity of solutions to contemporary organizational problems, or (c) are best regarded as signaling some fundamental defect in the Durkheimian formula that will ultimately reveal itself more widely and reverse previously dominant tendencies toward sectionalism, localism, and occupationalization. Although there is clearly much room here for debate and speculation, we are of course inclined toward (a) and (b) as the most plausible interpretations, all the more so because the distinctive institutional arrangements of Sweden and Japan are under increasing threat and are no longer as frequently held up by class analysts as alternatives to be emulated.

Contemporary class analysis

We have so far argued that Durkheim deserves some credit for anticipating both the demise of aggregate classes (i.e. the negative macro-level story) and the rise of local organization at the site of production (i.e. the positive micro-level story). If this Durkheimian interpretation of the course of recent history is accepted, it raises the question of how class analysis might now be pursued. We suggest that two changes in contemporary practice are warranted: (a) the search for big classes and the sociological principles underlying them should no longer be treated as the *sine qua non* of the class analytic enterprise, and (b) the focus of class analysis might usefully shift to a local level that has heretofore been dismissed as irrelevant to research and theorizing on social class. We develop below the case for each of these arguments.

The virtues of a realist account

As for the first point, our concern is that class analysis has become disconnected from the institutional realities of contemporary labor markets, with scholars positing class mappings that are represented as *analytically* meaningful even though they have no legal or institutional standing and are not salient to employers, workers, or anyone else (save a small cadre of academics). This criticism applies, for example, to such standard sociological categories as "semicredentialed supervisors" (Wright 1997), "operatives" (Featherman and Hauser 1978), "professionals and managers" (Ehrenreich and Ehrenreich 1977), and "routine non-manuals" (Erikson and Goldthorpe 1992). Although class categories of this conventional sort are only shallowly institutionalized in the labor market, the class analyst nonetheless attempts to build a case for them (a) by claiming that they are consistent with the class analytic "logic" of some revered theorist (i.e. the "exegetical" justification), (b) by arguing that such categories, while currently latent, will nonetheless reveal themselves in the future and ultimately become classes "für sich" (i.e. the "latency" claim), or (c) by suggesting that these categories capture much of the important variability in life chances, political behavior, or other outcomes of interest (i.e. the "explained variance" justification). The latter claim has at least the virtue of being testable, yet in practice the proffered tests have involved little more than demonstrating that the preferred class mapping has *some* explanatory value, leaving open the question of whether other mappings might perform yet better (e.g. Mills and Evans 1998; Marshall et al. 1988; Hout, Brooks, and Manza 1993; cf. Halaby and Weakliem 1993).

This conventional "analytic" approach often rests on the logic that scholars should look beyond surface appearances and somehow discern more fundamental forces at work. It is no accident, we suspect, that surface appearances came to be seen as misleading just as aggregate categories began to wither away. After all, the modern analyst who continues to serve up aggregate schemes in the modern context has no choice but to justify them via some deeper logic, thereby converting what would appear to be a defect (i.e. shallow institutionalization) into a virtue. This approach, while now dominant, is of course peculiarly modern. In characterizing stratification systems of the past, sociologists have typically relied on categories that were deeply institutionalized (e.g. estates, castes), thus rendering them sensible and meaningful to intellectuals and the lay public alike.

If sociologists were to return to this strategy today, it would lead them directly to the micro-level of production, where Durkheim presciently argued that deeply institutionalized categories will be found. The starting point for a modern Durkheimian analysis is accordingly the "unit occupation," which may be defined as a grouping of technically similar jobs that is institutionalized in the labor market through such means as (a) an association or union, (b) licensing or certification requirements, or (c) widely diffused understandings (among employers, workers, and others) regarding efficient or otherwise preferred ways of organizing production and dividing labor. The unit occupations so defined are often generated through jurisdictional struggles between competing groups over functional niches in the division of labor (e.g. Abbott 1988). As Granovetter and Tilly (1988) note, "Our encrusted and reified sense that one task is for orderlies, another for nurses, and yet another for doctors . . . is the result of legal, political, and economic struggles, just as are the names of the professions themselves" (p. 190). We have thus defined unit occupations in terms of the social boundaries that are constructed through closure-generating devices of various kinds. By contrast, statisticians often describe the task of constructing occupational classifications in narrowly technical terms, as if the categories defined in such schemes were merely aggregates of positions sharing "general functions and principal duties and tasks" (International Labour Office [1968] 1990: 5; also, Hauser and Warren 1997: 180). Although all unit occupations do indeed comprise technically similar tasks, this constraint hardly suffices in itself to account for the classification decisions that are embodied in conventional occupational schemes, given that the criterion of technical similarity could justify an infinity of possible combinations and aggregations of jobs. This is not to imply, of course, that socially constructed boundaries are always to be found; to the contrary, the technical division of labor is clearly "occupationalized" to varying degrees, with some sectors remaining disorganized because of minimal skill barriers or other impediments (see "Incomplete Occupation-alization" above). In these sectors, the task of defining unit occupations is perforce difficult, involving as it does the identification of social boundaries that are, at best, in incipient form and may never come to be well defended.[15]

Should class analysts care about local organization?

The preceding hopefully makes the case that scholars have over-invested in the search for aggregate classes and under-invested in the study of more deeply institutionalized groupings at the disaggregate level. The critic might well counter, however, that the study of local organization is perfectly suit-able for scholars of occupations and professions, but is hardly the heady stuff deserving of attention of class analysts proper (see Goldthorpe 2002; Kingston 2000). This reaction, while understandable, nonetheless fails to appreciate the class-like behavior that emerges at the local level. We have argued elsewhere (Grusky and Sørensen 1998: 1196–212) that occupations act collectively on behalf of their members, extract rent and exploit non-members, shape life chances and lifestyles, and otherwise behave precisely as class theorists have long thought aggregate classes should. If class analysts wish to demonstrate that advanced economies are "lumpy" amalgams of competing groups (rather than seamless neo-classical markets), they would accordingly do well to turn to the local level and analyze the occupational associations that emerge around functional niches in the division of labor. The purpose of this section is to elaborate the above argument for each of the social organizational processes (i.e. identification, closure, collective action, proximate structuration) that class analysts have sought, largely unsuccess-fully, to uncover at the aggregate level.

Identification and awareness

It is natural to begin by considering the subjective domain of class systems. Although both Marx and Durkheim anticipated a great clearing operation in which solidarities outside the productive realm (e.g. ethnic or regional ties) would wither away, they differed on whether aggregate or disaggregate groupings would be the main beneficiaries of this development. The aggre-gate account appears, of course, to have lost out. To be sure, some sociol-ogists remain convinced that contemporary identities are strongly shaped by aggregate affiliations (e.g. Marshall et al. 1988), but the prevailing post-Marxist position is that big classes now have only a weak hold over workers. For example, Emmison and Western (1990) report that only 7 percent of all Australians choose a big class as a "very important" identity, while other commentators (e.g. Saunders 1989) have stressed that open-ended queries about class identification tend to yield confused responses, refusals to answer, and even explicit denials that classes exist. This evidence has led many sociologists to conclude that class is now a "passive identity" (Bradley 1996: 72) and that the realm of production is no longer the dominant or principal locus of identity formation (e.g. Hall 1988; Pakulski and Waters 1996a). As we see it, the latter conclusion is overstated and fails to appreciate the continuing power of class analysis, at least in the expanded form that we are proposing here. The Emmison-Western results are again revealing on this point, since they indicate that detailed occupational groupings continue to be one of the main social identities for contemporary workers (Emmison and Western 1990: 247–8). Likewise, there is much qualitative research suggesting that individual identities and self-definitions are strongly affected by occupational affiliations, almost to the point of bearing out a Durkheimian "essentialist" view that such ties provide a master identity (e.g. Zabusky and Barley 1996; Mortimer and Lorence 1995; Freidson 1994: 89–91). These results are hardly surprising given that occupational affiliations are so routinely solicited in everyday interactions. For example, firms often request occupational information from clients and customers, while individuals proceed likewise in their opening gambits at parties, business meetings, and other social gatherings. The state also collects detailed occupational information when marriages, births, or deaths occur, when state benefits are requested and taxes collected, when censuses and labor force surveys are administered, and when immigrants, citizens, and jurors are admitted or selected. The disaggregate "language of occupation" is accordingly well-developed and widely diffused, whereas the aggregate language of class is spoken almost exclusively in academic institutions. This state of affairs, while perhaps too obvious to interest class analysts searching for deeper truths, is also too important to ignore when attention turns to the social organization of the labor market and subjective understandings of this organization.

Social closure

If subjectivist models of class were once dominant in sociology (e.g. Warner et al. 1949), they have now been superseded by approaches that focus on the social processes by which class membership is restricted to qualified eligibles (Freidson 1994: 80–4; Murphy 1988; Collins 1979; Parkin 1979; Weber [1922] 1968). These models emphasize not only the institutionalized means by which closure is secured (e.g. private property, credentials, licenses) but also the efforts of excluded parties to challenge these institutions and the inequality that they maintain. While closure theory provides, then, a new sociological language for understanding inter-class relations, the actual class mappings posited by closure theorists have proven to be standard aggregate fare. The two-class solution proposed, for example, by Parkin (1979: 58) features an exclusionary class comprising those who control productive capital or professional services and a subordinate class comprising all those who are excluded from these positions of control. This tendency to default to aggregate mappings reveals the hegemony of big-class formulations and the consequent inability of class analysts, even those armed with closure theory, to imagine any alternatives. Indeed, if closure theory were somehow reinvented without the coloration of class analytic convention, its authors would likely emphasize that the real working institutions of closure (e.g. professional associations, craft unions) are largely local associations "representing the credential-holders themselves" (Murphy 1988: 174). In most cases, the underlying mechanisms of closure (e.g. licensing, credentialing, apprenticeships) do not govern entry to aggregate classes, but instead serve only to control entry (and exit) at the more detailed occupational level. By contrast, there are no analogous organizations that represent aggregate classes, nor are there jurisdictional settlements or closure devices that are truly aggregate in scope.[16]

Collective action

For most neo-Marxists, social closure is of interest not because it provides a vehicle for pursuing purely local interests (e.g. "trade union consciousness"), but rather because it allegedly facilitates the development of classwide interests and grander forms of inter-class conflict. The aggregate classes identified by contemporary sociologists have so far shown a decided reluctance to act in accord with such theorizing. This quiescence at the aggregate level initially prompted various neo-Marxian salvage efforts (e.g. Poulantzas 1974; Wright 1985; Korpi 1983) and then provoked a more radical postmodernist reaction in which interests were held to be increasingly defined and established outside the realm of production (e.g. Laraña, Johnston, and Gusfield 1994). The latter form of postmodernism, popular as it is, overlooks the simple fact that much collective action flows unproblematically out of structurally defined groupings, albeit only when those groupings are defined in less aggregate terms than is conventionally the case. The three principal types of collective action at the level of unit occupations are (a) downwardly directed closure strategies designed to restrict access to occupational positions, (b) lateral competitive struggles between occupational associations over functional niches in the division of labor, and (c) upwardly directed collective action oriented toward securing occupation-specific benefits (e.g. monopoly protection) from the state and from employers. This emphasis on instrumental action at the micro-level is not inconsistent with a Durkheimian formulation. To be sure, Durkheim glossed over all discussion of the instrumental pursuits of occupational associations, but this was largely because he took them for granted and sought to cast light on more subtle and complicated extra-economic functions (Durkheim [1893] 1960: 15). For Durkheim, the purely instrumental action of occupational associations had neither complicated nor profound effects, as it was oriented toward straightforward sectional interests (e.g. pay, working conditions) rather than transformative or revolutionary objectives.[17] While we might conclude, then, that disaggregate class analysis is an intellectually modest project, it bears noting that aggregate class analysts have likewise scaled back their ambitions and effectively discarded comprehensive class-based theories of history (e.g. Goldthorpe and Marshall 1992: 385). As Holton and Turner (1989: 175) have noted, such theories have by now been largely abandoned, with the typical fallback position being a "reconceptualization of class around non-organic *gesellschaftlich* relations or a historicization of class analysis around the few contingent moments when economic class has seemed to correspond to social class" (also, Holton 1996; Goldthorpe and Marshall 1992: 383–5).

Proximate structuration

In this sense, the class analytic project has become more limited in its objectives, with most contemporary scholars now satisfied with merely documenting that class membership conditions individual-level outcomes of all kinds (e.g. attitudes, voting behavior, lifestyles). The resulting analyses of "proximate structuration" (Giddens 1973) proceed by examining either the categorical effects of aggregate classes or the gradational effects of variables that represent the many dimensions underlying jobs (e.g. "substantive complexity") or detailed occupations (e.g. socioeconomic status). Although these approaches have yielded important results, it is nonetheless troubling that they ignore the *gemeinschaftlich* character of (some) disaggregate occupations. As argued above, modern closure is secured principally at the detailed occupational level, with the resulting restriction of social interaction generating occupational subcultures that are correspondingly disaggregate. These constraints on interaction serve to preserve and elaborate occupation-specific cultures of the sort that Durkheim ([1893] 1960) described long ago (also, see Caplow 1954). By contrast, aggregate classes have no comparable influence or authority over secondary socialization, and such aggregate cultures as emerge are accordingly more diffuse and abstract (e.g. Lamont 2000, 1992; Bourdieu 1984; Bernstein 1971; Kohn and Slomczynski 1990). The great failing, then, of conventional analyses of lifestyles, dispositions, and attitudes is that *gemeinschaftlich* occupations are regarded as nominal categories and are therefore blithely aggregated or dimensionalized. Indeed, when critics of class analysis complain that "class effects" tend to be weak (esp. Kingston 2000; also, Pakulski and Waters 1996a), this argument likely capitalizes on the blunt and highly aggregate operationalization of class more than any true weakness in the effects of the site of production (see Weeden and Grusky (2004) for substantiating evidence).

Where does this leave us? We have sought to establish that the social organizational processes that are often ascribed to big classes in fact emerge more clearly at a lower analytic level. We have emphasized, for example, the tendency of occupational groupings to act collectively on behalf of their interests, to defend their boundaries and thereby secure (partial) closure, to define lifestyles and consumption practices that are binding on members, and to become subjectively meaningful categories through which workers perceive themselves as well as others. To be sure, class analysts are free to claim that such processes are of interest only when revealed at aggregate levels, but doing so closes off an important route for revitalizing class analysis and protecting it from postmodernists who have exploited the characteristic weakness of big classes to (misleadingly) advance broader claims about the irrelevance of the site of production. If class analysts can see beyond their obsession with big groupings and own up to the rise of smaller class-like groupings, it may become possible to develop more powerful accounts of social behavior (e.g. Weeden and Grusky 2004), to build more realistic models of social mobility and social closure (e.g. Sørensen and Grusky 1996), and to otherwise tend to the micro-level business of class analysis in much more persuasive ways (see Weeden and Grusky (2004) for details).

Is there a Durkheimian model of exploitation and rent?

The preceding discussion suggests that disaggregate occupations can be meaningful sociopolitical communities of precisely the sort that class analysts have long sought. By contrast, it has proven difficult to find equally well-developed sociopolitical communities at the aggregate level, and class analysts have accordingly adopted the more limited objective of mapping out aggregate "structural locations" that are alleged to have the potential to become such communities in the future. Under this formulation, much attention is conventionally focused on identifying the underlying axes of exploitation, since these are assumed to constitute the "objective bases of antagonistic interests" (see Wright 1985) that may ultimately come to be recognized and pursued through more established sociopolitical communities. The two objectives of the present section are to explore whether Durkheim anticipated such models of exploitation and to examine how they might be usefully adapted or modified in light of his work.

A Durkheimian provenance?

For these objectives, the substantial literature on skill-based exploitation is especially relevant, and we shall therefore focus on it. In the context of this literature, Wright (1985) and others (Sørensen 1994, 2000) have equated skill-based exploitation with the extraction of rent, where the latter refers to the returns to skill that are secured by limiting opportunities for training and thus artificially restricting the supply of qualified labor. If this definition is adopted, one can then test for exploitation by calculating whether the cumulated lifetime earnings of skilled labor exceeds that of unskilled labor by an amount larger than the implied training costs (e.g. school tuition, foregone earnings). In a perfectly competitive market, labor will presumably flow to the most rewarding occupations, thereby equalizing the lifetime earnings of workers and eliminating exploitative returns (after correcting for training costs).[18] However, when opportunities for mobility are limited by constructing barriers that preclude workers from freely assuming highly remunerative or otherwise desirable jobs, the equilibrating flow of labor is disrupted and the potential for rent-extraction and exploitation occurs. The relatively high pay of doctors, for example, may be understood as arising from "artificial" restrictions on the number of training positions offered through medical schools.

Although skill-based exploitation of this type is sometimes represented as a generalized form of classical Marxian exploitation, the concept also has a Durkheimian provenance that has gone largely unappreciated. This becomes apparent, for example, when Durkheim ([1893] 1960: 374–88) rails against the constraints on free mobility that emerge either because of (a) norms or laws placing restrictions on the occupations that certain individuals may assume (e.g. caste systems, gender typing of occupations), or because of (b) economic barriers or entry costs that preclude lower-class workers from considering jobs that involve extended search or training time. The effect of both types of "forced mobility" is to reduce the bargaining power of the affected workers by eliminating or weakening their exit threat. As Durkheim ([1893] 1960: 384) puts it, "If one class of society is obliged, in order to live, to take any price for its services, while another can abstain from such action thanks to resources at its disposal . . . , the second has an unjust advantage over the first." The resulting potential for exploitation can be addressed by opening up mobility opportunities through direct or indirect interventions in the labor market. That is, Durkheim would have us equalize market opportunities not only by directly removing normative and legal restrictions on the free flow of labor (e.g. removing prohibitions on the mobility of caste members), but also by prohibiting parents from transmitting wealth and assets that indirectly advantage their children in the competition for desirable jobs (Durkheim [1893] 1960: 30–1, 374–88).[19] This formulation anticipates contemporary understandings of exploitation insofar as it recognizes that the bargaining power of workers is a function of the supply and demand for labor within their occupations. At the same time, the modern conception of rent is only partly and imperfectly anticipated, not merely because Durkheim emphasized the unfairness and inefficiency of "forced mobility" more than the exploitative wage terms that it allowed, but also because he focused on the wages foregone by workers trapped in undesirable occupations more than the rent extracted when privileged workers act to restrict the supply of competitors.

Improving contemporary models of skill-based exploitation

Although Durkheim thus fell well short of anticipating a systematic model of rent, his emphasis on local organization is nonetheless instructive when considering how contemporary models of skill-based exploitation might be improved. Indeed, given that modern institutions of closure (e.g. professional associations, craft unions) generate local rather than classwide restrictions on labor supply, the logic of the Durkheimian position suggests that rent is principally extracted at the local level. As we have stressed, Durkheim was especially interested in the extra-economic functions of occupational associations, yet he appreciated that such associations also provided their members with the "force needed to safeguard their common interests" (Durkheim [1893] 1960: 11). This force may be used to restrict the number of new entrants to an occupation, to prohibit competing occupations from performing similar functions, and to otherwise generate pockets of monopoly control within the division of labor. For the most part, neo-Marxians have instead argued for big "exploitation classes" that encompass and cut across many occupations, with the rationale for such aggregation being the usual analytic one that workers in structurally similar positions are equivalently exploited, have interests that are accordingly shared, and may ultimately come to form solidary cross-cutting groups to press such shared interests. This approach is problematic because the posited classes typically have no institutional or social organizational standing; that is, the working institutions of closure are organized largely at the occupational level (see "Social closure" above), and the potential for rent therefore emerges at that level. As a result, the elementary units of skill-based exploitation are occupations themselves, while neo-Marxian classes are heterogeneous aggregations of jobs and occupations that have structurally similar capacities for exploitation. It is always possible, of course, that rent-extracting exploiters with "structurally similar" capacities will ultimately band together to protect the credentialing institutions that make closure and rent possible (see Grusky and Sørensen 1998: 1211–12). In this sense, disaggregate class mappings serve to characterize the contemporary structure of rent-extraction, whereas conventional big-class mappings serve as hypotheses about how that structure might simplify in the future.

The more fundamental question, of course, is whether the underlying structure of rent-extraction will come to shape how interests are understood and pressed. From a neo-Durkheimian standpoint, the conventional definition of skill-based rent might well be critiqued as too arcane and academic to become widely diffused, especially given that countervailing stories about the appropriateness and legitimacy of occupational wage differentials are so widely accepted. As Durkheim saw it, consensual beliefs about the "level of reward . . . appropriate to the various occupational groups" (Parkin 1992: 62) will inevitably emerge in all societies, with such beliefs holding sway even when forced mobility and exploitation account for the observed differentials (see, esp., Durkheim [1897] 1951: 126). The occupational structure should be regarded, then, as a double-edged sword that works simultaneously to create closure and extract rent (i.e. the "rent-extraction" side) and to legitimate that rent and convince us that it is appropriate and unproblematic (i.e. the "rent-legitimation" side). The latter legitimating efforts may rest on beliefs about the importance of filling the most important occupations with the best workers (i.e. "functionalism"), about the sacredness or inviolability of market-determined rewards (i.e. "market legitimation"), or about the appropriateness of compensating workers for completing difficult or unpleasant tasks (i.e. "compensating differentials").

Whatever the story, the result is that inter-occupational differentials in earnings are typically regarded as acceptable, whereas intra-occupational differentials are closely scrutinized and are sometimes taken as evidence of discrimination (especially when correlated with race, gender, or ethnicity). It is no accident, for example, that anti-discrimination legislation has flourished just as comparable worth legislation has languished. In explaining this outcome, we need only appreciate that anti-discrimination legislation seeks to outlaw intra-occupational disparities in wages, whereas comparable worth legislation seeks to prohibit entrenched inter-occupational disparities that are legitimated with cultural stories about functional importance, market forces, and compensating differentials (see Nelson and Bridges 1999). The institutionalization of an occupational classification scheme thus trains us to regard between-category disparities as appropriate and legitimate. Indeed, there is much rhetoric in Durkheim ([1897] 1951: 383) about the importance of developing well-legitimated "classification schemes," precisely because they rein in potentially disruptive aspirations and prevent the weakest from "endlessly multiplying their protests" (also, see Zeitlin 1968: 275). For many sociologists, a more palatable value-free position is simply that these legitimating forces are exceedingly well-developed, thus calling into question any theory of rent suggesting that rent-extraction will ultimately become exposed and activate antagonistic interests that were previously latent.

The upshot, then, of our commentary is that big-class formulations cannot be salvaged by simply shifting over to rent-based definitions of class. When conventional definitions of skill-based rent are applied, a neo-Durkheimian should immediately point out that (a) such rent is extracted at a more local level than most class analysts appreciate, and (b) the very institutionalization of occupational classification schemes works to legitimate occupational wage differentials and to suppress the development of antagonistic interests. It follows that the categories of a micro-class scheme may never come to be invested with those antagonistic properties that class analysts have long sought.

Is more disaggregation always better?

In arguing for our neo-Durkheimian approach, we have referred to all competing class analytic models in quite generic terms, labeling them variously as "big class," aggregate, or gradational approaches. Although it has been convenient to treat conventional approaches as a whole, it is worth considering at this point whether all class models are equally vulnerable to the criticisms that we have been advancing. As indicated in table 13.2, six general types of categorical schemes and scales may be usefully distinguished, each combining a particular level of measurement (i.e. continuous, categorical) with a preferred unit of analysis (i.e. unit occupation, occupational aggregate, job-level aggregate). In the foregoing sections, we have principally focused on models that either scale occupations (i.e. Type A and C models) or aggregate them (i.e. Type D models), making it possible to pitch our critique in terms of the heterogeneity that is suppressed when "similar" unit occupations are coded into a single class or into similar levels on a gradational scale. This emphasis is justifiable given that most sociologists default to class models of these general types (i.e. Types A, C, and D).[20] At the same time, some analysts have of course sought to understand the social organization of

Table 13.2 *Models of social organization at the site of production*

Level of measurement	Type of aggregation or disaggregation		
	Unit occupations	*Occupational aggregates*	*Job-level aggregates*
Continuous	Type A models: Prestige, socioeconomic, and cultural capital scales (e.g. Hauser and Warren 1997, Bourdieu 1984)	Type C models: Hollingshead occupational scale (e.g. Hollingshead and Redlich 1958)	Type E models: Scales of working conditions and job desirability (e.g. Kohn and Slomczynski 1990, Jencks et al. 1988)
Categorical	Type B models: Neo-Durkheimian micro-classes (Grusky and Sørensen 1998)	Type D models: Neo-Weberian classes (e.g. Erikson and Goldthorpe 1992, Featherman and Hauser 1978)	Type F models: Neo-Marxian "exploitation classes" (e.g. Wright 1985)

production by treating jobs (rather than occupations) as the elementary unit of analysis, thus raising the question of whether our concerns and arguments apply equally to such alternative approaches.

We may define a job as the "specific and sometimes unique bundle of activities carried out by a person in the expectation of economic remuneration" (Hauser and Warren 1997: 180). In conventional labor markets, there are at least as many jobs as there are workers, and analysts of job-level data can therefore choose to disaggregate even more radically than we have been advocating. We might usefully ask whether a neo-Durkheimian should be attracted to the possibility of such extreme disaggregation. In addressing this question, it should be recalled that unit occupations are socially constructed through various closure-generating mechanisms, such as associations, unions, and licensing or certification. It is this "social clothing" worn by functionally similar jobs that makes unit occupations relatively homogeneous categories. The sources of such homogeneity are threefold: (a) unit occupations select for workers who are consistent with preexisting occupational "stereotypes" (e.g. sociology attracts left-leaning recruits); (b) explicit training regimens introduce further homogeneity in the attitudes, behaviors, and worldviews of prospective incumbents (e.g. graduate school, vocational training, apprenticeships); and (c) social interaction occurs disproportionately within occupational boundaries and thus reinforces occupation-specific attitudes, values, and lifestyles. At some point, the explanatory returns to disaggregation should accordingly diminish, as the inveterate splitter disaggregates beyond the occupational boundaries that are institutionalized in the labor market and that generate homogeneity.

The class analysts advocating for Type E or F models will concede that some aggregation or dimensionalizing of jobs is required, but they of course opt against aggregating up to socially constructed occupational boundaries. Instead, an "analytical" approach is again preferred, with the objective thus being to identify the technical conditions of work (e.g. substantive complexity, autonomy) that structure interests, affect processes of social interaction, or otherwise condition the outcomes of interest. This approach has obviously yielded important results. However, because jobs that share the same abstract technical conditions (e.g. substantive complexity) are not socially organized into meaningful groups, such homogeneity as is found arises from the direct effects of technical conditions rather than the additional socially-induced effects of selection, shared training, and interactional closure. The explanatory losses involved in foregoing these social effects may be substantial.

The limitations of analytic approaches can be more closely examined by considering the familiar case of sociologists and their seemingly distinctive *habitus* (Bourdieu 1984). In seeking, for example, to account for the humanist, antimaterialist, and otherwise left-leaning culture and lifestyle of sociologists, a neo-Durkheimian would emphasize (a) the left-leaning reputation of sociology and the consequent self-selection of left-leaning recruits, (b) the liberalizing effects of lengthy professional training and socialization into the sociological worldview, and (c) the reinforcing effects of social interaction with like-minded colleagues. To be sure, sociologists also labor under distinctive working conditions (e.g. high autonomy, high complexity), but the effects of such abstract technical conditions would appear to be swamped by the foregoing social forces. The case of economists provides an instructive contrast here; after all, economists labor under quite similar job conditions (e.g. high autonomy, high complexity), yet are nonetheless comparatively conservative in their politics and lifestyles. It would be difficult to account for such conservatism without recognizing that economists are self-selected for conservatism, that their graduate training in neoclassical approaches only reinforces this pre-existing affinity for conservatism, and that their subsequent interaction with fellow economists further protects against any ideological "straying." The conservatism of economists would appear, then, to be socially produced rather than attributable to the technical conditions under which they labor.

The purely analytic approach of Type E and F models is thus weakened because the posited class categories are not held together by the homogenizing effects of selection, socialization, and interactional closure.

This line of argumentation is of course identical to that earlier advanced against Type A, C, and D models. Although our preferred micro-classes are not nested within job-level class categories (and hence the rhetoric of "disaggregation" cannot be strictly applied), this in no way alters or affects our larger argument about the virtues of sociological realism.

Conclusions

In his celebrated preface to the *Division of Labor*, Durkheim ([1893] 1960: 28) predicted that corporate occupations would gradually become "intercalated between the state and the individual," thereby solving the problem of order by regulating and institutionalizing industrial conflict and by creating new forms of solidarity at the detailed occupational level. This account is ritually rehearsed by scholars of Durkheim but has never been treated as a credible developmental model by class analysts. As neo-Marxian class models are subjected to increasing attack, class analysts have typically fallen back to some version of neo-Weberianism or postmodernism, neither of which pays much attention to the occupation-level structuration that Durkheim emphasized. There is, then, much room for exploring a neo-Durkheimian third road that refocuses attention on local organization within the division of labor.

This "third road" involves opening up new research questions more than providing ready or stock answers. As a sampling of such research, we list below five empirical questions of interest, each of which speaks to standard areas of inquiry within the class analytic tradition (see Grusky and Weeden (2001) for more details):

Are the effects of social class adequately captured by big-class categories? Although we have suggested that conventional classes fail to exploit the explanatory power available at the site of production, we have not provided any empirical evidence on behalf of this claim; and the burden of proof necessarily rests with scholars who seek to improve on existing approaches. In many conventional class schemes, the posited categories are merely aggregations of detailed occupations (see Table 13.2), and it becomes possible to test such aggregations by examining whether much explanatory power is lost by imposing them (see Weeden and Grusky 2004). These tests should of course be carried out for "class correlates" of all kinds (e.g. attitudes, consumption practices, life chances, lifestyles).

Is aggregation more defensible in some sectors of the class structure than in others? The costs of aggregation may be especially high in some classes. For example, the lifestyles of nonmanual workers are likely to be quite heterogeneous, since occupations in the nonmanual sector are well-formed and their incumbents are accordingly exposed to distinctive cultures and socializing experiences. The lower manual sector, by contrast, is typically represented as a relatively homogeneous zone in which occupationalization is only weakly developed. As plausible as it is, this standard account has not been pitted against any number of alternatives, most notably the null hypothesis that academics are simply more sensitive to occupational distinctions in sectors of the class structure with which they are most familiar.

Are some occupations especially well-formed? The contours of disaggregate structuration are likewise of interest. The conventional story here is that craft occupations are paradigmatic in their fusing of work and lifestyle (Mills 1956: 223), but we suspect that well-developed lifestyles also exist elsewhere in the occupational structure. The available evidence, such as it is, suggests that disaggregate structuration will be most pronounced when (a) training is harsh or lengthy (e.g. doctors, professors), (b) workers are isolated or stigmatized (e.g. sanitation workers, loggers, carnival workers), or (c) recruitment is highly self-selective by virtue of social networks (e.g. actors), economic barriers to entry (e.g. capitalist), or the unusual tastes and skills that an occupation requires (e.g. morticians). These hypotheses can be pursued by examining the heterogeneity of lifestyles and behaviors within unit occupations.

Are social classes decomposing as postmodernists allege? In postmodern circles, the main debates of interest implicitly address issues of trend, with the most extreme accounts implying that all forms of structure at the site of production are withering away. The evidence amassed in support of this claim is nonetheless quite limited. Indeed, virtually all relevant research pertains to trends in aggregate structuration, and even here the available evidence refers principally to voting behavior (e.g. Evans 1997), life chances (e.g. Erikson and Goldthorpe 1992), and a few other standard outcomes (see Grusky and Weeden 2001). The evidence thus falls well short of substantiating a "class destructuration" thesis in the broad and encompassing terms that it usually takes.

Is the underlying structure of social mobility misrepresented by big-class models? If social closure is secured mainly at the unit occupational level, then conventional aggregate analyses may underestimate the extent of rigidity and persistence in mobility regimes (Sørensen and Grusky 1996; Rytina 2000). Moreover, given that much of the cross-national variability in local structuration is concealed through aggregation, we may find that standard convergence hypotheses are no longer plausible once mobility data are disaggregated. The existing literature on social mobility, massive though it is, has been especially beholden to big-class formulations and is accordingly vulnerable when revisited at the micro-class level.

We are thus arguing that conventional research on "class effects" can be usefully re-examined. Although big-class formulations will likely remain dominant, the discipline should at least consider the possibility that a wrong turn has been taken and that much explanatory action will be found within big classes. It is well to bear in mind that big-class models were initially devised to account for macro-level transformative events and large-scale social change (see Grusky, Weeden, and Sørensen 2000). As class conflict became institutionalized, class theorists have gradually de-emphasized these macro-level theories of history and related developmental narratives (Holton and Turner 1989), preferring instead to deploy class categories for the more modest academic task of explaining contemporary micro-level behavior (e.g. voting behavior, lifestyles). The contemporary fascination with tinkering, adapting, and revising big-class formulations may be understood as the flailing efforts of a subfield coming to terms with this new agenda. It is altogether possible, of course, that no amount of tinkering will suffice. If the contemporary micro-level agenda is taken seriously, it may require new micro-class models that go beyond big-class nominalism and exploit such local social organization as can be found.

NOTES

For an earlier version of this chapter, see Grusky and Galescu (2005). This chapter also draws on previously published materials in Grusky and Sørensen (1998), Grusky and Weeden (2001), and Grusky, Weeden, and Sørensen (2000). We are grateful for the comments of Vivek Chibber, Dalton Conley, Paul DiMaggio, Kathleen Gerson, Guillermina Jasso, Michèle Lamont, Jeffery Paige, Philip Smith, Margaret Somers, George Steinmetz, Kim Weeden, Bruce Western, Erik Wright, and Yu Xie. In drafting the introduction to this chapter, we relied heavily on the inspired suggestions of Jeffrey Alexander, to whom we are especially grateful. We have also drawn extensively on the insightful comments of Philip Smith. The research reported here was supported in part by the National Science Foundation (SBS-9906419).

1 As Sørensen (2000) points out, commentators during this period adopted an exceedingly convenient reading of Weber ([1922] 1968), one that unconvincingly interpreted prestige and socioeconomic scales as an operationalization of the (Weberian) concept of status.

2 There is of course a long tradition of stratification scholarship recognizing that occupations are the "backbone" of the class system (Parkin 1971; Featherman, Jones, and Hauser 1975; Duncan 1968: 689–90; Parsons 1954: 326–9). It might be thought that scholars working within this tradition would celebrate Durkheim because he likewise stressed the importance of occupations. In explaining why Durkheim was instead ignored, it bears noting that contemporary stratification scholars have typically preferred to scale occupations in terms of a socioeconomic gradient, and the work of Durkheim does not provide any obvious justification for such a procedure. If mention of Durkheim is, then, conspicuously absent from

present-day commentary on class, it is largely because his project cannot be seen as presaging any conventional class analytic approaches, including those that map occupations or jobs into aggregate classes as well as those that map them into socioeconomic scales.

3 We should, however, note that a growing cast of contemporary scholars has sought to explicate Durkheim's class analysis without asking how such analysis, if taken seriously, might serve to reorient contemporary class models (Watts Miller 1996; Filloux 1993; Hawkins 1996, 1994; Müller 1993; Durkheim, 1993; Mouzelis 1993; Lockwood 1992; Pope and Johnson 1983; Thompson 1982; also, see Nisbet 1952; Giddens 1971, 1972, 1978; Lukes 1973).

4 In this regard, it is striking that class analysts have not only ignored the *Division of Labor*, but have more generally eschewed *any* analysis of the technical division of labor, even a non-Durkheimian one. Indeed, Wright (1979: 12) commented nearly 25 years ago on the "relatively few sustained theoretical reflections on the logic of linking class to positions within the technical division of labor," and the same conclusion probably holds with equal force today (also, see Kemper 1972: 739).

5 The categories of our micro-class scheme will, by virtue of being institutionalized, tend to be recognized by the lay public and appreciated as meaningful. In this sense, micro-class categories will often be subjectively salient, even though they are defined exclusively in terms of objective signals of institutionalization (e.g. the presence of occupational credentials or associations).

6 The views of Durkheim on occupational associations evolved and changed throughout his career (see Hawkins (1994) for an excellent exegesis). In the early 1890s, Durkheim began to lay out the positive functions of occupational associations, but at that time he regarded them as a largely "temporary antidote to contemporary social problems" (Hawkins 1994: 473). It was not until the late 1890s that his full-fledged "theory" of occupational associations was formulated.

7 As is well known, Parsons (1949; 1967) sought to interpret all of classical sociology, including the *Division of Labor*, as engaging directly with issues of social order. By contrast, other scholars (esp. Giddens 1983) have argued that Parsons imposed his own idiosyncratic problematic on the work of others, especially that of Durkheim.

8 If the terminology of Durkheim is strictly applied, it is inappropriate to refer to "mechanical solidarity" in this context, as the latter term is reserved for traditional societies in which the collective conscience consists of beliefs and sentiments shared by all. We have appropriated the term here only because it clarifies that intra-occupational solidarity arises from similarities among individuals (see Pope and Johnson 1983).

9 Although the skeptic might reasonably ask whether the banal collective ends of everyday life are inspiring enough to infuse the most routine jobs with much meaning, the Durkheimian position does become easier to appreciate when collectivities are oriented to especially dramatic or uplifting objectives (e.g. fighting a war, building socialism) that could render even the smallest of contributions morally significant and rewarding.

10 There is, to be sure, a contemporary literature on "post-occupationalism" that describes the gradual withering away of functionally-defined positions. This literature rests on the claim that contemporary organizations are relying increasingly

on teamwork, cross-training, and multi-activity jobs that break down conventional occupation-based distinctions (e.g. Casey 1995). These changes, if indeed they are underway, should be regarded as a recent and modest setback for the occupationalizing forces that have dominated the post-Durkheim period. Moreover, the post-occupationalist account is not without its critics, some of whom have argued that the "pressures for an occupational logic of organizing may in fact be rising" (Barley 1995: 40).

11 Unlike Tocqueville ([1835] 2000), Durkheim regarded the proliferation of multiple and overlapping intermediary groupings as maladaptive, indicating "the absence or weakness of central authority" (see Hawkins 1994: 476).

12 Moreover, even in regions of the occupational structure that are well-organized, one often finds complex combinations of nested and overlapping occupational associations that belie the simpler structure that Durkheim seemed to anticipate.

13 In conventional class analyses, the site of production is represented in *either* nominalist or realist terms, and the fundamentally hybrid character of modern class systems has therefore gone unappreciated.

14 However, given that aggregate classes persist in Germany as well-developed and deeply institutionalized groupings, the correspondence with the Durkheimian formulation is imperfect at best (see Table 13.1).

15 The concept of "unit occupation" is further an artifice given that one typically finds complex webs of nested and overlapping boundaries that are not easily reducible to an exhaustive set of mutually exclusive occupations. It follows that sociologists do violence to the data by assuming that each worker must be mapped into one and only one occupation. However, insofar as such simplifying assumptions continue to be relied upon, our approach requires class analysts to identify the dominant jurisdictional settlements at the disaggregate level.

16 The forces for aggregate closure are arguably better developed outside the workplace. For example, post-secondary schools generate closure within a broadly defined professional-managerial class, both by virtue of (a) the generalist post-secondary degrees that are "redeemable" for positions throughout this class, and (b) the classwide constriction of interaction that occurs within campus settings. Similarly, residential segregation may be seen as a force for aggregate closure, as neighborhoods typically are segregated by race, ethnicity, and income rather than detailed occupation. We are simply arguing here that such closure at the aggregate level produces boundaries that are blurrier, weaker, and less deeply institutionalized than those defining occupations and controlling entry into them.

17 Although occupational associations typically pursue sectional objectives, the spread of such associations nonetheless has unintended systemic effects, most notably the "squeezing out" of alternative classwide solidarities. We have sought to emphasize this linkage between Durkheim's micro-level and macro-level stories throughout our essay.

18 We are ignoring here the inequality that arises by virtue of effort, native ability, and compensating differentials.

19 It is conventional at this point to criticize Durkheim for failing to appreciate how upper-class parents also transmit social and cultural resources to their children. This critique clearly has merit, but also ought not be overstated. Although Durkheim does not emphasize non-economic inequalities to the extent that contemporary sociologists would, he does appreciate that some "illegitimate"

inequalities would perforce persist even if economic inheritance were eliminated (see Lehmann (1995) for a relevant discussion).

20 In their recent work, Erikson and Goldthorpe (1992) have sought to motivate their class scheme with reference to job-level properties (i.e. terms of employment), even though the scheme itself has always been operationalized at the occupational level.

REFERENCES

Abbott, Andrew. 1988. *The System of Professions: An Essay on the Division of Expert Labor.* Chicago: The University of Chicago Press.

Aronowitz, Stanley and William DiFazio. 1994. *The Jobless Future.* Minneapolis: University of Minnesota Press.

Barley, Stephen R. 1995. "The Technician as an Occupational Archetype: A Case for Bringing Work into Organizational Studies." Working Paper, Stanford University.

Barnes, Barry. 1995. *The Elements of Social Theory.* London: UCL Press.

Bernstein, Basil. 1971. *Class, Codes, and Control:, Theoretical Studies Toward a Sociology of Education.* Vol. 1. London: Routledge and Kegan Paul.

Blossfeld, Hans-Peter. 1992. "Is the German Dual System a Model for a Modern Vocational Training System?" *International Journal of Comparative Sociology* 33: 168–81.

Bourdieu, Pierre. 1984. *Distinction: A Social Critique of the Judgement of Taste.* Translated by Richard Nice. New York: Cambridge University Press.

Bouglé, Célestin. [1927] 1971. *Essays on the Caste System by Célestin Bouglé.* Translated by D. F. Pocock. Cambridge: Cambridge University Press.

[1926] 1971. *Essays on the Caste System.* Cambridge: Cambridge University Press.

1926. *The Evolution of Values.* Translated by Helen S. Sellars. New York: Henry Holt and Company.

Bottomore, Tom. 1981. "A Marxist Consideration of Durkheim." *Social Forces* 59: 902–17.

Bradley, Harriet. 1996. *Fractured Identities: Changing Patterns of Inequality.* Cambridge: Polity Press.

Caplow, Theodore. 1954. *The Sociology of Work.* Minneapolis, MN: University of Minnesota Press.

Casey, Catherine. 1995. *Work, Self, and Society.* London: Routledge.

Clark, Terry N. 1996. "The Debate over Are Social Classes Dying?" Working paper. Conference on Social Class and Politics, Woodrow Wilson Center, Washington, DC.

Clark, Terry Nichols and Seymour Martin Lipset. 2001. *The Breakdown of Class Politics.* Washington, DC: Woodrow Wilson Center Press.

1991. "Are Social Classes Dying?" *International Sociology* 6: 397–410.

Cole, Robert E. 1979. *Work, Mobility, and Participation.* Berkeley and Los Angeles: University of California Press.

Collins, Randall. 1979. *The Credential Society: An Historical Sociology of Education and Stratification.* New York: Academic Press.

Comte, Auguste. [1830] 1988. *Introduction to Positive Philosophy.* Edited by Frederick Ferré. Indianapolis, IN: Hackett.

Coser, Lewis A. 1992. "Introduction: Maurice Halbwachs, 1877–1945." pp. 1–34 in *On Collective Memory*. Edited and translated by Lewis A. Coser. Chicago: University of Chicago Press.

Dahrendorf, Ralf. 1959. *Class and Class Conflict in Industrial Society*. Stanford, CA: Stanford University Press.

Dore, Ronald P. 1973. *British Factory – Japanese Factory*. London: Allen and Unwin.

Duncan, Otis D. 1968. "Social Stratification and Mobility: Problems in the Measurement of a Trend." pp. 675–719 in *Indicators of Social Change*. Edited by Eleanor B. Sheldon and Wilbert E. Moore. New York: Russell Sage Foundation.

Durkheim, Emile. [1897] 1951. *Suicide, A Study in Sociology*. Translated by John A. Spaulding and George Simpson. Glencoe, IL: Free Press.

  [1893] 1960. *The Division of Labor in Society*. Translated by George Simpson. New York: Macmillan.

  1958. *Professional Ethics and Civic Morals*. Translated by C. Brookfield. Glencoe, IL: Free Press.

  [1897] 1970a. *Suicide*. London: Routledge and Kegan Paul.

  [1905] 1970b. *La Science Sociale et l'action*. Edited by J. C. Filloux. Paris: Presses Universitaires de France.

  1993. *Ethics and the Sociology of Morals*. Edited by Robert T. Hall. Amherst, NY: Prometheus Books.

Edwards, Richard. 1979. *Contested Terrain*. New York: Basic Books.

Ehrenreich, Barbara and John Ehrenreich. 1977. "The Professional-Managerial Class." *Radical America* 11: 7–31.

Emmison, Michael and Mark Western. 1990. "Social Class and Social Identity: A Comment on Marshall et al." *Sociology* 24: 241–53.

Erikson, Robert and John F. Goldthorpe. 1992. *The Constant Flux: A Study of Class Mobility in Industrial Societies*. Oxford: Clarendon Press.

Esping-Andersen, Gösta. 1988. "The Making of a Social Democratic Welfare State." pp. 35–66 in *Creating Social Democracy: A Century of the Social Democratic Labor Party in Sweden*. Edited by Klaus Misgeld, Karl Molin and Klas Amark. University Park, PA: The Pennsylvania State University Press.

Evans, Geoffrey. 1997. *The End of Class Politics? Class Voting in Comparative Perspective*. Oxford: Oxford University Press.

Featherman, David L. and Robert M. Hauser. 1978. *Opportunity and Change*. New York: Academic Press.

Featherman, David L., F. Lancaster Jones and Robert M. Hauser. 1975. "Assumptions of Mobility Research in the United States: The Case of Occupational Status." *Social Science Research* 4: 329–60.

Fenton, Steve. 1980. *Race, Class, and Politics in the Work of Emile Durkheim*. Paris: UNESCO.

Filloux, J. C. 1993. "Inequalities and Social Stratification in Durkheim's Sociology." pp. 211–28 in *Emile Durkheim: Sociologist and Moralist*. Edited by Stephen P. Turner. London and New York: Routledge.

Freidson, Eliot. 1994. *Professionalism Reborn: Theory, Prophecy, and Policy*. Chicago: The University of Chicago Press.

  1986. *Professional Powers: A Study of the Institutionalization of Formal Knowledge*. Chicago: University of Chicago Press.

Giddens, Anthony. 1983. "Classical Social Theory and the Origins of Modern Sociology." pp. 40–67 in *Profiles and Critiques in Social Theory* by Anthony Giddens. Berkeley, CA: University of California Press.

1978. *Emile Durkheim*. New York: Viking Press.

1973. *The Class Structure of the Advanced Societies*. London: Hutchinson.

1972. "Durkheim's Writings in Sociology and Social Philosophy." pp. 1–50 in *Emile Durkheim: Selected Writings*. Edited and translated by Anthony Giddens. Cambridge: Cambridge University Press.

1971. *Capitalism and Modern Social Theory*. Cambridge: Cambridge University Press.

Goldthorpe, John H. 2002. "Occupational Sociology, Yes: Class Analysis, No – A Comment on Grusky and Weedens' Research Agenda." *Acta Sociologica* 45: 211–17.

Goldthorpe, John H. and Gordon Marshall. 1992. "The Promising Future of Class Analysis: A Response to Recent Critiques." *Sociology* 26: 381–400.

Granovetter, Mark and Charles Tilly. 1988. "Inequality and Labor Processes." pp. 175–221 in *Handbook of Sociology*. Edited by Neil J. Smelser. Newbury Park, CA: Sage.

Grusky, David B. and Gabriela Galescu. 2005. "Foundations of Neo-Durkheimian Class Analysis" in *Approaches to Class Analysis*. Edited by Erik O. Wright. Cambridge: Cambridge University Press.

Grusky, David B. and Jesper B. Sørensen. 2001. "Are There Big Social Classes?" pp. 183–94 in *Social Stratification: Class, Race, and Gender in Sociological Perspective (Second Edition)*. Edited by David B. Grusky. Boulder, CA: Westview Press.

1998. "Can Class Analysis Be Salvaged?" *American Journal of Sociology* 103: 1187–234.

Grusky, David B. and Kim A. Weeden. 2002. "Class Analysis and the Heavy Weight of Convention." *Acta Sociologica* 45: 229–36.

2001. "Decomposition without Death: A Research Agenda for a New Class Analysis." *Acta Sociologica* 44: 203–18.

Grusky, David B., Kim A. Weeden and Jesper B. Sørensen. 2000. "The Case for Realism in Class Analysis." *Political Power and Social Theory* 14: 291–305.

Halaby, Charles N. and David L. Weakliem. 1993. "Ownership and Authority in the Earnings Function: Non-nested Tests of Alternative Specifications." *American Sociological Review* 58: 16–30.

Halbwachs, Maurice. 1958. *The Psychology of Social Class*. Glencoe, IL: Free Press.

[1945] 1992. *On Collective Memory*. Edited and translated by Lewis A. Coser. Chicago: University of Chicago Press.

Hall, Stuart. 2001. "The Meaning of New Times." pp. 859–65 in *Social Stratification: Class, Race, and Gender in Sociological Perspective (Second Edition)*. Edited by David B. Grusky. Boulder, CO: Westview Press.

1988. "Brave New World." *Marxism Today*, October: 24–9.

Hall, Stuart and Martin Jacques. 1989. *New Times: The Changing Face of Politics in the 1990s*. London: Lawrence and Wishart.

Hauser, Robert M. and John Robert Warren. 1997. "Socioeconomic Indexes of Occupational Status: A Review, Update, and Critique." pp. 177–298 in *Sociological Methodology 1997*. Edited by Adrian Raftery. Cambridge: Blackwell.

Hawkins, M. J. 1994. "Durkheim on Occupational Corporations: An Exegesis and Interpretation." *Journal of the History of Ideas* 20: 461–81.

Hollingshead, August and Frederick Redlich. 1958. *Social Class and Mental Illness.* New York: Wiley.

Holton, Robert. 1996. "Has Class Analysis a Future?" pp. 26–41 in *Conflicts About Class: Debating Inequality in Late Industrialism.* Edited by David J. Lee and Bryan S. Turner. London and New York: Longman.

Holton, Robert J. and Bryan S. Turner. 1989. *Max Weber on Economy and Society.* London: Routledge and Kegan Paul.

Hout, Michael, Clem Brooks and Jeff Manza. 1993. "The Persistence of Classes in Postindustrial Societies." *International Sociology* 8: 259–77.

International Labour Office. [1968] 1990. *International Standard Classification of Occupations: ISCO-88.* Geneva: ILO.

Ishida, Hiroshi. 1993. *Social Mobility in Contemporary Japan.* Stanford, CA: Stanford University Press.

Jencks, Christopher, Lauri Perman and Lee Rainwater. 1988. "What is a Good Job? A New Measure of Labor Market Success." *American Journal of Sociology* 93: 1322–57.

Joyce, Patrick. 1995. *Class.* Oxford: Oxford University Press.

Kingston, Paul W. 2000. *The Classless Society.* Stanford, CA: Stanford University Press.

1994. "Are There Classes in the United States?" pp. 3–41 in *Research in Social Stratification and Mobility,* vol. 13. Edited by Robert Althauser and Michael Wallace. Greenwich, CT.: JAI Press.

Kohn, Melvin L. and Kazimierz M. Slomczynski. 1990. *Social Structure and Self-Direction.* Oxford: Blackwell.

Korpi, Walter. 1983. *The Democratic Class Struggle.* London: Routledge.

Krause, Elliot A. 1971. *The Sociology of Occupations.* Boston, MA: Little, Brown.

Lamont, Michèle. 2000. *The Dignity of Working Men: Morality and the Boundaries of Race, Class, and Immigration.* Cambridge, MA: Harvard University Press.

1992. *Money, Morals, and Manners: The Culture of the French and American Upper-Middle Class.* Chicago: University of Chicago Press.

Laraña, Enrique, Hank Johnston and Joseph R. Gusfield. 1994. *New Social Movements: From Ideology to Identity.* Philadelphia: Temple University Press.

Lawrence, Paul R. and Davis Dyer. 1983. *Renewing American Industry.* New York: Free Press.

Lee, David J. 1995. "Class as a Social Fact." *Sociology* 28: 397–415.

Lee, David J. and Bryan S. Turner (eds.) 1996. *Conflicts about Class: Debating Inequality in Late Industrialism.* London: Longman.

Lehmann, Jennifer. 1995. "Durkheim's Contradictory Theories of Race, Class, and Sex." *American Sociological Review* 60: 566–85.

Lenin, Vladimir I. 1927. *Collected Works of V. I. Lenin.* New York: International Publishers.

Lockwood, David. 1992. *Solidarity and Schism.* Oxford: Clarendon Press.

Lukes, Steven. 1973. *Emile Durkheim: His Life and Work.* London: Allen Lane.

Marshall, Gordon, David Rose, Howard Newby and Carolyn Vogler. 1988. *Social Class in Modern Britain.* London: Unwin Hyman.

Marx, Karl. [1894] 1964. *Selected Works: Volume 1.* Moscow: Progress Publishers.

Meštrović, Stjepan G. 1992. *Durkheim and Postmodern Culture*. Hawthorne, NY: Aldine de Gruyter.

1988. *Emile Durkheim and the Reformation of Sociology*. Totowa, NJ: Rowman and Littlefield.

Mills, C. Wright. 1956. *White Collar*. New York: Oxford University Press.

Mills, Colin and Geoffrey Evans. 1998. "Identifying Class Structure: A Latent Class Analysis of the Criterion Related and Construct Validity of the Erikson-Goldthorpe Schema." *European Sociological Review* 14: 87–106.

Mortimer, Jeylan T. and Jon Lorence. 1995. "Social Psychology of Work." pp. 497–523 in *Sociological Perspectives on Social Psychology*. Edited by Karen S. Cook, Gary A. Fine and James S. House. Boston, MA: Allyn and Bacon.

Mouzelis, Nicos. 1993. "The Poverty of Sociological Theory." *Sociology* 27: 675–95.

Müller, Hans-Peter. 1993. "Durkheim's Political Sociology." pp. 211–28 in *Emile Durkheim: Sociologist and Moralist*. Edited by Stephen P. Turner. London and New York: Routledge.

Murphy, Raymond. 1988. *Social Closure: The Theory of Monopolization and Exclusion*. Oxford: Clarendon.

Nakane, Chie. 1970. *Japanese Society*. London: Weidenfeld and Nicolson.

Nelson, Robert L. and William P. Bridges. 1999. *Legalizing Gender Inequality: Courts, Markets, and Unequal Pay for Women in America*. Cambridge: Cambridge University Press.

Nisbet, Robert A. 1952. "Conservatism and Sociology." *American Journal of Sociology* 58: 167–75.

Pahl, R. E. 1989. "Is the Emperor Naked? Some Questions on the Adequacy of Sociological Theory in Urban and Regional Research." *International Journal of Urban and Regional Research* 13: 709–20.

Pakulski, Jan and Malcolm Waters. 1996a. *The Death of Class*. London: Sage Publications.

1996b. "The Death of Class." *Theory and Society* 25: 667–91.

1996c. "Misreading Class as Status: A Reply to Our Critics." *Theory and Society* 25: 667–91.

Parkin, Frank. 1992. *Durkheim*. Oxford: Oxford University Press.

1979. *Marxism and Class Theory: A Bourgeois Critique*. New York: Columbia University Press.

1971. *Class Inequality and Political Order: Social Stratification in Capitalist and Communist Societies*. New York: Praeger.

Parsons, Talcott. 1970. "Equality and Inequality in Modern Society, or Social Stratification Revisited." pp. 13–72 in *Social Stratification: Research and Theory for the 1970s*. Edited by Edward O. Laumann. Indianapolis, IN: Bobbs-Merrill Company.

1968. *The Structure of Social Action*. New York: Free Press.

1967. *Sociological Theory and Modern Society*. New York: Free Press.

1954. "An Analytical Approach to the Theory of Social Stratification." pp. 69–88 in *Essays in Sociological Theory* by Talcott Parsons. Glencoe, IL: Free Press.

Parsons, Talcott. 1949. *Essays in Sociological Theory, Pure and Applied*. Glencoe, IL: Free Press.

Pearce, Frank. 1989. *The Radical Durkheim*. London: Unwin Hyman.

Piore, Michael J. and Charles F. Sabel. 1984. *The Second Industrial Divide: Possibilities for Prosperity*. New York: Basic Books.

Poulantzas, Nicos. 1974. *Classes in Contemporary Capitalism*. London: Verso.

Pope, Whitney and Barclay D. Johnson. 1983. "Inside Organic Solidarity." *American Sociological Review* 48: 681–92.

Rytina, Steven. 2000. "Is Occupational Mobility Declining in the U.S.?" *Social Forces* 78: 1227–76.

Saunders, Peter. 1989. "Left Write in Sociology." *Network* 44: 3–4.

Smith, Adam. [1776] 1991. *The Wealth of Nations*. Amherst, NY: Prometheus.

Smith, Philip and Jeffrey C. Alexander. 1996. "Durkheim's Religious Revival." *American Journal of Sociology* 102: 585–92.

Sørensen, Aage B. 2001. "Toward a Sounder Basis for Class Analysis." *American Journal of Sociology* 105: 1523–58.

1996. "The Structural Basis of Social Inequality." *American Journal of Sociology* 101: 1333–65.

1994. "The Basic Concepts of Stratification Research: Class, Status, and Power." pp. 229–41 in *Social Stratification: Class, Race, and Gender in Sociological Perspective*. Edited by David B. Grusky. Boulder, CO: Westview.

Sørensen, Jesper B. and David B. Grusky. 1996. "The Structure of Career Mobility in Microscopic Perspective." pp. 83–114 in *Social Differentiation and Social Inequality*. Edited by James N. Baron, David B. Grusky and Donald J. Treiman. Boulder, CO: Westview.

Therborn, Göran. 1988. "A Unique Chapter in the History of Democracy: The Social Democrats in Sweden." pp. 1–34 in *Creating Social Democracy: A Century of the Social Democratic Labor Party in Sweden*. Edited by Klaus Misgeld, Karl Molin, and Klas Amark. University Park, PA: The Pennsylvania State University Press.

Thompson, K. 1982. *Emile Durkheim*. London and New York: Tavistock/Routledge.

Tiryakian, Edward A. 1975. "Neither Marx nor Durkheim . . . Perhaps Weber." *American Journal of Sociology* 81: 1–33.

de Tocqueville, Alexis. [1835] 2000. *Democracy in America*. New York: Bantam.

Treiman, Donald J. 1977. *Occupational Prestige in Comparative Perspective*. New York: Academic Press.

Van Maanen, John and Stephen R. Barley. 1984. "Occupational Communities: Culture and Control in Organizations." *Research in Organizational Behavior* 6: 287–365.

Visser, Jelle. 1988. "Trade Unionism in Western Europe: Present Situation and Prospects." *Labour and Society* 13: 125–82.

Warner, W. Lloyd, Marchia Meeker, and Kenneth Eells. 1949. *Social Class in America*. Chicago, IL: Science Research Associates.

Watts Miller, W. 1996. *Durkheim, Morals and Modernity*. London: UCI Press.

Weber, Max. [1922] 1968. *Economy and Society*. Berkeley, CA: University of California Press.

Weeden, Kim A. and David B. Grusky. 2004. "The Case for a New Class Map." Working paper, Dept. of Sociology, Cornell University.

Wilensky, Harold L. 1966. "Class, Class Consciousness, and American Workers." pp. 12–44 in *Labor in a Changing America*. Edited by William Haber. New York: Basic.

Wright, Erik O. 1997. *Class Counts: Comparative Studies in Class Analysis.* Cambridge: Cambridge University Press.

———. 1996. "The Continuing Relevance of Class Analysis." *Theory and Society* 25: 697–716.

———. 1985. *Classes.* London: Verso.

———. 1980. "Class and Occupation." *Theory and Society* 9: 177–214.

———. 1979. *Class Structure and Income Determination.* New York: Academic Press.

Zabusky, Stacia E. and Stephen R. Barley. 1996. "Redefining Success: Ethnographic Observations on the Careers of Technicians." pp. 185–214 in *Broken Ladders: Managerial Careers in the New Economy.* Edited by Paul Osterman. Oxford: Oxford University Press.

Zeitlin, Irving M. 1968. *Ideology and the Development of Sociological Theory.* Englewood Cliffs, NJ: Prentice-Hall.

14

ZYGMUNT BAUMAN

Durkheim's society revisited

Few of our contemporaries remember, and fewer still deserve to be rebuked if they do not, that when it first appeared in the vocabulary of incipient and inchoate sociology the word "society" was but a metaphor, and a metaphor of the most common, "here-like-there" kind, a kind usually deployed with the intention to domesticate something strange and make intelligible something heretofore unfamiliar and baffling. After all, two centuries or so have passed since that word had been deployed in metaphorical capacity. The mark of well-chosen and persuasive metaphors is that their metaphorical – interpretative – nature tends to be quickly forgotten and is no more noted. True to its metaphorical status, the word "society" was originally meant to focus attention on some otherwise blurry facets of the thing of which it claimed to be (newly) referent, thereby playing down the significance of that thing's confusing (and for that reason alarming) idiosyncrasy.

The facet of human experience which it was hoped would be laid bare or insinuated by the choice of "society" as the metaphor for the setting of human life-pursuits, was that of "being in company." According to the *Oxford English Dictionary*, "fellowship," "companionship," "association with one's fellow men, esp. in a friendly or intimate manner" were the oldest meanings of the word "society." There were other meanings too, all preceding the adoption of the word for metaphorical purposes – like "a number of persons associated together by some common interest and purpose" (first recorded in 1548); "the state or condition of living in association, company or intercourse with others of the same species"; "adopted by a body of individuals for the purpose of harmonious co-existence or for mutual benefit, defence, etc." (1553); "a corporate body of persons having a definite place of residence" (1588); or the "aggregate of persons living together with a more or less ordered community" (1639). All such other meanings were suggestive of groups set on purpose and groups having a purpose, of *purposeful* associations, *aware* of their togetherness, of forming a *group*. None of these original meanings is quite extinct. Under the rubric of *société*, current editions of *Larousse* list *"réunion d'individus vivant en groupes organisés"* and *"groupement de plusieurs personnes ayant mis quelque chose en commun,"* alongside *"milieu humain dans lequel une personne est intégrée."* It may be guessed that it has been the propinquity of the original, image-forming uses of the word, that supported and sustained over the years the perceived meaning of its sociological applications no less, if not more effectively than the sociologists' defining efforts.

It is not difficult to spot a joint theme in all primordial, pre-sociological uses of the concept in both its English and French renditions – "society" or "société." To whatever object they referred and to whatever use they had been put, they invariably conveyed an image or presentiment of proximity, closeness, togetherness and mutual engagement. The term "society" could be used as a metaphor because the kind of experience the sociologists struggled to grasp and to enclose in a conceptual frame was that of a certain number of people sharing a place, coming in and out of each other's presence and view, interacting in at least some of their activities and occasionally engaging in conversation. Connected in such a way, the people in question faced a prospect of living in each other's proximity for the long time to come. Given the growing density, though, and the unprecedented mobility of human population, one could not be sure what kind of the "others" might lay claim to the neighborhood. In some respects, this setting was reminiscent of that "companionship" whose image the orthodox meaning of "society" used to convey. It also differed from it, however, in some other important respects: the place was, unlike the old places, open to newcomers; the set of companions was poorly defined and changeable; and most of the people in view were unfamiliar.

As Émile Durkheim would have described that novelty – moral and physical density, once overlapping, had been now separated. By the established and habitualized standards, physical density was "incomplete" – it was not capped with moral density, with pre-reflexive sentiment of "belonging together," and of a bond of mutual obligations. Among people in each other's view and within the orbit of each other's action, a moral link was conspicuously missing. The idea of "society" would not come immediately to mind when the name for the new type of "togetherness" was sought. The term "society" could be applied only as a metaphor, and applying it was an act of interpretation; a yet-to-be-made-credible suggestion that despite its unfamiliar traits the new human environment is *like* the all-too-familiar "society."

Deployment of "society" as the name for the new form of human togetherness and cohabitation set the task which was to constitute, in the years to come, the prime business of sociology. That task was to fill the void left by the network of moral obligations, once the principal force holding society in its original meaning of companionship, together. The task stretched to the limits the powers of sociological imagination that in turn stretched to its limits the imagination of all the rest of the humans, now proclaimed to be "members of society."

From the start, "society" as used and prompted to be used by sociologists was an *imagined* entity. Let us note, however, that when Benedict Anderson (1983), to the universal applause of his fellow sociologists and the rest of social science practitioners, coined the term "imagined community," he supplied another vivid illustration to Heidegger's rule that the truth of an object is revealed to us only when something goes wrong. Anderson discovered the true status of "society," one of an imagined entity, just when that imagining – after a couple of centuries during which the imagining of society came to an average human mind matter-of-factly and with minimal effort – was becoming an ever more testing task. The gap between the image and the evidence of mundane experience widened at a rapidly accelerating pace. Alternatively, we may say that – like most of us most of the time – Anderson followed the habit of Minerva's owl: he enclosed reality in a fitting concept when the referent of that concept was just about to dissolve in the sunset twilights. It seems that the image of "society" could grip human imagination and raised few if any doubts only as long as it did not know being "imagined"; more to the point, as long as there were few if any occasions to discover that "being imagined" was indeed its case. Most of its life, perhaps the whole of it, society spent in the garb of *reality*, with disguise hardly ever seen for what it was, not being charged with imaginary provenance, let alone having its legitimacy questioned.

For Émile Durkheim, who did perhaps more than any other thinker to entrench "society" in social–scientific vocabulary as well as in that doxa which pre-shapes the common cognition-of-the-world, society was *everything but* an imagined entity. To Durkheim writing *Les Règles de la méthode sociologique* (1895) at the threshold of the now bygone century, society was *reality* – pure and simple, even if the admittedly unreliable human senses needed some prodding to notice it, while the admittedly confused human minds required some assistance to admit that what the eyes saw was true.

Durkheim offered such assistance, in the form of the argument that "society" meets, one by one, all the standards commonly recognized as the trademarks of "reality." Durkheim's society was a "thing-like," corporeal, palpable entity. Nothing "imaginary" about it; society was real, all-too-real. The setting in which human life is conducted – so Durkheim argued – is spattered by *social facts*, for all intents and purposes "thing-like." "Social facts," that would not be there if not for the society (facts that for all intents and purposes *are* society), behave like all other things solid, tough, impermeable, and resistant do. Like all other objects that we count among "real things," they would not soften, let alone disappear, just for being wished to do so. Like other things, they could be ignored only at our peril: bitter and painful awakening awaits all those who by ignorance or ill will behave as if "social facts" were but figments of imagination. We cannot go unpunished through the space they fill, just like we cannot try to pass through a locked door without bruising heads or knees. Reality, as Durkheim repeatedly pointed out, "is to be recognized by the power of external coercion which it exercises or is capable of exercising over individuals" (just how capable it is, the individuals would learn the hard way were they thoughtless or rash enough to ignore its toughness or play down its force). That coercive power of *social* facts stems from the "existence of some definite sanctions or by the resistance offered against every individual act that tends to contravene it" (1971: 102). You know reality when it hits you, inflicts pain or otherwise cramps your movements, and the reality of "social facts" you would know by the pain you would suffer once you ignore their "imperative and coercive power" (Durkheim 1971: 93). You would know that the "social facts" are there the moment you dare to act as if they were not.

Metaphors are good for thinking. They help to conjure up cohesive, legible forms out of the randomly scattered and shapeless blots of sensations. They allow to surmise order in a chaos. And so did the metaphor of "society." "Reality" might have been firmly set in human daily experience, clamoring to be found out and recognized – but without the metaphor of "society," imagination would spill and run out all over the vast expanses of the anything but shapely and cohesive *Erlebnisse* that sought desperately a fit-to-be-shared estuary, but were unable, unassisted, to find it. It is after all the familiar images supplied by metaphors that allow us to guess forms in fuzzy clouds, or constellations in the stars sprinkled haphazardly over the vast canopy of night heaven. Shapes do not emerge out of the flow of experience on their own. They are inserted into that flow from outside – by metaphors.

In Durkheim's time, however, the allegorical status of "society" could be easily overlooked. At the time the thoughts about coercive power of society (or rather about society *as* coercive power), were penned down, the *reality* of society could be easily (mis)taken for an *empirical* "given." The image of a hard and fast, tough and solid, all but corporeal society chimed well with the evidence supplied daily by common mundane experience. Daily life left little doubt about the coerciveness of powers, even if the location of powers was anything but obvious and remained contentious as well as difficult to pinpoint with certainty whenever guessed. It was that abundant and constantly replenished experience of coercion – of being kept in line, censured for stepping out of line and forcefully brought back into line – that could supply all the empirical proofs needed to establish and verify society's reality once the job of the metaphor had been done.

And to verify that reality was for an upstart discipline, a newcomer to the Academy, a matter of life and death. At any rate it was such a matter at a time like the end of nineteenth century, and in a place like the world of the French academy, with its protracted and firmly entrenched positivist canon that respected little else except tough and solid facts of tough and solid reality, and its belief in revealing and testing facts of a chosen section of reality as the one and only way of proceeding for all forms of cognition deserving the name of science. The world as seen through the positivist lens was divided into plots, each one allotted to a separate academic chair and a separate discipline of science (and so, no less if not more importantly yet, to a separate department inside the university). It was the allotment that made the discipline, and the land deed that made the discipline a part of scientific venture. No facts – no science; no possession/processing of a separate set of facts – no scientific discipline (and so no right to claim a university chair and department). If the chairs and departments of sociology were to sprawl in the French academy of the next century, the existence of a virgin, still "no man's" land of facts had to be, true to the spirit of the nineteenth-century voyages of discovery, found and mapped – and then claimed as the uncontested property of its founders. This was, roughly, the task that Émile Durkheim, young professor of *education* at Sorbonne wishing to be called to a chair of *sociology* and needing first to invent that chair, confronted. In fulfilling that task, the much floated around metaphor of "society" proved handy.

The task, to be sure, was twofold. The first part of the task – demonstrating the *reality* of "society," the solidity of its facts equal to that of the facts recycled by the older, better established branches of science and like that solidity undisputed – has been already mentioned. The other part was to draw a clear boundary between the claimed territory and all adjacent territories, so that exploitation of its natural resources – its "facts" – could be undertaken and go on undisturbed. The twofold nature of the task explains in large measure Durkheim's insistence on the strict separation of the new (more correctly, postulated) discipline of sociology from psychology, already well settled and fortified on a territory too close for comfort. It also explains why the case for separation was argued by him in terms of the "objective" or "natural" independence of "social" from "individual" facts. "Social facts are capable of objective representation to the degree that they are completely detached from individual facts expressing them." Social facts "reside exclusively in the very society itself which produces them, and not in its parts – that is, its members." "To understand the way in which a society represents itself and the world around it, we must consider the nature of the society and not that of the individuals." "The determining cause of a social fact must be sought among antecedent social facts and not among states of individual consciousness" (Durkheim 1971: 65, 69, 70, 74). These and many more similar statements combined into a declaration of independence composed on behalf of the new, up-and-coming and ambitious academic discipline.

Nevertheless, this was but one part of the story. Another part was the thinking people's response to the growing anxiety caused by the "melting the solids" and "profaning the sacreds" that, in many a distressed observer's view, threatened to sap the foundations of common life. The old joints and hinges seemed not to hold any more, and conditions of life in common seemed no more capable of self-reproducing. The centuries-long "gamekeeper posture" of kings and princes was obviously untenable. With the game no more trusted with either the intrinsic gift of self-preservation or the ability to self-reproduce if only protected against the balance-sapping poachers, a thoughtful gardener had to be put in charge, and a feasible design for a viable garden had to be worked out. The weakening grip of tradition needed to be replaced with another holding power. That need derived its overwhelming urgency from the widespread feeling of "without us, a deluge." Something had to be done quickly. The human world will not last unless the humans undertake the effort needed to secure its preservation.

The "managerial reason" combined with the managerial posture was the characteristically modern response to the gradual yet alarmingly relentless disintegration of the *ancien régime* – that archipelago of loosely linked and largely self-sustained local communities, capped by supra-local powers notorious for their insatiable greed but not known for their managerial ambitions and even less for their managerial capacity. *Ancien régime* was, in Ernest Gellner's witty description, the domain of the "dentistry State" – of supra-local power specializing in "extraction through torture." Indeed, the managerial ambitions of princes and managerial skills of their servants were by and large confined to the task of creaming-off the surplus product turned out by the prince's subjects. They stopped well short of all concern with how the product came to be there in the first place. "Wealth of the Nation" (that is, if such an idea cropped up – which it seldom did) was viewed by the pre-modern rulers as something one may enjoy in times of abundance or bewail in times of scarcity, but in both cases should placidly accept like one did all the other, benign or harsh, enjoyable or resented, but forever inscrutable verdicts of Providence. The idea of tending to the "wealth of the nation" occurred (simultaneously as a possibility within human reach and an imperative human task) only when the flying wheels of self-reproducing rural/craftsmen routine began to screech, threatening to grind to a halt altogether. We know from Alexis de Tocqueville (1853) that the *Ancien Régime* shook and started to collapse well before the French visionaries started to exhort the hoped-to-be-enlightened despots to boldly go where no rulers dared, or thought necessary or rewarding to go, before: into the strange, unmapped territory where an artificially designed, monitored and policed man-made order was to be forced into the messy and unwieldy affairs of humans. The modern condition, which Durkheim proposed to theorize as a coercive power of society no more needing or wishing to hide behind the broad shoulders of Divine Providence, was born under the sign of such order.

Modernity took off as a bold effort to manage the world of humans and to make it manageable. The need for such an effort was hardly in dispute, given the accumulating evidence that when left to their own care things tend to go awry or run amok. Modernity set about eliminating anything impenetrable, ambiguous, ambivalent, accidental and contingent. If the notoriously pleonastic idea of the "project of modernity" can be adumbrated at all, it can only be conceived as a retrospective gloss on the ongoing effort to implant determination into places where accidents and games of chance would have otherwise ruled. Also (by the same token?) as an effort to make the ambiguous *eindeutig*, the opaque transparent, the unexpected calculable and the uncertain predictable. Last but not least, as an attempt to insert meaning in things and then to force things to strive for the achievement of that meaning.

Reflecting on such modern experience, recycling it and re-processing, sociology (itself a modern invention) set about cracking the mystery of the deployment of free will in the production of necessity, regularity, norms and recurrent patterns of thought and action which Durkheim dubbed "social facts." Social thought shared with the rest of modern science the urge to "know nature in order to master it." In the case of social science though, "mastering of nature" meant primarily mastering of the human species itself, gaining control over the morbid predilection of its members to recalcitrance, over their desultory and random conduct that ignored the code of nature and the dictate of reason, nature's sole competent reader and interpreter.

In Durkheim's sociology, that purpose is pursued in two parallel, mutually complementary fashions. The first is denigration of the individual. The second is deification of society.

To start with the first. Just like Max Weber, his contemporary from the other side of the Rhine with whom he was at loggerheads in virtually every other detail of his vision of sociology, Durkheim insisted that individual actors are unreliable judges of the true causes of their actions and that therefore a science of "social facts" ought to start elsewhere and deem itself to be entitled (as well as to be advised) to ignore what the individuals believe. In one go, that decision begged the question of superiority of science over common sense, and of the right of the professionals of sociology to censure the blunders, correct the errors, and enlighten the minds of the lay actors. "Having been made uncritically and unmethodically," the representations that the ordinary, sociologically un-enlightened individuals "have been able to make in the course of their life" of the "facts properly so called" "are devoid of scientific value, and must be discarded. The facts of individual psychology themselves have this character and must be seen in this way. For although they are by definition purely mental, our consciousness of them reveals to us neither their real nature nor their genesis. It allows us to know them up to a certain point . . . [I]t gives us confused, fleeting, subjective impression of them, but not clear and scientific notions of explanatory concepts" (Durkheim 1971: 59).

The refusal to grant truth-value to lay individual judgments and denial of the individual cognitive authority was in tune with the preoccupation of the modern mind with "designed/ managed order." The sociologists' bird's eye view (external, and hence pre-defined as objective and value-free) of the springs, causes and effects of individual actions, can be plausibly interpreted as a theoretical gloss over the posture assumed by the designing/managing agencies towards the population under their jurisdiction, embraced by the concept of "society," as to the object of normative regulation, administration, and supervision. The strategy of sociological work had to be legislative and monological. Like on so many other occasions, knowledge and power, even if guided by factors of their own, landed in the end on a ground common to both.

Many years would pass, and Talcott Parsons (1968) would sum up the history of modern social thought as the perpetual effort to answer the "Hobbesian question" and so to unravel the mystery of "self-equilibrating social system." That is, to explain how voluntary actors follow by and large stable patterns instead of behaving haphazardly and at random. The mundane perception of the human world as primarily "external force," limiting individual freedom or channeling freely made choices in established patterns, collaborated closely with the managerial intention to design the patterns into which individual choices ought to be channeled. Influence of both can be found in that vision of "society" on which sociology was to focus during Durkheim's times and for almost a century after.

Let me repeat that the managerial posture characterizing modernity in its initial "solid" phase was a response to the multiplying signs of disintegration of the inherited and extant order. More exactly, the managerial posture was a reaction to the discovery of "order" as a problem and a task to be consciously undertaken and pursued. The reaction was self-reinforcing and self-intensifying, since each attempt to devise and impose new, monitored, and policed patterns to replace the old and no more reliable routines inserted more uncertainty into the setting of social life. It required the dismantling of some old habits and a massive retraining in the new – the task that called for yet more managerial acumen and initiative, adding to the overall impression of instability. The feverish pursuit of certainty had turned into the major and apparently inexhaustible source of uncertainty; this time, to use Anthony Giddens' (2000) felicitous expression, a "manufactured" one (grasped later in Ulrich Beck's (1992) concept of risks as inevitable by products of action).

Despite its reputedly indomitable force, the "society" of sociological narratives and managerial actions was viewed as an endemically fragile and unstable entity. It was believed to require constant attention and a steady flow of correctives. None of its forms could boast finality; none could be trusted to escape ageing and eventual demise, let alone to demand no intervention and allow no further improvement. Its unsteadiness and alterability could not but put on the agenda the question of "legitimation"; legitimacy of the coercion that society exerted on its members turned into a "problem" and a task, much as the issue of "order" did. Why should the individuals obey the demands with which "society" confronted them? On what ground was discipline demanded? Was not the power of society a matter of a surplus and uncalled-for coercion, serving particular and narrow interests at the expense of individual freedom? No more credibly claiming a status of the once-for-all Divine creation, the admittedly "social" (man-made, man-unmade, and man-remade) reality had to have its rights to command, to apply force, and to demand discipline recognized and accepted as legitimate. Only God, admittedly "the absolutely Other" of everything human, could cut short or better still pre-empt all questioning of legitimacy by abrupt declaration "I am who I am" and "this is My will." No such luxury was, is, or will ever be available to the institutions proclaiming human self-sufficiency in shaping and re-shaping the conditions of human life.

Longevity of "society" and all things "social," and even more their irrevocability, were notoriously moot questions. And yet, to argue the case for the legitimacy of society-originated coercion, Durkheim resorted to the value of durability. "Eternity" of society, unlike the ex-temporality of God's omnipotence, could not and was not (and could not, credibly, be) postulated. Even the admittedly historical society seemed however incomparably more durable than the abominably brief and incurably transient bodily life of the individuals. The argument could not be advanced at a better time: there were many gaping holes in the self-awareness of people bereaved of the *ancien régime* doxa and routines, clamoring to be filled and hoping to be filled with its help. The argument could indeed count on many ears willing to hear and many minds willing to absorb it.

The widest and deepest of holes came to be known and debated under the rubric of "life meaning." That question could have hardly arise under the tutelage of the Church, teaching the immortality of the soul and, more importantly, the exclusive responsibility of its mortal bodily casing for the quality of the soul's immortal life. The meaning of mundane, fleshy existence could be derivative, but was enormous, and above all indubitable – in spite of that existence's brevity. In the miserably short stopover on earth the fate of the soul's eternal life in Heaven or Hell was decided, and could be decided only then and there; no second chance nor right to appeal would be offered once the bodily life ended. Enthusiastic promoters of secularization reviled the alleged devaluation of bodily life resulting from its reduction to a purely instrumental status regarding the things proclaimed to be genuinely worthy. In fact, however much the ostensibly life-devaluating expedient invested bodily existence with gravity and significance it would later try to re-appropriate in vain.

The slow yet relentless "disenchantment of the world" has brought in its wake the suspicion and fear of the ultimate absurdity of the human condition. "When I consider the brief span of my life absorbed into the eternity which comes before and after . . . the small space I occupy and which I see swallowed up by the infinite immensity of spaces of which I know nothing and which know nothing of me, I take fright," noted Blaise Pascal (1968: 48). His words, anticipating the torments of men and women who refused the consolation of infinity ruled by God's providence, would have easily found understanding and resonance in innumerable lesser, less philosophically inclined minds. Infinity emptied of the after-life emanated horror, not a call to action; resignation, not *élan vital*. As if picking up this train of thought at the point where Pascal stopped, Durkheim insists ([1925] 1971: 110). that "we must discover the rational substitutes for those religious notions that have, for so long, served as the vehicle for the most essential moral ideas."

For men of action and men of thought alike, the most feared casualty of the "disenchantment" was expected to be the moral backbone holding together the assembly of humans. Moral bonds and obligations were secure among the people eager to earn spiritual salvation through lives filled with good deeds, compassion, and charity; and such redemptive concerns seemed to be the ethics' only security thus far and the only one morality could count on in the future. Also the line drawn between good and evil stayed firmly in place and provoked few doubts as long as it were sanctified rather than subjected to the judgments of reason, argued about, and "proved." Divine sanction made all other forms of vindication redundant. Would the separation of good from evil survive the withdrawal of Divine *imprimatur*? And first and foremost: in the name of what would men and women prefer doing good rather than evil?

Durkheim's ingenious idea to deify society meant under the circumstances killing with one stone the two most odious and sinister birds of prey threatening the security of human possessions.

Deification of society had been first disguised as socialization of God. Secularization, separation of the Church from the State, and the spread of atheistic skepticism did not portend after all an upheaval, let alone the catastrophe the guardians and preachers of morality feared. From the start and through the entire human history "God" was but a fanciful representation of the will of society; it concealed, rather than revealed, the true source and the permanent foundations of morality. Morality and the society whose will morality condensed into the norms of human interaction did not need such cover; now, thanks to the spectacular progress of scientific reason, they needed it less than at any other time. "Men did not begin by imagining gods . . . They began by linking themselves to the things which they made use of, or which they suffered from, in the same way as they linked each of these to the other – without reflection, without the least kind of speculation. The theory only came later, in order to explain and make intelligible to these rudimentary minds the modes of behavior which had thus been formed" (Durkheim [1887] 1971: 219–20). Our nineteenth-century minds being anything but "rudimentary," we can afford a better comprehension of the origins and the grounds of "social sentiments" – such as "bind me to the social entity as a whole." I may pierce through the flights of fantasy and realize that when I act under the influence of such sentiments "I am simply part of a whole, whose actions I follow, and whose influence I am subject to. This is why the latter alone can give rise to the idea of obligation." "In other words, it is inter-social factors which have given birth to the religious sentiment." To cut the long story short: what the new scientific era brought in its wake was not so much the destruction of the grounds on which morality was based all along as taking off the lid of illusory images that hid them for millennia. It is not "social facts" that changed, but our awareness of them, the clarity of our vision, and our ability to accept what that clarified vision reveals.

No major catastrophe, then; no need to worry on that account. The question remained, though, would the society pulled out of its divine armor be still able to draw and guard the boundary between good and evil? Would its verdicts be obeyed? And on what ground, if any, could society demand such obedience in its own name, to start with? It would and it could, if it itself managed to be "like God." That is, as irresistible, trusted to stay firmly by its verdicts, capable of passing the last judgment(s), and loftily remote from the space to which human daily bustle is confined. "This voice which speaks to us in such an imperative tone, which enjoins us to change our own nature, can only derive from a being which is distinct from ourselves, and which also dominates us" (Durkheim [1900] 1971: 133). Above all, however, if society manages to replace God and His works in the crucial task of servicing that eternity which the incurably mortal individual life, however rich in fascinating moment it could be made, sorely missed once *Deus* turned *absconditus*.

Indeed. For Émile Durkheim ([1887] 1971: 93–4) it was an "undoubted fact" that we need to believe that our actions have consequences reaching far beyond the immediate, fleeting moment. We would not settle, he believed, for anything less than that. We would not be happy unless we could ascribe to our actions results of a duration longer and a scope wider than the acts themselves (as Hans Jonas was to express it many years later, unless days counted, we would see no sense in counting them or feel urge to). Acts that are likely to consume themselves fully in the episode of action would seem to us too insignificant to care about. Only actions that leave traces likely to outlive them (and us, the actors) seem to be worthy of our effort and so imbue our mundane life with the meaning it would otherwise lack. Care of the immortal soul met this requirement; following God's commandments served the purpose very well. Could society on its own match that remarkable achievement of God?

All people, Durkheim insisted ([1887] 1971: 93–4), "aspire to detach themselves from the present." That applies to us all – to the child and the "savage" as much as to the adult "civilized man," whether "of average culture" or "more developed." All those types differ solely in the span of that "future" toward which they look for meaning. "The perspective of nothingness is an intolerable burden to us." This opinion seems to be derived directly from Pascal (1968). Unlike Pascal however, but in tune with the hopes and intentions of the spirit of modernity in its "solid" phase, Durkheim believed that rather than frantically seeking momentary diversions and trying to drown our terror of transience in the sea of fleeting concerns and pleasures, we would tend to fight back the dread by tending to the future and "living in the future." Diversion, to Durkheim, is not a solution: "what value are our individual pleasures, which are so empty and short?"

To cut the long story short: we may all be, as Pascal observed, mortal and miserable – but, fortunately, society is infinitely more long-lived than any of us. For each of us, given the brevity of our earthly existence, society represents eternity. To the mortals, society (met in the shape of "the family, the city and the nation" (Durkheim [1887] 1971: 92)) offers bridges to immortality. We may trust society as a secure shelter for our life accomplishments; indeed, as a shelter that miraculously re-forges our life-pursuits into accomplishments. Investing in the perpetuation of society, we may actually participate in things eternal. Through society we can re-cast our individual transience as perpetual duration. Who may say in good conscience "in thee, my society, I lay my trust," may also reasonably hope that the verdict "unto dust shalt thou return" will be, in his case at least, suspended or quashed.

And so it must be recognized as our good fortune that the individual, ephemeral pleasures of the mortal are not the only option. "Societies are infinitely more long-lived than individuals." They, therefore, "permit us to taste satisfactions which are not merely ephemeral." Also, utterly *gratifying* satisfactions – unlike any other pleasures that would do pretty little, in fact nothing, to quell the gnawing pain of meaninglessness. And often heard complaints of high costs in terms of sacrificed individual liberty are, to say the least, grossly exaggerated; whatever sacrifice might be required, should be entered on the "credit," not the "debit" side. If the individual "submits to society," so Durkheim insists ([1924] 1971: 115), "this submission is the condition of his liberation. For man freedom consists in deliverance from the blind, unthinking physical forces; he achieves this by opposing against them the great and intelligent force of society, under which protection he shelters. By putting himself under the wing of society, he makes himself also, to a certain extent, dependent upon it. But this is a liberating dependence; there is no contradiction in this."

The "no contradiction" verdict may sound bland today and hardly convincing – but it would not be just to lay the blame at Durkheim's door. Durkheim was the poet-laureate at the court of confident rulers of confident society. His privilege, as George Steiner (1971) said of Voltaire or Matthew Arnold, was his ignorance – he did not know what was to follow. The "liberating dependence" was yet to show its other ugly, pugnacious, totalitarian face, and at the time Durkheim eulogized on the benignity of society's embrace he could do it with a clear conscience, having romantic dreams and bohemian practices for sole opponents. Society could still be trusted to promote morality, to guard the cause of goodness against evil. An unswerving loyalty to the great and intelligent force of society could be still viewed as the best guarantee of the happy result of the moral crusade. It was difficult, if at all possible, to discern the Big Brother's self-promotional propaganda in the casting of "blind, unthinking physical forces" as the only target and prospective casualty of the battle and the only adversary doomed to be vanquished and trammeled. Nothing as yet had disturbed the harmony between "coercive social facts" and theorizing the ennobling impact of the society that produced them.

Coercion was not, as it were, the sole experience that had given flesh to the image of a "great and intelligent force" dubbed "society," that lent credibility to the work of imagination and usefulness to the metaphor it deployed. There were other equally common experiences that supported the veracity of the model – and their weight grew and became more salient by the year as the nineteenth century drew to its close and the twentieth century started. They joined forces with the daily experience of being on the receiving side of steady conformist pressures in the job of sustaining the vision of a cohesive, coherent, omnipotent and "aware of what was it doing" totality at the top. True, the image of "society" drew its credibility from the experience of ubiquitous, and difficult to avoid or escape, constraints. But the image was also believable thanks to the well-grounded sense of collective foundations of individual security, brought about and nourished daily by collectively sustained and guaranteed welfare provisions, and above all to the sense of solidity and durability of social institutions, endowed with life-expectation long enough to comfortably accommodate individual "whole-life projects." All experiences seemed to lead in the same direction. Imagination they spurred and set in motion converged on the legislating/executive/juridical powers of the State integrating the population under its rule into a "society" – a "whole that is greater than the sum of its parts." And a hospitable, caring and sharing whole – a genuine "company," as the metaphorical use of the term "society" implied from the beginning.

The point, though, is that all three types of experience listed above (of normative pressure, protection against vagaries of individual fate, and longevity of forms and collective parameters of life) began to fade fast in the last decades of the century that just ended. They have been gradually, yet relentlessly elbowed out by other experiences that suggested less a "company" than, in Keith Tester's (1997: 6) description, a world that has "separated from the individuals," that "has experientially become increasingly like a seamless web of overlapping institutions with independent existence;" but, let me add, an existence of an undefined and rather unreliable life-expectation, all too often shorter than the individual life-longevity and always "until further notice." The "we will meet again" conviction, the impressions of continuity and consistency over time that suggested a thinking/feeling (remember Durkheim's *conscience collective*), acting, occasionally quarrelsome yet on the whole cooperative company with shared purpose, joint interests and common destiny, have all but shrunk or vanished. Short of that conviction and those impressions, the idea of "society" was fast becoming, to use Ulrich Beck's (1992) term, a "zombie category," and was increasingly used, to deploy Jacques Derrida's (1976) concept, "*sous rature*," leading the shadowy existence of a name surviving its referent or a signifier that outlived its past signified.

A century had passed since Durkheim's synthesis of life concerns and experience of his contemporaries when the Great Transformation Mark Two arrived: a departure that took Durkheim legatees and descendants, the trained sociologists as much as the sociologically un-initiated, by surprise, and mentally unprepared.

Just as the great majority in the sociological profession were busy polishing off the finer points of scientific management disguised as "behavioral science," just as the "corporatist state," "administered society," and "Fordist factory" had become the most common talks of the sociologists' town, and just as Jeremy Bentham's Panopticon, recycled by Michel Foucault (1995)into universal model of modern power was celebrated as the ultimate representation of human condition – the social realities that made all that credible (indeed, "self-evident") started to dissipate and flow away, on a fast accelerating pace, from the conceptual net the sociologists had woven.

The hub of the present-day Great Transformation Mark Two is the collapse of the grand-scale social engineering ambitions and the agencies willing and resourceful enough to make them flesh. Well before François Lyotard ([1984] 1988) could declare the demise of "grand meta-narratives," the decline of grand, all-embracing models of a pre-designed and closely monitored and administered "societal order" or "orderly society" took off in earnest. A truly watershed-like shift in social practices began, soon (though with the benefit of hindsight) captured in Peter Drucker's (1978) blunt verdict: no more salvation by society and Margaret Thatcher's blunter yet quip: there is no such thing as society.

A little more than a half century ago, James Burnham (1966) proclaimed the true power to consist in the management of people; the access to management to be the prime stake of the power game; and the desire to manage to be the principal motivational force of the power-greedy. He could be right then, but in the light of the current experience that triple proclamation has little if any evidence to enlist for support and so sounds increasingly hollow. Whether or not the trends Burnham declared to have discovered were on the rise operation in the era of "solid" modernity, they are now in retreat. These days, the most coveted privilege of the managers (perhaps another "zombie category" used "*sous rature*") is to cede the chores of management to others. Responsibility entailed in direct engagement, in meticulous regulation and continuous policing of conduct, has become a "hot potato" rather than a coveted prize. The art of managing increasingly resorts to the principle of "subsidiarity" and relies on the refusal to assume managerial responsibilities and on obliging the yesterday subjects of insidious and pernickety managerial control to seek and find, following the example of currencies in the thoroughly deregulated exchanges, "their own level."

Domination has found now lighter, less burdensome, less absorbing and constraining strategies than ubiquitous surveillance and day-by-day, hour-by-hour and minute-by-minute interference that called for large administrative offices and legions of supervisors. The Panopticon-like structures of domination and control are fast falling out of fashion. If they survive in places other than prisons and even seek and acquire in such places new technical excellence, it is mostly to serve the task of keeping people *out* rather than *in*, of barring the entry to the excluded or destined for exclusion – a task directly opposite to the function for which panoptical structures had originally been designed. Following the lead of "Fordist factories" with their assembly lines and hierarchies of supervisors, and the army barracks crowded with mass conscripts, the clumsy, unwieldy, trouble-prone and costly panoptical structures are being phased out and dismantled.

It is no longer the job of the managers to keep their subordinates in line and bring them back into line in case of deviation. It is, rather, the job of the would-be subordinates to demonstrate their fitness for whatever task may come their way. They had to convince the managers of being self-propelling enough to spare the future bosses all trouble with supervision. Neither of the two sides considers their mutual engagement likely (let alone bound) to last for long. Neither is prepared to look beyond the momentary benefits that the current engagement brings. Long-term commitments might have made the managerial task easier "in the long run," as their subordinates learned and habitualized the monotonous routines that the managers had designed for them. But such commitments also tied the managers' hands. Dependence was mutual, binding both sides and cramping movements of each in equal measure.

Now it is the duty – the must – of the would-be subordinates to catch the eye of their would-be bosses and arouse their desire to purchase the services which in the now bygone times the bosses and the supervisors that the bosses hired used to force them to provide. As the Sorbonne economist Daniel Cohen put it (1999: 48), "there are no more white collars who give orders to blue collars – there are only collars of mixed colours who confront the task they have to resolve." Not much is left of the orthodox managerial job description if it is up to the "managed" (yet another "zombie category" used "*sous rature*") to prove their mettle and make their prospective employers believe that they would not regret taking the risk. We may say that the employees have been, as a result, "empowered" – but that empowerment manifests itself mostly in picking up the responsibility that the managers willingly, and joyously, shed: the responsibility for being relevant and profitable to the company. To quote Cohen again (1999: 56): "it is no more the company which supervises its employees. It is now the turn of the employees to demonstrate [their usefulness] to the company."

This is a mixed blessing. It prompted Robert Castel (1990) to comment that the new independence turns into a new vulnerability, while an apparent equality of power rebounds as uncertainty; whereas Jean-Paul Fitoussi and Pierre Rosanvallon (1996: 32–3) write of the endemic ambivalence of the new power relationship. On the one hand, the autonomy of individuals has grown spectacularly together with their rights; on the other, the experience of insecurity has deepened, as each individual is charged with responsibility for his/her future and is bound to "insert in life a meaning no more organised beforehand by anything outside."

The instability and short life-span of the external frame in which successive life-filling projects are inscribed results, to use Richard Sennett's term (1998: 43, 31, 25), in the experience of "disjointed time" which in turn threatens "the ability of people to form their characters into sustained narratives." The old-fashioned Fordist-factory style routine can demean, as Sennett points out, "but it can also compose a life." Not so the fleeting, admittedly short-term forms of association and engagement that have come to replace the long-term connections and obligations. As one of Sennett's interviewees confined, "You can't imagine how stupid I feel when I talk to my kids about commitment. It's an abstract virtue to them; they don't see it anywhere."

Indeed, the present-day departures are an ambiguous affair. One would be right to welcome them as the further, perhaps even ultimate triumph of individual self-assertion which modernity promised yet in its "solid" phase offered sparingly, in quantities far too small to benefit a great majority of modern men and women; instead, it turned out in huge volumes the obedient and cowardly, dull and routine conformity of the "other-directed." One would be also right, however, to agree with Luc Boltanski and Eve Chiapello (1999: 143ff.) that the same departures portend the end of security once associated with status, hierarchy, bureaucracy, fixed career tracks, and legally or customarily assured tenure. The void left by reliable long-term frames for life planning has been filled by the fast and accelerating succession of episodic projects, each one promising at best a slightly enhanced chance of being admitted to another, as short lived but in addition unpredictable, episodic project. All projects nowadays tend to be blatantly short term and until-further-notice, and so are the episodes into which they split individual life. The profusion, possibly excess, and growing variety of projects available for choice are to deputize for the missing certainty about the rules guiding identity-building. It is not easy however under the circumstances to trust that the sequence of initiated and quickly abandoned episodes would eventually compose a totality of life "greater than the sum of its parts . . ."

Boltanski and Chiapello (1999) suggest that it is a shifting allegiance to an *a priori* indefinable multitude of "projects" that replaces normative regulation as the principal vehicle of the individual integration into the social totality, whatever "integration" may mean under present conditions. Integration through a succession of short-term projects needs little, or no control from the top. No one needs to force the runners to keep running. Regarding the fitness to stay in the race, the burden of proof has shifted decisively to the runners themselves and to all those who would wish to join in the race. It could be argued that in terms of costs and effects or "value for money" no other form of social control has been more effective than the use of the specter of uncertainty and insecurity hovering over the heads of the controlled. As Ralph Waldo Emerson observed a long time ago – in skating over thin ice our safety is in our speed.

Today's "new and improved" power relations follow the pattern of a commodity market that puts allurement and seduction in the place once occupied by normative regulation. Public Relations has replaced command, while creation of new needs (more exactly, sustaining the desire and spurring the wishes) took over from surveillance and policing. True, the orthodox and time-tested techniques of surveillance-and-punishment-assisted integration continue to be deployed in keeping at a safe distance or in secure confinement and altogether out of mischief the "underclass" of the flawed consumers, of the publicity-deaf and seduction-blind or too poor to respond properly (that is, in market-rational fashion) to any, however insidious temptation and however sophisticated blandishment. To most of us, however, the new softer and aesthetically polished techniques of domination and discipline-eliciting feel as a huge stride forward; the "domination bit" turns all but invisible, neither obtrusive nor arousing anxiety. They chime well with life reorganized as a succession of short-term projects and the chase of new sensations, ever more exciting *Erlebnisse*. They feel, even if counter-factually, as a radical extension of the realm of individual freedom and a genuine chance of rationalizing one's otherwise risk-prone choices. As Ulrich Beck pithily summarized that new syndrome: "how one lives becomes a *biographical solution of systemic contradictions*" (1992: 137). Never mind that such solutions have not been found. The sheer impossibility of finding them is the best warrant of the continuity of the search.

The new techniques of power, favoring frequent rewriting of the game rules and changing of stakes too fast for any of the ends–means patterns to become routine, promotes as well the inconsequentiality of choices: no choice should limit the range of future choices, cut down the number of options, "mortgage the future." Fitting the choices, and in an orderly sequence, into a "whole life" project, still a couple of generations ago seen as a *conditio sine qua non* of sensible life, is under the new circumstances feared and resented. As an eighteen-year-old recently summarized her and her generation's sentiments "I don't want to look back on my life and see that I went into a job because it was safe and stayed there forever" (quoted by Burkeman 2001).

No wonder conformity to standards and the interest in trajectories extending far into the future, mapped in advance and leading to distant goals, have lost much of their past luster. Living in a poorly articulated "system" deprived of "headquarters" with a fixed and permanent address, one tends to receive diffuse and confusing, contradictory and hotly contested signals that do not add up into a cohesive "social fact" that one needs to obey or in which one would wish to invest one's trust. Flexible identity, constant readiness to change direction at short notice, avoiding commitments of the "till death do us part" kind appear to offer a life strategy much less risky than the conformity to once chosen tough-and-ready standards and staunch loyalty to the selected ways and means.

These are indeed seminal departures. Social reality is lived no more as it used to be experienced and perceived at the time when Durkheim set about unpacking the mysterious ways of the "society" hiding behind the individual life itineraries; and not as it used to be lived for a while later, when George Orwell (1949) and Aldous Huxley (1932) penned down the inventories of the nightmares of their time – the first of the totalitarian state bare-faced, and the second of the totalitarianism masquerading as universal duty of pre-fabricated and strictly rationed happiness; and not even as it appeared later yet to Hannah Arendt (1968) who spied out in modern society an endemic totalitarian inclination or Michel Foucault (1995) who found in Bentham's Panopticon the key to the clockwork of modern social reality. Life is not what it used to be for its users in Durkheim's, now largely bygone, times. The context in which life is lived, and so the meaning of a reasonable life-strategy, have radically changed. It could not but affect the plausibility, and cognitive usefulness, of Durkheim's grand vision.

Rather than as the master-designer and the chief umpire of the life-game, society appears to our contemporaries as one of the players. Like other players, it keeps its cards close to the chest, excels in the mischief of taking the other players by surprise and does not mind resorting to tricks and bluffing, using loaded dice or drawing cards from the sleeve. It "stands to reason" that "playing the system" is a more sensible life strategy than obeying it; but then it is far from clear, anyway, what exactly are the system's precepts to be obeyed. "Society" has lost the status of the ultimate ethical authority it might have had at the time when Durkheim embarked on the search for sources of morality. And it does not strike the observer any more as the lever that could lift the individuals, collectively, out of their individually suffered miseries. It no more seems evident, therefore, that capturing its control towers (if such could be found, that is) is worth the effort and the sacrifice required.

Michel Foucault anticipated this sort of development in the course of lectures read at the *Collège de France* in 1976 – or at least it may be argued that he did. Throughout that course, he struggled to re-arrange the notion of politics and government, personal and collective alike, around the metaphor of *pilotage*, aimed to capture the life-long strivings of the self; a series of, intermittently, "detachments from itself" and "returns to itself." "Piloting" is meant to grasp the logic of "*souci de soi*" self-attention, self-concern, self-care. "*Se soucier de soi,*" Foucault implies, does not consist, nor is it aimed at, the acquisition of a particular status inside society. Instead, it implies the "subject in its totality, the whole being": it is "coextensive with life as such."

It is easy to see that the metaphor of "piloting" appeals to altogether different associations than the metaphor of "society" (in Durkheim's rendering) with its confident norm-setting, tough and irresistible "social facts" and sole copyrights of ethical codes. The metaphor of "piloting" invokes the choice of destination, mastery of the technique of navigation, awareness of the risks involved in the journey, and uncertainty of the arrival. It also evokes readiness to change the course if conditions require or a more attractive destination looms, so that time and place of arrival cannot be fixed once for all at the point of departure. Finally, it emphasizes the travel rather than arrival; movement rather than rest.

It seems that social realities are catching up with Foucault's (some may say prophetic) suggestion.

Life-challenges, life-tasks, and life-pursuits tend to assume today colors and shapes quite different from those they bore in Durkheim's time or, for this matter, still a half-century ago. They used to be, essentially, outcomes of and responses to the order-design-and-order-built concerns and actions of societal power. They are today, essentially, outcomes of and responses to the fading, phasing-out, and demise of such concerns. They could be properly comprehended only if put and held in the context in which they have been born and to which they belong: that of the retreat of agencies striving to substitute pre-designed and ready-made routines for individual choices; and of the steady pressure to adopt biographical solutions (or private survival kits) for the problems arising out of unpredictability, incoherence, and capriciousness of the socially constructed conditions of action. To those striving as best they can to find or invent what find or invent they can *not*, sociology informed by the managerial reason, sociology narrating the omnipotence of "social facts" and haplessness of those who refuse to recognize their intractable authority, is of little use. The world lived by men and women of the early twenty-first century bears little resemblance to the world narrated by that sociology.

For what needs to be done in order to re-tie the broken links between sociological work and the social agenda, we may take a hint from Franz Rosenzweig (1961: 200, 199; 1999: 59), one of the more insightful yet less read modern thinkers, who suggested just a few years after the completion of Durkheim's oeuvre a sharp distinction between the "logical" and "grammatical" modes of thinking, both entrenched in the practice of intellectual work despite the difference of their roots and destinations.

The first, "logical" mode "means thinking for no one else and speaking to no one else" (Rosenzweig 1961: 200, 199; 1999: 59] – and so enjoys a good deal of independence from the mind of those it thinks about. This mode, let me comment, is a highly tempting option, since it offers the welcome shelter from the confusion and uncertainty with which the messy life of *hoi polloi* is fraught, and since it promises immunity against the risks and anxiety that all engagement with such a life is bound to produce. In addition, the high and mighty of this world are likely to lend a sympathetic ear to the kind of thought that suggests the orderliness of the world and the possibility of yet more order, thrives on the *hoi polloi* silence, and makes that silence yet more unlikely to be broken. This "logical" kind of thinking has been in Rosenzweig's view a dominant feature of the extant academic philosophy, a symptom of a terminal disease he called "apoplexia philosophica" and was considered the secret of the astonishing longevity of academic philosophy but also of its almost total irrelevance to life. Let me comment again that much of the orthodox academic sociology, particularly in its current "zombie" phase, can be with little distortion filed up in the same category.

The second, the "grammatical" thinking, is described by Rosenzweig as having a structure akin to speech. "Speaking," he says (1961: 200, 199; 1999: 59), "means speaking to some one and thinking for some one. And this some one is always a quite definite one, and he has not merely ears . . . but also a mouth." Its addressee having a mouth in addition to ears make thinking speech-like and has far reaching consequences for its course and its results. Speaking, as Rosenzweig points out, "is bound by time and nourished by time and it neither can nor wants to abandon this element. It does not know in advance just where it will end. It takes its cues from others. In fact, it lives by virtue of another's life, whether this other is the one who listens to a story, answers in the course of a dialogue, or joins in a chorus." "In actual conversation," Rosenzweig sums up (1961: 200, 199; 1999: 59), "something happens."

Sociological work that wants to be a conversation must be prepared that something happens in its course and admit that one cannot tell nor know in advance what that something will be. Such sociological work must be an open invitation for others to join in, a promise to listen, and an oath to listen not in order to censure, denigrate, and dismiss what has been heard. Such sociological work cannot ascribe to "social facts" an authority greater than the sum of problems confronted by the men and women striving to live in company. It must take these problems seriously, and take seriously the way its partners-in-dialogue talk about them; sufficiently seriously to put them in the focus of attention and make it the stuff of which its own narratives are woven. It needs to admit that "society" is the liminal, though never fully reached and never finished product of that dialogue. In conversation, authority of none of the partners is assured in advance; that authority is the outcome, not the starting point of the conversation. The seat at the round table for sociology is, like for the rest of the participants, a privilege that needs to be won, not a birthright.

REFERENCES

Anderson, Benedict. 1983. *Imagined Communities: Reflections on the Origin and Spread of Nationalism*. London: Verso.

Arendt, Hannah. 1968. *The Origins of Totalitarianism*. New York: Harcourt, Brace, Jovanovich.

Beck, Ulrich 1992. *Risk Society: Towards a New Modernity*. Translated by Mark Ritter. London: Sage.

Boltanski, Luc and Eve Chiapello. 1999. *Le Nouvel Ésprit du capitalisme*. Paris: Gallimard.

Burkeman, Oliver. 2001. "My dad is a living deterrent..." The *Guardian*, 21 March.

Burnham, James. 1966. *The Managerial Revolution*. Bloomington, IN: Indiana University Press.

Castel, Robert. 1990. "Le Roman de désaffiliation." *Le Débat*, September–October: xx–xxx.

Cohen, Daniel. 1999. *Nos temps modernes*. Paris: Flammarion.

de Tocqueville, Alexis. [1835] 1969. *Democracy in America*. Translated by George Lawrence. New York: Doubleday.

Derrida, Jacques. 1976. *Of Grammatology*. Translated by Gayatri Chakravorty Spivak. Baltimore, MD: John Hopkins University Press.

Drucker, Peter F. 1978. *Adventures of a Bystander*. New York: Harper and Row.

Durkheim, Émile. [1925] 1971. "Education morale" in *Émile Durkheim: Selected Writings*. Translated by Anthony Giddens. London: Nelson.

[1924] 1971. "Sociologie et Philosophie" in *Émile Durkheim: Selected Writings*. Translated by Anthony Giddens. London: Nelson.

[1900] 1971. "Deux lois de l'evolution penale" in *Émile Durkheim: Selected Writings*. Translated by Anthony Giddens. London: Nelson.

[1895]. *Les Règles de la methode sociologique*.

[1887] 1971. Review of Guyau's "L'Irreligion de l'avenir" in *Émile Durkheim: Selected Writings*. Translated by Anthony Giddens. London: Nelson.

[1887] 1971. "La Science Positive de la morale en Allemagne" in *Émile Durkheim: Selected Writings*. Translated by Anthony Giddens. London: Nelson.

Fitoussi, Jean-Paul and Pierre Rosanvallon. 1996. *Les Nouvel Age des inégalités*. Paris: Seuil.

Foucault, Michel. 1995. *Discipline & Punish*. New York: Vintage Books.

Giddens, Anthony. 2000. *Runaway World: How Globalization Is Reshaping our Lives*. New York: Routledge.

(ed.) 1971. *Émile Durkheim: Selected Writings*. London: Nelson.

Huxley, Aldous. 1932. *Brave New World*. New York: HarperCollins.

Lyotard, François. [1984] 1988. *The Postmodern Condition: A Report on Knowledge*. Translated by Geoff Bennington and Brian Massumi. Minneapolis, MN: University of Minnesota Press.

Orwell, George. 1949. *Nineteen Eighty-Four, a Novel*. London: Secker & Warburg.

Parsons, Talcott. [1937] 1968. *The Structure of Social Action*. 2 vols. New York: Free Press.

Pascal, Blaise. [1669] 1968. *Pensées*. Translated by A. J. Krailsheimer. New York: Penguin.

Rosenzweig, Franz. 1999. *Understanding the Sick and the Healthy*. Translated by Nahum Glatzer. Cambridge, MA: Harvard University Press.

1961. "The New Thinking" in *Franz Rosenzweig: His Life and Thought*, presented by Nahum Glatzer. New York: Schocken.

Sennett, Richard. 1998. *The Corrosion of Character*. New York: W. W. Norton.

Steiner, George. 1971. *In Bluebeard's Castle: Some Notes Towards the Redefinition of Culture*. New Haven, CT: Yale University Press.

Tester, Keith. 1997. *Moral Culture*. London: Sage.

382

15

MARK S. CLADIS

Beyond solidarity? Durkheim and twenty-first century democracy in a global age

When the World Trade Center collapsed, something like social solidarity radiated from its ashes. From New York, Washington, DC and Pennsylvania, a sense of common grief and shared bewilderment spread outward, engulfing the entire nation. The intensity of the anguish and the solidarity were perhaps strongest in New York City. Still, they were palpable throughout the nation – in small towns and large, in the countryside and urban centers. The attack struck three buildings in two cities, yet it was experienced as an assault on all. Just when we, US intellectuals, were most tempted to believe that we live in a nation of disparate individuals or disconnected groups, we were reminded, by terrible means, that we do indeed possess something like social solidarity. Evidently, it was there all along. We just did not have the eyes or occasion to see it.

Within weeks of September 11, the shared grief, outrage, and sense of unity also admitted diverse political commentary, national self-critique, and assorted views on why we were targeted and how we should respond. Does the rise of varied voices mark the eclipse of a short-lived solidarity? What difference might it make if we were to recognize solidarity in times of peace and not only in crisis or war? What role does and can solidarity play among us – citizens of liberal democracies?[1]

In this chapter, I consider the nature and place of solidarity in the work of Émile Durkheim, and what lessons that work may hold for pluralistic, democratic societies at the outset of the twenty-first century. In particular, I explore Durkheim's notion of solidarity in his work on moral individualism, democracy, pluralism, moral education, economic justice, and globalization. In the concluding section, I ask what role "otherness" plays in Durkheim's thought, by comparing his work to that of Giles Gunn.

I look to Durkheim because I believe he can help us think critically about the obstacles we face in achieving a genuinely multiracial, multicultural democracy. Such an achievement, I believe, is the hope – but thus far, not the reality – of the democratic experiment that has been taking place in the

USA. It is a worthy challenge to endeavor to fashion a democratic republic in which individual rights are protected and the public life is inclusive, lively, and just. We will often fail. Still, the endeavor is the way forward.

Solidarity, I will soon argue, need not be construed as sameness or uniformity. Rather, it can be akin to what Cornel West has expressed using the metaphor of the jazz band. "The interplay of individuality and unanimity," West declares, "is not one of uniformity and unanimity imposed from above but rather of conflict among diverse groupings that reach a dynamic consensus subject to questioning and criticism. As with a soloist in a jazz . . . band, individuality is promoted in order to sustain and increase the *creative* tension with the group – a tension that yields higher levels of performance to achieve the aim of the collective project" (West 2001: 150–1). Honoring both individual rights and common projects – these twin poles, with all the tension between them – mark Durkheim's work, his vision, his challenge. And this may capture the challenge of democracy in the twenty-first century. My fundamental question of Durkheim, then, is this: How can he assist us in formulating a model of solidarity that includes and supports diversity? Also, how can his work help us envision paradigms of cooperation on such shared projects as eradicating racism, protecting the environment, and achieving social justice?

Durkheim and solidarity

We associate the concept of social solidarity with the life and thought of Durkheim, and for good reason. He was committed to it, both theoretically and practically. In *The Elementary Forms of Religious Life* ([1912] 2001) (hereafter *Elementary Forms)*, arguably his most important book, Durkheim set himself the task of discovering an enduring source of human social identity and fellowship – *solidarité*. Durkheim treated religion, broadly understood, as dynamic social ideals, beliefs, and practices that shape a shared perception of, and therefore life in, a society's moral universe. One finds religion wherever public, normative concepts, symbols, or rites are employed. Religion, in this view, is variously found in modern and in (what we once called) postmodern societies. The upshot of this, morally and epistemologically, is that human life is, in a significant sense, life together. This is Durkheim's response, and challenge, to a long tradition of Cartesian and Spencerian individualistic thought.

Elementary Forms was Durkheim's last book, but from the start of his career the task of solidarity can be found: the task of understanding its various sources and forms, and of evaluating its appropriate shape or type for a society in light of sociohistorical circumstances. Durkheim's own sociohistorical circumstances account, in part, for his life-long interest in and commitment to solidarity. As a French Jew raised in the warmth and security of a tightly-knit Jewish community, David Émile Durkheim was early on exposed to the complex, often conflicting values of the Third Republic – liberty, equality, and solidarity. It is not much of an exaggeration to say that every major subject Durkheim investigated became for him a lens through which to examine the nature and condition of solidarity in contemporary democratic society.

In *Elementary Forms*, for example, Durkheim claimed that totemism among the aborigines of Australia was not in itself his principal object of study. Rather, it was an avenue "to yield an understanding of the religious nature of man, by showing us an essential and permanent aspect of humanity" (Durkheim 2001: 3). This "permanent aspect of humanity," as it turns out, is the human need and capacity to relate socially. Another example: Durkheim's sophisticated epistemology, or what is sometimes known as his sociology of knowledge, provided a way for philosophers and others to let go of the idea that reason is a transcendent, ahistorical faculty, yet without having to jettison all notions of objectivity. In Durkheim's mind, his work on epistemology – socializing the idealists and the empiricists – was especially significant insofar as it contributed to the view that there can be no radically private human existence. To exist in a world is to understand that world, and understanding is comprised of shared, collective representations. This is not only an empirical description of human cognition, but is also a normative position, for it challenges the atomistic assumptions of a methodological individualism that Durkheim found morally unacceptable. Epistemology, then, permitted Durkheim to feature once again the profoundly social nature of humankind.

Even Durkheim's investigations of modern individualism became a vehicle to explore social solidarity. Durkheim made the surprising claim that there is a form of contemporary individualism, what he called moral individualism, that emerges from the solidarity that marks North Atlantic democracies. Think of moral individualism as a cluster of dynamic beliefs and practices, symbols, and institutions that support the dignity and rights of the individual. This modern cult of the individual has all the attributes of traditional religion. It possesses robust, sacred symbols that express collective sentiments; it reaffirms and protects itself by means of both positive and negative rites, for example, public celebrations of defenders of individual rights or the prosecution of those who would violate such rights. Commitment to the rights and dignity of the individual is a principal thread, Durkheim argued, in the moral fabric that weaves together the diverse citizens of a modern democracy. It provides the shared moral identity of "we, the people." Moral individualism – as opposed to atomistic or utilitarian individualism – became for Durkheim an answer to the question: what can provide the basis of a common good in the democratic societies of his day?

The important task before me is to consider whether Durkheim's work on solidarity is still germane for reflection on present-day democratic societies – especially democracies marked by pluralism, multiculturalism, and globalization. My challenge is not to defend Durkheim's work – I am not dedicated to him – but rather to investigate his relevance for what I am dedicated to: robust, just, and inclusive democracies in an age of diversity and globalization.

Solidarity on trial

Solidarity is a concept widely held in suspicion today and often for good reason. On epistemological grounds, many doubt that there is a shared, universal human nature that could provide common ground among diverse human communities and individuals. And when solidarity does seem to emerge, it is often interpreted as either a contingent confluence of individuals with a shared cultural or ethnic inheritance, or an enforced uniformity that merely gives the impression of solidarity. In this latter view, solidarity is a form of imperialism or colonialism. Alien norms, practices, and symbols of identity are imposed by the powerful on those lacking power. Solidarity turns out to be hegemony. Debates in the USA over multiculturalism and what have come to be known as "cultural wars" have focused our attention on many insidious practices carried out in the name of solidarity. Yet these debates also have had the unintended consequence of leading us to think, once again, about the social significance and merit of solidarity. As we as a society wrestled with the importance of respecting "difference," we also asked about the shared context in which these debates took place. Who is the "we" engaged in these contests and disputes? Focusing on difference led to discussions about the possibility of common ground or solidarity. Moreover, as the language of human rights increasingly became something of a shared – though vague – global vocabulary, many social activists began speaking of a global or world solidarity centered on such goals as eradicating torture, hunger, racism, and the exploitation of women and children. Solidarity, today, is a contested concept. But this much is clear: solidarity is not simply a quaint term unworthy of our consideration. For better for worse, it remains a powerful notion. To think otherwise borders on self-deception.

Recent debates over the role and significance of solidarity are not without precedent. When Durkheim championed the need for solidarity and strategies to enhance it, he was addressing the entire French republic, but especially his fellow intellectuals, socialists, and other progressive peers. Solidarity, in Durkheim's vision, was to embrace all citizens, but it was based on a particular – far from neutral – set of goals and ideals: the protection and extension of human rights; an economy accountable to human welfare (as opposed to the maximization of profit); the freedom of critical inquiry; and a secular state that respected yet was not based on religion. Not long after Durkheim's death, however, his work was placed in a conservative canon of sociologists who, motivated by a nostalgic sense of by-gone days of community and uniformity, advanced solidarity for the sake of social control and order. It was Durkheim's commitment to solidarity, along with his historicist approach, that placed him in this conservative legacy.

This regrettable placement continues to distort our view of Durkheim's fundamental commitments and goals. Durkheim investigated the webs and patterns of social order for the sake of establishing social justice. Many have attributed conservatism to Durkheim because of his commitment to viewing humans and their moral principles and practices as ineluctably rooted in their social milieus. The logic here goes something like this: social theorists who begin and end with human situatedness can never rise above present or past social ideals, customs, and institutions. These allegedly conservative theorists are bound to the stagnant status quo. Yet Durkheim's sensitivity to the historical, far from tying him to a status quo, exposed him to social change and diversity. That exposure helped him to envision progressive social change, and also to recognize the fragility of many cultural and legal accomplishments. The rights and dignity of the individual, for Durkheim, are important pieces of moral, social progress. They are not, however, immutable. They are subject to immoral threats as well as to moral amelioration. Durkheim maintained that moral progress requires a social solidarity that is willing to wrestle with social problems and achieve social change. Human rights, for example, cannot be realized by the law or the courts alone, but rather they require shared social beliefs and practices that support the legal system.

Today, we still have progressive thinkers and activists who are committed to the work of achieving a dynamic, democratic solidarity that supports individual liberties and social justice. Such leaders as Ralph Nader, Cornel West, and Ann Richards encourage individuals and groups to develop their own, distinctive voices as they contribute to wider, on-going public dialogues. These public conversations acknowledge that, in spite of our differences, we do share a common history and future. The history of slavery in America, for example, is not a black issue. It is an American issue. Slavery is a basic, shared fact of American history that continues to inform our present. Due to shared sociohistorical events (and even a common grief that may spring from them) and shared social ideals (and a common hope that issues from them), some persist in thinking that we can achieve something like a public arena in which we honor diversity and discover commonality. This resolve need not be based on belief in a transcendent, universal morality. Rather, it can spring from the hope that – as sociohistorical creatures who by fate share common destinies and who by necessity need to cooperate – we can together create a flourishing social order.

It is not at all clear, then, that multiculturalism or the "fact of plural-ism" – to use John Rawls' characterization of contemporary, North Atlantic democratic societies – renders solidarity a quaint or inappropriate notion for us today. The fact of diversity need not entail moving beyond solidarity, as if solidarity and diversity were entirely oppositional, or as if "justice for all" could be accomplished by leaving solidarity behind. Of the three basic ideals of a democratic republic – liberty, equality, and solidarity – can we hazard to neglect the last of these? Can we pursue liberty and equality – which require much from us in the way of social resolve, collective wisdom, and financial commitment – without a tremendous sense of shared purpose? John Dewey, Martin Luther King, Jr., and Durkheim all agree that as social diversity and the need for social justice increase, so does the need for a robust yet appropriate form of solidarity.

The often assumed incompatibility, then, between social diversity and social solidarity deserves to be examined. What is solidarity? What does it mean to live in a shared social and geographic setting? What are the basic requirements of social life? What are the social implications of our shared need for shelter, nutritious food, clean air and water, work, repose, and safety? What kind of social cooperation is needed for citizens to move about unencumbered, to have access to public transportation, to drive or walk in peace? What are the requirements for achieving such collective goals as economic justice, environmental practices, and the eradication of discrimi-nation based on race, gender, or sexual orientation? Why should pluralism or globalization negate the need for cooperation in achieving basic, daily, shared human goods and future collective aims?

Durkheim affirmed that solidarity, in some form, is all but inevitable for any society, "if nothing abnormal occurs to disturb the natural course of things" (1992: 24). This claim is, of course, elementary. It says nothing about the various shapes or forms of solidarity – thick or thin, segmental or inclu-sive – or about the fragility or sturdiness of these varieties. Yet Durkheim's basic claim serves to remind us of what is dangerous to forget: we already have some form of solidarity. To think otherwise is to be absentminded and to accept an illusion. It is analogous to denying that in liberal democracies there are hierarchies and authoritative powers. It is unsafe to overlook what is there. This is how individuals and societies stumble.

We are a society of different yet also interdependent individuals and groups who share legal rights and moral obligations. We share a common history – regardless of when our diverse individual histories were played out on US soil – that informs a common future. Geographically, we belong to a well-defined territory. Symbolically, we share (albeit to different degrees) such powerful symbols as the American flag and the Bill of Rights; the image of John F. Kennedy, Sojourner Truth, and Martin Luther King, Jr.; the Vietnam Veterans Memorial, the Women's Rights National Historic Park, and the Crazy Horse Memorial. The rights and protection of the individual are a central tenet of a widely shared creed, as are the rights and protection of the nation in the international arena. This latter sign of solidarity is often overlooked by the academy, but not by most citizens. As Durkheim noted, the chief function of the military – national self-defense – implies that there is a national collectivity to be defended (1992: 70). When we ask fellow citizens to risk death in military service, we tacitly affirm that there is sufficient national solidarity such that these potential sacrifices are made on behalf of society as a whole by fellow members, and not simply made by this or that individual for this or that family or group. This accounts, in part, for our moral indignation when the military is used illegitimately for unwarranted political goals (such as in Vietnam or in Iraq) as opposed to being used for acceptable national or international goals of security and protection (such as in the case of the Second World War or in Bosnia).

When Durkheim wrote, "we do not belong to ourselves entirely: we owe something of ourselves to others," (1992: 122) he was attempting to remind us of a wide array of background beliefs, symbols, and practices that underlie our most basic institutions and daily activities. Although there are many human goods and activities that we seemingly pursue individually, most of these pursuits indirectly rely on a tapestry of interwoven assumptions, beliefs, and interdependencies that both spring from and constitute social solidarity. The question for us, then, is not: "Solidarity – should we have it?" The question is: "What kind of solidarity do we already have, and what kind should we have?" My own view is that an appropriate form of solidarity for contemporary democracies must not only tolerate diversity in the private space, but celebrate diversity as a precious public resource. I am convinced that the USA will not truly come to understand itself as a nation until it encounters and celebrates its rich social pluralism and diversity. Who we are as a people will only be found at the intersection of our distinctive backgrounds and beliefs, hopes and fears. The solidarity and identity of the

USA can, of course, be investigated and discovered from an empirical point of view. From a normative point of view, however, it still needs to be achieved. That achievement, I believe, can only be made at the plural crossroads of our nation, where we both affirm and risk our own personal identity for the sake of an enhanced sense of ourselves as private individuals and as members of a shared whole.

Moral individualism, pluralism, and education

In 1835 Tocqueville wrote, "individualism is a word recently coined to express a new idea. Our fathers only knew about egoism" (1969: 506). This provocative claim about "a new idea" is not entirely correct (think of the celebration of "individualism" in Montaigne's *Essays* or Rousseau's *Reveries of the Solitary Walker*). Moreover, it was not the case that everyone in Tocqueville's age would have agreed that there are forms of individualism that are not synonymous with egoism. Even in Durkheim's age – and still today – some identified individualism with egoism. "Individualism is the great sickness of the present time . . . Each of us has confidence only in himself, sets himself up as the sovereign judge of everything . . ." This quotation is not from MacIntyre's *After Virtue* but from Ferdinand Brunetière's "After the Trial," which appeared in the *Revue des deux mondes* (Brunetière 1898: 445). Brunetière, a Catholic literary historian and critic, denounced individualism and claimed that it was debilitating France's moral foundation and solidarity. It is the "intellectuals" who carry this disease, and if they are not checked, he warned, traditional virtue and values will wither as moral relativism and hedonism spread. In the same year Durkheim published a response entitled "Individualism and the Intellectuals." In it Durkheim discussed "the argument, always refuted and always renewed," that "intellectual and moral anarchy would be the inevitable result of liberalism" (1973: 49). Some varieties of liberalism, Durkheim conceded, are egoistic and threaten the common good of societies by encouraging the individual to become excessively consumerist and preoccupied with narrow self-interest. But there is a strand of liberalism, Durkheim argued, which is moral and social. This strand, I noted, Durkheim called moral individualism, and he claimed that "not only is [moral] individualism not anarchical, but it henceforth is the only system of beliefs which can ensure the moral unity of the country" (1973: 50). In liberal, democratic nations such as France, the people's character and their solidarity are promoted by the liberal practices and ideals of moral individualism.

This turns out to be a surprising and powerful defense of democratic liberalism. Durkheim did not appeal to universal principles derived from natural reason or from any other tap into an "objective," ahistorical moral reality. He situated his defense in history, specifically French history. France's modern, moral traditions, Durkheim argued, are largely constituted by liberal, pluralistic institutions and values that protect the rights and dignity of the individual. To neglect these traditions is to court moral anarchy. It is Brunetière then, the conservative who speaks of "solidarity above all" who, according to Durkheim, threatens the moral fabric of society.

This argument, like most of Durkheim's work, belongs to a distinctive French narrative, a narrative of struggle and accomplishment, of the Revolution and the Constitution. His arguments are not for all societies, even if they can be applied to many – certainly to our own. Mostly, however, his is an insider's argument: written for the French, by a Jewish Frenchman. Durkheim provided a distinctive reading of Rousseau and Kant, among others, attempting to locate them in a republican tradition that describes rights and duties as the result of a commitment to public, not only private, concerns. He worked to piece together his own account of his favorite varieties of liberalism (as well as offering complex criticisms of his least favorite forms of liberalism, for example, of what he called economic individualism and crass utilitarianism). This was no invention from scratch. A set of liberal, democratic traditions already existed. But Durkheim was well aware of competing liberal traditions, such as those of the classical economists and utilitarians, as well as competing solidarity traditions, such as those of the Royalists and the conservative Roman Catholics. Durkheim wanted to establish the authority of moral individualism by arguing that it, in fact, represented France's most morally progressive and legitimate traditions.

We can think of moral individualism as having two components. Moral individualism is characterized by (1) a set of social beliefs and practices that constitute a pervasive shared understanding which supports the rights and dignity of the individual; and (2) a plurality of social spheres that permits diversity and individual autonomy, and furnishes beliefs and practices which morally associate individuals occupying a particular sphere. The first component, briefly mentioned and then rejected in *The Division of Labor* (1893), was developed in the Dreyfusard article, "Individualism and the Intellectuals," after having been initially proposed in *Suicide* ([1897] 1951) the preceding year. The second component was explored in *The Division of Labor* and later enhanced in *Suicide* and especially in Durkheim's lectures published as *Professional Ethics and Civic Morals* ([1950] 1992) – lectures written around the same time as the Dreyfusard article.

A robust social defense of democratic liberalism requires both components. The first element ensures that a diverse citizenry cares for a common political community that is sustained by, among other things, beliefs pertaining to the sanctity of the individual. The second element ensures that as individuals pursue their rights, they reside within a multitude of relatively distinct and protected social spheres that provide shared meanings and identities. We can label this second component as Durkheim's understanding of moral pluralism and a plurality of morals, especially as described in *Professional Ethics and Civic Morals*. A plurality of morals refers to the diverse sets of goals and values, and the varying levels of homogeneity that characterize groups in the domestic, occupational, civic, and international spheres. Moral pluralism, in contrast, pertains to the relation between the beliefs and practices of the political community and the beliefs and practices of such associations or groups as churches and synagogues, ethnic organizations, and activist alliances. This can include associations that can be said to rest upon comprehensive religious, moral, or philosophical doctrines. The solidarity of the political community, in Durkheim's view, does not require broad agreement from these associations on every issue. Social solidarity, in other words, does not require social homogeneity. On some issues, however, such as the protection of diversity, widespread agreement is desirable. Moral pluralism, then, refers to a plurality of communities and associations that promote distinctive practices and beliefs, and yet also contribute to – or at least do not threaten – common public projects and goals.

Think of Durkheim's moral pluralism as standing in opposition to three models of society: society as (1) a group of disparate individuals; (2) a group of disparate, morally self-sustaining, homogeneous communities divorced from the larger political community; and (3) a single, national, homogeneous community. The moral pluralism that Durkheim envisioned captures the merits and avoids the limits of the three models. It sustains a multitude of diverse communities (model two), all sharing a common, albeit limited, set of obligations and goals (model three), including individual and group rights and liberties (model one). Durkheim would have agreed with progressive communitarians that human association is a social good that is necessary for well-being. With progressive liberals, however, he also would have agreed that no one community, including the political one, has a monopoly on virtue or the good life. Happiness and an ethical life are not contingent on participation in any single, privileged community, but are procurable in a variety of spheres and groups.

Nonetheless, moral pluralism, as Durkheim conceived it, does support the solidarity of a shared political community, a community that encompasses all others. This social realm aims for inclusion and open critical reflection. At times the most salient thing that needs to be agreed on may be what needs to be discussed. We can agree on the need to debate such pressing issues as how to pursue economic justice and environmental safeguards, balanced budgets and social services, citizens' security and global peace. Potential agreement rests on the fact that diverse citizens share a common history and future, and often care about the problems and promises that are germane, not only to a particular community, but to the broader community in which all participate. No secondary group should attempt to block its members from taking part in this wider life of common pursuits.

One of the best – and most misunderstood – examples of Durkheim's capacity to connect social solidarity with pluralism and conflict is his work on moral education (1961; 1956). Its heterogeneous character, embracing critical thought and shared traditions, autonomy and community, human diversity and social solidarity, offers a nuanced description of and challenge to liberal, democratic institutions. Durkheim championed various perspectives of society's shared understanding as a means to cultivate students' dispositions for critical thinking. Critical thought and the stories a people tells about itself go hand in hand, in Durkheim's view, because social critics, faced with changing circumstances, draw deeply from their social inheritances as they forge new paths and criticize old ones.

Durkheim held that future citizens of democracies need to know about styles of belief and practices other than those of the family or local group. He emphasized the need to accustom students to the unfamiliar in order that they can appreciate otherness and to identify the stranger as a fellow human. The study of history and literature is especially helpful in developing democratic skills and virtues, according to Durkheim. Studying history, for example, enables students to have an appreciation for the rich complexity of social life, and to develop a critical understanding of their own society's place in history. The study of history promotes critical thinking because it both discloses to students their society's distinctive shared understandings and exposes them to unfamiliar ways of life. Accustoming students to the unfamiliar enables them to value diversity and "the richness of life," and to acquire novel ways to cope with suffering.

History, then, plays a critical role in moral education: "It is by learning to become familiar with other ideas, other customs, other manners, other political constitutions, other domestic organizations, other moralities and logics than those which he is used to that the student will gain a sense of the richness of life within the bounds of human nature. It is, therefore, only by history that we can give an account of the infinite diversity of the aspects which human nature can take on" (Durkheim 1938 vol. 2: 208–9). Awareness of such pluralism is an essential aspect of moral education, because it thwarts the desire to designate a parochial moral vision as universal and then impose it on all humanity. Literature also figured importantly in Durkheim's approach to moral education, and for many of the same reasons.

General and abstract talk about the practices and hopes of a people will not make a vivid impression on students. Thick descriptions are required, and literature can deliver these. The detail found in literature allows the student "to touch [the manners, ideas, and institutions of a people] with his own hands," to "see them alive" (Durkheim 1977: 332).

Moral education, then, in Durkheim's view, takes place at the junctures of the familiar and the unfamiliar, the past and the present. Schools are to foster in students the capacity to evaluate contemporary practices in light of alternatives found in foreign or past cultures, in new developments taking place within contemporary society, and in long-standing ideals that need to be more fully realized in social practices.

The state has an active role to play in education, Durkheim insisted, lest, for example, the majority should attempt systematically "to impose its ideas on the children of the minority" (1956: 81). Durkheim recognized that in a pluralistic society, there is a moral obligation to resist the imposition of homogeneity. However, in his typically dialectical fashion, he also argued that education should not be "completely abandoned to the arbitrariness of private individuals." Since education is crucial to the common life of a nation, the state "cannot be indifferent to it." This is not to say that the state "must necessarily monopolize instruction," only that it must ensure the equal distribution of this crucial social good, education, and prevent it from falling under the domination of any particular group or class. Distressed by what he perceived to be a disintegrating set of shared moral aims and by the injustices that accompany it, Durkheim focused on the need for educating future citizens in their progressive traditions of moral individualism and democratic morality.

Surely some will ask: Is there such a thing as a shared understanding – or common ideals – that can be critically analyzed and appropriated by educational institutions? What is in it? What is missing from it? Is there only one? If not, whose version of "it" is to be considered? In the USA, for example, some may ask: Is "the" shared understanding the same for African Americans and White Americans, Hispanics and Native Americans, men and women, hetero- and homosexuals, lower, upper, and middle classes? What shared moral understanding is to be imparted to our youth? There are no easy answers to these good questions. That, in fact, was one of Durkheim's responses. These are not problems to be "easily determined, once and for all"; they are difficulties to be discussed through continual debate and argument in a democratic society. "It is not indeed up to the State to create this community of ideas and sentiments without which there is no society," Durkheim held (1956: 80–1). That community is made and remade continuously by a host of social activities, from parent–teacher associations to national debates to marches on Washington or Parliament.

Durkheim's educative philosophy follows one of his fundamental episte-mological premises, namely, that a shared vocabulary of some sort is neces-sary for genuine disagreement and social criticism. For Durkheim, the Drey-fusard is a case in point. His conscientious dissent from an anti-Semitic French populace is articulated in the shared moral languages of his day. Ini-tiation and participation in such public vocabularies are prerequisites for moral dissent. They in no way block social criticism. When articulating the public Dreyfusard cause, Durkheim spoke the language of human rights, human dignity, and of collective moral aspirations. He genuinely believed that there was common ground and a tacit solidarity regarding fundamental ideals and goals, while at the same time he recognized how such fundamen-tals were interpreted and pursued variously. Solidarity, in Durkheim's view, was both a present reality, however frail, and a future possibility, however distant, promising enhanced participation in what he deemed to be the best of France's dynamic and progressive moral identity. Was this a contested moral identity? Of course it was. But this sociological fact did not deter Durkheim from what he understood to be his duty – to encourage a social solidarity that both emerged from and supported just, reformist, progressive democratic institutions.

In 1898, in the midst of the Dreyfus Affair when France wrestled with and put on trial diversity and "otherness," Durkheim argued that there are varieties of individualism and pluralism – with all the diversity and risk that these terms signify – that constitute a salient aspect of France's moral charac-ter and social solidarity. Today in our academies, in contrast, individualism and diversity are not on trial, but rather solidarity is accused. Yet Durkheim's argument, I believe, works in both directions. It defends not only diversity but also solidarity, for it maintains that these two social goods need not threaten one another, but rather can mutually enhance one another.

Economic justice, the political community, and globalization

I have rehearsed Durkheim's notion of moral individualism and moral plural-ism, for these concepts are foundational for grasping Durkheim's basic posi-tion on solidarity and diversity. Further, I focused on his complex approach to moral education as an example of how he combined his commitment to both solidarity and diversity. I now wish to explore briefly how this pair of commitments informs his substantive positions on economic justice; the relation between secondary groups and the state; and globalization. My chief question of Durkheim, however, remains the same: Can he assist us in formulating a model of solidarity that acknowledges pluralism and globalization?

Durkheim's commitment to enhancing social solidarity was fueled, perhaps above all, by his worry over a private economy that put the maximization of profit above human social welfare. His multifaceted study on professional and civic ethics was motivated by his belief that economic institutions should be accountable to a society's civic life – at both the regional and national level. His worry was that as modern societies become increasingly individualistic, shared aims lack the strength to guide the economic life in light of prevailing conceptions of justice. So he imagined ways to broaden or extend democratic practices that could bring a moral influence to the economic life. This move is entirely consistent with Durkheim's belief that there are moral dimensions to our shared civic life. The economy, in his view, should not be understood as a discrete, amoral, private realm, but rather as an integral moral component of the public life. Hence, in Durkheim's lectures on professional ethics and civic morals, he concentrated on the economic sphere, for he believed that "the greater part of its existence is passed divorced from any moral influence" (1992: 12). The classical economists, Durkheim claimed, failed to see that "economic functions are not an end in themselves but only a means to an end; that they are one of the organs of social life and that social life is above all a harmonious community of endeavors" (1992: 16).

To make matters worse, the ethos of the economic sphere, marked by individual and corporate egoism, threatened to dominate other social spheres: "This amoral character of economic life amounts to a public danger" (1992: 12). Durkheim's fear was that, due to the prominence of the economic sphere in modern societies, its amoral character would spread to other spheres.

How did Durkheim account for this "moral vacuum" in the economic sphere? Social institutions, given their historical character, change. "For two centuries," Durkheim claimed, "economic life has taken on an expansion it never knew before" (1992: 11). While this sphere grew and began to dominate society, a new "ethic" emerged that sought to deliver society from the traditional regulation of popes and monarchs and guilds. These old monitors were to be replaced by a new, impartial one: the guiding hand of the spontaneous market. Durkheim, however, considered this spontaneous regulation as essentially no regulation. In *Suicide*, for example, he stated that "for a whole century, economic progress has mainly consisted in freeing industrial relations from all regulation . . . and government, instead of regulating economic life, has become its tool and servant" (1951: 254–5).

In his lectures on professional ethics and civic morals, while discussing the economic world which seems to lie "outside the sphere of morals," Durkheim asked, "Is this state of affairs a normal one? It has had the support of famous doctrines. To start with, there is the classical economic theory according to which the free play of economic agreements should adjust itself and reach stability automatically, without it being necessary or even possible to submit it to any restraining forces" (Durkheim 1992: 10). Yet Durkheim went on to note that a stable and just economic sphere "cannot follow of itself from entirely material causes, from any blind mechanism, however scientific it may be. It is a moral task" (Durkheim 1992: 12). Why a moral task? Because we should not expect just economic social practices to emerge spontaneously from private contracts or "supply and demand" or from any other liberal market devices. A moral task is at hand because people must do something to bring peace and justice to the economic sphere. Human effort and planning are required, but this in turn depends on some sense of shared purpose and common aims.

I will not discuss at length the most famous of Durkheim's solutions to the moral bankruptcy of the economic sphere, namely, his call for the formation of occupational groups – a new democratic space located between private lives and large, civic institutions. I do want to comment on, however, the premise of Durkheim's hope for the establishment of occupational groups. His premise was that ethical practices are a product of human association; that practical moral reasoning emerges from working together, from shared practices. Workers, isolated from each other and from the shared purposes of their work, cannot create for themselves a healthy working environment, for example, fashioning practices pertaining to workers' dignity, treatment, and fair compensation. Durkheim's solution was to infuse the economic sphere with moral principles internal to the various, particular activities of the various occupations – whether they be farming, banking, or factory work. The role of occupational groups, then, is to provide moral connections between vocational practices and the internal goods and external goods relevant to them.

In order that external goods support – as opposed to vitiate – internal goods, various economic activities that a Spencerian would call private would need to be viewed in a more public light. First, the workers involved in a particular occupation would have a greater voice concerning its just operations. Second, the economic sphere in general would no longer be seen as a radically private one but as a realm subject to the political community. This is not necessarily a call for socialism. But it is Durkheim's warning that moral economic practices will not develop under the present conditions of a Spencerian free market.

From one perspective occupational groups are centers of moral life which, although bound together, are distinct and relatively autonomous. In order that moral principles internal to each group emerge, the groups should, as Durkheim noted, "develop original characteristics." Together these groups form the economic sphere. From another perspective, however, these groups are tributaries fed by shared traditions and institutions, by common projects and interests, by social solidarity. This latter perspective needs mentioning lest we lose sight of Durkheim's conviction that the economic sphere needs to be accountable to the wider political community.

Without a sense of ourselves as a people with shared perspectives, problems, and goals, we will not be able to tackle such a pressing and massive problem as an economic sphere unaccountable to democratic institutions. Durkheim himself was not sanguine about the emergence of morally sustaining spheres of economic justice. He often wrote as if liberal society is taking on the character of a Hobbesian war of all against all. At such moments he seemed to doubt the possibility of robust shared commitments and aims. This pessimism, however, did not lead to moral paralysis but to increased commitment to the tasks at hand.

There is a social sphere, Durkheim tells us, which is greater in scope than the various secondary groups. It is the political community. Inquiry into the nature of this sphere and its relation to other social spheres and to the state is necessary for an intelligent reading of Durkheim's notion of a plurality of social spheres that are nourished by solidarity. If, for example, the domestic or the economic spheres are entirely independent of the political one, or even dominate it, that might suggest a precarious *laissez-faire* pluralism that could lead to a society's domination by a single sphere. On the other hand, if the other spheres are dominated by the political community or the state, that might suggest an open door to nationalism or fascism.

The political community, according to Durkheim's normative understanding of it, encompasses a plurality of secondary groups without becoming one itself. It includes all without being dominated by any. In Durkheim's idiom, the political community and the state are not the same. The state refers to "the agents of the sovereign authority," while the political community refers to a shared public space which includes all secondary groups. Far from being in radical opposition to the various secondary groups contained within the political sphere, Durkheim contends that "the state presupposes their existence . . . No secondary groups, no political authority, at least no authority which can legitimately be called political" (1992: 45). In his lectures on professional ethics and civic morals, Durkheim championed a model of the state that is neither *laissez-faire* liberal nor nationalistic. The state, if legitimately representing the ideals and goals of the democratic political community, supports moral individualism and pluralism.

In what ways, specifically, can the state support moral individualism and pluralism? First, "individual diversities can more easily have play" when the state checks various forms of "collective tyranny." Collective tyranny includes vicious crazes and majoritarian furies, though Durkheim was especially concerned about secondary groups that threaten to bring individuals within their "exclusive domination." The state, particularly its judicial branch, needs to worry about "all those secondary groups of family, trade and professional association, Church, regional areas and so on . . . which tend to absorb the personality of their members" (Durkheim 1992: 65). The state's moral task, as informed by the political community, is to remind secondary groups that they are a part of a whole and need to abide by the laws of that whole. This includes, Durkheim noted, rescuing "the child from patriarchal domination and from family tyranny," and the worker from corporate tyranny. The democratic state, then, far from assuming a negative or passive role, actively strives to foster the beliefs and practices of moral pluralism.

Between secondary groups and the state there will be conflict. In fact, Durkheim made the provocative claim that "it is out of this conflict of social forces that individual liberties are born" (Durkheim 1992: 63). Yet it is clear that, in Durkheim's view, there need not be a fatal antagonism between secondary groups and the liberal democratic state. The one, in fact, is a condition of the moral health of the other. Without secondary groups (including a variety of cultural and ethnic groups) to mediate between the state and the individual, the state would either be too distant from the individual and hence cease to be effective; or it would control too many aspects of the individual's life, and thus become autocratic. Secondary groups, on the other hand, require the moral authority of the state to protect them, lest some wage civil war of varying kinds and suppress minority voices. Moreover, the state safeguards the individual from potential group despotism.

There is, here, a dialectical relation between the state and its plural secondary groups. From this dialectic, in Durkheim's view, emerges the social solidarity of the political community, and such solidarity, in turn, sustains the dialectic. Solidarity is not the result of state sponsored coercion, nor of a natural harmony among secondary groups. Rather, it emerges from, and contributes to, the dialectical relation between the democratic state and its various secondary groups. Solidarity of the political community, then, does not work against pluralism, but rather is constitutive of its very existence. And the health of the political community requires a rich variety of secondary groups. Unlike Rousseau who feared secondary groups, Durkheim did not support the *Social Contract* model of the state in which diverse individuals have a direct relation to the state, but not to each other. Not only did Durkheim not fear secondary groups and the pluralism that they represent, but he defended their vital role in providing a variety of moral homes for individuals and in contributing diversity and dynamism to the political community.

Durkheim championed a democratic political community which engages in free and boundless critical debate and inquiry, and he held that such debate could engender radical social change. I say radical because the more a society can freely criticize and debate pressing issues and the multifarious content of its social traditions, the more it can probe, as Durkheim put it, "uncharted customs, the obscure sentiments and prejudices that evade investigation" (1992: 89). For such debate and reform to take place, however, there must be shared public space. Providing such a space is a primary role of the political community. The political community supports the conditions under which individuals and groups can learn from each other about diversity of aims, overlapping concerns, and genuinely shared beliefs and practices. Without debate and dialogue, the state operates without the check of a dynamic political community, and the state's authority becomes problematic. Such public conversations, in my view, will often take place on a more local, not national, arena. Nonetheless, these locally conducted conversations contribute to the political community, as long as wide-ranging national issues are discussed. Hence local, practical reasoning can contribute to inclusive, broad public conversations.

The more democratic a society, Durkheim claimed, "the more that deliberation and reflection and a critical spirit play a considerable part in the courses of public affairs" (Durkheim 1992: 89). Such robust deliberation does not simply advocate that nonconformists have their say, that is, are tolerated. Rather, it means the truly democratic nation establishes the conditions by which the political community can learn from vigorous dissent. The solidarity of the political community, in this view, is not about conformity, but active participation in public debate and reform.

What is the relation between the solidarity of the democratic nation-state and what some call the global community or village? Did Durkheim have a position on globalization or on the possibility of a social sphere larger than the nation's political community? Durkheim maintained that there is an international sphere that, in a limited sense, encompasses the political community. The political community, according to Durkheim, has no sovereign above it except that of the state. This sovereign, however, is relative and needs to be qualified. It is accountable to the political community, and Durkheim also insisted that it is also accountable to the international community.[2] In *Elementary Forms* Durkheim claimed that "there is no people, no state that is not involved with another society that is more or less unlimited and includes all peoples, or states with which they are directly or indirectly in contact. There is no national life that is not dominated by an inherently international collective life. As we go forward in history, these international groupings take on greater importance and scope" (2001: 321–2).

Durkheim provided two different yet related accounts for the rise of what could be called global ethics. In one account, global ethics emerges from the recognition of duties that apply to all individuals, regardless of national boundaries. In his lectures on professional ethics and civic morals, he claimed that there are "duties independent of any particular grouping. . . . This is the most general sphere in the whole of ethics, for it is independent of any local or ethnic conditions" (Durkheim 1992: 110). These duties pertain to protecting the rights and dignity of humans – for example, protection from cruel humiliation, mutilation, murder, or theft.

The second account is closely related to the first, for it is a sociohistorical explanation for the development of international human rights. He claimed that "the group no longer seems to have value in itself and for itself: it is only a means of fulfilling and developing human nature to the point demanded by the current ideals" (Durkheim 1992: 112). For example, increasingly nations justify their existence by their efforts to protect individuals from unnecessary suffering – "a hateful thing" – as opposed to in the past when the nation – a personification of God or the sacred – was the object of highest regard. Durkheim claimed that increased pluralism accounts for this transfer of sacred regard from the pride of the individual nation to the dignity of the individual – wherever she or he lives. He wrote, "with the increase of diversity among the members of all societies, there is no essential characteristic in common except those derived from the basic quality of their human nature. It is this quality that quite naturally becomes the supreme object of collective sensibility" (Durkheim 1992: 112).

We have already seen this logic in Durkheim's communitarian defense of moral individualism: our shared understanding is centered on the dignity and rights of the individual. Now, however, Durkheim has taken this logic from a national to a global level. Given the high level of human diversity in the international realm, shared beliefs and practices are thin, except for the overlapping commitment to the global ethic of human rights. Durkheim's prediction is that as members of diverse nations associate and work on common issues, international ethics will become more substantive. Increasingly, "national aims do not lie at the summit of the [moral] hierarchy – it is human aims that are destined to be supreme" (Durkheim 1992: 73).

Yet Durkheim was not entirely sanguine about what we today call globalization. As I noted above, he was deeply distressed about the economic sphere not being accountable to democratic institutions. Economic justice cannot be obtained by a global *laissez-faire* market place. Writing about economics and globalization, Durkheim claimed that "the lowering of tariffs and the ease of communications allow one country to get from others the supplies it happens to need," yet this economic boon cannot of itself justify the "commercial and industrial crises" of an unfettered global economy (Durkheim 1992: 16). Anomie on a global scale is the price paid for entry into a global economy that seeks the maximization of profit above all else. Hence Durkheim's worry that what might look like a promising "world state" may in fact turn out to be but another form of "egoistic individualism" (Durkheim 1992: 74).

Today, the notion of "egoistic corporatism" – not egoistic individualism – could be employed if one were constructing a Durkheimian critique of economic globalization. By economic globalization, I refer to developments that have contributed to the global expansion of free market capitalism. This expansion has entailed the deregulation and privatization of economies, including the removal of protective tariffs, foreign investment regulations, and many other obstacles to the flow of goods and currency. North and South, East and West, governments are adopting unrestricted market policies to compete in global markets and attract foreign investment.

There is another and more recent feature of globalization. With the fall of the Soviet Union and the rise of digital technology, an unprecedented global integration has taken place among nations, markets, corporations, and individuals. The information revolution – connecting the world inexpensively and instantly by way of computers, faxes, and telephones – has surmounted the confines of the local, putting within reach the expanse of the international. Never before in history have humans been able to reach and be reached by so many, so far away. Apparently, Durkheim understood much when referring to the revolution that accompanies the development of "the ease of communications."

At this point in history, globalization should cause at least as much alarm as celebration. Instead, however, it has been eagerly greeted or promoted by European and North American liberal democracies. Some governments are claiming that they want to adapt progressive and social democratic ideals to the global age. Their aim is to forge a "third way" that runs between and beyond *laissez-faire* liberalism and authoritarian socialism. However, insofar as this political agenda has embraced globalization, it has often endorsed questionable aspects of the very historical models that it supposedly sought to avoid. This agenda emulates *laissez-faire* liberalism insofar as it has granted unprecedented autonomy to transnational corporations, disassembling national, state, and local regulations. These transnational corporations, in turn, resemble authoritarian socialism in terms of vast concentrations of power that are not publicly accountable – except to private shareholders.

Earlier in US history, during eras of *laissez-faire* policy, corporations and individuals accrued much power through the accumulation of wealth. Yet such power pales when compared to the current concentrations of power of those transnational corporations whose financial holdings are greater than the GNP of many countries. Given this immense and unregulated concentration of power, support of corporate globalization by governments, supposedly wedded to "third way" politics, in fact promotes troubling aspects of the old two-way politics – *laissez-faire* capitalism and authoritarian socialism. This, in turn, has posed serious threats to democracy, community, and the natural environment.

Unregulated concentration of power subverts the sovereignty of citizens and the autonomy of local communities. Moreover, it drives a non-sustainable, extractive, polluting economic engine designed to maximize shareholder earnings. Increased profits require an ever expanding global economy, and global development has required the misuse of renewable and nonrenewable resources, the runaway extinction rate of animals and plants, the catastrophic loss of soil, fisheries, and forests, and unparalleled pollution of the planet's land, water, and air. Moreover, the creation of corporate wealth and the creation of global poverty are perversely connected. The noted political economist, Ankie Hoogvelt, recently reported that "today there are over 1.2 billion people in the world living in absolute poverty and misery, and their number is growing . . . Furthermore, the gap between the richest and the poorest quintile of the world's population is twice as big today than it was 30 years ago" (Hoogvelt 1977: xi).

Durkheim, of course, knew nothing about the environmental costs of a global economy unleashed from normative beliefs and practices. Yet he did anticipate the social harm and suffering that would flow from a global economy modeled on anomic national economies. What of a Durkheimian response? Does his suggestion for how democratic moral reasoning can govern *national* economies apply to today's new *global* economy? His proposal, you will recall, was to form local occupational groups that would promote practical moral reasoning, having emerged from shared work, that would govern particular industries. Again, the premise is to encourage a participatory democracy that directly engages with and shapes the economic realm. The premise, I believe, is for the most part sound, and can indeed be applied to global economies.

This Durkheimian approach to economic globalization would call for a transfer of power from transnational boards of directors and their stockholders to the local workers and communities whose lives are directly affected by the activities of large international corporations. It would also require a modified version of Durkheim's complex normative account of the dialectical relation among the state, secondary groups, and individuals. The revised Durkheimian model would entail an augmented dialectic that included the international realm. In this model, the progressive democratic nation would attempt to foster within the nation-state a social order that properly arranges and regards the domains of local community, the wider civic community, and global institutions.

Of special importance would be the support and maintenance of the local and civic community. The local community is where democracy and economies have a human face – in our daily activities, close to home. The civic community is where we come together, as a people, and deliberate about common hopes, projects, and such developments as globalization. Without strong local communities, our wider civic existence risks becoming abstract and hollow; without a strong civic community, our local existence risks becoming parochial and escapist. Government can promote institutions that foster a democratic culture, protecting individuals and their communities, and encouraging a robust civic life. And together, government and local communities can favor markets that fortify, rather than devastate, the relation among good work, strong community, and human flourishing.

Additionally, however, local and national institutions would need to acknowledge and participate in what Durkheim saw on the horizon – the arrival of international institutions and global social forces. As I have said, he was troubled by those global economic trends that fostered economic injustice and divided and alienated world populations. Yet he also thought he glimpsed the emergence of an international spirit committed to the protection and extension of human rights (and we might add, in particular, women's and children's rights). Yet even of this latter hope, Durkheim held that if global justice is to be achieved, then nation-states and local communities need to jointly cultivate in their members a commitment to international human rights and to global moral issues. Hence Durkheim claimed that the way to avoid a clash between national and global perspectives is for "each state to have as its chief aim, not to expand, or to lengthen its borders, but to set its own house in order and to make the widest appeal to its members for a moral life on an ever higher level . . . If the state had no other purpose than making men of its citizens, in the widest sense of the term, then civic duties would be only a particular form of the general obligations of humanity" (Durkheim 1992: 74).

Global justice, then, requires just states, and just states require sufficient solidarity to work jointly toward the common aims of justice at the local, national, and global level. The Durkheimian lesson is that if we want to achieve social and economic justice, whether we are living among civic or global diversity, we must remain committed to some form of solidarity. To neglect solidarity is to risk having our most cherished ideals, including the celebration of diversity, drained of their capacity to shape our lives, institutions, and communities.

Durkheim, Giles Gunn, and otherness

The title of this chapter was inspired by the recent book by Giles Gunn, *Beyond Solidarity: Pragmatism and Difference in a Globalized World* (2001). I confess that, given the title of his book, I had expected to disagree with his conclusions. I had assumed that "beyond solidarity" meant that, given our age of diversity and globalization, we should no longer be preoccupied with the concept of solidarity. I was wrong. Instead, Gunn argues convincingly that to achieve anything like solidarity in today's globalized environment, we need to embrace difference and otherness, and not aim for consensus or sameness. Solidarity, if it is to be successful and appropriate, must incorporate what he calls "the pragmatism of otherness" (Gunn 2001: 194). Gunn writes, "to think our way through the dilemmas that globalization, like its predecessors, have created for human community, we may need to look, as it were, 'beyond solidarity.'" What does it mean to go beyond solidarity? It is to both acknowledge difference and discover beneath or amid it a fundamental humanity. It entails looking "to those who have created their sense of humanity not out of the possibility of overcoming their differences with others, or even in the hope of regulating their relations with others, but rather out of their need (frequently amidst harrowing circumstances) to determine what constitutes their sense of fundamental kinship with others, despite their differences" (Gunn 2001: 47). The basis of this "fundamental kinship" is recognizing the "ethical claim of the 'other,'" resisting reductionism or essentialism that would implicitly shape the other in one's own image, and replacing "the hope of consensus" with the "need for 'comity'" (Gunn 2001: 194).

What is the relation between Gunn's "pragmatism of otherness" and Durkheim's philosophy of solidarity? Can a Durkheimian declare with Gunn that mutual understanding requires the self to place its beliefs and assumptions "at risk for the sake of encountering that which is inevitably different"? Can a Durkheimian support, as does Gunn, Richard Bernstein's claim that "it is only through an engaged encounter with the Other, with the otherness of the Other, that one comes to a more informed, textured understanding of the tradition to which 'we' belong" (Gunn 2001: 29)? Durkheim, we know, did not speak our turn-of-the-century language of "otherness" or "difference." Moreover, when he did speak of the maturation of the self, he was more likely to refer to the self being nurtured by tradition, history, or community, rather than to the self being challenged by the stranger, the alien, or the other. Giles Gunn introduces something new, and something extremely valuable, when he speaks of the process of discovering potentially shared (albeit contingent) grounds with the foreigner or even the enemy. Yet this new move, I will suggest, is not opposed to a Durkheimian approach. Indeed, it can be understood as an apt extension of Durkheim's philosophical and normative stances.

First, to learn from difference and otherness, some shared commitment to that process is required. Working beyond solidarity entails, on some level, the solidarity Durkheim recommended, namely, in this case, the cultivation of shared practices and beliefs that support respecting and learning from "otherness." Going beyond solidarity, then, does not necessarily take us beyond Durkheim. Also, there are substantive issues on which we should work for agreement or sameness. One of these is Judith Shklar's reasoned conviction that cruelty is the worst thing, that there are some things – such as torture or degrading humiliation – that no human should ever have to endure. This sensibility needs either to be part of the background beliefs which support a conversation among different parties, or, if the belief is not in place, agreement on this needs to be one of the aims of the conversation.

Moreover, Durkheim in his own way did move "beyond solidarity," in Gunn's sense of the term. Durkheim, I have argued, did not oppose moral pluralism or scorn all conflict. In his last written work, for example, he claimed that "only those periods which are divided over morality are morally inventive. And when traditional morality goes unchallenged, when there is no apparent need to renew it, moral thought falls into decline" (Durkheim 1979: 80–1). The premise behind this dynamic view is that moral "otherness" is not lamentable, and that moral growth is most likely to occur when one is willing to have one's beliefs and assumptions challenged by encountering fundamentally different moral points of view. Hence Durkheim often insisted that it is precisely during times of crisis, when a society's basic presumptions are most challenged, that newness and growth are most likely to be achieved.

In Durkheim's European world, the Jew was "the other." For this reason, the Jewish French officer, Captain Alfred Dreyfus, could be unjustly accused and convicted of high treason by a military tribunal. The background to this scapegoating by military and government officials was a fierce French nationalism inspired by the French military defeat by Germany in 1870. Like Muslims in the US after "September 11," Jews could not be trusted to be patriotic citizens. Hence Dreyfus could be found guilty of providing military secrets to Germany, even though the evidence against him was slim or else clearly fabricated. When Durkheim entered the public fray over Captain Dreyfus, he saw the controversy as an opportunity for democratic and moral renewal.

As France confronted the "otherness" of Dreyfus, Durkheim hoped that his nation could more fully realize its commitment to the rights and dignity of the individual – all individuals, regardless of ethnic or religious background. This was Durkheim's argument and hope, and at a time of intense national- ism, when many argued that solidarity was the most important thing, surely more important than the details of a treason case against a Jew. Durkheim, in contrast, held that French solidarity and its moral identity depended on upholding the protection of human rights and the safeguarding of diversity.

Again, this is not to suggest that Durkheim fully appreciated, as does Gunn, the problems and promises of encountering, respecting, and learning from the foreigner, the outsider, or the enemy. I am claiming, however, that Durkheim was a devoted champion of human rights, the protection of diversity, and the view that human maturity and enlightenment can come from encountering and honoring otherness. Morality, for Durkheim, did not rest on sameness. Nor did solidarity.

Beyond solidarity?

I now wonder if it wouldn't be more accurate to say that Giles Gunn doesn't go *beyond* solidarity, rather he goes *beneath* it – to a basic, fundamental human landscape on which any substantial solidarity is built. He travels to the extremities of human alienation to find remarkable examples where individuals have discovered kinship with their enemies or oppressors. In post-colonial writings, Holocaust literature, and the literature and thought of African-American slaves and their descendents, Gunn offers examples of when "alterity enables cultures, like selves, to learn from each other, to become constituents of each other's identity" (Gunn 2001: 194). While I may not be entirely comfortable with bringing back general lessons from such extreme cases, I want to suggest that this basic recognition of kinship – this acknowledgment of the other as a fellow human – is the starting point for a more substantive pursuit of human solidarity.

Durkheim's work and hope pertained not to what could emerge from extreme cases of human alienation, but to what forms of human flourishing could emerge in France and other democracies in light of their ideals (if not their actual grim histories). His moral hope was not neutral or shared univer- sally. It was particular and substantive: he imagined progressive democracies whose claim to greatness was not economic growth or military power, but rather their commitment to extending human rights and achieving social justice. Durkheim in France, like Martin Luther King, Jr. in the USA, spoke to his audience as if his listeners already shared such common ideals as equality, liberty, and social justice. Part of this strategy is to assume that a tacit solidarity is already in place, to assume that a nation of diverse individuals wants to work together and achieve common aims.

After the events of September 11, few can doubt that the USA possesses, and perhaps is seized by, some form of social solidarity. Little plastic flags abound. Support for the President's war efforts is overwhelming. Again, the question for the USA is not, do we have solidarity? It's already here. The question is: What is its form, and what does it do? What does our solidarity stand for? And then there is Durkheim's other question: What should it stand for? What can we hope it would stand for? Can the fierce solidarity that the USA is now experiencing during events of crisis and war be transformed and redirected to goals of peace and justice? I am convinced by Durkheim that progressive liberal democracies cannot afford to neglect or dispense with public solidarity. If we ignore the significance of solidarity, we may discover that solidarity is with us, but we cannot recognize our highest ideals in it.

In the months and years after September 11, the USA will wrestle with the question of what it means to be an American. Who are we? What is our origin, our history, our future? Do we share a common culture? There is no single answer to these questions. How we raise and address these questions will perhaps be the greatest indicator of who we are, what we share, and what we are becoming. My hope, inspired by Durkheim, is that we will honor our diversity and achieve a shared commitment to the founding ideals of "liberty and justice for all."

Toward the end of his life, Durkheim's world, inch by inch, was becoming unlivable. War, death, and degradation had stained it. In response, Durkheim increased his efforts to transform it, in particular, to mitigate human suffering. In one of his last publications, he wrote of a religious spirit that was gathering: a humane religion committed to justice, dedicated to human dignity. A global religion with which we could live. Whether Durkheim's vision or Weber's iron cage awaits us, who can say?

NOTES

1 In this chapter, when I refer to "citizens," I mean any who seek to participate in the shared public life of a nation-state regardless of whether she or he has legal status as a citizen.

2 See, for example, Durkheim 1915, esp. p. 7.

REFERENCES

Brunetière, Ferdinand. 1898. "Après le process." *Revue des deux mondes* 146 (15 mars): 428–46.

de Tocqueville, Alexis. [1835] 1969. *Democracy in America*. Translated by George Lawrence. New York: Doubleday.

Durkheim, Émile. 2001. *The Elementary Forms of Religious Life*. Edited by Mark Cladis. Translated by Carol Cosman. Oxford: Oxford University Press.

1992. *Professional Ethics and Civic Morals*. Translated by Cornelia Brookfield. London: Routledge. [I have slightly modified some of the translations from this edition].

1979. "Introduction to Ethics." pp. 77–96 in *Essays on Morals and Education*. Edited by W. S. F. Pickering. Translated by H. L. Sutcliffe. London: Routledge and Kegan Paul.

1977. *The Evolution of Educational Thought: Lectures on the Formation and Development of Secondary Education in France*. Translated by Peter Collins. London: Routledge and Kegan Paul.

1973. "Individualism and the Intellectuals." pp. 43–57 in *Émile Durkheim: On Morality and Society*. Edited by Robert Bellah. Translated by Mark Traugott. Chicago: University of Chicago Press.

1961. *Moral Education: A Study in the Theory and Application of the Sociology of Education*. Translated by Everett K. Wilson and Herman Schnurer. Glencoe, IL: Free Press.

1956. *Education and Sociology*. Translated and with an introduction by Sherwood D. Fox. Glencoe, IL: Free Press.

1951. *Suicide: A Study in Sociology*. Translated by John. A. Spaulding and George Simpson. Glencoe, IL: Free Press.

1938. *L'Évolution Pédagogique en France*. Vol. 2. Paris: Librairie Félix Alcan.

1915. *L'Allemagne au-dessus de tout*. Paris: Colin.

Gunn, Giles. 2001. *Beyond Solidarity: Pragmatism and Difference in a Globalized World*. Chicago: University of Chicago Press.

Hoogvelt, Ankie. 1977. *Globalization and the Postcolonial World*. Baltimore: John Hopkins Press.

West, Cornel. 2001. *Race Matters*. New York: Vintage Books.

SELECTED WORKS BY DURKHEIM AND
FURTHER READING

One can find a complete bibliography of Durkheim's own works and coverage of the secondary literature published before 1973, in Steven Lukes, *Émile Durkheim: His Life and Work*. This listing should be considered an update. We cover not only Durkheim's major works available in English, but also a selection of important recent articles and books on Durkheim. We have limited ourselves to writings which have as their primary objective the explication or critique of Durkheim's thinking. Obviously, a massive quantity of important material developing, illustrating, inspired by or applying Durkheim's ideas has been published over the years. This has not been included here. Readers will be able to locate this literature as needed through study of the chapters in this volume, each of which includes citation of relevant material.

Primary texts: works by Durkheim

Division of Labor in Society. Translated by George Simpson. New York: Free Press, 1964 [1933].

Division of Labor in Society. Translated by W. D. Halls. Introduction by Lewis A. Coser. New York: Free Press, 1984.

Durkheim and the Law. Edited by Steven Lukes and Andrew Scull. New York: St. Martin's Press, 1983.

Durkheim on Politics and the State. Edited and with an introduction by Anthony Giddens. Translated by W. D. Halls. Stanford, CA: Stanford University Press, 1986.

Durkheim on Religion: A Selection of Readings with Bibliographies. Edited by W. S. F. Pickering. Translated by Jacqueline Redding and W. S. F. Pickering. Boston, MA: Routledge and Kegan Paul, 1975.

Durkheim: Essays on Morals and Education. Edited and with introductions by W. S. F. Pickering. Translated by H. I. Sutcliffe. Boston, MA: Routledge and Kegan Paul, 1979.

Durkheim's Philosophy Lectures. Edited by Neil Gross. Cambridge: Cambridge University Press, 2004.

Education and Sociology. Translated and with an introduction by Sherwood D. Fox. Foreword by Talcott Parsons. Glencoe, IL: Free Press, 1956.

Elementary Forms of Religious Life. Translated and with an introduction by Karen E. Fields. New York: Free Press, 1995.

Elementary Forms of Religious Life. Translated by Carol Cosman with an introduction and notes by Mark S. Cladis. New York: Oxford University Press, 2001.

Elementary Forms of the Religious Life, a Study in Religious Sociology. Translated by Joseph Ward Swain. Glencoe, IL: Free Press, [1915] 1968.

Émile Durkheim on Morality and Society: Selected Writings. Edited and with an introduction by Robert N. Bellah. Chicago: University of Chicago Press, 1973.

Émile Durkheim: Contributions to L'Année sociologique. Edited by Yash Nandan. New York: Free Press, 1980.

Émile Durkheim: Selected Writings. Edited, translated, and with an introduction by Anthony Giddens. Cambridge: Cambridge University Press, 1972.

Ethics and the Sociology of Morals. Translated and with an introduction by Robert T. Hall. Buffalo, NY: Prometheus Books, 1993.

Evolution of Educational Thought: Lectures on the Formation and Development of Secondary Education in France. Translated by Peter Collins. Boston, MA: Routledge and Kegan Paul, 1977.

Incest: The Nature and Origin of the Taboo. Translated and with an introduction by Edward Sagarin. Together with "The Origins and the Development of the Incest Taboo" by Albert Ellis. New York: L. Stuart, 1963.

Montesquieu and Rousseau: Forerunners of Sociology. Foreword by Henri Peyre. With "Durkheim, Montesquieu, and Rousseau," by Georges Davy and "Note," by A. Cuvillier. Translated by Ralph Manheim. Ann Arbor, MI: University of Michigan Press, 1960.

Moral Education: A Study in the Theory and Application of the Sociology of Education. Foreword by Paul Fauconnet. Translated by Everett K. Wilson and Herman Schnurer. Edited and with a new introduction by Everett K. Wilson. New York: Free Press, [1961] 1973.

Pragmatism and Sociology. Translated by J. C. Whitehouse. Edited and with an introduction by John B. Allcock and a preface by A. Cuvillier. New York: Cambridge University Press, 1983.

Primitive Classification (with Marcel Mauss). Translated and edited with an introduction by Rodney Needham. London: Cohen and West, 1963.

Professional Ethics and Civic Morals. Translated by Cornelia Brookfield. London: Routledge and Kegan Paul, 1957.

The Radical Sociology of Durkheim and Mauss. Edited by Mike Gane. London: Routledge, 1992.

Readings from Émile Durkheim. Edited by Kenneth Thompson with new translations by Margaret A. Thompson. New York: Tavistock Publications, 1985.

Rules of Sociological Method and Selected Texts on Sociology and its Method. Edited and with an introduction by Steven Lukes. Translated by W. D. Halls. London: Macmillan Press, 1982.

Rules of Sociological Method. New York: Free Press, 1966.

Socialism and Saint-Simon. Edited and with an introduction by Alvin W. Gouldner. Translated by Charlotte Sattler from the version originally edited by Marcel Mauss. Yellow Springs, OH: Antioch Press, 1958.

Sociology and Philosophy. Translated by D. F. Pocock and with an introduction by J. G. Peristiany. Glencoe, IL: Free Press, 1953.

Suicide: A Study in Sociology. Translated by John A. Spaulding and George Simpson. Edited and with an introduction by George Simpson. New York: Free Press, [1951] 1966.

Textes. Vol. 1, *Eléments d'une théorie sociale.* Edited by Victor Karady. Paris: Éditions de Minuit [1889] 1975.

Textes. Vol. 2, *Religion, morale, anomie.* Paris: Éditions de Minuit, 1975.

Who Wanted War? The Origins of the War According to Diplomatic Documents (with E. Denis). Translated by A. M. Wilson-Garinei. Paris: Armand Colin, 1915.

Secondary literature: monographs about Durkheim and his work

Aimard, Guy. 1962. *Durkheim et la science économique.* Paris: Presses Universitaires de France.

Alexander, Jeffrey. C. 1989. *Structure and Meaning: Relinking Classical Sociology.* New York: Columbia University Press.

1982. *Theoretical Logic in Sociology.* Vol. 2, *The Antinomies of Classical Thought: Marx and Durkheim.* Berkeley, CA: University of California Press.

Alpert, Harry. 1939. *Émile Durkheim and his Sociology.* New York: Russell and Russell.

Aron, Raymond, Albert Demangeon, Jean Meuvret, et al. 1937. *Les Sciences Sociales en France: enseignement et recherché.* Paris: Presses Universitaires de France.

Baudelot, Christian and Roger Establet. 1984. *Durkheim et le suicide.* Paris: Presses Universitaires de France.

Berthelot, Jean-Michel. 1995. *Durkheim: L'avènement de la sociologie scientifique.* Joulouse: Presses Universitaires du Mirail.

Besnard, Philippe. 1987. *L'Anomie.* Paris: Presses Universitaires de France.

Bouglé, Célestin. 1938. *Humanisme, sociologie, philosophie: remarques sur la conception française de la culture générale.* Paris: Hermann et Cie.

Bureau, Paul. 1923. *La Science des mœurs: introduction à la méthode sociologique.* Paris: Bloud and Gay.

Challenger, D. 1995. *Durkheim through the Lens of Aristotle: Durkheimian, Postmodernist, and Communitarian Responses to the Enlightenment.* Lanham, MD: Rowman and Littlefield.

Clark, Terry N. 1973. *Prophets and Patrons: The French University and the Emergence of the Social Sciences.* Cambridge, MA: Harvard University Press.

Cotterrell, Roger. 1999. *Émile Durkheim: Law in a Moral Domain.* Stanford, CA: Stanford University Press.

Davy, Georges. 1950. *Sociologues d'hier et d'aujourd'hui.* Paris: Librairie Félix Alcan.

Digeon, Paul. 1959. *La Crise Allemande de la pensée française, 1870–1914.* Paris: Presses Universitaires de France.

Douglas, Jack D. 1967. *The Social Meanings of Suicide.* Princeton, NJ: Princeton University Press.

Evans-Pritchard, Edward E. 1965. *Theories of Primitive Religion.* Oxford: Clarendon Press.

Fenton, Steve. 1984. *Durkheim and Modern Sociology*. Cambridge: Cambridge University Press.

Filloux, Jean-Claude. 1977. *Durkheim et le socialisme*. Genève: Librairie Droz.

Fournier, Marcel. 1994. *Marcel Mauss*. Paris: Fayard.

n.d. *Durkheim*. Paris: Fayard, forthcoming.

Gane, Mike. 1988. *On Durkheim's Rules of Sociological Method*. London. Routledge.

Giddens, Anthony. 1971. *Capitalism and Modern Social Theory*. Cambridge: Cambridge University Press.

Habermas, Jürgen. 1987. *The Theory of Communicative Action*. Vol. 2, *Lifeworld and System: A Critique of Functionalist Reason*. Boston: Beacon Press.

Hughes, H. Stuart. 1958. *Consciousness and Society*. New York: Knopf.

Jones, Robert Alun. 1999. *The Development of Durkheim's Social Realism*. Cambridge: Cambridge University Press.

1984. *Émile Durkheim: An Introduction to Four Major Works*. Beverly Hills, California: Sage.

LaCapra, Dominick. 1972. *Émile Durkheim: Sociologist and Philosopher*. Ithaca, NY: Cornell University Press.

Lacombe, R. 1926. *La Méthode Sociologique de Durkheim*. Paris: Felix Alcan.

Lacroix, Bernard. 1981. *Durkheim et la politique*. Paris: Fondation des Sciences politiques and Montréal: Presses de l'Université de Montréal.

Lehman, N. J. 1993. *Deconstructing Durkheim: A Post-Post-Structuralist Critique*. London: Routledge.

Lukes, Steven. 1973. *Émile Durkheim: His Life and Work*. London: Allen Lane.

Meštrović, Stjepan G. 1988. *Durkheim and the Reformation of Sociology*. Totowa, NJ: Rowman and Littlefield.

Miller, W. Watts. 1996. *Durkheim, Morals and Modernity*. Montreal and Kingston: McGill-Queen's University Press.

Munch, Richard. 1982. *Theorie des Handelns: Zur Rekonstruktion der Beitrage von Talcott Parsons, Émile Durkheim und Max Weber*. Frankfurt am Main: Suhrkamp Verlag.

Nisbet, Robert A. 1965. *Émile Durkheim*. Englewood Cliffs, NJ: Prentice-Hall.

Parsons, Talcott. 1937. *The Structure of Social Action*. New York: McGraw-Hill.

Pearce, Frank. 1989. *The Radical Durkheim*. Boston, MA: Unwin Hyman.

Pickering, W. S. F. 1984. *Durkheim's Sociology of Religion: Themes and Theories*. Boston, MA: Routledge.

Poggi, Gianfranco. 1972. *Images of Society: Essays of the Sociological Theories of Tocqueville, Marx and Durkheim*. Stanford, CA: Stanford University Press.

Prades, Jose A. 1987. *Persistance et Metamorphose Du Sacré: Actualise Durkheim et repense la modernité*. Paris: Presses Universitaires de France.

Rawls, Anne Warfield. 2003. *Durkheim's Epistemology and the Elementary Forms*. New York: Cambridge University Press.

Seger, Imogen. 1957. *Durkheim and his Critics on the Sociology of Religion*. Monograph Series, Bureau of Applied Social Research. New York: Columbia University.

Smith, John. A. 2000. *Images of Community: Durkheim, Social Systems and the Sociology of Art*. Aldershot: Ashgate.

Stedman Jones, Susan. 2001. *Durkheim Reconsidered*. London: Polity Press.

Steiner, Philippe. 1994. *La Sociologie de Durkheim*. Paris: La Découverte.

Strenski, Ivan. 1997. *Durkheim and the Jews of France*. Chicago: University of Chicago Press.

Tarde, Gabriel de. 1895. *La Logique Social*. Paris: Librairie Félix Alcan.

Tarot, Camille. 1999. *De Durkheim à Mauss: L'invention du Symbolique: sociologie et science des religions*. Paris: La Découverte.

Wolin, Sheldon S. 1960. *Politics and Vision: Continuity and Innovation in Western Political Thought*. Boston, MA: Little, Brown.

Secondary literature: edited collections about Durkheim and his work

Alexander, Jeffrey C., ed. 1988. *Durkheimian Sociology: Cultural Studies*. Cambridge: Cambridge University Press.

Allen, N. J., W. S. F. Pickering, and W. Watts Miller, eds. 1998. *On Durkheim's Elementary Forms of Religious Life*. London: Routledge.

Besnard, Philippe, ed. 1983. *The Sociological Domain: The Durkheimians and the Founding of French Sociology*. Cambridge: Cambridge University Press.

Besnard, Philippe, Massimo Borlandi and Paul Vogt, eds. 1993. *Division du travail et lien social. La thèse de Durkheim un siècle après*. Paris: Presses Universitaires de France.

Borlandi, Massimo, and Mohamed Cherkaoui, eds. 2000. *Le suicide un siècle après Durkheim*. Paris: Presses Universitaires de France.

Cladis, Mark, ed. 2001. *Durkheim and Foucault: Perspectives on Education and Punishment*. New York: Berghahn Books.

Cuin, Charles-Henry, ed. 1997. *"Durkheim d'un siècle a l'autre: lectures actuelles des "Règles de la méthode sociologique"*. Paris: Presses Universitaires de France.

Gane, Mike, ed. 1992. *The Radical Sociology of Durkheim and Mauss*. London: Routledge.

Godlove, Terry F., ed. n.d. *Teaching Durkheim on Religion*. New York: Oxford University Press, forthcoming.

Martins, H. and W. S. F. Pickering, eds. 1994. *Debating Durkheim*. New York: Routledge.

Miller, W. Watts, ed. n.d. *Durkheimian Studies: Études Durkheimiennes*, vol. i–xx. Oxford: British Center for Durkheimian Studies.

Nisbet, Robert A., ed. 1965. *Émile Durkheim*. Englewood Cliffs, NJ: Prentice-Hall.

Pickering, W. S. F., ed. 2002. *Durkheim Today*. Introduction by Kenneth Thompson. New York: Berghahn Books.

   ed. 2000. *Emile Durkheim III: Critical Assessments of Leading Sociologists*. London: Routledge.

   ed. 1999. *Durkheim and Representations*. London: Routledge.

Pickering, W. S. F., and William Watts Miller, eds. 1993. *Individualism and Human Rights in the Durkheimian Tradition*. Oxford: British Centre for Durkheimian Studies.

Turner, Stephen, ed. 2003. *Émile Durkheim: Sociologist and Moralist*. New York: Routledge.

Wolff, Kurt, ed. 1960. *Emile Durkheim, 1858–1917: A Collection of Essays*. Columbus, OH: Ohio State University Press.

Walford, Geoffrey and W. S. F. Pickering, eds. 2000. *Durkheim's Suicide: a century of research and debate*. London: Routledge.
Walford, Geoffrey and Pickering, W. S. F., eds. 1998. *Durkheim and Modern Education*. London: Routledge.

Secondary literature: articles and book chapters

Adorno, Theodor W. 1967. "Introduction to Durkheim" in *Émile Durkheim, Soziologie und Philosophie*. Frankfurt: Suhrkamp.
Allardt, Erik. 1967. "Durkheim e la sociologia politica." *Rassegna italiana di sociologia* 8: 47–66.
Alpert, Harry. 1937. "France's First University Course in Sociology." *American Sociological Review* 2: 311–17.
Barbalet, Jack. 1994 "Ritual Emotion and Body Work: A Note on the Uses of Durkheim" in *Social Perspectives on Emotion*. Vol. 2. Edited by William Wentworth and John Ryan. Greenwich, CT: JAI Press.
Barnes, Harry E. 1920. "Durkheim's Contribution to the Reconstruction of Political Theory." *Political Science Quarterly* 35: 236–54.
Barnes, J. A. 1966. "Durkheim's Division of Labour in Society." *Man* 1: 158–75.
Bellah, Robert N. 1959. "Durkheim and History." *American Sociological Review* 24: 447–61.
Bendix, Reinhard. 1971. "Two Sociological Traditions" in *Scholarship and Partisanship*. Edited by Reinhard Bendix and Gunther Roth. Berkeley, CA: University of California Press.
Besnard, Philippe. 1988. "The True Nature of Anomie." *Sociological Theory* 6: 91–5.
  1979. "La Formation de l'équipe de *l'Année sociologique*." *Revue française de sociologie* 20: 7–31.
  1973. "Durkheim et les femmes ou *Le Suicide* inachevé." *Revue française de sociologie* 14: 27–61.
Clark, Terry N. 1968. "Émile Durkheim and the Institutionalization of Sociology in the French University System." *European Journal of Sociology* 9: 37–71.
Coser, Lewis A. 1988. "Primitive Classification Revisited." *Sociological Theory* 6: 85–90.
Cuvillier, Armand. 1961. "Émile Durkheim et le pragmatisme" in *Sociologie et Problèmes actuels*. Paris: Librairie Philosophique J. Vrin.
Davy, Georges. 1911. "La Sociologie de M. Durkheim." *Revue Philosophique* 72: 42–71.
Dohrenwend, Bruce Philip. 1959. "Egoism, Altruism, Anomie, and Fatalism: A Conceptual Analysis of Durkheim's Types." *American Sociological Review* 24: 466–72.
Emirbayer, Mustafa. 1996. "Useful Durkheim." *Sociological Theory* 14: 109–30.
Etzioni, Amitai. 2000. "Toward a Theory of Public Ritual." *Sociological Theory* 18: 44–59.
Fields, Karen E. 2002. "Individuality and the Intellectuals: An Imaginary Conversation between W. E. B. du Bois and Émile Durkheim." *Theory and Society* 31: 435–62.
  1996. "Durkheim and the Idea of Soul." *Theory and Society* 25: 193–203.

Gane, Mike. 1983. "Durkheim: The Sacred Language." *Economy and Society* 12: 1–47.

Geertz, Clifford. 1973. "Ritual and Social Change: A Javanese Example." pp. 142–69 in *The Interpretation of Cultures*. New York: Basic Books.

Greenberg, Louis M. 1976. "Bergson and Durkheim as Sons and Assimilators: The Early Years." *French Historical Studies* 9: 619–35.

Gross, Neil. 1997. "Durkheim's Pragmatism Lectures: A Contextual Interpretation." *Sociological Theory* 15: 126–49.

Halbwachs, Maurice. 1986. "Anomie and the Moral Regulation of Reality: The Durkheimian Tradition in Modern Relief." *Sociological Theory* 4: 1–19.

1939. "Individual Consciousness and the Collective Mind." *American Journal of Sociology* 44: 812–22.

1918. "La Doctrine d'Émile Durkheim." *Revue philosophique* 85: 353–411.

Horton, J. 1964. "The Dehumanization of Anomie and Alienation." *British Journal of Sociology* 15: 283–300.

Hughes, E. C. 1928. "Personality Types and the Division of Labor." *American Journal of Sociology* 33: 754–68.

Janssen, Jacques and Theo Verheggen. 1997. "The Double Center of Gravity in Durkheim's Symbol Theory: Bringing the Symbolism of the Body Back In." *Sociological Theory* 15: 294–306.

Johnson, B. D. 1964. "Durkheim's One Cause of Suicide." *American Sociological Review* 30: 875–86.

Jones, Robert Alun. 1994. "Ambivalent Cartesians: Durkheim, Montesquieu, and Method." *American Journal of Sociology* 100: 1–39.

1986. "Durkheim, Frazer, and Smith: The Role of Analogies and Exemplars in the Development of Durkheim's Sociology of Religion." *American Journal of Sociology* 92: 596–627.

Kemper, Theodore D. 1972. "The Division of Labor: A Post-Durkheimian Analytical View." *American Sociological Review* 37: 739–53.

Lehmann, Jennifer M. 1995. "Durkheim's Theories of Deviance and Suicide: A Feminist Reconsideration." *American Journal of Sociology* 100: 904–30.

Lemert, Charles. 1999. "The Might Have Been and Could Be of Religion in Social Theory." *Sociological Theory* 17: 240–63.

Lévi-Strauss, Claude. 1960. "Ce que l'ethnologie doit à Durkheim." *Annales de l'Université de Paris* 1: 3–54.

Lukes, Steven M. 1975. "Political Ritual and Social Integration." *Sociology* 9: 289–308.

1973. "On the Social Determination of Truth," in *Modes of Thought*. Edited by Robin Horton and Ruth Finnegan. London: Faber.

1971. "Prolegomena to the Interpretation of Durkheim." *European Journal of Sociology* 12: 183–209.

1968. "Methodological Individualism Reconsidered." *British Journal of Sociology* 19: 119–29.

Marshall, Douglas A. 2002. "Behavior, Belonging, and Belief: A Theory of Ritual Practice." *Sociological Theory* 3: 360–80.

Marske, Charles E. 1987. "Durkheim's 'Cult of the Individual' and the Moral Reconstitution of Society." *Sociological Theory* 5: 1–14.

Maryanski, Alexandra and Jonathan H. Turner. 1991. "The Offspring of Functionalism: French and British Structuralism." *Sociological Theory* 9: 106–15.

Matthews, Fred. 1989 "Social Scientists and the Cultural Concept, 1930–1950: The Conflict between Processual and Structural Approaches." *Sociological Theory* 7: 87–101.

Mawson, Anthony R. 1970. "Durkheim and Contemporary Pathology." *British Journal of Sociology* 21: 298–313.

Merton, Robert K. 1934. "Durkheim's Division of Labour in Society." *American Journal of Sociology* 40: 319–28.

Morrison, Ken. 2001. "The Disavowal of the Social in the American Reception of Durkheim." *Journal of Classical Sociology* 1: 95–125.

Nisbet, Robert A. 1943. "The French Revolution and the Rise of Sociology in France." *American Journal of Sociology* 49: 156–64.

Parsons, Talcott. 1968. "Émile Durkheim" in *International Encyclopedia of the Social Sciences*. New York: Macmillan Co. and the Free Press.

Pescosolido, Bernice A. and Sharon Giorgianna. 1989. "Durkheim, Suicide, and Religion: Toward a Network Theory of Suicide." *American Sociological Review* 54: 33–48.

Poggi, Gianfranco. 1971. "The Place of Religion in Durkheim's Theory of Institutions." *European Journal of Sociology* 12: 229–60.

Pope, Whitney and D. Barclay. 1983. "Inside Organic Solidarity." *American Sociological Review* 48: 681–92.

Pope, Whitney, Jere Cohen and Lawrence E. Hazelrigg. 1975. "On the Divergence of Weber and Durkheim: A Critique of Parsons' Convergence Thesis." *American Sociological Review* 40: 417–27.

Rawls, Anne Warfield. 2001. "Durkheim's Treatment of Practice: Concrete Practice vs. Representation as the Foundation of Reason." *Journal of Classical Sociology* 1: 33–68.

1998. "Durkheim's Challenge to Philosophy: Human Reason Explained as a Product of Enacted Social Practice." *American Journal of Sociology* 104: 887–901.

1997. "Durkheim and Pragmatism: An Old Twist on a Contemporary Debate." *Sociological Theory* 15: 5–29.

1996. "Durkheim's Epistemology: The Neglected Argument." *American Journal of Sociology* 102: 430–82.

Riley, Alexander Tristan. 2002. "Durkheim contra Bergson? The Hidden Roots of Postmodern Theory and the Postmodern 'Return' of the Sacred." *Sociological Perspectives* 45: 243–65.

Rossi, Peter H., ed. 1958. "Émile Durkheim – Georg Simmel 1858–1958." *American Journal of Sociology* 62: 579

Sawyer, R. Keith. 2002. "Durkheim's Dilemma: Toward a Sociology of Emergence." *Sociological Theory* 20: 227–47.

Simpson, George. 1933. "Émile Durkheim's Social Realism." *Sociology and Social Research* 28: 2–11.

Sorel, Georges. 1895. "Les Théories de M. Durkheim." *Le Devenir Social* 1: 1–26 and 148–50.

Stone, Gregory P. and Harvey A. Faberman. 1967. "On the Edge of Rapprochement: Was Durkheim Moving toward the Perspective of Social Interaction?" *Sociological Quarterly* 8: 149–64.

Takla, Tendzin N., and Whitney Pope. 1985. "The Force Imagery in Durkheim: The Integration of Theory, Metatheory, and Method." *Sociological Theory* 3: 74–88.

Tiryakian, Edward A. 2000. "Parsons's Emergent Durkheims." *Sociological Theory* 18: 60–83.

1965. "A Problem for the Sociology of Knowledge: The Mutual Unawareness of Émile Durkheim and Max Weber." *European Journal of Sociology* 7: 330–6.

1964. "Introduction to Biographical Focus on Émile Durkheim." *Journal for the Scientific Study of Religions* 3: 247–54.

INDEX

Formes élémentaires de la vie religieuse, Les
  (*see* Elementary Forms)
  duality of human nature, 81
  "dynamogenic quality of religion", 80
  and totemism, 85–97
  translation of
    devising equivalents, 165–73
    overview, 160–1
    translating familiar words, 173–7
Fortes, Meyer, 121
Foucault, Michel, 10, 11, 23, 196, 246, 268,
  290–2, 293–5, 374, 378, 379
Fouillée, Alfred, 57
Frank, Arthur, 211
Frazer, James George, 83–4, 85–7, 88–9, 90,
  91–2, 95, 114, 120, 121
Freeman, Walter, 189, 190, 191, 193
French General Staff, 52
French School of Sociology, 41
Freud, Sigmund, 56, 58, 94, 95, 172, 176,
  240, 250–8, 264
Friedland, Roger, 19, 22
Friedmann, Georges, 71
functionalism, *see* structural functionalism
Fustel, 82

Gambetta, Leon, 49
Garland, David, 25
Gaster, Moses, 87
Geertz, Clifford, 11, 12, 29
Gellner, Ernest, 365
Gennep, Arnold van, 11
Giddens, Anthony, 44, 368
Gift, The, 121
Gillen, Francis James, 86, 89, 90, 168, 170,
  249–50
Gitlin, Todd, 315
Glassman, Eugene, 163
globalization, 395–405
Goffman, Erving, 7–8, 17, 29, 122–4, 127–9,
  185, 189, 200–1, 207, 227–31, 232
Golden Bough, The, 83, 85, 87, 89, 96, 114
Goldenweiser, A. A., 95, 165
Gramsci, Antonio, 150
"grandes conclusions de la psychologie
  moderne, Les", 57
Granet, Marcel, 117, 288
Granovetter, Mark, 336
Groupe d'études socialistes, le, 55
Groupe d'étudiants révolutionnaires, 54
Groupe d'unité socialiste, 55
*Group Psychology and the Analysis of the
  Ego*, 255–6, 258

Grusky, David, 18, 21
Guizot, François, 118
Gunn, Giles, 383, 405–6, 407
Guyau, Jean-Marie, 81
Guyer, Paul, 166

Habermas, Jürgen, 23–4
Haddon, A. C., 87
Halbwachs, Maurice, 109, 116, 131, 329
Halévy, Elie, 144
Hawkins, Mike, 44, 51
Hegel, Georg Wilhelm Friedrich, 286–7
Heidegger, Martin, 246, 362
Heilbron, Johan, 284
Heimonet, Jean-Michel, 293
*Hellenistic Influences on Christian
  Asceticism*, 164
Hepworth, Mike, 232
Herr, Lucien, 53, 55
Hertz, Robert, 14, 55, 61, 115, 215, 277,
  280–2, 283, 286, 288, 290, 294
Hilbert, Richard, 129–30
Hitler, Adolph, 203, 265, 266
Hobbes, Thomas, 211
Holton, Robert, 340
Homo duplex, 212, 217–24, 234–5
Hoogvelt, Ankie, 403
Hubert, Henri, 61, 114–15, 117, 278–9, 280,
  281–2, 286, 288, 290
human nature, duality of, 81
Hume, David, 245
Huxley, Aldous, 378

Incest: The Nature and Origin of Taboo, 255
"Individualism and the Intellectuals", 52,
  390–1
Institue d'ethnologie, 117
interaction order and moral body, 228–33
impure (*see* pollution)
Isidor, Joseph Marx, 45
Isidor, Mélanie, 44–5
Izoulet, Jean, 109–10

"J'accuse", 53
Jakobson, Roman, 10
James, William, 56, 87, 88, 93–4, 162
Jamin, Jean, 285
Janet, Pierre, 60, 104
Jaurès, Jean, 52, 54, 55, 104, 312–13
"Jeunesse läique, La", 52
Jones, Robert Alun, 18, 43
Jouhaux, Léon, 312–13
July 1914, 312